Lecture Notes in Computer Science 1546

Edited by G. Goos, J. Hartmanis and J. van Leeuwen

Springer-Verlag Berlin Heidelberg GmbH

Bernhard Möller John V. Tucker (Eds.)

Prospects for
Hardware Foundations

ESPRIT Working Group 8533
NADA – New Hardware Design Methods
Survey Chapters

 Springer

Series Editors

Gerhard Goos, Karlsruhe University, Germany
Juris Hartmanis, Cornell University, NY, USA
Jan van Leeuwen, Utrecht University, The Netherlands

Volume Editors

Bernhard Möller
Department of Computer Science, University of Augsburg
Universitätsstr. 14, D-86135 Augsburg, Germany
E-mail: Bernhard.Moeller@informatik.uni-augsburg.de

John V. Tucker
Department of Computer Science, University of Wales at Swansea
Singleton Park, Swansea, SA2 8PP, Wales, UK
E-mail: J.V.Tucker@swansea.ac.uk

Cataloging-in-Publication data applied for

Die Deutsche Bibliothek - CIP-Einheitsaufnahme

Prospects for hardware foundations / ESPRIT Working Group 8533
NADA - New Hardware Design Methods Survey Chapters. Bernhard
Möller ; John V. Tucker (ed.). - Berlin ; Heidelberg ; New York ;
Barcelona ; Hong Kong ; London ; Milan ; Paris ; Singapore ; Tokyo
: Springer, 1998
(Lecture notes in computer science ; Vol. 1546)

CR Subject Classification (1998): F.1, F.3, D.2, F.4, B, C.1

ISBN 978-3-540-65461-2   ISBN 978-3-540-49254-2 (eBook)
DOI 10.1007/978-3-540-49254-2

© Springer-Verlag Berlin Heidelberg 1998
Originally published by Springer-Verlag Berlin Heidelberg New York in 1998

Typesetting: Camera-ready by author
SPIN 10693091   06/3142 – 5 4 3 2 1 0   Printed on acid-free paper

Preface

This volume, *Prospects for hardware foundations*, explores the theoretical foundations of hardware design. It contains twelve papers on

(*i*)   mathematical foundations of hardware modelling;
(*ii*) models of hardware and dynamical systems; and
(*iii*) verification and deductive design of systems.

The papers investigate some of the problems at the heart of our theoretical understanding of hardware systems, their design and their integration with other physical or biological systems. The volume aims to make a conceptual contribution to the theory of hardware and to offer prospects for its development.

Specifically, the articles address theoretical topics, including: stream processing, spatially extended systems, hierarchical structures, integration of analogue and digital models. There are case studies of superscalar processors, the Java Virtual Machine, and biological excitable media. There are design and verification techniques including higher order verification, process algebra, state charts, simulation and reasoning of analogue models. Also there are reflections on constructs for future generation hardware description languages.

This volume is also a scientific memoir of the NADA Working Group, the ESPRIT Basic Research Action 8533. The Action existed over the period April 1994 – October 1997. The Action brought together nine research groups, with interests in theoretical computer science, mathematical logic, formal methods for system design, dynamical systems, and hardware, to pursue a multidisciplinary research programme in the foundations of hardware. It held five general meetings and four specialist workshops, at which the groups met together, with some invited guests, for intensive exchanges; it also sponsored several visits between sites. The introduction to this volume gives further information about NADA; here we describe its origins and scientific purpose.

NADA

At the NATO Summer School at Marktoberdorf on *Logic and algebra of specification*, July 23 – August 4, 1991[1], the second of the foundations-

---

[1] F L Bauer, W Brauer and H Schwichtenberg (eds.), *Logic and algebra of specification*, NATO ASI Series F, Vol. 94, Springer-Verlag 1993

oriented "Blue Series" of this distinguished institution, there was enthusiastic discussion of hardware systems by people who were studying theoretical aspects of hardware, or were drawn to hardware systems in their work on design and verification. There was excitement about the wealth of problems and the possibilities of solving them. Discussions between John Tucker, Helmut Schwichtenberg, Hans Leiss, Bernhard Möller, Walter Dosch, Carlos Delgado Kloos and Manfred Broy created a common vision of a wide-ranging collaborative study of hardware systems, integrating knowledge of theoretical computer science, mathematical logic, formal methods, and hardware systems. After the Summer School, Jan Bergstra, Viggo Stoltenberg-Hansen and Arun Holden completed the team. Our group wanted to collaborate on research that might

(i) reveal the essential scientific structure of hardware systems;

(ii) shape a future generation of hardware description languages;

(iii) produce new mathematical methods for design and verification;

(iv) yield interesting theoretical and mathematical problems; and

(v) perform advanced case studies.

A first proposal for a Basic Research Action in the ESPRIT Programme, in October 1991, was rewarded with polite comments from referees and no funds. Undeterred and keen to collaborate, and with Keith Hanna joining the team, the revised application succeeded: the NADA Basic Research Action Working Group 8533 was awarded in 1993, with one of us (BM) as Coordinator, and held its inaugural meeting in April 1994 at TU Munich.

The aim of the Action was to collaborate in research on new, mathematically sound methods for the description and design of hardware systems. We interpreted the term "hardware systems" very generally to include circuits, architectures and the hardware/software interface. More controversially, we also included the interface between hardware and physical and biological systems.

One goal was the search for a next generation hardware description language having a high level of abstraction and a clean, formally defined semantics. NADA was to analyse the requirements for such an idealised language which was called NIL. Description aspects included general questions of timing, parameterisation and modularisation. The design techniques included verification, deductive design in the small, and structured design in the large.

The goal of the research on modelling hardware and dynamical systems was to elicit requirements on design methodologies and description languages. Architectures, circuits, and emerging new paradigms for hardware systems were studied, as well as various standard technologies, in the search for unified mathematical models of hardware. Representative case studies were also needed for demonstrations of the developed techniques.

The goal of the research on algebraic and logical foundations for hardware design was to support the above tasks. Appropriate mathematical methods were taken from computability theory, algebraic specifications, higher order algebra, proof theory and process algebra.

In publishing this volume we wish to bring together some of our results and make available our agenda and approach. It is interesting to reflect on progress in the theory of hardware. This volume may be compared with, for example, a volume[2] edited by one of us (JVT), almost ten years ago, on the then current state of hardware foundations. There has been clear progress on most fronts: mathematical tools, semantic frameworks, verification and specification techniques, deductive methods, and complexity of case studies have all been advanced. However, we are far from completing the important scientific task of creating a comprehensive theory of hardware.

Acknowledgements

We thank all the participants and guests of NADA for their contributions and support. Each paper submitted for this volume was allocated two referees from within NADA and one referee independent of NADA. We thank the external referees for their criticism: J Baeten, M von der Beeck, D Caucal, W J Fokkink, M Fourman, M Gordon, M Holcombe, T Margaria, A Setzer, D Spreen, Gh Ştefănescu, and K Weihrauch.

On behalf of the Group, we thank the European Commission for extending an award for our proposal and granting a five month extension. Working together has brought us forward in our research and led to fruitful interactions. The positive influence of NADA will be felt by its members for years to come.

Finally, on behalf of all the NADA participants, one editor (JVT) would like to thank the other editor (BM) for his outstanding contribution in establishing, sustaining and managing the project: Bernhard, you have our heartfelt gratitude and admiration.

November 1998   B Möller and J V Tucker

---

[2] K McEvoy and J V Tucker (eds.), *Theoretical foundations of VLSI design*, Cambridge Tracts in Theoretical Computer Science 10, Cambridge University Press, 1990.

Table of Contents

III VERIFICATION AND DEDUCTIVE DESIGN

Introduction: NADA and NIL

The NADA Group

Abstract. This introductory chapter provides a brief survey of the history and accomplishments of NADA. An extended section presents the recommendations of the NADA Group on future hardware description languages. Finally, the contents of the remaining chapters are briefly introduced. The chapter also lists some references to NADA-relevant work of those NADA members that have not contributed to one of the further chapters.

1   A Survey of Esprit Working Group 8533 NADA - New Hardware Design Methods

1.1   Aims and Scope

The topic of NADA was research on new, mathematically sound methods for the description and design of hardware systems. The term "hardware systems" was interpreted very generally to include architectures and circuits, the hardware/software interface and even biological systems. Three major subtopics were identified within the Inaugural Meeting in April 1994:

- modeling;
- hardware description languages and design techniques;
- foundations.

The goal of the research on modeling was to elicit requirements on design methodologies and description languages. It included studying architectures, circuits and emerging new paradigms for hardware systems, as well as various standard technologies.

The investigations around NIL ("NADA Integrated Language"), a fictitious next generation hardware description language, served to exhibit hardware specification and description concepts at a high level of abstraction for which a clean formal semantics can be given. The requirements on such a language were distilled out of the extensive body of case studies the NADA Group has performed.

The investigated design techniques included verification and deductive design.

The Group was also performing research on the mathematical foundations for hardware design. Appropriate mathematical methods were taken from computation theory, higher order algebra, proof theory, relation algebra and timed process algebra.

1.2   The NADA Participants

We give a table of the NADA participants as of the official project termination in October 1997. The University of Augsburg served as the Prime Contractor with B. Möller as the Coordinator of the Group. The responsible researcher at each site is marked by italic type font.

University of Amsterdam	*Jan A. Bergstra*, Alban Ponse
University of Augsburg	*Bernhard Möller*
University of Kent	*F. Keith Hanna*
University of Leeds	*Arun V. Holden*
Medical University of Lübeck	*Walter Dosch*
University Carlos III of Madrid	*Carlos Delgado Kloos*, Peter T. Breuer, Natividad Martínez Madrid, Luis Sánchez Fernández
Ludwigs-Maximilian-University Munich	*Helmut Schwichtenberg*, Hans Leiss, Ulrich Berger
Technical University Munich	*Manfred Broy*, Peter Scholz, Jan Philipps
Royal Technical Highschool Stockholm	*Karl Meinke*
University of Wales Swansea	*John V. Tucker*, Neal A. Harman, Matthew J. Poole, Karen Stephenson
Uppsala University	*Viggo Stoltenberg-Hansen*

Most of these participants have been with the Group from the very beginning. Some of them have moved locations during the duration of NADA: the Spanish partners switched from the ETSIT Madrid to their current university, W. Dosch left Augsburg to move to Lübeck and K. Meinke changed from Swansea to Stockholm. Earlier participants were J. Brunekreef at Amsterdam, M. Fuchs at TU Munich, B.C. Thompson at Swansea and P. Abdullah at Uppsala.

1.3   Main Overall Achievements

The first year was dominated by case studies in description and modeling as well as in verification and deductive design, building on and extending the partners' previous work, mainly concentrating on aspects in the small. Concerning NIL, the Group came up with a list of desirable language concepts and explored the possibilities of representing them within the generic theorem prover Isabelle; moreover, the selection of the language concepts was based on their suitability for the methodology of deductive design as employed in various case studies. On the side of foundations, a central theme was the use of streams based on various formal definitions of that concept. Moreover, there were investigations on modeling Synchronous Concurrent Algorithms (SCAs) using process algebra, effective algebras, models of time, tool-independent representation of algorithms and hardware, a framework for hardware-software codesign and technology independent specifications.

The second year was dominated by studies in modeling, on foundational issues and by further case studies. Concerning language issues, the Group started exploring MHDL for possibilities of serving as a basis for NIL. It turned out that many of the concepts exhibited in Year I were already accommodated there, although a coherent semantic framework was missing.

The third year significantly advanced the state of the art in the areas of modeling, deductive design and foundations. Concerning language issues, there was a severe backdrop imposed on the Group: the development of the language MHDL it had started exploring as a possible basis for NIL was abandoned. Meanwhile a new development is under way: SLDL (System level description language). However, this language is still in its requirements definition phase and so could not be used within the project duration. The Group's recommendations on NIL are detailed in Section 3.

1.4 Workshops and Conferences

Next to the NADA Inaugural Meeting in April '94, hosted by TU Munich, the formal milestones for NADA were the three Annual Meetings, organized by Swansea in March 1995, Uppsala in April 1996 and Madrid in April 1997, as well as the Final Meeting, organized by Lübeck in September 1997. In between these there were specialist workshops, viz. one on first case studies and an exploration of language concepts, organized by Madrid in October 1994, one on the central topic of streams, organized by LMU Munich in October 1995, and one on further case studies and language issues, organized by Amsterdam in October 1996.

Besides these NADA-specific meetings, NADA partners were also concerned with the organization of related conferences.

A lot of important material in the realm of deductive design was presented at the *Third International Conference on The Mathematics of Program Construction*, Kloster Irsee, Germany, July 17-21, 1995 [19,20], which was chaired and organized by NADA member B. Möller and partially sponsored by NADA.

On the side of foundations, two major events were the *Second* and *Third International Workshops on Higher Order Algebra, Logic and Term Rewriting*. The former of these took place at Paderborn, Sept. 21-22, 1995 [6], sponsored by the EACSL and with NADA members K. Meinke and B. Möller in the organizing committee. The latter of the workshops was held in conjunction with ALP (Algebra and Logic Programming) Southampton, Sept. 2–5, 1997 [8]. It was sponsored by the EACSL, and NADA members K. Meinke and B. Möller were again part of the organizing committee.

Finally, the NADA group had the opportunity to present its work to a broad audience at the *Third Annual NADA Meeting* held in conjunction with the conferences CHDL/VUFE/LCMQA '97 at Toledo, 20–25 April, 1997, and organized by NADA member C. Delgado Kloos. In particular, a tutorial on four central threads of NADA research was presented. All this was well-received and gave NADA considerable international visibility.

2 Project Achievements of the Individual Sites

2.1 Amsterdam

Amsterdam's participation in NADA triggered a lot of design and specification activity, ranging from refinement of the concept *early input* to design and application of Grid Protocols. Early input is a way of passing values between concurrent processes; it is primitive to formalize and used to model stream processing. Amsterdam's participation in NADA was driven by two general goals:

- To find simple and adequate primitives, and elegant algebraic methods to model data transfer between concurrent processes, and
- To give a process algebraic account of applications that are relevant to NADA, viz. the modeling of hardware phenomena, and development of respective analysis techniques.

As an example we mention the Amsterdam work on SCAs (Synchronous Concurrent Algorithms) as developed by Tucker et al. The following achievements of Amsterdam's participation in NADA can be distinguished:

- A better understanding of scientific work done elsewhere. This applies in particular to the modeling of hardware and other concurrent phenomena in which parallel input/output is a major ingredient.
- Much more focus on a systematic treatment of data manipulation in process algebra, as exemplified by the early input concept. Traditionally, process algebraic modeling often concentrated on operational aspects of concurrency, and treatment of data manipulation (by processes) was ad hoc or left implicit.
- Distinguishing primitives for file-transfer; further research on an algebraic treatment of (concurrent) assignment is being undertaken.
- A close observation of the development of μCRL ("process algebra with data") at CWI.
- Research on process algebra with recursive operations, such as binary Kleene star and nesting, in particular in combination with early input and value-passing.

2.2 Augsburg

The focus of the work at Augsburg has been on the method of *Deductive Design*, i.e., on the systematic construction of a system implementation, starting from its behavioural specification, according to formal, provably correct rules. The main advantages of this approach are:

- The resulting implementation is correct by construction.
- The rules can be formulated schematically, independent of the particular application area, and hence can be re-used for wide classes of similar problems.
- Since the rules are formal, the design process can be assisted by machine.

- Implementations can be constructed in a modular way, with emphasis on correctness first and subsequent transformation to increase performance.
- The formal derivation also serves as a record of the design decisions taken and hence is an explanatory documentation. Upon modification of the system specification it eases revision of the implementation.

This paradigm has successfully been applied to sequential and, to a lesser extent, also to parallel programs. Since hardware consists of "frozen" programs, it is an obvious idea to apply this method to hardware design. A large amount of work in this area has been done by M. Sheeran and others.

The major novel ingredients and achievements in the Augsburg work are the following:

- specification at the level of predicate logic, not necessarily algorithmic yet,
- a clearer disentangling of the abstract idea of an algorithm from the concrete layout that realizes it,
- in particular, introduction of wiring operators in a late stage of the derivations, thus avoiding a lot of burden and clutter,
- a simpler approach to retiming that avoids the concept of anti-delays,
- in the asynchronous case a strongly algebraic approach to streams, notably to questions about fairness.

While the first two items had been established already in the CIP group to which NADA members B. Möller and W. Dosch belonged, the latter three items were elaborated within the NADA project.

The case studies include many of the IFIP WG10.5 Benchmark Verification Problems [7]. Next to dealing with basic combinational and sequential circuits, a very simple treatment of systolic circuits was achieved. Finally, concerning higher-level hardware concepts, an easy formal account of pipelining became possible.

Special emphasis was laid on parameterization and re-usability aspects.

In the synchronous case, a major breakthrough was the switch to formalizing the specifications and derivations using the functional programming language *Gofer*, a subset of *Haskell*. The polymorphism of this language allows the use of Ştefănescu's network algebra and other algebraic laws both at the level of combinational and sequential circuits. Also fixpoint induction and related proof principles can be applied directly. Moreover, many derivations can be performed in a polymorphic way abstracting from concrete applications and hence achieving much better re-usability.

In the asynchronous case, the algebraic basis has been consolidated. This thread of work concerns more algebraic ways of specifying, reasoning about and transforming descriptions of (sets of) streams. Particular emphasis is laid on the use of regular algebra in describing stream patterns, notably in connection with questions of fairness. This algebraic approach has also been tied in with other specification formalisms such as temporal and modal logic.

2.3 Kent

The work undertaken at Kent has focused on two themes: the use of dependent types in specifications for digital systems and in extending formal verification from the digital domain towards the analog domain.

The motivation for using dependent types (loosely, types that are parameterized by values and/or other types) for formal specification is that they offer both greater expressiveness and greater generality. During the course of the NADA project, Kent have:

- Carried out an in-depth investigation of the use of dependent types in specifying and in formally verifying complex systolic array architectures;
- Shown how it is possible to capture, within a formal theory, the interrelation between the structural and the behavioural aspects of a circuit. Circuits are treated as typed graphs and their behavioural specifications as predicates. The key difficulty that has to be overcome is that, in a structural description, the types of ports have to be treated as values whereas, in the behavioural description, they appear as types. Using dependent types, it was found possible to devise a sufficiently expressive type for interfaces that guaranteed the consistency of structural and behavioural specifications. The approach was demonstrated using Veritas, an implementation of a dependently-typed higher-order logic.

The motivation for extending formal specification and verification techniques from the digital domain towards the analog domain is that, in practice, significant sections of a digital system often have to be designed at the analog electronics level of abstraction. By doing this, logically redundant signal conditioning and buffering stages can be eliminated, leading to circuitry which can be up to an order of magnitude faster, and with lower power consumption, than the corresponding circuitry designed (in terms of gates and flipflops, etc) at the digital level of abstraction. During the course of the NADA project, Kent have:

- Demonstrated how, using higher-order logic, the behavioural characteristics of typical electronic components (transistors, diodes, resistors) can be specified in terms of analog voltages and currents.
- Shown how the behavioural specification of an electronic circuit (for example, one that uses pass-transistor logic) can be inferred from the analog specifications of the component parts and their interconnections and how specifications at the analog and digital levels are related.
- Devised and implemented a decision procedure that, given a description of an analog circuit and behavioural specifications of its component parts, determines whether it correctly implements a given behavioural specification.

Kent believe that this work is likely to impact strongly upon the design of future generations of mixed-level hardware design languages which, at present, lack rigorous foundations.

2.4 Leeds

The focus of the work at Leeds has been on the development and evaluation of case studies, based on biomedical applications, that are practical illustrations of what current problems exist in the computational modeling of complicated, highly structured, spatially extended systems that are represented mathematically by different classes of models - cellular automata, coupled map lattices, coupled ordinary differential equation lattices, and partial differential equations, and that interact with data streams. The main idea of the approach is to use the theory of synchronous concurrent algorithms as a framework within which different types of model are embedded, and can be coupled. The advantage of this modular approach is that newer generation models can readily be incorporated, and the framework is applicable to modeling a wide range of hierarchical, structured system, not just the case studies, based on cardiac muscle, arryhthmias, and their control. The principal results of the Leeds work have been:

- The development of a family of partial differential equation models for different normal and pathological cardiac tissues, and the use of these models to simulate cardiac arryhthmias.
- The design of a novel means of controlling re-entrant cardiac arryhthmias, and the evaluation of its practicability.
- The development of a geometric, anisotropic model for the ventricles of the heart, and the coupling of this geometry with simple (coupled map lattice, simple ordinary differential equation models) of excitability and with partial differential equation models.
- The development of a formal approach, within the theory of synchronous concurrent algorithms, for coupling and verifying the above models.
- The application of the same approach to other biological systems - neural nets, and oceanic plankton population dynamics.

This approach has been primarily in collaboration with the Swansea group, and has led to extensive funding from UK research council and medical charities, in the applications of these models to clinical problems. It has also led to UK funding to continue the collaboration with the Swansea group.

2.5 Lübeck

The work in Lübeck concentrated on deductive design — both in the area of hardware and software [5]. This methodology aims at systematically deriving a system implementation from its behavioural specification following sound transformation rules. The derivation documents the design decisions and guides the redesign upon changing requirements. Within a structured design methodology, one initially abstracts from layout and timing issues and concentrate on algorithmic design principles. Synchronous descriptions are based on the algebra of finite sequences modeling the linear succession in space or in time; asynchronous descriptions employ stream processing functions. The major contributions in the work of Lübeck consist in

- isolating and formalizing important design steps [3],
- abstracting characteristic design patterns from specific case studies,
- deriving standard implementations for iterative and tree structured networks using higher-order functions,
- reasoning about ordered streams by set abstraction [4].

For a class of digit recurrence algorithms, W. Dosch has derived different implementations as combinational and sequential circuits in a schematic way. This class of iterative circuits was then generalized to tree structured networks originating from cascade recursive functions. The derivations are parameterized supporting their re-use in different applications.

2.6   Madrid

The Madrid work has been concentrated in three main areas. The first area is the semantics of hardware description languages, chiefly in connection with the formalization of VHDL and the development of specification, refinement and verification calculi for that language and real-time systems in general. Secondly, Madrid have been working with the specification language LOTOS. They have produced methods for designing hardware systems and generating VHDL code automatically from the design. Thirdly, Madrid have been researching in the area of codesign also using LOTOS as the system description language.

Madrid have given several presentations to the Group about the last two areas and have been actively developing the first area within the project itself. Participation in NADA has been specially useful to Madrid in the further development of their logic for real-time system design from their approach to VHDL semantics. With regard to the latter, Madrid have debugged the refinement calculus of VHDL, finally proving it to be complete with respect to their formal semantics for the language. Madrid have also taken the opportunity to investigate the problems of design in non-discrete regimes using their formalisms and those of others. The operational amplifier has been a particularly instructive example of an analog device operating in continuous time. From their attempts to describe it, Madrid have concluded that compositionality under these regimes derives from the constraints on a system and not from the solutions to (subsets of) those constraints. If one tries the latter approach one runs into problems with causality requirements. As a result of these investigations, Madrid have been able to suggest a semantic model for the analog extension to VHDL (now accepted by the IEEE), developing a prototype implementation.

2.7   LMU Munich

LMU have worked on a variety of subjects all subsumable under the heading 'applied proof theory'. This was done in conjunction with the development of an interactive prover MINLOG, well suited to the purpose and, in particular, for hardware verification and development. Most notably U. Berger and M. Eberl have been working on NADA-related questions.

LMU work in the area of program extraction from classical proofs. To this end they apply H. Friedman's A-translation followed by a modified realizability interpretation. However, to obtain a reasonable program it is essential to use a refinement of the A-translation introduced in Berger/Schwichtenberg 1995. This refinement makes it possible that not all atoms in the proof are A-translated, but only those with a "critical" relation symbol. Yannis Moschovakis suggested the following example of a classical existence proof with a quantifier-free kernel which does not obviously contain an algorithm: the gcd of two natural numbers a_1 and a_2 is a linear combination of the two. In that example only the divisibility relation $\cdot | \cdot$ turns out to be critical.

In addition, LMU worked on case studies in hardware description and verification, among which is the min/max-example from the IFIP WG 10.5 Hardware Verification Benchmarks [7].

2.8 TU Munich

In the past years, the design methodology Focus for distributed systems has been developed at TUM. As the original intention of Focus was to describe software systems, the NADA project has been a unique opportunity to verify to which extent Focus is applicable for the specification of hardware, too. To achieve this, a number of case studies, like the formal development of a production cell, a distributed min/max component, interfaces, modulo-n counter, and the Alpha AXP^{TM} shared memory have been carried out using Focus.

Apart from these case studies, which have shown that Focus is indeed suitable for the description of hardware oriented systems, it also turned out that Focus provides a mathematical framework for defining a formal semantics for hardware description languages like VHDL and system level languages like Statecharts. Furthermore, it was proven that Focus is not only appropriate to describe pure software or hardware components but in addition can be used to specify mixed hardware/software systems, i.e. can serve as a formal foundation for Hardware/Software Codesign.

2.9 Stockholm

Foundations of Hardware Specification K. Meinke has investigated the foundations of hardware specification using higher-order algebra. Roughly this corresponds with the equational fragment of many-sorted higher-order logic, where higher types are function types. Thus it is related to Church's system of finite types. This framework is natural for hardware description since it allows the direct representation of hardware devices as stream transformers. This observation has also been confirmed elsewhere, e.g. the HOL community. Significant achievements in this area have been:

- An exact characterization of the specification power of higher-order equations [14]. Earlier work on this problem was published in [12]. This power was shown to be Π_1^1, thus it properly includes the arithmetical hierarchy.

Furthermore, the expressive power of the hierarchy of specifications (second-order, third-order, etc.) collapses to second-order. In this sense, (quantifier free) second-order equational logic is slightly more powerful than first-order arithmetic.

- A proof theory for higher-order equations which exactly characterizes the case where higher-order equational reasoning is reducible to first-order equational reasoning through the existence of normal form proofs for higher-order equations. This result makes use of a particularly interesting topology on higher-order algebras which seems to capture a definition of observational equivalence for higher-order operations (e.g. stream transformers). Case study research [16] on Kung's systolic convolution algorithm found this to be a useful result for theorem proving and hardware verification.

Practical Case Studies Together with L.J. Steggles, K. Meinke studied some well known hardware algorithms in order to gain insight into their specification and verification requirements. These included a typical systolic algorithm (convolution) and a typical dataflow algorithm (Hamming Stream). The convolution algorithm lead to fundamental insights in the proof theory of verification for systolic algorithms (see above). The dataflow algorithm revealed the power of higher-order algebra for semantical verification.

L.J. Steggles extended the theory of higher-order algebraic specification to transfinite types, and showed that this formed a suitable framework to capture the parametricity of families of hardware algorithms [22]. He also developed a theory of parameterized higher-order algebraic specifications, which allowed taking advantage of the polymorphism inherent in the convolution algorithm to simplify the specification [23].

K. Meinke investigated the impact of the proof theory of higher-order equations on higher-order equational theorem proving, and verification of hardware by means of term rewriting in [13].

Software Tools Together with B.M. Hearn, K. Meinke designed and implemented a tool for parsing and executing higher-order algebraic specifications by rewriting of terms and types. This tool was based on earlier published research of K. Meinke. The tool and its input language is called ATLAS (A Typed Language for Algebraic Specification) and is based on many-level algebraic specifications, which can be used for equational specification both of data and types (by means of type equations). ATLAS [9] is implemented in C under UNIX and has a Motif graphical user interface. ATLAS was used to specify and verify hardware algorithms, as well as other case studies, including order-sorted, polymorphic and recursive types.

The research on ATLAS was also taken further by E. Visser at the CWI Amsterdam (outside the NADA project).

2.10   Swansea

Algebraic Models of Microprocessors Work on microprocessor modeling has progressed from basic representations of simple processors, at the level of the programmer, through models of microprogrammed implementations, to models of advanced processor implementations. In addition, considerable attention has been given to the problems of verifying the correctness of microprocessor implementations.

At the start of the NADA project, *iterated map* microprocessor models were restricted to a simple PDP-8-derived example, at the level of the programmer. An implementation of the PDP-8 was developed, and in parallel a technique was developed for substantially simplifying the process of formal verification. This required that a number of conditions be met, that were trivially satisfied by iterated map models of microprocessors, and their associated timing abstraction functions. A more sophisticated example, with input and output, was then developed. This was based on a standard example, *Gordon's Computer*.

The substantial body of work on microprocessor representation has been concerned with pipelined, and especially superscalar processors. The problems that these bring are (a) substantially increased complexity of implementations; and (b) a timing model that differs substantially from that of the programmer's level model, or architecture. Techniques were developed for representing superscalar microprocessors, and existing correctness conditions were modified. Work continues on developing techniques for simplifying the verification of superscalar processors.

An Algebraic Framework for Linking Program and Machine Semantics During the period 1994–1997, K. Stephenson and J.V. Tucker constructed an algebraic framework in which the process of executing a high-level program can be described at the level of hardware. There are many layers of abstraction involved between these two extremes. Each layer of the hierarchy consists of an algebraic specification for the semantics of the language at that level. To produce specifications for each layer requires the syntax and a semantic mapping of the language to be defined. In addition, to compare levels of the hierarchy and to define the relative correctness of levels to each other, these layers are structured further.

General methods of defining syntax are based on the notion of *filtering* context-free supersets to produce algebraic specifications of non-context-free languages. This work is set against a background of research into the relationship between context-free grammars and closed term algebras.

An operational model of semantics is used in which the sequences of states produced by the execution of programs are explicitly clocked by time. This enables computable models of operational semantics to be developed and hence algebraically specified. In particular, this provides an algebraic approach to structural operational semantics of high-level languages. The approach is also applicable to the semantics of low-level languages; this work is set against a background of research into machine semantics developed by J.V. Tucker and N.A. Harman within NADA.

In addition, each layer is structured so that the specifications have a common signature. This allows the process of compilation between the layers to be expressed as a homomorphism. Correctness of one level of the hierarchy with respect to another can then be stated in terms of commutative diagrams. This work is set against a background of research in algebraic semantics.

It has been shown, to deal with concepts at a higher level of abstraction, that the act of proving correctness can be reduced to establishing the correctness of the commutative diagram before execution (trivially) and at the end of the first time cycle. As these stages do not require structural induction to be used, this both dramatically reduces the work required, and also makes the process feasible for mechanical checking by a suitable theorem prover.

The first two levels of this hierarchy are specified and are (manually) shown to be correct relative to each other for a non-trivial case study of a simple while programming language and a very abstract machine-level language. This framework is now being extended to deal at lower levels of the hierarchy, with the aim of linking the work to that of N.A. Harman regarding the correctness of microprocessors.

SCAs and Dynamical Systems Work by J.V. Tucker and M.J. Poole, in collaboration with A.V. Holden (University of Leeds) has focused on algebraic models of spatially extended computational systems. The theory of synchronous concurrent algorithms (SCAs) has been applied and extended to unify the modeling of a range of different types of hardware system and biological system.

In their biological system applications, Tucker et al. have been primarily interested in coupled map lattice, cellular automaton, neural network, coupled ordinary differential equation and partial differential equation models of spatially extended biological phenomena. They have concentrated on models of electrical phenomena in cardiac tissue. On making discrete approximations of continuous spaces and times, the diverse range of available models of cardiac excitation are all examples of SCAs and may therefore be studied in a unified way, from the point of view of parallel deterministic computation. The notion of discrete space and local connectivity in cardiac models corresponds closely with the notion of parallel digital systems; continuous state systems are closely related to analogue computing systems.

Notions of hierarchies of spatially extended systems have been developed within the framework of SCAs. The formal concepts of hierarchy are derived from notions of abstraction and approximation between the structure and behaviour of two SCAs, which in turn are built upon abstractions of time, space and state. The general theory has been exploited in the investigation of systolic algorithms and, especially, of spatially extended biological systems. The concepts of hierarchy have led to the rigorous comparison of the behaviours of mathematically and biologically diverse models of cardiac electrical behaviour that are unified by SCA theory. Further, they have led to the construction of hierarchical and hybrid SCA models of cardiac activity combining many component models and reconstructing cardiac behaviour at many different, interacting, levels of biological detail.

2.11 Uppsala

The work of the Uppsala site has primarily been concerned with semantical foundations of data types, streams and stream transformers. The main tool used has been the theory of domains. Domain theory arose from generalizations of the theory of recursion and computability in the work of D. Scott, Yu. Ershov and others. Its use in denotational semantics is well known. Uppsala have also considered the use of formal spaces and of certain non-standard models.

Uppsala's work has been concentrated on considering domain theory as a theory of computation on data types or topological algebras, where approximations are the primary objects. That is, computations are performed on concrete approximations and the results are then transferred to ideal or non-concrete elements (the elements of the considered topological algebra) via a limit process. A domain captures this idea well. The method used is that of domain representability for topological algebras, developed by V. Stoltenberg-Hansen and J.V. Tucker starting in 1985. This general technique was applied to the processing of streams with discrete and continuous time and data.

Another tool useful for the study of computability for topological structures, and for obtaining constructive versions of non constructive theorems such as the Tychonoff or Hahn-Banach theorems, is the theory of formal spaces. Uppsala have made a comparison between this method and the method of domain representability showing their equivalence in certain precise senses for regular locally compact spaces. Uppsala have also found a connection between domain theory and model theory where saturation plays a key role. The have used this to give a logical presentation of the Kleene-Kreisel continuous functionals.

Finally, Uppsala have considered certain constructive non-standard models which they believe will be useful for foundational questions addressed by the NADA project.

3 Observations on NIL — The NADA Integrated Language

In this section we discuss the observations on requirements to future hardware description languages as they have arisen during the NADA work.

3.1 Introduction

The lack of a common hardware description language (HDL) with sound foundations and clear concepts hinder progress in high-level hardware design. HDLs in use support only the lower design level; their semantics are mostly simulator-based and hence awkwardly complex.

NIL is a fictitious next generation hardware description language. This section describes the concepts such a language would contain. It is based on the experience of extensive case studies on specification, verification and deductive design within NADA. Detailed reports on these case studies can be found in the subsequent chapters.

NIL employs concepts at a high level of abstraction and is based on a formally defined semantics. Description aspects include general questions of timing, parameterization and modularization. The design techniques include verification, deductive design in the small and structured design in the large.

During the duration of the NADA Working Group its members were looking at the functionally based language MHDL [21] as a possible basis for NIL. Unfortunately the development of that language was abandoned during the final phase of NADA.

At the same time efforts towards the definition of a *System Level Description Language SLDL* [24] as a successor to MHDL were set up. Currently this language is in its requirements definition phase. Many of the aims put forward by the SLDL committee fall well in line with observations by NADA. Therefore we shall freely quote the current SLDL requirements document to underline our views. Such citations are marked by slight indentation and a *slanted* type font. The mission statement of the SLDL effort is as follows:

> *To support the creation and/or standardization of a language or representation, or set of languages or representations, that will enable engineers to describe single and multi-chip silicon-based embedded systems to any desired degree of detail and that will allow engineers to verify and/or validate those systems with appropriate tools and techniques. The languages or representations will address systems under design and their operating environment, including software, mixed-signal, optical, and micro-electronic mechanical characteristics.*

The SLDL requirements document goes on to say:

> *Note that the mission statement does not necessarily require a specific language; a set of languages, or a meta-notation, or something of this sort is perfectly acceptable as long as it meets the requirements set forth in this document.*

This agrees very well with the actual road the NADA work took: the different groups have developed various formalisms, each suited to a particular problem domain. Due to lack of manpower, the complete design and definition of NIL could not have been achieved within NADA anyway.

3.2 Central Requirements on NIL

This section surveys the central requirements on NIL as they were identified within NADA. We deem the concepts essential for structured hardware description and design; however, they are only incompletely realized in existing HDLs such as VHDL, CIRCAL, ELLA, LTS. The reader is invited to compare the requirements with the SLDL ones.

Scope NIL is a general purpose language supporting the description of different types of hardware at several levels of abstraction, in particular, the behavioural, the structural and the layout levels.

Declarative Style NIL should have a clean declarative core which supports realization-independent behavioural specifications. Declarative hardware description abstracts from layout structure and computational process to functional behaviour.

Semantic Coherence NIL must provide a coherent semantic framework which, in the design, allows passing smoothly from specifications through component descriptions to concrete realizations. In particular, There have to be constructs for expressing non-functional aspects (resource bounds), among which are the allocation of computations both in space and time. The semantic model must coherently cover continuous and discrete notions of time as well as a notion of space.

Structuring and Parameterization NIL must support the decomposition of complex systems into subsystems in all design phases. For this purpose, it has to offer flexible component descriptions with clear interface specifications.

It must allow hierarchical design, large-scale parameterization and re-use of components.

Design Correctness NIL must support establishing the correctness of a design by formal methods. It has to encourage a modular and stepwise design process, based on sound notions of refinement.

In particular, the semantic model must allow concise transformation and verification rules that support deductive design and design verification. The refinement and abstraction concepts comprise timing, structure and layout. NIL supports the analysis of designs by providing rules how to infer properties from descriptions.

Extensibility NIL must be extensible so that users can tailor it to their particular needs. Such language extensions may capture specialized types of hardware (synchronous circuits, combinational circuits, associative memory) or particular realization levels (register transfer level, CMOS level).

The extension layers have to be explained in terms of the kernel language. In this way the language itself has a modular structure. This scheme has profitably and successfully been applied to the language CIP-L [1].

Tools and Graphics NIL has to be designed such that it interfaces with well-established tools such as VERILOG and VHDL simulators and compilers. In particular, NIL must designate operational sublayers for rapid prototyping, simulation and compilation. NIL also offers a standard interface to graphical tools supporting the visualization and visual manipulation of designs.

Use in Engineering and Education To gain wide acceptance, NIL cannot involve sophisticated concepts. The semantics and the type system should be as simple as possible. For the engineer, NIL must combine manipulative fluency with intuitive comprehension. For education, it should serve as a conceptually well-formed and clean vehicle for teaching hardware design methods. Moreover, NIL should attempt to bridge the gap between software and hardware design.

Let us conclude this section by another quotation from the SLDL document:

> The key activities of systems design include feasibility studies, concept selection, product selection and architectural (high-level) design. System design typically includes the following capabilities (as described in the section below on SCOPE):
>
> – Several levels of abstraction that are essential to support feasibility studies and concept selection.
> – Modularity in both functional and structural design to support product selection.
> – Verification, including analyses such as simulation modeling.
> – Provision for constraints and back annotation from downstream design stages.
> – Test planning to support architectural design.

3.3 Survey of NIL Core Concepts

Approach The approaches to formalization of hardware aspects used by NADA members are based on predicate logic and concepts from functional programming. Therefore it is natural that the core of NIL should essentially be a suitable fragment of logic and typed λ-calculus.

The core should stay close to standard algebraic and functional specification, i.e., use equational many-sorted logic, as long as possible. This will motivate the recommendations below on the various choice options.

An important question is whether to use total or partial functions as operators. Differing from the CoFI initiative [2], for simplicity NIL uses total functions because they lead to a much easier logical framework. Partial functions can be simulated through suitable totalization or by simulating relations by set-valued functions.

Basic Concepts The basic entities involved in any component are *data, time* and *space*.

Based on these, *streams*, also known as *traces* or *waveforms*, record the temporal succession of data at a given *input or output port*, whereas *states* record for each point in space and each time a data value. The computation by a module at a location in space is described by a *stream transformer*.

Data The data involved in the circuit level of hardware description mostly are of a very simple kind, such as Booleans or more refined logical values. At higher levels, particularly at the architecture level, also more involved data structures are needed. While equational axiomatizations using a generation principles are well-known, it may be advantageous to include certain standard data type constructors such as sums or products to allow recursive data types in the form known from functional programming languages.

All these data structures are discrete. It has to be determined whether continuous data make sense and how they would be described. This aspect certainly is a core concept.

Time NIL must include various concepts of time. Some options are

- discrete vs. continuous time;
- time with and without a starting point;
- linearly vs partially ordered time.

Discrete time usually is isomorphic to (an interval of) the natural numbers. It is easily axiomatized using an enumeration function or inductive definition.

Continuous time cannot be enumerated. It is best axiomatized using an order relation. This suggests use of predicate symbols other than just equality. Non-discreteness is axiomatized e.g. by requiring

$$\forall x, y : x < y \Rightarrow \exists z : x < z < y \, ,$$

which involves an existential quantifier. This can be avoided by introducing a Skolem function $between : Time \times Time \to Time$ with the axiom

$$x < y \Rightarrow x < between(x, y) < y \, .$$

Completeness is even worse, since it requires quantification over subsets to talk about infima/suprema. By the increasing importance of hybrid systems, however, continuous time cannot be neglected. For many hardware purposes discrete time will suffice, though.

Linear time is adequate for modeling systems with a global time. For asynchronous systems it may be advantageous to use a partial ordering of time.

Space Space serves to locate single subcomponents, which are entities with a well-defined extent. Hence the concept of continuous space is not relevant for NIL. Discrete space can be described via suitable enumeration functions or, in a more structured way, by inductive definition.

The elements of the space domain will be called *locations*.

For the description of placement and topologies the space domain needs to be equipped — in increasing degree of precision — with a neighbourhood relation, coordinates or even a metric.

Timing Disciplines Once a notion of space has been fixed, we can also talk about global or local time. For global time, a single sort *Time* is sufficient. To describe local time, one either needs to view *Time* as a sort constructor parameterized by elements of *Space*, or to reflect locality by retimings between the subcompoents.

For various retiming concepts see Lustre, Signal, Ruby as well as the SCA framework.

Connectivity The neighbourhood relation between locations can also be given by a function *Nbd* : *Space* × *Time* → *Set*(*Space*) that assigns to each point a *neighbourhood*, i.e., a set of other points. Depending on whether the underlying relation is symmetric, this models bi-directionality or uni-directionality.

The neighbourhood relation may even be time-dependent. This way one can describe dynamic structures as used e.g. in on-the-fly programming of FPGAs.

Another issue about connectivity is the treatment of channels. Options here are

- explicit naming/renaming/hiding of channels;
- use of special constants for interconnection networks.

Case studies have shown that both should be accommodated. Since they are inter-definable it is to be determined which option should go into the core.

Streams and Waveforms The options here are total vs. partial streams. Total streams are simply functions from time to data. Partial streams stop after a certain time. Among these one finally can distinguish between complete and incomplete. Total streams fit in nicely with the decision to use total operations.

Axiomatizations of partial streams are less direct in this setting. Possibilities are:

1. use a dummy element and inflate each partial stream to a total one that constantly yields the dummy after a certain initial part;
2. use higher-order concepts to distinguish the set of all (proper and improper) intervals of the time domain and have streams as functions from these intervals to data;
3. use domain-theoretic notions to characterize total streams as limits of the partial ones.

Of these, the first is the simplest.

As soon as continuous time is used, streams should better be called waveforms. For them, option 2 for describing partial waveforms becomes more interesting, since then quantification over subsets of the time domain are used anyway.

Stream Transformers This is probably the easiest concept: a stream transformer is a function from (tuples of) streams to (tuples of) streams. This is independent of all choices for the underlying domains of time, data and streams.

This notion suggests the use of higher types. As Möller [17, 18] and Meinke [11] have shown, this fits in well with equational logic, even if the axiom of extensionality is required to hold. Higher types would also easily accommodate a full typed λ-calculus, which is convenient in many formulations.

For the stream transformers further properties, such as monotonicity, continuity or causality, may be required.

Non-Determinacy There is quite a ramification in how NADA members model non-determinacy (if at all). The concepts used here are, in increasing semantic complexity,

- sets of streams (traces);
- sets of stream transformers;
- CCS/CSP-like processes.

Whereas the Amsterdam partners are using their well-established process algebra, essentially a first-order equational theory, the other two approaches heavily use higher-order concepts.

Uses of non-determinism in hardware description are e.g. modeling the accesses to a bus structure and handling of I/O events.

State Certain components, such as sequential circuits, depend on an internal state, whereas others, such as combinational circuits, do not. Depending on whether a component employs global or local time for its subcomponents, the state will be global or locally distributed. A global state can be modeled by a function $State : Space \times Time \rightarrow Data$, where $Time$ is the global time domain. If streams are simply functions from $Time$ to $Data$, one can, by currying, equivalently use $State : Space \rightarrow Stream$.

Another way to model states is to use a stream of states in a feedback loop.

In components with local time, local streams may be used to describe the local states. However, this would mean that $Stream$ now needs to be a parameterized data type constructor, and the $State$ function now needs to involve a dependent type:

$$State : (x : Space) \rightarrow Stream(Time(x), Data(x)) .$$

In components with global state, the stream transformer at each point in space may or may not depend on that state.

Architecture The *architecture* of a component is described by its connectivity, the timing discipline (global or local), the global state function (if any), the stream transformer or process at each location and the *parallel composition* of all these. If the definition of parallel composition is taken general enough it also comprises sequential composition and feedback.

Systems A system is the parallel composition of components. It will again involve a notion of space to locate the components, and a notion of connectivity. To allow hierarchical structuring, it would be most simple and coherent to view systems again as components. However, then parallel composition of stream transformers, which model the computation in subcomponents, has to be somehow unified with the "parallel composition" of algebras, which model the components.

In any case, there have to be concepts for expressing modularization, i.e., composition/decomposition of systems and hiding of internal structure; the semantics has to be compositional w.r.t. the correct implementation relation.

Possible Extensions Here we first list a few concepts that have proved valuable in some NADA case studies, but entail a certain semantic complexity, so that it is unclear whether they should be part of overall NIL. These are, above all, parameterization of types, polymorphism and dependent types. While each of these topics is well-understood by itself, their combination leads to problems with type checking that have not yet been resolved.

Another topic are formal descriptions of interfaces. While purely syntactic descriptions exist in many programming languages, in the overall line of NADA NIL would have to contain interface descriptions as "first-class citizens" that can be freely manipulated and formally reasoned about. Experiments have been performed to describe interfaces in the form of higher-order logic expressions, but no conclusive solution has been found.

The second group of concepts that would enter, but for which no case studies have been performed within NADA, are non-functional aspects, such as speed and size of components. Examples of this are the clock calculus in Lustre/Signal (which is used also for determining whether a stream-based specification can have a realization in bounded memory at all) or Skillicorn's cost calculus for parallel algorithms on lists.

3.4 Reasoning

One purpose of a formal system description is to allow precise reasoning about it. To this end, a precise formal semantics of the description language has to be given. A central notion is that of one component correctly *implementing* another.

Concepts of Correctness There are well-studied implementation relations both for the algebraic and the logical/functional/relational views of systems. In the presence of non-determinacy, the implementation must allow *behaviour refinement* (reduction of non-determinacy and/or increase of "definedness"). Further essential concepts are *abstraction* from layout/topology, *interface refinement* and *data refinement*. Moreover implementations via *retimings* have to be taken into account.

Reasoning Tools Since one of our basic aims is to keep the underlying logic as simple as possible, also our reasoning tools should be somewhat restricted:

- equational reasoning using the equational axioms or fixpoint properties of recursively defined entities;
- in the case of refinement, inequational reasoning using the refinement relation and monotonicity;

– induction principles, viz.
  • structural induction and
  • fixpoint induction for recursive definitions (using both least and greatest fixpoint semantics);
– uniqueness of the solution of certain fixpoint equations.

Design Verification In verification, one constructs the implementation by some independent proceeding and afterwards tries to show that it correctly implements the specification.

The methodical advantage of this is that one gives two views of a system; if they can be correctly related, this increases confidence in the overall formalization.

Relevant techniques here include model checking and equational reasoning over algebraic specifications.

Deductive Design In deductive design, one constructs the implementation from the specification by some systematic way. Current methods are stepwise transformation (refinement) or extraction of a program from a proof that the specification can be satisfied.

Interplay Verification and deductive design may be combined fruitfully. For instance, one can develop a library of components using deductive design and use their initial specifications for the verification of larger systems.

4 Survey of the Chapters of the Book

The chapters of this book have been grouped according to the main research themes within NADA. Besides the language aspects dealt with in the present chapter, these themes were Mathematical Foundations, Hardware and Dynamical Systems and Verification and Deductive Design.

4.1 Mathematical Foundations

As is clear from the discussion in previous sections, streams and stream transformers are a central topic in formal hardware description. The first two chapters of this part of the book provide mathematical treatments of this subject.

The chapter *Streams, stream transformers and domain representations* by J. Blanck, V. Stoltenberg-Hansen and J.V. Tucker presents a general theory for the computation of stream transformers of the form $F : (R \to B) \to (T \to A)$, where the domains T and R for time and A and B for data may be discrete or continuous. The authors show how methods for representing topological algebras by algebraic domains can be applied to transformations of continuous streams. A stream transformer is continuous in the compact-open topology on continuous streams if and only if it has a continuous lifting to a standard algebraic domain representation of such streams. The chapter also examines the important problem of representing discontinuous streams, such as signals $T \to A$ where time T is continuous and data A is discrete.

In the chapter *Ideal stream algebra*, B. Möller provides some mathematical properties of *behaviours* of systems, where the individual elements of a behaviour are modeled by *ideals* of a suitable partial order. It is well-known that the associated ideal completion provides a simple way of constructing algebraic cpos. An ideal can be viewed as a set of consistent finite or compact approximations of an object which itself may be infinite. A special case is the domain of streams where the finite approximations are the finite prefixes of a stream. The author defines a number of operators on ideals and behaviours and proves distributivity and monotonicity laws that are the basis for correct refinement of specifications into implementations. Various small examples illustrate that the operators lead to very concise while quite clear specifications. The chapter also gives a characterization of safety and liveness and generalizes the Alpern/Schneider decomposition lemma to arbitrary domains. An extended example concerns the specification and transformational development of an asynchronous bounded queue.

The final chapter of this part, *Normalisation by evaluation* by U. Berger, M. Eberl and H. Schwichtenberg, deals with a different area of the mathematical foundations of Hardware design. It extends normalization by evaluation from the pure typedλ-calculus to general higher type term rewrite systems. This work also gives a theoretical explanation of the normalization algorithm implemented in the verification system MINLOG.

4.2 Hardware and Dynamical Systems

In *Algebraic models of superscalar microprocessor implementations: a case study*, A.C.J. Fox and N.A. Harman extend a set of algebraic tools for microprocessor specification to model superscalar microprocessor implementations, and apply them to a case study. They develop existing correctness models to accommodate the more advanced timing relationships of superscalar processors, and consider formal verification. They illustrate their tools and techniques with an in-depth treatment of an example superscalar implementation. Clocks divide time into (not necessarily equal) segments, defined by the natural timing of the computational process of a device. The authors formally relate clocks by surjective, monotonic maps called retimings. In the case of superscalar microprocessors, the normal relationship between "architectural time" and "implementation time" is complicated by the fact that events that are distinct in time at the architectural level can occur simultaneously at the implementation level.

The chapter *Hierarchies of spatially extended systems and synchronous concurrent algorithms* by M.J. Poole, A.V. Holden and J.V. Tucker takes a very broad view of hardware, including even biological systems. First, the authors study the general idea of a spatially extended system (SES) and argue that many mathematical models of systems in computing and natural science are examples of SESs. They examine the computability and the equational definability of SESs and show that, in the discrete case, there is a natural sense in which an SES is computable if, and only if, it is definable by equations. The authors look at a simple idea of hierarchical structure for SESs and, using respacings and retimings, define how one SES abstracts, approximates, or is implemented by another SES. Secondly, the authors study a special kind of SES called a synchronous concurrent algorithm (SCA). They define the simplest kind of SCA with a global clock and unit delay which are computable and equationally definable by primitive recursive equations over time. The authors focus on two examples of SCAs: a systolic array for convolution and a non-linear model of cardiac tissue. The chapter investigates the hierarchical structure of SCAs by applying the earlier general concepts for the hierarchical structure of SESs. Th authors apply the resulting SCA hierarchy to the formal analysis of both the implementation of a systolic array and the approximation of a biologically detailed model of cardiac tissue.

In *Towards an algebraic specification of the Java virtual machine* K. Stephenson develops an algebraic specification of the architecture of an abstract and simplified version of the Java Virtual Machine (JVM). This concentration on the implementation-independent features of the machine allows her to build a clean and easily comprehensible model in which its structure is emphasized. The author then axiomatizes the semantics of programs on this architecture. She also considers how one can concretize this abstract model which provides a firm foundation for exploring the entire JVM and thus of analyzing the correctness of Java implementations.

In the next chapter, J.A. Bergstra and A. Ponse study *Grid protocol specifications*. A grid protocol models concurrent computation, and consists of one or more modules repeatedly performing parallel I/O and computation. The authors provide several concise specification formats and correctness results on (external) I/O behaviour and illustrate their approach by examples.

The aim of the chapter *The computational description of analogue system behaviour* by P.T. Breuer, N. Martínez Madrid and C. Delgado Kloos is to define a simple analogue hardware description language L and give it a sound semantics that supports formal reasoning about its properties. The syntax of L is that of a hybrid programming languages but the semantics has been derived from the analogue signal semantics of the upcoming IEEE VHDL-AMS extension to the IEEE standard digital hardware description language, VHDL. L is here given two semantics. Firstly, what may be termed an exact, or hardware, semantics and, secondly, an approximation, or simulation, semantics. The simulation semantics is computable and the hardware semantics is not. The authors show that the simulation semantics approximates the hardware semantics in a well-defined sense. This property is a "no surprises' guarantee with respect to simulation for the language.

4.3 Verification and Deductive Design

This part starts with *Reasoning about imperfect digital systems* by K. Hanna. The basis of his chapter is the observation that in order to realize digital systems that operate at high speeds or that have very low power consumption, it is necessary to work directly at the analog level of abstraction, that is, in terms of analog electronic components such as resistors and transistors. Although the external behaviour of such circuits can be described digitally, their internal operation can only be explained by working at the analog level and by taking account of both voltages and currents. This chapter describes how existing methods of specification and formal verification of digital systems can be extended so as to encompass such analog designs in a fully rigorous manner.

The chapter by J. Philipps and P. Scholz is about *Formal verification and hardware design with statecharts*. Statecharts extend the concept of Mealy Machines by parallel composition, hierarchy, and broadcast communication. While Statecharts in principle are widely accepted in industry, some semantical concepts, especially broadcasting, are still contested. In this contribution, the authors present a Statechart dialect that includes the basic concepts of the language and present a formal, relational semantics for it. They show that this semantics can be used for both formal verification by model checking and hardware synthesis.

The chapter *An exercise in conditional refinement* by K. Stølen and M. Fuchs is an attempt to demonstrate the potential of conditional refinement in step-wise system development. In particular, it emphasizes the ease with which conditional refinement allows boundedness constraints to be introduced in a specification based on unbounded resources. For example, a specification based on purely asynchronous communication can be conditionally refined into a specification using time-synchronous communication. The presentation is built around a small case-study: A step-wise design of a timed FIFO queue that is partly to be implemented in hardware and partly to be implemented in software. The authors first specify the external behaviour of the queue ignoring timing and synchronization. This overall specification is then restated in a time-synchronous setting and thereafter refined into a composite specification consisting of three subspecifications: A specification of a time-synchronous hardware queue, a specification of an asynchronous software queue, and a specification of an interface component managing the communication between the first two. The authors argue that the three overall specifications can be related by conditional refinement. By further steps of conditional refinement, additional boundedness constraints are introduced. The chapter explains how each step of conditional refinement can be formally verified in a compositional manner.

The final chapter by Möller presents *Deductive hardware design: a functional approach*. As stated earlier, the goal of deductive design is the systematic construction of a system implementation starting from its behavioural specification according to formal, provably correct rules. The author uses *Haskell* to formulate a functional model of directional, synchronous and deterministic systems with discrete time. The associated algebraic laws are then employed in deductive hardware design of basic combinational and sequential circuits as well as a brief account of pipelining. With this also several of the IFIP WG 10.5 benchmark verification problems are tackled. Special emphasis is laid on parameterization and re-usability aspects.

References

1. F.L. Bauer, R. Berghammer, M. Broy, W. Dosch, F. Geiselbrechtinger, R. Gnatz, E. Hangel, W. Hesse, B. Krieg-Brückner, A. Laut, T.A. Matzner, B. Möller, F. Nickl, H. Partsch, P. Pepper, K. Samelson, M. Wirsing, H. Wössner: The Munich project CIP. Volume I: The wide spectrum language CIP-L. Lecture Notes in Computer Science **183**. Berlin: Springer 1985

2. CoFI: The Common Framework Initiative for algebraic specification and development. Web document under http://www.brics.dk/Projects/CFI/

3. W. Dosch: Calculating digital counters. In: D. Bjørner, M. Broy, I.V. Pottosin (eds.): Perspectives of Systems Informatics. Second International Andrei Ershov Memorial Conference, Akademgorodok, June 25–28, 1996. Lecture Notes in Computer Science **1181**. Berlin: Springer 1996, 21–39

4. W. Dosch: Calculating Hamming streams. In: K. Yetongnon, S. Hariri (eds.): Proc. Ninth International Conference on Parallel and Distributed Computing Systems, Vol. I. Dijon, September 25–27, 1996. Raleigh, N.J.: International Society for Computers and Their Applications 1996, 529–534

5. W. Dosch, B. Möller: Calculating a functional module for binary search trees. In: W. Kluge (ed.): Implementation of functional languages. 8th International Workshop IFL'96, Bad Godesberg, September 16-18, 1996. Lecture Notes in Computer Science **1268**. Berlin: Springer 1997, 267–284

6. G. Dowek, J. Heering, K. Meinke, B. Möller (eds): Higher-order algebra, logic and term rewriting, (HOA '95). Lecture Notes in Computer Science **1074**. Berlin: Springer 1996

7. IFIP 94/97: IFIP WG 10.5 verification benchmarks. Web document under http://goethe.ira.uka.de/hvg/benchmarks.html

8. M. Hanus, J. Heering, K. Meinke (eds): Algebraic and logic programming (Joint ALP '97 and HOA '97). Lecture Notes in Computer Science **1298**. Berlin: Springer 1997

9. B.M. Hearn and K. Meinke, ATLAS: a typed language for algebraic specification. In [10], 146-168

10. J. Heering, K. Meinke, B. Möller, T. Nipkow (eds): Higher-order algebra, logic and term rewriting (HOA '93). Lecture Notes in Computer Science **816**. Berlin: Springer 1994

11. K. Meinke: Universal algebra in higher types. Theoretical Computer Science **100**, 385–417 (1992)

12. P. Kosiuczenko,K. Meinke: On the power of higher-order algebraic specifications. Information and Computation 124, 85-101 (1995)

13. K. Meinke: Higher-order equational logic for specification, simulation and testing. In [6], 124-143

14. K. Meinke: A completeness theorem for the expressive power of higher-order algebraic specifications, Journal of Computer and Systems Sciences 54, 502-518 (1997)

15. K. Meinke: Proof theory of higher-order equations, conservativity, normal forms and term rewriting, Information and Computation (to appear)

16. K. Meinke and L.J. Steggles: Specification and verification in higher-order algebra: a case study of convolution. In [10], 189-222

17. B. Möller: Algebraic specifications with higher-order operators. In L.G.L.T. Meertens (ed.): Proc. IFIP TC2 Working Conference on Program Specification and Transformation, Bad Tölz, April 14–17, 1986. Amsterdam: North-Holland 1987, 367–398

18. B. Möller: Ordered and continuous models of higher-order specifications. In [10], 223–255
19. B. Möller (ed.): Mathematics of program construction. Third International Conference, Kloster Irsee, July 17-21, 1995. Lecture Notes in Computer Science **947**. Berlin: Springer 1995
20. B. Möller (ed.): Mathematics of program construction. Special Issue. Science of Computer Programming **26**:1–3 (1996)
21. D.L. Rhodes: Analog modeling using MHDL. In: J.-M. Bergé (ed.): Current issues in electronic modeling, Issue #2 "Modeling in analog design. Kluwer 1995
22. L.J. Steggles, Higher-order algebra with transfinite types. In [6], 238-263
23. L.J. Steggles, Parameterised higher-order algebraic specifications. In [8], 76-98
24. Systems Level Design section of the Industry Standards Roadmap. Web document under http://www.intermetrics.com/SLDL/

Streams, Stream Transformers
and Domain Representations

Jens Blanck[1], Viggo Stoltenberg-Hansen[1], and John V. Tucker[2]

[1] Dept. of Mathematics, Uppsala University, Box 480, SE-751 06 Uppsala, Sweden
[2] Dept. of Computer Science, University of Wales Swansea, Swansea SA2 8PP, Wales

Abstract. We present a general theory for the computation of stream transformers of the form $F: (R \to B) \to (T \to A)$, where time T and R, and data A and B, are discrete or continuous. We show how methods for representing topological algebras by algebraic domains can be applied to transformations of continuous streams. A stream transformer is continuous in the compact-open topology on continuous streams if and only if it has a continuous lifting to a standard algebraic domain representation of such streams. We also examine the important problem of representing discontinuous streams, such as signals $T \to A$, where time T is continuous and data A is discrete.

1   Introduction

1.1   Background

Computing systems are implemented in physical systems, and physical systems are simulated by computing systems. Because of the importance of the applications, there is a need for theoretically sound methods for modelling computations involving the interface between the continuous models of physical processes and the discrete models of algorithmic processes on digital computers. The theory of hardware design can reveal a number of common features between certain classes of computing and physical systems (see [36]). Perhaps the simplest common feature is that computing and physical systems both process streams.

A stream is simply a sequence

$$\ldots, a_t, \ldots$$

of data $a_t \in A$ indexed by time $t \in T$, i.e., a function from T to A. Time may be discrete, when typically it is modelled by the set $\mathbb{N}$ of natural numbers; or time may be continuous, when typically it is modelled by the set $\mathbb{R}_+$ of non-negative real numbers. Time may also be modelled more abstractly.

Most computing systems are designed to operate in discrete time. Their underlying algorithms and architectures are designed to process infinite streams of data such as streams of bits and bytes. Numerous examples of such systems can be found among computers, application specific chips, operating systems and networks. The theoretical development of systolic arrays, dataflow architectures and distributed parallel systems in computing have motivated a great deal of research on stream processing with discrete time. See the recent survey [41], for example. It should also be noted that discrete time streams are basic for computer modelling methods such as neural networks [1], cellular automata [59], and coupled map lattices [8, 26, 28].

Most physical systems operate in continuous time. Their mathematical models can also be viewed as processing continuous streams. For example, partial differential equations specify a function that describes the behaviour of a system from an initial state under streams of input, such as wave forms, boundary conditions, etc. There has been relatively little research on computing with continuous streams though recently the subject has been studied as part of the design of hybrid systems (see e.g. [16]).

In numerical modelling both discrete and continuous stream processing are fundamental. Solution techniques for solving differential equations, such as finite difference and finite element methods, are based on the discretisation of time and space. They involve methods for approximating continuous streams by discrete streams. Both discrete and continuous streams are needed in modelling hybrid systems for control and instrumentation.

In the light of these observations the following problem is important:

> To create a computability theory for stream processing over abstract data types that can be applied to continuous and discrete models of physical and computing systems.

1.2 Domain representations of streams and stream transformers

In this paper we present a unified semantic treatment of discrete and continuous streams, and stream transformers. We will focus on problems concerning the continuity and computability of streams and stream transformers, and we will emphasise continuous streams. The framework is based on domain representation theory, which is a theory of representing topological algebras using domains [47]. The topological algebras are used to model data types, and the domains are used to model implementations of data types.

Domain theory is an abstract theory of approximation of spaces and functions, aimed at isolating the structures underlying computation. A domain is an ordered set of approximations on which functions that are continuous in an order-theoretic sense are defined. Of special importance is the fact that domain theory possesses elegant theories of (i) constructions of spaces of continuous functions; and (ii) effectively computable domains. At the heart of the subject is an intimate relation between computability and continuity.

Domain representation theory allows domains to model concrete representations of topological algebras. To a topological algebra A is associated an algebraic domain D_A from which a subset D_A^R is selected to make a representation of A via a continuous map $\nu: D_A^R \to A$. On choosing a domain representation, problems about the computability and continuity of functions on topological algebras are translated to corresponding problems about domains (for which there is an excellent theory).

Our unified semantic framework for stream computation is as follows. Let R and T be topological algebras of time, A and B topological algebras of data, and $(R \to B)$ and $(T \to A)$ sets of streams. A *stream transformer* is a function

$$F \colon (R \to B) \to (T \to A).$$

We will allow T and R to be both discrete and continuous models of time, and allow A and B to be discrete or continuous data types. There are 16 cases in total. Discrete time is identified with the natural numbers $\mathbb{N}$ or the integers $\mathbb{Z}$ (with the discrete topology) and continuous time with the real numbers $\mathbb{R}_+$ or $\mathbb{R}$ (with the Euclidean topology) depending on whether or not there is a starting time. In particular, the framework can be applied to a complete range of computing applications, including analogue-digital transformations of the form

$$F \colon (\mathbb{R} \to B) \to (\mathbb{N} \to A) \quad \text{and} \quad F \colon (\mathbb{N} \to B) \to (\mathbb{R} \to A).$$

First, to each of the four algebras R, T, A and B we associate a domain representation D_R, D_T, D_A and D_B respectively. The domains of continuous functions $[D_R \to D_B]$ and $[D_T \to D_A]$ naturally represent stream spaces $(R \to B)$ and $(T \to A)$. Most often we will consider spaces of continuous streams, denoted $C(R \to B)$ and $C(T \to A)$. We will also consider some spaces of non-continuous streams, in particular non-zeno signals (see Section 2.7).

Next, for a stream transformer F we show how to construct a continuous function on the domains

$$\bar{F} \colon [D_R \to D_B] \to [D_T \to D_A]$$

representing F. For example, we will show (Corollary 6.9):

> A stream transformer $F \colon C(\mathbb{R} \to \mathbb{R}) \to C(\mathbb{R} \to \mathbb{R})$ *is continuous with respect to the compact-open topology if, and only if, F has a continuous representation or lifting $\bar{F} \colon [\mathcal{R} \to \mathcal{R}] \to [\mathcal{R} \to \mathcal{R}]$, where $\mathcal{R}$ is the standard interval domain representation of $\mathbb{R}$.*

The study of properties of F, such as computability, is thus reduced to the study of properties of $\bar{F}$.

Despite the smooth theory of domains, this process is not straight-forward because of the relation:

$$\textit{computability implies continuity.}$$

One problem we must deal with is that our unified framework must cope with computing with non-continuous streams.

For example, consider the sets of continuous and discrete data streams in continuous time:

$$(\mathbb{R} \to [0,1]) \text{ and } (\mathbb{R} \to \{0,1\}).$$

In the first case, many applications require models based on the subset of continuous streams (e.g., wave functions). However, in the second case every non-trivial application involving discrete signals will need discontinuous functions (since the only continuous functions $\mathbb{R} \to \{0,1\}$ are constant functions). Thus, to explicate computability, we must find some reasonable notion of representation of non-continuous streams. In particular we consider non-zeno signals $NZ(\mathbb{R}_+ \to A)$ consisting of step functions, where A is a discrete space. We show that, for certain classes of stream transformers, $F: NZ(\mathbb{R}_+ \to B) \to NZ(\mathbb{R}_+ \to A)$ has a continuous *approximate* representation $\bar{F}: [\mathcal{R}_+ \to B_\perp] \to [\mathcal{R}_+ \to A_\perp]$.

In this paper we will explain the above mathematical framework. In Section 2 the basic ideas about streams and stream transformers will be defined and several examples of transformations of time and data in streams will be presented to motivate the technical development. In Section 3 we summarise the essential ideas about algebraic domains, function spaces and effective domains that we will use. In Section 4 we explain the method of domain representation for topological algebra, including the problem of approximate representations of discontinuous functions. In Section 5 we consider domain representations of stream spaces. Finally, in Section 6 we show how domain representations of stream transformations for continuous streams and for non-zeno signals are chosen and applied.

This paper is part of a series of articles on the theory of domain representations of topological algebras [43–47]. We first considered discrete time stream computation in [46]. We thank our colleagues in the NADA Working Group for the several stimulating debates on the problems of stream computation starting with the debate led by Jan Bergstra at the first NADA meeting at Munich 1994 and the NADA stream workshop 1995 hosted by Helmut Schwichtenberg and Hans Leiss at Elmau. We also have benefitted from discussions on the subject with Jeff Zucker (McMaster), and Neal Harman and Matthew Poole (Swansea).

2 Basic properties of streams and stream transformers

2.1 General definitions

There are several notions of streams and stream transformers in the literature. In this paper we will restrict ourselves to the simplest and, in our view, the most natural notion.

Definition 2.1. Let T be a set of data modelling time and let A be any non-empty set of data. A *stream* is a total function $\varphi: T \to A$. The set of all streams from T to A is called the *complete stream space* from T to A. A *stream space* from T to A is simply a subset of the complete stream space from T to A and is usually denoted $(T \to A)$.

This definition is quite open as to what requirements one should put on time T. There are many philosophical, physical and mathematical models of time [58]. Time can be discrete or continuous. To model discrete time we choose the ordered structure of natural numbers $\mathbb{N}$, in the case time has an initial starting point, or $\mathbb{Z}$, in case there is no starting point. For simplicity in the exposition we will usually model discrete time by $\mathbb{N}$. Thus a stream with discrete time is for us simply an infinite sequence of data.

To model continuous time we choose the ordered structure of non-negative real numbers $\mathbb{R}_+$, in the case time has an initial starting point, or $\mathbb{R}$, in case there is no starting point. For simplicity we will usually model continuous time by $\mathbb{R}$, except when an initial starting point is essential. A stream with continuous time is often called a *signal*.

There are well-established notions of computability on $\mathbb{N}$ and $\mathbb{R}$ and hence on our chosen models of discrete and continuous time. Classical models of computability on the natural numbers are well-known [9, 15, 40]. Computability models on $\mathbb{R}$ have been developed since the 1950's [7, 17, 29, 37].

Our data set A is in general simply a set or an algebra. In order to discuss computability of streams and stream transformers we need to have notions of computability on our data algebras as well.

For discrete algebras we have the usual notion of computability induced by the computability on $\mathbb{N}$ in the sense of computable algebra [12, 30, 38, 47, 49].

For uncountable algebras we need a notion of computability in terms of concrete approximations. Topology can be seen as an abstract theory of approximation where an open set approximates all its elements. Usually, but not always, our data type is a metric algebra. Of course, every discrete space can be given a discrete metric inducing the discrete topology.

Assumption 2.2. *All our data types are topological algebras.*

There are several approaches to computability on topological algebras including Type-2 computability by Weihrauch [57], recursive metric spaces by Moschovakis [34], and the approach chosen in this paper, domain representation. See [48] for a discussion of the relationship between these and other approaches.

Having topologies on both time and data allows us to talk about continuity of streams. Note that each discrete time stream $\varphi\colon \mathbb{N} \to A$ is continuous for any space A. Complete stream spaces with continuous time T and non-trivial data set A will contain non-continuous streams. When A is a continuous data set, such as $\mathbb{R}$, it is natural to consider the stream space $C(T \to A)$ of continuous streams. The stream space $C(T \to A)$ has a natural topology, viz. the the compact-open topology. Note that there is no obvious or canonical topology for the complete stream space $(T \to A)$ for continuous time T.

Consider streams from continuous time into a discrete data set, i.e., signals. Then the only continuous streams are the constant streams. Non-continuous streams from continuous time to discrete data exist in abundance in models used in computing. Thus our theory of streams and stream transformations must accommodate them. In order to model non-continuous streams we use *approximate* representations in the function space domains. In this way stream spaces containing non-continuous streams (more precisely quotients of such) obtain an induced topology from the representing domains. Thus we may, via the use of domains, speak about continuity of stream transformers also in this case.

We now turn to the notion of a stream transformer.

Definition 2.3. Let $(R_i \to B_i)$ and $(T_j \to A_j)$ be stream spaces for $1 \le i \le m$ and $1 \le j \le n$. A *stream transformer* is a functional $F \colon \prod_{1 \le i \le m}(R_i \to B_i) \to \prod_{1 \le j \le n}(T_j \to A_j)$.

Thus a stream transformer is a function which takes finitely many streams as input and gives finitely many streams as output. Usually, for the simplicity of the exposition, we will restrict ourselves to the case $m = n = 1$. This is not as restrictive as it first may appear. It is often the case that all input times R_i can be identified with some common input time R and similarly for T_j and T. In this case we have

$$\prod_{1 \le i \le m}(R_i \to B_i) \cong (R \to B_1 \times \cdots \times B_m), \text{ and}$$

$$\prod_{1 \le j \le n}(T_j \to A_j) \cong (T \to A_1 \times \cdots \times A_n)$$

and we may consider F to be a stream transformer having one stream as input and giving one stream as output.

The value $F(\varphi)(t)$ of a stream transformer $F \colon (R \to B) \to (T \to A)$ at time t may in general depend on the entire input stream φ. This is not reasonable for stream transformers modelling physical devices. Also from a computability point of view it is unreasonable to require infinite information in order to compute a finite object.

Assume that time R has an initial point 0. Then a stream transformer $F \colon (R \to B) \to (T \to A)$ is said to satisfy "causality", or is "finitely determined", if for each $t \in T$ there is an $r \in R$ such that the value of $F(\varphi)$ at t is determined by φ restricted to the interval between 0 and r.

It is clear that causality of a stream transformer F is intimately connected with the "continuity" of F. The latter will be defined via the domain representation of stream transformers.

2.2 Some examples of streams and stream transformers

First we consider some examples of streams. Then we give a few general forms of stream transformers in which the main idea is to separate time conversions from data conversions. We start with a simple model and then give some extensions. In each case the models will first be motivated by an example.

Discrete time streams. Streams of the form $f \colon \mathbb{N} \to A$, where A is a nonempty set, occur *throughout* computing. Hardware systems are modelled using streams and stream transformers: at low levels of digital design, the data sets of bits and k-bit words,

$$\text{Bit} = \{0, 1\} \text{ and } \text{Word}_k = \text{Bit}^k,$$

are used to represent integers, addresses, flags, reals, pixels, etc. Devices operate in time using one or more discrete clocks, each represented by ℕ. There input-output behaviours are modelled by stream transformations of the form

$$F: [\mathbb{N} \to \text{Bit}]^n \to [\mathbb{N} \to \text{Bit}]^m.$$

For example, a thorough study of modelling a digital correlator is given in [19]. Other examples are in [18,22]. Discrete time streams and stream transformers are widely used in modelling software. One comprehensive approach, FOCUS, has been developed by Broy and his co-workers [6]. There also finite partial streams are used.

Signals. Streams of the form $f: \mathbb{R} \to \{0, 1\}$ are used in digital signal processing and are drawn as square waves

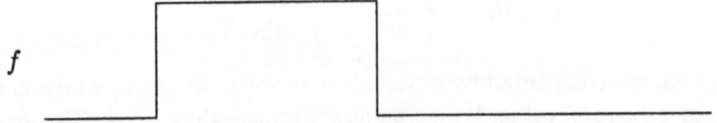

These streams do not exist in the physics of devices but are abstractions or specifications of certain streams of the form $\varphi: \mathbb{R} \to \mathbb{R}$. Transitions in voltage (or current) are "modelled" by discontinuities.

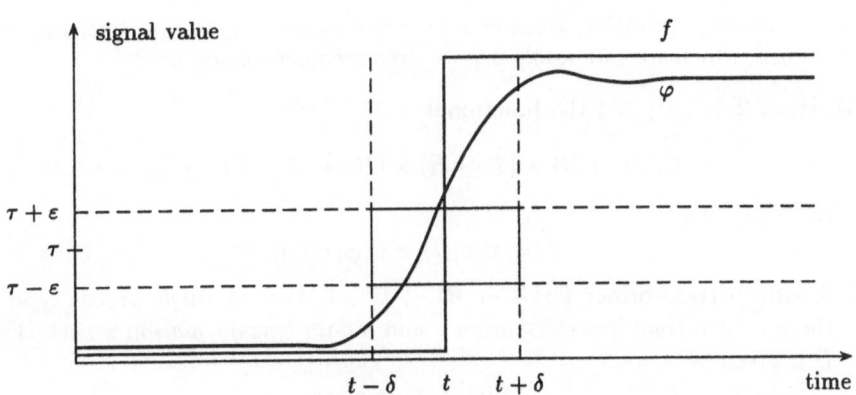

Fig. 1. A digital signal φ is modelled by a square wave form f.

A signal transition from low to high in f takes place at time t when the continuous wave φ passes a threshold value τ. Furthermore, the threshold value τ is a physical quantity that is not known exactly but to within a range

$$[\tau - \varepsilon, \tau + \varepsilon];$$

and the time t is not known exactly but within a range

$$[t - \delta, t + \delta].$$

Any waveform φ that enters the threshold range during the time range has the same square wave abstraction, see Figure 1. A device technology determines some ε and δ such that it is technically impossible to distinguish two (reasonable, steep) wave forms that pass through the box.

Single access stream transformers. Let us look at a very simple type of stream transformation. Suppose that a stream transformer simply transforms its input data at some point in time and outputs the result at some later time.

Example 2.4. Consider $G: (\mathbb{N} \to \mathbb{R}) \to (\mathbb{N} \to \mathbb{R})$, given by

$$G(\varphi)(t) = \begin{cases} 0, & \text{if } t = 0; \\ 2\varphi(t - 1), & \text{otherwise.} \end{cases}$$

Notice that we are confronted by a boundary problem at $t = 0$, which is handled by giving an arbitrary value. So let us now suppose that $t > 0$. The first thing to do when given a stream and a time at which to compute the new stream is to calculate the time of interest in the input stream by a function $\tau(t) = t - 1$. Secondly, use the input stream φ to get the input value at the appropriate time. Thirdly, calculate the output data from the input data by means of the function $\pi(n) = 2n$.

The following definition gives us a way of constructing stream transformers of this form, which we call *single access stream transformers*.

Definition 2.5. (i) Let the functional

$$\Phi: (R \to B) \times (T \to R) \times (B \to A) \to (T \to A),$$

be defined by

$$\Phi(\varphi, \tau, \pi)(t) = \pi(\varphi(\tau(t))).$$

(ii) A stream transformer $F: (R \to B) \to (T \to A)$ is of *single access* type if there exist a *time transformation* τ and a *data transformation* π such that F is given by

$$F(\varphi) = \Phi(\varphi, \tau, \pi).$$

The G of Example 2.4 can now be expressed as

$$G(\varphi) = \Phi(\varphi, \tau, \pi),$$

where τ and π are the transformations extracted in the example.

By varying the functions τ and π we get a whole family of stream transformers. Of course, not all stream transformers are of this form.

The important feature of the single access model is that it allows us to discuss time and data transformations independently.

Multiple access stream transformers. We model stream transformers that depend on the input data at several distinct times.

Example 2.6. Consider the Fibonacci stream transformer $G\colon (\mathbb{N} \to \mathbb{N}) \to (\mathbb{N} \to \mathbb{N})$, defined by

$$G(\varphi)(t) = \begin{cases} t, & \text{if } t \le 1; \\ \varphi(t-1) + \varphi(t-2), & \text{if } t \ge 2. \end{cases}$$

Clearly, G does not fit into the single access model described above since it accesses the input stream at two different times. Thus, we have two time transformations, τ_1 and τ_2, and a data transformation π taking two input data. The time and data transformations are

$$\tau_1(t) = t - 1,$$
$$\tau_2(t) = t - 2, \text{ and}$$
$$\pi(x, y) = x + y.$$

Here is a generalisation of Definition 2.5 to a finite number of accesses to the input stream.

Definition 2.7. (i) Let the functional

$$\Phi_n\colon (R \to B) \times (T \to R)^n \times (B^n \to A) \to (T \to A),$$

be defined by

$$\Phi_n(\varphi, \tau_1, \ldots, \tau_n, \pi)(t) = \pi(\varphi(\tau_1(t)), \ldots, \varphi(\tau_n(t))).$$

(ii) A stream transformer $F\colon (R \to B) \to (T \to A)$ is of *multiple access type* if there exist *time transformations* $\tau_1, \ldots, \tau_n$ and a *data transformation* π such that F is given by

$$F(\varphi) = \Phi_n(\varphi, \tau_1, \ldots, \tau_n, \pi).$$

Note that $\Phi = \Phi_1$ for Φ as in Definition 2.5.

The G of Example 2.6 can now be expressed as

$$G(\varphi) = \Phi_2(\varphi, \tau_1, \tau_2, \pi),$$

where τ_1, τ_2 and π are the transformations extracted in the example.

Accessing an interval of the input stream.

Example 2.8. Let $G\colon (\mathbb{R} \to \mathbb{R}) \to (\mathbb{R} \to \mathbb{R})$ be defined by

$$G(f)(t) = \max_{x \in [0,t]} f(x).$$

The stream transformer G depends on a continuum of values of the input stream so there is no possibility of modifying the single access model in the way done above for a finite number of accesses to the input stream.

If we generalise from the example above we could allow both endpoints of the interval to depend on t, making the data transformation to be of the following kind

$$\pi \colon (R \to B) \times R \times R \to A,$$

where π is defined by

$$\pi(f, a, b) = \max_{x \in [a,b]} f(x).$$

Instead of max we could have any of a number of common operations, e.g., the integral

$$\pi(f, a, b) = \int_b^a f(x)dx.$$

Definition 2.9.   (i) Let the functional

$$\Psi \colon (R \to B) \times (T \to R)^2 \times ((R \to B) \times R^2 \to A) \to (T \to A)$$

be defined by

$$\Psi(f, \tau_1, \tau_2, \pi)(t) = \pi(f, \tau_1(t), \tau_2(t)).$$

(ii) A stream transformer $F \colon (R \to B) \to (T \to A)$ is of *interval access* type if there exist *time transformations* τ_1, τ_2, and *data transformation* π with the property that $f = g$ on $[a, b]$ implies $\pi(f, a, b) = \pi(g, a, b)$, such that F is given by

$$F(f) = \Psi(f, \tau_1, \tau_2, \pi).$$

The stream transformer G of Example 2.8 can now be expressed as

$$G(f) = \Psi(f, \tau_1, \tau_2, \pi),$$

where τ_1, τ_2 and π are the transformations extracted in the example.

2.3   Time transformations

In the models exhibited so far we have extracted time and data transformations as parts of stream transformers. The data transformations considered are arbitrary functions on data. However, time transformations are of special interest and we will now look at some of the most fundamental time transformations.

Constant delay is modelled by a time transformation of the form

$$\tau(t) = t - d,$$

where d is the constant delay. Hence a simple delay node is

$$\Phi(\varphi, \tau, \mathrm{id}).$$

We can adjust for two clocks running at different speeds by a time transformation of the form

$$\tau(t) = kt,$$

where k is the number of time units that passes on the input clock during one time unit on the output clock. Hence, using the single access functional Φ of Definition 2.5, a stream transformer which outputs every other datum of a discrete stream is given by

$$\Phi(\varphi, \tau, \mathrm{id}),$$

where $\tau(t) = 2t$.

If the input and output clocks run at the same speed but are out of phase, then this can be modelled by

$$\tau(t) = t - m,$$

where m is the time offset. The offset is positive if the output time is ahead of the input time. There is a difference between a delay and the offset considered here since a delay cannot be negative whereas the time offset may be negative.

We have exhibited three different time transformations which are linear and can be used regardless of time being discrete or continuous. However, sometimes it is desirable to consider non-linear time transformations.

Here is a useful general class of time transformations.

Definition 2.10. A mapping $\tau : T \to R$ is a *retiming* if $\tau(0) = 0$ and τ is surjective and monotonic with respect to the orderings on T and R.

In the case that T and R are discrete clocks this notion of retiming is easy to understand and useful in both theoretical investigations and design exercises. It was introduced in a study of the design of digital correlators and further developed through applications to UARTs and micro processors, see [18, 19, 22, 23, 25].

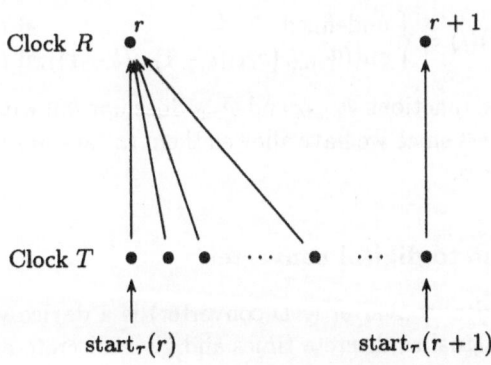

Fig. 2. A retiming τ.

A retiming $\tau: T \to R$ relates discrete clocks as in Figure 2. The figure illustrates the set

$$\tau^{-1}(r) = \{t \in T : \text{start}_\tau(r) \le t < \text{start}_\tau(r+1)\}$$

where $\text{start}_\tau(r) = (\text{least } t)[\tau(t) = r]$.

2.4 State transformations

Consider a server responding to requests. We assume that the requests appear at discrete times. The requests and the responses are easily seen to be streams, leaving us with the conclusion that the server should be modelled as a stream transformer.

The server typically has an internal state which governs the responses to the requests. We consider a server that has an internal state and is working in discrete time, i.e., $T = \mathbb{N}$.

Let I be a set of requests, O a set of responses and S a set of internal states. Suppose the server's transitions are governed by the functions

$$\text{out} : S \times I \to O, \text{ and}$$
$$\text{next} : S \times I \to S,$$

which determine the output and next state from the input and current state.

In responding to a stream of requests in discrete time, starting from some initial state, the dynamical behaviour of the server Φ is governed by

$$\Phi_{\text{state}}: S \times (T \to I) \to (T \to S)$$

$$\Phi_{\text{state}}(s, i)(t) = \begin{cases} s, & \text{if } t = 0; \\ \text{next}(\Phi_{\text{state}}(s, i)(t-1), i(t-1)), & \text{if } t > 0, \end{cases}$$

and

$$\Phi_{\text{out}}: S \times (T \to I) \to (T \to O)$$

$$\Phi_{\text{out}}(s, i)(t) = \begin{cases} \text{undefined}, & \text{if } t = 0; \\ \text{out}(\Phi_{\text{state}}(s, i)(t-1), i(t-1)), & \text{if } t > 0. \end{cases}$$

The typing of the functions Φ_{state} and Φ_{out} does not fall within our definition of stream transformers since we have allowed them to take arguments other than streams as parameters.

2.5 The analogue to digital converter

The analogue to digital converter (AD-converter) is a device which samples an analogue electrical signal at discrete times and gives discrete approximations of the analogue signal at those times.

We start by giving a very simple model of an idealistic AD-converter.

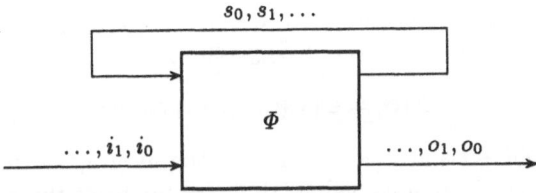

Fig. 3. Stream transformer with an internal state.

Example 2.11. Combining the use of the floor function both as a time transformation and as a data transformation in the single access model will give us a very simple model of an AD-converter. Let $G: (\mathbb{R}_+ \to \mathbb{R}) \to (\mathbb{N} \to \mathbb{Z})$ be defined by

$$G(\varphi) = \Phi(\varphi, \tau, \pi),$$

where $\tau(x) = \pi(x) = \lfloor x \rfloor$. Then G is a simple AD-converter.

We will now try to model a hardware AD-converter more faithfully. A hardware AD-converter will first bound the input signal to some closed interval. It will then sample the input stream at discrete points in time. More advanced converters will sample the input stream at several time points for every value it outputs, this is called *oversampling*. The output value is then calculated from the sampled values by some filtering algorithm.

Note that we have not made any effort to model the anomalous behaviour that hardware can exhibit if the input is widely out of range.

Example 2.12. We will model a 16-bit AD-converter with an output rate of 10 kHz, an oversampling factor of 100, and which converts the interval 0 V to 5 V.

The bounding step now amounts to bounding the input signal (stream) to the interval 0 V to 5 V. Let $B: (\mathbb{R}_+ \to \mathbb{R}) \to (\mathbb{R}_+ \to \mathbb{R})$ be defined by

$$B(\varphi) = \Phi(\varphi, \mathrm{id}, \pi),$$

where π is given by

$$\pi(x) = \max(0, \min(x, 5)).$$

Clearly, B is a stream transformer bounding the input stream in the desired way.

The sampling step can now be modelled similar to our trivial AD-converter example above. We model the sampling step by $S: (\mathbb{R}_+ \to \mathbb{R}) \to (\mathbb{N} \to \mathbb{Z})$ given by

$$S(\varphi) = \Phi(\varphi, \tau, \pi),$$

where $\tau(t) = \lfloor 10^6 \cdot t \rfloor$ and $\pi(x) = \lfloor \frac{2^{16} \cdot x}{5} \rfloor$. The constant 10^6 corresponds to the output frequency times the oversampling factor. The constant 2^{16} corresponds to 16 bit conversion. The constant 5 is the adjustment for the voltage interval.

The filtering step will become a multiple access stream transformer. We model the filtering by $F: (\mathbb{N} \to \mathbb{Z}) \to (\mathbb{N} \to \mathbb{Z})$ given by

$$F(\varphi) = \Phi_{100}(\varphi, \tau_0, \ldots, \tau_{99}, \pi),$$

where $\tau_i(t) = 100t + i$ and $\pi(x_0, \ldots, x_{99})$ is the filtering function. The filtering function will typically remove values that are far from the average value and then compute the average of the remaining values.

Our hardware AD-converter can now simply be modelled by composing the bounding, sampling and filtering stream tranformers given above. Thus we define our AD-converter $AD: (\mathbb{R}_+ \to \mathbb{R}) \to (\mathbb{N} \to \mathbb{Z})$ by

$$AD = F \circ S \circ B.$$

2.6 DA-conversion or curve fitting

A digital signal φ can be seen as a function from $\mathbb{N}$ to some discrete set (usually a finite set). We assume that the values of the digital signal form a finite subset of $\mathbb{R}$. We also assume that the discrete time is embedded into continuous time by an increasing function τ. Hence every pair $(\tau(n), \varphi(n))$ is a point in the space $\mathbb{R}_+ \times \mathbb{R}$. To convert a digital signal to an analogue signal we need to extend the enumerable set of points in $\mathbb{R}_+ \times \mathbb{R}$ to a function in $(\mathbb{R}_+ \to \mathbb{R})$. Figure 4 indicates a few alternatives of how a digital signal φ may be converted into a continuous signal. The first is to extend the point set to a step function (this is the normal description of a hardware DA-converter), the second makes a linear approximation and the third uses polynomials of degree three.

It is easy to describe the DA-converting stream transformers above. This is done for the linear case in the example below.

Example 2.13. The following stream transformer converts a digital signal to a linear analogue signal. Let $G: (\mathbb{N} \to \mathbb{Z}) \to (\mathbb{R} \to \mathbb{R})$ be given by

$$G(\varphi)(t) = \begin{cases} t\varphi(0), & \text{if } t < 1; \\ \varphi(\lfloor t-1 \rfloor) + (t - \lfloor t \rfloor)(\varphi(\lfloor t \rfloor) - \varphi(\lfloor t-1 \rfloor)), & \text{otherwise.} \end{cases}$$

It is easy to see that there are two time transformations in operation here, namely, $\tau_1(t) = \lfloor t-1 \rfloor$ and $\tau_2(t) = \lfloor t \rfloor$. However, the data transformation does not depend only on the input data at both of these times, but also on the time t. Hence this stream transformer does not fall into any of the previously discussed general forms of stream transformers.

2.7 Signal transformations

A *signal* is a stream with continuous time and discrete data. Normally, when considering signals, we consider time with a starting point, i.e. time is $\mathbb{R}_+$. Thus a signal is a function $\varphi: \mathbb{R}_+ \to A$ where A is a discrete data set. A *signal transformer* is a stream transformer taking signals to signals. Signal transformers are sometimes called *signal operators*.

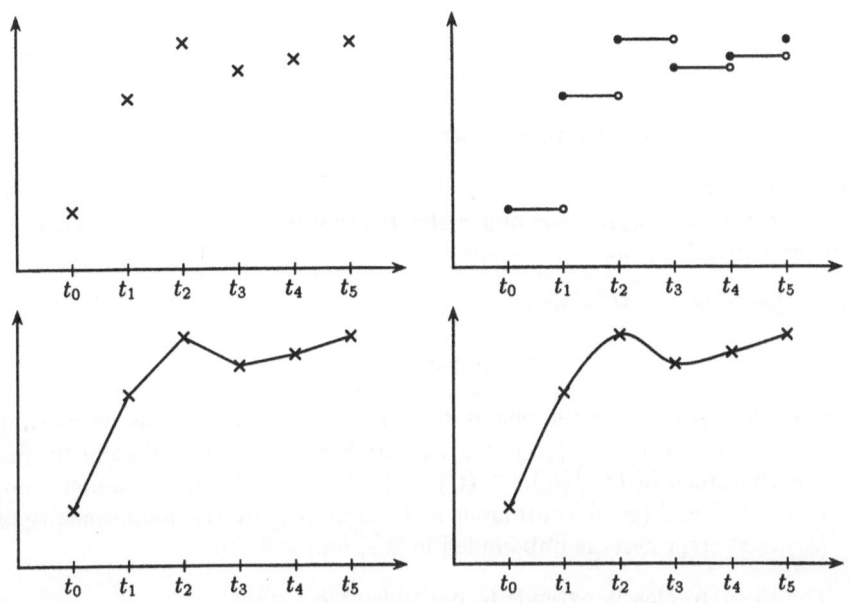

Fig. 4. DA-conversion of a digital signal φ.

Signals and operators on signals have been much studied in the literature from a computer science point of view, in particular in connection with hybrid systems [16]. Automata over continuous time is considered in [51, 39].

As mentioned earlier, the only continuous functions from $\mathbb{R}_+$ into a discrete data set A are the constant functions. Thus the class of continuous signals is no more interesting than the data set A. On the other hand it should be clear, and will be apparent later, that the class of all signals is too wide when considering signal operators. For example, the signal taking the value 0 at rational time points and the value 1 at irrational time points is too irregular to be distinguished by a reasonable operator.

From the discussion of signals in Section 2.2 we see that in order to model digital systems it suffices to consider the following subclass of signals.

Definition 2.14. Let A be a discrete countable set. A *non-zeno signal* over A is a stream $\varphi: \mathbb{R}_+ \to A$ such that φ is continuous at 0 and for each $t > 0$, φ has only finitely many discontinuities in $[0, t]$.

Thus a signal is a step function with finitely many jumps on $[0, t]$.

We now consider single and multiple access signal operators. We need to slightly strengthen the notion of retiming (Definition 2.10).

Definition 2.15. A mapping $\tau: \mathbb{R}_+ \to \mathbb{R}_+$ is a *strict retiming* if

(i) τ is surjective and monotonic;

(ii) $\tau(0) = 0$; and

(iii) $\tau(t) < \tau(t')$ whenever $\text{Init}(\tau) \leq t < t'$, where $\text{Init}(\tau) = \sup\{t \in \mathbb{R}_+ : \tau(t) = 0\}$.

Note that a strict retiming is continuous.

Theorem 2.16. *Let $F: (\mathbb{R}_+ \to B) \to (\mathbb{R}_+ \to A)$ be a single access signal operator with repect to $\pi: B \to A$ and a strict retiming $\tau: \mathbb{R}_+ \to \mathbb{R}_+$. Then F takes non-zeno signals to non-zeno signals.*

Proof. Let $\varphi: \mathbb{R}_+ \to B$ be non-zeno. Then

$$F(\varphi)(t) = \pi(\varphi(\tau(t))).$$

Assume that φ is discontinuous at $t_0 < t_1 < \ldots$. Then $\varphi\tau$ is discontinuous at precisely $\tau^{-1}(t_0) < \tau^{-1}(t_1) < \ldots$, and hence the set of discontinuities of $F(\varphi)$ is contained in $\{\tau^{-1}(t_0), \tau^{-1}(t_1), \ldots\}$. Now, $t_0 > 0$ since φ is non-zeno, so $\tau^{-1}(t_0) > 0$, i.e. $F(\varphi)$ is continuous at 0. Similarly, by the monotonicity of τ, $\tau^{-1}(t_0) < \tau^{-1}(t_1) < \ldots$ is unbounded in $\mathbb{R}_+$, unless finite. □

The theorem clearly extends to multiple access signal operators.

3 Domains

In this section we will briefly review some basic and relevant parts of domain theory. We concentrate on giving the notions and some results that are needed for our analysis. All proofs are omitted and can be found in the basic reference [42].

3.1 Preliminaries on domains

Let $D = (D, \sqsubseteq)$ be a partial order and let $A \subseteq D$. We will use the notation $\uparrow A$ to denote the set $\{y \in D : \exists x \in A(x \sqsubseteq y)\}$. The set $\uparrow\{x\}$ is abbreviated by $\uparrow x$. We define $\downarrow A$ and $\downarrow x$ dually. A is *directed* if $A \neq \emptyset$ and whenever $x, y \in A$ then there is $z \in A$ such that $x \sqsubseteq z$ and $y \sqsubseteq z$. The supremum, or least upper bound, of A (if it exists) is denoted by $\bigsqcup A$. As usual we write $x \sqcup y$ instead of $\bigsqcup\{x, y\}$.

A *complete partial order*, abbreviated *cpo*, is a partial order, $D = (D; \sqsubseteq, \bot)$, such that $\bot$ is the least element in D and any directed set $A \subseteq D$ has a supremum $\bigsqcup A$ in D.

Let D be a cpo. Then an element $a \in D$ is *compact* if whenever $A \subseteq D$ is a directed set and $a \sqsubseteq \bigsqcup A$, then $a \in \downarrow A$. The set of compact elements of D is denoted by D_c.

A cpo D is *algebraic* if for each $x \in D$, the set

$$\text{approx}(x) = \downarrow x \cap D_c$$

is directed and $x = \bigsqcup \text{approx}(x)$. A cpo D is *consistently complete* if $\bigsqcup A$ exists in D whenever $A \subseteq D$ is a consistent set, i.e., has an upper bound.

The domains we consider in this paper are of the following kind.

Definition 3.1. A *Scott–Ershov domain*, or simply *domain*, is a consistently complete algebraic cpo.

The topology normally used on domains is called the *Scott topology*. Let D be an algebraic cpo. Then $U \subseteq D$ is *open* if

(i) $x \in U$ and $x \sqsubseteq y$ implies $y \in U$, and
(ii) $x \in U$ implies that there exists $a \in \text{approx}(x)$ such that $a \in U$.

An easy observation is that the Scott topology on a non-trivial domain is T_0 but not T_1. Furthermore, the sets $\uparrow a$ for $a \in D_c$ constitute a base for the Scott topology on D. We will also write B_a for $\uparrow a$.

Let D and E be cpo's. A function $f \colon D \to E$ is continuous with respect to the Scott topology if, and only if, f is monotone and

$$f(\bigsqcup A) = \bigsqcup f[A],$$

for any directed set $A \subseteq D$.

Any continuous function between domains is determined by its values on the compact elements. In fact, let D and E be domains. Then a monotone function $f \colon D_c \to E$ has a unique extension to a continuous function $g \colon D \to E$ such that $f = g|_{D_c}$.

A *conditional upper semi-lattice with least element*, abbreviated *cusl*, is a partially ordered set where each finite bounded set has a least upper bound. The set of compact elements D_c of a domain D forms a cusl. Every domain is obtained as a completion of a cusl in the following way.

Definition 3.2. Let P be a cusl. Then $I \subseteq P$ is an *ideal* if

(i) $I \neq \emptyset$,
(ii) $a \in I$ and $b \sqsubseteq a$ implies $b \in I$, and
(iii) $a, b \in I$ implies $a \sqcup b$ exists and $a \sqcup b \in I$.

For $a \in P$ we let $[a]$ denote the principal ideal generated by a. The ideal completion of a cusl P is the set of all ideals over P, denoted $\text{Idl}(P)$. When ordered by set inclusion the ideal completion of a cusl is a domain. The compact elements of $\text{Idl}(P)$ are the principal ideals $[a]$, for $a \in P$.

The representation theorem for Scott–Ershov domains tells us that any domain is the ideal completion of a cusl.

Theorem 3.3. *Let D be a Scott–Ershov domain. Then* $\text{Idl}(D_c) \cong D$.

We clearly have the following equivalence, for $I \in \text{Idl}(P)$

$$[a] \subseteq I \iff a \in I.$$

Thus the basic open sets of $\text{Idl}(P)$ in the Scott topology are of the form $B_a = \{I \in \text{Idl}(P) : a \in I\}$ for $a \in P$.

The class of domains has pleasing closure properties. In particular, what is essential for our purposes, the category of domains is cartesian closed. Most importantly, this means that for any domains D and E, the function space

$$[D \to E] = \{f \colon D \to E \mid f \text{ is continuous}\}$$

is a domain, where the ordering $\sqsubseteq$ on $[D \to E]$ is given by $f \sqsubseteq g \iff (\forall x \in D)(f(x) \sqsubseteq g(x))$.

We recall some basic facts, and notations, of the compact elements in $[D \to E]$. For $a \in D_c$ and $b \in E_c$ we consider the "step function" $\langle a; b \rangle \colon D \to E$ defined by

$$\langle a; b \rangle(x) = \begin{cases} b, & \text{if } a \sqsubseteq x; \\ \bot, & \text{otherwise.} \end{cases}$$

Then $\langle a; b \rangle$ is continuous and compact. Furthermore, for any $f \in [D \to E]$ we have

$$\langle a; b \rangle \sqsubseteq f \iff b \sqsubseteq f(a).$$

The compact elements of $[D \to E]$ are those of the form

$$\bigsqcup_{i=1}^{n} \langle a_i; b_i \rangle,$$

where $\{\langle a_i; b_i \rangle : i = 1, \ldots, n\}$ is *consistent* (i.e. bounded) in $[D \to E]$. And the latter holds if, and only if, for each $I \subseteq \{1, \ldots, n\}$,

$$\{a_i : i \in I\} \text{ consistent} \implies \{b_i : i \in I\} \text{ consistent.}$$

Recall that consistent completeness is used to prove the above properties. In fact, the class of algebraic cpo's is *not* closed under the function space construction.

3.2   Effective domains

In this section we briefly recall some basic notions of effectivity or computability on domains. We start by recalling some general notions.

A *structure* A is a tuple $A = (A; R_1, \ldots, R_p; \sigma_1, \ldots, \sigma_q)$, where A is a non-empty set, $R_j \subseteq A^{n_j}$ is an n_j-ary relation and $\sigma_i \colon A^{n_i} \to A$ is an n_i-ary operation on A. A *numbering* of a structure A is a surjective function $\alpha \colon \Omega_\alpha \to A$, where $\Omega_\alpha \subseteq \omega$. Let $\equiv_\alpha$ denote the equivalence relation defined on Ω_α by

$$m \equiv_\alpha n \iff \alpha(m) = \alpha(n).$$

Definition 3.4. Let $\alpha \colon \Omega_\alpha \to A$ be a numbering of the structure $A = (A; R_1, \ldots, R_p; \sigma_1, \ldots, \sigma_q)$. Then α is a *weakly effective numbering* of A and the pair (A, α) is a *weakly effective structure* if (i) and (ii) below hold.

(i) For each $i = 1, \ldots, q$ there is an n_i-ary partial recursive function $\hat{\sigma}_i$ such that for each $m_1, \ldots m_{n_i} \in \Omega_\alpha$, $\hat{\sigma}_i(m_1, \ldots, m_{n_i})\!\downarrow$ (where $\downarrow$ means defined) and

$$\sigma_i\big(\alpha(m_1), \ldots, \alpha(m_{n_i})\big) = \alpha\big(\hat{\sigma}_i(m_1, \ldots, m_{n_i})\big).$$

(ii) For each $j = 1, \ldots, p$ there is an n_j-ary recursive relation $\hat{R}_j$ such that for each $m_1, \ldots, m_{n_j} \in \Omega_\alpha$,

$$R_j\big(\alpha(m_1), \ldots, \alpha(m_{n_j})\big) \iff \hat{R}_j(m_1, \ldots, m_{n_j}).$$

We say that $\hat{\sigma}_i$ and $\hat{R}_j$ *track* σ_i and R_j respectively.

Definition 3.5. A weakly effective numbering α of a structure A is *computable* if Ω_α is a recursive set and $\equiv_\alpha$ is a recursive relation. If α is computable then the pair (A, α) is a *computable structure*.

Let (A, α) and (B, β) be weakly effective structures. A function $f: A \to B$ is (α, β)-*computable* if there is a partial recursive function $\hat{f}$ such that $\Omega_\alpha \subseteq \text{dom}(\hat{f})$ and for each $m \in \Omega_\alpha$, $f(\alpha(m)) = \beta(\hat{f}(m))$.

A partial function $g: A \to B$ is (α, β)-*computable* if there is a partial recursive function $\hat{g}$ such that $\text{dom}(g \circ \alpha) \subseteq \text{dom}(\hat{g})$ and $g(\alpha(m)) = \beta(\hat{g}(m))$, for $m \in \text{dom}(g \circ \alpha)$.

A set $C \subseteq A$ is α-*decidable* (α-*semidecidable*) if there is a recursive (r.e.) set W such that $\alpha^{-1}[C] = W \cap \Omega_\alpha$. A recursive (r.e.) index for W, in the usual sense of recursion theory, is called a recursive (r.e.) α-index of C.

When regarding computability on a cusl we are often not only interested in having a decidable ordering but also having a decidable consistency relation and the ability to compute suprema of finite consistent sets. Therefore we consider a cusl to be a structure of the form

$$P = (P; \sqsubseteq, \text{Cons}, \sqcup, \bot).$$

Definition 3.6. Let P be a cusl. Then (P, α) is a *computable cusl* if α is a computable numbering of the structure $P = (P; \sqsubseteq, \text{Cons}, \sqcup, \bot)$. A domain D is an *effective domain* if there is α such that (D_c, α) is a computable cusl. We denote this effective domain by (D, α).

It is clear from earlier remarks about the function space that if D and E are effective domains then so is $[D \to E]$ with a numbering obtained uniformly from the numberings of D and E.

We now extend computability from the cusl of computable elements to the whole domain.

Definition 3.7. Let (D, α) be an effective domain. Then $x \in D$ is α-*computable* if approx(x) is α-semidecidable. An r.e. index of the set $\alpha^{-1}[\text{approx}(x)]$ is an α-*index* of the computable element x.

The prefix α will be dropped when the numbering is clear from the context. Let $D_k = \{x \in D : x \text{ is computable}\}$. Note that $D_c \subseteq D_k$.

Definition 3.8. Let (D, α) and (E, β) be effective domains. A continuous function $f: D \to E$ is (α, β)-*effective* if the relation $R \subseteq D_c \times E_c$ defined by

$$R(a, b) \iff b \sqsubseteq f(a)$$

is (α, β)-semidecidable, that is the relation

$$\hat{R}(m, n) \iff R(\alpha(m), \alpha(n))$$

is r.e. An r.e. index for $\hat{R}$ is an *effective index for f* with respect to α and β.

Lemma 3.9. *Let (D, α), (E, β) and (F, γ) be effective domains and let $f: D \to E$ and $g: E \to F$ be continuous and (α, β)-effective and (β, γ)-effective respectively.*

(i) *If $x \in D$ is α-computable then $f(x) \in E$ is β-computable.*
(ii) *The composition $h = g \circ f$ is (α, γ)-effective.*

We observe that the standard proof, see [42], is uniform. That is, we can uniformly obtain an index for $f(x)$ from indices for f and x. Similarly an index for h is obtained uniformly from indices of f and g.

We can extend computability via a numbering from D_c to the computable elements D_k in the following way.

Theorem 3.10. *Let (D, α) be an effective domain. Then there is a numbering $\bar{\alpha}: \omega \to D_k$ such that*

(i) *the inclusion mapping $\iota: D_c \to D_k$ is $(\alpha, \bar{\alpha})$-computable and,*
(ii) *the relation $R(n, m) \iff \alpha(n) \sqsubseteq \bar{\alpha}(m)$ is r.e., i.e.,* approx$(\bar{\alpha}(m))$ *is α-semidecidable uniformly in m.*

It can be shown that the numbering $\bar{\alpha}$ is the unique one satisfying (i) and (ii), up to recursive equivalence, see [42]. This numbering is the "correct" one since it identifies effectiveness and computability for functions.

Theorem 3.11. *Let (D, α) and (E, β) be effective domains. Then a continuous function $f: D \to E$ is (α, β)-effective if, and only if, $f|_{D_k}: D_k \to E_k$ is $(\bar{\alpha}, \bar{\beta})$-computable.*

In fact, the theorem in its stronger form says that any $(\bar{\alpha}, \bar{\beta})$-computable function $\bar{f}: D_k \to E_k$ extends to a continuous (α, β)-effective $f: D \to E$.

4 Domain representability

Our overall aim is to model streams and stream transformers using domains in a uniform way covering both discrete and continuous time and discrete and continuous data. The method we choose is *domain representation* in which time T and data A are represented by domains D_T and D_A, and a stream space is represented by the domain $[D_T \to D_A]$. First we recall the basic notions of domain representability and then we describe standard domain representations of metric spaces. Finally, in order to model non-continuous streams, we generalise the notion of domain representation to approximate representations. This is related to domain representations of structures with relations.

4.1 Basic definitions

We briefly recall some basic definitions and facts about domain representability. For motivation and details we refer to [47].

Let X and Y be topological spaces. Recall that function $\nu \colon X \to Y$ is a *quotient mapping* if $U \subseteq Y$ is open if, and only if, $\nu^{-1}[U]$ is open in X. In case ν is surjective we then have that $X/\sim$ and Y are homeomorphic spaces when the former is given the quotient topology and where $\sim$ is the equivalence relation induced on X by ν, i.e., $x \sim y \iff \nu(x) = \nu(y)$. Here is the basic definition.

Definition 4.1. Let X be a topological space, let D be a domain and D^R a subset of D. Then (D, D^R, ν) is a *domain representation* of X if $\nu \colon D^R \to X$ is a surjective quotient map when D^R is given the (relativised) Scott topology. In case (D, α) is an effective domain then (D, D^R, ν, α) is an *effective domain representation* of X.

Thus a domain representation (D, D^R, ν) of X contains both concrete and proper approximations of elements of X, the compact elements in D_c, and "total" elements in D^R containing sufficient information to represent elements of X exactly via ν. Since the function ν in the definition above is a quotient map we have

$$D^R/\sim \;\cong\; X.$$

Definition 4.2. A domain representation (D, D^R, ν) of a space X is

(i) *upwards closed* if whenever $x \in D^R$ and $x \sqsubseteq y$ then $y \in D^R$ and $\nu(x) = \nu(y)$;

(ii) *dense* if for each $a \in D_c$, $\uparrow a \cap D^R \neq \emptyset$;

(iii) *local* if $(\forall x, y \in D^R)(\nu(x) = \nu(y) \implies x$ and y are consistent$)$.

Upwards closed domain representations (D, D^R, ν) are natural when regarding the ordering $\sqsubseteq$ on D as an information ordering. If $x \in D^R$ completely determines $\nu(x) \in X$ and $x \sqsubseteq y$ then y contains all the information of x and hence also completely determines $\nu(x)$. All domain representations considered in this paper are upwards closed.

The usual way to construct a domain representation of a space X is to consider an *approximation structure* of concrete approximations of X. An approximation structure most often takes the form of a cusl $P = (P; \sqsubseteq, \bot)$. Then the representing domain is the ideal completion $\mathrm{Idl}(P)$ of P. A space X will have many domain representations. It is up to the "user" to choose a representation appropriate for his or her purposes. We refer to [47] for a discussion of approximation structures.

The next step is to represent continuous functions between topological spaces.

Definition 4.3. Let (D, D^R, ν) and (E, E^R, μ) be domain representations of X and Y respectively. A function $f \colon X \to Y$ is *represented* by (or *lifts* to) a continuous function $\bar{f} \colon D \to E$ if $\bar{f}(D^R) \subseteq E^R$ and $\mu(\bar{f}(x)) = f(\nu(x))$, for all $x \in D^R$.

This means that the following diagram commutes.

$$
\begin{array}{ccc}
D & \xrightarrow{\bar{f}} & E \\[4pt]
\uparrow & & \uparrow \\[4pt]
D^R & \xrightarrow{\bar{f}|_{D^R}} & E^R \\[4pt]
\nu \downarrow & & \downarrow \mu \\[4pt]
X & \xrightarrow{\quad f \quad} & Y
\end{array}
$$

Let (D, D^R, ν) and (E, E^R, μ) be domain representations of X and Y respectively. Suppose $\bar{f}: D \to E$ is such that $\bar{f}[D^R] \subseteq E^R$ and such that $\nu(x) = \nu(y) \implies \mu(\bar{f}(x)) = \mu(\bar{f}(y))$. Then $\bar{f}$ induces a unique function $f: X \to Y$ defined by $f(\nu(x)) = \mu(\bar{f}(x))$. In the terminology above, f is represented by $\bar{f}$.

Proposition 4.4. *If $f: X \to Y$ is represented by a continuous $\bar{f}: D \to E$ then f is continuous.*

The proof is simple and depends on the fact that ν is assumed to be a quotient (only continuity of μ is required).

Recall that D_k is the set of computable elements of the effective domain (D, α). Suppose the topological space X is represented by (D, D^R, ν, α). Then the set X_k of (D, D^R, ν, α)-*computable elements* of X is the set

$$
X_k = \{ x \in X : \nu^{-1}(x) \cap D_k \neq \emptyset \}.
$$

Let $\bar{\alpha}$ be the canonical numbering of D_k obtained from α as in Theorem 3.10 and let $\Omega = \{ n \in \omega : \nu(n) \in D^R \}$. Define $\tilde{\alpha}: \Omega \to X_k$ by

$$
\tilde{\alpha}(n) = \nu(\bar{\alpha}(n)).
$$

The numbering $\tilde{\alpha}$ is the *canonical numbering of X_k obtained from the domain representation* (D, D^R, ν, α).

Now suppose (E, E^R, μ, β) is a domain representation of Y and suppose $f: X \to Y$ has an (α, β)-*effective* representation $\bar{f}: D \to E$. Then we say that f is (α, β)-*effective*. It follows from the results for effective domains that $f[X_k] \subseteq Y_k$ and $f|_{X_k}: X_k \to Y_k$ is $(\tilde{\alpha}, \tilde{\beta})$-computable. Sufficient conditions for when an $(\tilde{\alpha}, \tilde{\beta})$-computable function $g: X_k \to Y_k$ can be extended to an $(\tilde{\alpha}, \tilde{\beta})$-effective function $f: X \to Y$ is established in [2, Theorem 2.27]. These conditions are met by the real numbers $\mathbb{R}$, as well as by many other recursive metric spaces.

We see that an effective domain representation of a topological space X induces effectivity on X. Thus the effectivity of X in the sense described here is dependent on the effective domain representation chosen. It is shown in [48] that other notions of effectivity considered in the literature for topological spaces and algebras, such as the algebra of real numbers $\mathbb{R}$, are obtainable from effective domain representations, showing that the method of domain representation is not only flexible and general but also has sufficient strength.

For a discrete space X we have a domain representation $(X_\perp, X, \mathrm{id})$. Here is another representation providing more information in the sense of having a richer set of approximations.

Example 4.5. Let X be a discrete topological space and let $E = \{X\} \cup \mathcal{P}_f(X) \setminus \{\emptyset\}$ be the domain of finite subsets of X ordered by reverse inclusion. Let E^R consist of all singleton sets in E. Then (E, E^R, ν) is a domain representation of X where $\nu(\{x\}) = x$, in fact,

$$E^R \cong X.$$

We will denote the domain E by $\mathcal{P}_f(X)$.

4.2 Standard representations of metric spaces

We will briefly describe how to construct a domain representation of a metric space X. The domain representation constructed here will be referred to as a *standard domain representation*.

Definition 4.6. Let X be a metric space and let P be a family of non-empty closed subsets of X, containing X but not $\emptyset$. Then P is a *closed neighbourhood system* for X if the following are satisfied:

(i) if $F, F' \in P$ and $F \cap F' \neq \emptyset$ then $F \cap F' \in P$, and
(ii) if $x \in U$, where U is open, then $(\exists F \in P)(x \in F^\circ \wedge F \subseteq U)$.

Here F° denotes the interior of F.

A closed neighbourhood system P is a cusl when ordered by reverse inclusion. Clearly each metric space has a closed neighbourhood system since metric spaces are regular.

Let X be a metric space with metric d and choose a closed neighbourhood system P for X. Let D be the ideal completion of the cusl $(P; \sqsubseteq, X)$, where $\sqsubseteq$ is reverse inclusion. For $F \in P$ we let

$$\text{diam}(F) = \sup_{x,y \in F} d(x, y).$$

Definition 4.7. An ideal $I \in D$ is *converging* if

$$(\forall \varepsilon > 0)(\exists F \in I)(\text{diam}(F) < \varepsilon).$$

It is easy to see that the intersection of a converging ideal is a singleton set. Let D^R be the set of converging ideals and define $\nu: D^R \to X$ by

$$\nu(I) = x \iff \bigcap I = \{x\}.$$

Theorem 4.8. *Let X be a metric space. Then (D, D^R, ν) constructed as above is a domain representation of X, which is upwards closed, dense and local.*

We say that (D, D^R, ν) is a *standard domain representation* of X.

Theorem 4.9. *Let (D, D^R, ν) and (E, E^R, μ) be standard domain representations of metric spaces X and Y respectively. Then every continuous function $f: X \to Y$ can be represented by a continuous function $\bar{f}: D \to E$.*

The proof of the theorems above can be found in [2].

For the real numbers $\mathbb{R}$ we choose in this paper the closed neighbourhood system

$$P = \{[a,b] : a \leq b \text{ and } a,b \in \mathbb{Q}\} \cup \{\mathbb{R}\}$$

and denote its ideal completion $\text{Idl}(P)$ by $\mathcal{R}$. Clearly, P is a computable cusl and hence $\mathcal{R}$ is an effective domain. Thus $\mathcal{R} = (\mathcal{R}, \mathcal{R}^R, \nu)$ is an effective domain representation of $\mathbb{R}$. It is shown in [47] that the computability on $\mathbb{R}$ induced by $\mathcal{R}$ coincides with the notions of computability usually considered in recursive analysis (e.g. in [37]).

It is easy to see that for an irrational point $x \in \mathbb{R}$ there exists only one converging ideal, namely the ideal $I_x = \{[a,b] : a < x < b\}$. However, for a rational point $r \in \mathbb{R}$ there exist four different converging ideals representing r. The existence of several ideals representing the same point in $\mathbb{R}$ is necessary for topological reasons. The converging ideals representing a rational point r are:

$$I_r = \{[a,b] : a < r < b\},$$
$$I_r^+ = \{[a,b] : a \leq r < b\},$$
$$I_r^- = \{[a,b] : a < r \leq b\}, and$$
$$I^r = \{[a,b] : a \leq r \leq b\}.$$

These are ordered as indicated in the following diagram.

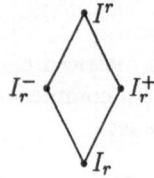

Effective representations exist for a large class of metric spaces. However, often a more intricate construction than the one above is needed; see [2].

A discrete topological space X can be given a discrete metric. Then $(X_\perp, X, \text{id})$ is (isomorphic to) a standard representation of X in the sense above. Similarly, the representation in Example 4.5 is a standard representation of X.

4.3 Representing relations and non-continuous functions

Streams need not be continuous. Thus, in order to represent such a stream space by a function space domain, we need a way to represent a non-continuous function by a continuous function between domains. By Proposition 4.4 we know that this is impossible. We have to settle for representing non-continuous functions *approximately*.

An analogous problem is how to represent a relation on a space. A canonical example is the space of real numbers $\mathbb{R}$. How do we represent the $\leq$ relation? The problem is that relations in terms of their characteristic functions are often not continuous.

Let X be a topological space and let $\mathbb{B} = \{\text{true, false}\}$ be the discrete boolean space. An n-ary relation P on X can be identified with its *characteristic function* $c_P : X \to \mathbb{B}$ defined by

$$c_P(a_1, \ldots, a_n) = \begin{cases} \text{true, if } P(a_1, \ldots, a_n); \\ \text{false, if } \neg P(a_1, \ldots, a_n). \end{cases}$$

The idea is to represent the possibly non-continuous characteristic function continuously in such a way that it gives exact values at points of continuity and only proper approximations at points of discontinuity. We know that this is the best possible.

Let (D, D^R, ν) be a domain representation of X and let P be an n-ary relation on X. Define $\bar{c}_P : D_c^n \to \mathbb{B}_\perp$ by

$$\bar{c}_P(a) = \begin{cases} \text{true, if } (\forall \boldsymbol{x} \in (D^R)^n)(a \sqsubseteq \boldsymbol{x} \implies P(\nu(\boldsymbol{x}))); \\ \text{false, if } (\forall \boldsymbol{x} \in (D^R)^n)(a \sqsubseteq \boldsymbol{x} \implies \neg P(\nu(\boldsymbol{x}))); \\ \perp, \quad \text{otherwise.} \end{cases}$$

$\bar{c}_P$ is clearly monotone and hence extends uniquely to a continuous function

$$\bar{c}_P : D^n \to \mathbb{B}_\perp.$$

We say that $\bar{c}_P$ *represents c_P or P approximately.*

Example 4.10. Consider the standard interval representation $\mathcal{R}$ of the reals and the relation $\leq$. Then

$$\bar{c}_\leq([a, b], [c, d]) = \begin{cases} \text{true, if } b \leq c; \\ \text{false, if } d < a; \\ \perp, \quad \text{otherwise.} \end{cases}$$

Note that $\bar{c}_\leq$ is effective. If $x < y$ in $\mathbb{R}$ then $\bar{c}_\leq(I_x, I_y) = \text{true}$ and if $y < x$ in $\mathbb{R}$ then $\bar{c}_\leq(I_x, I_y) = \text{false}$. In case $x = y$ then $\bar{c}_\leq(I_x, I_x) = \perp$.

The function $c_\leq : \mathbb{R}^2 \to \mathbb{B}$ is continuous on

$$\{(x, y) : x \neq y\} \subseteq \mathbb{R}^2,$$

and discontinuous on the diagonal. Thus $\bar{c}_\leq$ represents $c_\leq$ exactly on points of continuity. At points of discontinuity $\bar{c}_\leq$ only provides the trivial approximation of the value of $c_\leq$.

It is well-known that $\leq$ is not decidable or even semidecidable on the recursive reals $\mathbb{R}_k$, the problem being that equality on $\mathbb{R}_k$ is not semidecidable. (Equality is cosemidecidable, i.e., $\neq$ is semidecidable.) This is reflected by the discontinuity of $c_\leq$.

We now want to generalise the continuous representation of relations to continuous representations of non-continuous functions. The idea is the same. We want our representation to be exact at points of continuity and as good as possible in terms of approximations at points of discontinuity. Here is the definition.

Definition 4.11. Let (D, D^R, ν_X) and (E, E^R, ν_Y) be domain representations of the topological spaces X and Y, respectively. Then a function $f: X \to Y$ (not necessarily continuous) is said to be *represented approximately* by (or *lifts approximately* to) $\bar{f}: D \to E$ if

(i) $\bar{f}$ is continuous,
(ii) $(\forall x \in D^R)(f$ continuous at $\nu_X(x) \implies \bar{f}(x) \in E^R$ and $f\nu_X(x) = \nu_Y \bar{f}(x))$, and
(iii) $(\forall x \in D^R)(f$ not continuous at $\nu_X(x) \implies (\exists y \in \nu_Y^{-1}[f\nu_X(x)])(\bar{f}(x) \sqsubseteq y))$.

The following example illustrates the notion above.

Example 4.12. The floor function $\lfloor \cdot \rfloor: \mathbb{R} \to \mathbb{Z}$ is discontinuous at precisely the integer points. We shall represent the floor function by a continuous domain function in the above precise sense.

Let $\mathcal{R}$ be the standard interval domain representation of $\mathbb{R}$. We could choose $\mathbb{Z}_\perp$ as a representation of $\mathbb{Z}$ and proceed as in the case of representing relations. However we can do much better if we choose a domain representation with more care. Let $(\mathcal{P}_f(\mathbb{Z}), \mathcal{P}_f(\mathbb{Z})^R, \mu)$ be the domain representation of $\mathbb{Z}$ described in Example 4.5. Define $f: \mathcal{R}_c \to \mathcal{P}_f(\mathbb{Z})$ by

$$f([a, b]) = \{m \in \mathbb{Z} : \lfloor a \rfloor \leq m \leq \lfloor b \rfloor\}$$

and $f(\mathbb{R}) = \mathbb{Z}$ (i.e., f is strict). Clearly, f is monotone and hence extends uniquely to a continuous function $f: \mathcal{R} \to \mathcal{P}_f(\mathbb{Z})$.

Let $x \in \mathbb{R}$ and let $I_x \in \mathcal{R}^R$ be the smallest ideal representing x. If x is not an integer then $f(I_x) = \{\lfloor x \rfloor\}$. Thus f represents the floor function exactly for all points of continuity. Now consider an integer m. Recall the four different representations of m described in Section 4.2. It is easily seen that

$$f(I_m) = \{m - 1, m\},$$
$$f(I_m^-) = \{m - 1, m\},$$
$$f(I_m^+) = \{m\}, \text{ and}$$
$$f(I^m) = \{m\}.$$

It follows that f represents the floor function approximately in the sense of Definition 4.11. However, thanks to our choice of representation for $\mathbb{Z}$ we are able to obtain much information also at points of discontinuity. This illustrates the importance of choosing appropriate representations of the data types. Had we chosen $\mathbb{Z}_\perp$ to represent $\mathbb{Z}$ then the representation of the floor function would provide no information at points of discontinuity.

We close this section by showing that under rather general conditions, satisfied by the representations considered in this paper, there is a best continuous approximate representation of an arbitrary function, if there is one at all.

Theorem 4.13. *Let (D, D^R, ν_X) and (E, E^R, ν_Y) be domain representations of X and Y, respectively. Assume that D^R is dense in D, and that (E, E^R, ν_Y) is upwards closed and local. Let $f: X \to Y$ be a function and assume that f has one approximate representation in $[D \to E]$. Then there is a best approximate representation $\bar{f} \in [D \to E]$ in the sense of the domain ordering.*

It should be remarked that in the cases of streams that we consider we always have an approximate representation (see Theorem 5.2) and hence a best approximate representation. However, this representation is best only in the sense of the domain ordering. It may not be the best in the sense of computability, i.e. there may be a computable representation even though the best representation is not computable. Of course, the latter only affects the values at points of discontinuity.

Proof. Let $\mathcal{A}_f = \{\bar{f} \in [D \to E]: \bar{f} \text{ represents } f \text{ approximately}\}$. We show that $\mathcal{A}_f$ is directed. $\mathcal{A}_f \neq \emptyset$ by assumption. Suppose $\bar{f}_1, \bar{f}_2 \in \mathcal{A}_f$. We first show that $\bar{f}_1$ and $\bar{f}_2$ are consistent. For this it suffices by the density of D^R to show that $\bar{f}_1(x)$ and $\bar{f}_2(x)$ are consistent for each $x \in D^R$.

Fix $x \in D^R$ and assume f is continuous at $\nu_X(x)$. Thus $\bar{f}_1(x), \bar{f}_2(x) \in E^R$ and
$$\nu_Y(\bar{f}_1(x)) = \nu_Y(\bar{f}_2(x)) = f(\nu_X(x)).$$
But by the hypotheses on (E, E^R, ν_Y) the supremum $\bar{f}_1(x) \sqcup \bar{f}_2(x)$ exists and
$$\nu_Y(\bar{f}_1(x) \sqcup \bar{f}_2(x)) = f(\nu_X(x)).$$

Now assume f is discontinuous at $\nu_X(x)$. Then there are $y_1, y_2 \in E^R$ such that $\nu_Y(y_1) = \nu_Y(y_2) = f(\nu_X(x))$ and $\bar{f}_1(x) \sqsubseteq y_1$ and $\bar{f}_2(x) \sqsubseteq y_2$. Again, by the assumptions on (E, E^R, ν_Y),
$$\bar{f}_1(x) \sqcup \bar{f}_2(x) \sqsubseteq y_1 \sqcup y_2 \in E^R$$
and $\nu(y_1 \sqcup y_2) = f(\nu_X(x))$. We conclude that $\bar{f}_1$ and $\bar{f}_2$ are consistent and $\bar{f}_1 \sqcup \bar{f}_2 \in \mathcal{A}_f$, that is, $\mathcal{A}_f$ is directed.

Let $\bar{f} = \bigsqcup \mathcal{A}_f$. We need to show that $\bar{f} \in \mathcal{A}_f$. Let $x \in D^R$ be such that f is continuous at $\nu_X(x)$ and let $\bar{g} \in \mathcal{A}_f$. Then $\bar{g}(x) \sqsubseteq \bar{f}(x)$ and $\bar{g}(x) \in E^R$ so $\bar{f}(x) \in E^R$ and
$$\nu_Y(\bar{f}(x)) = \nu_Y(\bar{g}(x)) = f(\nu_X(x)).$$

Now suppose f is discontinuous at $\nu_X(x)$. Let $\bar{y} \in E^R$ be the maximal element such that $\nu_Y(\bar{y}) = f(\nu_X(x))$. The assumptions on (E, E^R, ν_Y) imply that such $\bar{y}$ exists. Thus $\bar{g}(x) \sqsubseteq \bar{y}$ and hence
$$\bar{f}(x) = \bigsqcup \{\bar{g}(x) : \bar{g} \in \mathcal{A}_f\} \sqsubseteq \bar{y},$$

proving that $\bar{f} \in \mathcal{A}_f$. □

5 Modelling streams

In this section we give a semantic model for a set of streams $T \to A$ using the function space of the representing domains.

Let (D_T, D_T^R, ν_T) and (D_A, D_A^R, ν_A) be domain representations of T and A respectively. Then, as described in Section 4.1, D_T and D_A capture the original topologies of T and A, or, alternatively, induce topologies on T and A. The domain $[D_T \to D_A]$ contains only continuous functions. Thus, by Proposition 4.4, any function $f \colon T \to A$ (totally) represented by $\bar{f} \in [D_T \to D_A]$ as in Definition 4.3 is continuous.

When time T is discrete it is natural to model T by $\mathbb{N}$ or $\mathbb{Z}$ (depending on the existence of an initial time) with the discrete topology. In this case every function from T to A is continuous, i.e., all streams from T to A are continuous.

Let us now consider continuous time T. In this case we model T by $\mathbb{R}_+$ or $\mathbb{R}$ with their usual topologies. Assume that A is a discrete set of data, i.e., A has the discrete topology. Then the continuous streams from T to A are precisely the constant streams since T is a connected space. Thus all interesting streams from continuous time to discrete data are non-continuous. One way to deal with such streams, necessary from a view of computability, is apparent via the use of domains. A stream f in the complete stream space $(T \to A)$ is represented by a continuous function $\bar{f} \colon D_T \to D_A$ which gives correct values at (the representation of) points of continuity of f and approximate values at points of discontinuity (see Definition 4.11).

Here is the formal definition.

Definition 5.1. Let time T and data A have domain representations (D_T, D_T^R, ν_T) and (D_A, D_A^R, ν_A) respectively and let $(T \to A)$ be a stream space. Then $[D_T \to D_A]$ is an *approximate domain representation* of $(T \to A)$ if each stream $\varphi \in (T \to A)$ has an approximate representation $\bar{\varphi}$ in $[D_T \to D_A]$.

To simplify the presentation we make the assumption that discrete time is modelled by $\mathbb{N}$ and continuous time is modelled by $\mathbb{R}$. The reader can easily modify all arguments for the mentioned variants of models for time.

As domain representation for time T we choose $(\mathbb{N}_\perp, \mathbb{N}, \mathrm{id})$ in the discrete case and the standard interval domain representation $\mathcal{R}$ of $\mathbb{R}$ for the continuous case. We denote either representation by D_T.

Theorem 5.2. *Let T be time, discrete or continuous, and let A be a data type. Assume that A is a metric space and let (D_A, D_A^R, ν_A) be a standard domain representation of A. Then each stream*

$$\varphi \colon T \to A$$

has an approximate representation $\bar{\varphi}$ in $[D_T \to D_A]$.

Thus the complete stream space from T to A has an approximate domain representation using the function space obtained from standard domain representations of time and data. Of course, a discrete space is a metric space when given a discrete metric.

Recall that $\mathcal{R}_c$, the cusl of compact elements of $\mathcal{R}$, consists of all closed intervals with rational endpoints and $\mathbb{R}$, ordered by reverse inclusion.

Proof. If T is discrete then each stream $\varphi: T \to A$ is continuous. By Theorem 4.9, φ lifts to a continuous function $\bar{\varphi}: D_T \to D_A$.

Now we assume that T is continuous time and is modelled by $\mathbb{R}$ with the standard interval domain representation $\mathcal{R}$.

Let $\varphi: T \to A$ be a stream. We define $\bar{\varphi}: \mathcal{R}_c \to D_A$ by

$$\bar{\varphi}([a, b]) = \{F \in (D_A)_c : \varphi([a, b]) \subseteq F^\circ\},$$

where F° denotes the interior of F. Then $\bar{\varphi}$ is monotone and extends uniquely to a continuous function $\bar{\varphi}: \mathcal{R} \to D_A$. In fact,

$$\bar{\varphi}(I) = \{F \in (D_A)_c : (\exists [a, b] \in I)(\varphi([a, b]) \subseteq F^\circ)\}.$$

Suppose φ is continuous at the point $x \in T$ and consider the ideal $I_x = \{[a, b] : a < x < b\} \in \mathcal{R}^R$. Recall that I_x is the smallest ideal representing x. Let $J = \bar{\varphi}(I_x)$. We need to show that $J \in D_A^R$ and that $\nu_A(J) = \varphi(x)$. Put differently, we need to show that $\bigcap J = \{\varphi(x)\}$. Obviously $\varphi(x) \in \bigcap J$. Given $\varepsilon > 0$, take $F \in (D_A)_c$ such that

$$\varphi(x) \in F^\circ \subseteq F \subseteq B(\varphi(x), \varepsilon),$$

where the latter is the open ε-ball around $\varphi(x)$. Since φ is continuous at x and F° is open there are $a', b' \in \mathbb{Q}$, $a' < x < b'$ and $\varphi[(a', b')] \subseteq F^\circ$. But then there is $[a, b] \in I_x$ such that

$$\varphi[\,[a, b]\,] \subseteq \varphi[(a', b')] \subseteq F^\circ,$$

i.e., $F \in J$. But $\text{diam}(F) < \varepsilon$ and ε was arbitrary. It follows that $\bigcap J = \{\varphi(x)\}$.

Now suppose $x \in T$ is a point of discontinuity of φ. It suffices to show

$$I \supseteq I_x \implies \bar{\varphi}(I) \sqsubseteq I_{\varphi(x)}.$$

But this follows directly from the definition of $\bar{\varphi}$. □

The theorem shows that the domain of continuous functions $[D_T \to D_A]$ contains representations of all streams from T to A. The representations are, however, only approximate on points of discontinuity. From a computational point of view this is quite reasonable. We cannot compute exactly on continuous data types, including continuous time, we can only compute on approximations of data. At points of continuity we obtain approximations of arbitrary precision. At points of discontinuity we can only expect proper approximations. However, with an appropriate choice of domain representation this may nonetheless produce important information.

Corollary 5.3. *Each stream $\varphi: T \to A$ has a best representation $\bar{\varphi}$ in $[D_T \to D_A]$.*

Proof. The hypotheses of Theorem 4.13 are satisfied for standard representations. □

From an approximate domain representation of the complete stream space $(T \to A)$ we define an equivalence relation $\sim$ on $(T \to A)$ by saying that $\varphi \sim \psi$ if they have the same best approximation. Thus we obtain a domain representation in the sense of Definition 4.1 of $(T \to A)/\sim$.

Finally we consider computability of streams. Note that by Ceitin's theorem [7] each computable stream $\varphi \colon T \to A$, where A is a computable metric space in the sense of [2], is continuous. Thus in order to consider "computability" of non-continuous streams it is necessary to consider approximate representations.

Definition 5.4. Let $(D_T, D_T^R, \nu_T, \alpha)$ and $(D_A, D_A^R, \nu_A, \beta)$ be effective domain representations of time T and data A, respectively. Then a stream $\varphi \colon T \to A$ is *computable* if there is an (α, β)-effective $\bar{\varphi} \in [D_T \to D_A]$ representing φ approximately.

As an example we consider non-zeno signals into a discrete space A. (Recall Definition 2.14.)

We choose the domain representation $\mathcal{P}_f(A)$ for A. This is clearly an effective domain when A is countable, and the set of maximal elements is decidable.

Let $\mathcal{R}_+$ be the standard interval domain representation of $\mathbb{R}_+$ obtained as the ideal completion of the cusl

$$\{[a, b] : 0 \leq a \leq b \text{ and } a, b \in \mathbb{Q}\} \cup \{\mathbb{R}_+\}$$

ordered by reverse inclusion.

Proposition 5.5. *If φ is a non-zeno signal represented by $\bar{\varphi} \in [\mathcal{R}_+ \to \mathcal{P}_f(A)]$ then*

$$Z \sqsubseteq \bar{\varphi}([a, b]) \implies \varphi[[a, b]] \subseteq Z.$$

Proof. Assume $Z \sqsubseteq \bar{\varphi}([a, b])$ and let $x \in [a, b]$. Note that $[a, b] \in I^x$, the largest ideal representing x. If φ is continuous at x then $\bar{\varphi}(I^x) = \{\varphi(x)\}$. But $[a, b] \in I^x$ so $Z \supseteq \bar{\varphi}([a, b]) \supseteq \{\varphi(x)\}$. If φ is not continuous at x then, by definition, we have $\bar{\varphi}(I^x) \sqsubseteq \{\varphi(x)\}$, i.e., again $\varphi(x) \in Z$. □

Proposition 5.6. *Suppose φ is a computable non-zeno signal represented by the effective $\bar{\varphi} \in [\mathcal{R}_+ \to \mathcal{P}_f(A)]$. Then each discontinuity of φ is a recursive real.*

Proof. Suppose $x \in \mathbb{R}_+$ is a point of discontinuity. Let $a < x < b$ be rational so that φ is constant on (a, x) and on (x, b). Let

$$I = \{[c, d] : (\exists c', d')(\exists m, n \in A)(a < c < c' < d' < d < b,$$
$$\bar{\varphi}([c, c']) = \{m\}, \bar{\varphi}([d', d]) = \{n\} \text{ and } m \neq n)\}.$$

Note that I is semidecidable. If $[c, d] \in I$ then $\varphi[(a, x)] = \{m\}$ and $\varphi[(x, b)] = \{n\}$ so $x \in (c, d)$. Let y be such that $a < y < x$. Then, by the continuity of φ at y, there is $[c, c'] \in I_y$ such that $\bar{\varphi}([c, c']) = \{m\}$. Similarly, we obtain appropriate $[d', d]$. That is, I generates the ideal I_x. We have shown that I_x is a computable element of D and hence that x is a recursive real. □

Finally we note that for a computable non-zeno signal φ, the set of recursive reals at which φ is continuous is semidecidable (recall the exact definition in Section 3.2). For φ is continuous at x if, and only if,

$$(\exists [a, b] \in I_x)(\bar{\varphi}([a, b]) \in \mathcal{P}_f(A)^R).$$

6   Modelling stream transformers

Now we consider stream transformers $F\colon (R \to B) \to (T \to A)$. We have already seen that some stream spaces naturally include non-continuous streams. It is equally clear that there are natural stream transformers which take continuous streams to non-continuous streams. For example, let $A = B$ be a non-trivial discrete data type, R discrete time and T continuous time. Let $\tau\colon T \to R$ and define $F\colon (R \to B) \to (T \to A)$ by

$$F(\varphi)(t) = \varphi(\tau(t)).$$

Then every stream in $(R \to B)$ is continuous and hence a non-trivial F takes some continuous streams to non-continuous streams, that is, natural stream transformers do not necessarily preserve continuity.

On the other hand there is an intuitive feeling that a stream transformer that we would want to model should be continuous in the sense that approximations to the value of an output stream at a specific time should only depend on a "finite" part or approximation of the input stream. In order to make this precise we need to model approximations of streams, and for this our method of domain representability is natural.

6.1   Transformations of continuous streams

In this subsection we consider the following question. When does a continuous stream transformer

$$F\colon \mathrm{C}(R \to B) \to \mathrm{C}(T \to A)$$

taking continuous streams to continuous streams have a continuous lifting

$$\bar{F}\colon [D_R \to D_B] \to [D_T \to D_A]?$$

More precisely, let $\mathrm{C}(R \to B)$ and $\mathrm{C}(T \to A)$ denote the spaces of *continuous* streams, where B and A are metric spaces and where R and T is any pair of our usual models of time. The spaces of continuous streams $\mathrm{C}(R \to B)$ and $\mathrm{C}(T \to A)$ are given the *compact-open topology*. On $\mathrm{C}(T \to A)$ this is the topology generated by the subbasic open sets

$$\mathrm{W}(K, U) = \{ f \in (T \to A) \mid f[K] \subseteq U \},$$

where $K \subseteq T$ is compact and $U \subseteq A$ is open. By a continuous stream transformer $F\colon \mathrm{C}(R \to B) \to \mathrm{C}(T \to A)$ we mean that F is continuous with respect to the compact-open topologies.

Let (D_A, D_A^R, ν_A) and (D_B, D_B^R, ν_B) be standard domain representations of A and B respectively. For simplicity in the exposition we choose $\mathbb{N}$ to model discrete time and $\mathbb{R}$ to model continuous time. The domain representations we consider for time are $(\mathbb{N}_\perp, \mathbb{N}, \mathrm{id})$ and $(\mathcal{R}, \mathcal{R}^R, \mu)$, respectively, where $\mathcal{R}$ is the standard interval domain representing $\mathbb{R}$.

Given time T and data set A, with the chosen domain representations as above, let

$$[D_T \to D_A]^R = \{f \in [D_T \to D_A] : f[D_T^R] \subseteq D_A^R\}.$$

We know by Proposition 4.4 that each $f \in [D_T \to D_A]^R$ induces a unique continuous function $\tilde{f} : T \to A$. Denoting $\tilde{f}$ by $\nu(f)$ we obtain the following theorem.

Theorem 6.1. $([D_T \to D_A], [D_T \to D_A]^R, \nu)$ *is an upwards closed domain representation of* $\mathrm{C}(T \to A)$, *when the latter is given the compact-open topology.*

The theorem follows from the fact that T is locally compact and that standard domain representations of T and A are used. The proof of the general fact appears in Blanck [3]. The special case of $T = A = \mathbb{R}$ appears in di Gianantonio [14].

In order to answer the question initially posed in this section, we first prove the following general lifting theorem.

Theorem 6.2. *Let X be a topological space with a dense domain representation (E, E^R, ν). Let T and A be time and data as above with domain representations D_T and D_A. Then each continuous*

$$\varphi : X \to \mathrm{C}(T \to A)$$

has a continuous lifting

$$\bar{\varphi} : E \to [D_T \to D_A].$$

Proof. We consider the case $T = \mathbb{R}$ and $D_T = \mathcal{R}$. The proof for $T = \mathbb{N}$ is similar but simpler.

For $a \in E_c$ let $B_a = \{x \in E : a \sqsubseteq x\}$, the basic open set determined by a. Define $\bar{\varphi} : E_c \to [\mathcal{R} \to D_A]$ by

$$\bar{\varphi}(a) = \bigsqcup \{ \bigsqcup_{i=1}^{n} \langle [c_i, d_i]; G_i \rangle : n \geq 1 \text{ and}$$

$$(\forall i = 1, \ldots, n)(\varphi\nu[B_a \cap E^R] \subseteq \mathrm{W}([c_i, d_i], G_i^o)) \}.$$

To see that $\bar{\varphi}(a)$ is well-defined consider $\langle [c_i, d_i]; G_i \rangle$ for $i = 1$ and 2 where $\varphi\nu[B_a \cap E^R] \subseteq \mathrm{W}([c_i, d_i], G_i^o)$. We must show that $\langle [c_1, d_1]; G_1 \rangle$ and $\langle [c_2, d_2]; G_2 \rangle$ are consistent. Suppose $[c_1, d_1] \cap [c_2, d_2] \neq \emptyset$ with $y \in \mathbb{R}$ as a witness. Let $x \in B_a \cap E^R$, which exists by the density of E^R. Then $\varphi\nu(x)(y) \in G_1 \cap G_2$ so $\langle [c_1, d_1]; G_1 \rangle$ and $\langle [c_2, d_2]; G_2 \rangle$ are consistent. Generalising the argument to arbitrary elements in $[\mathcal{R} \to D_A]_c$ proves that φ is well-defined.

It is clear from its definition that φ is monotone and hence extends uniquely to a continuous function $\bar{\varphi} : E \to [\mathcal{R} \to D_A]$. We now show that $\bar{\varphi}$ represents φ. Let $\bar{x} \in E^R$ and suppose $\nu(\bar{x}) = x \in X$. We need to show that $\upsilon(\bar{\varphi}(\bar{x})) = \varphi(x)$

where $([\mathcal{R} \to D_A], [\mathcal{R} \to D_A]^R, v)$ is the domain representation of $C(\mathbb{R} \to A)$. For this it suffices to show, for $y \in \mathbb{R}$,

$$I_{\varphi(x)(y)} \sqsubseteq \bar{\varphi}(\bar{x})(I_y).$$

Let $G \in I_{\varphi(x)(y)}$, that is, $\varphi(x)(y) \in G^\circ$. By the continuity of $\varphi(x)$ there is $[c, d] \in I_y$ such that $\varphi(x) \in W([c, d], G^\circ)$. By the continuity of φ the set $\nu^{-1}\varphi^{-1}[W([c, d], G^\circ)]$ is open. Choose $a \in E_c$ such that

$$\bar{x} \in B_a \cap E^R \subseteq \nu^{-1}\varphi^{-1}[W([c, d], G^\circ)].$$

Thus $a \sqsubseteq \bar{x}$ and

$$\varphi(x) = \varphi\nu(\bar{x}) \in \varphi\nu[B_a \cap E^R] \subseteq W([c, d], G^\circ).$$

But then

$$\langle [c, d]; G \rangle \sqsubseteq \bar{\varphi}(a) \sqsubseteq \bar{\varphi}(\bar{x})$$

and hence, since $[c, d] \in I_y$, $G \sqsubseteq \bar{\varphi}(\bar{x})(I_y)$. This shows that $I_{\varphi(x)(y)} \sqsubseteq \bar{\varphi}(\bar{x})(I_y)$. $\square$

In view of the above theorem it suffices, for the problem at hand, to consider sufficient conditions for density of the domain representation $[D_R \to D_B]$ of the space of continuous streams $C(R \to B)$. We first consider the case when R is discrete, i.e., $R = \mathbb{N}$.

Lemma 6.3. $[\mathbb{N}_\perp \to D_B]$ *is a dense representation of* $C(\mathbb{N} \to B)$.

Proof. Suppose $\bigsqcup_{i=1}^{k} \langle n_i; F_i \rangle \in [\mathbb{N}_\perp \to D_B]_c$. Without loss of generality, recalling the definition of a closed neighbourhood system, we can assume the n_i are distinct. Choose $x_0 \in B$ and $x_i \in F_i$. Then define $f: \mathbb{N}_\perp \to D_B$ by

$$f(n) = \begin{cases} I_{x_i} \sqcup [F_i], & \text{if } n = n_i; \\ I_{x_0}, & \text{if } n \neq n_i, \text{for } i = 1, \ldots, k; \end{cases}$$

and $f(\perp) = \perp$. Clearly $\bigsqcup_{i=1}^{k} \langle n_i; F_i \rangle \sqsubseteq f$ and $f \in [\mathbb{N}_\perp \to D_B]^R$.

In case $\langle \perp; F \rangle$ appears in the compact element we alter the definition of f by choosing $x_i \in F \cap F_i$, $x_0 \in F$, and setting $f(\perp) = [F]$. $\square$

An effective domain representation (D, D^R, ν, α) is *effectively dense* if there is a total recursive function d which given an α-index of $a \in D_c$ computes an $\bar{\alpha}$-index of some $x \in D^R$ such that $a \sqsubseteq x$. That is, for each $n \in \omega$,

$$\alpha(n) \sqsubseteq \bar{\alpha}d(n) \in D^R.$$

It follows from the proof of Lemma 6.3 that if D_B is an effective domain representation of B then the domain representation

$$([\mathbb{N}_\perp \to D_B], [\mathbb{N}_\perp \to D_B]^R, \nu)$$

of $C(\mathbb{N} \to B)$ is effectively dense.

Corollary 6.4. *Let R be discrete time, let T be discrete or continuous time, and let A and B be metric spaces. Then each continuous stream transformer*

$$F: C(R \to B) \to C(T \to A)$$

lifts to a continuous

$$\bar{F}: [D_R \to D_B] \to [D_T \to D_A].$$

The case when R is continuous time, i.e. R is modelled by $\mathbb{R}$, is more delicate. The density of the domain representation $[\mathcal{R} \to D_B]$ depends on topological properties of the metric space B and the standard domain representation D_B of B. Note that if B is a discrete metric space, say $\mathbb{N}$ with standard domain representation $(\mathbb{N}_\perp, \mathbb{N}, \mathrm{id})$, then $[\mathcal{R} \to \mathbb{N}_\perp]$ is not a dense representation. For example,

$$\langle [0,1]; 1 \rangle \sqcup \langle [2,3]; 2 \rangle$$

has no representing element above it.

Below we let $\mathcal{R}$ be the standard interval domain representation of $\mathbb{R}$ and we let (E, E^R, μ) be a standard domain representation of a metric space X. For each $[a,b] \in \mathcal{R}_c$ and $F \in E_c$ we use the notation

$$\langle\!\langle [a,b]; F \rangle\!\rangle = \{ f: \mathbb{R} \to X \mid f \text{ is continuous and } f([a,b]) \subseteq F \}.$$

Lemma 6.5. *Let $f \in \bigcap_{i=1}^{n} \langle\!\langle [a_i, b_i]; F_i \rangle\!\rangle$. Then $\{ \langle [a_i, b_i]; F_i \rangle : i = 1, \ldots, n \}$ is consistent in $[\mathcal{R} \to E]$ and there is $\tilde{f} \in [\mathcal{R} \to E]^R$ representing f such that*

$$\bigsqcup_{i=1}^{n} \langle [a_i, b_i]; F_i \rangle \sqsubseteq \tilde{f}.$$

Proof. If $x \in \bigcap_{i \in I} [a_i, b_i]$ for $I \subseteq \{1, \ldots, n\}$ then $f(x) \in \bigcap_{i \in I} F_i$ proving the consistency statement.

Let $\tilde{f} \in [\mathcal{R} \to E]$ represent f. The function space representation is upwards closed so it suffices to show that $\tilde{f}$ and $\bigsqcup_{i=1}^{n} \langle [a_i, b_i]; F_i \rangle$ are consistent. For the latter it suffices to consider consistency with each compact approximation of $\tilde{f}$. So suppose $\bigsqcup_{i=1}^{m} \langle [c_i, d_i]; G_i \rangle \sqsubseteq \tilde{f}$. Let $I \subseteq \{1, \ldots, n\}$ and $J \subseteq \{1, \ldots, m\}$, and suppose

$$\left(\bigcap_{i \in I} [a_i, b_i] \right) \cap \left(\bigcap_{j \in J} [c_j, d_j] \right) \neq \emptyset$$

with x as a witness. Then $f(x) \in \bigcap_{i \in I} F_i$ by hypothesis. Consider the maximal ideal I^x representing x. Thus $\tilde{f}(I^x)$ represents $f(x)$. But for each $j \in J$, $x \in [c_j, d_j]$ and $\langle [c_j, d_j]; G_j \rangle \sqsubseteq \tilde{f}$ so $G_j \in \tilde{f}(I^x)$. But then $f(x) = \mu(\tilde{f}(I^x))$, that is, $f(x) \in G_j$. We have shown that $(\bigcap_{i \in I} F_i) \cap (\bigcap_{j \in J} G_j) \neq \emptyset$. $\square$

Definition 6.6. A space X is *arcwise connected* if for every pair of distinct points $x_1, x_2 \in X$ there is a continuous embedding $h: [0,1] \to X$ such that $h(0) = x_1$ and $h(1) = x_2$.

Lemma 6.7. *Let X be a metric space with a standard representation (E, E^R, μ). Suppose X is arcwise connected and each $F \in E_c$ is arcwise connected. Then the function space representation $([\mathcal{R} \to E], [\mathcal{R} \to E]^R, \gamma)$ is dense.*

Note that the representation $\mathcal{R}$ of $\mathbb{R}$ satisfies the hypotheses. Similarly there is a standard representation of $\mathbb{R}^n$ satisfying the hypotheses.

Proof. It suffices to find $f \in \bigcap_{i=1}^n \langle\!\langle [a_i, b_i]; F_i \rangle\!\rangle$ for each $\bigsqcup_{i=1}^n \langle [a_i, b_i]; F_i \rangle \in E_c$, by Lemma 6.5. Fix such a compact element. Partition $\{1, \ldots, n\}$ into $I_1, \ldots, I_k$ such that $\bigcup_{i \in I_j} [a_i, b_i]$ is connected but

$$\left(\bigcup_{i \in I_j} [a_i, b_i] \right) \cap \left(\bigcup_{i \in I_l} [a_i, b_i] \right) = \emptyset$$

for $j \neq l$. Then $\bigcup_{i \in I_j} [a_i, b_i] = [\bar{a}_j, \bar{b}_j]$ and we may assume that $\bar{b}_j < \bar{a}_{j+1}$ for $j = 1, \ldots, k-1$.

Assume we have constructed $f_j \in \bigcap_{i \in I_j} \langle\!\langle [a_i, b_i]; F_i \rangle\!\rangle$ for $j = 1, \ldots, k$. Since the space X is arcwise connected there are continuous functions g_j for $j = 1, \ldots, k-1$ such that $g_j(\bar{b}_j) = f_j(\bar{b}_j)$ and $g_j(\bar{a}_{j+1}) = f_{j+1}(\bar{a}_{j+1})$. These functions can now be glued together to define

$$f(x) = \begin{cases} f_1(\bar{a}_1), & \text{if } x \leq \bar{a}_1; \\ f_j(x), & \text{if } \bar{a}_j \leq x \leq \bar{b}_j, j = 1, \ldots, k; \\ g_j(x), & \text{if } \bar{b}_j \leq x \leq \bar{a}_{j+1}, j = 1, \ldots, k-1; \\ f_k(\bar{b}_k), & \text{if } \bar{b}_k \leq x. \end{cases}$$

Clearly f is continuous and $f \in \bigcap_{i=1}^n \langle\!\langle [a_i, b_i]; F_i \rangle\!\rangle$.

Thus it suffices to consider the case when $\bigcup_{i=1}^n [a_i, b_i]$ is connected. Let $c_1 < c_2 < \cdots < c_k$ be a strictly increasing listing of the set $\{a_1, \ldots, a_n\} \cup \{b_1, \ldots, b_n\}$. For each j, choose $d_j \in \bigcap_{c_j \in [a_i, b_i]} F_i$ and let $I_j = \{i : (c_j, c_{j+1}) \subseteq [a_i, b_i]\}$. Then $I_j \neq \emptyset$ and $d_j, d_{j+1} \in \bigcap_{i \in I_j} F_i$. By assumption $\bigcap_{i \in I_j} F_i$ is arcwise connected, since E_c is closed under intersection, so there is a continuous function g_j such that $g_j(c_j) = d_j$, $g_j(c_{j+1}) = d_{j+1}$, and $g_j([c_j, c_{j+1}]) \subseteq \bigcap_{i \in I_j} F_i$. Now we define $f : \mathbb{R} \to X$ by

$$f(x) = \begin{cases} d_1, & \text{if } x \leq c_1; \\ g_j(x), & \text{if } c_j \leq x \leq c_{j+1}, j = 1, \ldots, k-1; \\ d_k, & \text{if } c_k \leq x. \end{cases}$$

Then f is continuous and $f \in \bigcap_{i=1}^n \langle\!\langle [a_i, b_i]; F_i \rangle\!\rangle$. $\qquad \square$

It is worth noting that for $X = \mathbb{R}$ and $E = \mathcal{R}$, the representation

$$([\mathcal{R} \to \mathcal{R}], [\mathcal{R} \to \mathcal{R}]^R, \nu)$$

of $C(\mathbb{R} \to \mathbb{R})$ is effectively dense.

Theorem 6.8. *Let R be continuous time, let T be discrete or continuous time, and let A and B be metric spaces with standard domain representations D_A and D_B. Assume B is arcwise connected and each $F \in (D_B)_c$ is arcwise connected. Then a stream transformer*

$$F \colon \mathrm{C}(R \to B) \to \mathrm{C}(T \to A)$$

is continuous if, and only if, F has a continuous lifting

$$\bar{F} \colon [D_R \to D_B] \to [D_T \to D_A].$$

Proof. By Proposition 4.4, Lemma 6.7 and Theorem 6.2. □

In particular we have

Corollary 6.9. *A functional $F \colon \mathrm{C}(\mathbb{R} \to \mathbb{R}) \to \mathrm{C}(\mathbb{R} \to \mathbb{R})$ is continuous with respect to the compact-open topology if, and only if, F has a continuous lifting $\bar{F} \colon [\mathcal{R} \to \mathcal{R}] \to [\mathcal{R} \to \mathcal{R}]$.*

D. Normann [35] has recently extended our results about density and lifting to the whole finite type structure over $\mathcal{R}$.

To summarise, we have shown that a continuous stream transformer

$$F \colon \mathrm{C}(R \to B) \to \mathrm{C}(T \to A)$$

has a continuous lifting

$$\bar{F} \colon [D_R \to D_B] \to [D_T \to D_A].$$

if R is discrete time or if R is continuous time and $B = \mathbb{R}$ or $\mathbb{R}^n$.

In the remaining case when R is continuous time and B is a discrete space then $\mathrm{C}(R \to B)$ is homeomorphic to B.

6.2 Simple transformations of non-continuous streams

The characterisation theorems in Section 6.1 provide domain representation methods for many examples of transformations acting on *continuous* streams $\mathrm{C}(R \to B)$. However, transformations of signals with discrete data, such as signals from $\mathbb{R}_+$ to $\mathbb{N}$, which are necessarily discontinuous when non-constant, are not covered though they are important in system modelling.

In Section 5 we saw how to provide domain representations of discontinuous streams (Theorem 5.2) and, in particular, the class of non-zeno signals. Now we will look at their transformations: we will show how to provide domain representations for stream transformations that are single or multiple access on non-zeno signals, see Section 2.2.

First we need to be precise about what we mean by a stream transformer on non-zeno signals having a domain representation.

Below we let $\mathcal{R}_+$ denote the standard closed interval domain representation of $\mathbb{R}_+$ and we let A and B denote discrete spaces with, for simplicity, flat domain representations. The stream space of non-zeno signals over A is denoted by

$$\mathrm{NZ}(\mathbb{R}_+ \to A).$$

For non-zeno signals it is reasonable to modify the notion of approximate representation as follows.

Definition 6.10. The function $\bar{\varphi} \in [\mathcal{R}_+ \to A_\perp]$ is a *non-zeno representation* of $\varphi \in \mathrm{NZ}(\mathbb{R}_+ \to A)$ if

(i) for each $t > 0$, the set $\{t' \in [0, t]: \bar{\varphi}(I_{t'}) = \perp\}$ is finite and does not contain 0, and

(ii) $\bar{\varphi}$ represents φ exactly for all t such that $\bar{\varphi}(I_t) \neq \perp$.

The set $\{t \in \mathbb{R}_+: \bar{\varphi}(I_t) = \perp\}$ is called the *exceptional set* for the representation $\bar{\varphi}$ of φ.

Definition 6.11. Let $F: \mathrm{NZ}(\mathbb{R}_+ \to B) \to \mathrm{NZ}(\mathbb{R}_+ \to A)$ be a stream transformer on non-zeno signals. Then

$$\bar{F}: [\mathcal{R}_+ \to B_\perp] \to [\mathcal{R}_+ \to A_\perp]$$

is an *approximate non-zeno representation* or *lifting* of F if $\bar{F}$ is continuous and whenever $\bar{\varphi} \in [\mathcal{R}_+ \to B_\perp]$ is a non-zeno representation of $\varphi \in \mathrm{NZ}(\mathbb{R}_+ \to B)$ then $\bar{F}(\bar{\varphi})$ is a non-zeno representation of $F(\varphi)$.

Recall from Section 2.7 that single or multiple access signal operators with strict retimings take non-zeno signals to non-zeno signals.

Theorem 6.12. *Let* $F: \mathrm{NZ}(\mathbb{R}_+ \to B) \to \mathrm{NZ}(\mathbb{R}_+ \to A)$ *be a single access stream transformer with respect to* $\pi: B \to A$ *and a strict retiming* $\tau: \mathbb{R}_+ \to \mathbb{R}_+$, *where* A *and* B *are discrete spaces. Then* F *has an approximate non-zeno representation*

$$\bar{F}: [\mathcal{R}_+ \to B_\perp] \to [\mathcal{R}_+ \to A_\perp]$$

Proof. Define $\bar{F}: [\mathcal{R}_+ \to B_\perp]_c \to [\mathcal{R}_+ \to A_\perp]$ by

$$\bar{F}\left(\bigsqcup_{i=1}^{k} \langle [a_i, b_i]; x_i \rangle\right) = \bigsqcup\left\{\langle [c, d]; \pi(x) \rangle: (\exists i)(x = x_i \ \& \right.$$

$$[0 < a_i \ \& \ [c, d] \subseteq (\tau^{-1}(a_i), \tau^{-1}(b_i)) \text{ or}$$

$$\left. a_i = 0 < b_i \ \& \ [c, d] \subseteq [0, \tau^{-1}(b_i))])\right\}.$$

It is routine to verify that $\bar{F}$ is well-defined and monotone and hence $\bar{F}$ extends continuously to

$$\bar{F}: [\mathcal{R}_+ \to B_\perp] \to [\mathcal{R}_+ \to A_\perp].$$

Let $\bar{\varphi} \in [\mathcal{R}_+ \to B_\perp]$ be a non-zeno representation of $\varphi \in \mathrm{NZ}(\mathbb{R}_+ \to B)$. Let $t_1 < t_2 < \ldots$ be the exceptional set for the representation $\bar{\varphi}$ of φ. We claim that $\bar{F}(\bar{\varphi})$ is a non-zeno representation of $F(\varphi)$ with exceptional set $\tau^{-1}(t_1) < \tau^{-1}(t_2) < \ldots$.

Suppose $\varphi(0) = x$ and choose δ such that $0 < \delta < t_1$. Then $\langle [0, \delta]; x \rangle \sqsubseteq \bar{\varphi}$ so there is d such that

$$\langle [0, d]; \pi(x) \rangle \sqsubseteq \bar{F}(\langle [0, \delta]; x \rangle) \sqsubseteq \bar{F}(\bar{\varphi}).$$

Thus

$$\pi(x) = \langle [0, d]; \pi(x) \rangle (I_0) \sqsubseteq \bar{F}(\bar{\varphi})(I_0),$$

that is, $\bar{F}(\bar{\varphi})(I_0) = F(\varphi)(0)$.

Similarly, $\bar{F}(\bar{\varphi})(I_t) = F(\varphi)(t)$ when $t \neq \tau^{-1}(t_i)$ for any i.

Now suppose $t = \tau^{-1}(t_i)$ for some i. Then $\bar{\varphi}(I_{t_i}) = \perp$. It then follows from the definition of $\bar{F}$ that $\bar{F}(\bar{\varphi})(I_t) = \perp$. □

Suppose (A, α) and (B, β) are computable structures. Then $(A_\perp, \tilde{\alpha})$ and $(B_\perp, \tilde{\beta})$ are effective domains with numberings obtained from α and β in a canonical way. It follows that $[\mathcal{R}_+ \to A_\perp]$ and $[\mathcal{R}_+ \to B_\perp]$ are effective domains with numberings obtained from α, β and a standard numbering of $\mathcal{R}_+$. Analysing the proof of Theorem 6.12, in particular the definition of $\bar{F}$, we obtain the following theorem (with numberings suppressed).

Theorem 6.13. *Let A and B be computable structures and let $F: \mathrm{NZ}(\mathbb{R}_+ \to B) \to \mathrm{NZ}(\mathbb{R}_+ \to A)$ be a single access stream transformer with respect to $\pi: B \to A$ and a strict retiming $\tau: \mathbb{R}_+ \to \mathbb{R}_+$. Assume that π is computable and τ is effective. Then F has an effective approximate non-zeno representation*

$$\bar{F}: [\mathcal{R}_+ \to B_\perp] \to [\mathcal{R}_+ \to A_\perp]$$

Remark 6.14. Theorems 6.12 and 6.13 easily extend to multiple access stream transformers on non-zeno signals with essentially the same proof.

7 Concluding remarks

We have given an introduction to streams and stream transformations with an emphasis on transformations of both discrete and continuous time streams and their connections. We have posed the problem of creating a unified semantic framework for analysing the computability of the 16 different kinds of stream transformations

$$F: (R \to B) \to (T \to A)$$

that depend upon whether time T and R, and data A and B, are discrete or continuous.

In this paper we have given a solution to the problem. It is based on the theory of algebraic domain representations for topological spaces and algebras.

Specifically, we have demonstrated that the domain methods can be successfully applied to all cases of transformations of continuous streams.

In addition, we have explored the problem of representing discontinuous streams, such as commonly arise in models based on signals $T \to A$, where time T is continuous and data A is discrete. The computability of transformations of discontinuous streams is an interesting subject about which little is known, at present.

Other general approaches to computability in topological spaces may provide alternate solutions to the problem of creating a general theory of stream computability. For example, effective metric space theory [34] or Weihrauch's TTE [57] may be applied, although these approaches are known to be equivalent with algebraic domain representations [48].

References

1. J. A. ANDERSON AND E. ROSENFELD (eds.), *Neurocomputing*, MIT Press, 1988.
2. J. BLANCK, Domain representability of metric spaces, *Annals of Pure and Applied Logic* 83 (1997), 225–247.
3. J. BLANCK, Domain representations of topological spaces, *U.U.D.M. Report* 1997:26, 1997. *Theoretical Computer Science*, to appear.
4. L. BLUM, M. SHUB AND S. SMALE, On a theory of computation and complexity over the real numbers: NP-completeness, recursive functions, and universal machines, *Bulletin of the American Mathematical Society* 21 (1989), 1-46.
5. V. BRATTKA, Recursive characterisation of computable real valued functions and relations, *Theoretical Computer Science* 162 (1996), 45-77.
6. M. BROY, F. DEDERICHS, C. DENDORFER, M. FUCHS, T. F. GRITZNER AND R. WEBER, The design of distributed systems — An introduction to FOCUS, *Technical Report TUM* 19202-2, Institut für Informatik, Technical University Munich, 1993.
7. G. S. CEITIN, Algorithmic operators in constructive complete separable metric spaces, *Doklady Akademii Nauk SSSR* 128, 49–52, 1959.
8. J. P. CRUTCHFIELD AND K. KANEKO, Phenomenology of spatio-temporal chaos, in H Bai-lin (ed.), *Directions in Chaos*, World Scientific, 1987.
9. N. J. CUTLAND, *Computability: An Introduction to Recursive Function Theory*, Cambridge University Press, 1980.
10. S. M. EKER AND J. V. TUCKER, Specification and verification of synchronous concurrent algorithms: a case study of the Pixel Planes architecture, in P. M. Dew et al. (eds.), *Parallel processing for computer vision and display*, Addison-Wesley, 1989, 16-49.
11. S. M. EKER, V. STAVRIDOU AND J. V. TUCKER, Verification of synchronous concurrent algorithms using OBJ3. A case study of the Pixel Planes architecture, in G Jones and M Sheeran (eds.), *Designing Correct Circuits*, Springer, 1991, 231-252.
12. YU. L. ERSHOV, Theorie der Numerierungen III, *Zeitschrift für Mathematische Logik und Grundlagen der Mathematik* 23 (1977), 289-371.
13. F. FOGELMAN SOULIE, Y. ROBERT AND M. TCHUENTE (eds.), *Automata networks in computer science*, Manchester University Press, 1986.
14. P. DI GIANANTONIO, Real number computability an domain theory, *Information and Computation* 127 (1996) 11-25.

15. E. R. GRIFFOR (ed.), *Handbook of Computability Theory*, Elsevier, to appear.

16. R. L. GROSSMAN, A. NERODE, A. P. RAVN AND H. RISCHEL (eds.), *Hybrid Systems*, Lecture Notes in Computer Science vol. 736, Springer-Verlag, 1993.

17. A. GRZEGORCZYK, Computable functionals, *Fundamenta Mathematicae* 42, 168–202, 1955.

18. N. A. HARMAN AND J. V. TUCKER, Clocks, retimings, and the formal specification of a UART, in G Milne (ed.), *The fusion of hardware design and verification (Proceedings of IFIP Working Group 10.2 Working Conference)*, North-Holland, 375-396.

19. N. A. HARMAN AND J. V. TUCKER, The formal specification of a digital correlator I : User specification process, in K McEvoy and J V Tucker (eds.), *Theoretical foundations of VLSI design*, Cambridge University Press, 1990, 161-262.

20. N. A. HARMAN AND J. V. TUCKER, Consistent refinements of specifications for digital systems, in: P Prinetto and P Camurati (eds.), *Proceedings of ESPRIT BRA CHARME Advanced Research Workshop on Correct hardware design methodologies*, Elsevier, Amsterdam, 1991, 281-304.

21. N. A. HARMAN AND J. V. TUCKER, Algebraic models computers and the correctness of micro processors, in G J Milne and L Pierre (eds.), *Correct hardware design and verification methods (Proceedings of IFIP Working Group 10.2, May 1993)*, Springer Lecture Notes in Computer Science 683, Berlin, 1993, 92-108.

22. N. A. HARMAN AND J. V. TUCKER, Algebraic models of microprocessors: architecture and organisation, *Acta Informatica* 33 (1996) 421-456.

23. N. A. HARMAN AND J. V. TUCKER, Algebraic models of microprocessors: the verification of a simple computer, in V Stavridou (ed.), *Mathematics for dependable systems II, Proceedings of the Second IMA Conference*, Oxford University Press, 1997, 135-169

24. K. M. HOBLEY, B. C. THOMPSON AND J. V. TUCKER, Specification and verification of synchronous concurrent algorithms: a case study of a convolution algorithm, in G Milne (ed.), *The fusion of hardware design and verification (Proceedings of IFIP Working Group 10.2 Working Conference)*, North-Holland, 347-374.

25. K. HOBLEY AND J. V. TUCKER, Clocks, retimings and the transformation of synchronous concurrent algorithms. in G Megson (ed.), *Transformational approaches to systolic design*, Chapman Hall, 1994, 99-132.

26. A. V. HOLDEN, J. V. TUCKER, H. ZHANG AND M. POOLE, Coupled map lattices as computational systems, *American Institute of Physics - Chaos* 2 (1992) 367-376.

27. G. KAHN, The semantics of a simple language for parallel processing, in *Proceedings IFIP Congress* 74, IFIP, 1974, 471-475

28. K. KANEKO (ed.), *Coupled Map Lattices - Theory and Applications*, Wiley, 1993.

29. D. LACOMBE, Extension de la notion de fonction récursive aux fonctions d'une ou plusieurs variables réelles I, II, III, *Comptes Rendus de l'Académie des Sciences, Série A* 240, 2478–2480, and 241, 13–14, 151–153, 1955.

30. A. I. MAL'CEV, *The Metamathematics of Algebraic Systems. Collected Papers: 1936-1967*, North-Holland, Amsterdam, 1971, 148-212.

31. K. MCEVOY AND J. V. TUCKER, Theoretical foundations of hardware design, in K McEvoy and J. V. Tucker (eds.), *Theoretical foundations of VLSI design*, Cambridge University Press, 1990, 1-62.

32. G. MEGSON, *An introduction to systolic algorithm design*, Oxford University Press, 1992.

33. K. MEINKE AND J. V. TUCKER, Scope and limits of synchronous concurrent computation, in F. H. Vogt (ed.), *Concurrency '88*, Springer Lecture Notes in Computer Science 335, Springer-Verlag, 163-180.

34. Y. N. MOSCHOVAKIS, Recursive metric spaces, *Fundamenta Mathematicae* 55 (1964), 215-238.

35. D. NORMANN, The continuous functionals of finite types over the reals, manuscript, 1998.

36. M. J. POOLE, J. V- TUCKER AND A. V. HOLDEN, Hierarchies of spatially extended systems and synchronous concurrent algorithms, this volume.

37. M. B. POUR-EL AND J. I. RICHARDS, *Computability in Analysis and Physics*, Perspectives in Mathematical Logic, Springer-Verlag, Berlin, 1989.

38. M. O. RABIN, Computable algebra, general theory and theory of computable fields, *Transactions of the American Mathematical Society* 95 (1960), 341-360.

39. A. RABINOVICH, Automata over continuous time, manuscript,1997.

40. H. ROGERS, JR., *Theory of Recursive Functions and Effective Computability*, McGraw-Hill, New York, 1967.

41. R. STEPHENS, A survey of stream processing, *Acta Informatica* 34 (1997), 491-541.

42. V. STOLTENBERG-HANSEN, I. LINDSTRÖM AND E. R. GRIFFOR, *Mathematical Theory of Domains*, Cambridge University Press, 1994.

43. V. STOLTENBERG-HANSEN AND J. V. TUCKER, Complete local rings as domains, CTCS Report 1.85, University of Leeds, 1985.

44. V. STOLTENBERG-HANSEN AND J. V. TUCKER, Complete local rings as domains, *Journal of Symbolic Logic* 53 (1988), 603-624.

45. V. STOLTENBERG-HANSEN AND J. V. TUCKER, Algebraic and fixed point equations over inverse limits of algebras, *Theoretical Computer Science* 87 (1991), 1-24.

46. V. STOLTENBERG-HANSEN AND J. V. TUCKER, Infinite systems of equations over inverse limits and infinite synchronous concurrent algorithms, in J. W. de Bakker and W.-P. de Roever and G. Rozenberg (eds.), *Semantics - Foundations and Applications*. Lecture Notes in Computer Science vol 666, 1993, 531-562.

47. V. STOLTENBERG-HANSEN AND J. V. TUCKER, Effective algebra, in S. Abramsky et al. (eds.), *Handbook of Logic in Computer Science*, vol. IV, Oxford University Press, 1995, 357–526.

48. V. STOLTENBERG-HANSEN AND J. V. TUCKER, Concrete models of computation for topological algebras, *Theoretical Computer Science* , to appear.

49. V. STOLTENBERG-HANSEN AND J. V. TUCKER, Computable rings and fields, in E. R. Griffor (ed.), *Handbook of Computability Theory*, Elsevier, to appear.

50. B. C. THOMPSON AND J. V. TUCKER, Equational specification of synchronous concurrent algorithms and architectures, *Computer Division Research Report CSR* 9-91, University College of Swansea, 1991. Second Edition 1994.

51. B. TRAKHTENBROT, Origins and metamorphoses of the Trinity: Logics, Nets, Automata, in *Proceedings of Logic in Computer Science*, IEEE Computer Society Press, 1995, 506-507.

52. J. V. TUCKER AND J. I. ZUCKER, *Program Correctness over Abstract Data Types with Error-State Semantics*, North-Holland, Amsterdam, 1988.

53. J. V. TUCKER AND J. I. ZUCKER, Theory of computation over stream algebras, and its applications, in I. M. Havel and V. Koubek (eds.), *Mathematical Foundations of Computer Science* 1992, 17th International Symposium, Prague, Springer Lecture Notes in Computer Science 629, Berlin, 62-80.

54. J. V. TUCKER AND J. I. ZUCKER, Computable functions on stream algebras, in H. Schwichtenberg (ed.), *Proof and Computation*, Proceedings of NATO Advanced Study Institute, International Summer School 1993 at Marktoberdorf, Springer, 1994, 341-382.

55. J. V. TUCKER AND J. I. ZUCKER, Computable functions and semicomputable sets on many sorted algebras, in S. Abramsky et al. (eds.), *Handbook of Logic in Computer Science*, vol. V, Oxford University Press, to appear.

56. J. V. TUCKER AND J. I. ZUCKER, Computation by "While" programs on topological partial algebras, *University of Wales Swansea Computer Science Report* 10.97, 1997. *Theoretical Computer Science*, to appear.

57. K. WEIHRAUCH, *Computability*, EATCS Monographs on Theoretical Computer Science 9, Springer-Verlag, Berlin, 1987.

58. G. J. WHITROW, *The natural philosophy of time*, Second Edition, 1980.

59. S. WOLFRAM (ed.), *Theory and applications of cellular automata*, World Scientific, Singapore, 1986.

Ideal Stream Algebra

Bernhard Möller

Institut für Informatik, Universität Augsburg, D-86135 Augsburg, Germany,
e-mail: moeller@uni-augsburg.de

Abstract. We provide some mathematical properties of *behaviours* of
systems, where the individual elements of a behaviour are modeled by
ideals, ie. downward closed directed subsets of a suitable partial order.
It is well-known that the associated ideal completion provides a simple
way of constructing algebraic cpos. An ideal can be viewed as a set of
consistent finite or compact approximations of an object which itself
may be infinite. A special case is the domain of streams where the finite
approximations are the finite prefixes of a stream.
We introduce a special way of characterizing behaviours through sets
of relevant approximations. This is a generalization of the technique we
have used earlier for the case of streams. Given a set $P \subseteq M$ of a partial
order $(M, \leq)$, we define

$$\text{ide}\, P := \{Q^{\leq} : Q \subseteq P \text{ directed}\} \,,$$

where $Q^{\leq} := \{x \in M : \exists y \in Q : x \leq y\}$ is the downward closure of Q. So
$\text{ide}\, P$ is the set of all ideals "spanned" by directed subsets of P. We prove
a number of distributivity and monotonicity laws for ide and related
operators. They are the basis for correct refinement of specifications into
implementations. Various small examples illustrate that the operators
lead to very concise while quite clear specifications.
Finally, we give a characterization of safety and liveness and generalize
the Alpern/Schneider decomposition lemma to arbitrary domains.
An extended example concerns the specification and transformational
development of an asynchronous bounded queue.

Part I: Introduction

1 Origin and Goals

The context of this work is deductive program design, in which implementations
are derived from specifications by semantics-preserving deduction rules. Examples of this paradigm are transformational program development (eg. [53, 8]) and

This research was partially sponsored by Esprit Working Group 8533 NADA — New
Hardware Design Methods

the refinement calculus (eg. [16, 23, 5, 2, 46, 47]). There is a growing conviction that this paradigm is most efficient when based on algebraic rather than purely logical frameworks. The aim there is to make program specification and calculation more concise and perspicuous by compacting logic into algebra as much as possible. For sequential programs this is demonstrated eg. in [39, 41, 8].

In the parallel case, to some extent the work reported in [50, 14] can be viewed as falling into the algebraic realm; purely algebraic approaches are presented in [31, 56]. The present paper presents a particular approach to streams (see eg. [30, 49, 12] and [62] for a recent survey). It centers around the order-theoretic view of streams and other semantic objects as used in denotational semantics. In addition to order theory we use a suitable algebra of formal languages [39] in reasoning about streams.

To exhibit a certain uniformity we use the same calculational style of reasoning in the parts treating the mathematical background as in the program derivations proper.

2 Streams and Ideals

The basic tool in our approach is the prefix order on finite words in A^* over some alphabet A of basic actions, data or states. These words are considered as initial parts of system traces. A trace language is directed w.r.t. this order iff it is totally ordered by it. Therefore ideals, ie. prefix closed directed sets of traces, are a suitable representation of finite and infinite streams.

It is well known that the space of streams under the prefix ordering is isomorphic to the ideal completion of the set of finite streams. Since, however, ideals are just particular trace languages, we can use all operations on formal languages for their manipulation. A large extent of this is covered by conventional regular algebra. Moreover, we can apply the tools developed for quite different purposes in a number of papers on algebraic calculation of graph, pointer and sorting algorithms (see [39, 41] and the references there). Finally, we do not need additional mechanisms for dealing with fairness; rather, fairness is made explicit within the generating expressions for trace languages.

Using regular expressions rather than automata or transition systems gives considerable gain in conciseness and clarity, both in specification and calculation. While this has long been known in the field of syntax analysis, most approaches to the specification of concurrency stay with the fairly detailed level of automata, thus leading to cumbersome and imperspicuous expressions. Other approaches use logical formulas for describing sets of traces; these, too, can become very involved. By extracting a few important concepts and coming up with closed expressions for them one can express things in a more structured and concise form. This is done here using regular and regular-like expressions with their strong algebraic properties. The approach can also be nicely tied in with temporal and modal operators (see [45]).

Another advantage of our approach is that we can do with simple set-theoretic notions thus avoiding most of the overhead of domain theory. By this, the approach also is completely orthogonal w.r.t. nesting of data structures, ie. it admits streams of functions, streams of sets, sets of streams, streams of streams etc. without problems.

3   A Simple Soda Machine

To show the style of our approach and in order to better motivate the technicalities to come we first give a number of examples with informal explanations. The precise definitions will be given in later sections.

We start with the description of a simple soda machine. It accepts half dollars and quarters and emits a can of soda after having received a half dollar's worth in coins. Let h and q denote the events of receiving a half dollar and a quarter, respectively, and c the event of emitting a can of soda. Then the behaviour of that machine is described by the regular-like expression

$$((h \cup q \bullet q) \bullet c)^\omega ,$$

where $\bullet$ is concatenation and $\_^\omega$ denotes infinite repetition. Each expression of this kind denotes a set of (finite or infinite) streams; in the case of the soda machine all these streams are infinite.

In the above expression, the iterated subexpression $(h \cup q \bullet q) \bullet c$ states the following safety properties: the customer must insert the correct amount of money and is not allowed to insert further money before delivery of the can. The infinite repetition $\_^\omega$ combines safety and liveness aspects: it expresses the correct order of insert/deliver cycles, a safety property, and expresses the temporal aspect of eventuality (see eg. [22]): it guarantees that after insertion of a sufficient amount of money eventually a can is delivered and the machine is ready to accept further orders.

We prefer to leave states implicit as long as possible, since frequently regular expressions are clearer and more concise than the corresponding descriptions by accepting automata (Büchi automata in the case of infinite repetition, see eg. [52, 65, 66]).

4   Fairness

Other eventuality properties can already be expressed by Kleene's finite repetition operators $\_^*$ and $\_^+$. To exemplify this, we describe a scheduler for unboundedly fair merging of input from two channels. It is modeled as an infinite stream over the alphabet $\{0, 1\}$, where 0 denotes choice from the left and 1 choice from the right input channel of the merge module. A sequence in which there is at least once a choice from the left followed eventually by a choice from the right is described by the regular expression $0^+ \bullet 1$. By adding the symmetric requirement and, again, infinite repetition to drive the single cycles, we get the following description of the set of streams that model the behaviour of a fair scheduler:

$$SCHED \overset{\text{def}}{=} (0^+ \bullet 1 \cup 1^+ \bullet 0)^\omega .$$

The "local eventuality" is here expressed by the finiteness of $\_^+$, whereas the infinite repetition $\_^\omega$ again adds liveness and "global eventuality".

Arbitrary (and hence possibly non-fair) merge would be obtained by replacing this scheduler by $(0 \cup 1)^\omega$.

The reason why fairness does not cause problems in our approach is that fairness constraints are expressed using the star operation which has a simple recursive definition using least fixpoints w.r.t. the inclusion ordering on sets of streams, whereas there are continuity problems w.r.t. extensions of the prefix order to sets of streams. This is due to the fact that the prefix order has operational traits and unbounded fairness is operationally not feasible, whereas the inclusion ordering is purely descriptive and hence does not face this problem. It is adequate for proving properties of sets of streams; when it comes to implementation, of course operationally feasible descendants have to be used.

We prefer to state fairness assumptions explicitly, since this gives much greater flexibility than building them into the underlying semantic framework (such as eg. in [17]).

5 Channels

Another aspect of fairness and eventuality is exhibited in the description of channels as used in many protocol specifications. The channels are faulty, but fair in the sense that after an unbounded but finite number of faulty transmissions they will at least once transmit correctly.

We will describe their behaviour using streams of functions. Each such function models the transmission behaviour at one particular instance of time. The identity function *id* models correct transmission, *fail* transforms any message into an "error element" and *skip* transforms any message into empty output. Let in the sequel stand the sub/superscript i for $*$ (unbounded but finite repetition) or $\leq k$ for some $k \in \mathbb{N}$ (bounded repetition). Then the following specifications express unbounded and bounded fairness, respectively.

A possibly corrupting but fair channel is described by

$$cchan_i \stackrel{\text{def}}{=} (fail^i \bullet id)^\omega ,$$

a possibly lossy but fair channel by

$$lchan_i \stackrel{\text{def}}{=} (skip^i \bullet id)^\omega$$

and a possibly lossy and corrupting but fair channel by

$$lcchan_i \stackrel{\text{def}}{=} ((skip \cup fail)^i \bullet id)^\omega .$$

An unfair corrupting channel is

$$arbchan \stackrel{\text{def}}{=} (fail \cup id)^\omega .$$

This kind of channel descriptions has been used in [42] for a very concise algebraic correctness proof of the alternating bit protocol.

6 Two Stream-Based Models of Systems

6.1 Modules as Stream-Processing Functions

A stream-processing function (SPF) is a function from tuples of input streams to tuples of output streams (see eg. [30, 12]). In the case of synchronous systems this may equivalently be replaced by a function from a stream of input tuples to a stream of output tuples.

In the SPF view each module is described as an SPF. The advantage of this model is that it allows easy definitions of various composition operations for modules and hence lends itself to a modular structuring of large systems.

The disadvantage in the description of asynchronous systems is that the separation between input and output streams loses causal information, viz. which input triggered which output. This gives rise to the (in)famous merge anomaly [9] which can be fixed by re-introducing time information into the streams. It has to be expressed which elements of a stream are considered to belong to the same time interval. This can be done using explicit time ticks [11, 63] or streams of sequences where each sequence lists the elements that belong to one time interval [32].

6.2 Trace Models

In the trace view, the overall system is described by admissible sequentializations of actions during system runs (interleaving semantics). If the structure of non-deterministic branching is preserved, one obtains tree-like semantic domains such as used in CCS [36], CSP [26] and process algebra [3]. In the simplest case, however, the trace structure is a *set* of streams (see also [29]) which we term a *behaviour*. In this view, a stream in A^∞ is a complete record of one possible system run with all system actions interleaved.

Eg. for a CSP-like view one uses the alphabet $A = C \times V$ of basic actions, where C is a set of channel names and V a set of values that are transmitted along the channels. Then the streams in A^∞ are complete records of system runs with all channel activities interleaved.

The advantage of this view is that it keeps track of the causality between input and output; hence the merge anomaly does not arise.

The disadvantage is a loss in modularity, since only the overall system is described directly. Modularization can be re-introduced, though, by restricting attention to subsets of channels.

Part II: The Algebra of Ideals

This part reviews a few order-theoretic notions and provides some auxiliary facts. It then goes on to develop the ideal-theoretic basis of our approach. On first reading, this part may be skipped and consulted later for details as the need arises.

7   Mathematical Background

7.1   Order-Theoretic Preliminaries

In this section we repeat some basic notions from the theory of partial orders. Some useful properties of the operations introduced are given in the Appendix. Proofs not contained in the present paper can be found in [42].

For partially ordered set $(M, \leq)$ and $N \subseteq M$ we define the *proper* and *improper downward closure* by

$$N^< \overset{\text{def}}{=} \{y \in M : \exists\, x \in N : y < x\}$$
$$N^\leq \overset{\text{def}}{=} \{y \in M : \exists\, x \in N : y \leq x\} = N \cup N^<$$

where $y < x \Leftrightarrow y \leq x \wedge x \neq y$.

The set of *maximal* elements of $N \subseteq M$ is defined by

$$\max N \overset{\text{def}}{=} N \backslash N^< .$$

We now extend the order $\leq$ to a relation on subsets of M by

$$N \leq P \overset{\text{def}}{\Leftrightarrow} N \subseteq P^\leq .$$

This is the angelic half of the Egli-Milner pre-order [54]. In particular, $N^\leq \leq N$.

Since $\leq$ generally is only a pre-order between sets, we are interested in the induced equivalence relation

$$N \sim P \overset{\text{def}}{\Leftrightarrow} N \leq P \wedge P \leq N .$$

A subset $N \subseteq M$ is a *cone* if it is downward closed, ie. if $N^\leq \subseteq N$. Hence on cones $\leq$ and $\subseteq$ coincide; in particular, $\leq$ is a partial order on cones.

Since M is a cone and the intersection of cones is a cone again, the set of all cones forms a complete lattice under inclusion. It is isomorphic to the angelic or Hoare power domain [58] over $(M, \leq)$. However, we are not going to use that domain.

7.2   Pointwise Extension

In the sequel we will define many functions on single points of M and lift them to subsets of M by *pointwise extension*, ie. by setting, for $f : M \to M$ and $N \subseteq M$,

$$f(N) \overset{\text{def}}{=} \{f(x) : x \in N\} .$$

These pointwise extended functions distribute through arbitrary unions and hence are monotonic w.r.t. inclusion and strict w.r.t. $\emptyset$. We will also use this mechanism to lift these functions a further level to sets of subsets of M.

Pointwise extensions inherit *linear laws*. These are laws of the following form:

- Equational laws in which all variables occur exactly once on both sides of the equality sign. Examples are the laws of neutrality, associativity and commutativity over a groupoid.
- Implications with element relations as atoms in which all variables occur exactly once on both sides of the implication sign. In the inherited form the variables for elements turn into variables for non-empty sets and the element relations turn into inclusions. An example is

$$s \bullet t \in \varepsilon \Rightarrow s \in \varepsilon \wedge t \in \varepsilon$$

which lifts to

$$S \neq \emptyset \wedge T \neq \emptyset \wedge S \bullet T \subseteq \varepsilon \Rightarrow S \subseteq \varepsilon \wedge T \subseteq \varepsilon.$$

7.3 Directed Sets and the Ideal Completion

A subset $N \subseteq M$ is *directed* if every finite subset of N has an upper bound in N. Equivalently, N is directed if $N \neq \emptyset$ and any two elements of N have a common upper bound in N. Hence every two elements of a directed set are consistent in that they approximate a common element.

For $P \subseteq M$ we denote by dir P the set of all directed subsets of P. Note that the operation dir is monotonic w.r.t. inclusion. Some further properties of dir can be found in the Appendix.

To tie our approach in with domain-theoretic notions (see eg. [64] we recall the ideal completion (cf. eg. [6, 19]). Consider an ordered set $(M, \leq)$. An *ideal* is a directed cone. The set of all ideals is denoted by $I(M)$.

The partial order $(M, \leq)$ is called *complete* or a *cpo* iff every directed set $D \subseteq M$ has a supremum (or least upper bound) $\sqcup D \in M$. An element x of M is *finite* (*compact*) iff for every directed set $D \subseteq M$ with $x \leq \sqcup D$ we have also $x \leq z$ for some $z \in D$. Equivalently, x is finite iff for every ideal $I \subseteq M$ with $x \leq \sqcup I$ we have $x \in I$. $(M, \leq)$ is *algebraic* iff every element of M is the supremum of a directed set of finite elements. A non-finite element of an algebraic set is called a *limit point* or an *infinite element*. With these notions one has

Theorem 7.1. *1. The set $(I(M), \subseteq)$ ordered by set inclusion is a cpo and algebraic, the finite elements being the principal ideals $x^{\leq}$ for $x \in M$. The mapping $\iota : x \mapsto x^{\leq}$ is an embedding of M into $I(M)$.*

2. For every monotonic mapping $h : M \to P$ into a cpo $(P, \leq)$ there is a unique continuous mapping $\overline{h} : I(M) \to P$ extending h, ie. with $\overline{h}(x^{\leq}) = h(x)$. $\overline{h}$ is given by $\overline{h}(I) = \sqcup h(I)$ for $I \in I(M)$; hence $\overline{h}(D^{\leq}) = \sqcup h(D)$ for directed $D \subseteq M$.

The ordered set $(I(M), \subseteq)$ is called the *ideal completion* of $(M, \leq)$. We set $M^{\infty} \stackrel{\text{def}}{=} I(M)$. An ideal in M^{∞} is non-compact iff it does not have a maximal (and hence greatest) element.

8   Streams as Ideals

We now make our notion of streams precise. Assume an alphabet A of atomic actions, data or states. Then, as usual, A^* is the set of all finite words over A. By ε we denote the empty word, whereas concatenation is denoted by $\bullet$. A subset of A^* is called a *(formal) language*.

A word u is a *prefix* of a word v, written $u \sqsubseteq v$, iff there is a word w such that $u \bullet w = v$. It is well-known that this defines a partial order on words which is even well-founded. Moreover, ε is the least element in this order. The corresponding strict-order is denoted by $\sqsubset$. A *cone* of $(A^*, \sqsubseteq)$ is then a prefix-closed language. Note that every non-empty cone contains ε.

A few properties we shall use are the following (where $x, y, u, v, w \in A^*$ and $U, V \subseteq A^*$):

$$v \sqsubseteq w \Leftrightarrow u \bullet v \sqsubseteq u \bullet w , \tag{1}$$

$$u \sqsubseteq w \wedge v \sqsubseteq w \Rightarrow u \sqsubseteq v \vee v \sqsubseteq u , \tag{2}$$

$$V \neq \emptyset \Rightarrow (U \bullet V)^{\sqsubseteq} = U^{\sqsubseteq} \cup U \bullet V^{\sqsubseteq} . \tag{3}$$

Poperty (2) is also called *local linearity*.

Informally, a stream over A is a finite or infinite sequence of elements of A. The basis of our approach is the observation that such a stream is completely characterized by the set of its finite prefixes. This set is downward closed w.r.t. $\sqsubseteq$, ie. a cone. Moreover, it is directed, since in the partial order $(A^*, \sqsubseteq)$ by local linearity the directed sets can be characterized another way:

Lemma 8.1. *$D \subseteq A^*$ is directed w.r.t. $\sqsubseteq$ iff D is totally ordered by $\sqsubseteq$, ie. iff for any two elements $u, v \in D$ we have $u \sqsubseteq v$ or $v \sqsubseteq u$.*

Hence an *ideal* of $(A^*, \sqsubseteq)$ is a totally and prefix-closed non-empty language. Note that every ideal contains ε. Therefore an ideal is a set of words of increasing length "growing at the right end". This set may be finite or infinite. A simple example is, for $a \in A$, the infinite ideal

$$a^* = \{\varepsilon, a, a \bullet a, a \bullet a \bullet a, a \bullet a \bullet a \bullet a, \ldots\} .$$

We identify a stream with the set of its finite prefixes. By the above, this set is an ideal of $(A^*, \sqsubseteq)$. Therefore we call the elements of A^∞ *streams* over A. It should be noted that the compact elements of A^∞ correspond to the elements of A^*; hence, for countable A, the set $(A^\infty, \subseteq)$ has a countable basis of finite elements and therefore is countably algebraic. The *length* of stream S is denoted by $|S|$; it coincides with its cardinality minus one. Let us give a characterization of infinite streams:

Lemma 8.2. *A stream S is infinite iff $\max S = \emptyset$.*

Proof. First, by linearity of the prefix order on a stream and by its well-foundedness, an infinite stream cannot have a maximal element. The reverse implication is provided by Lemma 12.1.2.   □

The compact elements of A^∞ correspond to the elements of A^*, whereas the non-compact elements are precisely the (cardinally) infinite ideals. They correspond to infinite sequences over A.

To resume our previous example, the ideal

$$a^* = \{\varepsilon,\ a,\ a \bullet a,\ a \bullet a \bullet a,\ a \bullet a \bullet a \bullet a,\ \ldots\}$$

is the limit (supremum) of the set of finite ideals

$$\{\{a^i : i \leq n\} : n \in \mathbb{N}\}$$

corresponding to the $\sqsubseteq$-increasing set

$$\{a^n : n \in \mathbb{N}\}$$

of finite words. It may thus be viewed as a representation of the infinite stream of as. This observation is the main motivation for our approach; it allows us to work with infinite streams by manipulating their sets of finite approximations, since in the ideal completion each (finite or infinite) element is *identified* with the set of its finite approximations. This allows carrying over all laws from the algebra of formal languages to streams. Of course, the fact that the set of finite and infinite streams is isomorphic to the ideal completion of the set of finite streams is well-known; what is new here is the direct algebraic manipulation of the ideals using those laws.

While our approach was motivated by the particular case of streams, we will perform the mathematical development as far as possible for general ideal completions.

9   A Setting for Non-Interleaving Semantics

To stress that latter point and to illustrate our approach with a different setting we now sketch how partial-order semantics, allowing true concurrency, can be accommodated in our setting.

Let E be a set of *events*. Then a *history* over E is a partial order $(F, \preceq)$ with a finite subset $F \subseteq E$ of events. The order $\preceq$ models temporal/causal dependence. Two events not related by $\preceq$ are considered as parallel/concurrent.

Let now $H(E)$ be the set of all histories over E. We define an approximation ordering $\leq$ on $H(E)$ by

$$(F_1, \preceq_1) \leq (F_2, \preceq_2) \stackrel{\text{def}}{\Leftrightarrow} F_1 \subseteq F_2\ \wedge$$
$$\preceq_1\ =\ \preceq_2 \cap F_1 \times F_2\ \wedge$$
$$\forall\, x \in F_1 : x^{\preceq_1} = x^{\preceq_2}\ \wedge$$
$$\forall\, y \in F_2 : \exists\, x \in F_1 : x \preceq_2 y\ .$$

This is the appropriate generalization of the prefix relation on words to histories. It means that F_1 is embedded as a cone into F_2 and F_2 may only add "later" events. It is straightforward to check that this indeed defines a partial order. The least element is $(\emptyset, \emptyset)$.

A *chronicle* now is an ideal in $(H(E), \leq)$, and infinite chronicles generalize infinite streams. The case of streams is retrieved if one only considers histories that are linearly ordered by $\preceq$; in that case $\preceq$ corresponds directly to $\sqsubseteq$. In the present paper, we shall not pursue this example further, though.

10   Behaviours and Refinement

Our application of ideals will be the description of systems. To model non-determinacy, we define a *behaviour* to be a set of ideals.

It should be noted that using *sets* of ideals as behaviours allows only "trace-like" semantics in which there is no distinction between internal and external non-determinacy. The algebraic reflection of this is that concatenation, our sequencing operation, distributes through union both from the left and from the right. In algebraic approaches to CCS-like systems (see eg. [36, 3]) only one of these distributivities holds. This results in models with tree-like objects that reflect the non-deterministic branching structure in time. This detailed record is lost by admitting both distributivities rather than just one.

The set of finite prefixes of a behaviour $\mathcal{B}$ is

$$\mathsf{pref}\, \mathcal{B} \stackrel{\mathrm{def}}{=} \bigcup \mathcal{B}\ .$$

Clearly, **pref** distributes through union and hence is $\subseteq$-monotonic.

As our refinement relation we choose inclusion, ie. behaviour $\mathcal{B}$ *refines* behaviour $\mathcal{C}$ if $\mathcal{B} \subseteq \mathcal{C}$. For instance, given a property $P \subseteq M$, the set ide P of ideals satisfying P, is a behaviour. To allow correct local refinements one therefore has to ensure monotonicity of all operations w.r.t. inclusion.

Example 10.1. We resume the example from Section 4 and show that bounded fairness refines unbounded fairness: since all operators involved are monotonic w.r.t. inclusion, we obtain from $a \bullet a^{\leq k} \subseteq a^+$ for $a \in A$ that

$$(0 \bullet 0^{\leq k} \bullet 1 \cup 1 \bullet 1^{\leq k} \bullet 0)^{\omega} \subseteq \mathcal{SCHED}\ .$$

$\square$

11   Describing Behaviours by Properties

We want to characterize ideals by certain sets of "relevant" er "admissible" finite approximations. Such a set, ie. a subset of our overall partially ordered set M, is called a *property* in this connection.

In the particular case of streams the finite approximations are "snapshots" in the form of finite words in A^*. Assume a set $U \subseteq A^*$ of admissible snapshots. If a stream contains snapshots from a subset $D \subseteq U$ then D has to be directed. However, there may be arbitrary "gaps" between the snapshots in D. To reconstruct the stream we therefore have to "fill in the details" between the snapshots. This is done by taking the prefix closure $D^{\sqsubseteq}$. Hence we define the set of streams, ie. the behaviour, spanned by snapshot set U as

$$\text{str } U \stackrel{\text{def}}{=} \{D^{\sqsubseteq} : D \in \text{dir } U\} .$$

This is the set of streams that "interpolate" consistent snapshots in U. A related notion occurs in [20]; the connection will be made precise in Section 12.

We generalize this to arbitrary partial orders and their ideal completions. Let $(M, \leq)$ be the partial order of finite approximations. For property $P \subseteq M$ we now define by

$$\text{ide } P \stackrel{\text{def}}{=} \{D^{\leq} : D \in \text{dir } P\}$$

the set of all ideals "spanned" by directed subsets of P. Note that $\text{ide } M = I(M)$. Moreover, ide is monotonic w.r.t. inclusion. A different characterization of ide is given by

Lemma 11.1. *For $I \in I(M)$ and $Q \subseteq M$ the following statements are equivalent:*

1. *$I \in \text{ide } Q$.*
2. *$I \subseteq (I \cap Q)^{\leq}$.*
3. *$I = (I \cap Q)^{\leq}$.*

Proof. The equivalence of 2 and 3 is obvious by monotonicity of $\leq$ and downward closedness of I.
$(1 \Rightarrow 2)$ Suppose $I = D^{\leq}$ for $D \in \text{dir } Q$.

$$
\begin{aligned}
& I \\
= \quad & \{\!\!\{ \text{ assumption } \}\!\!\} \\
& D^{\leq} \\
= \quad & \{\!\!\{ \text{ since } D \subseteq Q \}\!\!\} \\
& (D \cap Q)^{\leq} \\
\subseteq \quad & \{\!\!\{ \text{ monotonicity } \}\!\!\} \\
& (D^{\leq} \cap Q)^{\leq} \\
= \quad & \{\!\!\{ \text{ assumption } \}\!\!\} \\
& (I \cap Q)^{\leq} .
\end{aligned}
$$

$(3 \Rightarrow 1)$ Since I is directed, so is $(I \cap Q)^{\leq}$. By Lemma 30.5.3 also $I \cap Q$ is directed and the claim follows. □

We have the following distributivity property for ide:

Lemma 11.2. *Consider $N, P \subseteq M$. Then*

$$\mathrm{ide}\,(N \cup P) = \mathrm{ide}\,N \cup \mathrm{ide}\,P\ .$$

Proof. $I \in \mathrm{ide}\,(N \cup P)$

> $\Leftrightarrow$ $\{\!\!\{$ by Lemma 11.1 $\}\!\!\}$
>
> $I = (I \cap (N \cup P))^{\leq}$
>
> $\Leftrightarrow$ $\{\!\!\{$ distributivity of $\cap$ over $\cup$ and Lemma 30.1.1 $\}\!\!\}$
>
> $I = (I \cap N)^{\leq} \cup (I \cap P)^{\leq}$
>
> $\Rightarrow$ $\{\!\!\{$ by directedness of I, Lemma 30.5.2 and Lemma 30.3.3 $\}\!\!\}$
>
> $I = (I \cap N)^{\leq} \vee I = (I \cap P)^{\leq}$
>
> $\Leftrightarrow$ $\{\!\!\{$ by Lemma 11.1 $\}\!\!\}$
>
> $I \in \mathrm{ide}\,N \vee I \in \mathrm{ide}\,P\ .$

The reverse inclusion follows by monotonicity of ide.
Another proof can be given using Lemma 30.5.5. $\square$

This also shows once again the monotonicity of ide. We have even

Corollary 11.3. $N \subseteq P \Leftrightarrow \mathrm{ide}\,N \subseteq \mathrm{ide}\,P$.

Proof. The inclusion from right to left is part of Theorem 7.1.1 via the principal ideals $x^{\leq}$ for $x \in M$. $\square$

It should be noted, however, that ide only distributes through finite unions and hence is not "continuous". For an instance of this see Example 13.3 below.

Lemma 11.4. *We have the following properties concerning downward closure:*

1. $I \in \mathrm{ide}\,(P^{\leq}) \Leftrightarrow I \subseteq P^{\leq}$.
2. $\mathrm{pref}\,\mathrm{ide}\,P = P^{\leq}$.
3. $\mathrm{ide}\,Q \subseteq \mathrm{ide}\,Q^{\leq}$. *The reverse inclusion is not valid.*

Proof. 1. ($\Rightarrow$) Assume $I = D^{\leq}$ for $D \in \mathrm{dir}\,(P^{\leq})$. Then, by monotonicity and idempotence of $\leq$ we get $D^{\leq} \subseteq (P^{\leq})^{\leq} = P^{\leq}$, ie. $I \subseteq P^{\leq}$.
($\Leftarrow$) Straightforward, since $I \subseteq P^{\leq}$ implies $I \in \mathrm{dir}\,(P^{\leq})$ and $I = I^{\leq}$.
2. The inclusion $\subseteq$ is straightforward. For the reverse consider $y \in P^{\leq}$. There is $x \in P$ with $y \leq x$. But then $y \in x^{\leq} \in \mathrm{ide}\,P$.
3. Immediate from $Q \subseteq Q^{\leq}$ and monotonicity of ide. For a counterexample to the reverse inclusion see Example 13.1. $\square$

12   Maximal and Infinite Ideals

12.1   Maximal Ideals

Frequently one is interested in processes that continue as long as possible. These are modeled by ideals which are maximal w.r.t. $\leq$ or, equivalently, w.r.t. inclusion. We therefore give a characterization of maximal ideals. For a behaviour $\mathcal{B}$ we denote the subset of maximal ideals by $\max \mathcal{B}$; this agrees with the definition in Section 7.1, and hence all our laws in the Appendix apply.

Lemma 12.1. *Suppose* $I \in I(M)$ *and* $N \subseteq M$. *Then*

1. $x \in \max I \Leftrightarrow I = x^{\leq}$.
2. $\max I = \emptyset \Rightarrow I$ *infinite.*
3. $\max N = \emptyset \wedge I \in \max \text{ide } N \Rightarrow \max I = \emptyset$.

Proof. 1. ($\Rightarrow$) We only need to show $I \subseteq x^{\leq}$; the other inclusion follows from downward closure of I. Suppose $y \in I$. By directedness of I there is $z \in I$ with $x \leq z$ and $y \leq z$. Maximality of x implies $z = x$ and hence $y \leq x$.
($\Leftarrow$)

$$\max I$$
$$= \quad \{\!\!\{ \text{ by assumption } \}\!\!\}$$
$$\max x^{\leq}$$
$$= \quad \{\!\!\{ \text{ by Lemma 30.2.1 } \}\!\!\}$$
$$(x^{\leq})^{\leq} \backslash (x^{\leq})^{<}$$
$$= \quad \{\!\!\{ \text{ by Lemma 30.1.2 } \}\!\!\}$$
$$x^{\leq} \backslash x^{<}$$
$$= \quad \{\!\!\{ \text{ by Lemma 30.2.1 } \}\!\!\}$$
$$\max x$$
$$= \quad \{\!\!\{ \text{ irreflexivity of } < \}\!\!\}$$
$$\{x\} .$$

2. Every non-empty finite set has a maximal element.
3. Suppose $\max I \neq \emptyset$, say $x \in \max I$. By 1 then $I = x^{\leq}$ and by $I \in \text{ide } N$ we get $x \in N$. Since $\max N = \emptyset$, there is $y \in N$ with $x \leq y$ and $y \neq x$. But then $y^{\leq} \in \text{ide } N$ and hence, by Theorem 7.1.1, we have $x^{\leq} \subseteq y^{\leq} \wedge x^{\leq} \neq y^{\leq}$. This is a contradiction to $I \in \max \text{ide } N$.

□

12.2   Infinite Ideals

Motivated by Lemma 12.1.2 we define, for a behaviour $\mathcal{B}$, the set of its infinite ideals as

$$\inf \mathcal{B} \stackrel{\text{def}}{=} \{I \in \mathcal{B} : \max I = \emptyset\} \ .$$

For general domains, this is a bit of a misnomer, since there may well be infinite ideals *with* maximal elements. However, we will single out a particular class of domains where this cannot occur and work mostly with these, so that the terminology will be justified. Clearly, inf distributes through arbitrary union and intersection:

$$\inf \left(\bigcup_{i \in I} \mathcal{B}_i\right) = \bigcup_{i \in I} \inf \mathcal{B}_i \ , \tag{4}$$

$$\inf \left(\bigcap_{i \in I} \mathcal{B}_i\right) = \bigcap_{i \in I} \inf \mathcal{B}_i \ . \tag{5}$$

Now Lemma 12.1.3 can be restated as

$$\max N = \emptyset \ \Rightarrow \ \max \mathrm{ide}\, N \subseteq \inf \mathrm{ide}\, N \ .$$

The reverse inclusion is generally not valid. For a counterexample choose $M = \mathbb{N} \cup \{\infty\}$ with the usual ordering and consider the ideal $\mathbb{N} \in I(M)$. We have $\max \mathbb{N} = \emptyset$, but $\mathbb{N} \notin \max I(M)$, since $\mathbb{N} \subseteq M \in I(M)$ and $\mathbb{N} \neq M$.

We call a partial order $(M, \leq)$ *max-determined* if

$$\inf I(M) \subseteq \max I(M) \ .$$

12.3   Refinement Laws

Now we clarify the relation between inf ide and max ide and investigate monotonicity and distributivity of the max ide, inf ide and max inf operations, which is important for refinement. First we note

Lemma 12.2. *For $N, P \subseteq M$,*

$$\inf \mathrm{ide}\, N \cup P = \inf \mathrm{ide}\, N \cup \inf \mathrm{ide}\, P \ .$$

In particular, inf ide *is monotonic w.r.t. inclusion.*

Proof. Immediate from Lemma 11.2 and equation (4). ☐

Concerning maximal ideals we have

Lemma 12.3. *Let $(M, \leq)$ be max-determined. Then, for $N, P \subseteq M$,*

1. $\inf \mathrm{ide}\, N \ \subseteq \ \mathrm{ide}\, N \cap \max I(M) \ \subseteq \ \max \mathrm{ide}\, N$.
2. $\max \mathrm{ide}\, N \ = \ \inf \mathrm{ide}\, N \cup \mathrm{ide}\max N$.
3. $\max N = \emptyset \ \Rightarrow \ \inf \mathrm{ide}\, N \ = \ \mathrm{ide}\, N \cap \max I(M) \ = \ \max \mathrm{ide}\, N$.

4. $\operatorname{inf ide} N \cup P = \operatorname{inf ide} N \cup \operatorname{inf ide} P$.
   In particular, $\operatorname{inf ide}$ is monotonic w.r.t. inclusion.
5. $N = \operatorname{saf} N \Rightarrow \operatorname{inf ide}(N \cap P) = \operatorname{inf ide} N \cap \operatorname{inf ide} P$.
6. $\max N = \emptyset \wedge N \subseteq P \Rightarrow \operatorname{max ide} N \subseteq \operatorname{max ide} P$.
7. $\max N = \max P = \emptyset \Rightarrow \operatorname{max ide}(N \cup P) = \operatorname{max ide} N \cup \operatorname{max ide} P$.
8. *If N and P are cones with $\max N = \max P = \max(N \cap P) = \emptyset$ then*
   $\operatorname{max ide}(N \cap P) = \operatorname{max ide} N \cap \operatorname{max ide} P$.

Proof.   1. $I \in \operatorname{inf ide} N$

$\Leftrightarrow$ { definition }

    $I \in \operatorname{ide} N \wedge \max I = \emptyset$

$\Rightarrow$ { since $(M, \leq)$ is max-determined }

    $I \in \operatorname{ide} N \wedge I \in \max I(M)$

$\Rightarrow$ { by Lemma 30.2.3, since $\operatorname{ide} N \subseteq I(M)$ }

    $I \in \operatorname{max ide} N$.

2. ($\subseteq$) Suppose $I \in \operatorname{max ide} N$. If $\max I = \emptyset$, then $I \in \operatorname{inf ide} N$ by definition. Otherwise $\max I$ is a singleton, say $\max I = \{x\}$, and $I = x^{\leq}$. It follows that $x \in N$. For $y \in N$ with $x \leq y$ we have $x^{\leq} \subseteq y^{\leq} \in \operatorname{ide} N$, so that $x^{\leq} = y^{\leq}$ by maximality of $I = x^{\leq}$. Hence also $x = y$. This shows $x \in \max N$, so that $I = x^{\leq} \in \operatorname{ide} \max N$.
   ($\supseteq$) $\operatorname{inf ide} N \subseteq \operatorname{max ide} N$ was shown in 1. Suppose now $I \in \operatorname{ide} \max N$, say $I = x^{\leq}$ with $x \in \max N$, and $I \subseteq J \in \operatorname{ide} N$, say $J = D^{\leq}$ for $D \in \operatorname{dir} N$. Consider $y \in J$. By directedness of J there is a $z \in J$ with $x, y \leq z$. By $J = D^{\leq}$ there is a $u \in D$ with $z \leq u$. Hence also $x, y \leq u$. By $D \subseteq N$ and $x \in \max N$ we get $x = u$. So $y \leq x$ and hence $y \in x^{\leq} = I$. Altogether, $J \subseteq I$ and hence $J = I$. So $I \in \operatorname{max ide} N$.

3. Assume $\max N = \emptyset$. Then by Lemma 12.1.3 $\operatorname{max ide} N \subseteq \operatorname{inf ide} N$ and the equalities follow from 1.

4. $\operatorname{max ide} N$

$=$ { by 3 }

    $\operatorname{ide} N \cap \max I(M)$

$\subseteq$ { by assumption $N \subseteq P$ and monotonicity of ide }

    $\operatorname{ide} P \cap \max I(M)$

$\subseteq$ { by 3 }

    $\operatorname{max ide} P$.

5. We aim at an application of Lemma 30.2.4. Assume $I \in \operatorname{max ide} N \cap (\operatorname{ide} P)^{C}$. By 3 we have $I \in \max I(M)$. But by $I \in (\operatorname{ide} P)^{C}$ there is $J \in \operatorname{ide} P$ with $I \subset J$, a contradiction to maximality of I. Hence $\operatorname{max ide} N \cap (\operatorname{ide} P)^{C} = \emptyset$. By symmetry, also $\operatorname{max ide} P \cap (\operatorname{ide} N)^{C} = \emptyset$. Now the claim is immediate from Lemma 30.2.4.

6. ($\subseteq$) follows from 6.

($\supseteq$) Assume $I \in \max\text{ide}\,N \cap \max\text{ide}\,P$. Then by 3 we have $I \in \max I(M)$. Hence, again by 3, we only need to show $I \in \text{ide}\,(N \cap P)$. Since N and P are cones we get $I \subseteq N$ and $I \subseteq P$ and hence $I \subseteq N \cap P$ as well, showing the claim.

$\square$

The next lemma allows simplification of the defining property of a behaviour.

Lemma 12.4. *Consider* $N, P \subseteq M$. *Then*

$$\max\text{ide}\,(N \cup P) = \max\text{ide}\,P \iff \text{ide}\,N \leq \text{ide}\,P .$$

Proof. ($\Leftarrow$)

$$\text{ide}\,N \leq \text{ide}\,P$$
$$\Rightarrow \quad \{\!\!\{ \text{ by Lemma 30.3.4} \}\!\!\}$$
$$\max\,(\text{ide}\,N \cup \text{ide}\,P) = \max\text{ide}\,P$$
$$\iff \quad \{\!\!\{ \text{ by Lemma 11.2} \}\!\!\}$$
$$\max\text{ide}\,(N \cup P) = \max\text{ide}\,P .$$

($\Rightarrow$) If $N = \emptyset$, the claim holds trivially, since $\text{ide}\,\emptyset = \emptyset$. Hence we now assume $N \neq \emptyset$.

We now need the so-called *Maximal Principle*, a variant of the Axiom of Choice (see eg. [19]): *Assume a partial order in which every non-empty chain has an upper bound. Then every element has a maximal element above it.*

We apply this to the partial order $(\text{ide}\,N, \subseteq)$. It satisfies the assumption, since $\text{ide}\,N$ is closed under directed unions and hence, in particular, under unions of chains. Consider now $I \in \text{ide}\,N \subseteq \text{ide}\,(N \cup P)$. By the maximal principle there is a $J \in \max\text{ide}\,(N \cup P) = \max\text{ide}\,P$ with $I \leq J$. $\square$

Under additional assumptions we can simplify the assertion:

Lemma 12.5. *Assume* $P \in \text{dir}\,M$. *Then*

$$\max\text{ide}\,(N \cup P) = \max\text{ide}\,P \iff N \leq P .$$

Proof. To apply Lemma 12.4 we show that $P \in \text{dir}\,M$ implies

$$\text{ide}\,N \leq \text{ide}\,P \iff N \leq P .$$

($\Rightarrow$) Assume $x \in N$. Then $x^{\leq} \in \text{ide}\,N$ and so there is $I \in \text{ide}\,P$, say $I = D^{\leq}$ for $D \in \text{dir}\,P$, with $x^{\leq} \leq I$. By Lemma 30.3.1-2 we get $x \leq P$.

($\Leftarrow$) For $I \in \text{ide}\,N$ we have $I \leq P \in \text{dir}\,P$ and hence, by Lemma 30.3.1, also $I \leq P^{\leq} \in \text{ide}\,P$. $\square$

For a counterexample when P is not directed see Example 14.2 in connection with Corollary 12.6.2 below.

Recalling the equivalence $\sim$ associated with the pre-order $\leq$, we obtain from the previous two lemmas

Corollary 12.6. *Consider* $N, P \subseteq M$. *Then*

1. $\mathrm{ide}\, N \sim \mathrm{ide}\, P \Rightarrow \mathrm{max}\,\mathrm{ide}\, N = \mathrm{max}\,\mathrm{ide}\, P$.
2. *If* $N, P \in \mathrm{dir}\, M$ *then*

$$N \sim P \Rightarrow \mathrm{max}\,\mathrm{ide}\, N = \mathrm{max}\,\mathrm{ide}\, P \ .$$

12.4 An Alternative Characterization of Infinite Ideals

We conclude this section by an alternative characterization of the set $\mathrm{inf}\,\mathrm{ide}\, P$ for property $P \subseteq M$. First we define

$$\lim P \overset{\mathrm{def}}{=} \{I \in I(M) : I \cap P \in \mathrm{dir}\, M \wedge \mathrm{max}\,(I \cap P) = \emptyset\} \ .$$

This generalizes the corresponding definition for infinite words or streams in [55, 60, 61, 65, 66] (to cite just a few), which is based on [20]. Other notations for $\lim P$ found in the literature are P^δ or $\boldsymbol{P}$. We can then show

Lemma 12.7. *1.* $\mathrm{inf}\,\mathrm{ide}\, P \subseteq \lim P$.
2. *If* $(M, \leq)$ *is* max-*determined then the reverse inclusion holds as well.*

Proof. We first note that

$\qquad I \in \mathrm{inf}\,\mathrm{ide}\, P$

$\Leftrightarrow \qquad \{\!\!\{\ \text{definition}\ \}\!\!\}$

$\qquad I \in \mathrm{ide}\, P \wedge \mathrm{max}\, I = \emptyset$

$\Leftrightarrow \qquad \{\!\!\{\ \text{by Lemma 11.1}\ \}\!\!\}$

$\qquad I = (I \cap P)^{\leq} \wedge \mathrm{max}\, I = \emptyset$

$\Leftrightarrow \qquad \{\!\!\{\ \text{equality}\ \}\!\!\}$

$\qquad I = (I \cap P)^{\leq} \wedge \mathrm{max}\,(I \cap P)^{\leq} = \emptyset$

$\Leftrightarrow \qquad \{\!\!\{\ \text{Lemma 30.2.2}\ \}\!\!\}$

$\qquad I = (I \cap P)^{\leq} \wedge \mathrm{max}\,(I \cap P) = \emptyset \ . \qquad\qquad (*)$

Now we prove our claims as follows:

1. $\qquad\qquad (*)$

$\qquad \Rightarrow \qquad \{\!\!\{\ \text{by Lemma 30.5.3}\ \}\!\!\}$

$\qquad I \cap P \in \mathrm{dir}\, M \wedge \mathrm{max}\,(I \cap P) = \emptyset$

$\qquad \Leftrightarrow \qquad \{\!\!\{\ \text{definition}\ \}\!\!\}$

$\qquad I \in \lim P \ .$

2. Let $(M, \leq)$ be max-determined and assume $I \in \lim P$. By $(*)$ it remains to show $I = (I \cap P)^{\leq}$. First, by monotonicity of downward closure we have $(I \cap P)^{\leq} \subseteq I^{\leq} = I$. Using Lemma 30.2.2 we obtain $\max (I \cap P)^{\leq} = \max (I \cap P) = \emptyset$, so that by max-determinedness $(I \cap P)^{\leq} \in \max I(M)$ and hence $(I \cap P)^{\leq} = I$.

$\square$

12.5 About max-Determinedness

To investigate under which conditions a partial order is max-determined, we introduce some auxiliary notions. Let $F : \mathcal{P}(M) \rightarrow \mathcal{P}(M)$ be some function, such as dir or ide. We say that $N \subseteq M$ has F-maxima if every set in $F(N)$ has a maximal element. In addition to the functions mentioned we shall use

$$\text{ne}\, N \overset{\text{def}}{=} \{ C \subseteq N : C \neq \emptyset \} \,,$$
$$\text{chai}\, N \overset{\text{def}}{=} \{ C \subseteq N : C \text{ non-empty chain} \} \,.$$

Lemma 12.8. *If $N \subseteq M$ has* chai-*maxima, then it also has* ne-*maxima.*

Proof. Assume $\emptyset \neq D \subseteq N$ and $\max D = \emptyset$. Construct a chain $C \subseteq N$ as follows: Choose $x_0 \in D$ arbitrarily. Assume now that x_i has been found. Since $x_i \notin \emptyset = \max D$, there is $x_{i+1} \in D$ with $x_i < x_{i+1}$. Now for $C \overset{\text{def}}{=} \{ x_i : i \in \mathbb{N} \}$ we have $\max C = \emptyset$, a contradiction. $\square$

Corollary 12.9. *If $N \subseteq M$ has* chai-*maxima, then it also has* dir-*maxima.*

Proof. Every directed set is non-empty. $\square$

We say that $(M, \leq)$ *separates ideals* if for all $I, J \in I(M)$ with $I \neq J$ the intersection $I \cap J$ has chai-maxima. The connection with max-determinedness is given by

Theorem 12.10. *$(M, \leq)$ is* max-*determined iff $(M, \leq)$ separates ideals.*

Proof. ($\Rightarrow$) Suppose $I \neq J$ and $C \in \text{chai}\, (I \cap J)$, but $\max C = \emptyset$. Then $C^{\leq}$ is an ideal with $\max C^{\leq} = \emptyset$. By max-determinedness then $C^{\leq} \in \max \text{ide}\, M$. Since by downward closedness of I and J we have $C^{\leq} \subseteq I$ and $C^{\leq} \subseteq J$ it follows that $I = C^{\leq} = J$, a contradiction.
($\Leftarrow$) Assume $\max I = \emptyset$ and $I \notin \max \text{ide}\, M$. Then there is $J \neq I$ with $I \subseteq J$. Since $(M, \leq)$ separates ideals, and by Corollary 12.9, then $I = I \cap J$ has dir-maxima. In particular, $\max I \neq \emptyset$, a contradiction. $\square$

This has the following surprising consequence:

Corollary 12.11. *Let $(M, \leq)$ be* max-*determined. Then all elements of M are compact.*

Proof. By the previous theorem, $(M, \leq)$ separates ideals.

We now first show $\sqcup I \subseteq I$ for all $I \in I(M)$. Assume $y \in \sqcup I$ and set $J \overset{\text{def}}{=} y^{\leq}$. We have $I \subseteq J$. If $I \neq J$ then $I = I \cap J$ has a maximal and hence, by directedness, greatest element z. But then $z = \sqcup I = y$ so that $J = I$, a contradiction. Consider now $x \in M$ and $I \in I(M)$ such that $x \leq \sqcup I \in I$. By downward closedness of I we get $x \in I$ and x is compact. $\qquad\square$

The reverse implication is not valid as the following example shows. Consider the partial order

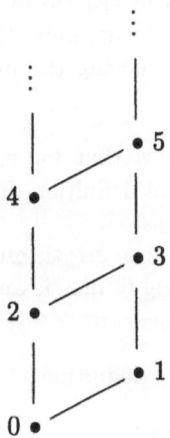

in which all elements are compact. However, for $I \overset{\text{def}}{=} \{0, 2, 4, \ldots\}$ we have $\max I = \emptyset$ and $I \subset J \overset{\text{def}}{=} \{0, 1, 2, 3, 4, \ldots\}$, ie. I is not maximal. Concerning separation of ideals, $I = I \cap J$ doesn't have a maximal element.

It will be interesting to find further, more "manageable" characterizations of max-determinedness.

Part III: A Particular Case: Streams

We now specialize to a particular partial order. We shall represent streams using sets of finite traces. These are finite words over an alphabet A of atomic actions; they are ordered by the prefix relation.

13   Streams and Properties

Whenever we are working in the particular domain A^{∞}, we rename ide into str to emphasize that fact. So the set of streams spanned by property $P \subseteq A^*$ is

$$\text{str}\, P \overset{\text{def}}{=} \text{ide}\, P \,.$$

Note that it would not be adequate to work with the set $\mathrm{str}\,(P^{\sqsubseteq})$, the so-called *adherence* of P (see eg. [49, 60]), instead of $\mathrm{str}\,P$. The reason is that by prefix-closure infinite substreams may "sneak" into a cone although it results from a language of mutually $\sqsubseteq$-incomparable words which represent systems with finite behaviour only.

Example 13.1. The language $L \overset{\text{def}}{=} 0^* \bullet 1$ represents a behaviour with arbitrarily long but finite sequences of 0s terminated by the "explicit endmarker" 1. The words in L are mutually incomparable w.r.t. $\sqsubseteq$. Hence all directed subsets of L are singletons and their downward closures are principal ideals and hence finite. So $\mathrm{str}\,L$ consists of finite ideals only. However, the prefix closure $L^{\sqsubseteq}$ contains the infinite ideal 0^* representing the infinite stream 0^ω of 0s. So $\mathrm{str}\,L^{\sqsubseteq} = \mathrm{str}\,L \cup \{0^\omega\}$. □

Using König's Lemma one can show that for finite A *every* infinite cone contains an infinite stream. The general definition of ide omits these undesired streams.

So, using ide we can distinguish between erratic and angelic non-determinacy and talk about fairness without resorting to metric and topological spaces as eg. in [4].

Example 13.2. Consider the recursive definition

$$B = 0 \circ B \,[\!]\, 1 \,,$$

where $\circ$ denotes stream concatenation (see Section 15 for a precise definition) and $[\!]$ denotes non-deterministic choice. In an angelic interpretation of $[\!]$ always eventually the terminating branch 1 is chosen, and so B would equal $\mathrm{str}\,L$ of Example 13.1.

In an erratic interpretation of $[\!]$, on the other hand, no guarantee is given that the terminating branch will ever be chosen, and so B would equal $\mathrm{str}\,L^{\sqsubseteq}$ of Example 13.1. □

We want to show now that str (and hence ide) does not distribute through general union:

Example 13.3. Take $U = 0^*$. Then $U = \bigcup_{i \in \mathbb{N}} 0^i$. However, $\mathrm{str}\,U = \{0^*\} \cup \{(0^i)^{\sqsubseteq} : i \in \mathbb{N}\}$, whereas $\bigcup_{i \in \mathbb{N}} \mathrm{str}\,0^i = \{(0^i)^{\sqsubseteq} : i \in \mathbb{N}\}$. □

14 Maximal and Infinite Streams

As already mentioned, maximal ideals model processes that go on as long as possible. For streams we have a more pleasant situation than for general ideals:

Lemma 14.1. $(A^*, \sqsubseteq)$ *is* max-determined.

Proof. Assume $I \in \text{ide}\, A^* \wedge \max I = \emptyset$ and consider $J \in \text{ide}\, A^*$ with $I \subseteq J$. By Lemma 30.4 and downward closure of I, J it suffices to show $J \leq I$. Consider $y \in J$. Since $\max I = \emptyset$ there is some $x \in I \subseteq J$ with $||y|| \leq ||x||$, where $||u||$ denotes the length of word u. Moreover, by directedness of J, there is $z \in J$ with $x \sqsubseteq z \wedge y \sqsubseteq z$. From linearity of $z^{\sqsubseteq}$ it therefore follows that $x \sqsubseteq y \vee y \sqsubseteq x$. However, since $||y|| \leq ||x||$, we must have $y \sqsubseteq x$. □

This allows us to use all laws from Section 12 for streams. At this point it is also convenient to give the counterexample to the simplified version of Corollary 12.6:

Example 14.2. Set $U \stackrel{\text{def}}{=} 0^* \bullet 1$ and $V \stackrel{\text{def}}{=} U \cup 0^* = U^{\sqsubseteq}$ by (3). Then $U \sim V$, but $\max \text{str}\, U \neq \max \text{str}\, V$, since $0^* \in (\max \text{str}\, V) \backslash (\max \text{str}\, U)$. □

Concerning infinite streams, we note that by Lemma 8.2 we have

$$\inf \text{ide}\, P = \{I \in \text{ide}\, P : I \text{ infinite}\} \,.$$

To establish the relation with [60] we also show

Lemma 14.3. *For $P \subseteq A^*$ we have*

$$\lim P = \{I \in A^\infty : I \cap P \text{ infinite}\} \,.$$

Proof. $\quad I \in \lim P$

$\quad \Leftrightarrow \quad \{\!\!\{ \text{ definition } \}\!\!\}$

$\quad\quad I \cap P \in \text{dir}\, M \wedge \max(I \cap P) = \emptyset$

$\quad \Leftrightarrow \quad \{\!\!\{ \text{ by } I \cap P \subseteq I \text{ and Lemma 8.1 } \}\!\!\}$

$\quad\quad I \cap P \neq \emptyset \wedge \max(I \cap P) = \emptyset \,.$

We show now that, for linearly ordered $L \subseteq A^*$,

$$L \text{ infinite } \Leftrightarrow L \neq \emptyset \wedge \max L = \emptyset \,.$$

($\Rightarrow$) $L \neq \emptyset$ is immediate. Suppose $x \in \max L$. By linearity then $L \subseteq x^{\sqsubseteq}$. But then $|L| \leq ||x|| + 1$, a contradiction.

($\Leftarrow$) Every non-empty finite set has a maximal element. □

To end this section, we write out specializations of some of our laws for the case of streams, since they will be used in the bounded buffer example below:

Corollary 14.4.

$$\inf \text{str}\,(N \cup P) = \inf \text{str}\, P \Leftarrow N \sqsubseteq P \wedge P \text{ directed}$$
$$\inf \text{str}\, N = \inf \text{str}\, P \Leftarrow N \sim P \wedge N, P \text{ directed}$$

Proof. Immediate from Lemma 14.1, Lemma 12.5 and Corollary 12.6. □

Example 14.5. Since $(a \bullet b)^* \bullet a) \sim (a \bullet b)^*$ and both languages are directed, we obtain $(\inf \text{str}\,(a \bullet b)^* \bullet a) = \inf \text{str}\,(a \bullet b)^*$. □

15   Stream Concatenation

As a prerequisite for defining infinite repetition we need stream concatenation which, for streams S, T is defined by

$$S \circ T \stackrel{\text{def}}{=} S \cup (\max S) \bullet T .$$

Let us explain this definition. If S is finite then $\max S$ is a singleton. This part of the overall behaviour then is prefixed to all traces in T to represent the concatenated behaviour. If S is infinite then $\max S = \emptyset$ and hence, by strictness of $\circ$, we get $S \circ T = S$, as is intuitively expected. We have

$$\max (S \circ T) = (\max S) \bullet (\max T) .$$

It is straightforward to show that $S \circ T$ is indeed a stream and that $(A^\infty, \circ, \varepsilon)$ is a monoid. As a shorthand notation we shall also allow words as first argument of $\circ$. This is made precise by setting

$$u \circ T \stackrel{\text{def}}{=} u^\sqsubseteq \circ T = u^\sqsubseteq \cup u \bullet T .$$

Again, $\circ$ is extended pointwise to behaviours and, in the case of the above shorthand, to languages.

16   Infinite Repetition

We now give the usual greatest fixpoint definition of the set U^ω of streams that result from infinite repetition of words from a language $U \subseteq A^*$:

$$U^\omega = U \circ U^\omega \;\wedge$$
$$\mathcal{X} = U \circ \mathcal{X} \;\Rightarrow\; \mathcal{X} \subseteq U^\omega .$$

According to the Knaster-Tarski fixpoint theorem this is well-defined by monotonicity of $\circ$. Note that by this definition $\emptyset^\omega = \emptyset$. However, if $\varepsilon \in U$ then $U^\omega = A^\infty$. For that reason, U^ω is usually considered only for $\varepsilon \notin U$.

It should be noted that for $|U| \geq 2$ and $\varepsilon \notin U$ there are nontrivial solutions of $\mathcal{X} = U \circ \mathcal{X}$ properly less than U^ω. As an example consider the behaviour $U^* \circ \bigcup_{u \in U} u^\omega$ of all eventually periodic streams.

To tie this in with the str-operation, we quote [60], p. 433:

$$\varepsilon \notin U \;\Rightarrow\; \lim U^* = U^\omega \cup U^* \circ \lim U ,$$

or, using Lemma 12.7 and max -determinedness,

$$\varepsilon \notin U \;\Rightarrow\; \inf \operatorname{str} U^* = U^\omega \cup U^* \circ \inf \operatorname{str} U .$$

From this, by strictness of $\circ$ it is immediate that

$$\varepsilon \notin U \wedge \inf \operatorname{str} U = \emptyset \;\Rightarrow\; U^\omega = \inf \operatorname{str} U^* . \tag{6}$$

A sufficient condition to establish the premise is given by

Lemma 16.1. *If $U \subseteq A^* \backslash \varepsilon$ satisfies the Fano condition, ie. the words in U are mutually incomparable w.r.t. $\sqsubseteq$, then*

$$U^\omega = \inf \operatorname{str} U^* \, .$$

Proof. By the Fano condition, all directed subsets of U are singletons. Hence $\operatorname{str} U = \{u^{\leq} : u \in U\}$ consists of finite streams only. □

Note that if $\varepsilon \in U$ then U satisfies the Fano condition iff $U = \varepsilon$; for this case the above equation doesn't hold, since then $\inf \operatorname{str} U^* = \emptyset$. It should also be mentioned that U satisfies the Fano condition iff $U = \max U$. To see what happens if the Fano condition is not satisfied, consider

Example 16.2. Let $A = \{a, b\}$ and $U \stackrel{\text{def}}{=} \{a \bullet b^n : n \in \mathbb{N}\} \subseteq A^*$. Then $U \in \operatorname{dir} U^*$, since $U \subseteq U^*$ and U is directed. Hence $U^{\sqsubseteq} = \varepsilon \cup U \in \operatorname{str} U^*$ and, since $U^{\sqsubseteq}$ is infinite, even $U^{\sqsubseteq} \in \inf \operatorname{str} U^*$. Now, $U^{\sqsubseteq}$ represents an a followed by infinitely many bs; but this behaviour clearly does not arise from repeated concatenation of words in U. It is "sneaked in" by the fact that simply considering directed subsets of U^* throws away too much structural information. □

To allow a characterization of U^ω for languages that do not satisfy the Fano condition, one can artificially enforce it by attaching a special endmarker to all words in U and remove it after singling out the infinite streams. Let $\# \notin A$ be a new letter and consider streams over the extended alphabet $A \cup \#$. Moreover, denote by $A \triangleleft u$ the word that results from u by removing all occurrences of $\#$ and extend the operation $A\triangleleft$ pointwise to languages and behaviours. Then we have

Lemma 16.3. *For $U \subseteq A^* \backslash \varepsilon$,*

$$U^\omega \stackrel{\text{def}}{=} A \triangleleft \inf \operatorname{str} (U \bullet \#)^* \, .$$

For the somewhat tedious proof see [43].

The streams in $\operatorname{str}(U \bullet \#)^*$ correspond to finite and infinite sequences that result from concatenating arbitrary elements of U with the separator $\#$ in between. The operation $\inf$ then selects the infinite ones of these; if $\varepsilon \notin U$ these are precisely the infinite words resulting from repeatedly concatenating words from U. The separators are used to record the "construction history" of the streams; they are finally thrown away again by the filter $A\triangleleft$. In this way subsets of U^* which are directed "by accident" are ignored. A similar mechanism for defining iteration is employed in [50] in the finite case and in [11] in the infinite case.

17 Streams of Functions

We have made no assumptions about our alphabet A. Hence it may even be a set of functions. Then streams over A model components with time-dependent behaviour. We have seen examples of this in the description of various faulty channels in Section 5.

A stream $S \in A^\infty$ of arguments is fed into a stream $F \in (A \to A^*)^\infty$ of functions by the operator $\gg$. The images $f(a)$ of the elements a of A under the individual functions f in F are concatenated into an overall output stream. A wordwise definition of this is

$$\varepsilon \gg w \stackrel{\text{def}}{=} \varepsilon ,$$
$$s \gg \varepsilon \stackrel{\text{def}}{=} \varepsilon ,$$
$$a \bullet s \gg f \bullet w \stackrel{\text{def}}{=} f(a) \bullet (s \gg w) .$$

This operation is extended pointwise to languages and behaviours.

Example 17.1. For finite stream S we have

$$(S \bullet T) \gg cchan_* = (S \gg arbchan) \bullet (T \gg cchan_*) .$$

This reflects the unbounded fairness of $cchan_*$: we have no guarantee *when* correct transmission occurs, and hence the elements of S may or may not be transmitted correctly. $\square$

With bound assumptions one gets more precise information:

Example 17.2. We have

$$m > k \Rightarrow (a^m \bullet T) \gg cchan_{\le k} \in A^{\le k} \bullet a \bullet A^\infty .$$

A channel with fairness bound k *must* transmit a correctly at least once if it receives more than k copies of a. $\square$

18 Feedback and State-Based Systems

18.1 The Feedback Operation

An essential operation on SPFs is *feedback* of some outputs to the inputs. Assume an SPF $F : A^\infty \times B^\infty \to A^\infty \times C^\infty$. Then its feedback $feed\, F : B^\infty \to C^\infty$ is given by

$$(feed\, F)(S) = T \text{ where } (Z, T) = F(Z, S) .$$

It may be depicted as

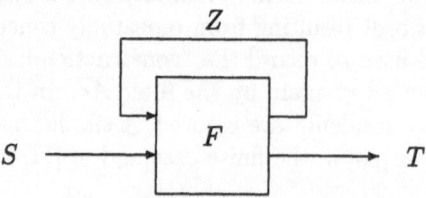

The semantics of this recursive declaration is the usual least-fixpoint one. This version of the feedback operator hides the feedback stream. If this is to made visible one simply copies it and feeds one copy back whereas the other is transmitted to the outside.

18.2 State-Based Systems and Automata

This operation together with streams of functions allows a very convenient and concise description of state-based systems.

Assume a set Q of states, an input alphabet A and an output alphabet B. Then a *time-dependent automaton* is given by a stream $H \in (Q \times A \to Q \times B)^\infty$.

We may now feed this automaton with a starting state $q_0 \in Q$ and a stream $S \in A^\infty$ of input values to produce a stream of output values in B^∞. The stream of states entered during the processing of the input is constructed by a feedback and hidden from the outside. This is described by

$$auto(H, q_0, S) = T \text{ where } (Z, T) = (q_0 \bullet Z, S) >> H \ .$$

By placing various restrictions on the entities involved, we can distinguish a hierarchy of automata:

- If no further restrictions are made, we obtain a *timed and state-dependent* automaton.
- If we require $|Q| = 1$ then we have a *timed and state-independent* automaton.
- If we take $H = f^\omega$ for some $f : Q \times A \to Q \times B$, we obtain a *timeless and state-dependent* automaton.
- If we again take $H = f^\omega$ but also require $|Q| = 1$, we have a *timeless and state-independent* automaton.

For example, an easy proof by induction over the structure of the finite words shows

Lemma 18.1. *If* $|Q| = 1$ *then*

$$auto(f^\omega, q_0, S) = S >> g^\omega \ ,$$

where $g(i) = \pi_2(f(q_0, i))$.

We now illustrate the general case by the following

Example 18.2. We give a description of a one-place asynchronous buffer. The example is taken from [10]. Consider a set D of data. The input alphabet is

$$A \stackrel{\text{def}}{=} D \cup \{!\} \ .$$

An input $d \in D$ means that d is to be stored in the buffer, whereas ! means a request for the current contents of the buffer.

At each time point the buffer may accept or reject its input which is shown by a Boolean value. In addition to that the buffer will output data if it accepts the request signal. So we choose the output alphabet

$$B \stackrel{\text{def}}{=} (D \cup \{\varepsilon\}) \times \mathbb{B} \ ,$$

where ε models the case of no proper output.

As the set of states we choose

$$Q \stackrel{\text{def}}{=} D \cup \{\varepsilon\}$$

where ε models the state of being empty whereas $d \in D$ models the state of containing value d.

Now we define two transition functions

$$acc, rej : Q \times A \rightarrow Q \times B$$

which model acceptance and rejection of the input. We have

$$
\begin{aligned}
acc(q, d) &= (\text{if } q = \varepsilon \text{ then } d \text{ else } q, (\varepsilon, q = \varepsilon)) \ , \\
acc(q, !) &= (\varepsilon, (q, q \neq \varepsilon)) \ , \\
rej(q, x) &= (q, (\varepsilon, \text{false})) \ .
\end{aligned}
$$

The behaviour of a fair buffer, ie. one which rejects inputs only finitely many times before eventually accepting one is the specified as

$$auto((rej^* \bullet acc)^\omega, \varepsilon) \ .$$

In particular, we can avoid the use of prophecy variables (see eg. [10]) in this style. □

19 Processes and Synchronized Parallel Composition

While the previous two sections are appropriate for the SPF view of distributed systems, we now define operators that are adequate for the trace view (cf. Section 6). The particular definitions given here draw strongly on the corresponding ones in [25].

Assume an overall alphabet A for our streams. A *process* is a pair $(B, \mathcal{B})$ where $B \subseteq A$ is the *alphabet* of the process and $\mathcal{B} \subseteq B^\infty$ is a behaviour. We set

$$\alpha(B, \mathcal{B}) \stackrel{\text{def}}{=} B \ , \qquad \beta(B, \mathcal{B}) \stackrel{\text{def}}{=} \mathcal{B} \ .$$

An auxiliary operation is the *projection* † of words to an alphabet $B \subseteq A$. It is defined inductively as follows:

$$
\begin{aligned}
\varepsilon \dagger B &\stackrel{\text{def}}{=} \varepsilon \\
(a \bullet s) \dagger B &\stackrel{\text{def}}{=} \begin{cases} a \bullet (s \dagger B) & \text{if } a \in B \\ s \dagger B & \text{otherwise.} \end{cases}
\end{aligned}
$$

Projection is extended pointwise to languages and behaviours. The projection of a stream is a stream again.

Using projection we can characterize processes in another way: the pair $(B, \mathcal{B})$ is a process iff $\forall S \in \mathcal{B} : S \dagger B = S$.

We need to lift the notion of refinement to processes. We allow that a process is refined by another one that has additional "internal" actions. Since then refinement amounts to inclusion of (the projection of) the behaviour, we abuse notation and write again $\subseteq$ for the refinement relation:

$$P \subseteq Q \stackrel{\text{def}}{\Leftrightarrow} \alpha P \supseteq \alpha Q \,\wedge\, (\beta P) \dagger \alpha Q \subseteq \beta Q \,.$$

In this case we say that P *refines* Q. It is easily checked that $\subseteq$ is a partial order on processes.

If behaviours are "loose enough" in that they allow arbitrary actions in between the "interesting" ones, one can model synchronized parallel composition very simply by intersection (see eg. [26]). For general behaviours this works well only if they are "loosened" by interspersing arbitrary actions between the proper ones; this is again taken from [25]. The intersection then allows only traces in which the actions interesting to both partners occur in a sequence that is acceptable to both partners (ie. allowed in both behaviours) whereas the private actions of each partner are not constrained by the other partner.

Hence, for processes P and Q, we define the parallel composition $P\|Q$ by

$$
\begin{aligned}
\alpha(P\|Q) &\stackrel{\text{def}}{=} \alpha P \cup \alpha Q \,, \\
S \in \beta(P\|Q) \stackrel{\text{def}}{\Leftrightarrow} \,\, & S = S \dagger \alpha(P\|Q) \,\wedge \\
& S \dagger \alpha P \in \beta P \,\wedge \\
& S \dagger \alpha Q \in \beta Q \,.
\end{aligned}
$$

Note, in particular, that $\|$ is commutative, associative and idempotent then. Moreover,

$$P \subseteq Q \,\Leftrightarrow\, P\|Q = P \,.$$

If $\alpha P = \alpha Q$ then $\beta(P\|Q) = \beta P \cap \beta Q$.

This parallel composition operator will be used in our extended example in Section 22.3.

Part IV: Safety and Liveness

We have already informally discussed safety and liveness (see eg. [33, 1, 21]). We want to show how these notions can be expressed algebraically. In [1] and subsequent papers, a *property* is a set of infinite sequences of states. The appropriate counterpart in our setting is therefore a set of streams, more generally, ideals, ie. a *behaviour*.

20 Safety

20.1 Definition and Topological Properties

In [1] a behaviour $B \subseteq A^\omega$ over infinite streams is called *safe* if the following holds:

$$\forall\, S \in A^\omega : S \notin B \,\Rightarrow\, (\exists\, s \in S : \forall\, T \in A^\omega : s \circ T \notin B) \,.$$

This means that for every stream not in the behaviour there is a decisive finite prefix s where something went "irreparably wrong" in that *no* continuation of s can bring the computation back to the "good path".

We want to simplify the formal definition above by moving from logic to algebra. First, using contraposition, the formula can be transformed to

$$\forall\, S \in A^\omega : (\forall\, s \in S : \exists\, T \in A^\omega : s \circ T \in B) \Rightarrow S \in B\ .$$

Now, recalling the definition $\mathsf{pref}\,B = \cup B$ from Section 10, we have

$$\exists\, T \in A^\omega : s \circ T \in B \Leftrightarrow s \in \mathsf{pref}\,B\ . \tag{7}$$

Hence the safety condition reduces to

$$\forall\, S \in A^\omega : (\forall\, s \in S : s \in \mathsf{pref}\,B) \Rightarrow S \in B$$

$$\Leftrightarrow \quad \{\!\!\{\ \text{set theory}\ \}\!\!\}$$

$$\forall\, S \in A^\omega : S \subseteq \mathsf{pref}\,B \Rightarrow S \in B$$

$$\Leftrightarrow \quad \{\!\!\{\ \text{by prefix-closedness of } \mathsf{pref}\,B \text{ and Lemma 11.4.1}\ \}\!\!\}$$

$$\forall\, S \in A^\omega : S \in \mathsf{str\,pref}\,B \Rightarrow S \in B$$

$$\Leftrightarrow \quad \{\!\!\{\ \text{defining should}\,B \stackrel{\mathrm{def}}{=} \mathsf{str\,pref}\,B\ \}\!\!\}$$

$$\mathsf{should}\,B \subseteq B\ .$$

This simplified form involves only order-theoretic notions and hence generalizes easily to arbitrary ideal completions. Consider a partial order $(M, \leq)$ and a behaviour $B \subseteq M^\infty$. Then we call B safe iff $\mathsf{should}\,B \subseteq B$, where

$$\mathsf{should}\,B \stackrel{\mathrm{def}}{=} \mathsf{ide\,pref}\,B\ .$$

By $\subseteq$-monotonicity of pref and ide also should is $\subseteq$-monotonic. Note that for all $B \subseteq M^\infty$ we have $B \subseteq \mathsf{should}\,B$. So a behaviour $B \subseteq M^\infty$ is safe iff $B = \mathsf{should}\,B$. Moreover,

Lemma 20.1. *1. Safe behaviours are closed under arbitrary intersections and finite unions.*
2. should is idempotent.
3. should$\,B$ is the least safe behaviour containing B.

Proof. 1. Assume a family $(B_j)_{j \in J}$ of safe behaviours. Then for all $j \in J$ we have by monotonicity of should and safety of B_j that

$$\mathsf{should}\,\Big(\bigcap_{j \in J} B_j\Big) \subseteq \mathsf{should}\,B_j \subseteq B_j\ ,$$

so that

$$\mathsf{should}\,\Big(\bigcap_{j \in J} B_j\Big) \subseteq \bigcap_{j \in J} B_j\ ,$$

ie. $\bigcap_{j \in J} B_j$ is safe again.

For union we calculate, for $I \in M^\infty$,

$I \in \text{should}\,(\mathcal{B} \cup \mathcal{C})$

$\Leftrightarrow$ $\{\!\!\{$ definition and distributivity of pref $\}\!\!\}$

$I \subseteq \text{pref}\,\mathcal{B} \cup \text{pref}\,\mathcal{C}$

$\Leftrightarrow$ $\{\!\!\{$ Boolean algebra $\}\!\!\}$

$I = (I \cap \text{pref}\,\mathcal{B}) \cup (I \cap \text{pref}\,\mathcal{C})$.

Set now $I_B \stackrel{\text{def}}{=} I \cap \text{pref}\,\mathcal{B}$ and $I_C \stackrel{\text{def}}{=} I \cap \text{pref}\,\mathcal{C}$. Since I is directed, by Lemma 30.5.2 we have $I_B \le I_C$ or $I_C \le I_B$. So by downward closedness of I_B and I_C and Lemma 30.3.3 we have $I_B \subseteq I_C$ or $I_C \subseteq I_B$ and hence $I = I_B$ or $I = I_C$. But then, by Boolean algebra and the definition, we get $I \in \text{should}\,\mathcal{B} \vee I \in \text{should}\,\mathcal{C}$, so that by safety of $\mathcal{B}$ and $\mathcal{C}$ also $I \in \mathcal{B} \cup \mathcal{C}$.

2. For $I \in M^\infty$ we have

$I \in \text{should}\,\text{should}\,\mathcal{B}$

$\Leftrightarrow$ $\{\!\!\{$ definitions $\}\!\!\}$

$I \subseteq \bigcup \{J \in M^\infty : J \subseteq \text{pref}\,\mathcal{B}\}$

$\Leftrightarrow$ $\{\!\!\{$ using the principal ideals $J = x^{\le}$ for $x \in \text{pref}\,\mathcal{B}$ $\}\!\!\}$

$I \subseteq \text{pref}\,\mathcal{B}$

$\Leftrightarrow$ $\{\!\!\{$ definitions $\}\!\!\}$

$I \in \text{should}\,\mathcal{B}$.

3. Let $\mathcal{C}$ be safe with $\mathcal{B} \subseteq \mathcal{C}$. Then

$\text{should}\,\mathcal{B}$

$\subseteq$ $\{\!\!\{$ monotonicity $\}\!\!\}$

$\text{should}\,\mathcal{C}$

$=$ $\{\!\!\{$ safety of $\mathcal{C}$ $\}\!\!\}$

$\mathcal{C}$.

But $\text{should}\,\mathcal{B}$ is safe by 2.

$\square$

By these properties, the safe behaviours coincide with the closed sets of a topology on M^∞ (cf. eg. [59]) and should is the topological closure operator.

20.2 Safety and Snapshot sets

Let us now study how safety is reflected in snapshot sets. In other words, we want to know when for $P \subseteq M$ the behaviour $\text{ide}\,P$ is safe. We calculate, for $I \in M^\infty$,

$I \in$ should ide P

$\Leftrightarrow$ 〔 definition of should 〕

$I \in$ ide pref ide P

$\Leftrightarrow$ 〔 by Lemma 11.4.2 〕

$I \in$ ide $(P^{\leq})$

$\Leftrightarrow$ 〔 by Lemma 11.4.1 〕

$I \subseteq P^{\leq}$

and hence

ide P is safe

$\Leftrightarrow$ 〔 by the above 〕

$\forall I \in M^{\infty} : I \subseteq P^{\leq} \Rightarrow I \in$ ide P

$\Rightarrow$ 〔 $\forall u \in P : u^{\leq} \subseteq P^{\leq}$ 〕

$\forall u \in P^{\leq} : u^{\leq} \in$ ide P

$\Rightarrow$ 〔 since for $D \in$ dir P we have $D^{\leq} = u^{\leq} \Leftrightarrow u \in D$ 〕

$P^{\leq} \subseteq P$.

On the other hand,

$$P^{\leq} \subseteq P \Rightarrow \forall I \in M^{\infty} : I \subseteq P^{\leq} \Rightarrow I \subseteq P .$$

Altogether we have shown

Lemma 20.2. *The behaviour* ide P *is safe iff* $P^{\leq} \subseteq P$, *ie. iff* P *is downward closed.*

For that reason we call a snapshot set $P \subseteq M$ a *safety property* iff it is downward closed. We have

Corollary 20.3. *If* $I \in M^{\infty}$ *and* P *is a safety property, then*

$$I \in \text{ide } P \Leftrightarrow I \subseteq P .$$

Proof. Immediate from Lemma 11.4.1. □

For a safety property P the behaviour ide P is closed under unions (ie. suprema) of $\subseteq$-ascending chains of streams. In the special case of streams, safety properties are simply prefix-closed subsets of A^{*}.

21 Continual Satisfaction

21.1 The General Case

In connection with safety issues one is interested in the set of all objects that satisfy a property also in all their finite approximations. Given a property $P \subseteq M$ we define the property saf P by

$$\text{saf } P \overset{\text{def}}{=} \{x \in M : x^{\leq} \subseteq P\} \, .$$

The set saf P has also been termed the *prefix kernel* of P in [50, 67]. We have

Lemma 21.1. *1.* saf $P \subseteq P$.
2. saf $P = P$ *iff* P *is a safety property. In particular,* saf $P^{\leq} = P^{\leq}$.
3. saf P *is the greatest safety property contained in* P.
4. saf *is monotonic and strict w.r.t.* $\emptyset$.
5. saf $(P \cap Q) = $ saf $P \cap$ saf Q.
6. $I \in$ ide saf $P \Leftrightarrow I \subseteq P$.

Proof. 1. $x \in$ saf P

$\qquad \Leftrightarrow \qquad \{\!\!\{ \text{ definition } \}\!\!\}$

$\qquad \qquad x^{\leq} \subseteq P$

$\qquad \Rightarrow \qquad \{\!\!\{ \, x \in x^{\leq} \, \}\!\!\}$

$\qquad \qquad x \in P \, .$

2. ($\Rightarrow$)

$\qquad \qquad x \in P$

$\qquad \Leftrightarrow \qquad \{\!\!\{ \text{ assumption } \}\!\!\}$

$\qquad \qquad x \in$ saf P

$\qquad \Leftrightarrow \qquad \{\!\!\{ \text{ definition } \}\!\!\}$

$\qquad \qquad x^{\leq} \subseteq P \, .$

($\Leftarrow$)

$\qquad \qquad x \in P$

$\qquad \Rightarrow \qquad \{\!\!\{ \text{ assumption } \}\!\!\}$

$\qquad \qquad x^{\leq} \subseteq P$

$\qquad \Leftrightarrow \qquad \{\!\!\{ \text{ definition } \}\!\!\}$

$\qquad \qquad x \in$ saf P

so $P \subseteq$ saf P; the reverse inclusion was shown in 1.
3. It is obvious that saf P is a safety property. Let $Q \subseteq P$ be a safety property and $x \in Q$. By definition then $x^{\leq} \subseteq Q \subseteq P$ and hence $x \in$ saf P.

4. Immediate from the definition.

5.
$$x \in \text{saf}\,(P \cap Q)$$

$\Leftrightarrow$ $\{\!\{$ definition $\}\!\}$

$$x^{\leq} \subseteq P \cap Q$$

$\Leftrightarrow$ $\{\!\{$ infimum property of intersection $\}\!\}$

$$x^{\leq} \subseteq P \wedge x^{\leq} \subseteq Q$$

$\Leftrightarrow$ $\{\!\{$ definition $\}\!\}$

$$x \in \text{saf}\,P \wedge x \in \text{saf}\,Q\ .$$

6.
$$I \in \text{ide}\,\text{saf}\,P$$

$\Leftrightarrow$ $\{\!\{$ by Lemma 11.1 $\}\!\}$

$$I \subseteq (I \cap \text{saf}\,P)^{\leq}$$

$\Leftrightarrow$ $\{\!\{$ since $\text{saf}\,P \subseteq P$ $\}\!\}$

$$I \subseteq \text{saf}\,P^{\leq}$$

$\Leftrightarrow$ $\{\!\{$ by downward closedness of $\text{saf}\,P$ $\}\!\}$

$$I \subseteq \text{saf}\,P$$

$\Leftrightarrow$ $\{\!\{$ by downward closedness of I $\}\!\}$

$$I \subseteq P\ .$$

$\square$

Note that saf does not distribute through union. We can now state further distributivity properties for ide:

Lemma 21.2. *Consider $N, P \subseteq M$. Then*

1. $N = \text{saf}\,N \Rightarrow \text{ide}\,(N \cap P) = \text{ide}\,N \cap \text{ide}\,P$.
2. $N = \text{saf}\,N \Rightarrow \inf \text{ide}\,(N \cap P) = \inf \text{ide}\,N \cap \inf \text{ide}\,P$.
3. $\text{ide}\,Q \cap \text{ide}\,P \subseteq \text{ide}\,(Q^{\leq} \cap P^{\leq})$.

Proof. 1. We only need to show ($\supseteq$), since the reverse inclusion follows from monotonicity of ide.
Assume $S \in \text{ide}\,N \cap \text{ide}\,P$, say $S = D^{\leq} = E^{\leq}$ with $D \in \text{dir}\,N \wedge E \in \text{dir}\,P$. By Lemma 30.4 then $E \leq D$, and by Lemma 30.3.2 we get $E \leq N$, since $D \subseteq N$. Now $N = N^{\leq}$ shows $E \subseteq N$. Since $E \subseteq P$ we get $E \subseteq N \cap P$ and, since E is directed, even $E \in \text{dir}\,(N \cap P)$. This shows that $S = E^{\leq}$ and hence $S \in \text{ide}\,(N \cap P)$.
2. immediate from 2 and equation (5).
3. Immediate from 1, Lemma 21.1.2 and monotonicity of ide.

$\square$

21.2 Deriving a Recursion for saf

Next, for the particular case of streams we want to derive a grammar-like or automaton-like representation for safety properties of the form saf P for some $P \subseteq A^*$. We use induction on the words involved. For the induction base we calculate

$$\varepsilon \in \text{saf } P$$

$\Leftrightarrow$ { definition }

$$\varepsilon^{\sqsubseteq} \subseteq P$$

$\Leftrightarrow$ { $\varepsilon^{\sqsubseteq} = \varepsilon$ }

$$\varepsilon \in P .$$

For the induction step, we have, for arbitrary $c \in A$,

$$c \bullet s \in \text{saf } P$$

$\Leftrightarrow$ { definition }

$$(c \bullet s)^{\sqsubseteq} \subseteq P$$

$\Leftrightarrow$ { by (3) }

$$c^{\sqsubseteq} \cup c \bullet s^{\sqsubseteq} \subseteq P$$

$\Leftrightarrow$ { set theory }

$$c^{\sqsubseteq} \subseteq P \wedge c \bullet s^{\sqsubseteq} \subseteq P$$

$\Leftrightarrow$ { $c^{\sqsubseteq} = \varepsilon \cup c$ }

$$\varepsilon \in P \wedge c \in P \wedge c \bullet s^{\sqsubseteq} \subseteq P .$$

We assume now that P itself is already given in the form of an automaton-like recursion. Then there is a systematic way for passing from that to a recursion for saf P. Suppose that P satisfies, for all $c \in A$ and $U \subseteq A^*$,

$$c \bullet U \subseteq P \Leftrightarrow U \subseteq F_c(P) \tag{8}$$

for some function $F : A \to (\mathcal{P}(A^*) \to \mathcal{P}(A^*))$. In other words, we assume that the "recursive call" $F_c(P)$ depends only on the first symbol of the word to be analyzed. Note that this assumption means a Galois connection between $c\bullet$ and F_c.

Under this assumption we can continue as follows:

$$c \bullet s^{\sqsubseteq} \subseteq P$$

$\Leftrightarrow$ { by assumption (8) }

$$s^{\sqsubseteq} \subseteq F_c(P)$$

$\Leftrightarrow$ { definition }

$$s \in \text{saf } F_c(P) .$$

Note that a bi-implication linear in s results. To sum up, we have shown

Lemma 21.3. *Suppose property* $P \in \mathcal{P}(A^*)$ *satisfies*

$$c \bullet U \subseteq P \Leftrightarrow U \subseteq F_c(P) .$$

Then, for $U \neq \emptyset$,

$$\varepsilon \in \mathsf{saf}\, P \Leftrightarrow \varepsilon \in P ,$$
$$c \bullet U \subseteq \mathsf{saf}\, P \Leftrightarrow \varepsilon \in P \wedge c \in P \wedge U \subseteq \mathsf{saf}\, F_c(P) .$$

Assume now that we are given two properties P and Q and seek a recursion for $\mathsf{saf}\, P \cap \mathsf{saf}\, Q = \mathsf{saf}\,(P \cap Q)$. The following result is immediate from Lemma 21.1.5 and Lemma 21.3:

Lemma 21.4. *Suppose* P, Q *satisfy*

$$(c \bullet U \subseteq P \Leftrightarrow U \subseteq F_c(P)) \wedge (c \bullet U \subseteq Q \Leftrightarrow U \subseteq G_c(P)) .$$

Then, for $U \neq \emptyset$,

$$\varepsilon \in \mathsf{saf}\,(P \cap Q) \Leftrightarrow \varepsilon \in P \cap Q ,$$
$$c \bullet U \subseteq \mathsf{saf}\,(P \cap Q) \Leftrightarrow c^{\leq} \subseteq P \cap Q \wedge U \subseteq \mathsf{saf}\,(F_c(P) \cap G_c(Q)) .$$

This corresponds to the construction of a product automaton.

22 Liveness

22.1 Definition and Topological Properties

Following again [1] we call a behaviour $\mathcal{B}$ over streams *live* iff

$$\forall\, s \in A^* : \exists\, T \in A^{\omega} : s \circ T \in \mathcal{B} .$$

Using again (7) we can reduce this to

$$\forall\, s \in A^* : s \in \mathsf{pref}\, \mathcal{B}$$

and hence to

$$A^* \subseteq \mathsf{pref}\, \mathcal{B} .$$

Since A^* is the set of compact elements of A^{∞} we can again easily generalize this to arbitrary ideal completions. Consider a partial order $(M, \leq)$ and a behaviour $\mathcal{B} \subseteq M^{\infty}$. Then $\mathcal{B}$ is called *live* iff

$$M \subseteq \mathsf{pref}\, \mathcal{B} .$$

We show now (see again [1])

Lemma 22.1. *$\mathcal{B}$ is live iff it is topologically dense in M^{∞}, ie. iff should $\mathcal{B} = M^{\infty}$.*

Proof. $M \subseteq \operatorname{pref} B$

$\Leftrightarrow$ {{ for ($\Rightarrow$) use transitivity of inclusion,
            for ($\Leftarrow$) the principal ideals $J = x^{\leq}$ for $x \in \operatorname{pref} B$ }}

$\forall \ J \in M^{\infty} : J \subseteq \operatorname{pref} B$

$\Leftrightarrow$ {{ by Corollary 20.3 and the definition of should }}

$\forall \ J \in M^{\infty} : J \in \operatorname{should} B$

$\Leftrightarrow$ {{ set theory }}

$M^{\infty} \subseteq \operatorname{should} B$

$\Leftrightarrow$ {{ set theory }}

$M^{\infty} = \operatorname{should} B$.

$\square$

Now we obtain

Lemma 22.2. *Every behaviour is the intersection of a live and a safe behaviour.*

Proof. We could copy the proof of the respective theorem in [1] verbatim, since it proceeds purely in topological terms. However, we give a simpler proof that avoids most of the topological reasoning in [1].
Assume $B \subseteq M^{\infty}$. We have

B

$=$ {{ since $B \subseteq \operatorname{should} B$ }}

$\operatorname{should} B \backslash (\operatorname{should} B \backslash B)$

$=$ {{ definition of $\backslash$, where $\overline{C}$ denotes the complement
            of C w.r.t. M^{∞} }}

$\operatorname{should} B \cap \overline{\operatorname{should} B \cap \overline{B}}$

$=$ {{ de Morgan and double complement }}

$\operatorname{should} B \cap (\overline{\operatorname{should} B} \cup B)$.

Since $\operatorname{should} B$ is safe, the claim is shown if $\overline{\operatorname{should} B} \cup B$ is live. We calculate

$\operatorname{should} (\overline{\operatorname{should} B} \cup B)$

$\supseteq$ {{ since $\subseteq$-monotonic and hence superdistributive over $\cup$ }}

$\operatorname{should} (\overline{\operatorname{should} B}) \cup \operatorname{should} B$

$\supseteq$ {{ since should is extensive }}

$\overline{\operatorname{should} B} \cup \operatorname{should} B$

$=$ {{ definition of complement }}

M^{∞} ,

so that we are done by Lemma 22.1.

$\square$

Inspection of the proof leads to the following abstraction. Consider a Boolean algebra $(K, \leq)$ with greatest element $\top$. Call a function $f : K \rightarrow K$ a *pre-closure* if it is extensive, ie. satisfies $\forall x : x \leq f(x)$, and monotonic. Next, say that $y \in K$ is f-*dense* if $f(y) = \top$. Then we have

Corollary 22.3. *Every element x of K is the meet of an f-image and an f-dense element, viz.*

$$x = f(x) \sqcap (\overline{f(x)} \sqcup x) .$$

Another way of replacing the topological proof of Lemma 22.2 in [1] by a proof over Boolean algebras is presented in [24]. However, our proof is simpler still.

22.2 Liveness and Snapshot Sets

As in the case of safety, we now investigate when a property P spans a live behaviour. We calculate

   ide P is live

$\Leftrightarrow$ 〔 definition 〕

   $M \subseteq$ pref ide P

$\Leftrightarrow$ 〔 by Lemma 11.4.2 〕

   $M \subseteq P^{\leq}$

$\Leftrightarrow$ 〔 definition of $\leq$ 〕

   $M \leq P$.

Hence we call $P \subseteq M$ a *liveness property* iff $M \leq P$.

22.3 Spanning Infinite Behaviours by Snapshot Sets

We now define that part of a snapshot set that is relevant for the infinite streams. We call a set $Q \subseteq M$ *lively* iff $Q \neq \emptyset \wedge \max Q = \emptyset$.

Lemma 22.4. *1. If Q is lively and $x \in Q$ then there is an $I \in$ inf ide Q with $x \in I$.*
2. If Q is lively then inf ide $Q \neq \emptyset$.
3. If M itself is lively then for every B we have $M^{\infty} \subseteq B$ iff inf $M^{\infty} \subseteq$ inf B.

Proof. 1. We construct a chain $(x_i)_{i \in \mathbb{N}}$ as follows. Choose $x_0 \stackrel{\text{def}}{=} x$. Assume now that x_i has been chosen. Since $x_i \notin \max Q = \emptyset$, there is an $x_{i+1} \in Q$ with $x_i < x_{i+1}$.

By construction then $K \stackrel{\text{def}}{=} \{x_i : i \in \mathbb{N}\} \in$ dir Q and hence $I \stackrel{\text{def}}{=} K^{\leq} \in$ ide Q. Moreover, $\max I = \max K = \emptyset$, i.e, $I \in$ inf ide Q.

2. Immediate from 1.
3. Immediate from 1.

$\square$

In connection with the results below, property 3. will allow easier liveness proofs. Note that this is particularly relevant for the case of streams, since the set A^* of compact elements itself is lively.

Now we define the *live part* of $P \subseteq M$ as

$$\text{liv } P \stackrel{\text{def}}{=} \bigcup \mathcal{L}_P$$

where

$$\mathcal{L}_P \stackrel{\text{def}}{=} \{Q \subseteq P : Q \text{ lively}\} .$$

This operation enjoys the following properties:

Lemma 22.5. *1.* liv $P \subseteq P$.
2. max liv $P = \emptyset$.
3. P *is lively iff* $P \neq \emptyset \wedge P = \text{liv } P$.
4. liv *is* $\subseteq$*-monotonic.*
5. liv liv $P = \text{liv } P$.
6. liv $P \neq \emptyset \Rightarrow \text{inf ide } P \neq \emptyset$.
7. $\mathcal{L}_P \neq \emptyset \Rightarrow \text{inf ide } P \neq \emptyset$.
8. inf ide $P = \text{inf ide liv } P$.
9. pref inf ide $P = (\text{liv } P)^{\leq}$.

Proof. 1. Clear from the definition.
2. Assume $x \in \text{max liv } P \subseteq \text{liv } P$. Then there is a $Q \in \mathcal{L}_P$ with $x \in Q$. Since $x \notin \emptyset = \max Q$, there is $y \in Q \subseteq P$ with $x < y$. Contradiction!
3. The implication ($\Rightarrow$) is clear.
   For the converse we use that $\max P = \text{max liv } P = \emptyset$ by 2.
4. We have $P \subseteq Q \Rightarrow \mathcal{L}_P \subseteq \mathcal{L}_Q \Rightarrow \bigcup \mathcal{L}_P \subseteq \bigcup \mathcal{L}_Q$.
5. By 1 and 4 we have liv liv $P \subseteq \text{liv } P$. For the converse we calculate

$$Q \subseteq P \wedge Q \text{ lively}$$

$\Rightarrow \quad \{\!\!\{ \text{ definition of liv } P \}\!\!\}$

$$Q \subseteq \text{liv } P \wedge Q \text{ lively}$$

$\Rightarrow \quad \{\!\!\{ \text{ definition of } \mathcal{L} \}\!\!\}$

$$\mathcal{L}_P \subseteq \mathcal{L}_{\text{liv } P}$$

$\Rightarrow \quad \{\!\!\{ \text{ monotonicity of } \bigcup \text{ and definition of liv } \}\!\!\}$

$$\text{liv } P \subseteq \text{liv liv } P .$$

6. By 6 we have max liv $P = \emptyset$. Now from Lemma 22.4 and using $\subseteq$-monotonicity of the inf ide-operation we get $\emptyset \neq \text{inf ide liv } P \subseteq \text{inf ide } P$.
7. First note that $\emptyset \notin \mathcal{L}_P$. But then $\bigcup \mathcal{L}_P \neq \emptyset$ iff $\mathcal{L}_P \neq \emptyset$. Now apply 6.

8. By 1 and $\subseteq$-monotonicity of inf ide we get $\supseteq$. Assume, conversely, $I \in$ inf ide P. Then there is a $D \in \operatorname{dir} P$ with $I = D^{\leq}$. Since D is directed, we have $D \neq \emptyset$. Moreover, $\max D = \max I = \emptyset$. So $D \in \mathcal{L}_P$ and hence also $D \subseteq \operatorname{liv} P$, ie. $D \in \operatorname{dir} \operatorname{liv} P$. So $I \in \operatorname{inf} \operatorname{str} \operatorname{liv} P$ as well.

9.   pref inf ide P

$=$ $\{\!\!\{$ definitions $\}\!\!\}$

$\bigcup\{D^{\leq} : D \in \operatorname{dir} P \wedge \max D = \emptyset\}$

$=$ $\{\!\!\{$ distributivity $\}\!\!\}$

$(\bigcup\{D : D \in \operatorname{dir} P \wedge \max D = \emptyset\})^{\leq}$

$\subseteq$ $\{\!\!\{$ definition of $\mathcal{L}$ $\}\!\!\}$

$(\bigcup \mathcal{L}_P)^{\leq}$

$=$ $\{\!\!\{$ definition of liv $\}\!\!\}$

$(\operatorname{liv} P)^{\leq}$.

Assume conversely $y \in \operatorname{liv} P^{\leq}$. There is a $Q \in \mathcal{L}_P$ and an $x \in Q$ with $y \leq x$. By 22.4.1 there is an $I \in \operatorname{inf} \operatorname{ide} Q \subseteq \operatorname{inf} \operatorname{ide} P$ with $x \in I$.

$\square$

So in particular, liv is again a kernel operator. Moreover, by 7, to show that a snapshot set P spans infinite ideals, it suffices to exhibit a lively $Q \subseteq P$. Such Qs can frequently be constructed by induction.

Part V: Extended Example: Buffers and Queues

23   Specification of a Bounded Buffer

As an example of the use of our constructs, we give a specification of bounded buffer and queue modules. For this we use the particular domain $A^{\infty} = A^* \cup A^{\omega}$ of finite and infinite streams over a set A of atomic actions. This example uses the trace view (cf. Section 6) of streams. It was motivated by the asynchronous bounded queue implementation in the collection of the IFIP WG10.5 benchmark problems in hardware verification [28].

The buffer module has one input and one output port. In describing such modules, we choose the letters a for the action of inputting and b for outputting and set $A \stackrel{\text{def}}{=} \{a, b\}$. Boundedness of a module can be enforced by requiring the number of input actions to exceed the number of output actions by at most some $n \in \mathbb{N}$ which then is the *capacity* of the device.

We denote by s_c the number of occurrences of $c \in A$ in $s \in A^*$. Formally,

$$\varepsilon_c \stackrel{\text{def}}{=} 0 ,$$
$$(a \bullet s)_c \stackrel{\text{def}}{=} \delta_{ac} + s_c ,$$

where δ is the Kronecker symbol defined by

$$\delta_{xy} \stackrel{\text{def}}{=} \begin{cases} 1 \text{ if } x = y\,, \\ 0 \text{ otherwise}\,. \end{cases}$$

Generalizing the above informal description slightly, we define, for $n \in \mathbb{Z}$ and $a, b \in A$, the set

$$\text{EX}_n^{ab} \stackrel{\text{def}}{=} \{s \in A^* : s_a \le s_b + n\}$$

of snapshots. Then $s \in \text{EX}_n^{ab}$ may be pronounced as "a exceeds b by at most n in s". The specification is, however, very loose in that the balance between as and bs might be struck only at the very end of a word. For instance, $a^{k+n} \bullet b^k \in \text{EX}_{ab}^n$. So the restriction may be violated in prefixes and only established in the end. For bounded devices, this is not possible. They need a stronger specification. Therefore we strengthen our snapshot set to the safety property

$$\text{B}_n^{ab} \stackrel{\text{def}}{=} \text{saf EX}_n^{ab}\,.$$

Now ide B_n^{ab} is the set of all finite and infinite streams that satisfy EX_n^{ab} in all prefixes. However, we are interested in devices that work for an unbounded time. This is specified by considering as overall behaviour of such a device the set

$$\mathcal{B}_n^{ab} \stackrel{\text{def}}{=} \text{inf str B}_n^{ab}$$

consisting only of infinite admissible streams.

A buffer is a device in which the number of outputs must not exceed the number of inputs. Hence we define

$$\mathcal{BF}^{ab} \stackrel{\text{def}}{=} \mathcal{B}_0^{ba}\,.$$

Note the reversal of the arguments in the superscript. The finitary property B_0^{ba} spells out to $s_b \le s_a$, as required. This describes an unbounded buffer. A bounded buffer of capacity n then is described by

$$\mathcal{BB}_n^{ab} \stackrel{\text{def}}{=} \mathcal{BF}^{ab} \cap \mathcal{B}_n^{ab}\,.$$

This specifies the set of all infinite streams for which, in all finite prefixes, the number of outputs does not exceed the number of inputs and the number of inputs does not exceed the number of outputs by more than n.

24 Transformation to Automaton Form

We consider now again the family of properties EX_n^{ab}. From its predicative definition in the previous section we want to calculate a more "operational" description corresponding to a generating grammar or accepting automaton. This can be done by a simple unfold/fold transformation using induction on the words in A^*. For the induction basis we calculate

$$\varepsilon \in EX_n^{ab}$$

$\Leftrightarrow$ $\quad \{\!\!\{$ definition of EX $\}\!\!\}$

$$\varepsilon_a \leq \varepsilon_b + n$$

$\Leftrightarrow$ $\quad \{\!\!\{$ definition of count $\}\!\!\}$

$$0 \leq 0 + n$$

$\Leftrightarrow$ $\quad \{\!\!\{$ arithmetic $\}\!\!\}$

$$0 \leq n \ .$$

For the induction step, we consider an arbitrary $c \in A$:

$$c \bullet s \in EX_n^{ab}$$

$\Leftrightarrow$ $\quad \{\!\!\{$ definition of EX $\}\!\!\}$

$$(c \bullet s)_a \leq (c \bullet s)_b + n$$

$\Leftrightarrow$ $\quad \{\!\!\{$ definition of count $\}\!\!\}$

$$\delta_{ca} + s_a \leq \delta_{cb} + s_b + n$$

$\Leftrightarrow$ $\quad \{\!\!\{$ arithmetic $\}\!\!\}$

$$s_a \leq s_b + n + \delta_{cb} - \delta_{ca}$$

$\Leftrightarrow$ $\quad \{\!\!\{$ definition of EX $\}\!\!\}$

$$s \in EX_{n+\delta_{cb}-\delta_{ca}}^{ab} \ ,$$

Note that the recursion relations are linear bi-implications. Therefore we obtain, for $U \neq \emptyset$,

$$\varepsilon \in EX_n^{ab} \Leftrightarrow 0 \leq n \ ,$$
$$c \bullet U \subseteq EX_n^{ab} \Leftrightarrow U \subseteq EX_{n+\delta_{cb}-\delta_{ca}}^{ab} \ .$$

This corresponds to an infinite grammar with nonterminals EX_n^{ab} or an infinite automaton with states EX_n^{ab} $(n \in \mathbb{Z})$.

25 Counting Resumed

Next we want a similar representation for

$$B_n^{ab} \stackrel{\text{def}}{=} \text{saf } EX_n^{ab} \ .$$

This can be done quite systematically using Lemma 21.3. We obtain, for $U \neq \emptyset$,

$$\varepsilon \in B_n^{ab} \Leftrightarrow 0 \leq n \ ,$$
$$c \bullet U \subseteq B_n^{ab} \Leftrightarrow 0 \leq n \wedge 0 \leq n \wedge U \subseteq B_n^{ab} \text{ for } c \in A \backslash \{a, b\} \ ,$$
$$a \bullet U \subseteq B_n^{ab} \Leftrightarrow 0 \leq n \wedge 0 \leq n - 1 \wedge U \subseteq B_{n-1}^{ab} \ ,$$
$$b \bullet U \subseteq B_n^{ab} \Leftrightarrow 0 \leq n \wedge 0 \leq n + 1 \wedge U \subseteq B_{n+1}^{ab} \ .$$

which simplifies to

$$\varepsilon \in B_n^{ab} \Leftrightarrow 0 \leq n ,$$
$$c \bullet U \subseteq B_n^{ab} \Leftrightarrow 0 \leq n \wedge U \subseteq B_n^{ab} \text{ for } c \in A\backslash\{a,b\} ,$$
$$a \bullet U \subseteq B_n^{ab} \Leftrightarrow 0 \leq n-1 \wedge U \subseteq B_{n-1}^{ab} ,$$
$$b \bullet U \subseteq B_n^{ab} \Leftrightarrow 0 \leq n \wedge U \subseteq B_{n+1}^{ab} .$$

In particular, $B_n^{ab} = \emptyset$ for $n < 0$.

Now we consider the bounded buffer behaviour. We calculate:

$$BB_n^{ab}$$

= $\quad$ { definition }

$$BF^{ab} \cap B_n^{ab}$$

= $\quad$ { definition }

$$B_0^{ba} \cap B_n^{ab}$$

= $\quad$ { definition }

$$\text{inf str } B_0^{ba} \cap \text{inf str } B_n^{ab}$$

= $\quad$ { by Lemma 12.3.5, since the B sets have been specified as safety properties }

$$\text{inf str } (B_0^{ba} \cap B_n^{ab}) .$$

So the problem has been reduced to finding an explicit representation for $B_0^{ba} \cap B_n^{ab}$, which is a simple product automaton construction. It is a special case of the automaton for

$$G_{mn} \stackrel{\text{def}}{=} B_m^{ba} \cap B_n^{ab} .$$

26 Decomposition

Let us now define a buffer process by setting

$$BB_m^{ab} \stackrel{\text{def}}{=} (\{a,b\}, BB_m^{ab}) .$$

Then using parallel composition we can state the following nice decomposition properties:

Lemma 26.1. *1.* $EX_m^{ab} \cap EX_n^{bc} \subseteq EX_{m+n}^{ac}.$
2. $B_m^{ab} \cap B_n^{bc} \subseteq B_{m+n}^{ac}.$
3. $S \restriction \{a,b\} \in BB_m^{ab} \wedge S \restriction \{b,c\} \in BB_n^{bc} \Rightarrow S \restriction \{a,c\} \in BB_{m+n}^{ac}.$
4. $BB_m^{ab} \parallel BB_n^{bc} \subseteq BB_{m+n}^{ac}.$

Proof. 1. $\quad s \in EX_m^{ab} \cap EX_n^{bc}$

$\Leftrightarrow \quad$ { definition }

$$s_a \leq s_b + m \wedge s_b \leq s_c + n$$

$\Rightarrow$ ⦃ transitivity and monotonicity ⦄

$$s_a \leq s_c + m + n$$

$\Leftrightarrow$ ⦃ definition ⦄

$$s \in \text{EX}^{ac}_{m+n} \ .$$

2. immediate from 1.,Lemma 21.1.5 and Lemma 21.1.4.
3. immediate from 2.
4. immediate from 3.

□

This allows decomposing a buffer of capacity n into a parallel composition of n buffers of capacity 1. Of course, it needs to be shown that the intersections/parallel compositions are non-empty. This follows from our results in Section 22: first, it is easy to show that

$$(a \bullet b)^* \subseteq \text{EX}^{ab}_n \quad \Leftarrow \quad n \geq 0 \ ,$$
$$\inf \text{str} \, (a \bullet b)^* \subseteq \mathcal{BB}^{ab}_n \quad \Leftarrow \quad n \geq 1 \ .$$

From this we get

$$\inf \text{str} \, (a \bullet b \bullet c)^* \subseteq \beta(\text{BB}^{ab}_m \parallel \text{BB}^{bc}_n) \quad \Leftarrow \quad m, n \geq 1 \ .$$

Since $(a \bullet b \bullet c)^*$ is lively, $\inf \text{str} \, (a \bullet b \bullet c)^*$ and hence $\text{BB}^{ab}_m \parallel \text{BB}^{bc}_n$ are non-empty.

27 The One-Place Buffer

For the special case of $n = 1$ we have

$$\mathcal{BB}^{ab}_1 = \inf \text{str} \, G_{01} \ ,$$

where, for $U \neq \emptyset$,

$$\varepsilon \in G_{01} \Leftrightarrow \text{TRUE} , \qquad \varepsilon \in G_{10} \Leftrightarrow \text{TRUE} ,$$
$$a \bullet U \subseteq G_{01} \Leftrightarrow U \subseteq G_{10} , \qquad a \bullet U \subseteq G_{10} \Leftrightarrow \text{FALSE} ,$$
$$b \bullet U \subseteq G_{01} \Leftrightarrow \text{FALSE} , \qquad b \bullet U \subseteq G_{10} \Leftrightarrow U \subseteq G_{01} .$$

This corresponds to a two-state accepting automaton for the bounded buffer property, which is sufficient for purposes of implementation.

However, the above can also be seen as a regular grammar or system of equations for languages. We can calculate from it a regular expression for G_{01} using twice

$$\textbf{(Arden's Rule)} \quad \frac{\varepsilon \neq U \quad X = V \cup U \bullet X}{X = U^* \bullet V} \ .$$

This gives

$$G_{01} = (a \bullet b)^* \bullet (\varepsilon \cup a) \ .$$

Using Example 14.5 and Corollary 14.4, we obtain

$$BB_1^{ab} = \text{inf str}\,(a \bullet b)^* .$$

Finally we use the fact that the language $a \bullet b$ as a singleton trivially satisfies the Fano condition, so that Lemma 16.1 gives

$$BB_1^{ab} = (a \bullet b)^\omega ,$$

as expected.

28   From Buffers to Queues

So far we have only talked about the relative order of input and output *events*. For queues also the relative order of input and output *values* is relevant. We use now the refined alphabet $A = C \times V$ where C is the set of channel names and V the set of values. An element of A will be denoted as $c\langle v \rangle$. As a shorthand we introduce

$$c = \{ c\langle x \rangle : x \in V \} . \tag{9}$$

For a word $w \in A^*$ we define the word $chans(w)$ of channels on which activity occurred and for each $c \in C$ the word $vals_c(W)$ of values transmitted along c. Their inductive definitions read

$$chans(\varepsilon) = \varepsilon ,$$
$$chans(b\langle x \rangle \bullet w) = b \bullet chans(w) ,$$

$$vals_c(\varepsilon) = \varepsilon ,$$
$$vals_c(b\langle x \rangle \bullet w) = \begin{cases} x \bullet vals_c(w) & \text{if } b = c , \\ vals_c(w) & \text{otherwise} . \end{cases}$$

These operations are extended pointwise to languages and behaviours.

With these operations we may specify the behaviour of a *faithful* component, ie. a component which does not re-order or lose messages when transmitting from channel a to channel b, as

$$\mathcal{FA}^{ab} \stackrel{\text{def}}{=} \{ S : vals_a(S) = vals_b(S) \} .$$

A bounded queue is then specified as a faithful bounded buffer:

$$\mathcal{BQ}_n^{ab} \stackrel{\text{def}}{=} \mathcal{FA}^{ab} \cap BB_n^{ab} .$$

Here a, b in BB_n^{ab} are to be understood according to abbreviation (9).

The decomposition properties for buffers carry over to queues, so that again a queue of capacity n can be refined into the parallel composition of n queues of capacity 1. Moreover, a similar calculation as before, using again Arden's rule, yields for the refinement

$$\mathcal{BQ}_1^{ab} = (\bigcup_{x \in V} a\langle x \rangle \bullet b\langle x \rangle)^\omega .$$

29   Conclusion

We have introduced some algebraic operators and laws that can be used in the specification and derivation of systems. By abstracting from the domain of streams for which most of the notions were coined originally, we have obtained a rich set of laws which hold for a variety of domains. The order-theoretic approach lends itself well to an algebraic treatment. The point-free formulation eases and compacts specifications, proofs of the basic properties and the actual derivations. Further research along these lines should search for similar algebraic characterizations of other important notions about systems and to explore their algebraic properties.

Concerning the underlying theory, our domain-theoretic notions should be tied in more closely with the topological view (see eg. [55, 59]). Moreover, in the stream domain there obviously is a close connection with temporal operators: str P is related to intermittent assertions [15] and hence the formula $\Box\Diamond P$ (always eventually P) in temporal logic, while saf P corresponds to $\boxed{i}\,P$ (P holds in all initial subintervals [48]). These connections are made precise and carried over to arbitrary domains in [44, 45]. The resulting "modal algebra" as well as the ideal and stream algebra developed in the present paper need to be tried out in larger and more realistic case studies of deductive design of parallel systems.

Acknowledgement: Many helpful remarks on this paper were provided by J. Baeten, A. Ponse and V. Stoltenberg-Hansen.

References

1. B. Alpern, F.B. Schneider: Defining liveness. Information Processing Letters **21**, 181–185 (1985)
2. R.-J.R. Back: A calculus of refinements for program derivations. Acta Informatica **25**, 593–624 (1988)
3. J.C.M. Baeten, W.P. Wijland: Process algebra. Cambridge Tracts in Theoretical Computer Science **18**. Cambridge: Cambridge University Press 1990
4. J.W. de Bakker, J.I. Zucker: Compactness in semantics for merge and fair merge. In: E. Clarke and D. Kozen (eds.): Logics of Programs. Lecture Notes in Computer Science **164**. Berlin: Springer 1983, 18-33
5. F.L. Bauer, B. Möller, H. Partsch, P. Pepper: Formal program construction by transformations — Computer-aided, Intuition-guided Programming. IEEE Transactions on Software Engineering **15**, 165–180 (1989)
6. G. Birkhoff: Lattice theory, 3rd edition. American Mathematical Society Colloquium Publications, Vol. XXV. Providence, R.I.: AMS 1967
7. R. Bird: Lectures on constructive functional programming. In: M. Broy (ed.): Constructive methods in computing science. NATO ASI Series. Series F: Computer and Systems Sciences **55**. Berlin: Springer 1989, 151–216
8. R.S. Bird, O. de Moor: Algebra of programming. Prentice-Hall 1996
9. J.D. Brock, W.B. Ackerman: Scenarios: a model of non-determinate computation. In: J. Diaz, I. Ramos (ed.): Formalization of programming concepts. Lecture Notes in Computer Science **107**. Berlin: Springer 1981, 252–259

10. M. Broy: Specification and refinement of a buffer of length one. In: M. Broy (ed.): Deductive program design. NATO ASI Series, Series F: Computer and Systems Sciences **152**. Berlin: Springer 1996, 273–304

11. M. Broy: Functional specification of time sensitive communicating systems. In: M. Broy (ed.): Programming and mathematical method. NATO ASI Series, Series F: Computer and Systems Sciences **88**. Berlin: Springer 1992, 325–367

12. M. Broy, F. Dederichs, C. Dendorfer, M. Fuchs, T.F. Gritzner, R. Weber: The design of distributed systems — an introduction to FOCUS. Revised Version. Institut für Informatik der TU München, Report TUM-I9202-2 (SFB-Bericht Nr. 342/2-2/92 A), 1993

13. M. Broy, G. Ştefănescu: The algebra of stream processing functions. Institut für Informatik, TU München, Report TUM-I9620, 1996

14. M. Broy, K. Stølen: Specification and refinement of finite dataflow networks — a relational approach. In: H. Langmaack, W.-P. de Roever, J. Vytopil (eds.): Formal techniques in real-time and fault-tolerant computing. Lecture Notes in Computer Science **863**. Berlin: Springer 1994, 247–267

15. R.M. Burstall: Program proving as hand simulation with a little induction. Proc. IFIP Congress 1974. Amsterdam: North-Holland1974, 308–312

16. R.M. Burstall, J. Darlington: A transformation system for developing recursive programs. J. ACM **24**, 44–67 (1977)

17. K.M. Chandy, J. Misra: Parallel program design: a foundation. Reading, Mass.: Addison Wesley 1988

18. J.H. Conway: Regular algebra and finite machines. London: Chapman and Hall 1971

19. B.A. Davey, H.A. Priestley: Introduction to lattices and order. Cambridge: Cambridge University Press 1990

20. M. Davis: Infinitary games of perfect information. In: M. Dresher, L.S. Shapley, A.W. Tucker (eds.): Advances in game theory. Princeton, N.J.: Princeton University Press 1964, 89–101

21. F. Dederichs, R. Weber: Safety and liveness from a methodological point of view. Information Processing Letters **36**, 25–30 (1990)

22. E.A. Emerson: Temporal and modal logic. In: J. van Leeuwen (ed.): Handbook of theoretical computer science. Volume B: Formal models and semantics. Amsterdam: Elsevier 1990, 995–1072

23. M.S. Feather: A survey and classification of some program transformation approaches and techniques. In L.G.L.T. Meertens (ed.): Proc. IFIP TC2 Working Conference on Program Specification and Transformation, Bad Tölz, April 14–17, 1986. Amsterdam: North-Holland 1987, 165–195

24. H.P. Gumm: Another glance at the Alpern-Schneider characterization of safety and liveness in concurrent executions. Information Processing Letters **47**, 291–294 (1993)

25. C.A.R. Hoare: Communicating sequential processes. London: Prentice Hall 1985

26. C.A.R. Hoare: Conjunction and concurrency. PARBASE 90, 1990

27. J.K. Huggins: Kermit: specification and verification. In: E. Börger (ed.): Specification and validation methods. Oxford: Clarendon Press 1995

28. IFIP 94/97: IFIP WG 10.5 Verification Benchmarks. Web document under http://goethe.ira.uka.de/hvg/benchmarks.html

29. B. Jonsson: A fully abstract trace model for dataflow and asynchronous networks. Distributed Computing **7**, 197–212 (1994)

30. G. Kahn: The semantics of a simple language for parallel processing. In: J.L. Rosenfeld (ed.): Information Processing 74. Proc. IFIP Congress 1974. Amsterdam: North-Holland 1974, 471–475

31. B. Von Karger, C.A.R. Hoare: Sequential calculus. Information Processing Letters **53**, 123–130 (1995)

32. J.N. Kok: A fully abstract semantics for data flow nets. In: J.W. de Bakker, A.J. Nijman, P.C. Treleaven (eds.): PARLE, Parallel languages and architectures Europe, Volume I. Lecture Notes in Computer Science **259**. Berlin: Springer 1987, 351–368

33. L. Lamport: Proving the correctness of multiprocess programs. IEEE Trans. Software Eng. **SE-3**, 125–143 (1977)

34. L. Lamport: Specifying concurrent program modules. ACM TOPLAS **5**, 190–222 (1983)

35. L.G.L.T. Meertens: Algorithmics — Towards programming as a mathematical activity. In: J. W. de Bakker et al. (eds.): Proc. CWI Symposium on Mathematics and Computer Science. CWI Monographs Vol 1. Amsterdam: North-Holland 1986, 289–334

36. R. Milner: Communication and concurrency. London: Prentice Hall 1989

37. B. Möller: Relations as a program development language. In [38], 373–397

38. B. Möller (ed.): Constructing programs from specifications. Proc. IFIP TC2/WG 2.1 Working Conference on Constructing Programs from Specifications, Pacific Grove, CA, USA, 13–16 May 1991. Amsterdam: North-Holland 1991, 373–397

39. B. Möller: Derivation of graph and pointer algorithms. In: B. Möller, H.A. Partsch, S.A. Schuman (eds.): Formal program development. Lecture Notes in Computer Science **755**. Berlin: Springer 1993, 123–160

40. B. Möller: Algebraic calculation of graph and sorting algorithms. In: D. Bjørner, M. Broy, I.V. Pottosin (eds.): Formal Methods in Programming and their Applications. Lecture Notes in Computer Science **735**. Berlin: Springer 1993, 394–413

41. B. Möller, M. Russling: Shorter paths to graph algorithms. In: R.S. Bird, C.C. Morgan, J.C.P. Woodcock (eds.): Mathematics of Program Construction. Lecture Notes in Computer Science **669**. Berlin: Springer 1993, 250–268. Science of Computer Programming **22**, 157–180 (1994)

42. B. Möller: Ideal streams. In: E.-R. Olderog (ed.): Programming concepts, methods and calculi. IFIP Transactions A-56. Amsterdam: North-Holland 1994, 39–58

43. B. Möller: Refining ideal behaviours. Institut für Mathematik der Universität Augsburg, Report Nr. 345, 1995

44. B. Möller: Temporal operators on partial orders. Proc. 3rd Domain Workshop, Munich, May 29-31, 1997. Ludwig-Maximilian-Universität München (to appear)

45. B. Möller: Modal and Temporal Operators on Partial Orders. In: R. Berghammer (ed.): Programmiersprachen und Grundlagen der Programmierung. Institut für Informatik und Praktische Mathematik, Universität Kiel (to appear). Extended version: Institut für Informatik der Universität Augsburg, Report 97-02, 1997

46. C.C. Morgan: Programming from Specifications. Prentice-Hall, 1990.

47. J.M. Morris: A theoretical basis for stepwise refinement and the programming calculus. Science of Computer Programming **9**, 287–306 (1987)

48. B. Moszkowski: Some very compositional temporal properties. In: E.-R. Olderog (ed.): Programming concepts, methods and calculi. IFIP Transactions A-56. Amsterdam: North-Holland 1994, 307–326

49. M. Nivat: Behaviors of processes and synchronized systems of processes. In: M. Broy, G. Schmidt (eds.): Theoretical foundations of programming methodology. Dordrecht: Reidel 1982, 473–551

50. E.-R. Olderog: Nets, terms and formulas. Cambridge: Cambridge University Press 1991
51. E.-R. Olderog, C.A.R. Hoare: Specification-oriented semantics for communicating processes. Acta Informatica **23**, 9–66 (1986)
52. D. Park: On the semantics of fair parallelism. In D. Bjørner (ed.): Abstract software specifications. Lecture Notes in Computer Science **86**. Berlin: Springer 1980, 504–526
53. H.A. Partsch: Specification and transformation of programs — A formal approach to software development. Berlin: Springer 1990
54. G.D. Plotkin: A powerdomain construction. SIAM J. Computing **5**, 452-487 (1976)
55. R. Redziejowski: Infinite-word languages and continuous mappings. Theoretical Computer Science **43**, 59–79 (1986)
56. F.J. Rietman: A relational calculus for the design of distributed algorithms. Dissertation, University of Utrecht, 1995
57. R. Sharp: Principles of Protocol design. London: Prentice Hall 1994
58. M.B. Smyth: Power domains. J. Computer Syst. Sciences **16**, 23–36 (1978)
59. M.B. Smyth: Topology. In: S. Abramsky, D.M. Gabbay, T.S.E. Maibaum (eds.): Handbook of logic in computer science. Vol. 1, Background: Mathematical structures. Oxford: Clarendon Press 1992, 641–761
60. L. Staiger: Research in the theory of ω-languages. J. Inf. Process. Cybern. EIK **23**, 415–439 (1987)
61. L. Staiger: ω-languages. In: G. Rozenberg, A. Salomaa (eds.): Handbook of formal languages. Vol. 3: Beyond words. Berlin: Springer 1997, 339–387
62. R. Stephens: A survey of stream processing. Acta Informatica **34**, 491–541 (1997)
63. K. Stølen, M. Fuchs: An exercise in conditional refinement. In: B. Möller, J.V. Tucker (eds.): Prospects for hardware foundations. Lecture Notes in Computer Science **1546**. Berlin: Springer (this volume)
64. V. Stoltenberg-Hansen, I. Lindström and E.R. Griffor: Mathematical theory of domains. Cambridge Tracts in Theoretical Computer Science, Vol. 22. Cambridge: Cambridge University Press 1994
65. W. Thomas: Automata on infinite objects. In: J. van Leeuwen (ed.): Handbook of theoretical computer science. Vol. B: Formal models and semantics. Amsterdam: Elsevier 1990, 133–191
66. W. Thomas: Languages, automata and logic. In: G. Rozenberg, A. Salomaa (eds.): Handbook of formal languages. Vol. 3: Beyond words. Berlin: Springer 1997, 389–455
67. J. Zwiers: Compositionality, concurrency and partial correctness. Lecture Notes in Computer Science **321**. Berlin: Springer 1989

30 Appendix: Auxiliary Lemmas

30.1 Cones and Maximal Elements

Lemma 30.1. *Consider $N, P \subseteq M$. Then*

1. $(N \cup P)^< = N^< \cup P^< \wedge (N \cup P)^\leq = N^\leq \cup P^\leq$ *(distributivity)*.
2. $(N^\leq)^< = N^< \wedge (N^\leq)^\leq = N^\leq$.

Lemma 30.2. *Consider $N, P \subseteq M$. Then*

1. $\max N = N^{\leq} \backslash N^{<}$.
2. $\max N = \max N^{\leq}$.
3. $N \subseteq P \Rightarrow N \cap \max P \subseteq \max N$.
4. $\max N \cap P^{<} = \emptyset \Rightarrow \max (N \cup P) = \max N \cup (\max P) \backslash N^{<}$.

Lemma 30.3. *Consider $N, P \subseteq M$. Then*

1. $N \leq P \Leftrightarrow N \leq P^{\leq}$.
2. $L \subseteq N \wedge N \leq P \wedge P \subseteq Q \Rightarrow L \leq Q$.
3. $N \leq P \Leftrightarrow N^{\leq} \subseteq P^{\leq}$.
4. $N \leq P \Rightarrow \max (N \cup P) = \max P$.

Lemma 30.4. *Consider $N, P \subseteq M$. Then $N \sim P \Leftrightarrow N^{\leq} = P^{\leq}$.*

Proof. Immediate from Lemma 30.3.3. □

30.2 Directed Sets

Lemma 30.5. *Consider $N, P \subseteq M$. Then*

1. $N \cup P \in \mathrm{dir}\, M \wedge N \leq P \Rightarrow P \in \mathrm{dir}\, M$.
2. $N \cup P \in \mathrm{dir}\, M \Rightarrow (N \leq P \vee P \leq N) \wedge (N \in \mathrm{dir}\, M \vee P \in \mathrm{dir}\, M)$.
3. $Q^{\leq} \in \mathrm{dir}\, M \Leftrightarrow Q \in \mathrm{dir}\, M$.
4. $N \leq P \wedge P \in \mathrm{dir}\, M \Rightarrow N \cup P \in \mathrm{dir}\, M$.
5. $\mathrm{dir}\, (N \cup P) = \{K \cup L : (K \in \mathrm{dir}\, N \wedge L \subseteq P \wedge L \leq K)\} \cup$
   $\{K \cup L : (L \in \mathrm{dir}\, P \wedge K \subseteq N \wedge K \leq L)\}$.

Proof. 1. Assume $x, y \in P$. By directedness of $N \cup P$ there is a $z \in N \cup P$ with $x \leq z$ and $y \leq z$. If $z \in P$, we are done. Otherwise, by $N \leq P$ there is a $u \in P$ with $z \leq u$ so that by transitivity also $x \leq u$ and $y \leq u$.

2. For $N = \emptyset$ or $P = \emptyset$ the claim is trivial. So consider $N, P \neq \emptyset$ and suppose $N \not\leq P$. Then there is $x \in N$ with $x \not\leq P$. Assume now $y \in P$. By directedness of $N \cup P$ there is a $z \in N \cup P$ with $x, y \leq z$. Since $x \not\leq P$, it follows that $z \in N \backslash P \subseteq N$. Since y was arbitrary, we have shown $P \leq N$.
The second disjunct is immediate from the first and 1.

3. Immediate from 1 by setting $N = Q^{\leq}$, $P = Q$ and using $Q^{\leq} \leq Q$.

4. Assume $x, y \in N \cup P$. By $N \leq P$ and $P \leq P$ there are $u, v \in P$ with $x \leq u \wedge y \leq v$. Since P is directed, there is $z \in P$ with $u \leq z$ and $v \leq z$. Hence also $x \leq z$ and $y \leq z$ by transitivity.

5. We show $(\subseteq)$; the reverse inclusion is immediate from 4.

   Consider $Q \in \mathrm{dir}\, (N \cup P)$. We have $Q = K \cup L$ where $K \overset{\mathrm{def}}{=} Q \cap N$ and $L \overset{\mathrm{def}}{=} Q \cap P$. By 2 we know $K \leq L \vee L \leq K$. If $K \leq L$ then $L \in \mathrm{dir}\, P$ by 1. If $L \leq K$ then $K \in \mathrm{dir}\, N$ by 1. This shows the claim.

□

Normalization by Evaluation

Ulrich Berger, Matthias Eberl and Helmut Schwichtenberg

Mathematisches Institut der Universität München

Abstract. We extend normalization by evaluation (first presented in [4]) from the pure typed λ-calculus to general higher type term rewrite systems. This work also gives a theoretical explanation of the normalization algorithm implemented in the MINLOG system.

1 Introduction

In interactive proof systems it is crucial to have a term rewriting machinery available, in order to ease the burden of equational reasoning. Quite often term rewriting can be reduced to normalization and therefore it is essential to implement normalization of terms efficiently. By the same token, one then can also effectively normalize whole proofs (which can be written as derivation terms, using the CURRY-HOWARD correspondence). Normalization is used when extracting terms from formal proofs. For an application concerning circuits cf. [12].

It is well known that implementing normalization of λ-terms in the usual recursive fashion is quite inefficient. However, it is possible to compute the long normal form of a λ-term by evaluating it in an appropriate model (cf. [4]). When using for that purpose the built-in evaluation mechanism of e.g. SCHEME (a pure LISP dialect) one obtains an amazingly fast algorithm called "normalization by evaluation". The essential idea is to find an inverse to evaluation, converting a semantic object into a syntactic term. This normalization procedure is used and tested in the proof system MINLOG developed in Munich (cf. [2]).

Obviously, for applications pure typed λ-terms are not sufficient, but it is necessary to have constants in it. These were not considered in [4], but will be treated in this paper.

Let us begin with a short explanation of the essence of the method for normalizing typed λ-terms by means of an evaluation procedure of some functional programming language such as SCHEME. For simplicity we return to the simplest case, simply typed λ-calculus without constants.

Simple types are built from ground types τ by $\rho \to \sigma$ (later also products $\rho \times \sigma$ will be included). The set Λ of terms is given by x^τ, $(\lambda x^\rho M^\sigma)^{\rho \to \sigma}$, $(M^{\rho \to \sigma} N^\rho)^\sigma$. The set LNF of terms in long normal form (i.e. normal w.r.t. β-reduction and η-expansion) is defined inductively by $(x M_1 \ldots M_n)^\tau$, $\lambda x M$ (we abbreviate $x M_1 \ldots M_n$ by $x\mathbf{M}$ and similar a list $M_1 \ldots M_n$ by $\mathbf{M}$). By $\mathsf{lnf}(M)$ we denote the long normal form of M, i.e. the unique term in long normal form $\beta\eta$-equal to M.

Now we have to choose our model. A simple solution is to take terms of ground type as ground type objects, and all functions as possible function type objects:

$$\llbracket \tau \rrbracket := \Lambda_\tau, \quad \llbracket \rho \to \sigma \rrbracket := \llbracket \sigma \rrbracket^{\llbracket \rho \rrbracket} \quad \text{(the full function space)}.$$

It is crucial that all terms (of ground type) are present, not just the closed ones. Next we need an assignment $\uparrow$ lifting a variable to an object, and a function $\downarrow$ giving us a normal term from an object. They should meet the following condition, which might be called "correctness of normalization by evaluation":

$$\downarrow(\llbracket M \rrbracket_\uparrow) = \mathsf{lnf}(M)$$

where $\llbracket M^\rho \rrbracket_\uparrow \in \llbracket \rho \rrbracket$ denotes the value of M under the assignment $\uparrow$. Two such functions $\downarrow$ and $\uparrow$ can be defined simultaneously, by induction on the type. It is convenient to define $\uparrow$ on all terms (not just on variables). Hence for every type ρ we define $\downarrow_\rho : \llbracket \rho \rrbracket \to \Lambda_\rho$ and $\uparrow_\rho : \Lambda_\rho \to \llbracket \rho \rrbracket$ (called reify and reflect) by

$$\downarrow_\tau(M) := M, \qquad\qquad\qquad \uparrow_\tau(M) := M,$$
$$\downarrow_{\rho \to \sigma}(a) := \lambda x \downarrow_\sigma(a(\uparrow_\rho(x))) \quad \text{"x new"}, \quad \uparrow_{\rho \to \sigma}(M)(a) := \uparrow_\sigma(M \downarrow_\rho(a)).$$

Here a little difficulty appears: what does it mean that x is new? We will solve this problem by slightly modifying the model and defining $\llbracket \tau \rrbracket$ to be the set of families of terms of type τ (instead of single terms) and setting $\downarrow_{\rho \to \sigma}(a)(k) := \lambda x_k(\downarrow_\sigma(a(\uparrow_\rho(x_k^\infty)))(k+1))$, where x_k^∞ is the constant family x_k. The definition of $\uparrow_{\rho \to \sigma}$ has to be modified accordingly. This idea corresponds to a representation of terms in the style of DE BRUIJN [9]. An advantage of this approach is that we get the same normal form even if the terms are only equal up to renaming of bound variables.

The proof of correctness is easy: Since for the typed lambda calculus without constants we have preservation of values, i.e. $\llbracket M \rrbracket_\xi = \llbracket \mathsf{lnf}(M) \rrbracket_\xi$ for all terms M and environments ξ, we only have to verify $\downarrow(\llbracket N \rrbracket_\uparrow) = N$ for normal terms N, which is straightforward. The situation is different when we add constants together with rewrite rules, since then preservation of values (in our model) is false in general. However, correctness of normalization by evaluation still holds, but needs to be proven by a different method.

The structure of the paper is as follows. In section 2 we present the simply typed λ-calculus with constants and pairing and give some examples of higher order rewrite systems. Then we inductively define a relation $M \longrightarrow Q$, with the intended meaning that M is normalizable with long normal form Q, and prove in section 4 the correctness of normalization by evaluation by showing that $M \longrightarrow Q$ implies $\downarrow(\llbracket M \rrbracket_\uparrow) = Q$. Hence the mapping $M \mapsto \downarrow(\llbracket M \rrbracket_\uparrow)$ is a normalization function. In order to define the semantics $\llbracket M \rrbracket$ of a term M properly we use domain theory. This is described briefly in section 3.

In subsection 4.2 we show how to interpret a constant c more efficiently if all its rules are of some special forms. In fact, most of the rewrite rules in the

MINLOG system have one of these forms. Again, normalization by evaluation is shown to remain correct.

The final section 5 contains a review of the relevant literature [1, 5, 7, 8], and also a comparison of the run-times of our algorithm with those coming from the other setups. The results clearly support our claim that the present approach (with function spaces as higher type domains) leads to a much faster implementation.

Acknowledgements. The present work has benefitted considerably from ideas of Felix Joachimski and Ralph Matthes concerning strategies for normalization proofs, including η-expansion and primitive recursion. In particular, the idea to employ the inductive definition of the relation $M \longrightarrow Q$ is essentially due to them. We also want to thank Holger Benl for illuminating discussions.

2 A simply typed λ-calculus with constants

2.1 Types and terms; rewrite rules

We start from a given set of *ground types*. *Types* are inductively generated from ground types τ by $\rho \to \sigma$ and $\rho \times \sigma$. *Terms* are

x^ρ	typed variables,
c^ρ	constants,
$(\lambda x^\rho M^\sigma)^{\rho \to \sigma}$	abstractions,
$(M^{\rho \to \sigma} N^\rho)^\sigma$	applications,
$\langle M_0^\rho, M_1^\sigma \rangle^{\rho \times \sigma}$	pairing,
$\pi_0(M^{\rho \times \sigma})^\rho,\ \pi_1(M^{\rho \times \sigma})^\sigma$	projections.

Ground types will always be denoted by τ. We sometimes write $M0$ for $\pi_0(M)$ and $M1$ for $\pi_1(M)$. Two terms M and N are called *α-equal* – written $M =_\alpha N$ – if they are equal up to renaming of bound variables. Λ_ρ denotes the set of all terms of type ρ. $M\boldsymbol{N}$ denotes $(\ldots(MN_1)N_2 \ldots)N_n$, where some of the N_i's may be 0 or 1. By $\mathsf{FV}(M)$ we denote the set of variables occurring free in M. By $M_x[N]$ we mean substitution of every free occurrence of x in M by N, renaming bound variables if necessary. Similarly $M_{\boldsymbol{x}}[\boldsymbol{N}]$ denotes simultaneous substitution. Finally $\boldsymbol{\rho} \to \sigma$ stands for $\rho_1 \to (\rho_2 \to \ldots(\rho_n \to \sigma)\ldots)$ and $\lambda \boldsymbol{x} r$ abbreviates $\lambda x_1 \ldots \lambda x_n r$.

For the constants c^ρ we assume that some rewrite rules of the form $c\boldsymbol{K} \longmapsto N$ are given, where $\mathsf{FV}(N) \subseteq \mathsf{FV}(\boldsymbol{K})$ and $c\boldsymbol{K}, N$ have the same type (not necessarily a ground type). Moreover, for any two c-rules $c\boldsymbol{K} \longmapsto N$ and $c\boldsymbol{K}' \longmapsto N'$ with equal projection markers $0, 1$ we require that $\boldsymbol{K}$ and $\boldsymbol{K}'$ are of the same length. For example, if c is of type $(\tau \to \tau \to \tau) \times (\tau \to \tau)$, then the rules $c0x_1x_1 \longmapsto a$ and $c1x \longmapsto b$ are admitted.

Since we allowed almost arbitrary rewrite rules, it may happen that a term can be rewritten by different rules. In order to obtain a deterministic procedure we assume that for every constant $c^{\rho \to \sigma}$ we are given a function sel_c computing for every tuple of terms $\boldsymbol{M}^{\boldsymbol{\rho}}$ either a rule $c\boldsymbol{K} \longmapsto N$, in which case $\boldsymbol{M}$ is an instance of K, i.e. $M = K_x[L]$, or else the message "no-match", in which case M doesn't match any rule, i.e. there is no rule $cK \longmapsto N$ such that M is an instance of K. Clearly sel_c should be compatible with α-equality.

For readability a rule $cK \longmapsto \lambda y N$ with y distinct variables not free in K will be written $cKy \longmapsto N$.

2.2 Examples

(a) Usually we have the ground type ι of natural numbers available, with constructors 0^ι, $\mathrm{Suc}^{\iota \to \iota}$ and *recursion operators* $R_\rho^{\iota \to \rho \to (\iota \to \rho \to \rho) \to \rho}$. The rewrite rules for R are

$$R0yz \longmapsto y,$$
$$R(\mathrm{Suc}\, x)yz \longmapsto zx(Rxyz),$$

i.e. $R0 \longmapsto \lambda y \lambda z y$ and $R(\mathrm{Suc}\, x) \longmapsto \lambda y \lambda z(zx(Rxyz))$. A simplified scheme of the same form gives a cases construct:

$$\text{if } 0yz \longmapsto y,$$
$$\text{if } (\mathrm{Suc}\, x)yz \longmapsto z.$$

We may also add a rewrite rule (due to McCarthy [11])

$$\text{if } (\text{if } xyz)uv \longmapsto \text{if } x(\text{if } yuv)(\text{if } zuv).$$

Moreover we can write down rules according to the usual recursive definitions of addition and multiplication, and then also the rewrite rule

$$\mathsf{mult}(\mathsf{add}\, xy)z \longmapsto \mathsf{add}(\mathsf{mult}\, xz)(\mathsf{mult}\, yz).$$

Simultaneous recursion may be treated as well, e.g.

$$\mathsf{odd}\, 0 \longmapsto \mathrm{Suc}\, 0 \qquad\qquad \mathsf{even}\, 0 \longmapsto 0,$$
$$\mathsf{odd}(\mathrm{Suc}\, x) \longmapsto \mathsf{even}\, x \qquad\qquad \mathsf{even}(\mathrm{Suc}\, x) \longmapsto \mathsf{odd}\, x.$$

(b) We can also deal with infinitely branching trees like the Brouwer ordinals of type $\mathcal{O}$. We have constructors $0^{\mathcal{O}}$ and $\mathrm{Sup}^{(\iota \to \mathcal{O}) \to \iota}$, and for recursion constants $\mathrm{REC}_\rho^{\mathcal{O} \to \rho \to ((\iota \to \mathcal{O}) \to (\iota \to \rho) \to \rho) \to \rho}$. The rewrite rules for REC are:

$$\mathrm{REC}0yz \longmapsto y,$$
$$\mathrm{REC}(\mathrm{Sup}\, x)yz \longmapsto zx(\lambda u\, \mathrm{REC}(xu)yz).$$

(c) It is well known that by the Curry-Howard correspondence natural deduction proofs can be written as λ-terms with formulas as types. To use normalization by evaluation for normalizing proofs we may also introduce a ground type ex with constructors and destructors

$$(\exists^+_{\rho_0,\rho_1})^{\rho_0 \to \rho_1 \to \mathsf{ex}} \quad \text{and} \quad (\exists^-_{\rho_0,\rho_1,\sigma})^{\mathsf{ex} \to (\rho_0 \to \rho_1 \to \sigma) \to \sigma};$$

these are called *existential constants*. The rewrite rule for $\exists^-$ is

$$\exists^-(\exists^+ x_0 x_1)y \longmapsto yx_0x_1.$$

The (constructive) existential quantifier can then be dealt with conveniently by means of axioms

$$\exists^+ : \forall x(A \to \exists xA),$$
$$\exists^- : \exists xA \to \forall x(A \to B) \to B \quad \text{with } x \notin \mathsf{FV}(B).$$

If x has type ρ_0 and the formulas A and B are associated with the types ρ_1 and σ, respectively, the rewrite rule above is clear. It seems that the existential type ex could be replaced by $\rho_0 \times \rho_1$ and the constants $\exists^+_{\rho_0,\rho_1}$ and $\exists^-_{\rho_0,\rho_1,\sigma}$ by the terms $\lambda x_0 \lambda x_1 \langle x_0, x_1 \rangle$ and $\lambda z \lambda f(f\pi_0(z)\pi_1(z))$ respectively. However, the latter term does not correspond to a derivation in first order logic, since it is impossible to pass from an arbitrary derivation d (possibly with free assumptions) of $\exists xA$ to a term $\pi_0(d)$ and a derivation $\pi_1(d)$ of $A_x[\pi_0(d)]$.

2.3 Normalizable terms and their normal forms

We inductively define a relation $M \longrightarrow Q$ for terms M, Q. The intended meaning of $M \longrightarrow Q$ is that M is normalizable with (long) normal form Q. Here it is convenient to identify α-equal terms.

ETA.

$$\frac{My \longrightarrow Q}{M^{\rho \to \sigma} \longrightarrow \lambda yQ} \text{ for } y \notin \mathsf{FV}(M) \qquad \frac{\pi_0(M) \longrightarrow Q_0 \quad \pi_1(M) \longrightarrow Q_1}{M^{\rho \times \sigma} \longrightarrow \langle Q_0, Q_1 \rangle}$$

For the next rules it is enough that they all have a conclusion $M \longrightarrow Q$ with M, Q of a ground type τ.

BETA.

$$\frac{M_x[N]P \longrightarrow Q}{(\lambda xM)NP \longrightarrow Q} \qquad \frac{M_iP \longrightarrow Q}{\pi_i(\langle M_0, M_1 \rangle)P \longrightarrow Q} \text{ for } i \in \{0,1\}$$

VARAPP.

$$\frac{M \longrightarrow M'}{xM \longrightarrow xM'}$$

$M \longrightarrow M'$ abbreviates the list $M_1 \longrightarrow M'_1, \dots, M_n \longrightarrow M'_n$ of assumptions. Moreover, for every constant c we have the following rules.

RED.

$$\frac{M \longrightarrow M' \quad N_x[L]P \longrightarrow Q}{cMP \longrightarrow Q} \text{ if } \mathsf{sel}_c(M') = cK \longmapsto N \text{ and } M' = K_x[L]$$

PASSAPP.

$$\frac{M \longrightarrow M' \quad P \longrightarrow P'}{cMP \longrightarrow cM'P'} \text{ if } \mathsf{sel}_c(M') = \text{no-match}$$

For readability we will write RED in the following form and always assume that $cK \longmapsto N$ is the selected rule.

$$\frac{M \longrightarrow K_x[L] \qquad N_x[L]P \longrightarrow Q}{cMP \longrightarrow Q} \quad \text{if } cK \longmapsto N$$

The set LNF of terms in long normal form is defined as follows: $\lambda x M$, $\langle M, N \rangle$, xM and cMN are in LNF if $M, N, \boldsymbol{M}, \boldsymbol{N}$ are and $\mathsf{sel}_c(cM) = \text{no-match}$. It is obvious that $M \longrightarrow Q$ implies that $Q \in$ LNF. Furthermore it can be shown that in this case M normalizes to Q in the usual sense w.r.t. β-reduction, η-expansion and the rewrite rules for the constants. Conversely, if M is strongly normalizable w.r.t. these reductions (i.e. every reduction sequence terminates) then $M \longrightarrow Q$ for some Q. We omit the proofs of these facts since they will not be needed in the sequel. Although $M \longrightarrow Q$ implies that Q is a normal form of M, the converse is not true in general. To see this, consider the non-terminating rewrite rules $\mathsf{mult} x^\iota 0 \longmapsto 0$ and $\bot^\iota \longmapsto \bot$. Then 0 is a normal form of $\mathsf{mult}\bot 0$, but $\mathsf{mult}\bot 0 \longrightarrow 0$ does not hold. Moreover, the relation $M \longrightarrow Q$ clearly is not closed under substitution. However, it is closed under substitution of variables.

Lemma 1. *If $M \longrightarrow Q$, then $M_x[z] \longrightarrow Q_x[z]$ with a derivation of the same height.*

Proof. We use induction on the height of the derivation of $M \longrightarrow Q$, and only treat the rule ETA

$$\frac{My \longrightarrow Q}{M \longrightarrow \lambda y Q} \quad \text{for } y \notin \mathsf{FV}(M)$$

with M of type $\rho \to \sigma$. In case $x = y$ there is nothing to show, since then x does not occur free in the conclusion $M \longrightarrow \lambda y Q$. So assume $x \neq y$.

Subcase $y \neq z$. We must show $M_x[z] \longrightarrow \lambda y Q_x[z]$. By induction hypothesis $M_x[z]y \longrightarrow Q_x[z]$, since $x \neq y$. Therefore by ETA $M_x[z] \longrightarrow \lambda y Q_x[z]$, since $y \notin \mathsf{FV}(M_x[z])$ (because of $y \neq z$).

Subcase $y = z$. We must show $M_x[y] \longrightarrow (\lambda y Q)_x[y] = \lambda u Q_{x,y}[y, u]$ with a new variable u. By induction hypothesis $Mu \longrightarrow Q_y[u]$ with a derivation of the same height as that for $My \longrightarrow Q$, hence again by induction hypothesis $M_x[y]u \longrightarrow Q_{x,y}[y, u]$. Therefore by ETA $M_x[y] \longrightarrow \lambda u Q_{x,y}[y, u]$.

2.4 Term families

Since normalization by evaluation needs to create bound variables when "reifying" abstract objects of higher type, it is useful to follow DE BRUIJN's [9] style of representing bound variables in terms. This is done here – as in [4] – by means of *term families*. A term family is a parametrized version of a given term M. The idea is that the term family of M at index k reproduces M with bound variables renamed starting at k. For example, for

$$M := \lambda u \lambda v. c(\lambda x. v x)(\lambda y \lambda z. z u)$$

the associated term family M^∞ at index 3 yields

$$M^\infty(3) := \lambda x_3 \lambda x_4.c(\lambda x_5.x_4 x_5)(\lambda x_5 \lambda x_6.x_6 x_3).$$

We denote terms by $M, N, K, \ldots$, and term families by $r, s, t, \ldots$.
    To every term M^ρ we assign a term family $M^\infty : \mathbb{N} \to \Lambda_\rho$ by

$$x^\infty(k) := x,$$
$$(\lambda y M)^\infty(k) := \lambda x_k(M_y[x_k]^\infty(k+1)), \quad \langle M_0, M_1 \rangle^\infty(k) := \langle M_0^\infty(k), M_1^\infty(k) \rangle,$$
$$(MN)^\infty(k) := M^\infty(k)N^\infty(k), \qquad \pi_i(M)^\infty(k) := \pi_i(M^\infty(k)).$$

Application of a term family $r : \mathbb{N} \to \Lambda_{\rho \to \sigma}$ to a term family $s : \mathbb{N} \to \Lambda_\rho$ is the family $rs : \mathbb{N} \to \Lambda_\sigma$ defined by $(rs)(k) := r(k)s(k)$, and similarly for pairing $\langle r_0, r_1 \rangle(k) := \langle r_0(k), r_1(k) \rangle$ and projections $\pi_i(r)(k) := \pi_i(r(k))$. Hence e.g. $(MN)^\infty = M^\infty N^\infty$.

    Note that in contrast to our convention to consider terms up to bound renaming, the definition of $(\lambda y M)^\infty$ refers to a particular choice of the bound variable y. Part a of the following lemma shows that nevertheless this definition is compatible with our convention. In the rest of this subsection we drop the convention to identify α-equal terms. Hence $M = N$ means that M and N are literally identical as opposed to $M =_\alpha N$, which means equality up to bound renaming.

    We let $k > \mathsf{FV}(M)$ mean that k is greater than all i such that $x_i^\rho \in \mathsf{FV}(M)$ for some type ρ.

Lemma 2.   *a. If $M =_\alpha N$, then $M^\infty = N^\infty$.*
    b. If $k > \mathsf{FV}(M)$, then $M^\infty(k) =_\alpha M$.

Proof. a. Induction on the height of M. Only the case where M and N are abstractions is critical. So assume $\lambda y^\rho M =_\alpha \lambda z^\rho N$. Then $M_y[P] =_\alpha N_z[P]$ for all terms P^ρ. In particular $M_y[x_k] =_\alpha N_z[x_k]$ for arbitrary $k \in \mathbb{N}$. Hence $M_y[x_k]^\infty(k+1) = N_z[x_k]^\infty(k+1)$, by induction hypothesis. Therefore

$$(\lambda y M)^\infty(k) = \lambda x_k(M_y[x_k]^\infty(k+1)) = \lambda x_k(N_z[x_k]^\infty(k+1)) = (\lambda z N)^\infty(k).$$

b. Induction on the height of M. We only consider the case $\lambda y M$. The assumption $k > \mathsf{FV}(\lambda y M)$ implies $x_k \notin \mathsf{FV}(\lambda y M)$ and hence $\lambda y M =_\alpha \lambda x_k(M_y[x_k])$. Furthermore $k + 1 > \mathsf{FV}(M_y[x_k])$, and hence $M_y[x_k]^\infty(k+1) =_\alpha M_y[x_k]$, by induction hypothesis. Therefore

$$(\lambda y M)^\infty(k) = \lambda x_k(M_y[x_k]^\infty(k+1)) =_\alpha \lambda x_k(M_y[x_k]) =_\alpha \lambda y M. \qquad \Box$$

    Let $\mathsf{ext}(r) := r(k)$, where k is the least number greater than all i such that some variable of the form x_i^ρ occurs (free or bound) in $r(0)$.

Lemma 3. $\mathsf{ext}(M^\infty) =_\alpha M$.

Proof. Use part b of the lemma above, and the fact that $\mathsf{ext}(M^\infty) =_\alpha M^\infty(k)$ where $k > \mathsf{FV}(M)$.

3 Domain theoretic semantics of simply typed λ-calculi

In this section we shall discuss the domain theoretic semantics of simply typed lambda calculi in general. Although the constructions below are standard (see e.g. the books of LAMBEK/SCOTT [10] or CROLE [6]), we discuss them in some detail in order to make the paper accessible also for readers not familiar with this subject. Most constructions make sense in an arbitrary cartesian closed category (ccc). However we will confine ourselves to the domain semantics and will only occasionally comment on the categorical aspects.

It is well-known that SCOTT-domains with continuous functions form a cartesian closed category DOM. The product $D \times E$ is the set-theoretic product with the component-wise ordering. The exponential $[D \to E]$ is the continuous function space with the pointwise ordering. The terminal object is the one point space $1 := \{\bot\}$ (there is no initial object and there are no coproducts). In order to cope with the categorical interpretation we will identify an element x of a domain D with the mapping from 1 to D with value x.

Besides the cartesian closedness we also use the fact that DOM is closed under infinite products and that there is a fixed point operator $\text{FIX}: (D \to D) \to D$ assigning to every continuous function $f: D \to D$ its least fixed point $\text{FIX}(f) \in D$. Furthermore we will use that partial families of terms form a domain and some basic operations on terms and term families are continuous and hence exist as morphisms in the category. Any other ccc with these properties would do as well.

Elements of a product domain $D_1 \times \cdots \times D_n$ are written $[a_1, \ldots, a_n]$. If $f \in [D_1 \to [D_2 \to \ldots [D_n \to E] \ldots]]$ and $a_i \in D_i$, then $f(a_1, \ldots, a_n)$ or $f(a)$ stands for $f(a_1) \ldots (a_n)$.

An *interpretation* for a given system of ground types is a mapping $\mathcal{I}$ assigning to every ground type τ a domain $\mathcal{I}(\tau)$. Given such an interpretation we define domains $[\![\rho]\!]^{\mathcal{I}}$ for every type ρ by

$$[\![\tau]\!]^{\mathcal{I}} := \mathcal{I}(\tau), \quad [\![\rho \to \sigma]\!]^{\mathcal{I}} := [[\![\rho]\!]^{\mathcal{I}} \to [\![\sigma]\!]^{\mathcal{I}}], \quad [\![\rho \times \sigma]\!]^{\mathcal{I}} := [\![\rho]\!]^{\mathcal{I}} \times [\![\sigma]\!]^{\mathcal{I}}.$$

We write $[\![\rho_1, \ldots, \rho_n]\!]^{\mathcal{I}} := [\![\rho_1 \times \cdots \times \rho_n]\!]^{\mathcal{I}} = [\![\rho_1]\!]^{\mathcal{I}} \times \cdots \times [\![\rho_n]\!]^{\mathcal{I}} =: [\![\rho]\!]^{\mathcal{I}}$. An *interpretation of a typed lambda calculus* (specified by a set of ground types and a set of constants) is a mapping $\mathcal{I}$ assigning to every ground type τ a domain $\mathcal{I}(\tau)$ (hence $\mathcal{I}$ is an interpretation of ground types), and assigning to every constant c^ρ a value $\mathcal{I}(c) \in [\![\rho]\!]^{\mathcal{I}}$ (i.e. a morphism from 1 to $[\![\rho]\!]^{\mathcal{I}}$).

In order to extend such an interpretation to all terms we use the following continuous functions, i.e. morphisms (in the sequel a continuous function will be called morphism if its role as a morphism in the ccc DOM is to be emphasized):

$$!_D : D \to 1, \quad !_D(d) := \bot$$

$$\pi_i : D_1 \times \cdots \times D_n \to D_i, \quad \pi_i([a]) := a_i,$$

$$\text{curry} : [D \times E \to F] \to [D \to [E \to F]], \quad \text{curry}(f, a, b) := f([a, b]),$$

$$\text{eval} : [D \to E] \times D \to E, \quad \text{eval}(f, a) := f(a).$$

Furthermore we use the fact that morphisms are closed under composition ∘ and (since DOM is a ccc) under pairing $\langle .,. \rangle$, where for $f \colon D \to E$ and $g \colon D \to F$ the function $\langle f, g \rangle \colon D \to E \times F$ maps a to $[f(a), g(a)]$. For every type ρ and every list of distinct variables $\boldsymbol{x}^{\boldsymbol{\rho}} = x_1^{\rho_1}, \ldots, x_n^{\rho_n}$ we let $\Lambda_\rho(\boldsymbol{x})$ denote the set of terms of type ρ with free variables among $\{\boldsymbol{x}\}$. Let $\mathcal{I}$ be an interpretation. Then for every $M \in \Lambda_\rho(\boldsymbol{x}^{\boldsymbol{\rho}})$ we define a morphism $[\![M]\!]_{\boldsymbol{x}}^{\mathcal{I}} \colon [\![\boldsymbol{\rho}]\!] \to [\![\rho]\!]$ by

$$[\![c]\!]_{\boldsymbol{x}}^{\mathcal{I}} := \mathcal{I}(c) \circ !_{[\![\boldsymbol{\rho}]\!]},$$
$$[\![x_i]\!]_{\boldsymbol{x}}^{\mathcal{I}} := \pi_i,$$
$$[\![\lambda x M]\!]_{\boldsymbol{x}}^{\mathcal{I}} := \mathsf{curry}([\![M]\!]_{\boldsymbol{x},x}^{\mathcal{I}}),$$
$$[\![M N]\!]_{\boldsymbol{x}}^{\mathcal{I}} := \mathsf{eval} \circ \langle [\![M]\!]_{\boldsymbol{x}}^{\mathcal{I}}, [\![N]\!]_{\boldsymbol{x}}^{\mathcal{I}} \rangle,$$
$$[\![\langle M, N \rangle]\!]_{\boldsymbol{x}}^{\mathcal{I}} := \langle [\![M]\!]_{\boldsymbol{x}}^{\mathcal{I}}, [\![N]\!]_{\boldsymbol{x}}^{\mathcal{I}} \rangle,$$
$$[\![\pi_i(M)]\!]_{\boldsymbol{x}}^{\mathcal{I}} := \pi_i \circ [\![M]\!]_{\boldsymbol{x}}^{\mathcal{I}}.$$

This definition works in any ccc. For our purposes it will be more convenient to evaluate a term in a global environment and not in a local context. Let

$$\mathrm{ENV} := \prod_{x^\sigma \in \mathrm{VAR}} [\![\sigma]\!]^{\mathcal{I}} \in \mathrm{DOM}.$$

For every term $M \in \Lambda_\rho(x_1, \ldots, x_n)$ we define a continuous function

$$[\![M]\!]^{\mathcal{I}} \colon \mathrm{ENV} \to [\![\rho]\!]^{\mathcal{I}}, \quad [\![M]\!]_\xi^{\mathcal{I}} := [\![M]\!]_{\boldsymbol{x}}^{\mathcal{I}}([\xi(x_1), \ldots, \xi(x_n)]).$$

Formally this definition depends on a particular choice of the list of variables $x_1, \ldots, x_n$. However, because of the well-known coincidence property in fact it does not.

Lemma 4. *If $M \in \Lambda_\rho(y_1, \ldots, y_m)$ then*

$$[\![M]\!]_\xi^{\mathcal{I}} = [\![M]\!]_{\boldsymbol{y}}^{\mathcal{I}}(\xi(y_1), \ldots, \xi(y_m)).$$

From this we easily get the familiar equations

$$[\![c]\!]_\xi^{\mathcal{I}} = \mathcal{I}(c),$$
$$[\![x]\!]_\xi^{\mathcal{I}} = \xi(x),$$
$$[\![\lambda x M]\!]_\xi^{\mathcal{I}}(a) = [\![M]\!]_{\xi[x \mapsto a]}^{\mathcal{I}},$$
$$[\![M N]\!]_\xi^{\mathcal{I}} = [\![M]\!]_\xi^{\mathcal{I}}([\![N]\!]_\xi^{\mathcal{I}}),$$
$$[\![\langle M, N \rangle]\!]_\xi^{\mathcal{I}} = [[\![M]\!]_\xi^{\mathcal{I}}, [\![N]\!]_\xi^{\mathcal{I}}],$$
$$[\![\pi_i(M)]\!]_\xi^{\mathcal{I}} = \pi_i([\![M]\!]_\xi^{\mathcal{I}}).$$

In many cases the interpretation $\mathcal{I}$ of the constants will have to be defined recursively, by e.g. referring to $[\![M]\!]^{\mathcal{I}}$ for several terms M. This causes no problem, since the functionals $[\![M^\rho]\!]^{\mathcal{I}} \colon \mathrm{ENV} \to [\![\rho]\!]$ depend continuously on $\mathcal{I}$, where $\mathcal{I}$ is to be considered as an element of the infinite product $\Pi_{c^\rho}[\![\rho]\!]$. This can be seen as follows: Looking at their definitions we see that the functions $[\mathcal{I}, a] \mapsto [\![M]\!]_x^{\mathcal{I}}(a)$ are built by composition from the continuous functions

$$\pi_{c^\sigma} : \Pi_{c^\rho}[\![\rho]\!] \to [\![\sigma]\!], \quad \pi_{c^\sigma}(\mathcal{I}) := \mathcal{I}(c),$$
$$\cdot \circ \cdot : [E \to F] \times [D \to E] \to [D \to F],$$
$$\langle \cdot, \cdot \rangle : [D \to E] \times [D \to F] \to [D \to E \times F],$$

as well as the functions $!_D, \pi_i,$ curry and eval above. Hence $[\mathcal{I}, a] \mapsto [\![M]\!]_x^{\mathcal{I}}(a)$ is continuous. But then also $[\mathcal{I}, \xi] \mapsto [\![M]\!]_\xi^{\mathcal{I}}$ is continuous, since we have $[\![M]\!]_\xi^{\mathcal{I}} = [\![M]\!]_x^{\mathcal{I}}([\pi_{x_1}(\xi), \ldots, \pi_{x_n}(\xi)])$, where $\pi_{x^\rho} : \text{ENV} \to [\![\rho]\!]$, $\pi_x(\xi) := \xi(x)$.

Hence the value $\mathcal{I}(c)$ may be defined as a least fixed point of a continuous function on the domain $\Pi_{c^\rho}[\![\rho]\!]$. – In the sequel we will omit the superscript $\mathcal{I}$ when it is clear from the context.

The following facts hold in any ccc.

Lemma 5.

$$[\![M_x[N]]\!]_\xi = [\![M]\!]_{\xi[x \mapsto [\![N]\!]_\xi]} \qquad \textit{(substitution lemma)}$$
$$[\![(\lambda x M)N]\!]_\xi = [\![M_x[N]]\!]_\xi \qquad \textit{(beta 1)}$$
$$[\![\pi_i(\langle M_0, M_1 \rangle)]\!]_\xi = [\![M_i]\!]_\xi \qquad \textit{(beta 2)}$$
$$[\![M]\!]_\xi = [\![\lambda y(My)]\!]_\xi \quad (y^\rho \notin \mathsf{FV}(M^{\rho \to \sigma})) \qquad \textit{(eta 1)}$$
$$[\![M]\!]_\xi = [\![\langle \pi_0(M), \pi_1(M) \rangle]\!]_\xi \qquad \textit{(eta 2)}$$

Lemma 6. *If $[\![P]\!]_\xi = [\![Q]\!]_\xi$ for all environments ξ, and M is transformed into N by replacing an occurrence of P in M by Q, then $[\![M]\!]_\xi = [\![N]\!]_\xi$ for all environments ξ.*

Proof. Induction on M.

Lemma 7. *If $M \xrightarrow{1}_\beta N$ or $M \xrightarrow{1}_\eta N$, then $[\![M]\!]_\xi = [\![N]\!]_\xi$.*

4   Normalization by evaluation

We now consider a special model, whose ground type objects are made from syntactic material. We let $\mathbb{N} \xrightarrow{\cup} \Lambda_\rho$ denote the set of partial term families, i.e. partial functions from the integers to the set of terms of type ρ. $\mathbb{N} \xrightarrow{\cup} \Lambda_\rho$ partially ordered by inclusion of graphs is a domain. We interpret the ground types by

$$\mathcal{I}(\tau) := \mathbb{N} \xrightarrow{\cup} \Lambda_\tau.$$

This gives us an interpretation $[\![\rho]\!] = [\![\rho]\!]^{\mathcal{I}} \in \text{DOM}$ for every type ρ. In order to define the interpretation of the constants, some preparations are necessary.

4.1 Reification and reflection; interpretation of the constants

For every type ρ we define two continuous functions

$$\downarrow_\rho: [\![\rho]\!] \to (\mathbb{N} \overset{\cup}{\to} \Lambda_\rho) \quad (\text{``reify''}) \qquad \uparrow_\rho: (\mathbb{N} \overset{\cup}{\to} \Lambda_\rho) \to [\![\rho]\!] \quad (\text{``reflect''}).$$

These functions will be used when defining the interpretation of the constants as well as in our final goal, normalization by evaluation. $\downarrow_\rho$ and $\uparrow_\rho$ are defined simultaneously by induction on the type ρ.

$$\downarrow_\tau(r) := r, \qquad\qquad\qquad\qquad \uparrow_\tau(r) := r,$$
$$\downarrow_{\rho\to\sigma}(a)(k) := \lambda x_k^\rho \downarrow_\sigma \big(a(\uparrow_\rho(x_k^\infty))\big)(k{+}1), \quad \uparrow_{\rho\to\sigma}(r)(b) := \uparrow_\sigma(r\downarrow_\rho(b)),$$
$$\downarrow_{\rho\times\sigma}([a,b]) := \langle \downarrow_\rho(a), \downarrow_\sigma(b)\rangle, \qquad\qquad \uparrow_{\rho\times\sigma}(r) := [\uparrow_\rho(\pi_0(r)), \uparrow_\sigma(\pi_1(r))].$$

Note that for $a_i \in [\![\rho_i]\!]$ we have $\uparrow_{\rho\to\sigma}(r)(a_1,\ldots a_n) = \uparrow_\sigma(\downarrow_{\rho_1}(a_1)\ldots\downarrow_{\rho_n}(a_n))$, to which we refer by

$$\uparrow(r)(a) = \uparrow(r\downarrow(a)). \tag{1}$$

We now define the values of the constants c in our special model. Note that we can view $\uparrow$ as an environment: it assigns to every variable x of type ρ the value $\uparrow(x^\infty) \in [\![\rho]\!]$.

$$\mathcal{I}(c)(a) := \begin{cases} [\![N]\!]^{\mathcal{I}}_{[x\mapsto[L]^{\mathcal{I}}_\uparrow]} & \text{if } \mathsf{sel}_c(\mathsf{ext}(\downarrow(a))) = cK \longmapsto N \text{ and } \mathsf{ext}(\downarrow(a))=K_x[L] \\ \uparrow(c^\infty \downarrow(a)) & \text{if } \mathsf{sel}_c(\mathsf{ext}(\downarrow(a))) = \mathsf{no\text{-}match} \\ \bot & \text{otherwise, i.e. } \mathsf{ext}(\downarrow(a)) \text{ is undefined.} \end{cases}$$

Note that this in general is a recursive definition, since the terms N and L may contain c. We now obtain the correctness of normalization by evaluation:

Theorem 1. *If* $M \longrightarrow Q$, *then* $\downarrow([\![M]\!]_\uparrow) = Q^\infty$.

Proof. By induction on the height of the derivation of $M \longrightarrow Q$. For brevity we leave out the rules concerning product types, since their treatment does not bring up any new issues.

Case ETA, i.e.

$$\frac{My \longrightarrow Q}{M \longrightarrow \lambda y Q} \quad \text{for } y \notin \mathsf{FV}(M)$$

with M of type $\rho \to \sigma$. By lemma 1 we then have $Mx_k \longrightarrow Q_y[x_k]$ with a derivation of the same height as that of the given derivation of $My \longrightarrow Q$, hence by induction hypothesis $\downarrow([\![Mx_k]\!]_\uparrow) = Q_y[x_k]^\infty$. We obtain

$$\downarrow([\![M]\!]_\uparrow)(k) = \lambda x_k \left(\downarrow([\![M]\!]_\uparrow(\uparrow(x_k^\infty)))(k+1) \right)$$
$$= \lambda x_k \left(\downarrow([\![Mx_k]\!]_\uparrow)(k+1) \right)$$
$$= \lambda x_k \left(Q_y[x_k]^\infty(k+1) \right) \qquad \text{by IH}$$
$$= (\lambda y Q)^\infty(k).$$

In the following cases the rules are of ground type τ, so we use that $\downarrow(\llbracket M \rrbracket_\uparrow) = \llbracket M \rrbracket_\uparrow$ for $M \in \Lambda_\tau$.

Case BETA, i.e.

$$\frac{M_x[N]P \longrightarrow Q}{(\lambda x M)NP \longrightarrow Q}$$

$$
\begin{aligned}
\llbracket (\lambda x M)NP \rrbracket_\uparrow &= \llbracket M_x[N]P \rrbracket_\uparrow && \text{by lemma 7}\\
&= Q^\infty && \text{by IH.}
\end{aligned}
$$

Case RED, i.e.

$$\frac{M \longrightarrow K_x[L] \qquad N_x[L]P \longrightarrow Q}{cMP \longrightarrow Q}$$

where $cK \longmapsto N$ is the selected rule, i.e. $\mathsf{sel}_c(K_x[L]) = cK \longmapsto N$. Recall

$$\llbracket cMP \rrbracket_\uparrow = \mathcal{I}(c)(\llbracket M \rrbracket_\uparrow)(\llbracket P \rrbracket_\uparrow).$$

By induction hypothesis $\downarrow(\llbracket M \rrbracket_\uparrow) = K_x[L]^\infty$. By definition of $\mathcal{I}(c)$ we have to compute $\mathsf{sel}_c(\mathsf{ext}(\downarrow(\llbracket M \rrbracket_\uparrow)))$. By lemma 3 $\mathsf{ext}(K_x[L]^\infty) = K_x[L]$. Hence $\mathsf{sel}_c(\mathsf{ext}(\downarrow(\llbracket M \rrbracket_\uparrow))) = \mathsf{sel}_c(K_x[L]) = cK \longmapsto N$, and therefore

$$
\begin{aligned}
\llbracket cMP \rrbracket_\uparrow &= \mathcal{I}(c)(\llbracket M \rrbracket_\uparrow)(\llbracket P \rrbracket_\uparrow) \\
&= \llbracket N \rrbracket_{[x \mapsto [L]_\uparrow]}(\llbracket P \rrbracket_\uparrow) && \text{by definition of } \mathcal{I}(c) \\
&= \llbracket N_x[L] \rrbracket_\uparrow(\llbracket P \rrbracket_\uparrow) && \text{by the substitution lemma} \\
&= \llbracket N_x[L]P \rrbracket_\uparrow \\
&= Q^\infty && \text{by IH.}
\end{aligned}
$$

Case VARAPP, i.e.

$$\frac{M \longrightarrow M'}{xM \longrightarrow xM'}$$

$$
\begin{aligned}
\llbracket xM \rrbracket_\uparrow &= \uparrow(x^\infty)(\llbracket M \rrbracket_\uparrow) \\
&= x^\infty \downarrow(\llbracket M \rrbracket_\uparrow) && \text{by (1)} \\
&= x^\infty (M')^\infty && \text{by IH} \\
&= (xM')^\infty.
\end{aligned}
$$

Case PASSAPP, i.e.

$$\frac{M \longrightarrow M' \quad P \longrightarrow P'}{cMP \longrightarrow cM'P'}$$

where there is no rule $cK \longmapsto N$ such that M' is of an instance of K, i.e. $\mathsf{sel}_c(M') = \mathsf{no\text{-}match}$. We obtain by induction hypothesis $\downarrow(\llbracket M \rrbracket_\uparrow) = M'^\infty$ and hence $\text{sel}_c\big(\downarrow([\![M]\!]_\uparrow)\big) = \text{sel}_c\big(\text{ext}(M'^\infty)\big) = \text{sel}_c(M') = \text{no-match}$. Hence

$$
\begin{aligned}
[\![cMP]\!]_\uparrow &= \mathcal{I}(c)([\![M]\!]_\uparrow)([\![P]\!]_\uparrow) \\
&= \uparrow\!\big(c^\infty\!\downarrow([\![M]\!]_\uparrow)\big)([\![P]\!]_\uparrow) \quad \text{by definition of } \mathcal{I}(c) \\
&= c^\infty\!\downarrow([\![M,P]\!]_\uparrow) \quad\quad\quad \text{by (1)} \\
&= c^\infty (M')^\infty (P')^\infty \quad\quad\quad \text{by IH} \\
&= (cM'P')^\infty.
\end{aligned}
$$
$\hfill\square$

4.2 Special rewrite rules

We will now consider special cases of our general form of rewrite rules – to be called d-, e- and f-rules –, where the interpretation function $\mathcal{I}$ and hence normalization by evaluation is more efficient. It will be shown that theorem 1 continues to hold.

d-rules. One problem with the interpretation of the constants in 4.1 is a certain inefficiency inherent in it: after computing a syntactic reification of a by $\text{ext}(\downarrow(a))$, determining the relevant rule $cK \longmapsto N$ as $\text{sel}_c(\text{ext}(\downarrow(a)))$ and reading off L such that $\text{ext}(\downarrow(a)) = K_{\boldsymbol{x}}[L]$, we must go back to semantics and compute $[\![L]\!]_\uparrow$.

However, in many cases we have rules of the special form

$$dN_z[K] \longmapsto P_z[K], \tag{2}$$

with K of ground types and $\text{FV}(P) \subseteq z$. Notice that $N_z[K]_{\boldsymbol{x}}[L] = N_z[K_{\boldsymbol{x}}[L]]$ and $P_z[K]_{\boldsymbol{x}}[L] = P_z[K_{\boldsymbol{x}}[L]]$. So for instance $R0 \longmapsto \lambda y, z.y$ and $R(\text{Suc}x) \longmapsto \lambda y, z.zx(Rxyz)$ are instances of this kind of rules. Then it is tempting to define

$$
\mathcal{I}(d)(a) := \begin{cases}
[\![P]\!]_{[z \mapsto K_{\boldsymbol{x}}[L]^\infty]} & \text{if } \text{sel}_d(\text{ext}(\downarrow(a))) = dN_z[K] \longmapsto P_z[K] \\
& \text{and } \text{ext}(\downarrow(a)) = N_z[K_{\boldsymbol{x}}[L]] \\
\uparrow(d^\infty\!\downarrow(a)) & \text{if } \text{sel}_d(\text{ext}(\downarrow(a))) = \text{no-match} \\
\bot & \text{otherwise.}
\end{cases}
$$

Here the necessity to evaluate L no longer exists; rather, we can work with the term family $K_{\boldsymbol{x}}[L]^\infty$ directly.

e-rules. One may still not be satisfied with the d-rules, since each time $\mathcal{I}(d)(a)$ is evaluated we need to compute $\text{sel}_d(\text{ext}(\downarrow(a)))$ in order to determine the rule to be applied. Now for a_i of ground type each $r_i := \downarrow(a_i)$ is a term family, and the computation of $\text{ext}(r_i) = r_i(k)$ involves computing k from the set of all free and bound variables of the term $r_i(0)$. However, in many cases it suffices to evaluate the term family r_i at a fixed index, say 0.

Consider e-rules of the form

$$eK \longmapsto P_z[K] \tag{3}$$

with K of ground types and $\mathrm{FV}(P) \subseteq z$, and assume that for normal terms M

$$\mathsf{sel}_e(M^\infty(0)) = \mathsf{sel}_e(M). \tag{4}$$

This is particularly likely to hold if the terms K are λ-free, since the formation of term families $K_x[L]^\infty$ only affects names of λ-bound variables. Now define

$$\mathcal{I}(e)(r) := \begin{cases} [\![P]\!]_{[z \mapsto r]} & \text{if } \mathsf{sel}_e(r(0)) = eK \longmapsto P_z[K] \\ \uparrow(e^\infty r) & \text{if } \mathsf{sel}_e(r(0)) = \text{no-match} \\ \bot & \text{otherwise.} \end{cases}$$

Note that if we would interpret e according to the d-rules, we would have $[\![P]\!]_{[z \mapsto \mathrm{ext}(r)^\infty]}$ in the first case. But $\mathrm{ext}(r)^\infty$ and r will be different in general.

Rules of the form (3) satisfying (4) are particularly possible if we work within the ground type ι of natural numbers and have the predecessor function available, as a fixed constant with a fixed interpretation.

f-rules. There is a final type of rules – to be called f-rules – which we want to consider. Their usefulness comes up when we work with concrete data types like the type ι of natural numbers and want to employ e.g. the usual polynomial normal form of terms. For instance, the term $(n+3)(n^2+2n+5)$ should normalize to $n^3+5n^2+11n+15$. Abstractly, what we have here is a function norm: $\Lambda_\tau \to \Lambda_\tau$ for a ground type τ, and it will turn out that all we need to prove theorem 1 are the following properties:

$$\mathsf{norm}^2 = \mathsf{norm} \tag{5}$$

$$\mathsf{norm}(M^\infty(k)) = \mathsf{norm}(M)^\infty(k) \tag{6}$$

$$\text{if } M \text{ is } cde\text{-normal, then } \mathsf{norm}(M) \text{ is } cde\text{-normal} \tag{7}$$

where cde-normal refers to the c-rules, the d-rules and the e-rules (and of course the β-rule). Given such a function norm, we add all rules of the form

$$fM \longmapsto \mathsf{norm}(fM) \quad \text{provided both are different.} \tag{8}$$

with M and fM of ground types; these should be the only rules for f. We define the sel_f function by

$$\mathsf{sel}_f(M) := \begin{cases} fM \longmapsto \mathsf{norm}(fM) & \text{if } fM \text{ and } \mathsf{norm}(fM) \text{ are different,} \\ \text{no-match} & \text{otherwise.} \end{cases}$$

The interpretation is defined by

$$\mathcal{I}(f)(r)(k) := \mathsf{norm}(fr(k)).$$

Extension of theorem 1. We will show that theorem 1 (i.e. $M \longrightarrow Q$ implies $\downarrow([\![M]\!]_\uparrow) = Q^\infty$) continues to hold for such constants d, e and f with interpretations as given above.

Lemma 8. *For normal terms M we have*

$$\downarrow([\![M]\!]_\uparrow) = M^\infty.$$

Proof. Induction on the height of M.

Case $\lambda y^\rho M^\sigma$. This is similar to, but a little simpler than the case ETA in theorem 1.

$$\downarrow([\![\lambda y M]\!]_\uparrow)(k) = \lambda x_k \left(\downarrow([\![\lambda y M]\!]_\uparrow(\uparrow(x_k^\infty)))(k+1) \right)$$
$$= \lambda x_k \left(\downarrow([\![M_y[x_k]]\!]_\uparrow)(k+1) \right)$$
$$= \lambda x_k (M_y[x_k]^\infty(k+1)) \qquad \text{by IH}$$
$$= (\lambda y M)^\infty(k).$$

Case $\langle M, N \rangle$. Easy.

Case $(x M)^\tau$.

$$[\![x M]\!]_\uparrow = \uparrow(x^\infty)([\![M]\!]_\uparrow)$$
$$= x^\infty \downarrow([\![M]\!]_\uparrow) \qquad \text{by (1)}$$
$$= x^\infty M^\infty \qquad \text{by IH}$$
$$= (x M)^\infty.$$

Case $(c M P)^\tau$. Since $c M P$ is normal, we have $\mathsf{sel}_c(M) = $ no-match by our general requirements on sel_c, and by induction hypothesis and lemma 3 $\mathsf{sel}_c(\mathsf{ext}(\downarrow([\![M]\!]_\uparrow))) = \mathsf{sel}_c(\mathsf{ext}(M^\infty)) = \mathsf{sel}_c(M) = $ no-match, hence

$$[\![c M P]\!]_\uparrow = \mathcal{I}(c)([\![M]\!]_\uparrow)([\![P]\!]_\uparrow)$$
$$= \uparrow(c^\infty \downarrow([\![M]\!]_\uparrow))[\![P]\!]_\uparrow$$
$$= c^\infty \downarrow([\![M]\!]_\uparrow)\downarrow([\![P]\!]_\uparrow) \qquad \text{by (1)}$$
$$= c^\infty M^\infty P^\infty \qquad \text{by IH}$$
$$= (c M P)^\infty.$$

Case $(d M P)^\tau$. We have only used that the interpretation of the constants c satisfies $\mathcal{I}(c)(a) = \uparrow(c^\infty \downarrow(a))$ if $\mathsf{sel}_c(\mathsf{ext}(\downarrow(a))) = $ no-match, and this also holds for the constants d.

Case $(e M P)^\tau$. Since $e M P$ is normal, we again have $\mathsf{sel}_e(M) = $ no-match. By induction hypothesis and (4) $\mathsf{sel}_e([\![M]\!]_\uparrow(0)) = \mathsf{sel}_e(M^\infty(0)) = \mathsf{sel}_e(M) = $ no-match. The proof then proceeds as before.

Case $(fM)^\tau$. Since fM is normal, we have $fM = \text{norm}(fM)$, hence

$$\begin{aligned}
[\![fM]\!]_\uparrow(k) &= \mathcal{I}(f)([\![M]\!]_\uparrow)(k) \\
&= \text{norm}(f[\![M]\!]_\uparrow(k)) \\
&= \text{norm}(fM^\infty(k)) \qquad \text{by IH} \\
&= \text{norm}((fM)^\infty(k)) \\
&= \text{norm}(fM)^\infty(k) \qquad \text{by (6)} \\
&= (fM)^\infty(k).
\end{aligned}$$
□

Theorem 2. *If* $M \longrightarrow Q$ *w.r.t. all types of rules above, then* $\downarrow([\![M]\!]_\uparrow) = Q^\infty$.

Proof. As for theorem 1; we only have to add an argument for the new rules in case RED.

Case $dN_z[K] \longmapsto P_z[K]$ for RED, i.e.

$$\frac{M \longrightarrow N_z[K_x[L]] \qquad P_z[K_x[L]]P \longrightarrow Q}{dMP \longrightarrow Q}$$

where $\text{sel}_d(N_z[K_x[L]]) = dN_z[K] \longmapsto P_z[K]$, i.e. $dN_z[K] \longmapsto P_z[K]$ is the selected rule. Recall

$$[\![dMP]\!]_\uparrow = \mathcal{I}(d)([\![M]\!]_\uparrow)([\![P]\!]_\uparrow).$$

By induction hypothesis we have $\downarrow([\![M]\!]_\uparrow) = N_z[K_x[L]]^\infty$. Now by lemma 3 $\text{ext}(N_z[K_x[L]]^\infty) = N_z[K_x[L]]$, so

$$\text{sel}_d(\text{ext}(\downarrow([\![M]\!]_\uparrow))) = \text{sel}_d(N_z[K_x[L]]) = dN_z[K] \longmapsto P_z[K].$$

Hence

$$\begin{aligned}
[\![dMP]\!]_\uparrow &= \mathcal{I}(d)([\![M]\!]_\uparrow)([\![P]\!]_\uparrow) \\
&= [\![P]\!]_{[z \mapsto K_x[L]^\infty]}([\![P]\!]_\uparrow) \qquad \text{by definition of } \mathcal{I}(d) \\
&= [\![P]\!]_{[z \mapsto [\![K_x[L]]\!]_\uparrow]}([\![P]\!]_\uparrow) \qquad \text{see below} \\
&= [\![P_z[K_x[L]]]\!]_\uparrow([\![P]\!]_\uparrow) \qquad \text{by the substitution lemma} \\
&= [\![P_z[K_x[L]]P]\!]_\uparrow \\
&= Q^\infty \qquad \text{by IH.}
\end{aligned}$$

It remains to show that $K_x[L]^\infty = [\![K_x[L]]\!]_\uparrow$. Now $M \longrightarrow N_z[K]_x[L]$, hence $N_z[K_x[L]] \in \text{LNF}$, and so all subterms of ground type, in particular $K_x[L]$, are also in LNF. Hence $[\![K_x[L]]\!]_\uparrow = \downarrow([\![K_x[L]]\!]_\uparrow) = K_x[L]^\infty$ by lemma 8.

Case $eK \longmapsto P_z[K]$ for RED, i.e.

$$\frac{M \longrightarrow K_x[L] \qquad P_z[K_x[L]]P \longrightarrow Q}{eMP \longrightarrow Q}$$

where $eK \longmapsto P_z[K]$ is the selected rule, i.e. $\mathsf{sel}_e(K_x[L]) = eK \longmapsto P_z[K]$. By induction hypothesis we have $[\![M]\!]_\uparrow = K_x[L]^\infty$, hence $\mathsf{sel}_e([\![M]\!]_\uparrow(0)) = \mathsf{sel}_e(K_x[L]^\infty(0)) = \mathsf{sel}_e(K_x[L]) = eK \longmapsto P_z[K]$ by (4). Therefore

$$
\begin{aligned}
[\![eMP]\!]_\uparrow &= \mathcal{I}(e)([\![M]\!]_\uparrow)([\![P]\!]_\uparrow) \\
&= [\![P]\!]_{[z \mapsto [\![M]\!]_\uparrow]}([\![P]\!]_\uparrow) && \text{by definition of } \mathcal{I}(e) \\
&= [\![P]\!]_{[z \mapsto K_x[L]^\infty]}([\![P]\!]_\uparrow) && \text{by IH} \\
&= [\![P]\!]_{[z \mapsto [\![K_x[L]]\!]_\uparrow]}([\![P]\!]_\uparrow) && \text{since } [\![K_x[L]]\!]_\uparrow = K_x[L]^\infty \text{ by lemma 8} \\
&= [\![P_z[K_x[L]]]\!]_\uparrow([\![P]\!]_\uparrow) && \text{by the substitution lemma} \\
&= [\![P_z[K_x[L]]P]\!]_\uparrow \\
&= Q^\infty && \text{by IH.}
\end{aligned}
$$

Case $fK \longrightarrow \mathsf{norm}(fK)$ for RED, i.e.

$$
\frac{M \longrightarrow K \qquad \mathsf{norm}(fK) \longrightarrow Q}{fM \longrightarrow Q}
$$

Note that fK is cde-normal, hence by (7) $\mathsf{norm}(fK)$ is cde-normal as well. Moreover because of (5) we have $\mathsf{norm}^2(fK) = \mathsf{norm}(fK)$, so $\mathsf{norm}(fK)$ is also normal w.r.t. the f-rules. Now by induction on the rules for $\longrightarrow$ one can see at once that for normal M, $M \longrightarrow Q$ implies $M = Q$. Therefore, in our instance of the rule RED above we actually have $\mathsf{norm}(fK) = Q$. Now we obtain

$$
\begin{aligned}
[\![fM]\!]_\uparrow(k) &= \mathcal{I}(f)([\![M]\!]_\uparrow)(k) \\
&= \mathsf{norm}(f[\![M]\!]_\uparrow(k)) && \text{by definition of } \mathcal{I}(f) \\
&= \mathsf{norm}(fK^\infty(k)) && \text{by IH} \\
&= \mathsf{norm}((fK)^\infty(k)) \\
&= \mathsf{norm}(fK)^\infty(k) && \text{by (6)} \\
&= Q^\infty(k). && \qquad\qquad \square
\end{aligned}
$$

5 Comparison

The difference of the present approach to those of other authors is mainly that $\longrightarrow$ is modelled simply by the function space. This means that we only use the properties of application and abstraction given in the definition of a cartesian closed category. Due to this fact we can use an internal evaluation of a programming language like SCHEME. In other approaches [1, 5, 7] evaluation has to be defined by hand. A comparison between an internal and a hand made evaluation shows that the former is much more efficient. We tested this in SCHEME and present a table with the run-times for some appropriate examples below.

5.1 Related work

In [1] ALTENKIRCH, HOFMANN and STREICHER give a categorical explanation of normalization by evaluation. Therefore they describe terms as morphisms from a context to their types. The model is not an arbitrary cartesian closed category but a presheaf over a category W of weakenings with contexts as objects. Roughly speaking weakenings are projections on finite sequences of variables and a presheaf can be seen as a variable set or a proof relevant KRIPKE structure. In the interpretation of $\Lambda_{\rho \to \sigma}$ objects depend on $[\![\Lambda_\rho]\!]$ as well as on the morphisms of W (cf. the implication in a KRIPKE structure). In their proof they make use of a category that has both, a semantical and a syntactical component, called glueing model. They also describe a correspondence between intuitionistic completeness proofs and normalization.

CUBRIC, DYBJER and SCOTT [7] have a similar aim, namely to give a normalization proof with as little syntactic properties as possible. They also describe terms as morphisms and use a presheaf model over these terms, but here categories are equipped with a partial equivalence relation. So the function ↓ (called quote in [1, 5, 7]) appears as natural isomorphism between the YONEDA embedding and an interpretation, that interprets atoms by YONEDA. The function quote and its inverse are used when the universal property of the category of terms is shown. In the appendix they investigate some λ-theories, but it seems that these are too restricted for practical purposes.

COQUAND and DYBJER [5] also interpret terms in a model and reconstruct the normal forms via the function quote. The λ-calculus is given by S- and K-combinators, so they get slightly different normal forms. The model is a glueing model, therefore it is not extensional and application is application of the semantic part. They emphasize that they use an intuitionistic metalanguage and have implemented the algorithm in ALF.

DANVY [8] successfully uses the ↓ and ↑ functions for partial evaluation, in particular for compiler construction. His setting is the two-level λ-calculus.

5.2 Comparison of algorithms

We tested different ways to normalize simply typed λ-terms. The first is normalization by evaluation using an internal eval function of the given programming language. The second is normalization by evaluation with a user defined eval function. The third is normalization by means of a user defined β-conversion. In situations where application is not the usual one, e.g. in presheaf models or in glueing models, and for typed programming language like Standard ML, whose eval is not accessible to the user, the first way is excluded.

To test the different normalization algorithms we used iterated functions, i.e. $M_{nm} := (\text{it}_n^3 \text{it}_m^2)(\lambda x^0 x)^1$, where $\text{it}_n^{i+2} := \lambda f^{i+1} \lambda x^i (f \ldots (fx) \ldots)$ with n occurrences of f. Here the type 0 is any ground type and $i + 1 := i \to i$. So it_n^i is of type i and M_{nm} is of type 1 with $\lambda x^0 x$ as its normal form. The point in these examples is that the result is small (always $\lambda x^0 x$), but due to iterated function applications it takes many steps to reach the normal form. The table shows that normalization by evaluation with an internal evaluation is about twenty times faster than the version with self-made evaluation, and this again is faster than a recursively defined normalization. The run-times are given in seconds resp. minutes and seconds:

	normalization by an internal evaluation	normalization by a defined evaluation	recursive normalization
M_{45}	0	1	3
M_{55}	0	2	14
M_{56}	0	6	stack overflow
M_{66}	2	36	
M_{67}	4	1:27	
M_{76}	10	3:34	
M_{77}	31	10:13	
M_{78}	1:16	25:28	
M_{88}	10:12	207:59	

Now we give the main definitions of an implementation in SCHEME. We restrict ourselves to the case of closed terms since by λ-abstraction we can bind all free variables. First our $\downarrow$ and $\uparrow$-functions:

```
(define (reify type)
  (if (ground-type? type)
      (lambda (x) x)
      (let ((reflect-rho (reflect (arg-type type)))
            (reify-sigma (reify (val-type type))))
        (lambda (a)
          (lambda (k)
            (let ((xk (mvar k)))
              (abst xk ((reify-sigma
                              (a (reflect-rho (lambda (l) xk))))
                        (+ k 1)))))))))

(define (reflect type)
  (if (ground-type? type)
      (lambda (x) x)
      (let ((reify-rho (reify (arg-type type)))
            (reflect-sigma (reflect (val-type type))))
        (lambda (r)
          (lambda (a)
            (reflect-sigma
             (lambda (k)
               (app (r k) ((reify-rho a) k)))))))))
```

Normalization with internal evaluation:

```
(define (ev1 x) (eval x (the-environment)))
```

```
(define (norm1 r rho) (((reify rho) (ev1 r)) 0))
```

Normalization with defined evaluation:

```
(define (ev2 M)
  (lambda (env)
    (cond ((variable? M) (cadr (assq M env)))
          ((application? M)
           (((ev2 (operator M)) env) ((ev2 (argument M)) env)))
          ((abstraction? M)
           (lambda (a) ((ev2 (kernel M))
                        (cons (list (abstvar M) a) env))))
          (else #f))))
```

```
(define (norm2 r rho) (((reify rho) ((ev2 r) ())) 0))
```

Finally a recursive normalization:

```
(define (norm3 r)
  (cond ((variable? r) r)
        ((application? r)
         (let ((op (norm3 (operator r)))
               (arg (norm3 (argument r))))
           (if (abstraction? op)
               (let ((x (abstvar op))
                     (s (kernel op)))
                 (norm3 (substitute s x arg)))
               (app op arg))))
        ((abstraction? r)
         (abst (abstvar r) (norm3 (kernel r))))))
```

The auxiliary definitions are not mentioned and hopefully obvious. So for instance mvar produces variables x_k from k, abst constructs a λ-abstraction $\lambda x_k M$ from x_k and M, app constructs an application MN from M and N, and abstvar resp. kernel gets out x_k resp. M of $\lambda x_k M$.

References

1. Thorsten Altenkirch, Martin Hofmann, and Thomas Streicher. Categorical reconstruction of a reduction free normalization proof. In *CTCS'95, Cambridge*, volume 953 of *Lecture Notes in Computer Science*, pages 182–199. Springer Verlag, Berlin, Heidelberg, New York, 1995.

2. Holger Benl, Ulrich Berger, Helmut Schwichtenberg, Monika Seisenberger, and Wolfgang Zuber. Proof theory at work: Program development in the Minlog system. To appear: Automated Deduction – A Basis for Applications (eds W. Bibel and P. Schmitt), Volume I: Foundations, Kluwer Academic Publishers, 1998.

3. Ulrich Berger. Continuous functionals of dependent and transfinite types. Habilitationsschrift, Mathematisches Institut der Universität München, 1997.

4. Ulrich Berger and Helmut Schwichtenberg. An inverse of the evaluation functional for typed λ–calculus. In R. Vemuri, editor, *Proceedings of the Sixth Annual IEEE Symposium on Logic in Computer Science*, pages 203–211. IEEE Computer Society Press, Los Alamitos, 1991.

5. Thierry Coquand and Peter Dybjer. Intuitionistic model constructions and normalization proofs. *Mathematical Structures in Computer Science*, 7:73–94, 1997.

6. Roy L. Crole. *Categories for Types*. Cambridge University Press, 1993.

7. Djordje Cubric, Peter Dybjer, and Philip Scott. Normalization and the Yoneda embedding. To appear: Mathematical Structures in Computer Science, 1998.

8. Olivier Danvy. Pragmatics of type-directed partial evaluation. In O. Danvy, R. Glück, and P. Thiemann, editors, *Partial Evaluation*, volume 1110 of *LNCS*, pages 73–94. Springer Verlag, Berlin, Heidelberg, New York, 1996.

9. N.G. de Bruijn. Lambda calculus notation with nameless dummies, a tool for automatic formula manipulation, with application to the Church–Rosser theorem. *Indagationes Math.*, 34:381–392, 1972.

10. J. Lambek and P. Scott. *Introduction to higher order categorical logic*, volume 7 of *Cambridge Studies in Advanced Mathematics*. Cambridge University Press, 1986.

11. John McCarthy. Recursive functions of symbolic expressions and their computation by machine. *Communications of the ACM*, 3(4):184–195, 1960.

12. Helmut Schwichtenberg and Karl Stroetmann. From higher order terms to circuits. In M.L. Dalla Chiara, K. Doets, D. Mundici, and J. van Benthem, editors, *Logic and Scientific Methods. Proceedings (Vol. 1) of the Tenth International Congress of Logic, Methodology and Philosophy of Science, Florence, August 1995*, volume 259 of *Synthese Library*, pages 209–220, Dordrecht, Boston, London, 1997. Kluwer Academic Publishers.

Algebraic Models of Superscalar Microprocessor Implementations: A Case Study

A. C. J. Fox and N. A. Harman

Computer Science, University of Wales, Swansea,
Swansea SA2 8PP, United Kingdom

Abstract. We extend a set of algebraic tools for representing microprocessors to model superscalar microprocessor implementations, and apply
them to a case study. We develop existing correctness models to accommodate the more advanced timing relationships of superscalar processors,
and consider formal verification. We illustrate our tools and techniques
with an in-depth treatment of an example superscalar implementation.
We use *clocks* to divide time into (not necessarily equal) segments, defined by the natural timing of the computational process of a device. We
formally relate clocks by surjective, monotonic maps called retimings. In
the case of superscalar microprocessors, the normal relationship between
'architectural time' and 'implementation time' is complicated by the fact
that events that are distinct in time at the architectural level can occur
simultaneously at the implementation level.

1 Introduction

In this chapter, we extend a set of algebraic tools for microprocessors
[HT96, HT97, FH96] to model *superscalar* microprocessor implementations, and apply them to a case study. In superscalar microprocessors, the
timing of events in an implementation can be substantially different from
that of the architecture that they implement. We develop the existing
correctness models of [HT96, HT97] to accommodate the more advanced
timing relationships of superscalar processors, and consider formal verification. We illustrate our tools and techniques with an in-depth treatment
of an example superscalar implementation, first seen in a simpler form in
[FH96].

We are particularly interested in models of time and temporal abstraction. *Clocks* divide time into (not necessarily equal) segments, defined by
the natural timing of the computational process of a device: for example,
the execution of machine instructions, or some system clock. We formally
relate clocks by surjective, monotonic maps called *retimings*. In the case
of superscalar microprocessors, the normal relationship between 'architectural time' and 'implementation time' is complicated by the fact that

events that are distinct in time at the architectural level can occur simultaneously at the implementation level.

Interesting recent work on pipelined microprocessors includes [WC94] on UINTA, a processor of moderate complexity, and its verification in HOL [GM93]; [MS95a, MS95b] on AAMP5, a more complex processor, and its verification in PVS [ORSS94]; and [BD94] on a fragment of the DLX architecture [HP96]. More recently, superscalar processors have been addressed: in particular, the increased complexity of verification in the face of complex timing behaviour [WB96, Bur96, SDB96, Cyr96].

The intuitive models used in both UINTA and AAMP5 are conceptually similar to our own [HT96, HT97, FH96]. However, there are substantial differences, particularly in the approach to time, and timing abstraction. The main focus of attention of related work is on the engineering realities of developing techniques to successfully address more complex, and impressive, examples (almost always in conjunction with specific software tools). Our own work is concerned with developing a general formal framework for representing and verifying microprocessors within a uniform and well-developed algebraic theory.

In [WC94] systems are modelled as *state streams*: functions from time to state. Temporal and data abstraction functions are used to map between different levels of abstraction. In earlier work [Win93], data and timing abstraction functions are separated (as in this paper). However, in [WC94], and related work on pipelined systems, they are combined. This is because the view is taken that the values of specification state components are distributed in time at the level of abstraction of the implementation. For example, the value of a data register reg in an implementation may correspond with a specification state at time t, and the value of the program counter pc with a specification state $t+n$, where n pipeline stages are required for an instruction to progress from initiation to completion. We take the view that, rather than being temporally shifted, such state components are fundamentally different at the levels of specification and implementation. Consequently, we maintain a separation between data and temporal abstraction functions.

The techniques of [MS95a, MS95b] derive from the earlier work of [BS90, SB91], in which specification and implementation are modelled as state sequences, but time is not explicitly present. To synchronise the specification and implementation state sequences, multiple copies of specification states are inserted. In [MS95a, MS95b] a *visible state* predicate is introduced which identifies those implementation states that should correspond to a specification state. This approach is modified, in a manner similar to that of [WC94], to cope with pipelining by distributing data in time. Again, time is not explicitly present. A recent account of this and related work is [CRS97].

In [BD94] a simple three-stage ALU pipeline and a fragment of DLX are considered. Given a state Q or a pipelined implementation, a new state Q' is generated after executing one step of an instruction I. Both Q and Q' are then *flushed* by repeatedly *stalling* further execution (effectively, filling with no-ops). This results in two new states Q_f representing the (flushed) pipeline and Q'_f representing the (flushed) pipeline after executing instruction I. Q_f and Q'_f can be compared with appropriate specification states by projecting out the specification state elements. Note that there is no timing abstraction in this model: specification and implementation are both considered to take a single cycle to execute an instruction. This method is applicable if some mechanism for stalling the pipeline is available, which is generally the case.

Also of interest is [Mel93] which again has a somewhat similar model of time. An injective, monotonic function f_P maps *abstract* time to *concrete* time, and is defined in terms of a predicate P. If $P(t_c)$ for some concrete time t_c, then there is an abstract time t_a such that $f_P(t_a) = t_c$. Predicate P is required to be true at an infinite number of times. The map f_P is similar to the *immersion* of Sect. 3.1.

Other, earlier, work on microprocessors includes the following. *Gordon's Computer* [Gor83], since considered, in various forms, by others [Joy87, Sta93, HT97]. *Viper* [Coh87, Cul87], which has also been considered in [ALL$^+$93]. Landin's SECD machine [Lan63], considered in [Gra92, BG90]. The FM8501, a processor based on the PDP-11, and its more advanced successor FM9001 are discussed in [Hun89, Hun92, Hun94, BJ93].

The structure of this paper is as follows. In Sect. 2 we introduce the basic *iterated map* model of a microprocessor. In Sect. 3 we consider how we may express the correctness of one model of a (non-superscalar) microprocessor with respect to another, at a different level of abstraction, when both are represented as iterated maps. In Sect. 4 we informally introduce the fundamental aspects of superscalar microprocessors. In Sect. 5 we consider how our correctness model from Sect. 3 must be modified for superscalar microprocessors. In Sect. 6 we introduce a simple machine architecture. In Sect. 7 we informally introduce *ACS*, a superscalar implementation of our simple architecture. In Sect. 8 we formalise *ACS* in detail. Although we include the majority of the formal representation of *ACS*, space considerations force us to omit certain parts. A full treatment can be found in [Fox98]. Finally, in Sect. 9, we consider the correctness of *ACS*, and the problems of the formal verification of superscalar processors.

2 Basic Models of Microprocessors

In general, we model a microprocessor using an *iterated map State*, of the form:

$$State : T \times STATE \rightarrow STATE,$$
$$State(0, state) = init(state),$$
$$State(t + 1, state) = next(State(t, state)).$$

1. T is a copy of the natural numbers **N**, representing discrete time intervals, or *clock cycles*.
2. *STATE* is the state-set of the microprocessor. Generally, this will be a Cartesian product of components representing registers, memory, etc.
3. $init : STATE \rightarrow STATE$ is an *initialisation function*, that enforces internal consistency of the initial state of the microprocessor (e.g. given memory m, program counter pc and instruction register ir, we expect: $ir = m(pc)$) and acts as an invariant in formal verification: see Sect. 9. In the case of an architectural-level model, $init$ will often be the identity function. Furthermore, when considering $init$ as an invariant, it should be as *weak* as possible (Sect. 9).
4. $next : STATE \rightarrow STATE$ is the *next-state function*, determining state evolution.

For simplicity, we have chosen to omit inputs and outputs as they are not needed in our case study. In practice, their inclusion causes no difficulty [HT97, Fox98].

The choice of T, *STATE*, $init$ and $next$ controls the level of abstraction of the formal representation. For example, the choice of clock T controls the level of *timing abstraction*. We can choose clock cycles of T to represent *system clock* cycles, which would be appropriate in the case of a low-level representation of an implementation; or we could choose cycles of T to represent instruction execution, with each clock cycle lasting precisely one instruction. This latter choice (an *instruction clock*) would be more appropriate for a high-level, architectural description. Notice in the latter case that clock cycles would typically vary in length, since in general different instructions will have different execution times. Additionally, the choice of *STATE* controls the level of *data abstraction*. If we wish to represent a microprocessor at the architectural level, we will choose *STATE* to represent those components visible to the programmer. If we wish to represent an implementation, *STATE* will additionally include components not visible to the programmer (e.g. *buffer registers, cache memories,* etc.).

In addition to timing and data abstraction, we can consider *structural abstraction*, where a formal representation is sub-divided into component parts, representing a the physical structure of the implementation. We may partition, or *decompose*, state-set *STATE*, iterated map *State* and next-state function *next* to reflect both the physical partitioning of the microprocessor, and the conceptual sub-tasks that must be performed in instruction execution.

We may consider many different levels of abstraction when modeling microprocessors. However, we will restrict our attention to two. The *programmer's model PM*, corresponding to the user-visible architectural level, and the *abstract circuit model AC*, corresponding with a high-level view of the implementation, commonly called the *organisation*.

3   Simple Correctness Models

Given two descriptions of microprocessors

$$State_{PM} : T \times STATE_{PM} \to STATE_{PM},$$
$$State_{AC} : S \times STATE_{AC} \to STATE_{AC},$$

how do we formulate the statement:
            "*State$_{AC}$ correctly implements State$_{PM}$*"?

3.1   Retimings

First, we must consider how we can relate times on two different clocks. Given two clocks T and S, a function $\lambda : S \to T$ is called a *retiming* if it is: (*i*) monotonic, ensuring time always runs forwards on T and S; and (*ii*) surjective, ensuring that each time $t \in T$ corresponds with some time $s \in S$. We denote the set of all such retimings by $Ret(S,T)$. In the case of microprocessors, we can construct *state-dependent* retimings $\lambda : STATE \to Ret(S,T)$ that are functions of the state-set of a microprocessor representation. For example, in the case that T represents an instruction clock, and S a system clock, then λ would map times on S to the time on T corresponding to the execution of the current machine instruction. A simple retiming is illustrated in Fig. 1.

We can build a number of formal tools based on retimings. In this paper, we require the following.

1. The *immersion*: $\overline{\lambda} : T \to S$, defined by

$$\overline{\lambda}(r) = (least\ t)[\lambda(t) = r].$$

2. The *start* function $start : Ret(S, T) \to [S \to S]$, defined by

$$start(\lambda)(s) = \overline{\lambda}\lambda(s).$$

Further discussion of retimings can be found in [Har89, HT90, HT93, HT96].

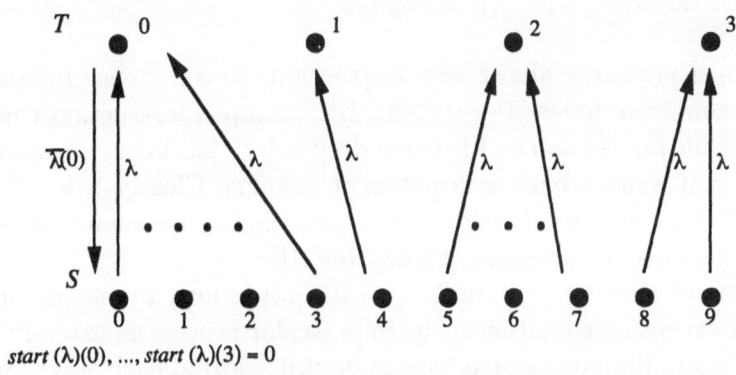

$$start\ (\lambda)(0), ..., start\ (\lambda)(3) = 0$$

Fig. 1. A simple retiming.

3.2 Correctness Statement

We construct a commutative diagram representing the correctness of $State_{AC}$ with respect to $State_{PM}$ as follows:

$$
\begin{array}{ccc}
T \times STATE_{PM} & \xrightarrow{State_{PM}} & STATE_{PM} \\
\Big\uparrow {\scriptstyle (\lambda, \psi)} & & \Big\uparrow {\scriptstyle \psi} \\
S \times STATE_{AC} & \xrightarrow{State_{AC}} & STATE_{AC},
\end{array}
$$

where:

1. $\lambda : STATE_{AC} \rightarrow Ret(S,T)$ is a state-dependent retiming, mapping the system clock and state of $State_{AC}$ to the instruction clock of $State_{PM}$.

2. $\psi : STATE_{AC} \rightarrow STATE_{PM}$ is a projection function, discarding the elements of $State_{AC}$ not visible in $State_{PM}$.

We say that $State_{PM}$ is correct with respect to $State_{AC}$ if the above diagram commutes, for all times $s \in S$ such that:

$$s = start(\lambda(state))(s);$$

that is, for all times corresponding with the end of a machine instruction, and for all states $state \in STATE_{AC}$.

4 Superscalar Microprocessors

A *pipelined processor* allows new instructions to commence before their predecessors have finished execution. For example, instruction i may be fetched while instruction $i-1$ is being decoded, $i-2$ is being executed, and $i-3$'s result written back to registers or memory. Clearly, it is necessary to ensure that the relationships, or *dependencies*, between instructions permit this (see, for example, [Sto93, Joh91]).

Pipelined processors permit several instructions to be in different stages of execution simultaneously. Superscalar processors extend this by allowing more than one instruction to be processed at each stage. Several instructions may start execution simultaneously, and finish together, or even out of program order. To achieve this the processor must contain multiple pipeline units at each stage. Machines capable of parallel instruction execution have existed since the 1960s. For example, the CDC 6600 [Tho61], and the IBM 360/91 [AST67]. These machines were not superscalar, though they did contain parallel functional units: necessary because of the advanced pipelining techniques they used. The IBM 360/91 used *Tomasulo's algorithm* for the issuing logic [Tom67], commonly used in modern superscalar microprocessors for scheduling instruction execution. Superscalar processors first appeared in the late 1980s: for example the IBM RISC System/6000 [Gro90]. Subsequent superscalar processors include, among others: Sun Microsystems *Ultra SPARC-I*; IBM/Motorola *PowerPC 620*; Intel *Pentium* and *Pentium Pro*; MIPS/NEC *R10000*; and DEC *Alpha 21064* and *Alpha 21164*.

The level of parallelism achievable by superscalar (and pipelined) processors is determined by the *dependencies* between instructions [Sto93,

Joh91]. There are five types of dependency: the first three apply to both superscalar and pipelined processors.

1. *Data dependency* occurs when an instruction needs the result of a preceding instruction.
2. *Procedural dependency* occurs when a branch instruction disrupts the normal (sequential) flow of execution; requiring any work done on subsequent instructions to be discarded. This can be a particularly significant source of delay in the case of conditional branches, where the outcome may not be known until late in the pipeline.
3. *Resource conflicts* occur when two instructions simultaneously require the same hardware resources (functional units, etc.). This problem can often be reduced by duplicating hardware, at a cost. For example, providing two addition units removes the resource conflict between a pair of add instructions.

The remaining two dependencies apply only to superscalar processors.

1. *Antidependency* occurs when an instruction overwrites the arguments of a preceding instruction. This is significant if instructions are allowed to execute out of order.
2. *Output dependency* occurs when two instructions wish to store results at the same destination, which, again, is significant if instructions are allowed to execute out of order.

These dependencies must be resolved if the processor is to function correctly. That is, to be functionally indistinguishable from a non-superscalar *sequential architecture* model. In a sequential architecture, each instruction is assumed to finish before its successor. This is a natural model for instruction-level computation at the *PM* level of abstraction. Furthermore, it is also the model used by older implementations of currently-popular architectures. In order to preserve the natural model, and maintain backward compatibility, it is necessary for superscalar processors to retain, or be able to reconstruct, a state which corresponds exactly with a state of the *PM* level. A *precise architectural state* is a processor state which meets this condition. A processor can generate precise states if dependencies are correctly resolved and results are written to *PM*-level state components in program order. This is particularly important in the case of *exceptions*. For example, if instruction i causes an exception because of an error, it is reasonable to expect that instruction $i + 1$ has not yet executed.

There are a number of techniques used to maximise throughput, whilst observing dependencies and maintaining a precise architectural state. The most common method is some form of *register renaming*, where additional registers are used to resolve instruction dependencies, and to temporarily store results. A common form of register renaming is a *reorder buffer*. This consists of a circular buffer of registers, used to (temporarily) store the results of computations before they are are *committed*, or *retired*, to *PM*-level state components. Whenever an instruction is *dispatched* for execution, the next available slot in the buffer is reserved to store the result. Results are inserted into the buffer, in the appropriate location, when they become available. They are then removed from the head of the buffer, and are stored in architectural components, in program order. For example, suppose instructions i, $i + 1$ and $i + 3$ generate results at time t, but that $i + 2$ has yet to finish. The results of i and $i + 1$ can be transferred to *PM*-level components, but $i + 3$ must wait until $i + 2$ has also finished. This ensures a precise architectural state: if the machine is interrupted at this point, execution will restart with instruction $i+2$, and $i+3$ will be re-executed. In order to speed up execution, implementations generally permit *bypassing*. That is, results in the reorder buffer can be used by subsequent instructions (subject to dependencies) *before* they are moved to the relevant *PM*-level components.

5   Superscalar Correctness

The correctness model in Sect. 3 is applicable to simple, *microprogrammed* implementations, and to more complex *pipelined* implementations, where each system clock cycle corresponds with the termination of at most one machine instruction. In a superscalar implementation, it is possible for multiple instructions to terminate on a single clock cycle. That is, there may be cycles of clock T that correspond with no cycle of clock S. Hence there is no retiming from S to T. To solve this problem, we introduce a new *retirement clock* R. Cycles of clock R mark the committal of one or more machine instructions. We can construct two retimings $\lambda_1 : T \rightarrow R$, mapping instruction clock cycles to retirement clock cycles, and $\lambda_2 : S \rightarrow R$, mapping system clock cycles to retirement clock cycles. We can construct the map $\rho : S \rightarrow T$ from system clock cycles to instruction clock cycles by composition:

$$\rho(t) = \overline{\lambda}_1 \lambda_2(t).$$

Function ρ is illustrated in Fig. 2. Note that ρ is not a retiming since it need not be surjective. If, for example, instructions i and $i + 1$ commit simultaneously, it is not meaningful to talk about the correctness of

State$_{AC}$ after instruction i, since there is no time at which instruction i has terminated, and instruction $i+1$ has not.

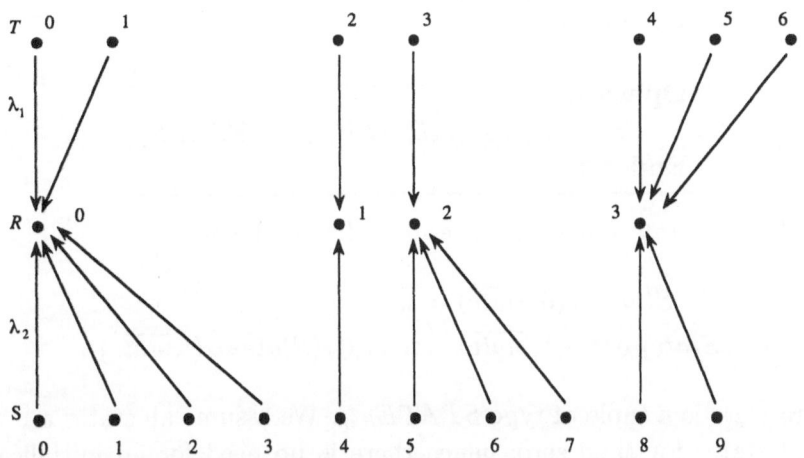

Fig. 2. Retimings from T to R and from S to R.

6 PM: A Simple Architecture

To illustrate our algebraic tools, we will introduce a simple machine architecture *PM*, consisting of: separate data and instruction memories; a set of registers; and five instructions, with the following informal meanings.

1. add reg$_a$, reg$_b$, reg$_c$ — Add register reg$_a$ to register reg$_b$, store the result in register reg$_c$ and increment the program-counter.
2. branch addr — If register reg$_0$ is zero then add the program-counter to addr and store the result in the program-counter; otherwise increment the program-counter.
3. load reg$_a$, addr — Load the contents of the data memory, at location addr, into register reg$_a$, and increment the program-counter.
4. store reg$_a$, addr — Store the contents of register reg$_a$ in the data memory at location addr, and increment the program-counter.
5. set reg$_a$, val — Store the constant val in register reg$_a$, and increment the program-counter.

We will first describe the *state algebra* of *PM*, defining the state-space, clock and state function. We then describe the *next state algebra*, defining the initialisation and the next-state function.

The *PM* state algebra is as follows:

Algebra *PM* State
Carrier Sets
$T, STATE_{PM}$
Constants
$-$

Operations
$State_{PM} : T \times STATE_{PM} \rightarrow STATE_{PM}$
End Algebra.

The *PM* state function $State_{PM}$ is defined below

$$State_{PM}(0, \overrightarrow{state}) = \overrightarrow{state},$$
$$State_{PM}(t+1, \overrightarrow{state}) = next_{PM}(State_{PM}(t, \overrightarrow{state})),$$

where $\overrightarrow{state}$ is a tuple of type $STATE_{PM}$. We assume all states are valid initial states for time zero: hence there is no need for an initialisation function. Each cycle of clock T corresponds with one machine instruction.

The state-space of the architecture is

$$STATE_{PM} = Mem \times Mem \times PC \times Reg.$$

The various components, and subcomponents, of $STATE_{PM}$ are defined as follows.

$RC = W_a$ (where $a \in \mathbf{N}^+$ is the number of *PM* registers),

$PC = W_b$ (where $2^b \in \mathbf{N}^+$ is the number of *PM* memory addresses),

$R = W_c$ (where $c \in \mathbf{N}^+$ is the *PM* register width),

$OP = W_3$ (where OP is the operation code field of an instruction,

$Reg = [RC \rightarrow R],$

$Mem = [PC \rightarrow R],$

and $W_n = Bit^n$ $(n \in \mathbf{N}^+)$ is the set of n-bit words ($Bit = \{0, 1\}$).

The typical state element will be of the form $(mp, md, pc, reg) \in STATE_{PM}$ where: $mp \in Mem$ is the program memory; $md \in Mem$ is the data memory; $pc \in PC$ is the program-counter; and $reg \in Reg$ is the set of registers.

The *PM* next-state algebra is as follows:

Algebra *PM* Next-State
Carrier Sets
$$T, STATE_{PM}$$
Constants
$$0 \in T$$
Operations
$$\cdot + 1 : T \to T$$
$$next_{PM} : STATE_{PM} \to STATE_{PM}$$
End Algebra.

The function $\cdot + 1$ is the successor clock cycle function which enumerates time from the initial cycle $0 \in T$. The next-state function $next_{PM}$ is defined as follows

$$next_{PM}(mp, md, pc, reg) =$$

$$
\begin{cases}
(mp, md, pc + 1, & \text{if } op(ins) = \text{add}; \\
\quad reg[reg_{ra(ins)} + reg_{rb(ins)}/rc(ins)]), & \\
(mp, md, pc + addr(ins), reg), & \text{if } op(ins) = \text{branch} \\
& \text{and } reg_0 = 0; \\
(mp, md, pc + 1, reg), & \text{if } op(ins) = \text{branch} \\
& \text{and } reg_0 \neq 0; \\
(mp, md, pc + 1, reg[md(addr(ins))/ra(ins)]), & \text{if } op(ins) = \text{load}; \\
(mp, md[reg_{ra(ins)}/addr(ins)], pc + 1, reg), & \text{if } op(ins) = \text{store}; \\
(mp, md, pc + 1, reg[pad(val(ins))/ra(ins)]), & \text{if } op(ins) = \text{set}.
\end{cases}
$$

where $ins = mp(pc)$ is the next instruction to be executed. There are six cases; one for each type of instruction with the exception of branch, which has two cases (taken and not taken). The generic notation $r[v/a]$ is an abbreviation for functions of the form:

$$sub : [A \to V] \times V \times A \to [A \to V],$$

$$sub(r, v, a)(i) = \begin{cases} v, & \text{if } a = i; \\ r(a), & \text{otherwise.} \end{cases}$$

The functions $op : R \to OP$, $ra, rb, rc : R \to RC$, and $addr, val : R \to PC$ extract the *op-code*, *register* and *address/value* fields of an instruction, respectively.

The definitions of op, ra, rb, rc, $addr$ and val are omitted. The *pad* function simply extends bit strings by padding with zeros. The definition is omitted.

7 ACS: An Informal Description

We introduce an implementation *ACS* of *PM* that will include component parts, typical of a superscalar microprocessor, in a somewhat simplified form. We will permit *out-of-order instruction issue and execution*, and will enforce *in-order instruction retirement* by means of a *scoreboarding* algorithm, implemented using a *re-order buffer*, thus preserving a *precise architectural state*. We will permit a maximum of four instructions to execute simultaneously, dependencies permitting.

The implementation presented lacks some features, such as register renaming, present in many superscalar machines (see for example [SS95]). Instructions can execute out-of-order and are committed in-order. Thornton's algorithm is used to resolve dependencies instead of the more complex Tomasulo's algorithm [WS84]. In addition, we do not permit bypassing of results from the reorder buffer. However, our example does have the essential property of a superscalar implementation: the ability to commit more than one instruction in a single cycle. The intention is to present a pedagogical example, that is not obscured by unnecessary complexity. None of the omitted features would be difficult to introduce.

First we describe the *physical structure* of the microprocessor and its component parts. Then we consider the *conceptual operations* performed by groups of physical components, operating together. We discuss the relationship between physical components and conceptual operations in Sect. 8.

7.1 Processor Organisation

The *ACS* processor consists of the eight physical units shown in Fig. 3.

1. *The Instruction Cache* stores machine instructions, performing the same function as the *PM* program memory. For simplicity, we will assume that the instruction cache is the same size as the *PM* program memory. In reality, it will be much smaller, and an attempt to fetch an instruction not in the cache will cause a *cache miss*. This will cause a block of memory containing the missing instruction to be fetched into the instruction cache. Steps will need to be taken to decide which *cache replacement strategy* to use, and the operation of the processor may *stall* while the new instruction is fetched. Modeling this algebraically causes no difficulties. However, in *ACS*, it will complicate the representation in an unhelpful way, and is hence omitted.

2. *The Instruction Buffer* contains a *fetch program counter* and a buffer. The buffer stores a small number of instructions, fetched from the instruction cache using the fetch program counter. The buffer maintains a reserve of instructions available for processing in the event of a cache miss. We have eliminated cache misses in *ACS*, but the instruction buffer is a necessary part of a superscalar processor, and hence we have retained it.

3. *The Decode Unit* breaks down instructions into component parts: operation codes, and operand specifiers. The *ACS* processor has a very simple, fixed instruction format, and hence the decode unit is very simple. Real processors, with more complex instruction sets, will generally require a more sophisticated decode unit.

4. *The Issue Unit* contains four *reservation stations* [Tom67], one for each functional unit. These schedule program execution, by determining dependencies, and then forward instructions that are free to execute to the appropriate functional units.

5. *The Functional Units* compute results based on instructions and their operands. There are two *adders* (allowing **add** instructions to execute in parallel), a *load-store* unit and a *branch* unit.

6. *The Reorder Buffer Unit* stores instruction results prior to their committal to *PM*-level components (data cache, registers and program counter). Results from instructions that finish execution out of program order are held in a buffer until their predecessors have finished execution, at which point they are written back (*committed*) to the appropriate *PM*-level components.

7. *The Register Unit* contains *PM* registers, *PM* program counter, and a *reset* flag for clearing the pipeline. It also contains an array of bits indicating which registers are currently in use, and a list of memory locations currently in use.

8. *The Data Cache* performs the same function as the *PM* data memory. As with the instruction cache, the data cache is assumed to be the same size as the *PM* model data memory, eliminating cache misses. Again, there is no difficulty in modeling a smaller cache algebraically; though we would have to deal with the additional question of the *cache write strategy*, since, unlike the instruction cache, it is possible to write to the data cache.

We briefly describe each unit below. Each of these units are involved in one or more processor operations.

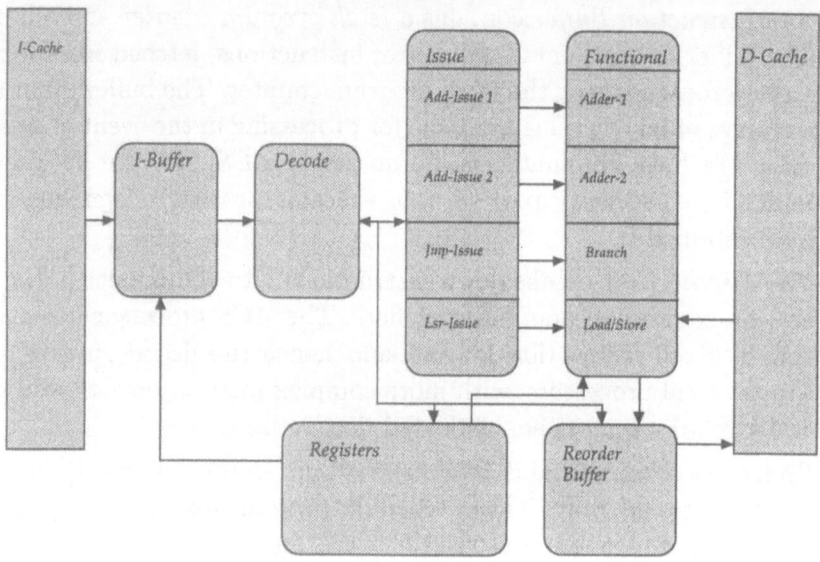

Fig. 3. A simple organisation.

7.2 Processor Operations

There are six operations involved in instruction execution, outlined below.

1. *Instruction Fetch.* Instructions are read from the current *fetch program counter* value, which attempts to predict the future evolution of the *PM program counter*, assuming there are no branches taken. Clearly, any taken branches will render subsequently-fetched instructions invalid. To simplify *ACS*, branches are *not* treated differently: that is branches are predicted as not taken. Correctly predicating branch destinations significantly improves performance, because branching to the 'wrong' destination requires the pipeline to be emptied. In practice, it may be more effective to predict branches to be taken; and maintaining a history of previous behaviour would certainly be better. Modifying *ACS* to accommodate either of these (or other) strategies would present no difficulties.

2. *Instruction Decode.* Instructions are decoded into five *fields*: an opcode, three register indexes and an address/value field. Not all fields are required for all instructions.

3. *Instruction Dispatch and Issue.* Instruction dependencies are resolved at run-time before issue, so that the *reorder buffer* can always recover a precise architectural state. There are a number of alternative methods

available. *ACS* uses Thornton's algorithm for the issue logic [Tho70]. When resources are available instructions are *dispatched* (added) to the end of the appropriate reservation station's buffer, and a place is reserved in the reorder buffer to hold the result. Instructions can then be *issued* (removed), *in any order*, from the reservation station, when all dependencies are resolved.

4. *Instruction Execution.* The implementation contains two adders, a load-store unit and a branch unit, for executing: add and set; load and store; and branch instructions respectively. Two add instructions may be executed simultaneously, or one add and one set.

5. *Instruction Reorder.* Instruction results (from the functional units) are inserted into their pre-reserved slots in the reorder buffer.

6. *Instruction Committal.* Once results reach the top of the reorder buffer they are removed and committed to *PM* state components (register, program counter or data cache). This means that the *PM* state components always contain a precise architectural state, because instruction i is not allowed to commit until all instructions i', $i' < i$ have generated results in the reorder buffer, and have themselves committed.

8   *ACS*: A Formal Description

We will formally represent *ACS* as follows.

1. We describe the *state algebra* of *ACS* in Sect. 8.1. This algebra defines the state-space, *AC* clock and state function of *ACS*.

2. We then describe the *next state algebra* in Sect. 8.2. This algebra defines the initialisation and next-state functions of *ACS*. There is one next-state function for each of the physical units in *ACS*.

3. Finally, we describe the *processor operation algebra* in Sect. 8.3. Each of the next-state functions for the *units* described in Sect. 8.2 is defined in terms of processor *operations*, for example, instruction decode. Each operation will typically affect a number of processor units.

The relationships between processor operations and units is shown in Figure 4. Operations are represented by rectangular boxes and machine units are represented by rounded boxes. For example, the operation *Execute* affects the issue unit (from which instructions are removed) and the functional units (where instruction results are computed). *Execute* receives input from the issue unit, the register unit and the data cache.

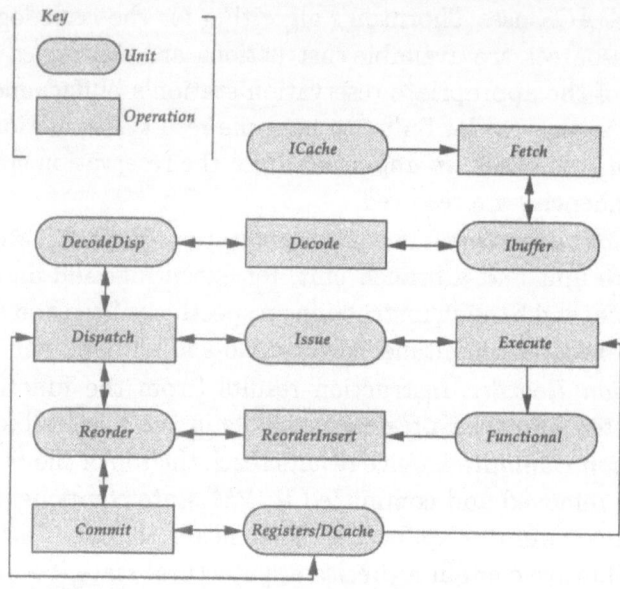

Fig. 4. Dependencies of the microprocessor operations.

8.1 The State Algebra

The state algebra for the ACS processor consists of carrier sets for time S and the state of the processor $STATE$, and the state function $State_{ACS}$, which returns a new state of the processor, given a time and an initial state.

Algebra ACS State
Carrier Sets
  $S, STATE$
Constants

  $-$

Operations
  $State_{ACS} : S \times STATE \rightarrow STATE$
End Algebra.

The state function is defined below.

$$State_{ACS}(0, \overrightarrow{state}) = init_{ACS}(\overrightarrow{state}),$$
$$State_{ACS}(s + 1, \overrightarrow{state}) = next_{ACS}(State_{ACS}(s, \overrightarrow{state})).$$

The hidden function $next_{ACS} : STATE \rightarrow STATE$ is defined below.

$$next_{ACS}(\overrightarrow{state}) = (Icache, Ibuffer(\overrightarrow{state}),$$
$$DecodeDisp.(\overrightarrow{state}), Issue(\overrightarrow{state}), Functional(\overrightarrow{state}),$$
$$Reorder(\overrightarrow{state}), Registers(\overrightarrow{state}), Dcache(\overrightarrow{state})).$$

The initialisation function $init_{ACS}$, and next-state functions for the ACS units $Ibuffer$, $DecodeDisp.$, $Issue$, $Functional$, $Reorder$, $Registers$ and $Dcache$ are defined in Sect. 8.2.

8.2 Processor Initialisation and Next-State Functions

The next-state algebra for ACS consists of carrier sets for time S and the state of the processor $STATE$, together with carrier sets for individual units (the Cartesian product of which constitutes the overall state set $STATE$). The operations in the next-state algebra are the successor function for time, the initialisation function for the processor $init_{ACS}$, and the individual next-state functions for each of the units.

Algebra ACS Next-State
Carrier Sets
$\quad$ $S, STATE$, Ibuffer, Decode, Issue, Functional, ReorderBuf,
$\quad$ Registers, Dcache
Constants
$\quad$ $0 \in S$
Operations
$$s + 1 : S \rightarrow S$$
$$init_{ACS} : STATE \rightarrow STATE$$
$$Ibuffer : STATE \rightarrow \text{Ibuffer}$$
$$DecodeDisp. : STATE \rightarrow \text{Decode}$$
$$Issue : STATE \rightarrow \text{Issue}$$
$$Functional : STATE \rightarrow \text{Functional}$$
$$Reorder : STATE \rightarrow \text{ReorderBuf}$$
$$Registers : STATE \rightarrow \text{Registers}$$
$$Dcache : STATE \rightarrow \text{Dcache}$$
End Algebra.

The components of this algebra are defined in the following sections.

Processor State-Space and Clock. The machine state-space is made up of Cartesian product of the state-spaces for each of the eight main

ACS units.

$$STATE = \mathsf{Icache} \times \mathsf{Ibuffer} \times \mathsf{Decode} \times \mathsf{Issue} \times \mathsf{Functional}$$
$$\times \mathsf{ReorderBuf} \times \mathsf{Registers} \times \mathsf{Dcache}.$$

A typical vector will be of the form.

$$\overrightarrow{state} = (\overrightarrow{Icache}, \overrightarrow{ibuffer}, \overrightarrow{decode}, \overrightarrow{issue}, \overrightarrow{functional},$$
$$\overrightarrow{reorderbuf}, \overrightarrow{registers}, Dcache).$$

Figure 5 gives a pictorial representation of the AC state of the processor.

The state-space of ACS is *hierarchical* in that each physical unit has its own state, which is constructed of simpler state sets, that may in turn be made up of yet more primitive components. The *full name* of a state component is of the form $x_1 \cdot x_2 \cdot x_3 \cdots x_n$. For example, $\overrightarrow{issue} \cdot$ AddIssue1 $\cdot \overrightarrow{regopnd}_1 \cdot ready$ is the ready bit of the first operand, of the first adder reservation station in the issue unit. To simplify the definitions, and where no ambiguity results (the vast majority of cases), we will omit name elements.

The state-space of ACS makes heavy use of *buffers* and *lists*. We assume the existence of a general-purpose *finite buffer algebra*, and a general-purpose *finite list algebra*, which we will not define here: see [Fox98]. In general, $\mathsf{Buffer}_{(bufsize,Data)}$ and $\mathsf{List}_{(bufsize,Data)}$ are the sets of finite buffers and lists respectively, of size *bufsize* containing elements from the set *Data*. We will informally introduce buffer and list operations as required.

In Figure 5, we imply concrete buffer and list operations, based on register files, with *head* and *tail* pointers (and *usage bits* in the case of lists). In the case of the *Dispatch* only (Sect. 8.3), we *require* such a concrete definition. Given we are specifying hardware, this is not unreasonable.

The processor state-space is parameterised by eight constants, defining the sizes of the buffers and reservation stations in the processor:

$ibufsize$ = instruction buffer entries;

$decsize$ = decode unit entries;

$addsize1$ = reservation station entries for the first adder;

$addsize2$ = reservation station entries for the second adder;

$brsize$ = reservation station entries for the branch unit;

$lsrsize$ = reservation station entries for the load-store unit;

$reordersize$ = reorder buffer entries; and

$memusize$ = memory address usage entries.

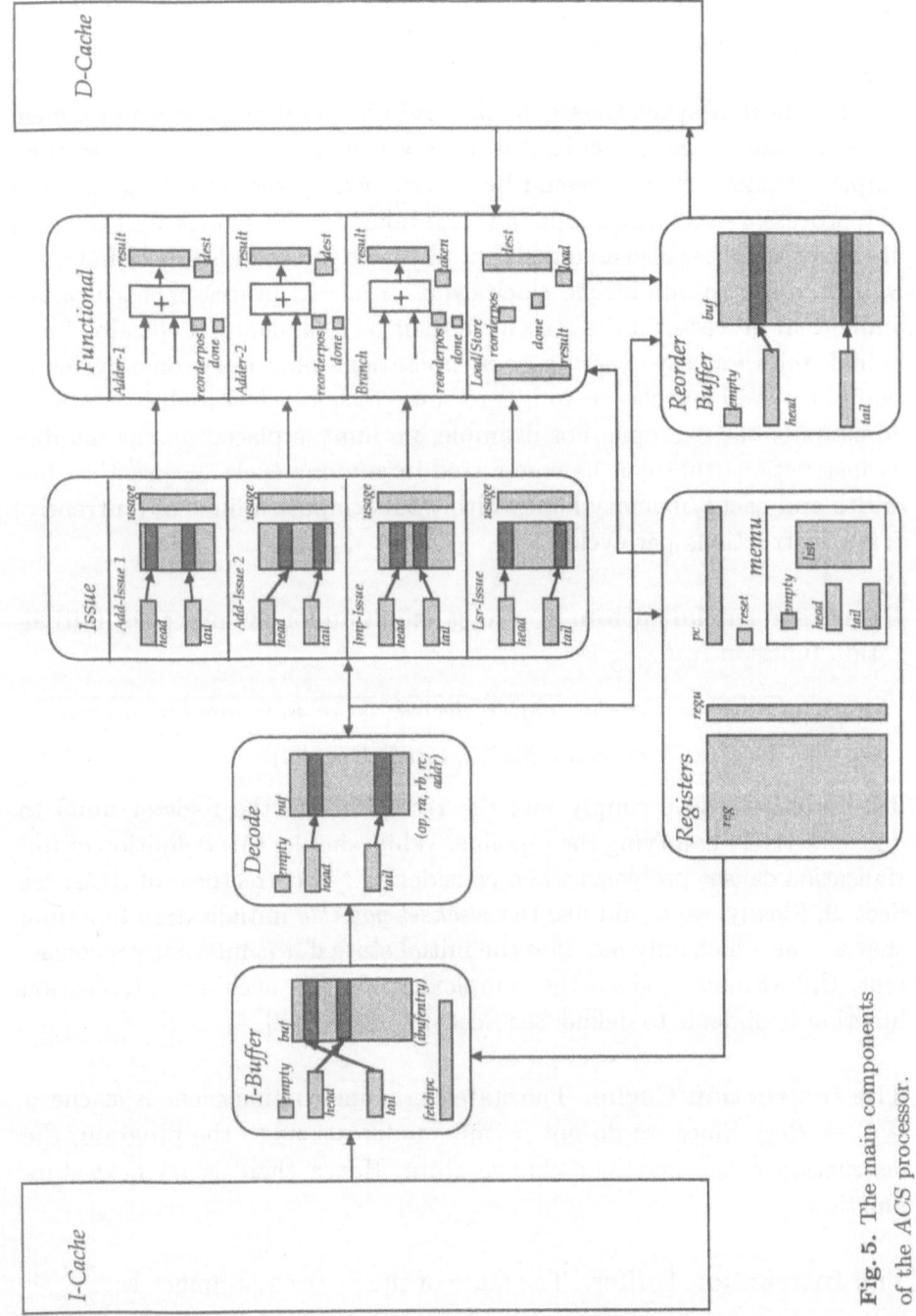

Fig. 5. The main components of the *ACS* processor.

These constants would be instantiated for any given concrete implementation of the processor and, in practice, are limited by technological constraints.

The clock S synchronises the processor's operations and is not a measure of absolute time: that is, it is not a *system clock*. The clock rate of an implementation of *ACS* would be determined by the minimum speed of the processor units: the maximum time taken for the slowest unit to reach its next state. It is also assumed that all of the processor's functional units will compute results in one clock cycle. In a real processor, each of the individual processor units may have their own pipelines. Typically, functional units for, say, *floating point* operations may take some cycles to compute. We have chosen to ignore some technological realities in order to simplify the example. For example, no limit is placed on the number of instructions that can be committed in any one cycle. In practice, bus width and cache/memory bandwidth would impose a limit of (currently) a few instructions per cycle.

Processor Initialisation. A strong definition for the processor initialisation function $init_{ACS}$ is:

$$init_{ACS}(\overrightarrow{state}) = (Icache, \overrightarrow{ibuffer}, \overrightarrow{decode}, \overrightarrow{issue}, \overrightarrow{functional}, \overrightarrow{reorderbuf},$$
$$(reg, regu, \overline{memu}, 1, pc), Dcache).$$

The function above simply sets the reset flag (in the register unit) to one, effectively emptying the pipeline. While simple, this definition of initialisation causes problems when considering the correctness of *ACS*: see Sect. 9. Ideally, we would like the *weakest possible* initialisation function; that is, one which only modifies the initial state if it is internally inconsistent. Unfortunately, given the complexity of *ACS*, such an initialisation function is difficult to define: see Sect. 9 and [Fox98].

The Instruction Cache. The state of the instruction cache is Icache = $[PC \rightarrow Reg]$. Since we do not permit modifications to the program, the instruction cache does not change state. Hence there is no next-state function.

The Instruction Buffer. The state of the instruction buffer is:

$$\text{Ibuffer} = \text{Buffer}_{(ibufsize, Reg)} \times PC,$$

with component names:

$$\overrightarrow{ibuffer} = (\overrightarrow{instbuf}, fetchpc).$$

The fetch buffer $\overrightarrow{instbuf}$ stores instruction words fetched from the instruction cache. The register $fetchpc$ holds the address of the next instruction to be fetched, 'guessing' the future value of the PM program counter by assuming the absence of branches.

The next-state function $Ibuffer : STATE \rightarrow \mathsf{Ibuffer}$ is defined below.

$$Ibuffer(\overrightarrow{state}) =$$

$$\begin{cases} IBuffMrg(\pi^{Fetch}_{\overrightarrow{ibuffer}}(Fetch(Icache, \overrightarrow{ibuffer})), & \text{if } reset = 0; \\ \quad \pi^{Decode}_{\overrightarrow{ibuffer}}(Decode(\overrightarrow{ibuffer}, \overrightarrow{decode}))), & \\ \pi^{Fetch}_{\overrightarrow{ibuffer}}(Fetch(Icache, < Reset(\overrightarrow{instbuf}), pc >)), & \text{otherwise.} \end{cases}$$

If the pipeline is not being reset then instruction buffer entries at the head of $\overrightarrow{ibuffer}$ are removed by the operation $Decode : \mathsf{Ibuffer} \times \mathsf{Decode} \rightarrow \mathsf{Ibuffer} \times \mathsf{Decode}$ (Sect. 8.3), and new ones inserted at the tail of $\overrightarrow{ibuffer}$ by the operation $Fetch : \mathsf{Icache} \times \mathsf{Ibuffer} \rightarrow \mathsf{Icache} \times \mathsf{Ibuffer}$ (Sect. 8.3). If the pipeline is being reset (i.e. after a branch), then the instruction buffer is cleared with the buffer operation $Reset$, which empties the buffer. It is then filled with entries fetched from the instruction cache using the current PM program counter value pc, rather than the fetch program counter $fetchpc$. Note that $< Reset(\overrightarrow{instbuf}), pc >$ is a tuple of type $\mathsf{Ibuffer}$. We use $< \cdots >$ to identify tuples, here and elsewhere, to avoid confusion over the numbers and types of arguments of functions.

The projection functions $\pi^{Decode}_{\overrightarrow{ibuffer}} : \mathsf{Ibuffer} \times \mathsf{Decode} \rightarrow \mathsf{Ibuffer}$ and $\pi^{Fetch}_{\overrightarrow{ibuffer}} : \mathsf{Icache} \times \mathsf{Ibuffer} \rightarrow \mathsf{Ibuffer}$ are defined as follows:

$$\pi^{Decode}_{\overrightarrow{ibuffer}}(\overrightarrow{ibuffer}, \overrightarrow{decode}) = \overrightarrow{ibuffer},$$

$$\pi^{Fetch}_{\overrightarrow{ibuffer}}(Icache, \overrightarrow{ibuffer}) = \overrightarrow{ibuffer}.$$

In general, projection functions of the form π^y_x project out the state element named x from some tuple represented by y, where y may either be state element, or a function returning a state element. We will omit the definitions of such projections from now on.

The hidden function $IBuffMrg : \mathsf{Ibuffer} \times \mathsf{Ibuffer} \rightarrow \mathsf{Ibuffer}$ combines the results of instruction decode and instruction fetch.

$$IBuffMrg(\overrightarrow{instbuf}_1, fetchpc_1, \overrightarrow{instbuf}_2, fetchpc_2) =$$
$$(Merge(\overrightarrow{instbuf}_1, \overrightarrow{instbuf}_2), fetchpc_1).$$

The fetch program counter is affected by the $Fetch$ operation but not by the $Decode$ operation; hence $fetchpc_2$ is discarded. Instruction buffers

$\overrightarrow{instbuf}_1$ and $\overrightarrow{instbuf}_2$ are combined using the buffer function *Merge*, which concatenates the contents of two buffers.

The Decode and Dispatch Unit. The state of the decode and dispatch unit is:

$$\mathsf{Decode} = \mathsf{Buffer}_{(decsize, \mathsf{DecEntry})},$$

where

$$\mathsf{DecEntry} = OP \times RC^3 \times PC,$$

with component names:

$$\overrightarrow{decentry} = (op, ra, rb, rc, addr).$$

The fields correspond with op-code, registers and address/value field respectively.

The next-state function $DecodeDisp. : STATE \rightarrow \mathsf{Decode}$ is defined below.

$$DecodeDisp.(\overrightarrow{state}) = $$
$$\begin{cases} Merge(\pi\xrightarrow[decode]{Decode}(Decode(\overrightarrow{ibuffer}, \overrightarrow{decode})), & \text{if } reset = 0; \\ \quad \pi\xrightarrow[decode]{Dispatch}(Dispatch(\overrightarrow{decode}, \overrightarrow{issue}, \overrightarrow{reorderbuf}, \\ \quad \overrightarrow{registers}, Dcache))), \\ Reset(\overrightarrow{decode}), & \text{otherwise.} \end{cases}$$

If the pipeline is not being reset then entries are dispatched to the issue unit *Issue* by the operation $Dispatch$: Decode × Issue × ReorderBuf × Registers → Decode × Issue × ReorderBuf × Registers (Sect. 8.3), and decoded from the instruction buffer *IBuffer* by *Decode*, with results combined by *Merge*. If the pipeline is being reset then the decode and dispatch unit is emptied by the buffer operation *Reset*.

The Issue Unit. The state of the issue unit is:

$$\mathsf{Issue} = \mathsf{AddIssue1} \times \mathsf{AddIssue2} \times \mathsf{BrIssue} \times \mathsf{LsrIssue},$$

where

$$\mathsf{AddIssue1} = \mathsf{List}_{(addsize1, \mathsf{AddEntry})},$$
$$\mathsf{AddIssue2} = \mathsf{List}_{(addsize2, \mathsf{AddEntry})},$$
$$\mathsf{BrIssue} = \mathsf{List}_{(brsize, \mathsf{BrEntry})},$$
$$\mathsf{LsrIssue} = \mathsf{List}_{(lsrsize, \mathsf{LsrEntry})},$$

and

$$\mathsf{AddEntry} = \mathsf{RegOpnd}^2 \times RC \times W_{\log_2(reordersize)},$$

$$\mathsf{BrEntry} = Bit \times Reg \times W_{\log_2(reordersize)} \times PC$$

$$\times W_{\log_2(reordersize)},$$

$$\mathsf{LsrEntry} = \mathsf{RegOpnd} \times \mathsf{MemOpnd} \times PC \times RC \times Bit$$

$$\times W_{\log_2(reordersize)},$$

$$\mathsf{RegOpnd} = Bit \times RC \times Reg,$$

$$\mathsf{MemOpnd} = Bit \times PC \times Reg,$$

with component names:

$$\overrightarrow{issue} = (\overrightarrow{addissue}_1, \overrightarrow{addissue}_2, \overrightarrow{brissue}, \overrightarrow{lsrissue}),$$

where

$$\overrightarrow{addentry} = (\overrightarrow{regopnd}_1, \overrightarrow{regopnd}_2, dr, reorderpos),$$

$$\overrightarrow{brentry} = (ready, opnd, offset, addr, reorderpos),$$

$$\overrightarrow{lsrentry} = (\overrightarrow{regopnd}, \overrightarrow{memopnd}, da, dr, load, reorderpos),$$

and

$$\overrightarrow{regopnd} = (ready, sr, opnd),$$

$$\overrightarrow{memopnd} = (ready, sa, opnd).$$

The issue unit contains reservation stations for each of the functional units: AddIssue1, AddIssue2, BrIssue and LsrIssue. Each reservation station is modeled using the *finite list algebra*. An adder reservation station entry consists of two register operand entries ($\overrightarrow{regopnd}_1$ and $\overrightarrow{regopnd}_2$), a destination register dr, and an assigned location in the reorder buffer *reorderpos*.

The register operand entries each consist of a ready flag *ready*, a register location sr, and a machine word *opnd*. If the flag *ready* is set then the operand will already be stored in *opnd*, otherwise it will be fetched later from register location sr.

The branch unit reservation station consists of a flag *ready*, a machine word *opnd*, a reorder buffer offset *offset*, a memory address *addr*, and an assigned location in the reorder buffer *reorderpos*. If the flag *ready* is set then *opnd* will contain the current contents of register zero. Otherwise, this will be fetched later. The *offset* field is used to ensure the *pc*-relative branch is made to the correct address. If the reorder buffer is not empty when the branch is dispatched then the *PM* program counter value upon dispatch will be inconsistent with the branch instruction address. The *offset* field compensates for this.

A load-store reservation station entry consists of a register operand $\overrightarrow{regopnd}$ (identical to an adder reservation station's operand entry), an address operand $\overrightarrow{memopnd}$, a memory destination address da, a destination register dr, a flag $load$, and an assigned location in the reorder buffer $reorderpos$. The address operand $\overrightarrow{memopnd}$ consists of ready flag $ready$, a data-cache memory location sa and a machine word $opnd$. If the ready flag is set, then the operand to be loaded/stored is already present in the $opnd$ field of $\overrightarrow{memopnd}$ or $\overrightarrow{regopnd}$ as appropriate. Otherwise, it is fetched later from register location sr (in $\overrightarrow{regopnd}$) in the case of a store instruction, or data cache location sa (in $\overrightarrow{memopnd}$) in the case of a load instruction. The flag $load$ is set when a load instruction is to be executed.

The next-state function $Issue : STATE \rightarrow \mathsf{Issue}$ is defined below.

$$Issue(\overrightarrow{state}) =$$

$$\begin{cases} IssueRmv(< \pi_{issue}^{Dispatch}(Dispatch(\overrightarrow{decode}, \overrightarrow{issue}, & \text{if } reset = 0; \\ \overrightarrow{reorderbuf}, \overrightarrow{registers}, Dcache)) >, \\ < \pi_{execs}(Execute(\overrightarrow{issue}, \overrightarrow{registers}, Dcache)) >), \\ (Reset(\overrightarrow{addissue_1}), Reset(\overrightarrow{addissue_2}), Reset(\overrightarrow{brissue}), \text{otherwise.} \\ Reset(\overrightarrow{lsrissue})), \end{cases}$$

If the pipeline is not being reset then entries are pushed onto the reservation station by $Dispatch$ and removed by the operation $Execute :$ $\mathsf{Issue} \times \mathsf{Registers} \times \mathsf{Dcache} \rightarrow \mathbf{N}^4 \times \mathsf{Functional}$ (Sect. 8.3).

The projection $\pi_{execs} : \mathbf{N}^4 \times \mathsf{Functional} \rightarrow \mathbf{N}^4$ gives a 4-tuple of natural numbers identifying the instructions that have been issued from each of the four reservation stations $(\overrightarrow{addissue_1}, \dots, \overrightarrow{lsrissue})$. The issued functions are then removed from the reservation stations by the hidden function $IssueRmv : \mathsf{Issue} \times \mathbf{N}^4 \rightarrow \mathsf{Issue}$.

$$IssueRmv(< \overrightarrow{addissue_1}, \overrightarrow{addissue_2}, \overrightarrow{branch}, \overrightarrow{loadstore} >,$$
$$< ex_1, ex_2, ex_3, ex_4 >) =$$
$$(Remove(\overrightarrow{addissue_1}, ex_1), Remove(\overrightarrow{addissue_2}, ex_2)$$
$$Remove(\overrightarrow{brissue}, ex_3), Remove(\overrightarrow{lsrissue}, ex_4)).$$

Each reservation station has the entries of executed instructions removed by the list operation $Remove$, which removes a specified element from a list.

The Functional Units. The states of the functional units are:

$$\text{Functional} = \text{Adder}^2 \times \text{Branch} \times \text{LoadStore},$$

where

$$\text{Adder} = Reg \times RC \times Bit \times W_{\log_2(reordersize)},$$
$$\text{Branch} = PC \times Bit \times Bit \times W_{\log_2(reordersize)},$$
$$\text{LoadStore} = Reg \times PC \times Bit \times Bit \times W_{\log_2(reordersize)},$$

with component names:

$$\overrightarrow{functional} = (\overrightarrow{adder}_1, \overrightarrow{adder}_2, \overrightarrow{branch}, \overrightarrow{loadstore}),$$

where

$$\overrightarrow{adder} = (result, dest, done, reorderpos),$$
$$\overrightarrow{branch} = (result, taken, done, reorderpos),$$
$$\overrightarrow{loadstore} = (result, dest, load, done, reorderpos).$$

The adder functional units consist of a result word *result*, a destination register address *dest*, a flag *done*, and a reorder buffer location *reorderpos*. The flag *done* is set when the unit has finished computing a result to be inserted into the reorder buffer. The branch functional unit consists of a memory address *result*, flags *taken* and *done*, and a reorder buffer location *reorderpos*. The flag *taken* is set when the condition for the branch holds. The flag *done* serves the same purpose as that in the adder functional units. The load-store functional unit consists of a result word *result*, a destination address *dest*, flags *load* and *done*, and a reorder buffer location *reorderpos*. The *load* flag distinguishes between `load` and `store` instructions; the *done* flag serves the same purpose as in the adder and branch units.

The next-state function $Functional : STATE \rightarrow \text{Functional}$ is defined below.

$$Functional(\overrightarrow{state}) =$$
$$\begin{cases} \pi\frac{Execute}{functional}(Execute(\overrightarrow{issue}, \overrightarrow{registers}, Dcache)), & \text{if } reset = 0; \\ ((0,0,0,0), (0,0,0,0), (0,0,0,0), (0,0,0,0,0)), & \text{otherwise.} \end{cases}$$

If the pipeline is not being reset then instructions are executed, otherwise all registers are set to zero. Note that clearing just the *done* flags would be sufficient to reset each functional unit, since this would prevent results from the functional units being moved to the reorder buffer (Sect. 8.3).

The Reorder Buffer Unit. The state of the reorder buffer unit is:

$$\text{ReorderBuf} = \text{Buffer}_{(reordersize,\text{ReorderEntry})},$$

where

$$\text{ReorderEntry} = W_3 \times PC \times Reg,$$

with component names:

$$\overrightarrow{reorderentry} = (type, dest, word).$$

The reorder buffer entry consists of a three-bit content-type word *type*, a destination word *dest*, and a result word *word*. Valid *type* values will be represented by unique constants `wait`, `skip`, `dcache`, `reg` and `count`.

The next-state function $Reorder : STATE \rightarrow \text{ReorderBuf}$ is defined below.

$$Reorder(\overrightarrow{state}) =$$
$$
\begin{cases}
ReorderIns(Merge(\pi\frac{Dispatch}{reorderbuf}(Dispatch(\overrightarrow{decode}, & \text{if } reset = 0; \\
\overrightarrow{issue}, \overrightarrow{reorderbuf}, \overrightarrow{registers}, Dcache)), & \\
\pi\frac{Commit}{reorderbuf}(Commit(\overrightarrow{reorderbuf}, & \\
\overrightarrow{registers}, Dcache))), \overrightarrow{functional}), & \\
Reset(\overrightarrow{reorderbuf}), & \text{otherwise.}
\end{cases}
$$

If the pipeline is not being flushed, entries are removed from the buffer by the operation $Commit : \text{ReorderBuf} \times \text{Registers} \times \text{Dcache} \rightarrow \text{ReorderBuf} \times \text{Registers} \times \text{Dcache}$ (Sect. 3), place-holding entries are added (to hold future results) by *Dispatch*, and available results from the functionals units are inserted into their assigned entries by the operation $ReorderIns : \text{ReorderBuf} \times \text{Functional} \rightarrow \text{ReorderBuf}$ (Sect. 8.3). If the pipeline is being flushed then the reorder unit is cleared using the buffer operation *Reset*.

The Register Units. The state of the register unit is:

$$\text{Registers} = Reg \times [RC \rightarrow Bit]$$
$$\times \text{List}_{(W_{\log_2(memusize)},PC)} \times Bit \times PC,$$

with component names:

$$\overrightarrow{registers} = (reg, regu, \overrightarrow{memu}, reset, pc).$$

This unit consists of the register array *reg*, a register usage table *regu*, a memory address usage list $\overrightarrow{memu}$, a flag *reset*, and the program counter *pc.* The components *regu* and *memu* are used to keep track of registers and memory locations that are to be written to by instructions that have been *dispatched* and have not yet *committed*. This information is used to resolve dependencies in instruction dispatch.

The next-state function *Registers* : *STATE* → Registers is defined below.

$$
Registers(\overrightarrow{state}) =
\begin{cases}
\pi\frac{Commit}{registers}(Commit(\overrightarrow{reorderbuf}, & \text{if } reset = 0; \\
\qquad \pi\frac{Dispatch}{registers}(Dispatch(\overrightarrow{decode}, \overrightarrow{issue}, \overrightarrow{reorderbuf}, \\
\qquad \overrightarrow{registers}, Dcache), Dcache))) \\
(reg, emptyregu, Reset(\overrightarrow{memu}), 0, pc), & \text{otherwise.}
\end{cases}
$$

If the pipeline is not being reset, then the register usage table and memory usage list is updated by *Dispatch*. After this, all components may be altered by *Commit*. Dispatch and commit results are combined by simple composition. If the pipeline is being reset then the register usage table and the memory usage list are cleared, and the reset flag set to zero.

The hidden constant $emptyregu \in [RC \rightarrow Bit]$ is defined by

$$
emptyregu(i) = 0, \text{ for all } i \in RC.
$$

The Data Cache. The state of the data cache is Dcache $= [PC \rightarrow Reg]$, and the next-state function *Dcache* : *STATE* → Dcache is defined below.

$$
Dcache(\overrightarrow{state}) =
\begin{cases}
\pi_{Dcache}^{Commit}(Commit(\overrightarrow{reorderbuf}, & \text{if } reset = 0; \\
\qquad \overrightarrow{registers}, Dcache)), \\
Dcache, & \text{otherwise.}
\end{cases}
$$

If the pipeline is not being reset then the data cache is only affected by *Commit*. If the pipeline is being reset, the data cache remains unchanged.

8.3 Processor Operations

The next-state functions for each of the *physical units* of *ACS* are defined in terms of *conceptual operations*. The six operation stages form the *ACS Operations algebra*, defined below.

Algebra *ACS* Operations
Carrier Sets
 Icache, Ibuffer, Decode, Issue, Functional, ReorderBuf,
 Registers, Dcache
Constants
 —

Operations
   $Fetch$: Icache $\times$ Ibuffer $\rightarrow$ Icache $\times$ Ibuffer
   $Decode$: Ibuffer $\times$ Decode $\rightarrow$ Ibuffer $\times$ Decode
  $Dispatch$: Decode $\times$ Issue $\times$ ReorderBuf $\times$ Registers $\rightarrow$
        Decode $\times$ Issue $\times$ ReorderBuf $\times$ Registers
   $Execute$: Issue $\times$ Registers $\times$ Dcache $\rightarrow$ $\mathbf{N}^4$ $\times$ Functional
   $Commit$: ReorderBuf $\times$ Registers $\times$ Dcache $\rightarrow$
        ReorderBuf $\times$ Registers $\times$ Dcache
 $Reorder Ins$: ReorderBuf $\times$ Functional $\rightarrow$ ReorderBuf
End Algebra.

The components of this algebra are defined in the following sections.

Instruction Fetch. The operation $Fetch$: Icache $\times$ Ibuffer $\rightarrow$ Icache $\times$ Ibuffer is defined below.

$$Fetch(Icache, \overrightarrow{ibuffer}) =$$
$$\begin{cases} Fetch(Icache, < Push(\overrightarrow{instbuf}, & \text{if not } Full(\overrightarrow{instbuf}); \\ \quad Icache(fetchpc)), fetchpc + 1 >), \\ (Icache, \overrightarrow{ibuffer}), & \text{otherwise.} \end{cases}$$

Instructions are repeatedly fetched from the instruction cache, and added to the instruction buffer using the buffer operation *Push*, until the instruction buffer is full (tested by the buffer operation *Full*). In *ACS*, the operation is bounded by the size of the instruction buffer. In a real microprocessor, the bandwidth of the bus between the instruction cache and the instruction buffer will also bound the number of instructions that can be transferred in a clock cycle.

Instruction Decode. The operation

$$Decode : \text{Ibuffer} \times \text{Decode} \rightarrow \text{Ibuffer} \times \text{Decode}$$

is defined below.

$$Decode(\overrightarrow{ibuffer}, \overrightarrow{decode}) =$$
$$\begin{cases} Decode(< Pop(\overrightarrow{instbuf}), fetchpc >, & \text{if not } Empty(\overrightarrow{instbuf}) \\ \quad < Push(\overrightarrow{decode}, & \text{and not } Full(\overrightarrow{decode}); \\ \quad DecodeEntry(Top(\overrightarrow{instbuf}))) >), & \\ (\overrightarrow{ibuffer}, \overrightarrow{decode}), & \text{otherwise.} \end{cases}$$

Instructions are removed from the instruction buffer using the buffer operation *Pop*, decoded by *DecodeEntry*, and then added to the decode-dispatch unit buffer using the buffer operation *Push*, until either the instruction buffer is emptied (tested by the buffer operation *Empty*), or the decode-dispatch unit buffer is full. The operation is bounded by the sizes of these two buffers.

The hidden function $DecodeEntry : Reg \rightarrow OP \times RC^3 \times PC$ decodes an instruction word.

$$DecodeEntry(ibufentry) = (op(ibufentry), ra(ibufentry),$$
$$rb(ibufentry), rc(ibufentry), addr(ibufentry)).$$

There are five fields: an op-code, three register addresses and a data memory address; each of these fields is extracted using the functions *op*, *ra*, *rb*, *rc* and *addr* from Sect. 6.

Instruction Dispatch. The operation $Dispatch : \text{Decode} \times \text{Issue} \times \text{ReorderBuf} \times \text{Registers} \rightarrow \text{Decode} \times \text{Issue} \times \text{ReorderBuf} \times \text{Registers}$ affects decode-dispatch and issue units, reorder buffer, and registers.

$$Dispatch(\overrightarrow{decode}, \overrightarrow{issue}, \overrightarrow{reorderbuf}, \overrightarrow{registers}, Dcache) =$$

$$\begin{cases} Dispatch(DispatchAdd1(\overrightarrow{decode}, \ldots, \overrightarrow{registers}), Dcache), \\ \qquad \text{if } CanDispatchAdd1(\overrightarrow{decode}, \overrightarrow{addissue_1}, \overrightarrow{addissue_2}, \\ \qquad \overrightarrow{reorderbuf}, regu); \\[4pt] Dispatch(DispatchAdd2(\overrightarrow{decode}, \ldots, \overrightarrow{registers}), Dcache), \\ \qquad \text{if } CanDispatchAdd2(\overrightarrow{decode}, \overrightarrow{addissue_1}, \overrightarrow{addissue_2}, \\ \qquad \overrightarrow{reorderbuf}, regu); \\[4pt] Dispatch(DispatchBr(\overrightarrow{decode}, \ldots, \overrightarrow{registers}), Dcache), \\ \qquad \text{if } CanDispatchBr(\overrightarrow{decode}, \overrightarrow{brissue}, \overrightarrow{reorderbuf}); \\[4pt] Dispatch(DispatchLoad(\overrightarrow{decode}, \ldots, \overrightarrow{registers}), Dcache), \\ \qquad \text{if } CanDispatchLoad(\overrightarrow{decode}, \overrightarrow{lsrissue}, \overrightarrow{reorderbuf}, \\ \qquad \overrightarrow{registers}); \\[4pt] Dispatch(DispatchStore(\overrightarrow{decode}, \ldots, \overrightarrow{registers}, Dcache), Dcache), \\ \qquad \text{if } CanDispatchStore(\overrightarrow{decode}, \overrightarrow{lsrissue}, \overrightarrow{reorderbuf}, \\ \qquad \overrightarrow{registers}); \\[4pt] Dispatch(DispatchSet(\overrightarrow{decode}, \ldots, \overrightarrow{registers}), Dcache), \\ \qquad \text{if } CanDispatchSet(\overrightarrow{decode}, \overrightarrow{addissue_1}, \overrightarrow{reorderbuf}, regu); \\[4pt] (\overrightarrow{decode}, \ldots, \overrightarrow{registers}, Dcache), \qquad \text{otherwise.} \end{cases}$$

The first six cases correspond with instruction dispatch for each of the five types of instruction. (There are two cases for the **add** instruction, since there are two addition functional units.) In each of these cases the reservation station is filled and the decode unit entry removed. This process is repeated until the seventh case applies and no further instructions are dispatched. *Dispatch* is bounded in *ACS* by the size of the decode-despatch unit buffer, and/or the sizes of the functional unit buffers.

Dispatching Add Instructions to the First Adder Unit. The hidden function *DispatchAdd1* controls instruction dispatch to the first addition unit's reservation station, and is defined below.

$$DispatchAdd1 : \text{Decode} \times \text{Issue} \times \text{ReorderBuf}$$
$$\times \text{Registers} \rightarrow \text{Decode}$$
$$\times \text{Issue} \times \text{ReorderBuf} \times \text{Registers},$$

$$DispatchAdd1(\overrightarrow{decode}, \overrightarrow{issue}, \overrightarrow{reorderbuf}, \overrightarrow{registers}) =$$
$$(Pop(\overrightarrow{decode}), \tag{1}$$
$$Push(\overrightarrow{addissue}_1, AddIssEnt(Top(\overrightarrow{decode}), \overrightarrow{registers}, \tag{2}$$
$$\quad reorderbuf \cdot tail + 1)),$$
$$\overrightarrow{addissue}_2, \overrightarrow{brissue}, \overrightarrow{lsrissue},$$
$$Push(\overrightarrow{reorderbuf}, (\texttt{wait}, 0, 0)), \tag{3}$$
$$(reg, regu[1/\pi_{rc}^{\overrightarrow{decentry}}(Top(\overrightarrow{decode}))], \overrightarrow{memu}, reset, pc)). \tag{4}$$

When an **add** instruction is dispatched, the following steps are taken.

1. The decode-dispatch unit buffer is popped.
2. A reservation station entry is constructed by $AddIssEnt$, and pushed onto the reservation station list of the first adder. This entry includes the address of the next free reorder buffer entry $(reorderbuf \cdot tail + 1)$. Note, it is assumed that the concrete implementation of the buffer described in [Fox98] is being used.
3. An entry for the result of the addition in the reorder buffer (labeled 'wait') is pushed onto the reorder buffer.
4. The destination register rc is in use $(regu[1/\pi_{rc}^{\overrightarrow{decentry}}(Top(\overrightarrow{decode}))])$.

The hidden function

$$AddIssEnt : \mathsf{DecEntry} \times \mathsf{Registers} \times W_{\log_2(reordersize)} \rightarrow \mathsf{AddEntry}$$

is defined below.

$$AddIssEnt(\overrightarrow{decentry}, \overrightarrow{registers}, reorderpos) =$$
$$\quad (DispatchOperand(ra, \overrightarrow{registers}), DispatchOperand(rb, \overrightarrow{registers}),$$
$$\quad rc, reorderpos).$$

The operands ra and rb are fetched (if ready; see $DispatchOperand$ below), the destination register is set to rc and the reorder position becomes the successor to the current reorder buffer tail.

The hidden function $DispatchOperand : RC \times \mathsf{Registers} \rightarrow \mathsf{RegOpnd}$ is defined below.

$$DispatchOperand(sr, \overrightarrow{registers}) = \begin{cases} (0, sr, 0), & \text{if } regu(sr) = 1; \\ (1, 0, reg_{sr}), & \text{otherwise.} \end{cases}$$

If the source register sr is reserved (that is, the register sr is already in use), then the ready bit is set to zero and sr is stored in the reservation station; the contents of sr will be fetched later. If the register is not in use then the ready bit is set to one, and the contents of sr are stored in the reservation station.

The hidden function

$$CanDispatchAdd1 : \text{Decode} \times \text{AddIssue1} \times \text{AddIssue2}$$
$$\times \text{ReorderBuf} \times [RC \rightarrow Bit] \rightarrow \mathbf{B}$$

is defined below.

$$CanDispatchAdd1(\overrightarrow{decode}, \overrightarrow{addissue}_1, \overrightarrow{addissue}_2, \overrightarrow{reorderbuf}, \overrightarrow{regu}) =$$

$$\begin{cases} tt, \text{ if not } Empty(\overrightarrow{decode}) \text{ and } \pi_{op}^{\overrightarrow{decentry}}(Top(\overrightarrow{decode})) = \mathbf{add} \quad (1) \\ \quad \text{and not } Full(\overrightarrow{addissue}_1) \text{ and not } Full(\overrightarrow{reorderbuf}) \quad (2) \\ \quad \text{and } regu(\pi_{rc}^{\overrightarrow{decentry}}(Top(\overrightarrow{decode}))) = 0 \quad (3) \\ \quad \text{and } (Size(\overrightarrow{addissue}_1) \leq Size(\overrightarrow{addissue}_2) \quad (4) \\ \quad \text{or } Full(\overrightarrow{addissue}_2)); \\ ff, \text{ otherwise.} \end{cases}$$

In order to dispatch an **add** instruction to the first adder unit:

1. there must be an **add** instruction at the top of the (non empty) decode unit;
2. the first adder reservation station and reorder buffer must not be full;
3. the destination register for the **add** must not be in use; and
4. the first adder reservation station must have fewer or the same number of instructions pending execution as the second adder station, or the second adder reservation station must be full. This prevents the same instruction from being dispatched to both adder reservation stations.

The process of dispatching **branch**, **store**, **load** and **set** instructions, and of dispatching **add** instructions to the second adder unit, is similar, and we omit the definitions.

Instruction Execution. The $Execute$: Issue $\times$ Registers $\times$ Dcache $\rightarrow$ $\mathbf{N}^4 \times$ Functional operation returns a 4-tuple of reservation station locations, representing instructions that have been executed, together with the state of each of the functional units, and is defined below.

$$Execute(\overrightarrow{issue}, \overrightarrow{registers}, Dcache) =$$
$$(\pi_{exec}(Adder(\overrightarrow{addissue_1}, \overrightarrow{registers})),$$
$$\pi_{exec}(Adder(\overrightarrow{addissue_2}, \overrightarrow{registers})),$$
$$\pi_{exec}(Branch(\overrightarrow{brissue}, \overrightarrow{registers})),$$
$$\pi_{exec}(LoadStore(\overrightarrow{lsrissue}, \overrightarrow{registers}, Dcache)),$$
$$\pi_{unit}(Adder(\overrightarrow{addissue_1}, \overrightarrow{registers})),$$
$$\pi_{unit}(Adder(\overrightarrow{addissue_2}, \overrightarrow{registers})),$$
$$\pi_{unit}(Branch(\overrightarrow{brissue}, \overrightarrow{registers})),$$
$$\pi_{unit}(LoadStore(\overrightarrow{lsrissue}, \overrightarrow{registers}, Dcache))).$$

The functions *Adder*, *Branch*, and *LoadStore* each return a reservation station location and functional unit state as a pair. The projection

$$\pi_{exec} : \{0, \ldots, \max(addsize_1, \ldots, lsrsize)\}$$
$$\times (\mathsf{Adder} \cup \mathsf{Branch} \cup \mathsf{LoadStore})$$
$$\rightarrow \{0, \ldots, \max(addsize_1, \ldots, lsrsize)\}$$

projects out the reservation station location, and the projection

$$\pi_{unit} : \{0, \ldots, \max(addsize_1, \ldots, lsrsize)\}$$
$$\times (\mathsf{Adder} \cup \mathsf{Branch} \cup \mathsf{LoadStore}) \rightarrow (\mathsf{Adder} \cup \mathsf{Branch} \cup \mathsf{LoadStore})$$

projects the functional unit state.

Executing Add and Set Instructions. The hidden function *Adder* is defined below.

$$Adder : (\mathsf{List}_{(addsize_1, \mathsf{AddEntry})} \cup \mathsf{List}_{(addsize_2, \mathsf{AddEntry})}) \times \mathsf{Registers} \rightarrow$$
$$\{0, \ldots, \max(addsize_1, addsize_2)\} \times \mathsf{Adder},$$

$$Adder(\overrightarrow{addissue}, \overrightarrow{registers}) =$$
$$\begin{cases} (toexec, AddExecute(Eval(\overrightarrow{addissue}, toexec), reg)), & \text{if } toexec > 0; \\ (toexec, (0, 0, 0, 0)), & \text{otherwise,} \end{cases}$$

where $toexec = Find(\overrightarrow{addissue}, CanExecuteAdd_{regu})$ is the reservation station location of an **add** instruction that may be able to execute. The list operation *Find* is defined in [Fox98]. If an **add** instruction is able to execute ($toexec > 0$), then $toexec$ is returned together with the state of the adder functional unit after executing reservation station entry *toexec*. Note that the oldest instructions in a reservation station list will be executed first, subject to dependencies: see the definition of *Find* in [Fox98].

At this stage of the instruction pipeline, **set** instructions are indistinguishable from **add** instructions of the form $0 + x$: see [Fox98]. Therefore, we need take no special steps to execute them.

The hidden function $AddExecute$: AddEntry $\times$ Reg $\rightarrow$ Adder is defined below.

$$AddExecute(\overrightarrow{addentry}, reg) =$$
$$(GetOperand(\overrightarrow{regopnd}_1, reg)$$
$$+ GetOperand(\overrightarrow{regopnd}_2, reg), dr, 1, reorderpos).$$

The two register operands are added, the destination address dr and reorder unit position are copied, and the *done* flag is set to one.

The hidden function $GetOperand$: RegOpnd $\times$ Reg $\rightarrow$ Reg is defined below.

$$GetOperand(\overrightarrow{regopnd}, reg) = \begin{cases} opnd, & \text{if } ready = 1; \\ reg_{sr}, & \text{otherwise.} \end{cases}$$

If $ready = 1$ then the operand has already been fetched, and is stored in $opnd$. Otherwise the operand is fetched from the appropriate PM-level register reg_{sr}.

The family of sets $CanExecuteAdd$ of executable **add** instructions is defined below.

$$< CanExecuteAdd_{regu} \subseteq \text{AddEntry} \mid regu \in [PC \rightarrow Bit] >,$$

$$CanExecuteAdd_{regu} =$$
$$\{\overrightarrow{addentry} \in \text{AddEntry} \mid Ready(addentry \cdot \overrightarrow{regopnd}_1, regu) \text{ and}$$
$$Ready(\overrightarrow{addentry} \cdot \overrightarrow{regopnd}_2, regu)\}.$$

An **add** instruction may be executed if both its register operands are *ready*.

The function $Ready$: RegOpnd $\times$ $[RC \rightarrow Bit]$ $\rightarrow$ **B** is defined below.

$$Ready(\overrightarrow{regopnd}, regu) = \begin{cases} tt, & \text{if } ready = 1 \text{ or } regu(sr) = 0; \\ ff, & \text{otherwise.} \end{cases}$$

The operand is ready if it has already been fetched ($ready = 1$) or it is no longer being used as the destination of a waiting instruction ($regu(sr) =$

0). Note, if an **add** instruction is using the same register as destination and operand, then the *ready* bit will not be set until after its operands have been dispatched: see *DispatchAdd1*, *AddIssEnt* and *DispatchOperand* in Sect. 8.3. Therefore, an instruction will not attempt to wait for itself to commit before being executed.

The process of executing **branch**, **store** and **load** instructions is similar, and we omit the definitions.

Filling the Reorder Buffer. The operation

$$ReorderIns : \mathsf{ReorderBuf} \times \mathsf{Functional} \rightarrow \mathsf{ReorderBuf}$$

is defined below.

$$ReorderIns(\overrightarrow{reorderbuf}, \overrightarrow{functional}) =$$
$$ReorderAdd(ReorderAdd(ReorderBranch(ReorderLsr(\overrightarrow{reorderbuf},$$
$$\overrightarrow{loadstore}), \overrightarrow{branch}), \overrightarrow{adder_2}), \overrightarrow{adder_1}).$$

Results are inserted into the reorder buffer from each of the four functional units.

The hidden function $ReorderAdd : \mathsf{ReorderBuf} \times \mathsf{Adder} \rightarrow \mathsf{ReorderBuf}$ is defined below.

$$ReorderAdd(\overrightarrow{reorderbuf}, \overrightarrow{adder}) =$$
$$\begin{cases} Insert(\overrightarrow{reorderbuf}, (\mathbf{reg}, pad(dest), result), & \text{if } done = 1; \\ \quad reorderpos), \\ \overrightarrow{reorderbuf}, & \text{otherwise.} \end{cases}$$

The reorder buffer entry consists of (*i*) a destination flag, set to **reg** in the case of an **add** or **set** instruction; (*ii*) the (padded) register destination; and (*iii*) the result of the addition (*result*). The position at which the entry is inserted within the reorder buffer (*reorderpos*) is stored within the adder functional unit. If no instruction has been executed by the addition unit (*done* = 0), the reorder buffer is unchanged. The buffer operation *Insert* is defined in [Fox98].

The hidden function

$$ReorderBranch : \mathsf{ReorderBuf} \times \mathsf{Branch} \rightarrow \mathsf{ReorderBuf}$$

is defined below.

$$ReorderBranch(\overrightarrow{reorderbuf}, \overrightarrow{branch}) =$$

$$\begin{cases} Insert(\overrightarrow{reorderbuf}, (\mathbf{count}, result, 0), & \text{if } done = 1 \text{ and } taken = 1; \\ \quad reorderpos), \\ Insert(\overrightarrow{reorderbuf}, (\mathbf{skip}, 0, 0), & \text{if } done = 1 \text{ and } taken = 0; \\ \quad reorderpos), \\ \overrightarrow{reorderbuf}, & \text{otherwise.} \end{cases}$$

There are two types of reorder buffer entries for **branch** instructions. A branch which is taken is flagged with **count**, whereas a branch which is not taken is flagged **skip**. In the case of a taken branch, the branch unit result (i.e. the branch address) is stored in the destination field of the reorder buffer entry.

The hidden function

$$ReorderLsr : \mathsf{ReorderBuf} \times \mathsf{LoadStore} \to \mathsf{ReorderBuf}$$

is defined below.

$$ReorderLsr(\overrightarrow{reorderbuf}, \overrightarrow{loadstore}) =$$

$$\begin{cases} Insert(\overrightarrow{reorderbuf}, (\mathbf{reg}, dest, result), & \text{if } done = 1 \\ \quad reorderpos), & \text{and } load = 1; \\ Insert(\overrightarrow{reorderbuf}, (\mathbf{dcache}, dest, result), & \text{if } done = 1 \\ \quad reorderpos), & \text{and } load = 0; \\ \overrightarrow{reorderbuf}, & \text{otherwise.} \end{cases}$$

If the instruction executed was a **load** then the reorder buffer entry is flagged with **reg**. If the instruction was a **store** then the reorder buffer entry is flagged with **dcache**.

Instruction Committal. The operation

$$Commit : \mathsf{ReorderBuf} \times \mathsf{Registers} \times \mathsf{Dcache} \to$$
$$\mathsf{ReorderBuf} \times \mathsf{Registers} \times \mathsf{Dcache}$$

is defined below.

$$Commit(\overrightarrow{reorderbuf}, < \overrightarrow{registers}, Dcache >) =$$

$$\begin{cases} (\overrightarrow{reorderbuf}, \overrightarrow{registers}, & \text{if } (\text{not } Empty(\overrightarrow{reorderbuf}) \text{ and} \qquad (1) \\ \quad Dcache), & \pi_{type}^{\overrightarrow{reorderentry}}(Top(\overrightarrow{reorderbuf})) = \texttt{wait}) \\ & \text{or } Empty(\overrightarrow{reorderbuf}); \\ (Reset(\overrightarrow{reorderbuf}), CommitResult(Top(\overrightarrow{reorderbuf}), \overrightarrow{registers}, \\ \quad Dcache)), & \text{if not } Empty(\overrightarrow{reorderbuf}) \text{ and} \qquad (2) \\ & \pi_{type}^{\overrightarrow{reorderentry}}(Top(\overrightarrow{reorderbuf})) = \texttt{count}; \\ Commit(Pop(\overrightarrow{reorderbuf}), < CommitResult(Top(\overrightarrow{reorderbuf}), \\ \quad \overrightarrow{registers}, Dcache >)), \quad \text{otherwise.} \qquad\qquad\qquad (3) \end{cases}$$

There are three cases to consider.

1. There are no results to be committed, either because the reorder buffer is empty or because the topmost entry is waiting for instruction results. In this case, the reorder buffer, registers and data cache are unchanged.
2. A branch has been taken. The branch is committed and the reorder buffer is reset.
3. A functional unit result is to be committed. The topmost reorder buffer entry is committed and an attempt is made to commit the next result.

The commit function is bounded by the size of the reorder buffer.

The hidden function

$$CommitResult : \text{ReorderEntry} \times \text{Registers} \times \text{Dcache} \rightarrow \text{Registers} \times \text{Dcache}$$

is defined below.

$$CommitResult(\overrightarrow{reorderentry}, \overrightarrow{registers}, Dcache) =$$

$$\begin{cases} (reg[word/trim(dest)], regu[0/trim(dest)], & \text{if } type = \texttt{reg}; \quad (1) \\ \quad \overline{memu}, reset, pc + 1, Dcache), \\ (reg, regu, Remove(\overline{memu}, & \text{if } type = \texttt{dcache}; (2) \\ \quad Find(\overline{memu}, =_{dest})), reset, pc + 1, \\ \quad Dcache[word/dest]), \\ (reg, regu, \overline{memu}, 1, dest, Dcache), & \text{if } type = \texttt{count}; \quad (3) \\ (reg, regu, \overline{memu}, reset, pc + 1, Dcache), & \text{if } type = \texttt{skip}; \quad (4) \end{cases}$$

There are four cases to consider.

1. A result is to committed to a register. The value is written to the register, the register usage table is modified such that the register location *dest* is no longer active, and the program counter is incremented. The *trim* function removes the field-padding zeros added by *pad* in *ReorderAdd* (Sect. 8.3).
2. A result is to be committed to the data cache. The memory address usage list is updated by removing the entry with address *dest*, the program counter is incremented, and the result written to the data cache.
3. A branch was taken. The program counter is set to the destination of the branch (*dest*), and the *reset* flag is set to one.
4. A branch was not taken (`skip`). The program counter is incremented.

9 Correctness and Verification

We will formulate the correctness conditions for our superscalar implementation with respect to its architectural description, using the techniques described in Sect. 3 and Sect. 5. We will then discuss the process of verification, and consider why the usual technique is problematic in the case of superscalar processors.

9.1 A Correctness Definition for *ACS*

The implementation ACS is correct if (given maps $\rho : STATE_{ACS} \to [S \to T]$ and $\psi : STATE_{ACS} \to STATE_{PM}$ defined below) the following diagram commutes for all clock cycles $s = start(\lambda(\overrightarrow{state}))(s)$ and $\overrightarrow{state} \in STATE_{ACS}$:

$$
\begin{array}{ccc}
T \times STATE_{PM} & \xrightarrow{\ State_{PM}\ } & STATE_{PM} \\[4pt]
\Big\uparrow {\scriptstyle (\rho,\psi)} & & \Big\uparrow {\scriptstyle \psi} \\[4pt]
S \times STATE_{ACS} & \xrightarrow{\ State_{ACS}\ } & STATE_{ACS}
\end{array}
$$

The map $\psi : STATE_{ACS} \to STATE_{PM}$ is defined below.

$$\psi(\overrightarrow{state}) = (Icache, Dcache, pc, reg),$$

where *Icache*, *Dcache*, *pc* and *reg* are those parts of $\overrightarrow{state}$ also present in $STATE_{PM}$. Let R be a retirement clock; each cycle of clock R corresponds with the committal of a number of instructions. The map $\rho : STATE \to [S \to T]$ is defined by $\rho(b) = \overline{\lambda}_1(b)\lambda_2(b)$, with the retimings

$\lambda_1 : STATE_{PM} \rightarrow Ret(T, R)$ and $\lambda_2 : STATE_{ACS} \rightarrow Ret(S, R)$ defined by their respective immersions below.

$$\bar{\lambda}_1(\overrightarrow{state})(0) = 0,$$
$$\bar{\lambda}_2(\overrightarrow{state})(0) = 0,$$
$$\bar{\lambda}_1(\overrightarrow{state})(r + 1) = dur_1(State_{ACS}(\bar{\lambda}_2(\overrightarrow{state})(r), \overrightarrow{state})) + \bar{\lambda}_1(\overrightarrow{state})(r),$$
$$\bar{\lambda}_2(\overrightarrow{state})(r + 1) = dur_2(State_{ACS}(\bar{\lambda}_2(\overrightarrow{state})(r), \overrightarrow{state})) + \bar{\lambda}_2(\overrightarrow{state})(r).$$

The duration functions $dur_1 : STATE \rightarrow T^+$ and $dur_2 : STATE \rightarrow S^+$, where $T^+ = \{t \in T \mid t > 0\}$ and $S^+ = \{s \in S \mid s > 0\}$ are defined below.

$$dur_1(\overrightarrow{state}) = Committed(next_{ACS}^{dur_2(\overrightarrow{state})}(\overrightarrow{state})),$$
$$dur_2(\overrightarrow{state}) = \text{least } s \in S^+ \text{ such that } CanCmt(next_{ACS}^{s}(\overrightarrow{state})).$$

Duration function dur_1 counts the number of instructions committed for each cycle of clock R. Duration function dur_2 counts the number of system clock cycles for each cycle of event clock R.

The function $Committed : STATE_{ACS} \rightarrow T^+$ gives the number of instructions committed from a given state.

$$Committed(\overrightarrow{state}) =$$
$$\begin{cases} 0, & \text{if not } CanCmt(\overrightarrow{reorderbuf}); \\ 1 + \text{greatest } n \in \mathbf{N}, & \text{otherwise.} \\ \quad \text{such that: } \forall\, m \leq n, \\ \quad CanCmt(Pop^m(\overrightarrow{reorderbuf})), \end{cases}$$

The function $CanCmt : \mathsf{ReorderBuf} \rightarrow \mathbf{B}$ is defined below.

$$CanCmt(\overrightarrow{reorderbuf}) = \begin{cases} tt, \text{ if not } \overrightarrow{Empty(reorderbuf)} \\ \quad \text{and } \pi_{type}^{\overrightarrow{reorderentry}}(Top(\overrightarrow{reorderbuf})) \neq \mathtt{wait}; \\ ff, \text{ otherwise.} \end{cases}$$

9.2   Verifying ACS

Space precludes a full formal discussion of the normal process of verifying the correctness of a microprocessor, expressed as an iterated map in the form above. However, informally, the argument proceeds as follows. Microprocessors expressed as iterated maps are functions only of their initial state, some number of clock cycles, and (possibly) some inputs. They do not depend on the numeric value of time. That is, given an initial state σ_0, and neglecting inputs, suppose we run a microprocessor representation F for $t_1 + t_2$ clock cycles, and finish (at time $t = t_1 + t_2 - 1$ in state σ_n). We would reach the same state σ_n as if we first ran F for t_1 cycles, reaching state σ_t, reset time to zero, and then ran F for t_2 cycles, now starting in state σ_t.

Logically extending this argument, given $State_{PM} : T \times STATE_{PM} \rightarrow STATE_{PM}$, and $State_{AC} : S \times STATE_{ACS} \rightarrow STATE_{ACS}$, together with retiming $\lambda : STATE_{ACS} \rightarrow Ret(S,T)$ and projection function $\psi : STATE_{ACS} \rightarrow STATE_{PM}$, to show that $State_{AC}$ is a correct implementation of $State_{PM}$ it is sufficient to establish the following for all $\overrightarrow{state} \in STATE_{ACS}$.

1. $State_{PM}(0, \psi(\overrightarrow{state})) = \psi(State_{AC}(0, \overrightarrow{state}))$.
2. $State_{PM}(1, \psi(\overrightarrow{state})) = \psi(State_{AC}(\overline{\lambda(\overrightarrow{state})}(1), \overrightarrow{state}))$.
3. At time $\overline{\lambda(\overrightarrow{state})}(1)$, the state of $State_{AC}$ is consistent with correct future execution. The easiest way to establish this is to use $init_{AC}$ as an invariant, and show that

$$State_{AC}(\overline{\lambda(\overrightarrow{state})}(1), \overrightarrow{state}) = init_{AC}(State_{AC}(\overline{\lambda(\overrightarrow{state})}(1), \overrightarrow{state})).$$

This requires that $init_{AC}$ is as *weak* as possible: that is, $init_{AC}(\overrightarrow{state})$ will leave elements of $\overrightarrow{state} \in STATE_{ACS}$ unchanged unless they are inconsistent (e.g. $m(pc) \neq ir$: see Sect. 2).

This can significantly simplify formal verification. A more formal discussion can be found in [FH98], and a full account in [Fox98] (including the conditions $STATE_{PM}$, $STATE_{ACS}$, λ and ψ must satisfy). The same simplification has also been observed, within the framework of their own formalisms, by others working on microprocessor verification; for example, [WC94, MS95b, MS95a, WB96, Bur96, SDB96, Cyr96].

There are several difficulties in the case of superscalar microprocessors.

1. The size of the state-space makes establishing that

$$State_{PM}(1, \psi(\overrightarrow{state})) = \psi(State_{AC}(\overline{\lambda(\overrightarrow{state})}(1), \overrightarrow{state}))$$

difficult, simply because of the number of cases to consider. A large proportion of the possible cases will be disallowed by $init_{AC}$; but even so, the number remaining is very large [Fox98].
2. The complexity of the relationships within the state-space makes it difficult to construct an appropriately-weak initialisation function. The current initialisation function (Sect. 8.2) for ACS simply resets

the pipeline, and is very strong. However, given the size of the state-space, the complexity of the relationships between state components, and the consequent number of possible, consistent values for each of the state elements, a weak initialisation function is extremely complex [Fox98].

3. As well as being complex to construct and check, such an initialisation function will consume considerable resources in automated verification attempts because of the need to check

$$State_{AC}(\overrightarrow{\lambda(state)}(1), \overrightarrow{state}) = init_{AC}(State_{AC}(\overrightarrow{\lambda(state)}(1), \overrightarrow{state})).$$

It is not clear how to address these problems. In [Fox98] a systematic method for constructing initialisation functions for pipelined processors is described, where the state of the pipeline can be uniquely determined by the immediately-preceding instructions. This will not work for ACS, where the state of the pipeline may be influenced by instructions that passed though in the (potentially distant) past. (For example, the choice of which addition unit to send an add instruction to will be influenced by, among other things, the sizes of the queues at each unit, which in turn will be influenced by the number and distribution of add instructions in the past.) The problems essentially stem from the 'complexity' of the state-space, where 'complexity' in this context is some measure of (i) the number of separate state components; and (ii) the relationships between the state components. Point (i) leads to a large number of cases to be checked. Point (ii) makes establishing that the processor is in a legal state, corresponding to one of the cases, complex and time consuming.

We are considering two possible approaches to reducing state-space complexity. Firstly, making concessions in the implementation to simplify the complexity of the state-space. This obviously could negatively affect performance, and, at first sight, seems to imply a return to less advanced implementations. However, this need not be the case. The aim is more subtle than simply making the state-space 'smaller': recall that a monolithic memory can be very large, yet is conceptually simple. It may be possible to reduce the number of discrete state components, and the complexity of their interrelationships, while still maintaining the potential for high instruction throughput. The second approach involves inserting a new level of abstraction between the current PM and AC levels. By doing this, it may be possible to conceal some of the complexities of the current AC level and hence simplify the representation of the processor. It would, of course, still be necessary to verify that the AC level is correct with respect to this new level of abstraction. However, we could consider each of the physical units of the processor in isolation, which would make verification more tractable.

10 Concluding Remarks

We have shown that the algebraic tools developed for representing simple, non-superscalar microprocessor implementations are equally applicable to complex superscalar examples. The algebraic techniques are not specific to any particular software, but are adaptable to a range of currently-available tools. We have developed, in considerable detail, a superscalar implementation. We have formulated the correctness conditions for the implementation with respect to an architecture. We have also briefly discussed the problems of formal verification. Future work will consider simplifying formal verification, by studying possible alternative techniques for reducing complexity. In addition, we intend to consider levels of abstraction higher than the current *PM* level. [Ste96, Ste98] consider algebraic models of *high-level languages*, *compilers* and *abstract machine languages* in a form very similar to our models of hardware. We wish to bridge the gap between abstract machine languages, and the current *PM* level, in order to construct a unified algebraic model of computer systems, from high level languages to abstract hardware.

References

[ALL+93] T Arora, T Leung, K Levitt, T Schubert, and P Windley. Report on the UCD microcoded Viper verification project. In *Higher-Order Logic Theorem Proving and its Applications*, pages 239 – 252. Lecture Notes in Computer Science 780, Springer-Verlag, 1993.

[AST67] D. W. Anderson, F. J. Sparacio, and R. M. Tomasulo. The IBM System/360 model 91: Machine philosophy and instruction handling. *IBM Journal of Research and Development*, 11:8–24, January 1967.

[BD94] J Burch and D Dill. Automatic verification of pipelined microprocessor control. In D Dill, editor, *Proceedings of the 6th International Conference, CAV'94: Computer-Aided Verification*, pages 68 – 80. Lecture Notes in Computer Science 818, Springer-Verlag, 1994.

[BG90] G Birtwistle and B Graham. Verifying SECD in HOL. In J Staunstrup, editor, *Formal Methods for VLSI Design*, pages 129 – 177. North-Holland, 1990.

[BJ93] B Bose and S D Johnson. DDD-FM9001: Derivation of a verified microprocessor. In L Pierre G Milne, editor, *Correct Hardware Design and Verification Methods*, pages 191 – 202. Lecture Notes in Computer Science 683, Springer-Verlag, 1993.

[BS90]   M Bickford and M Srivas. Verification of a pipelined processor using
             Clio. In M Leeser and G Brown, editors, *Proceedings of the Mathemat-
             ical Sciences Institute Workshop on Hardware Specifcation, Verification
             and Synthesis: Mathematical Aspects*, pages 307 – 332. Lecture Notes in
             Computer Science 408, Springer-Verlag, 1990.

[Bur96]   J Burch. Techniques for verifying superscalar microprocessors. In *Design
             Automation Conference*, 1996.

[Coh87]   A Cohn. A proof of correctness of the Viper microprocessor: the first lev-
             els. In G Birtwistle and P A Subrahmanyam, editors, *VLSI Specification,
             Verification and Synthesis*, pages 27 – 72. Kluwer Academic Publishers,
             1987.

[CRS97]   D Cyrluk, J Rushby, and M Srivas. Systematic formal verification of
             interpreters. In *IEEE International Conference on Formal Engineering
             Methods (ICFEM'97*, pages 140 – 149, 1997.

[Cul87]   W J Cullyer. Implementing safety critical systems: the Viper microproces-
             sor. In G Birtwistle and P A Subrahmanyam, editors, *VLSI Specification,
             Verification, and Synthesis*, pages 1 – 26. Kluwer Academic Publishers,
             1987.

[Cyr96]   D Cyrluk. Inverting the abstraction mapping: A methodology for hard-
             ware verification. In A Camilleri M Srivas, editor, *Formal Methods in
             Computer-Aided Design*, pages 172 – 186. Lecture Notes in Computer Sci-
             ence 1166, Springer-Verlag, 1996.

[FH96]   A C J Fox and N A Harman. An algebraic model of correctness for su-
             perscalar microprocessors. In *Formal Methods in Computer-Aided Design*,
             pages 346 – 361. Lecture Notes in Computer Science 1166, Springer-Verlag,
             1996.

[FH98]   A C J Fox and N A Harman. Algebraic models of correctness for mi-
             croprocessors. Technical Report CSR 8-98, University of Wales Swansea,
             1998.

[Fox98]   A C J Fox. *Algebraic Representation of Advanced Microprocessors*. PhD
             thesis, Department of Computer Science, University of Wales Swansea,
             1998.

[GM93]   M J C Gordon and T F Melham. *Introduction to HOL*. Cambridge
             University Press, 1993.

[Gor83]   M J C Gordon. Proving a computer correct with the LCF-LSM hardware
             verification system. Technical report, Technical Report No. 42, Computer
             Laboratory, University of Cambridge, 1983.

[Gra92]   B Graham. *The SECD Microprocessor: a Verification Case Study*. Kluwer,
             1992.

[Gro90]   G. F. Grohoski. Machine organisation of the IBM RISC System/6000
             processor. *IBM Journal of Research and Development*, 34:37–58, January
             1990.

[Har89]   N A Harman. *Formal Specifications for Digital Systems*. PhD thesis,
             School of Computer Studies, University of Leeds, 1989.

[HP96]   J L Hennessy and D A Patterson. *Computer Architecture: A Quantative
             Approach*. Morgan Kaufman, 1996.

[HT90]   N A Harman and J V Tucker. The formal specification of a digital corre-
             lator I: Abstract user specification. In K McEvoy and J V Tucker, editors,
             Theoretical Foundations for VLSI Design, pages 161 – 262. Cambridge
             University Press Tracts in Theoretical Computer Science 10, 1990.

[HT93]   N A Harman and J V Tucker. Algebraic models and the correctness of microprocessors. In L Pierre G Milne, editor, *Correct Hardware Design and Verification Methods*. Lecture Notes in Computer Science 683, Springer-Verlag, 1993.

[HT96]   N A Harman and J V Tucker. Algebraic models of microprocessors: Architecture and organisation. *Acta Informatica*, 33:421 – 456, 1996.

[HT97]   N A Harman and J V Tucker. Algebraic models of microprocessors: the verification of a simple computer. In V Stavridou, editor, *Proceedings of the 1995 IMA Conference on Mathematics for Dependable Systems*. Oxford University Press, 1997.

[Hun89]   W A Hunt. Microprocessor design verification. *Journal of Automated Reasoning*, 5(4):429 – 460, 1989.

[Hun92]   W Hunt. A formal HDL and its use in the FM9001 verification. In C A R Hoare and M Gordon, editors, *Mechanized Reasoning in Hardware Design*. Prentice-Hall, 1992.

[Hun94]   W Hunt. *FM8501: A Verified Microprocessor*. Lecture Notes on Artificial Intelligence 795, Springer Verlag, 1994.

[Joh91]   M Johnson. *Superscalar microprocessor design*. Prentice Hall, Englewood Cliffs, N. J., 1991.

[Joy87]   J Joyce. Formal verification and implementation of a microprocessor. In G Birtwistle and P A Subrahmanyam, editors, *VLSI Specification, Verification and Synthesis*, pages 129 – 159. Kluwer Academic Publishers, 1987.

[Lan63]   P Landin. On the mechanical evaluation of expressions. *Computer Journal*, 6:308 – 320, 1963.

[Mel93]   T F Melham. *Higher Order Logic and Hardware Verification*. Cambridge University Press Tracts in Theoretical Computer Science 31, 1993.

[MS95a]   S Miller and M Srivas. Formal verification of an avionics microprocessor. Technical report, SRI International Computer Science Laboratory CSL-95-04, 1995.

[MS95b]   S Miller and M Srivas. Formal verification of the AAMP5 microprocessor: a case study in the industrial use of formal methods. In *Proceedings of WIFT 95, Boca Raton*, 1995.

[ORSS94]   S Owre, J Rushby, N Shankar, and M Srivas. A tutorial on using PVS. In *Proceedings of TPCD 94*, pages 258–279. Lecture Notes in Computer Science 901, Springer-Verlag, 1994.

[SB91]   M Srivas and M Bickford. Formal verification of a pipelined microprocessor. *IEEE Software*, 7(5):52 – 64, 1991.

[SDB96]   J Su, D Dill, and C Barrett. Automatic generation of invariants in processor verification. In A Camilleri M Srivas, editor, *Formal Methods in Computer-Aided Design*, pages 377 – 388. Lecture Notes in Computer Science 1166, Springer-Verlag, 1996.

[SS95]   J. E. Smith and G. S. Sohi. The microarchitecture of superscalar processors. In *Proceedings of the IEEE*, volume 83, pages 1609–1624, December 1995.

[Sta93]   V Stavridou. *Formal Specification of Digital Systems*. Cambridge University Press Tracts in Theoretical Computer Science 37, 1993.

[Ste96]   K Stephenson. *An Algebraic Approach to Syntax, Semantics and Compilation*. PhD thesis, University of Wales Swansea Computer Science Department, 1996.

[Ste98]   K Stephenson. Algebraic specification of the Java virtual machine. In B Möller and J V Tucker, editors, *Prospects for Hardware Foundations*. Lecture Notes in Computer Science 1546, Springer-Verlag, 1998.

[Sto93]   H S Stone. *High Performance Computer Architecture*. Addison-Wesley, 1993.

[Tho61]   J. E. Thornton. Parallel operation in the Control Data 6600. In *Proceedings of the Fall Joint Computer Conference*, volume 26, pages 33–40, 1961.

[Tho70]   J. E. Thornton. *Design of a Computer — The Control Data 6600*. Glenview, IL: Scott, Foresman and Co., 1970.

[Tom67]   R. M. Tomasulo. An efficient algorithm for exploiting multiple arithmetic units. *IBM Journal of Research and Development*, pages 176–188, January 1967.

[WB96]   P Windley and J Burch. Mechanically checking a lemma used in an automatic verification tool. In A Camilleri M Srivas, editor, *Formal Methods in Computer-Aided Design*, pages 362 – 376. Lecture Notes in Computer Science 1166, Springer-Verlag, 1996.

[WC94]   P Windley and M Coe. A correctness model for pipelined microprocessors. In *Proceedings of the 2nd Conference on Theorem Provers in Circuit Design*, 1994.

[Win93]   P Windley. A theory of generic interpreters. In L Pierre G Milne, editor, *Correct Hardware Design and Verification Methods*, pages 122 – 134. Lecture Notes in Computer Science 683, Springer-Verlag, 1993.

[WS84]   S. Weiss and J. E. Smith. Instruction issue logic in pipelined supercomputers. *IEEE Transactions on Computers*, c-33(11):1013–1022, November 1984.

Hierarchies of Spatially Extended Systems and Synchronous Concurrent Algorithms

M J Poole[1], J V Tucker[1] and A V Holden[2]

[1] Department of Computer Science,
University of Wales Swansea, Swansea SA2 8PP, Wales
[2] Department of Physiology,
University of Leeds, Leeds LS2 9JT, England

Abstract. First, we study the general idea of a *spatially extended system* (SES) and argue that many mathematical models of systems in computing and natural science are examples of SESs. We examine the computability and the equational definability of SESs and show that, in the discrete case, there is a natural sense in which an SES is computable if, and only if, it is definable by equations. We look at a simple idea of hierarchical structure for SESs and, using respacings and retimings, we define how one SES abstracts, approximates, or is implemented by another SES. Secondly, we study a special kind of SES called a *synchronous concurrent algorithm* (SCA). We define the simplest kind of SCA with a global clock and unit delay which are computable and equationally definable by primitive recursive equations over time. We focus on two examples of SCAs: a systolic array for convolution and a non-linear model of cardiac tissue. We investigate the hierarchical structure of SCAs by applying the earlier general concepts for the hierarchical structure of SESs. We apply the resulting SCA hierarchy to the formal analysis of both the implementation of a systolic array and the approximation of a biologically detailed model of cardiac tissue.

1 Introduction

Modern computing hardware comprises a great range of devices, including digital and analogue components, which are studied at a number of levels of abstraction, determined by the physical technologies, circuit layouts and the architectures seen by programmers. A comprehensive theory of hardware design should encompass both this diversity and hierarchy of levels of abstraction. It should accommodate changes caused by the emergence of new physical technologies and programming techniques. A comprehensive theory of hardware design might also integrate the digital and analogue components of systems, bridging computers and electro-mechanical devices, from signal processing systems to biological tissue.

We are far from having a comprehensive theory of hardware. The design of transistors and circuits requires many mathematical models aimed at different levels of abstraction. Architectures have only recently become accessible to mathematical modelling, and we are struggling to support their design and programming with formal techniques. Technology independence and software-hardware codesign are popular research areas. The theoretical unification and integration of digital systems with analogue environments is a challenge.

In contemplating and seeking a theory of hardware, we are led to some significant scientific problems, not least among which is the following:

Integrative hierarchy problem. *Develop a mathematical theory that is able to relate and integrate different mathematical models at different levels of abstraction.*

In the case of conventional hardware this involves relating and combining methods for the modelling of physical systems which are normally continuous, with the methods for modelling architectures which are normally discrete.

It turns out that this integrative hierarchy problem is not only a problem for hardware: it is a problem for the scientific modelling of physical systems *in general*. The levels of hierarchy are often determined by specific scientific or engineering ideas, which vary with the problem area and its state of the art. In some areas, such as the non-linear dynamical properties of physiological excitable media (e.g., neural and muscular tissue), the hierarchical nature is evident in the science of neurones and cardiac cells. It is particularly clear in the case of hardware because of the pre-eminent role of the hierarchy.

All types of systems, from microprocessors to neural or muscular tissue, are modelled at different levels of abstraction for different purposes. Inevitably we need to compare models. In microprocessor design we often see this comparison as a *correctness problem*. In the case of, say, models of cardiac tissue, the existence of two partial differential equations that model a system at different levels of abstraction leads to two algorithms that ought to be related. In scientific modelling we often see this comparison as an *approximation problem*.

In understanding a complex system, a *portfolio* of models is needed, representing the system at different levels of abstraction. The family of models might range from abstract qualitative models of the system that are computationally efficient to concrete quantitative models that are computationally intensive. They might also offer different views of the system relevant to different users.

In this paper we will describe an approach to the integrative hierarchy problem in general. It is limited by the assumptions that

> *all the mathematical models in the hierarchy are algorithmic models of spatially extended systems,* and

> *all the algorithmic models of spatially extended systems are synchronous concurrent algorithms.*

We begin, in Section 2, by studying the concept of a spatially extended system (SES). We give some simple mathematical definitions that encompass examples of continuous physical models and discrete computing systems. The gap between the continuous and discrete models can be bridged by appropriate abstract concepts, such as spatially extended system.

In Section 3 we discuss the computable representations of SESs and their mathematical characterisation by means of equations. Using the algebraic theory of data, we show that

> *a countable spatially extended system can be computably modelled if, and only if, it can be uniquely characterised by a small finite set of equations.*

In Section 4 we formulate notions of hierarchy for SESs by giving simple refinements of space, time, data, and behaviour.

Primarily, the aim of this paper is to study the hierarchical structure in a special class of algorithmic models of SESs called synchronous concurrent algorithms (SCAs), and to show the applicability of the hierarchical SCA framework to both computing and physical systems.

A synchronous concurrent algorithm (SCA) is a network constructed from modules, channels, data and clocks. The modules are distributed in space and are connected by channels. The modules process data and the data moves around the network, from module to module, via the channels. The modules and channels operate simultaneously and are governed by one or more clocks. Thus the network is an algorithm that is *synchronous* and *concurrent*. "Synchronous" means "with time". The algorithm can operate continually over periods of time and can process sequences or streams of input data. A formal definition of a simple kind of SCA is given in Section 5.

Algorithms that match this loose description of an SCA can be found in abundance. In computer science, SCAs are a fundamental structure that can be found in the design of digital hardware that include:

- general purpose hardware (e.g., microprocessors);
- special purpose hardware (e.g., graphics machines, systolic arrays);
- parallel computer architectures (e.g., hypercubes); and
- general parallel models of computation (e.g., PRAMs).

Information on SCA-related models of microprocessors can be found in [HT96]. SCA models of systolic algorithms and graphics machines are discussed in [HTT88] and [EST90], respectively. SCAs can also be found in other parts of computer science, although sometimes less obviously. A general introduction to models of parallel computation is [Sav98].

In mathematics and the natural and engineering sciences, SCAs arise in *algorithmically approximating* the solutions of:

- coupled ordinary differential equations (CODEs); and
- partial differential equations (PDEs).

Approximation techniques, like the finite difference method (FDM) and finite element method (FEM), are based on spatial intuitions and can lead to algorithms that qualify as SCAs. In addition to approximation algorithms for differential equations, a number of discrete and more algorithmic approaches to modelling systems have been created, perhaps most notably:

- neural networks;
- cellular automata; and
- coupled map lattices.

These subjects are surveyed in [RM86], [Wol86] and [Kan92], respectively. In Section 5 we give examples of SCAs from hardware and physiological excitable media.

These SCA methods of modelling physical systems have several features in common. They start from a view of space and time that is discrete. They focus on the local behaviour of a point or small area in space and postulate rules for the interactions at that site. The algorithms synthesise global behaviour from the local behaviour. The parallelism is the result of calculating local behaviour at all sites in the space simultaneously.

In Section 6 we address the question that lies at the heart of the paper:

How does one SCA abstract, approximate, or implement another SCA?

Using the principles given for spatially extended systems in Section 4, we will analyse the relationship between two SCAs at different levels of spatial, temporal and data abstraction.

We then apply our analysis to the formal description of the relationship existing between SCAs in hardware and excitable media. We treat the cases of systolic array architectures for convolution, and models of electrical behaviour in cardiac tissue. For both case studies, we compare models at two levels of abstraction.

The pre-requisites for this paper are the elements of the algebraic theory of data and some interest in non-linear systems. References will be given in the appropriate places.

2   Spatially Extended Systems

An aim of our theory is to show that a variety of deterministic systems in computing, mathematics, natural science and engineering have a common algorithmic structure. First, here and in Section 3, we demonstrate that the conceptions of deterministic systems found in these disparate areas have a common algebraic form that can be defined by equations. The algorithmic models arise from these algebraic models.

2.1   Spatially Extended Deterministic Systems

To model a system, we must choose properties of the system and characterise its behaviour over time in terms of these properties. The chosen properties are used to define a notion of state for the system, and a set of all possible states of the system.

Let X be a set of points, or sites, where the properties of the system are measured. The set X provides names for locations in some geometric space. Let A be a set of data used to measure the properties of the system at each location in X. Then a state of the system is a function $s : X \to A$ such that for $x \in X$,

$$s(x) = \text{data characterising the system's state at point } x.$$

The set of all possible states of the system is, therefore, a subset $S(X, A)$ of the set $[X \to A]$ of all functions with domain X and codomain A. In many cases $S(X, A) = [X \to A]$. In other cases, such as the vibrating string in Section 2.3, $S(X, A) \subset [X \to A]$. For simplicity, we have chosen the single-sorted case in which the set A is used to describe possible states of all points; it is not difficult to extend the approach to the many-sorted case.

The set T of times at which we wish to know the behaviour of the system is defined by a clock that may, in general, be discrete or continuous. The key requirement is that time is modelled by an infinite, linearly ordered set with an initial cycle or instant. For discrete time we take $T = \mathbb{N}$, the natural numbers, and for continuous time we take $T = \mathbb{R}^+$, the non-negative real numbers.

In addition, there may be a set P of parameters that are inputs to the system and affect its behaviour at each time instant. The parameters may change over time and so a stream $\ldots, p_t, \ldots$ of parameters, with $p_t \in P$ for each time instant $t \in T$, is involved in the operation of the system. A stream of parameters is a map $p : T \to P$ such that, for all $t \in T$,

$$p(t) = parameter\ value\ at\ time\ t.$$

The set of all possible parameter streams for the system is, in general, a subset $S(T, P)$ of $[T \to P]$. Often, in the case $T = \mathbb{R}^+$, the stream p is called a *signal*.

The fact that the system is deterministic means that

at each time point the system can be in one and only one state, and this state is uniquely determined by the time point, the initial state of the system, and a stream of parameters for the system.

In fact, the state depends only on the initial segment of the parameter stream defined by the current time point, rather than on the entire stream.

These ideas are expressed mathematically as follows.

Definition: spatially extended system. A *spatially extended deterministic system model S* consists of:

- a non-empty set X of *points* distributed in space;
- a non-empty set A of *data*;
- a set $S(X, A) \subseteq [X \to A]$ of *global states*;
- a non-empty set T of *time points*;
- a non-empty set P of *input parameters*;
- a non-empty set $S(T, P) \subseteq [T \to P]$ of *input parameter streams*; and
- a *system function*

$$F : T \times S(T, P) \times S(X, A) \to S(X, A)$$

defined for all $t \in T$, $p \in S(T, P)$ and $s \in S(X, A)$, by

$F(t, p, s) =$ *state of the system at time t evolving under input pa-rameter stream p from initial state s.*

The system state at time t is determined by an initial segment of the input stream: for all $p_1, p_2 \in S(T, P)$ where $p_1(t') = p_2(t')$ for all $t' < t$, $F(t, p_1, s) = F(t, p_2, s)$.

The spatially extended deterministic system model is a 6-sorted algebra

$$S = (X, A, T, P, S(T, P), S(X, A) \mid F).$$

Definition: closed spatially extended system. A *closed spatially extended deterministic system model S* is a spatially extended system without input parameter streams. A closed system has space set X, data set A, global state set $S(X, A)$, time set T and system function $F : T \times S(X, A) \to S(X, A)$. A closed spatially extended system model is a 4-sorted algebra

$$S = (X, A, T, S(X, A) \mid F).$$

Examples of SESs are given shortly, in Section 2.3.

Generalisation to multi-valued local states. We will call a *local state* the data that characterise the state of a system at any point x. In practice, a local state will often have many components, and these components may be of different units (and different sorts) across the system. Thus, variable names and identifiers will be used in states. Here we extend the basic model to allow each point to have a finite number of named properties or measurements of the same sort. Extending this idea to the many-sorted case is straightforward.

Let Var be a set of *names* that may be used to identify the components of local states. Let $var : X \to Powerset_f(Var) - \{\emptyset\}$ be a map that assigns each point $x \in X$ with a non-empty finite set $var(x) \subseteq Var$ of names that identify each of the state-components of point x. A local state at point x is described by a mapping of the form $s_x \in A^{var(x)}$ where, for $v \in var(x)$, $s_x(v) \in A$ is the v-*component* of the local state at x. The set of all possible local states at x is $A^{var(x)}$. Let

$$S(X, A) \subseteq \{s \in [X \to \bigcup_{x \in X} A^{var(x)}] \mid s(x) \in A^{var(x)} \text{ for all } x \in X\}$$

denote the set of all possible global states of the system. For $s \in S(X, A)$, $s(x) \in A^{var(x)}$ is the local state at point x and $s(x)(v) \in A$ is the v-component of this local state.

This simple naming of state components allows us to describe systems with *vector-valued* local states. Let $\mathbb{N} \subseteq Var$ and let $var(x) = \{1, \ldots, n(x)\}$ for each $x \in X$, where $n : X \to \mathbb{N}$ determines the length of local state vectors at each point throughout the system (we require that $n(x) > 0$ for all $x \in X$). A local state of each point $x \in X$ is a vector of the form $s_x \in A^{n(x)}$ where $s_x(i) \in A$ (for $1 \leq i \leq n(x)$) is the i-th *element* of the local state of x.

It is useful to be able to identify a state component across the space X. Let $C \subseteq X \times Var$ be a set of global state *coordinates* defined by

$$C = \{(x, v) \mid x \in X \text{ and } v \in var(x)\}$$

where coordinate (x, v) refers to the v-component of the local state at point x. Let

$$S(X, A) \subseteq [C \to A]$$

denote the set of all possible global states of the system, where for $s \in S(X, A)$, $s(x, v) \in A$ is the v-component of the local state at point x.

Observable and hidden states. Another generalisation to the basic SES model is to distinguish between those points of a system whose states are external or *observable*, and those that are internal or *hidden*.

Let $X_{obs} \subseteq X$ be the set of points in the system whose states are observable, and let $X_{hid} = X - X_{obs}$ be the set of remaining points, whose states are hidden. The set $S_{obs}(X, A) \subseteq [X_{obs} \to A]$ of all possible *global observable states* of the system is defined by

$$S_{obs}(X, A) = \{s_{obs} \in [X_{obs} \to A] \mid s_{obs} = s|_{X_{obs}} \text{ for some } s \in S(X, A)\}.$$

An *observable state function*

$$F_{obs} : T \times S(T, P) \times S(X, A) \to S_{obs}(X, A)$$

is easily defined from the system function F, for all $t \in T$, $p \in S(T, P)$ and $s \in S(X, A)$, by

$$F_{obs}(t, p, s) = F(t, p, s)|_{X_{obs}}.$$

For a system with multi-valued local states, we can define a set $C_{obs} \subseteq C$ to be those state coordinates whose values are observable, and let $C_{hid} = C - C_{obs}$ be those remaining coordinates whose states are hidden. The set $S_{obs}(X, A)$ of global observable states, and global observable state function F_{obs} are defined in a straightforward manner.

2.2 A Classification of Spatially Extended Systems

We illustrate these general definitions by noting some common terminology for their components in computing and physical systems:

Elements of System	Computing System	Physical System
X	locations, variables, identifiers, names, registers	points, sites, locations, cells, nodes
A	data	data
T	discrete time points, instants, cycles, intervals	continuous and discrete time points, instants
P	input data, instructions, parameters, events, messages, button presses	physical parameters, boundary conditions, perturbations, tolerances

In continuous space systems, usually X is a geometric object, such as a compact smooth manifold, which can be embedded as a subspace of $\mathbb{R}^n$.

In discrete space systems, X can be a discrete subset of points from a geometric object (for example, a subset of the integer lattice $\mathbb{Z}^n \subset \mathbb{R}^n$ or a finite element mesh).

The components X, T, and A (and P) are used to classify models of physical systems in terms of space, time and state (and parameters). For example, the primary characteristic of a component X, T or A (or P) is whether it is *discrete* or *continuous*. There are 8 (or 16) cases; those of interest to us are listed in the table below, where "D" denotes "discrete" and "C" denotes "continuous":

Space	Time	State	Parameters	Example
C	C	C	C	Solutions to PDEs
D	C	C	C	Solutions to CODEs
D	D	C	C	Coupled Map Lattices
D	D	D	D	Cellular Automata

2.3 Examples

Consider briefly some simple examples of spatially extended systems from hardware and mechanics to illustrate the definitions.

Example (Computer). A computer is a spatially extended discrete system. Consider a simple l-bit machine, illustrated in Figure 1.

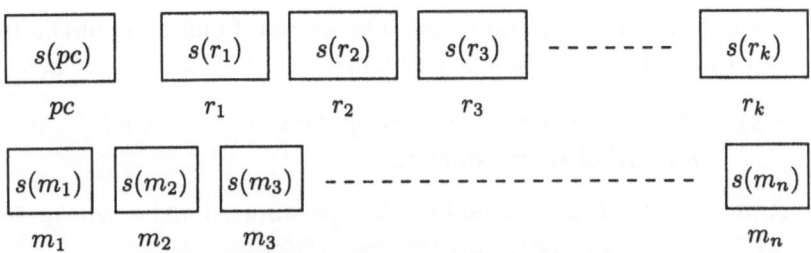

Fig. 1. A simple computer.

The space X is the set

$$I = \{pc, r_1, r_2, \ldots, r_k, m_1, m_2, \ldots, m_n\}$$

of names for the program counter pc, registers $r_1, r_2, \ldots, r_k$ and memory locations $m_1, m_2, \ldots, m_n$. The computer is characterised by the data at these locations. Let $W_l = \{0, 1\}^l$ be the set of l-bit words. A state of the computer is a function $s : I \to W_l$ such that for $i \in I$, $s(i) = l$-*bit word stored at location* i. Let $[I \to W_l]$ be the set of all states. Time T is discrete and is represented by the set $\mathbb{N}$ of natural numbers. Furthermore, let P be the set of input data; the computer reads a datum at each clock cycle. The operation of the computer in time is specified by $F : T \times [T \to P] \times [I \to W_l] \to [I \to W_l]$ where, for $t \in T$, $p \in [T \to P]$, $s \in [I \to W_l]$ and $i \in I$,

$$F(t, p, s)(i) = l\text{-}bit \ word \ stored \ in \ the \ computer \ at \ location \ i \ at \ time$$
$$t \ on \ starting \ the \ machine \ with \ input \ stream \ p \ from$$
$$initial \ state \ s.$$

The system function is specified by a system of equations.

Example (Vibrating String). An elastic vibrating string, fixed at either end, is a closed spatially extended continuous system; see Figure 2. The space X is the interval $[a, b]$ which represents the length of the string at rest, and the string is characterised by its displacement from the horizontal and its velocity. Let $var(x) = \{d, v\}$ for all $x \in [a, b]$ so that values of the state coordinates (x, d) and (x, v) give the displacement and velocity of the string at location x. Let the set $S([a, b], \mathbb{R})$ of all possible states be the subset of $[[a, b] \times \{d, v\} \to \mathbb{R}]$ for which displacements and velocities are continuously differentiable across $[a, b]$ and have zero values at a and b. Time is continuous and is represented by the set $\mathbb{R}^+$ of non-negative real numbers. The system function is of the form $F : \mathbb{R}^+ \times S([a, b], \mathbb{R}) \to S([a, b], \mathbb{R})$ where, for $t \in \mathbb{R}^+$ and $s \in S([a, b], \mathbb{R})$

$F(t, s) =$ *displacement and velocity of the string at time t from the initial string state s.*

The system function F is specified by the one-dimensional wave equation

$$\frac{\partial^2 y}{\partial t^2} = c^2 \frac{\partial^2 y}{\partial x^2}$$

(where y, t and x are displacement, time and space variables respectively, and c is a constant derived from the string's mass and tension) in the following way: if y is a solution to the wave equation with initial string position $y(x, 0) = s(x, d)$ for $x \in [a, b]$, and initial string velocity

$$\frac{\partial y}{\partial t}(x, 0) = s(x, v),$$

for $x \in [a, b]$, then for all $t \in \mathbb{R}^+$ and $x \in [a, b]$, $F(t, s)(x, d) = y(x, t)$.

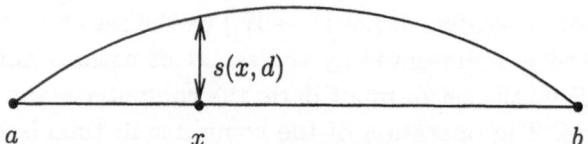

Fig. 2. A vibrating string.

3 Computability and Equational Specification of Spatially Extended Systems

The general definitions in Section 2 specify the mathematical form of a large class of models of deterministic spatially extended systems and their behaviour in time. Both computing systems and physical systems are well represented in this class. In this section we reflect on general methods of:

(i) defining the models using systems of equations; and
(ii) defining the models using algorithms.

Obviously, such methods are central in the modelling of both computing and physical systems. We believe that they have a common form. For this section, we assume the reader is familiar with the theory of algebraic specifications, as described in [Wir91] and [MT92], for example. The contents of this section are not used in the rest of the paper.

3.1 Modelling Systems

Among the aims of mathematically modelling a system are simulation and analysis; specifically, the following stand out:

Computing. *To compute the system function F.*

Reasoning. *To prove properties of the system function F.*

For a computer system, the computation of F is its *raison d'être*: the system is intended to compute. In natural science, where a dynamical system models an aspect of a physical system, often the practice is to compute F in order to explore possible causes of the known behaviour of the system, to make predictions, and to discover new properties of the system. In applied science and engineering design, often the practice is to compute F in order to answer quantitative questions needed in solving a specific design problem.

In both cases, we reason about the system to establish properties of its behaviour over time. Does it accomplish certain tasks, or exhibit certain properties? Is it fast, stable, error prone, etc.?

For the design or investigation of a deterministic system, it is necessary to devise a mathematical model of the following form and answer the basic questions:

System Characterisation Problem. *Let*

$$S = (X, A, T, P, S(T, P), S(X, A) \mid F)$$

be a spatially extended deterministic system model with system function

$$F : T \times S(T, P) \times S(X, A) \to S(X, A).$$

Computing. *Does there exist an algorithm to compute F, or an approximation to F?*

Reasoning. *Does there exist an axiomatic specification to characterise F uniquely, or to reason about F or an approximation of F?*

The problem of representing space, time, data, states, parameters and system functions on a computer involves both algorithms and specifications.

In computer science, a system model is usually discrete. The theoretical analysis of computing systems has led to equational techniques for their mathematical description, using methods based on Mathematical Logic and Abstract Algebra.

In particular, equations can be found that provide an axiomatic specification of the system F, such that:

(i) the equations express key properties of the system;
(ii) the function F satisfies the equations; and, often,
(iii) F is the only solution of the equations, given certain constraints determined mainly by the semantics/model theory and proof theory of equations.

In science and engineering, a system model is usually continuous, and a theoretical analysis of a system uses differential equations. Mathematical Analysis provides a great deal of information about the solutions to differential equations. The differential equations constitute an axiomatic specification of the system function F, such that:

(i) the equations express key properties of the system;
(ii) the function F satisfies the equations; and, often,
(iii) F is the only solution of the equations, given certain constraints determined mainly by the theory of continuity and differentiability.

Since the model has continuous states, an approximation F_0 to F must be computed, and algorithms for F_0 are needed.

In both cases, there is a need for theoretical understanding of mathematical models that comes from an individual's curiosity and the wish to solve practical design problems. Axiomatic specifications, such as equations, express the system dynamics, have F as a solution, and are used for reasoning. Algorithms for computation are needed, whether the function F is computable exactly or approximately.

3.2 Equational Specification of Computable Data Types

The algebraic theory of data is concerned with computability and axiomatic specifications and can help provide answers to the System Characterisation Problem in Section 3.1.

Many sorted algebras are used to model data and operations on data. For an account of the subject, see [MT92]. A many sorted algebra can be represented on a computer if there exist appropriate data and algorithms to represent the sets and operations of the algebra. Let us say that such an algebra is *effective*. There are various mathematical concepts that characterise which algebras can be represented on a computer. For an account of the subject see [SHT95].

In the case of countable algebras viewed as discrete structures, there are principally:

- *computable algebras,*
- *semicomputable algebras, and*
- *co-semicomputable algebras*

which have been well-studied. A computable algebra is one which possesses a representation by an algebra of natural numbers in which the carrier sets, basic operations and equality relation are all recursive. Semicomputable and co-semicomputable algebras are weaker in that their equality relations are recursively enumerable and co-recursively enumerable respectively; see [SHT95].

In the case of uncountable algebras, viewed as continuous or topological structures, the situation is more complex. Effective topological algebras are defined by means of effective countable discrete structures that provide effective approximations. There are various methods for defining algorithmic approximations to topological algebras including: *recursive metric spaces* [Mos64], *type two enumerability* [Wei87], and *domain representability* [SHT88,SHT95,Bla97]. The approaches converge and there is emerging a stable theory of computation on topological algebras: see [SHT97].

At the heart of the theory of data there are axiomatic specification methods for defining countable algebras uniquely up to isomorphism, principally:

- *equations with initial algebra semantics,*
- *equations with various pre-initial algebra semantics based on term rewriting semantics, and*
- *equations with final algebra semantics.*

Concepts of computability and equational definability have been combined in a series of classification theorems, due to J A Bergstra and J V Tucker. These characterise those *countable* algebras that can be represented on a computer using equations. Roughly speaking, the theorems have the following form:

> Let A be a many sorted algebra. The following are equivalent:
> (i) A is definable by algorithms; and
> (ii) A is uniquely definable by a finite set of equations.

Here is one such theorem that we will apply to dynamical systems shortly, in Section 3.3:

Theorem [BT82]. *Let A be a many sorted minimal Σ-algebra with n sorts. The following are equivalent:*

1. *A is computable.*
2. *There is an equational specification (Σ', E') such that*
   (i) $Sorts(\Sigma') = Sorts(\Sigma)$;
   (ii) $\Sigma' - \Sigma$ contains $3(n+1)$ hidden functions;
   (iii) E' contains $2(n+1)$ equations;
   (iv) $A \cong Initial(\Sigma', E') \cong Final(\Sigma', E')$.

The power of equations to capture, in principle, all we require of a data type can be illustrated in many ways; in the case of the theorem above we need only contemplate the following table of sizes of equational specification:

Sorts	1	2	3	4	5	6	7	8
Hidden Functions	6	9	12	15	18	21	24	27
Equations	4	6	8	10	12	14	16	18

3.3 Systems as Data Types

A spatially extended system is a data type and is modelled by an algebra. The Characterisation Problem of Section 3.1 can be reformulated algebraically in the light of the ideas in Section 3.2:

Algebraic System Characterisation Problem. *Let*

$$S = (X, A, T, P, S(T, P), S(X, A) \mid F)$$

be a spatially extended deterministic system model.

Computability. *Is the algebra effective?*

Reasoning. *Does there exist an axiomatic specification to characterise uniquely and reason about the algebra, or about an approximation to the algebra?*

To address this algebraic problem we must look closely at the algebraic structure of a spatially extended system. Clearly, the system algebra S simply captures the system behaviour. Obviously, there are more functions on the carrier sets that are of importance in the design of a model. The purpose and nature of these functions vary greatly over the different models—only the system function is common to all models.

For example, in the case of the space X there might be functions that construct a discrete grid or mesh, specify a directed multigraph, or define the sub-basis of a topology on X. In the case of the data set A there might be logical operations on n-bit words, or continuous functions on the real numbers; and similarly for the input parameter set P. In the case of time, functions expressing system delays might be present. Among the operations on states and streams will be evaluation and substitution functions.

The key point is that from the basic assumptions about the spatially extended system, a family of functions will be developed from which the system function will be definable by systems of equations.

Let us introduce some terminology.

Definition. An algebra S_0 is a *construction* of the system algebra S if S is a reduct of S_0, i.e., $S_0|_\Sigma = S$ where Σ is the signature of S.

Obviously, these ideas are very general and a great deal of variation in a construction S_0 of S is possible. However, with the help of the theory of data, some general facts can be proved, at least in the countable case.

Here are some further properties of a construction S_0 of S that are important.

First, there is the property that S_0 has exactly the same carrier sets as S and so S_0 does not introduce new sets of data.

Secondly, there is the property that S_0 is a *minimal algebra*, which means all the elements of the algebra can be constructed from the operations of the algebra applied to the constants of the algebra. It is not difficult to show that any infinite countable n sorted algebra can be expanded into a minimal algebra by adding at most $k < n + 2$ functions.[1]

Note that system algebras are infinite since time T is assumed to be an infinite set.

Consider the question in the case of countable systems using the strong notions of a computable algebra and an equational specification under initial and final algebra semantics. We can apply the Bergstra-Tucker theorem in the case of 6 sorts:

System Characterisation Theorem. *Let*

$$S = (X, A, T, P, S(T, P), S(X, A) \mid F)$$

be a spatially extended deterministic system, and let S_0 be any minimal construction algebra for S. Then the following are equivalent:

(i) The system S_0 is computable.

(ii) The system S_0 can be uniquely characterised by 14 equations and 21 hidden operators under initial algebra semantics and final algebra semantics.

4 Abstraction and Approximation Between Spatially Extended Deterministic Systems

A spatially extended system can be viewed at different levels of abstraction. This leads to a *portfolio* of models of the system that analyse dif-

---

[1] There are two cases for the expansion of A to a minimal algebra A' as follows. Let A_s be a carrier of A. We say that carrier A_s is minimal if it is generated by the operations and constants of A; otherwise it is non-minimal.

Suppose A contains an infinite minimal carrier A_s, then for each carrier A_t that is non-minimal we add to the operations of A a surjection $\phi_t : A_s \to A_t$ to make A'; and so $k = $ the number of non-minimal carriers.

Suppose A does not contain an infinite minimal carrier but contains an infinite carrier A_s. Then we pick an element a of A_s and a function $f : A_s \to A_s$ that can generate the set $A_s = \{f^n(a) \mid n = 0, 1, 2, \ldots\}$ and add a and f to the algebra A to make A'. Thus, in the "worst" case that an infinite algebra A has no minimal carrier we need to add $n - 1 + 2 = n + 1$ operations.

If A is computable then it is possible to choose operations of the above form such that A' is computable. Such simple algebraic tricks may be used to ensure that a computable system construction algebra can be expanded to a minimal and computable system construction algebra.

ferent aspects with different degrees of detail. Some of these models may have clear relations and form a hierarchy. The purpose of a hierarchy is to better understand the system by analysing different properties at "appropriate" levels of detail. In particular, the hierarchy typically contains models of the spatially extended system at different *scales* of space, time and data.

In computer science, the use of hierarchy is firmly established in both theory and practice. For example, if the system is a microprocessor then the levels range from the physical device to the programmer's model of the machine. Furthermore, there are several layers of software that are built on top of the architecture ranging from operating systems to user interfaces. We think of the levels as independent autonomous systems that have increasingly complex relationships with one another as one approaches the physical system. We do not normally think of the user interface, the operating system or the architecture as *simply* imperfect approximations of the system. Modern computer science, in practice, is the study of everything but the "real" system (which is the province of electrical engineers and physicists).

The same is true of physical systems. Here models of different aspects of systems are abstractions of a real physical system. Depending on properties of the system that are known experimentally, more commonly they are described as *simply* imperfect approximations of the system. For example, cardiac tissue can be modelled at the cellular level—with different degrees of detail or accuracy—or more abstractly as wave propagation in an excitable medium—again with different degrees of detail or accuracy. Hierarchy is important in scientific practice but at present we know of relatively little to serve as a theory of hierarchical structure of mathematical models. The concepts of abstraction and approximation overlap in discussions of mathematical modelling. Here we use the term abstraction except where the behaviour of a model is approximated by another to some known numerical bound.

In this section, we will present concepts that define formally the relationship between two SESs at different levels of space, time, state and system behaviour. Later, we will use these ideas to develop a theory of hierarchical structure for our algorithmic models.

Let

$$S_1 = (X_1, A_1, T_1, P_1, S_1(T_1, P_1), S_2(X_1, A_1) \mid F_1)$$
$$S_2 = (X_2, A_2, T_2, P_2, S_1(T_2, P_2), S_2(X_2, A_2) \mid F_2)$$

be spatially extended deterministic systems, and suppose that S_1 is a more detailed model or is at a lower level of abstraction than S_2. First we define component abstractions, then we consider behaviour abstractions and approximations.

4.1 Abstractions of Components

We compare the spaces X_1 and X_2, the sets T_1 and T_2 of time points, the global state sets $S_1(X_1, A_1)$ and $S_2(X_2, A_2)$ and the sets $S_1(T_1, P_1)$ and $S_2(T_2, P_2)$ of parameter streams.

Space abstraction. A *respacing* between X_1 and X_2 is a surjective map $\pi : X_1 \to X_2$. The intention is that each S_1 point $x \in X_1$ is abstracted in S_2 by $\pi(x) \in X_2$. Let $\pi^{-1} : X_2 \to Powerset(X_1)$ be defined by $\pi^{-1}(y) = \{x \in X_1 \mid \pi(x) = y\}$ so that $\pi^{-1}(y) \subseteq X_1$ is the set of all points in X_1 abstracted by $y \in X_2$. Maps π and π^{-1} are illustrated in Figure 3. There are further natural properties of a respacing that we will not need here.

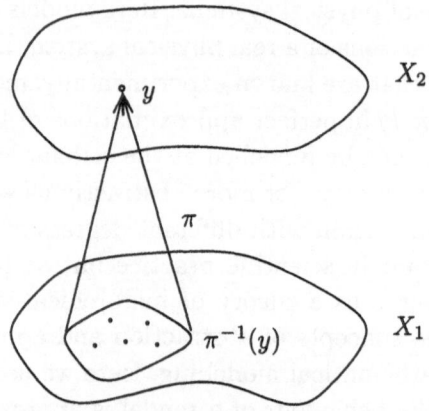

Fig. 3. Abstraction between spaces X_1 and X_2.

Time abstraction. A *retiming* between the sets T_1 and T_2 of time points is a surjective, monotonic map $\lambda : T_1 \to T_2$ with the intention that each time point $t \in T_1$ is abstracted in T_2 by $\lambda(t)$. A retiming provides a simple temporal abstraction in which a time instant or cycle $t \in T_2$ is represented by the set $\lambda^{-1}(t) \subset T_1$. Although this notion is not suitable for the case that $T_1 = \mathbb{N}$ and $T_2 = \mathbb{R}^+$, since the condition of surjectivity is impossible, it and its refinements are useful in many situations. A typical refinement is in the case that T_1 and T_2 are both $\mathbb{N}$ or both $\mathbb{R}^+$, where we can say that T_1 is *faster* than T_2 if, for each interval $[t, t'] \subseteq T_1$, we have $t' - t \geq \lambda(t') - \lambda(t)$.

State abstraction. Global states are compared using a map of the form

$$\phi : S_1(X_1, A_1) \to S_2(X_2, A_2)$$

with the intention that the global state $s \in S_1(X_1, A_1)$ of S_1 is abstracted in S_2 by $\phi(s) \in S_2(X_2, A_2)$.

A state abstraction mapping ϕ is *spatially consistent* with the respacing π if, for any point $y \in X_2$, the abstracted local state $\phi(s)(y)$ at y depends only on the state of the subspace $\pi^{-1}(y) \subseteq X_1$ abstracted by y. Formally, ϕ is consistent with π if, and only if, for all states $s, s' \in S_1(X_1, A_1)$, and all points $y \in X_2$,

$$s(x) = s'(x) \text{ for all } x \in \pi^{-1}(y) \Rightarrow \phi(s)(y) = \phi(s')(y).$$

Abstraction of observable states. Where we define sets $X_{1,obs} \subseteq X_1$ and $X_{2,obs} \subseteq X_2$ of observable points in the two systems, we say that ϕ is *consistent with respect to observable states* if, and only if, for all states $s, s' \in S_1(X_1, A_1)$, and all points $y \in X_{2,obs}$,

$$s(x) = s'(x) \text{ for all } x \in X_{1,obs} \Rightarrow \phi(s)(y) = \phi(s')(y).$$

A state abstraction map ϕ that is consistent with respect to observable states determines an *observable state abstraction map*

$$\phi_{obs} : S_{1,obs}(X_1, A_1) \to S_{2,obs}(X_2, A_2)$$

as follows. Let $s \in S_1(X_1, A_1)$ be any global state of S_1 and let $s_{obs} = s|_{X_{1,obs}} \in S_{1,obs}(X_1, A_1)$ be its observable part. Then, for all $y \in X_{2,obs}$,

$$\phi_{obs}(s_{obs})(y) = \phi(s)(y).$$

We say that ϕ_{obs} is the *observable part* of ϕ.

Parameter abstraction. Parameter streams are compared using a function of the form

$$\Theta : S_1(T_1, P_1) \rightarrow S_2(T_2, P_2)$$

with the intention that an S_1 parameter stream $p \in S_1(T_1, P_1)$ is abstracted in S_2 by $\Theta(p) \in S_2(T_2, P_2)$. The function Θ is *temporally consistent* with the retiming λ if, for all $p, p' \in S_1(T_1, P_1)$ and $t \in T_2$,

$$p(c) = p'(c) \text{ for all } c \in \lambda^{-1}(t) \Rightarrow \Theta(p)(t) = \Theta(p')(t).$$

4.2 Abstraction and Approximation of Behaviour

We now define how system behaviours are related using abstraction concepts for time, states and parameter streams. There are four basic notions dealing with abstraction and approximation for global and observable behaviour. We will define notions that are suited to our later case studies: abstraction of global behaviour and approximation of observable behaviour. It is straightforward to define the other two notions.

Abstraction of global behaviour. The behaviour of system S_2 is an *abstraction* of S_1 with respect to retiming λ, parameter abstraction map Θ and state abstraction map ϕ if, for all $t \in T_1$, $p \in S_1(T_1, P_1)$ and $s \in S_1(X_1, A_1)$,

$$\phi(F_1(t, p, s)) = F_2(\lambda(t), \Theta(p), \phi(s)),$$

or, equivalently, if the following diagram commutes:

$$
\begin{array}{ccc}
T_2 \times S_2(T_2, P_2) \times S_2(X_2, A_2) & \xrightarrow{\quad F_2 \quad} & S_2(X_2, A_2) \\
\Big\uparrow{\lambda} \quad \Big\uparrow{\Theta} \quad \Big\uparrow{\phi} & & \Big\uparrow{\phi} \\
T_1 \times S_1(T_1, P_1) \times S_1(X_1, A_1) & \xrightarrow{\quad F_1 \quad} & S_1(X_1, A_1)
\end{array}
$$

Approximation of observable behaviour. Let $F_{1,obs}$ and $F_{2,obs}$ be the observable state functions of S_1 and S_2 respectively. Let

$$d : S_{2,obs}(X_2, A_2) \times S_{2,obs}(X_2, A_2) \rightarrow \mathbb{R}^+$$

be a metric that compares two observable states of system S_2. We say that the observable behaviour of S_2 *approximates* that of S_1 with respect to retiming λ, parameter abstraction map Θ, state abstraction map ϕ with observable part ϕ_{obs}, state comparison metric d and tolerance $\varepsilon \in \mathbb{R}^+$, if for all $t \in T_1$, $p \in S_1(T_1, P_1)$ and $s \in S_1(X_1, A_1)$,

$$d(\phi_{obs}(F_{1,obs}(t, p, s)), F_{2,obs}(\lambda(t), \Theta(p), \phi(s))) < \varepsilon.$$

Generalisations of abstraction and approximation notions. It is often the case that S_1 exhibits behaviours that are not abstracted or approximated by S_2. For example, a detailed model S_1 of a physical system might display complex spatio-temporal behaviours that are *observable* at the abstract level (via a state abstraction map ϕ), but are not *reproduced* by a simpler model S_2 of the same physical system.

One method to deal with such cases is to consider ϕ as a function that maps states of S_1 onto *partial states* of S_2, where if $\phi(s)(y) \downarrow$ then $\phi(s)(y) \in A_2$ is the local state of $y \in X_2$ abstracted from $s \in S_1(X_1, A_1)$, and $\phi(s)(y) \uparrow$ denotes that the state s is not abstracted by ϕ for S_2 point y. Let

$$S_{2,p}(X_2, A_2) = \{s_p \in [X_2 \nrightarrow A_2] \mid$$
$$(\exists s \in S_2(X_2, A_2))(\forall y \in X_2)[s_p(y) = s(y) \text{ or } s(y) \uparrow]\}$$

be the set of all partial global states of S_2 (where $\nrightarrow$ denotes partial functions) and let $\phi : S_1(X_1, A_1) \rightarrow S_{2,p}(X_2, A_2)$ be a state abstraction map. Let $dom_p(\phi) \subseteq S_1(X_1, A_1)$ be the set of all S_1 states that map to total S_2 states under ϕ.

To be able to define notions of observable approximation or abstraction using ϕ it is sufficient to require that $dom_p(\phi)$ is non-empty and that its observable part ϕ_{obs} always maps to fully defined states (that is, it must be of the form $\phi_{obs} : S_{1,obs}(X_1, A_1) \rightarrow S_{2,obs}(X_2, A_2)$).

It is often also the case that the set $S_1(T_1, P_1)$ of parameter streams for S_1 might contain elements that are not abstracted by elements in the set $S_2(T_2, P_2)$. In such a case we allow Θ to be a partial function with domain $dom(\Theta)$ which we require to be non-empty.

We say that the observable behaviour of S_2 *approximates* that of S_1 with respect to retiming λ, global state abstraction map ϕ with observable part ϕ_{obs} that maps only onto total states, parameter stream abstraction map Θ, state comparison metric d and tolerance $\varepsilon \in \mathbb{R}^+$, if for all $t \in T_1$, $p \in dom(\Theta)$ and $s \in dom_p(\phi)$,

$$d(\phi_{obs}(F_{1,obs}(t, p, s)), F_{2,obs}(\lambda(t), \Theta(p), \phi(s))) < \varepsilon.$$

Further, we may consider the case that S_2 abstracts or approximates S_1 only for a subset $sub(T_1) \subseteq T_1$ of time points (typically, for an initial segment, or at regular time points) and on subsets $sub(T_1, P_1) \subseteq S_1(T_1, P_1)$ of parameter streams and $sub(X_1, A_1) \subseteq S_1(X_1, A_1)$ of initial states. For example, we say that the observable behaviour of S_2 approximates that of S_1 with respect to the abstraction maps, the above subsets, the state comparison metric d and tolerance $\varepsilon \in \mathbb{R}^+$, if the above inequality holds for all $t \in sub(T_1)$, $p \in sub(T_1, P_1)$ and $s \in sub(X_1, A_1)$.

5 Synchronous Concurrent Algorithms

We now turn our attention to a concrete model of computation for spatially extended systems. Synchronous concurrent algorithms (SCAs) are algorithms distributed discretely in space and operating in discrete time. The concept of an SCA was introduced in 1985 to model parallel deterministic computing systems, especially hardware; see [TT94]. Many mathematical models of physical and biological systems have also been shown to be SCAs, including cellular automata [HTT91], coupled map lattices [HTZP92,HPTZ94,HPT96a], neural networks [HPT96b], and discrete approximations of PDEs and CODEs. SCAs are easily seen to be equationally specifiable and computable; SCA theory is built upon the theory of primitive recursive functions over many-sorted algebras [Tuc91,TZ92]. SCAs have also been studied using process algebra [BHP97,BP99].

In this section we define the simplest type of SCA which has a single clock. In Section 5.2 we relate the general notion of an SCA to that of an SES. We present two examples of SCAs in Sections 5.3 and 5.4: a systolic array and a model of electrical activity in a strand of cardiac tissue.

5.1 Formal Definition

An SCA N is characterised by its global clock, the data it processes, and its architecture of modules, channels and sources. For simplicity, we describe SCAs where modules compute on a single data set, although it is not difficult to extend the definition to the the many-sorted case.

Data and time. We assume that the algorithm N computes over data from a non-empty set A and is synchronised by a discrete clock $T = \{0, 1, 2, \ldots\}$.

Modules and channels. Let I be a finite non-empty set of *modules*. A module is an atomic computing device capable of some specific internal processing. Let each module $i \in I$ have $p(i)$ inputs and a finite set

$$Ch_i = \{(i, v), (i, u), \ldots\}$$

of output *channels*, where $u, v, \ldots$ are identifiers chosen from a set Var. Channels have unit bandwidth with respect to A (i.e., at any time they hold a single datum) and are unidirectional. Let Ch denote the set of all network channels, and is defined by

$$Ch = \bigcup_{i \in I} Ch_i.$$

A typical module i may be depicted:

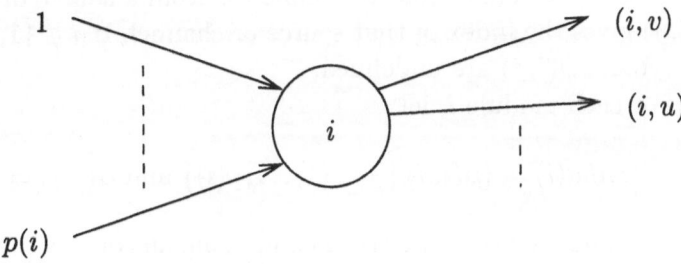

Let each module $i \in I$ compute a function

$$f_{i,v} : A^{p(i)} \to A$$

for each of its output channels $(i, v) \in Ch_i$ with the intention that if values $b_1, \ldots, b_{p(i)} \in A$ arrive on its $p(i)$ inputs (each of which may be a channel from another module, or an input source supplying data from the external environment) then module i outputs the value $f_{i,v}(b_1, \ldots, b_{p(i)})$ along channel (i, v). For clarity, when the relationship between module functions and channel names is well understood, we might denote $f_{i,v}$ by f_i, $f_{i,u}$ by g_i etc..

Sources and output channels. An SCA N may operate on infinite sequences or streams of data from the set $[T \to A]$. Let In be a finite (possibly empty) set of network inputs or *sources*. Each source supplies the network with a single stream of input data. An SCA without sources is termed *closed*.

Network N processes a set of input streams of the form $a \in [T \to A]^{In}$ where $a(i) \in [T \to A]$ (often written a_i) is the stream supplied by source i, and $a_i(t) \in A$ is the value supplied by source i at time t.

Data is read from N at its *output channels*. Let $Out \subseteq Ch$ be a set of all network output channels.

Architecture. The architecture of a network N is its topological structure of modules, channels and sources. We define two *wiring maps* to formalise the connections between modules, channels and sources. Let

$$\alpha : I \times \mathbb{N} \rightarrowtail \{source, channel\}$$

$$\beta : I \times \mathbb{N} \rightarrowtail In \cup Ch$$

be partial functions that enumerate inputs to modules in the following way: for any module $i \in I$, for $j \in \{1, \ldots, p(i)\}$, $\alpha(i, j)$ says whether the j-th input connection to module i is from a source or a channel, and $\beta(i, j)$ gives the index of that source or channel. If $j \notin \{1, \ldots, p(i)\}$, then $\alpha(i, j)$ and $\beta(i, j)$ are undefined.

For each module i, let

$$snhd(i) = \{\beta(i, j) \mid j \in \{1, \ldots, p(i)\} \text{ and } \alpha(i, j) = source\}$$

be the *source neighbourhood* of i comprising all sources that supply i with data. Similarly, let

$$cnhd(i) = \{\beta(i, j) \mid j \in \{1, \ldots, p(i)\} \text{ and } \alpha(i, j) = channel\}$$

be the *channel neighbourhood* of i comprising all channels that supply i with data.

SCA Equations. An SCA N as described above computes on streams $a \in [T \rightarrow A]^{In}$ from a state $s \in A^{Ch}$ of initial channel values, where $s(i, v) \in A$ (often written $s_{i,v}$) is the initial value held on channel (i, v). For each channel $(i, v) \in Ch$ we define a *channel state function*

$$V_{i,v} : T \times [T \rightarrow A]^{In} \times A^{Ch} \rightarrow A$$

where $V_{i,v}(t, a, s)$ denotes the datum held on (i, v) at time t when the network is executed on input streams a from initial state s. We define $V_{i,v}$ by induction on the clock T, as follows:

Time 0. At time 0, each channel is initialised with the datum $s_{i,v} \in A$; thus

$$V_{i,v}(0, a, s) = s_{i,v}.$$

Time $t + 1$. The value held by channel (i, v) at time $t + 1$ is evaluated by module i with function $f_{i,v} : A^{p(i)} \to A$. If $b_1, \ldots, b_{p(i)}$ are the values held on the inputs of module i at time t, then the value of (i, v) at time $t + 1$ is $f_{i,v}(b_1, \ldots, b_{p(i)})$. The channels and sources bearing the input values $b_1, \ldots, b_{p(i)}$ are determined by the wiring maps α and β. Thus,

$$V_{i,v}(t + 1, a, s) = f_{i,v}(b_1, \ldots, b_{p(i)})$$

where for $j \in \{1, \ldots, p(i)\}$,

$$b_j = \begin{cases} a_{\beta(i,j)}(t) & \text{if } \alpha(i,j) = source \\ V_{\beta(i,j)}(t, a, s) & \text{if } \alpha(i,j) = channel. \end{cases}$$

Global state functions. The channel state functions $V_{i,v}$ tell us the value of a particular channel, given a time, input streams and initial data. We may combine these functions into a *global state function*

$$V : T \times [T \to A]^{In} \times A^{Ch} \to A^{Ch}$$

that gives the state of the entire network. The function V is defined for all $t \in T$, $a \in [T \to A]^{In}$ and $s \in A^{Ch}$, by

$$V(t, a, s) = (V_{i,v}(t, a, s) \mid (i, v) \in Ch).$$

Output functions. The global state function tells us the values at all the network's channels. Restricting this to output channels gives us an *output function*

$$V_{out} : T \times [T \to A]^{In} \times A^{Ch} \to A^{Out}$$

where $V_{out}(t, a, s)$ is the output of N at time t given input streams a and initial data s. We define V_{out}, for all $t \in T$, $a \in [T \to A]^{In}$ and $s \in A^{Ch}$, by

$$V_{out}(t, a, s) = (V_{i,v}(t, a, s) \mid (i, v) \in Out).$$

It is often useful to regard N as a *stream transformer*. We define a stream transformer version

$$\hat{V}_{out} : [T \to A]^{In} \times A^{Ch} \to [T \to A]^{Out}$$

of V_{out} with coordinates $\hat{V}_{out,(i,v)}$ for all output channels $(i, v) \in Out$ defined for all $a \in [T \to A]^{In}$, $s \in A^{Ch}$ and $t \in T$, by

$$\hat{V}_{out,(i,v)}(a, s)(t) = V_{i,v}(t, a, s)$$

such that $\hat{V}_{out}(a, s)$ is the *Out*-indexed set of streams that are output from N given input streams a and initial state s.

5.2 SCAs as Spatially Extended Systems

An SCA is essentially a spatially extended system with a discrete clock whose system function is definable by primitive recursive equations of the form of Section 5.1.

Identifying elements of a general SCA with the space, state, parameter stream, system function, and observable state function components of a spatially extended system is straightforward.

We can identify either the set Ch of channels or the set I of modules with space. In the former case, each point (channel) in the space has a single state at any time instant. In the latter each point (module) is, in general, multi-valued where each output channel is identified with a component of the point's local state. In both cases the set of global state coordinates is given by Ch. In the remainder of the paper, we identify the set I with space, although it is not difficult to reformulate the ideas using Ch as the space set.

The set of possible global states of the system is A^{Ch}. The set of parameter values is A^{In} and the set of all possible parameter streams is $[T \to A^{In}]$ although we often prefer to use the equivalent set $[T \to A]^{In}$.

The SCA's global state function V is identified as the system function. The set $Out \subseteq Ch$ of output channels is identified as the set of observable state coordinates, and V_{out} as the observable state function.

5.3 Example: Systolic Convolver

We consider a first example of an SCA: a systolic convolver introduced in [Kun82]; convolution has many important applications in digital signal processing. In this section we define the task of convolution, and specify the convolver as an SCA in the style of Section 5.1. The algorithm has been studied as an SCA in [HTT88], where its correctness was proven.

Task. Let A be a commutative ring and let $r = (r_1, \ldots, r_n) \in A^n$ be an n-vector which we call a *reference word*. Let $conv_r : A^n \to A$ be the *inner product* or *convolution* function defined with respect to r, for all n-vectors $a = (a_1, \ldots, a_n) \in A^n$, by

$$conv_r(a_1, \ldots, a_n) = r_1 \cdot a_1 + \cdots + r_n \cdot a_n.$$

(For simplicity, we will assume $n \geq 2$). Let $C = \{0, 1, 2, \ldots\}$ be a clock. We specify formally the task of convolution by means of a stream transformer

$$\Phi : [C \to A] \to [C \to (A \cup \{unspec\})]$$

defined, for all $a \in [C \to A]$ and $c \in C$, by

$$\Phi(a)(c) = \begin{cases} unspec & \text{if } c < n \\ conv_r(a(c-n), \ldots, a(c-1)) & \text{if } c \geq n \end{cases}$$

so that the value output at time c is the inner product of r and the previous n values of the input stream. The value $unspec \notin A$ means "unspecified" and is used here to denote the fact that we are not concerned with the specification's output until time n. We illustrate Φ in the table below. The first two columns give the output for the general specification. The final two columns give the output of the specification in the case that $A = \mathbb{Z}$, $n = 3$, $r = (1, 2, 3)$ and where the input stream $a : C \to A$ begins with elements $a(0) = 2$, $a(1) = 1$, $a(2) = 3$, $a(3) = 1$, $a(4) = 3$, $a(5) = 2$, $a(6) = 3$, ...

c	$\Phi(a)(c)$	c	$\Phi(a)(c)$
0	$unspec$	0	$unspec$
1	$unspec$	1	$unspec$
2	$unspec$	2	$unspec$
$\vdots$	$\vdots$	3	13
$n-1$	$unspec$	4	10
n	$conv_r(a(0), \ldots, a(n-1)))$	5	14
$n+1$	$conv_r(a(1), \ldots, a(n)))$	6	13
$n+2$	$conv_r(a(2), \ldots, a(n+1)))$	7	16
$\vdots$	$\vdots$	$\vdots$	$\vdots$

Algorithm. Consider the network illustrated in Figure 4.

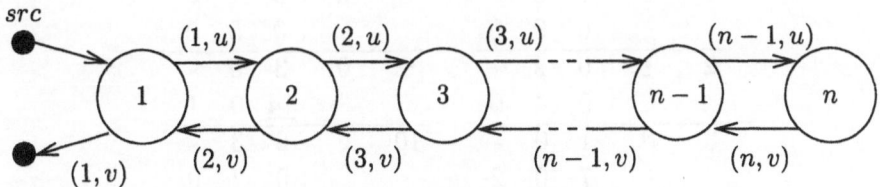

Fig. 4. A systolic convolver.

During every clock cycle, each module operates as follows. Module 1 reads some value a from the network's input source src, and some value b

from channel $(2, v)$; it outputs the value $r_n \cdot a + b$ onto channel $(1, v)$ and a onto channel $(1, u)$. Module j, for $j = 2, \ldots, n - 1$, reads two values a and b from channels $(j - 1, u)$ and $(j + 1, v)$ respectively, and outputs the value $r_{n-j+1} \cdot a + b$ onto channel (j, v) and the value a along channel (j, u). Module n reads some value a from channel $(n-1, u)$ and outputs the value $r_1 \cdot a$ onto channel (n, v). Elements from the single input stream travel along the right-facing channels $(1, u), (2, u), \ldots$ of the network where they are multiplied by each element r_j of the reference word r. Partial results travel from right to left via channels $(n, v), (n - 1, v), \ldots$ and appear as inner-products at the output channel $(1, v)$.

Elements of a stream $a : C \to A$ must be supplied by the network source only at even numbered clock cycles; padding values (e.g., 0) should be supplied at odd cycles. We define the algorithm to compute with respect to a network clock T, which is twice as fast as the specification's clock C. From the example stream $a : C \to A$ above, we can define a network input stream $a' : T \to A$ padded with alternate 0's, that begins with $a'(0) = 2$, $a'(1) = 0$, $a'(2) = 1$, $a'(3) = 0$, $a'(4) = 3$, $a'(5) = 0, \ldots$. Taking $A = \mathbb{Z}$, $n = 3$, $r = (1, 2, 3)$, and initial channel states to be 0, we trace the execution of the convolver on the network input stream a' in the following table, where the upper row for each time gives the values on the two u channels and the lower row gives the three v channels' values. Notice that we obtain results (shown underlined) from the convolver at times $2n - 1 = 5, 2n + 1 = 7, 2n + 3 = 9, \ldots$.

t	$a'(t)$	1	2	3		t	$a'(t)$	1	2	3
0	2	0	0	-		7	0	1	0	-
		0	0	0				<u>10</u>	0	3
1	0	2	0	-		8	3	0	1	-
		6	0	0				0	5	0
2	1	0	2	-		9	0	3	0	-
		0	4	0				<u>14</u>	0	1
3	0	1	0	-		10	2	0	3	-
		7	0	2				0	7	0
4	3	0	1	-		11	0	2	0	-
		0	4	0				<u>13</u>	0	3
5	0	3	0	-		12	3	0	2	-
		<u>13</u>	0	1				0	7	0
6	1	0	3	-		13	0	3	0	-
		0	7	0				<u>16</u>	0	2

We use the basic SCA model to formalise the convolver and its operation over a commutative ring A with respect to clock T.

Channels and Modules. The index sets for the modules, sources, channels and output channels are easily determined from Figure 4:

$$I = \{1, \ldots, n\}$$
$$In = \{src\}$$
$$Ch = \{(1, u), (1, v), (2, u), (2, v), \ldots, (n-1, u), (n-1, v), (n, v)\}$$
$$Out = \{(1, v)\}.$$

Module functions. For modules $j = 1, \ldots, n-1$, we define $g_j : A^2 \to A$ and $f_j : A^2 \to A$, associated with channels (j, u) and (j, v) respectively, for all $a, b \in A$, by

$$g_j(a, b) = a \quad \text{and} \quad f_j(a, b) = r_{n-j+1} \cdot a + b.$$

For the rightmost module n we define $f_n : A \to A$, associated with channel (n, v), for all $a \in A$, by $f_n(a) = r_1 \cdot a$.

Architecture. Let α and β be wiring maps that define the following neighbourhoods in a straightforward manner:

$$snhd(1) = \{src\}$$
$$snhd(j) = \emptyset \qquad\qquad\qquad j = 2, \ldots, n$$
$$cnhd(1) = \{(2, v)\}$$
$$cnhd(j) = \{(j-1, u), (j+1, v)\} \quad j = 2, \ldots, n-1$$
$$cnhd(n) = \{(n-1, u)\}.$$

SCA equations. The formal specification of the convolver's components determines channel state functions

$$V_{j,w} : T \times [T \to A] \times A^{Ch} \to A$$

for each $(j, w) \in Ch$, defined for all $a \in [T \to A]$ and $s \in A^{Ch}$, at time 0 by $V_{j,w}(0, a, s) = s(j, w)$, and at time $t + 1$ as follows:

$$V_{1,u}(t+1, a, s) = g_1(a(t), V_{2,v}(t, a, s))$$
$$V_{1,v}(t+1, a, s) = f_1(a(t), V_{2,v}(t, a, s))$$
$$V_{2,u}(t+1, a, s) = g_2(V_{1,u}(t, a, s), V_{3,v}(t, a, s))$$
$$V_{2,v}(t+1, a, s) = f_2(V_{1,u}(t, a, s), V_{3,v}(t, a, s))$$

$$\vdots \qquad \vdots \qquad \vdots$$

$$V_{n-1,u}(t+1,a,s) = g_{n-1}(V_{n-2,u}(t,a,s), V_{n,v}(t,a,s))$$
$$V_{n-1,v}(t+1,a,s) = f_{n-1}(V_{n-2,u}(t,a,s), V_{n,v}(t,a,s))$$
$$V_{n,v}(t+1,a,s) = f_n(V_{n-1,u}(t,a,s)).$$

Stream transformer specification. We specify the input-output behaviour of the convolver as a stream transformer

$$\hat{V}_{out} : [T \rightarrow A] \times A^{Ch} \rightarrow [T \rightarrow A]$$

defined, for all $a \in [T \rightarrow A]$, $s \in A^{Ch}$ and $t \in T$, by

$$\hat{V}_{out}(a,s)(t) = V_{1,v}(t,a,s).$$

Algorithm correctness. We now consider the correctness of the convolver, specified by $\hat{V}_{out}$, with respect to the task specification Φ. Since the algorithm computes with respect to clock T rather than C, on padded input streams, and supplies valid output only at times $2n-1, 2n+1, \ldots$, we need to *schedule* streams into and out-from the algorithm.

We define an input scheduling function $\theta_{in} : [C \rightarrow A] \rightarrow [T \rightarrow A]$, for all specification input streams $a : C \rightarrow A$ and network clock cycles $t \in T$, by

$$\theta_{in}(a)(t) = \begin{cases} a(t/2) & \text{if } t \text{ even} \\ 0 & \text{if } t \text{ odd.} \end{cases}$$

We define an output scheduling function $\theta_{out} : [T \rightarrow A] \rightarrow [C \rightarrow (A \cup \{unspec\})]$, for all network output streams $a \in [T \rightarrow A]$ and specification times $c \in C$, by

$$\theta_{out}(a)(c) = \begin{cases} unspec & \text{if } c < n \\ a(2c-1) & \text{if } c \geq n. \end{cases}$$

We consider the convolver to be correct with respect to Φ, if for all specification input streams $a \in [C \rightarrow A]$ and initial network states $s \in A^{Ch}$, at each time $c \in C$,

$$\theta_{out}(\hat{V}_{out}(\theta_{in}(a), s))(c) = \Phi(a)(c).$$

See [HTT88] for a proof of correctness.

5.4   Example: Model of Cardiac Tissue

We now consider an example SCA from biology: a model of electrical behaviour in cardiac tissue. The SCA is derived from a biophysically detailed, high-order ODE model of a single guinea pig ventricular cell (see [Nob90]) that provides a quantitative description of the intracellular processes and ionic concentrations and currents that determine the cell membrane potential. It has 17 dynamic variables, with kinetics derived from voltage clamp experiments. It is an example of a number of biophysical excitation equations for heart muscle [PH97].

Linking together copies of this model into a one-dimensional coupled ODE (CODE) lattice reconstructs a strand of tissue (where the coupling between ODEs represents the cell-to-cell junctional conductance). The CODE lattice itself is not an SCA, but many algorithmic approximations to the model are SCAs. As a full description of the biological details of the model itself would be too involved for our purposes, we will consider only the essential details of an SCA approximation, derived using the *finite difference method*.

Consider the figure below, where each box represents a single module (cardiac cell) with nearest neighbour connections, a local source supplying a stream of electrical stimuli, and an observable output channel. The network computes on the set $\mathbb{R}$ of real numbers.

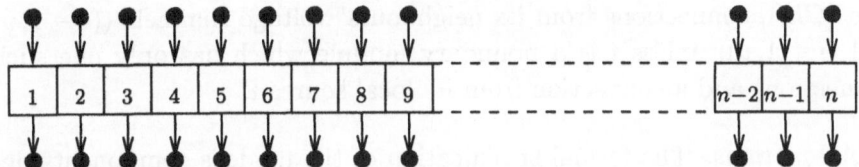

Modules and Channels. We use the set $I = \{1, \ldots, n\}$ to index both the modules and the stimulation sources. Each module has 17 output channels which hold its local state. Channel values include representations of membrane potential or voltage, and various ionic concentrations and processes. Details concerning these states are not relevant to the present discussion; we only need bear in mind that the model encompasses considerable biological detail. We will use the set

$$Ch_i = \{i\} \times (\{v\} \cup dyn)$$

to index the channels of cell i where v denotes voltage and dyn denotes a set of 16 names used to identify each of the other dynamic states. The sets Ch_i determine a set Ch of $17n$ network channels.

Of primary interest are the voltages of the cells across the network, and thus we define the set *Out* of observable or output channels to be

$$Out = \{(1, v), (2, v), \ldots, (n, v)\}.$$

Module functions. At each clock cycle, every cell computes on its 17-valued state, the voltages of its two nearest neighbours (boundary cells 1 and n each have only one nearest neighbour), and on the current local stimulation value. The module functions, determined by a finite difference approximation technique, thus take the form

$$f_{i,v}, \ldots : \mathbb{R}^{17} \times \mathbb{R}^2 \times \mathbb{R} \to \mathbb{R} \qquad i = 2, \ldots, n - 1$$
$$f_{i,v}, \ldots : \mathbb{R}^{17} \times \mathbb{R} \times \mathbb{R} \to \mathbb{R} \qquad i = 1, n.$$

Architecture. Let α and β be wiring maps that define the following neighbourhoods in a straightforward way:

$$cnhd(i) = Ch_i \cup \{(i - 1, v), (i + 1, v)\} \qquad i = 2, \ldots, n - 1$$
$$cnhd(1) = Ch_1 \cup \{(2, v)\}$$
$$cnhd(n) = Ch_n \cup \{(n - 1, v)\}$$
$$snhd(i) = \{i\} \qquad\qquad\qquad\qquad\qquad i = 1, \ldots, n$$

so that each module i has feedback connections from all its output channels (Ch_i), connections from its neighbours' voltage channels $((i - 1, v)$ and $(i + 1, v)$, unless i is a boundary module which has only one such connection) and a connection from its local source i.

SCA equations. The formal specification of the model's components determines channel state functions

$$V_{i,w} : T \times [T \to \mathbb{R}]^I \times \mathbb{R}^{Ch} \to \mathbb{R}$$

for each $(i, w) \in Ch$, defined for all stimulation streams $a \in [T \to \mathbb{R}]^I$ and initial states $s \in \mathbb{R}^{Ch}$, at time 0 by $V_{i,w}(0, a, s) = s(i, w)$ and at time $t + 1$ as follows:

$$V_{i,w}(t + 1, a, s) = f_{i,w}(V_{i,v}(t, a, s), \ldots, V_{i-1,v}(t, a, s), V_{i+1,v}(t, a, s), a_i(t))$$

for $i = 2, \ldots, n - 1$, and

$$V_{1,w}(t + 1, a, s) = f_{1,w}(V_{1,v}(t, a, s), \ldots, V_{2,v}(t, a, s), a_1(t))$$
$$V_{n,w}(t + 1, a, s) = f_{n,w}(V_{n,v}(t, a, s), \ldots, V_{n-1,v}(t, a, s), a_n(t)).$$

Observable behaviour. We define the observable (i.e., voltage) behaviour of the CODE model as a function

$$V_{out} : T \times [T \to \mathbb{R}]^I \times \mathbb{R}^{Ch} \to \mathbb{R}^{Out}$$

for all $t \in T$, $a \in [T \to \mathbb{R}]^I$ and $s \in \mathbb{R}^{Ch}$, by

$$V_{out}(t, a, s) = (V_{1,v}(t, a, s), V_{2,v}(t, a, s) \dots, V_{n,v}(t, a, s)).$$

To demonstrate the observable behaviour of the CODE model, consider a system of $n = 2000$ coupled cells which, taking $80\mu m$ as the length of a cardiac cell, represents a 160mm strand of tissue. This unreasonably long strand is to allow for illustration of the fully spatially extended travelling wave; in reality a wave propagates in a medium that is smaller than its wavelength. Each clock cycle in the model represents 0.01ms of real time, which gives a numerically stable solution to the CODE. Figure 5 illustrates snapshots of an *action potential* propagating along the system at 50ms (5000 clock cycle) intervals following a $30nA$ stimulation of the four left-most cells for an initial period of 2ms (given by parameter streams $a_i(t) = -30$ for $1 \leq i \leq 4$ and $t < 200$; $a_i(t) = 0$ otherwise), given that the model begins in a uniformly resting state (given by an appropriate value of s). Figure 5 illustrates only one aspect of the biological detail reconstructed by the CODE model; we could easily trace the values of each of the other 16 state coordinates at any cell.

6 Abstraction and Approximation Between SCAs

Suppose we have two SCAs N_1 and N_2 with components I_1, I_2, Ch_1, Ch_2 etc.. We wish to compare the operation of the SCAs and define formally the notion that the behaviour of N_2 (given by V_2) is an *abstraction* or *approximation* of the behaviour of N_1 (given by V_1). In Section 6.1, we show how components of N_1 can be related formally to those of N_2. Then, in Section 6.2, we present a formal definition of behaviour abstraction for SCAs. The component and behaviour abstractions and approximations for SCAs are special cases of those for general spatially extended systems given in Sections 4.1 and 4.2.

6.1 Comparing Components of SCAs

We compare the finite spaces or module sets I_1 and I_2, the discrete clocks T_1 and T_2, the sets $A_1^{Ch_1}$ and $A_2^{Ch_2}$ of global states, and the sets $[T_1 \to A_1]^{In_1}$ and $[T_2 \to A_2]^{In_2}$ of input streams.

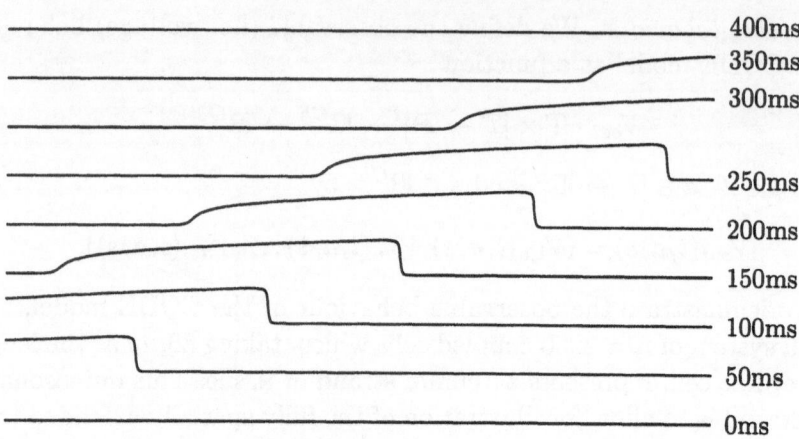

400ms
350ms
300ms

250ms

200ms

150ms

100ms

50ms

0ms

Fig. 5. An action potential travelling from left-to-right along the CODE model following a single stimulus at the four left-most cells. Voltage is plotted against space at 50ms intervals.

Spaces. We begin by comparing the sets I_1 and I_2 of modules. An SCA *respacing*

$$\pi : I_1 \to I_2$$

is a surjective function, with the intention that each N_1 module $i \in I_1$ is abstracted in N_2 by module $\pi(i) \in I_2$. The inverse $\pi^{-1} : I_2 \to Powerset_f(I_1)$ of π is defined by $\pi^{-1}(j) = \{i \in I_1 \mid \pi(i) = j\}$ where $\pi^{-1}(j)$ is the *subspace* of all N_1 modules abstracted in N_2 by module $j \in I_2$. Figure 6 illustrates an SCA respacing π and its inverse π^{-1}.

Clocks. Next consider the SCAs' global clocks T_1 and T_2. An SCA *retiming*

$$\lambda : T_1 \to T_2$$

is a surjective, monotonic function with the intention that each clock cycle $t \in T_1$ abstracts clock cycle $\lambda(t) \in T_2$. From a retiming λ, we determine an *immersion* $\overline{\lambda} : T_2 \to T_1$ defined, for all $t \in T_2$, by

$$\overline{\lambda}(t) = \min c \in T_1 \text{ such that } \lambda(c) = t.$$

Let the range of $\overline{\lambda}$ be denoted $Start_\lambda \subseteq T_1$; this set comprises clock cycles of T_1 that correspond with the "beginning" of each cycle of clock T_2. The

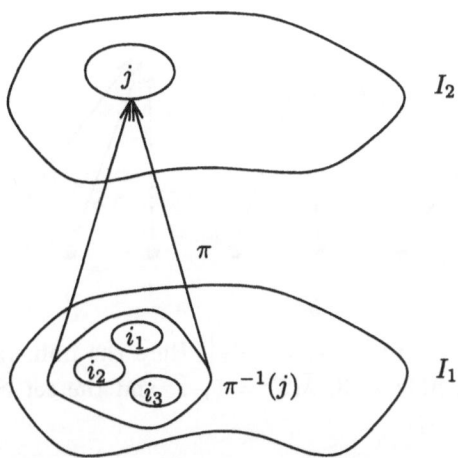

Fig. 6. An SCA respacing $\pi : I_1 \to I_2$ and its inverse $\pi^{-1} : I_2 \to Powerset_f(I_1)$.

inverse $\lambda^{-1} : T_2 \to Powerset_f(T_1)$ of λ is defined, for all $t \in T_2$, by

$$\lambda^{-1}(t) = \{\overline{\lambda}(t), \overline{\lambda}(t) + 1, \ldots, \overline{\lambda}(t+1) - 1\}.$$

Often, we are interested in expressing the idea that clock T_1 is r times faster than clock T_2 for some $r \in \mathbb{R}$ where $r \geq 1$. This is accomplished by means of a *linear retiming*, which takes the form

$$\lambda(t) = \left\lfloor \frac{t}{r} \right\rfloor.$$

The linear retiming for the case $r = 2.5$ is illustrated in Figure 7.

Global states. An SCA global state abstraction map is of the form

$$\phi : A_1^{Ch_1} \to A_2^{Ch_2}$$

with the intention that a global state $s \in A_1^{Ch_1}$ of SCA N_1 is abstracted in SCA N_2 by $\phi(s) \in A_2^{Ch_2}$.

The map ϕ is *spatially consistent* with π if, and only if, for all states $s, s' \in A_1^{Ch_1}$ and channels $(j, u) \in Ch_2$,

$$s(i, v) = s'(i, v) \text{ for all } i \in \pi^{-1}(j), v \in Ch_i \Rightarrow \phi(s)(j, u) = \phi(s')(j, u).$$

The map ϕ is *consistent with respect to observable states* if, and only if, for all states $s, s' \in A_1^{Ch_1}$ and output channels $(j, u) \in Out_2$,

$$s(i, v) = s'(i, v) \text{ for all } (i, v) \in Out_1 \Rightarrow \phi(s)(j, u) = \phi(s')(j, u).$$

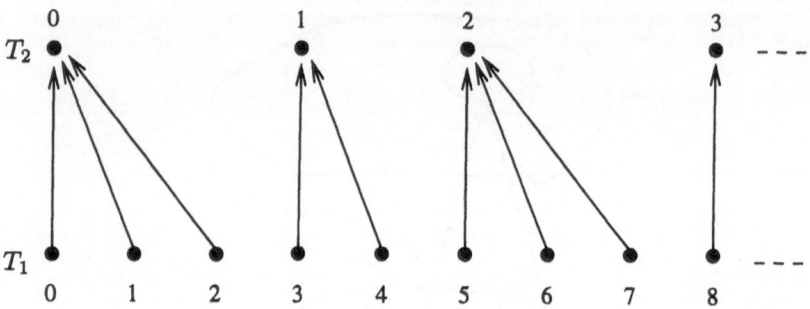

Fig. 7. The linear retiming $\lambda(t) = \lfloor \frac{t}{2.5} \rfloor$. Here the immersion $\overline{\lambda} : T_2 \to T_1$ is given by $\overline{\lambda}(0) = 0$, $\overline{\lambda}(1) = 3$, $\overline{\lambda}(2) = 5, \ldots$ and the set $Start_\lambda$ is defined by $Start_\lambda = \{0, 3, 5, 8, \ldots\}$.

Given a map ϕ that is consistent with respect to observable states, we can derive an observable state abstraction map $\phi_{obs} : A_1^{Out_1} \to A_2^{Out_2}$ as follows. For any state $s \in A_1^{Ch_1}$, let $s_{obs} = s|_{Out_1} \in A_1^{Out_1}$ denote that part of s that is observable or output. Let ϕ_{obs} be defined, for all output channels $(j, u) \in Out_2$, by

$$\phi_{obs}(s_{obs})(j, u) = \phi(s)(j, u).$$

Input streams. We map input streams for SCA N_1 onto input streams for N_2 by means of a stream abstraction function

$$\Theta : [T_1 \to A_1]^{In_1} \to [T_2 \to A_2]^{In_2}$$

with the intention that streams $a \in [T_1 \to A_1]^{In_1}$ for SCA N_1 are abstracted in SCA N_2 by $\Theta(a) \in [T_2 \to A_2]^{In_2}$.

Let $\Theta_j : [T_1 \to A_1]^{In_1} \to [T_2 \to A_2]$ be the j-coordinate of Θ, which abstracts streams for the N_2 source $j \in In_2$. The map Θ is *temporally consistent* with the retiming λ if, for all $a, a' \in [T_1 \to A_1]^{In_1}$, $t \in T_2$ and $j \in In_2$,

$$a_i(c) = a'_i(c) \text{ for all } i \in In_1, c \in \lambda^{-1}(t) \Rightarrow \Theta_j(a)(t) = \Theta_j(a')(t).$$

It is often the case that each source of N_1 is abstracted by a single source in N_2; such a relationship is expressed by a surjective *source abstraction map* $\eta : In_1 \to In_2$ defined with the intention that data supplied by a source $i \in In_1$ is abstracted by data supplied by source $\eta(i) \in In_2$. The inverse $\eta^{-1} : In_2 \to Powerset_f(In_1)$ of η is defined by $\eta^{-1}(j) = \{i \in I_1 \mid \pi(i) = j\}$ where $\eta^{-1}(j)$ is the set of N_1 sources abstracted in N_2 by source $j \in In_2$.

We say that Θ is consistent with both λ and η if for all $a, a' \in [T_1 \to A_1]^{In_1}$, $t \in T_2$ and $j \in In_2$,

$$a_i(c) = a'_i(c) \text{ for all } i \in \eta^{-1}(j), c \in \lambda^{-1}(t) \Rightarrow \Theta_j(a)(t) = \Theta_j(a')(t).$$

6.2 Notions of Abstraction and Approximation for SCAs

For each of the notions of abstraction and approximation of behaviours for spatially extended systems given in Section 4.2, we can define special cases for SCAs. As an example, consider abstraction of global behaviour for SCAs.

Typically, we wish to express the notion that the state of N_2 at each time $t \in T_2$ abstracts that of N_1 not at all clock cycles $\overline{\lambda}(t), \overline{\lambda}(t) + 1, \ldots, \overline{\lambda}(t+1) - 1 \in T_1$ that t abstracts, but only at the first cycle $\overline{\lambda}(t)$. The set of all of such clock cycles is given by $Start_\lambda$. The notion of SCA abstraction now follows directly from Section 4.2: we say that the global behaviour of N_2 is an abstraction of that of N_1 if the following diagram commutes:

$$
\begin{array}{ccccccc}
T_2 & \times & [T_2 \to A_2]^{In_2} & \times & A_2^{Ch_2} & \xrightarrow{\ V_2\ } & A_2^{Ch_2} \\
\big\uparrow{\lambda} & & \big\uparrow{\Theta} & & \big\uparrow{\phi} & & \big\uparrow{\phi} \\
Start_\lambda & \times & [T_1 \to A_1]^{In_1} & \times & A_1^{Ch_1} & \xrightarrow{\ V_1\ } & A_1^{Ch_1}
\end{array}
$$

6.3 Example: Abstraction Between Systolic Convolvers

In this section we consider a bit-level implementation of the systolic convolver of Section 5.3, and define formally the notion that the behaviour of the first SCA abstracts that of the bit-level algorithm.

A bit-level convolver. We begin the specification of the new SCA by defining a bit-level implementation of the ring A over which the convolver of Section 5.3 computes. We shall assume that A can be represented by k-bit words for some $k > 0$. Specifically, we will assume the existence of an algebra $(\{0,1\}^k \mid r_1^B, \ldots, r_n^B, \cdot^B, +^B)$ and an epimorphism $h : \{0,1\}^k \to A$ from this algebra to the algebra $(A \mid r_1, \ldots, r_n, \cdot, +)$ comprising the reference word elements and operations $\cdot$ and $+$ used in the construction of the abstract convolver in Section 5.3.

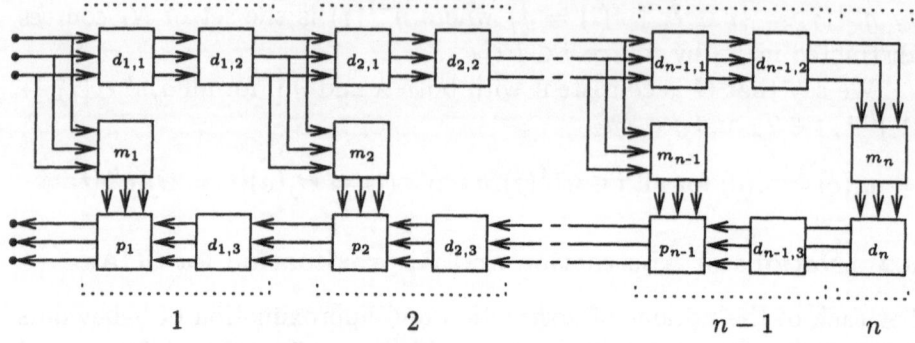

Fig. 8. A bit-level implementation of the convolver of Section 5.3.

Consider the SCA depicted in Figure 8 where each dotted box $j = 1,\ldots,n$ comprises those modules that implement module j of the first convolver; each module has k bit-valued output channels, and there are k sources (for clarity, we have used $k = 3$ in Figure 8). Each d module computes the identity function on $\{0,1\}^k$, and hence serves as a delay module; each p module computes $+^B$; and each module m_j computes $r_{n-j+1}^B \cdot a$ given input $a \in \{0,1\}^k$. (By the terminology of Section 5.1, each module actually computes k coordinate functions, one for each of its output channels.)

The relationship to the first convolver is straightforward. Each k-vector of channels that pass from box j to $j+1$ represents channel (j,u); those that pass from dotted box j to $j-1$ represent (j,v); the k output channels represent $(1,v)$; and the k sources represent the single source src. Data entering a box at time t determines data output from the box at time $t+2$. Thus each clock cycle of the abstract convolver is represented by two clock cycles: input stream and channel values of the abstract convolver at times $0,1,2,\ldots,t,\ldots$ are represented on the appropriate sources and channels here at times $0,2,4,\ldots,2t,\ldots$.

To distinguish clearly between the two systems and their components, let us denote the bit-level convolver by N_1 and the abstract convolver by N_2. We rename the components T, I, In, Ch and Out of Section 5.3 by T_2, I_2, In_2, Ch_2 and Out_2.

Using the sets

$$I_1 = \{d_{j,1}, d_{j,2}, d_{j,3}, p_j, m_j \mid j = 1,\ldots,n-1\} \cup \{m_n, d_n\}$$
$$In_1 = \{1,\ldots,k\}$$

$$Ch_1 = \{(i,1),\ldots,(i,k) \mid i \in I_1\}$$
$$Out_1 = \{(p_1,1),\ldots,(p_1,k)\}$$

to index the modules, sources, channels and output channels of the bit-level convolver, we define channel state functions

$$V_{i,r} : T_1 \times [T_1 \to \{0,1\}]^k \times \{0,1\}^{Ch_1} \to \{0,1\}$$

for each channel $(i,r) \in Ch_1$ in terms of vectorised functions

$$V_i : T_1 \times [T_1 \to \{0,1\}]^k \times \{0,1\}^{Ch_1} \to \{0,1\}^k$$

for each module $i \in I_1$, where

$$V_i(t,a,s) = (V_{i,1}(t,a,s),\ldots,V_{i,k}(t,a,s)) \in \{0,1\}^k$$

denotes the k-bit word held on the output channels $(i,1),\ldots(i,k)$ of module i at time t. For all $a \in [T_1 \to \{0,1\}]^k$ and $s \in \{0,1\}^{Ch_1}$, let

$$
\begin{aligned}
V_i(0,a,s) &= (s(i,1),\ldots s(i,k)) & i \in I\\
V_{d_1,1}(t+1,a,s) &= (a_1(t),\ldots,a_k(t))\\
V_{d_j,1}(t+1,a,s) &= V_{d_{j-1},2}(t,a,s) & j = 2,\ldots,n-1\\
V_{d_j,2}(t+1,a,s) &= V_{d_j,1}(t,a,s) & j = 1,\ldots,n-1\\
V_{d_j,3}(t+1,a,s) &= V_{p_{j+1}}(t,a,s) & j = 1,\ldots,n-2\\
V_{d_{n-1},3}(t+1,a,s) &= V_{d_n}(t,a,s)\\
V_{d_n}(t+1,a,s) &= V_{m_n}(t,a,s)\\
V_{m_1}(t+1,a,s) &= r_n^B \cdot^B (a_1(t),\ldots,a_k(t))\\
V_{m_j}(t+1,a,s) &= r_{n-j+1}^B \cdot^B V_{d_{j-1},2}(t,a,s) & j = 2,\ldots,n\\
V_{p_j}(t+1,a,s) &= V_{m_j}(t,a,s) +^B V_{d_j,3}(t,a,s) & j = 1,\ldots,n-1.
\end{aligned}
$$

Component abstraction. To compare the behaviours of N_1 and N_2 we first define mappings between their components.

Spaces. The respacing $\pi : I_1 \to I_2$, illustrated by the dotted boxes in Figure 8, is defined by

$$\pi(d_{j,1}) = \pi(d_{j,2}) = \pi(d_{j,3}) = \pi(m_j) = \pi(p_j) = j \qquad 1 \le j < n$$
$$\pi(d_n) = \pi(m_n) = n.$$

Clocks. Each clock cycle of the abstract convolver N_2 is represented by two clock cycles of the bit-level algorithm N_1; we thus define a retiming $\lambda : T_1 \to T_2$, for all $t \in T_1$, by $\lambda(t) = \lfloor t/2 \rfloor$. The corresponding immersion $\overline{\lambda} : T_2 \to T_1$ is defined, for all $t \in T_2$, by $\overline{\lambda}(t) = 2t$, and $Start_\lambda$ is defined by $Start_\lambda = \{0,2,4,\ldots\}$.

Data. Using the data abstraction map h, we define a space consistent global state abstraction map $\phi : \{0,1\}^{Ch_1} \to A^{Ch_2}$ for all N_1 states $s \in \{0,1\}^{Ch_1}$ as follows:

$$\phi(s)(j,u) = h(s(d_{j,2},1),\ldots,s(d_{j,2},k)) \qquad j < n$$
$$\phi(s)(j,v) = h(s(p_j,1),\ldots,s(p_j,k)) \qquad j < n$$
$$\phi(s)(n,v) = h(s(d_n,1),\ldots,s(d_n,k)).$$

Input streams. We define an input stream abstraction map $\Theta : [T_1 \to \{0,1\}]^k \to [T_2 \to A]$, for all $a \in [T_1 \to \{0,1\}]^k$ and $t \in T_2$, by

$$\Theta(a)(t) = h(a_1(2t),\ldots,a_k(2t)).$$

We see that the data supplied by the k sources of N_1 at even valued clock cycles is abstracted using the data abstraction map h. This map is consistent with the retiming λ and the (trivial) source abstraction map $\eta : In_1 \to In_2$ defined for all $i \in In_1$ by $\eta(i) = src$.

Abstraction of global behaviour. We now formalise the notion that the global behaviour of the first convolver abstracts that of the bit-level convolver N_1 defined above. Let V_1 and V_2 be the global state functions determined from the channel state functions of these two SCAs. It is possible for the correctness of this SCA abstraction to be proven mathematically.

Theorem. The global operation of N_2 abstracts that of N_1 with respect to the component abstraction maps defined above for any initial state and input streams, at all clock cycles in $Start_\lambda = \{0,2,4\ldots\}$; that is, the following diagram commutes:

$$
\begin{array}{ccccccc}
T_2 \times & [T_2 \to A] & \times & A^{Ch_2} & \xrightarrow{\;\;V_2\;\;} & A^{Ch_2} \\
\big\uparrow{\lambda} & \big\uparrow{\Theta} & & \big\uparrow{\phi} & & \big\uparrow{\phi} \\
Start_\lambda \times [T_1 \to \{0,1\}]^k & \times \{0,1\}^{Ch_1} & & & \xrightarrow{\;\;V_1\;\;} & \{0,1\}^{Ch_1}
\end{array}
$$

6.4 Example: Approximation Between Models of Cardiac Tissue

In this section we define a second model of the electrical activity of the heart, and compare its behaviour with that of the CODE model of Section 5.4. The PDE model we will define has been introduced in [AP96] to reconstruct some basic properties of *electrical wave propagation* in cardiac tissue, including action potential shape, dispersion and restitution properties. Unlike the CODE model, the PDE does not model behaviour at the cellular level, although we might regard it as approximating biophysical processes at a very abstract level. Compared with biophysically detailed models such as the CODE of Section 5.4, the computing resources required for simulating the behaviour of large volumes of muscle with simple models like this are modest, which is one reason for their popularity. In fact, it will not be feasible to perform whole-heart simulations using cellular models for some time to come; recent computations using a supercomputer were limited to modelling the behaviour in a tiny two-dimensional portion of tissue [WKVN93]. Phenomenological PDE models such as the one defined here are commonly used for simulations of whole-heart behaviour [AP96,PH97].

In [HPT95,HPT98] the concepts of hierarchy for SCAs discussed in this paper are extended to allow *multi-level, hybrid* models of cardiac activity to be defined, where different regions of tissue are modelled using different, interacting, SCAs. Modelling small regions of tissue with biophysically derived, but computationally demanding CODEs embedded within a large-scale (e.g. whole-heart) phenomenological PDE system reconstructs both global wave behaviour (by the PDE), as well as local biophysics within the given regions (by the CODEs), and experimentation with the model requires only modest computing power.

A PDE model of wave propagation. The PDE model comprises two equations:

$$\frac{\partial v}{\partial t} = -8v(v - 0.1)(v - 1) - vu + e + \frac{\partial^2 v}{\partial x^2}$$

$$\frac{\partial u}{\partial t} = \varepsilon(v, u)(-u - 8v(v - 1.1)).$$

The first equation approximates the tissue's fast excitation processes, which we will identify with voltage. The second equation approximates slow processes which we refer to as tissue "recovery". Here, t and x are time and space variables, and e is a time- and space-dependent variable that models electrical stimuli. The map $\varepsilon(v, u) = 0.002 + 0.01u/(v + 0.14)$ represents the excitability of the tissue.

We define a finite difference approximation to this model as an SCA depicted:

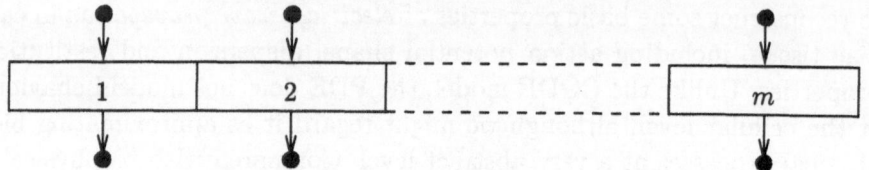

that computes over the set $\mathbb{R}$, with numerical parameters Δt (time step) and Δx (space step). To distinguish clearly between the CODE and PDE models and their components, we denote the CODE SCA by N_1 and the new PDE SCA by N_2, and rename the components T, I, In, Ch and Out of Section 5.4 by T_1, I_1, In_1, Ch_1 and Out_1, and the observable state function V_{out} by $V_{1,out}$. We will also assume that N_1 comprises a network of $n = 4m$ modules.

The model computes on data from the set $\mathbb{R}$ with respect to a clock T_2. Let $I_2 = \{1, \ldots, m\}$ index the modules and stimulation sources of the PDE model N_2, and let $Ch_2 = \{(j, v), (j, u) \mid j \in I_2\}$ index its channels where v denotes voltage and u denotes recovery. Since we are interested in observing the voltages of the system, let $Out_2 = \{(j, v) \mid j \in I_2\}$ be the set of output channels.

The module functions are determined by the finite difference method and the numerical parameters Δt and Δx. Let each (non-boundary) cell $j = 2, \ldots, m - 1$ compute

$$f_{j,v}, f_{j,u} : \mathbb{R}^2 \times \mathbb{R}^2 \times \mathbb{R} \to \mathbb{R}$$

for channels (j, v) and (j, u) respectively, defined, for all cell states $(a, b) \in \mathbb{R}^2$, left and right neighbour's voltages $a_l, a_r \in \mathbb{R}$, and input stimuli $e \in \mathbb{R}$, by

$$f_{j,v}(a, b, a_l, a_r, e) = a + \Delta t(-8a(a - 0.1)(a - 1) - ab + e)$$
$$+ \frac{\Delta t}{\Delta x^2}(a_l - 2a + a_r)$$
$$f_{j,u}(a, b, a_l, a_r, e) = b + \Delta t(\varepsilon(a, b)(-b - 8a(a - 1.1))).$$

(The left- and rightmost cells $j = 1, m$ share module functions $f_{j,v}, f_{j,u} : \mathbb{R}^2 \times \mathbb{R} \times \mathbb{R} \to \mathbb{R}$ defined using equations similar to the above, but dependent on a single nearest neighbour's voltage.)

For each $(j, w) \in Ch_2$ we define a channel state function

$$V_{j,w} : T_2 \times [T_2 \to \mathbb{R}]^{I_2} \times \mathbb{R}^{Ch_2} \to \mathbb{R}$$

for all stimulation streams $a \in [T_2 \to \mathbb{R}]^{I_2}$ and initial states $s \in \mathbb{R}^{Ch_2}$, at time 0 by $V_{j,w}(0, a, s) = s(j, w)$, and at time $t + 1$ for $j = 2, \ldots, m - 1$, by

$$V_{j,w}(t+1, a, s) = f_{j,w}(V_{j,v}(t, a, s), V_{j,u}(t, a, s),$$
$$V_{j-1,v}(t, a, s), V_{j+1,v}(t, a, s), a_j(t))$$

and

$$V_{1,w}(t+1, a, s) = f_{1,w}(V_{1,v}(t, a, s), V_{1,u}(t, a, s), V_{2,v}(t, a, s), a_1(t))$$
$$V_{m,w}(t+1, a, s) = f_{m,w}(V_{m,v}(t, a, s), V_{m,u}(t, a, s), V_{m-1,v}(t, a, s), a_m(t)).$$

Observable behaviour. We define the observable behaviour

$$V_{2,out} : T_2 \times [T_2 \to \mathbb{R}]^{I_2} \times \mathbb{R}^{Ch_2} \to \mathbb{R}^{Out_2}$$

of the PDE, for all $t \in T_2$, $a \in [T_2 \to \mathbb{R}]^{I_2}$ and $s \in \mathbb{R}^{Ch_2}$, by

$$V_{2,out}(t, a, s) = (V_{1,v}(t, a, s), V_{2,v}(t, a, s) \ldots, V_{m,v}(t, a, s)).$$

We illustrate the model's observable behaviour using a simulation similar to that of the CODE model in Figure 5. Consider a system comprising $m = 500$ cells representing a 160mm strand of cardiac tissue as for the CODE model, thus assuming a PDE cell represents a 0.32mm sequence of 4 cardiac (and CODE) cells. Numerical parameter values $\Delta t = 0.112$ and $\Delta x = 1.57$ give a stable solution to the PDE and a good approximation to the action potential duration, restitution and wave propagation velocity of the CODE model, taking each clock cycle to represent 0.05ms or 5 CODE clock cycles. Figure 9 shows the voltages along the space at 50ms (1000 clock cycle) intervals following an initial stimulus of value 0.2 at the left-most cell for a period of 2ms or 40 clock cycles (achieved by taking $a_1(t) = 0.2$ for $t < 40$ and $a_j(t) = 0$ for all other j and t) for an initially resting system ($s(j, w) = 0$ for all $(j, w) \in Ch_2$).

Component abstraction. We compare the components of the PDE model N_2 with those of the CODE model N_1 in order to compare their behaviours.

Spaces. Each PDE cell represents four neighbouring CODE cells; this fact is formalised by a respacing $\pi : I_1 \to I_2$ defined, for all CODE cells $j \in I_1$, by $\pi(j) = \lceil j/4 \rceil$. Thus each PDE cell $j \in I_2$ abstracts CODE cells $\pi^{-1}(j) = \{4j - 3, 4j - 2, 4j - 1, 4j\}$.

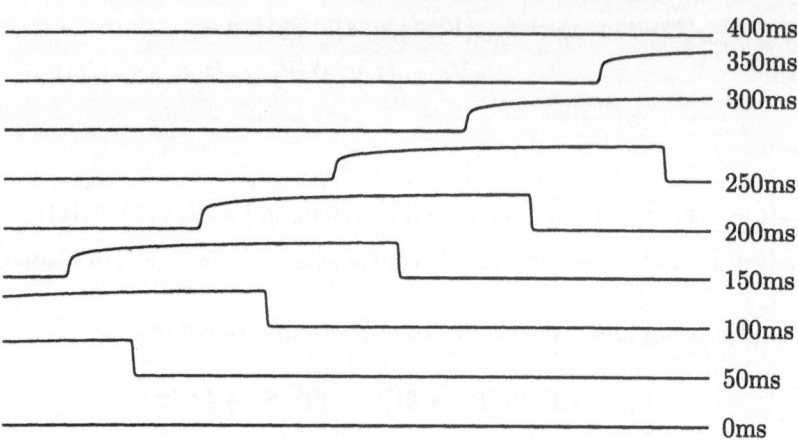

400ms
350ms
300ms

250ms

200ms

150ms

100ms

50ms

0ms

Fig. 9. An action potential propagating from left-to-right along the PDE model following a single stimulus at the left-most cell. Voltage is plotted against space at 50ms intervals.

Clocks. We define a linear retiming $\lambda : T_1 \to T_2$ by $\lambda(t) = \lfloor t/5 \rfloor$ with the intention that the CODE clock T_1 is five times faster than the PDE clock T_2.

Data. We now define the state abstraction map $\phi : \mathbb{R}^{Ch_1} \to [Ch_2 \rightarrowtail \mathbb{R}]$ relating global states of the CODE model N_1 with those of the PDE model N_2. Notice that ϕ maps onto partial PDE states since we cannot compare fully the global states of the two models.

Values on each PDE voltage channel (j, v) abstract values on the voltage channels of the set $\pi^{-1}(j) = \{4j - 3, 4j - 2, 4j - 1, 4j\}$ of four CODE cells abstracted by j. We use a simple averaging/scaling technique to map voltages, determined from the minimum and maximum voltage values that ordinarily occur in each of the models. For the CODE model, a propagating action potential generates minimum and maximum voltage values of -94.25 and 48.25 (mV) respectively; in the PDE model the normal minimum and maximum values are 0 and 1. (In some circumstances, voltage values can fall outside these limits, by small amounts, in both models.) Using these values we define ϕ, for all global CODE states $s \in \mathbb{R}^{Ch_1}$ and PDE voltage channels $(j, v) \in Ch_2$ by

$$\phi(s)(j, v) = (average(s(i, v) \mid i \in \pi^{-1}(j)) + 94.25)/142.5$$
$$= (average(s(4j - 3, v), \ldots, s(4j, v)) + 94.25)/142.5.$$

The second equation in the PDE model N_2 represents slow processes, which includes everything in the CODE model with the exception of voltage. Due to the biological detail of the CODE model N_1, expressed largely by the computation of each CODE cell's 16 local non-voltage states, it is pointless to attempt to completely formulate an abstraction map. Almost always, values on each PDE recovery channel (j, u) will not approximate the state of the set $\pi^{-1}(j) \times dyn$ of 64 channels, even for fairly weak notions of approximation. By Section 6.1 however, there must exist at least one CODE state $s \in \mathbb{R}^{Ch_1}$ for which $\phi(s) \in \mathbb{R}^{Ch_2}$ is totally defined. The most useful state for comparing the two models' behaviours is one corresponding to uniformly resting (or completely recovered) tissue (such a state was used as the initial state in the simulation illustrated in Figure 5). Let us define a state $s \in \mathbb{R}^{\pi^{-1}(j)}$ of the subspace $\pi^{-1}(j)$ to be at rest with respect to non-voltage channels if, for all $i \in \pi^{-1}(j)$ and $w \in dyn$, $s(i, w) = rest_w$ where $rest_w \in \mathbb{R}$ is termed the *resting value* for w-channels. Resting tissue in the PDE model N_2 is represented by the value 0. We therefore define ϕ, for all N_1 states $s \in \mathbb{R}^{Ch_1}$ and N_2 recovery channels $(j, u) \in Ch_2$, by

$$\phi(s)(j, u) = \begin{cases} 0 & \text{if } s(i, w) = rest_w \text{ for all } i \in \pi^{-1}(j) \text{ and } w \in dyn \\ \uparrow & \text{otherwise.} \end{cases}$$

The map ϕ is obviously space consistent, and since its observable (voltage) part $\phi_{obs} : \mathbb{R}^{Out_1} \to \mathbb{R}^{Out_2}$ maps only onto totally defined observable states of N_2, we can define a notion of observable approximation between the two models.

Input streams. Finally, we define a function $\Theta : [T_1 \to \mathbb{R}]^{I_1} \to [T_2 \to \mathbb{R}]^{I_2}$ that compares global streams of stimuli between the two models. We define Θ to be consistent with λ, and with π viewed as a source abstraction map: for each coordinate $\Theta_j : [T_1 \to \mathbb{R}]^{I_1} \to [T_2 \to \mathbb{R}]$ of Θ (for $j \in I_2$) the value $\Theta_j(a)(t) \in \mathbb{R}$ abstracted for source j at time $t \in T_2$ from a set $a \in [T_1 \to \mathbb{R}]^{I_1}$ of CODE input streams should depend only on the 20 values supplied at times $\lambda^{-1}(t) = \{5t, \ldots, 5t + 4\}$ by the set $\pi^{-1}(j) = \{4j - 3, \ldots, 4j\}$ of sources.

It is difficult to meaningfully define each Θ_j as a total function, and not really necessary to compare the models: stimuli streams are a somewhat artificial mechanism for initiating action potentials in models of tissue not integrated into the whole-heart (in the heart, a special region of tissue, the sino-atrial node, generates action potentials which propagate throughout the muscle). We define the map Θ to be partial with non-empty domain

$dom(\Theta)$. The map Θ is defined where, for all $j \in I_2$ and $t \in T_2$, the above 20 values are (i) all 0, representing an absence of stimulation; or (ii) all -30, representing a uniform stimulation of 30nA suitable for generating (at least for resting tissue) an action potential. Corresponding suitable values in the PDE model N_2 are 0 and 0.2. The domain of Θ is given by

$$dom(\Theta) = \{a \in [T_1 \to \mathbb{R}]^{I_1} \mid$$
$$(\forall j \in I_2)(\forall t \in T_2)(\forall i \in \pi^{-1}(j))(\forall c \in \lambda^{-1}(t))$$
$$[a_i(c) = 0 \text{ or } a_i(c) = -30]\}$$

and we define each Θ_j, for all $a \in dom(\Theta)$ and $t \in T_2$, by

$$\Theta_j(a)(t) = \begin{cases} 0 & \text{if } a_i(c) = 0 \text{ for all } i \in \pi^{-1}(j) \text{ and } c \in \lambda^{-1}(t) \\ 0.2 & \text{if } a_i(c) = -30 \text{ for all } i \in \pi^{-1}(j) \text{ and } c \in \lambda^{-1}(t). \end{cases}$$

Approximation of observable behaviour. We now define one notion in which the observable behaviour of the PDE model N_2 can be said to approximate that of the CODE model N_1.

Let $d : \mathbb{R}^{Out_2} \times \mathbb{R}^{Out_2} \to \mathbb{R}^+$ be a metric that compares two global observable states of the PDE model, and is defined, for all $s_1, s_2 \in \mathbb{R}^{Out_2}$, by

$$d(s_1, s_2) = \sum_{(j,v) \in Out_2} \mid s_1(j, v) - s_2(j, v) \mid$$

such that $d(s_1, s_2)$ is the sum of the differences of cell voltages across the space.

Due to the biological complexity of the CODE model, there are some streams, initial states and times for which its observable behaviour will not be approximated by the PDE model, even for reasonably large tolerances. For example, the PDE model does not accurately reproduce the *vulnerability* properties of the CODE model, which deal with the effects of stimulating tissue a short distance behind a travelling action potential. Depending on the strength and position of the stimulus, either (i) no new action potential is initiated, (ii) a single action potential is generated which travels in the opposite direction from the original wave; or (iii) two action potentials are generated, one travelling in either direction. An input stream that gives rise to one of these cases in the CODE model may (when abstracted) result in a different case for the PDE model. If so, after a short time period, the action potential positions will not match between the two models, giving large values of d.

However, for *many* cases the observable behaviour of the PDE model *will* approximate that of the CODE model. A simple example is given by the values used in the simulations of Figures 5 and 9. This does not yield a mathematically provable theorem, but we do obtain, from experimentation, a useful result.

Experimental result. There exist subsets $sub(T_1) \subseteq Start_\lambda$, $sub([T_1 \to \mathbb{R}]^{I_1}) \subset [T_1 \to \mathbb{R}]^{I_1}$ and $sub(\mathbb{R}^{Ch_1}) \subseteq dom_p(\phi)$ useful for practical modelling purposes, such that for all clock cycles $t \in sub(T_1)$, stream sets $a \in sub([T_1 \to \mathbb{R}]^{I_1})$ and initial states $s \in sub(\mathbb{R}^{Ch_1})$,

$$d(\phi_{obs}(V_{1,out}(t, a, s)), V_{2,out}(\lambda(t), \Theta(a), \phi(s)) < \varepsilon$$

for an acceptably small value of $\varepsilon \in \mathbb{R}^+$. A fact important for practical purposes, is that when all the subsets are finite, approximation can be exhaustively tested for.

7   Concluding Remarks

Our conception of a theory of hardware is very broad. In particular, it includes within its scope applications to the analysis of digital hardware, and of physical and biological systems. For example, we would wish to include in the desiderata for a theory the capability of integrating digital and biological systems. This integration is needed in applications where an implantable cardiac device is coupled to cardiac tissue, forming a single system. More ambitiously perhaps, we would wish the theory to account for similarities and differences between hardware, firmware and wetware. We are far from such a comprehensive theory at present.

We posed, in the Introduction, the Integrative Hierarchy Problem for a theory of hardware which requires a mathematical theory that can relate and integrate a range of mathematical models of systems at different levels of abstraction. This means that we need formal concepts that embrace models of hardware, physical and biological systems and that explain how to compare, couple, and partially substitute such models.

The aim of this paper is to pose this general hierarchy problem and to report on some initial progress of our theoretical analysis of its solution.

In the paper we have introduced a simple definition of spatially extended system which clearly embraces a broad range of computing, physical and biological models. We have used the general theory of data types to show that computable systems, and computable systems that approximate continuous systems, can be defined very simply by small finite sets of equations. Thus we have established a prima facie case that the algebraic theory of data and equational specifications can successfully attack the general problem. We also gave some simple definitions of hierarchical structure between two SESs.

In the second half of the paper we studied synchronous concurrent algorithms (SCAs). We showed that SCAs are indeed SESs, and that they model both computer hardware and biological systems. We applied the hierarchical notions about SESs to derive appropriate hierarchical notions for SCAs. These notions were then used to hierarchically analyse algorithms for signal processing and cardiac tissue.

Our intention is to make a conceptual contribution to the theory of hardware. Within the confines of our algebraic approach, we have concentrated on the narrow task of exploring the essential scientific structure of the Integrative Hierarchy Problem, while emphasising the full generality of its application. This theoretical analysis is far from over, of course. For example, there are many problems hidden in case studies, such as the hierarchical relationship between discrete digital and continuous electrical models of chips, and the coupling of digital and biological systems.

Outside the algebraic approach, there are questions concerning the relationship between our models and the various theories of hybrid control systems (see the various approaches in [GNRR93], for example). This field of applications is blessed with a landscape of models and logics for reasoning about the behaviour and control of timed state systems, timed automata, and abstract machines.

Furthermore, work is needed on questions concerning the hierarchy, including the refinement, parameterisation, modularity and scalability of our models. These are basic concerns underlying hardware description languages, of course.

On a practical front the SCA approach has been used in the modelling and specification of examples of increasing size in both hardware and biological systems. For example, the methods for the study of microprocessors, started in [HT93], has been applied to complex examples in [Fox98] and [FH99], and to the JAVA virtual machine in [Ste99]. The methods for the study of biological excitable media have been used in our programme on heart simulation [HPT95,HPT96a].

Acknowledgements

We thank W Dosch, M Holcombe and A Stümpel for many helpful comments made on a draft of this paper.

References

[AP96]   R R Aliev and A V Panfilov. A simple two-variable model of cardiac excitation. *Chaos, Solitons and Fractals*, 7:293–301, 1996.

[BHP97]   J A Bergstra, J A Hillebrand, and A Ponse. Grid protocols based on synchronous communication. *Science of Computer Programming*, 29(1–2):199–233, 1997.

[Bla97]   J Blanck. Domain representability of metric spaces. *Annals of Pure and Applied Logic*, 83:225–247, 1997.

[BP99]   J A Bergstra and A Ponse. Grid protocol specifications. 1999. In this volume.

[BT82]   J A Bergstra and J V Tucker. The completeness of the algebraic specification methods for computable data types. *Information and Control*, 54:186–200, 1982.

[EST90]   S M Eker, V Stavridou, and J V Tucker. Verification of synchronous concurrent algorithms using OBJ3. A case study of the pixel planes architecture. In *Proceedings of a Workshop on Designing Correct Circuits*. Springer-Verlag, 1990.

[FH99]   A C J Fox and N A Harman. Algebraic models of superscalar microprocessor implementations: A case study. 1999. In this volume.

[Fox98]   A C J Fox. *Algebraic Models for Advanced Microprocessors*. PhD thesis, Department of Computer Science, University of Wales Swansea, 1998.

[GNRR93]   R L Grossman, A Nerode, A P Ravn, and H Rischel, editors. *Hybrid systems*. Lecture Notes in Computer Science 736. Springer-Verlag, 1993.

[HPT95]   A V Holden, M J Poole, and J V Tucker. Reconstructing the heart. *Chaos, Solitons and Fractals*, 5:691–704, 1995.

[HPT96a]   A V Holden, M J Poole, and J V Tucker. An algorithmic model of the mammalian heart: propagation, vulnerability, re-entry and fibrillation. *International Journal of Bifurcation and Chaos*, 6:1623–1635, 1996.

[HPT96b]   A V Holden, M J Poole, and J V Tucker. A theoretical framework for analysis and synthesis of networks of neurones. In R Moreno-Díaz and J Mira-Mira, editors, *Brain Processes, Theories and Models*, pages 320–329. MIT Press, 1996.

[HPT98]   A V Holden, M J Poole, and J V Tucker. Hierarchical reconstructions of cardiac tissue. Technical Report CSR 6-98, Department of Computer Science, University of Wales Swansea, 1998.

[HPTZ94]   A V Holden, M J Poole, J V Tucker, and H Zhang. Coupling CMLs and the synchronisation of a multilayer neural computing system. *Chaos, Solitons and Fractals*, 4:2249–2268, 1994.

[HT93]   N A Harman and J V Tucker. Algebraic specifications and the correctness of microcomputers. In G J Milne and E L Pierre, editors, *Correct hardware design and verification methods*, Lecture Notes in Computer Science 683, pages 92–108. Springer-Verlag, 1993.

[HT96]   N A Harman and J V Tucker. Algebraic models of microprocessors: Architecture and organisation. *Acta Informatica*, 33:421–456, 1996.

[HTT88]   K M Hobley, B C Thompson, and J V Tucker. Specification and verification of synchronous concurrent algorithms: a case study of a convolution algorithm. In G Milne, editor, *The Fusion of Hardware Design and Verification*, pages 347–374. North-Holland, 1988.

[HTT91]   A V Holden, J V Tucker, and B C Thompson. Can excitable media be considered as computational systems? *Physica D*, 49:240–246, 1991.

[HTZP92]   A V Holden, J V Tucker, H Zhang, and M J Poole. Coupled map lattices as computational systems. *Chaos*, 2:367–376, 1992.

[Kan92]   K Kaneko, editor. *Coupled Map Lattices: Theory and Applications*. John Wiley, 1992.

[Kun82]   H T Kung. Why systolic architectures? *Computer*, pages 37–46, January 1982.

[Mos64]   Y N Moschovakis. Recursive metric spaces. *Fundamenta Mathematicae*, 55:215–238, 1964.

[MT92]   K Meinke and J V Tucker. Universal algebra. In D Gabbay S Abramsky and T S E Maibaum, editors, *Handbook of Logic in Computer Science*, volume 1, pages 189–411. Oxford University Press, 1992.

[Nob90]   D Noble. Oxsoft Heart program, Oxsoft Ltd, Oxford, 1990.

[PH97]   A V Panfilov and A V Holden, editors. *Computational Biology of the Heart*. John Wiley & Sons, 1997.

[RM86]   D E Rumelhart and J L McClelland, editors. *Parallel Distributed Processing. Explorations in the Microstructure of Cognition. (Two volumes)*. MIT Press, 1986.

[Sav98]   J E Savage. *Models of Computation*. Addison-Wesley, 1998.

[SHT88]   V Stoltenberg-Hansen and J V Tucker. Complete local rings as domains. *Journal of Symbolic Logic*, 53:603–624, 1988.

[SHT95]   V Stoltenberg-Hansen and J V Tucker. Effective algebras. In D Gabbay S Abramsky and T S E Maibaum, editors, *Handbook of Logic in Computer Science*, volume 4, pages 357–526. Oxford University Press, 1995.

[SHT97]   V Stoltenberg-Hansen and J V Tucker. Concrete models of computation for topological algebras. Technical Report 34, University of Uppsala, Mathematics Department, 1997.

[Ste99]   K Stephenson. Towards an algebraic specification of the JAVA virtual machine. 1999. In this volume.

[TT94]   B C Thompson and J V Tucker. Equational specification of synchronous concurrent algorithms and architectures (2nd edition). Technical Report CSR 15-94, Department of Computer Science, University of Wales Swansea, 1994.

[Tuc91]   J V Tucker. Theory of computation and specification over abstract data types and its applications. In F L Bauer, editor, *Logic, Algebra and Computation*, pages 1–39. Springer-Verlag, 1991.

[TZ92]   J V Tucker and J I Zucker. Theory of computation over stream algebras, and its applications. In I M Havel and V Koubek, editors, *Mathematical Foundations of Computer Science*, Lecture Notes In Computer Science 629. Springer-Verlag, 1992.

[Wei87]   K Weihrauch. *Computability*. EATCS Monographs on Theoretical Computer Science 9. Springer-Verlag, 1987.

[Wir91]   M Wirsing. Algebraic specification. In J van Leeuwen, editor, *The Handbook of Theoretical Computer Science*, pages 675–788. Elsevier, 1991.

[WKVN93] R L Winslow, A L Kimball, A Varghese, and D Noble. Simulating cardiac sinus and atrial network dynamics on the Connection Machine. *Physica D*, 64:282–298, 1993.

[Wol86]   S Wolfram. *Theory and applications of cellular automata*. World Scientific, 1986.

Towards an Algebraic Specification of the Java Virtual Machine

K Stephenson

Department of Computer Science
University of Wales Swansea
Swansea SA2 8PP UK

Abstract. We develop an algebraic specification of the architecture of an abstract and simplified version of the Java Virtual Machine (JVM). This concentration on the implementation-independent features of the machine allows us to build a clean and easily comprehensible model in which its structure is emphasised. We then axiomatise the semantics of programs operating on this architecture. We also consider how we can concretise this abstract model which provides us with a firm foundation for exploring the entire JVM and thus of analysing the correctness of Java implementations.

1 Introduction

Virtual machines are software emulations of physical, or physically realisable, machines; they act as "synthetic computers" (Liu [1996]). Virtual machines are used to describe and standardise the behaviour of a variety of applications across a range of platforms and so must abstract from architectural-dependent details.

For example, the operational semantics of programming languages, from the SECD machine (Landin [1964]) through to the abstract rewriting machine (Kamperman and Walters [1993]), explain the behaviour of programs in terms of their effect on abstract or virtual machines. This idea has been extended and applied to the implementation of a number of languages, for example, the Warren Abstract Machine for Prolog (Warren [1983]), the Java Virtual Machine for Java (Gosling [1995], Lindholm and Yellin [1997]).

Related to this implementation theme, the universal intermediate language UNCOL (Strong *et al.* [1958]) was envisaged as a general intermediate language for abstract machines. This goal has been realised for particular compiler front-ends, with, for example, P-Code for Pascal (described in Nori *et al.* [1981]) and the Register Transfer Language (Davidson and Fraser [1984]) which has been used for a number of languages.

Other application areas revolve around that of operating systems. The IBM VM operating system series (for example, the VM/370 (Seawright and MacKinnen [1979])) and Microsoft Windows 95 (King [1994]) both implement virtual machines to facilitate compatibility between product versions. Virtual machines are now also being used to enable executable code to be emulated on different platforms, for example, MS-DOS based products running on INTEL processors.

Recently, there has been renewed interest in virtual machines through their use in implementing the Java programming language: it is the ability of Java applets to deliver code across the internet which will execute on different platforms, that has driven this interest in employing an architecturally neutral model of execution in the form of the Java Virtual Machine (JVM). We take the JVM as a case study for the application of general techniques to the semantic modelling of deterministic machines. We show that these methods apply smoothly to virtual machines, helping to close the gap between semantic models of programs, systems and hardware.

Specifically, in this paper, we take the methods of algebraically modelling microprocessors described in Harman and Tucker [1996, 1997] and Fox and Harman [1998], and

(i) axiomatise the modelling process to yield an algebraic specification framework in Section 2 for defining the semantics of machines;

(ii) apply these techniques to the algebraic specification of the architecture (Section 3) and semantics (Sections 4) of an abstract (and simplified) version of the JVM; and

(iii) explain how we can concretise our abstract JVM model to provide a specification of the JVM in Section 5.

We axiomatise the semantics of the JVM by describing how the system evolves over time. We iterate a next-state function on a specification of an algebraic model of the JVM and enumerate with a clock the sequence of states produced. We specify this iteration by means of primitive recursive equations.

One of our major concerns is how we can manage the scale of this large example (the concrete JVM has 201 instructions). We first produce a more abstract model of the JVM in Section 3, by removing implementation dependent features. Then we build a specification of the architecture of this abstract JVM by linking together and instantiating generic specifications of abstract data types that describe commonly occurring structures.

These abstractions percolate through to the instruction set, reducing its size to 20 instructions (or rather families of instructions which are indexed by the sort set of the underlying abstract data type that we compute over). We define the next-state function on each of these instructions in Section 4, to produce an axiomatisation of the semantics of the JVM.

Our final task in Section 5 is to relate our abstract model to that of the JVM.

One aim of this work is to continue this modelling process upwards (to Java) and downwards (towards a particular platform). Such models can be integrated within a common framework testing for trusted compilation. This would allow us to trace the progress of the execution of Java programs from their conception in software to their implementation in hardware.

The reader is assumed to have some familiarity with algebraic specifications (Meinke and Tucker [1992]) and the Java Virtual Machine (Lindholm and Yellin [1997]).

Related Work There have been a number of approaches to specifying the JVM.

In Börger and Schulte [1998], the JVM and its instructions are subdivided into incremental sets, and their semantics are modelled using abstract state machines. In addition, compilers from subsets of Java to these languages are constructed.

Hartel *et al.* [1998] produce an executable specification of the semantics of the Java Secure Processor; this is essentially a modified subset of the JVM designed to be sufficiently small to fit onto a smart card.

Pusch [1998] also describes an executable specification of the JVM. An abstract model of the JVM is produced, although she does not exploit the abstractions to as full as an extent as we do. A principle feature of our work is handling the issue of scale; we employ the principles of abstraction and modularisation wherever possible.

Some of the literature on the semantics of the JVM is more biased towards type-checking. For example, Qian [1998] is concerned with producing a static type inference system, and Cohen [1997] uses run-time checks to ensure type-correctness. Much work has focused on typing constraints; see for example, Goldberg [1998], Freund and Mitchell [1998] and Stata and Abadi [1998]. This is an area which we do not concentrate on (to enable the dynamic semantics to be viewed with greater clarity); we presume that the instructions have already been type-checked. However, a thorough investigation could be made using the work in this paper as a foundation.

2 Modelling and Specification Preliminaries

In this section we describe the algebraic specification framework that we use to define the semantics of machines.

2.1 Machine Semantics

We shall define the behaviour of a machine in terms of how the system evolves from one state to another over time. Thus, we consider the execution of a machine from an initial state τ_0 to produce a finite

$$\tau_0, \tau_1, \ldots, \tau_t$$

or infinite sequence

$$\tau_0, \tau_1, \ldots, \tau_t, \ldots$$

of machine states. We shall encode finite sequences $\tau_0, \tau_1, \ldots, \tau_t$ as infinite ones $\tau_0, \tau_1, \ldots, \tau_t, *, *, \ldots$, where $*$ is a distinguished machine state specifically introduced for this purpose.

Time We use a clock $Time$ to enumerate our state sequences. As we use a discrete clock to record events, we can specify the generation of the ticks of the clock with:

specification $TIME$
import
sorts $time$
constants $Zero : \rightarrow time$
operations $Succ : time \rightarrow time$
equations

Next-State Function To define the behaviour of machines, we introduce a function

$$Next : machine\_state \rightarrow machine\_state$$

such that $Next(\tau_t)$ gives the next state τ_{t+1} that results from executing the machine on the state τ_t.

Thus, we can define machine semantics using the iterated map $Next^t$, which we specify by:

```
specification  MACHINE_SEMANTICS
import         MACHINE_STATE, TIME
sorts
constants
operations     Next : machine_state → machine_state
               Sem :  machine_state × time → machine_state
equations
                    Sem(τ, Zero) = τ
                    Sem(τ, Succ(t)) = Sem(Next(τ), t)
```

2.2   Machine States

Thusfar in our model of semantics, we have just assumed that we have some specification *MACHINE_STATE* of the set of states of the machine which includes the distinguished state ∗. We now extend the modelling process as far as we can whilst striving to maintain generality.

Programmable Machine States We want to consider how a machine behaves in response to the execution of programs.

First, we observe that the distinction between programs and states is somewhat blurred; the program is stored within the state, and certain aspects of the state are typically determined by the program to be executed. However, it is useful to be able to separate out these concerns as distinct entities so that we do not consider the program as being hardwired into the state.

Let *PROG* be a specification of the set of programs for the machine (for example, as described later in this section) and *STATE* that of the set of all states of the machine without the program component (for example, the von Neumann general architecture specification given in Section 2.3). We suppose that we have a function

$$Install : prog × state → machine\_state$$

such that $Install(P, \sigma)$ gives the state of the machine which results from loading the program P into memory for execution on the state whose initial values are determined by σ.

We can now specify the concept of a programmable machine state:

specification	*MACHINE_STATE*
import	*PROG, STATE*
sorts	*machine_state*
constants	$* : \rightarrow machine\_state$
operations	$Install : prog \times state \rightarrow machine\_state$
	$\pi^{prog} : \quad machine\_state \rightarrow prog$
equations	
	$\pi^{prog}(Install(P,\sigma)) = P$

Note that projecting out the state component of a machine state $Install(P,\sigma)$ will not necessarily yield σ. (The construction of machine states is not, in general, that of forming a Cartesian product, which we specify in Section 2.3.)

General Architecture Model In order to add further structure to our model, we have to make certain assumptions about the architecture of the machines that we want to perform this process for. We shall take the class of von Neumann machines, whose architecture follows the classical structure illustrated in Figure 1, (although note that we consider the program to be a separate entity from that of the memory).

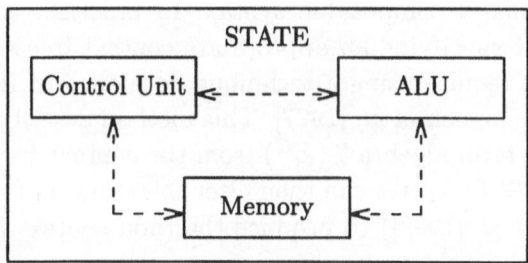

Fig. 1. Von Neumann architecture. The dotted arrows indicate the flow of data between components.

We produce an algebra *State* below that models the architecture of von Neumann machines; we will give a succinct specification *STATE* of this model in Section 2.3 when we have introduced appropriate generic specifications that make this task more manageable.

algebra	*State*
import	*Memory, CU, ALU*
carriers	*State = Memory × CU × ALU*
constants	
operations	δ^{Memory} : *Memory × State → State*
	δ^{CU} : *CU × State → State*
	δ^{ALU} : *ALU × State → State*
definitions	
	$\delta^{Memory}(M',(M,C,A)) = (M',C,A)$
	$\delta^{CU}(C',(M,C,A)) = (M,C',A)$
	$\delta^{ALU}(A',(M,C,A)) = (M,C,A')$

where *Memory*, *CU* and *ALU* are algebraic models of the memory, control unit, and arithmetic and logic unit. We can change these components of *State* with the operations of δ^{Memory}, δ^{CU} and δ^{ALU}. This will allow us to describe how the machine behaves in response to the execution of a program.

Programs We now turn our attention to the program component of machine states.

By application of a result of Bergstra and Tucker [1987], we know that it is possible to algebraically specify the programs of any programming language which has a computable syntax. In practice, we can achieve this effect by first specifying an appropriate context-free superset of the language that we require using a technique developed in Rus [1971] and independently in Goguen *et al.* [1977]. This method describes how we can generate a closed term algebra $T(\Sigma^G)$ from the context-free grammar G, such that $T(\Sigma^G) \cong L(G)$. We can then filter this superset (van Deursen *et al.* [1996], Rees *et al.* [1998]) to produce the (non-context-free) language $L \subseteq L(G)$ that we require.

Example In Section 4, we shall model the semantics of an instruction set for an abstract version of the Java Virtual Machine, which includes:

$$\text{<instrn>} ::= \ldots | \text{Return}_{void} | \text{Goto <instrn\_index>} | \ldots$$

We model these instructions algebraically with the constant

$$\text{Return}_{void} :\to instrn$$

and the function

$$\text{Goto} : instrn\_index \to instrn.$$

In addition though, we have to specify the non-context-free constraints imposed on JVM programs, such as requiring that Goto instructions refer to some instruction of the program.

2.3 Specification Framework

In order to manage the complexity of our models we need to be able to describe the architecture of machines at different levels of abstraction. Furthermore, to manage the scale of the models produced, we shall impose a modular structure on the design; we model the interconnections between components by using simple parameterising mechanisms (flattening) that allow specifications to be instantiated with other specifications.

In this section we specify the structures that we shall find useful for describing the architecture of machines at a high level of abstraction.

Cartesian Products Typically, we can model machine states as certain Cartesian products $CP(A_1, \ldots, A_n)$ of sub-components $A_1, \ldots, A_n$; for example, we can specify the general von Neumann architecture of Section 2.2 by

$$STATE = CP(MEMORY, CU, ALU)$$

where $MEMORY$, CU and ALU are specifications of the memory, control unit and ALU components.

We specify the general construction by:

specification $CP(A_1, \ldots, A_n)$
import $\quad A_1, \ldots, A_n, INDEX_n$
sorts $\quad A$
constants
operations $\quad v: \quad A_1 \times \cdots \times A_n \to A$
$\qquad \ldots, \pi^i : A \to A_i, \ldots$
$\qquad \ldots, \delta^i : A_i \times A \to A, \ldots$
equations
$\qquad \ldots, \pi^i(v(a_1, \ldots, a_n)) = a_i, \ldots$
$\ldots, Equals(i, j) = True \implies \pi^i(\delta^j(a_j, a)) = a_j, \ldots$
$\ldots, Equals(i, j) = False \implies \pi^i(\delta^j(a_j, a)) = \pi^i(a), \ldots$

(To make the presentation more concise, we have used a specification $INDEX_n$ of the indexing set $\{1, \ldots, n\}$, which contains a test for equality.)

Thus, given specifications $A_1, \ldots, A_n$, we can

(*i*) form tuples of elements;

(*ii*) project out the component elements; and

(*iii*) change the values of any tuple component.

Lists One of the simplest structuring mechanisms is that of forming a list of elements from a given data type; the only complication that arises is that we want to be able to have lists that are composed of elements that are of different sorts from an arbitrary specification A with sort set S (which for ease of notation, we denote by $S = \{\ldots, s, \ldots\}$):

```
specification  LIST(A)
import         A,
sorts          list(S)
constants      Empty : → list(S)
operations     ..., Lst_s : s × list(S) → list(S), ...
equations
```

Stacks A central structure of the JVM is the stack; we specify the generic stack structure by:

```
specification  STACK(A)
import         A
sorts          ..., stack_s, ...
               ..., s_stack_underflow, ...
constants      ..., EmptyStack_s : → stack_s, ...
               ..., Underflow_s :    → s_stack_underflow, ...
operations     ..., Push_s : s × stack_s → stack_s, ...
               ..., Pop_s :   stack_s → stack_s, ...
               ..., Top_s :   stack_s → s_stack_underflow, ...
               ..., ι_s :       s → s_stack_underflow, ...
equations
               ..., Top_s(EmptyStack_s) = Underflow_s, ...
               ..., Top_s(Push_s(d, S)) = ι_s(d), ...
               ..., Pop_s(EmptyStack_s) = EmptyStack_s, ...
               ..., Pop_s(Push_s(d, S)) = S, ...
```

Note that later we shall consider how we can concretise this structure to provide a model of the concrete JVM. In particular, at some point in this process we shall merge the family of S-sorted stacks into a single stack. As a consequence, we shall need to know the order in which we take elements of different sorts from the stack. Thus, in our later descriptions of the semantics of the abstract model of the JVM, where such considerations will affect the concrete model, we indicate the relative order of the elements on the stack.

Tables We shall use tables to store arbitrary data types which allow direct access to the data through an indexing mechanism. We impose the restriction that the specification *INDEX* of the indexing scheme comes complete with a specification of the Booleans, and an equality function

$$Equals_{index} : index \times index \rightarrow bool$$

on indices.

---

specification $TABLE(A, INDEX)$
import $A, INDEX,$
sorts $\dots, s_{uninitialised}, \dots$
$\dots, table_s, \dots$
constants $\dots, Empty_s : \quad\quad \rightarrow table_s, \dots$
$\dots, Uninitialised_s : \rightarrow s_{uninitialised}, \dots$
operations $\dots, Read_s : index \times table_s \rightarrow s_{uninitialised}, \dots$
$\dots, Store_s : s \times index \times table_s \rightarrow table_s, \dots$
$\dots, \iota_s : \quad\quad s \rightarrow s_{uninitialised}, \dots$
equations
$\dots, Read_s(i, Empty_s) = Uninitialised_s, \dots$

$\dots, Equals_{index}(i, j) = true \Rightarrow$
$Read_s(i, Store_s(d, j, T)) = \iota_s(d), \dots$

$\dots, Equals_{index}(i, j) = false \Rightarrow$
$Read_s(i, Store_s(d, j, T)) = Read_s(i, T), \dots$

Error-Handling The generic specifications of stacks and tables given above can both return error elements ($Underflow_s$ and $Uninitialised_s$, respectively) in certain circumstances. As these specifications will form the basis of the architectural components of the JVM, these error elements will percolate through to most aspects of the model of the JVM. (For example, the JVM is a stack-based machine, so the execution of the majority of the instructions can potentially create errors.)

We would like our specifications to be strict in their error-handling, but we would like to deal with the propagation of these errors in a manageable fashion.

We could introduce equations to specifically propagate the errors through the specifications, or alternatively, we could introduce some algebraic machinery (for example, Goguen and Meseguer [1992] or Haveraaen and Wagner [1995]) that would automatically deal with the errors. In order to avoid the problems with the explosion of equations that result from the first route, and the introduction of an additional algebraic overhead of the second, we shall adopt a pragmatic view; henceforth, we deliberately omit the additional equations that would be required to give a complete specification.

To illustrate the conventions that we adopt, consider the definition of the instruction

$$Dup_s :\rightarrow instrn$$

from Section 4.1, that duplicates the top value of the operand stack by:

$$[\![Dup_s]\!](\sigma) = \Delta_{+1}^{PC}(Load_s(Fetch_s(\sigma), \sigma))$$

The function

$$Fetch_s : jvm\_state \rightarrow s_{stack\_underflow}$$

takes the top element of the operand stack, and so can produce an error. The functions $Load_s$ (that places an element onto the top of the element stack) and Δ^{PC+1} (that increments the program counter) however, do not produce errors when they are applied, *except* when they simply propagate errors. Thus, we give the type of these functions as

$$Load_s : s \times jvm\_state \rightarrow jvm\_state$$

and

$$\Delta^{PC+1} : jvm\_state \rightarrow jvm\_state$$

so withholding the error propagation typing information:

$$Load_s : \quad s_{stack\_underflow} \times jvm\_state \rightarrow jvm\_state_{stack\_underflow}$$
$$\Delta^{PC+1} : jvm\_state_{stack\_underflow} \rightarrow jvm\_state_{stack\_underflow}$$

In addition, we suppress the error-propagating conditional equations:

$$Equals_{s_{stack\_underflow}}(Fetch_s(\sigma), \iota_s(Underflow)) = True$$
$$\Rightarrow \quad [\![Dup_s]\!](\sigma) = \iota_{jvm\_state}(Underflow)$$

$$Equals_{s_{stack\_underflow}}(Fetch_s(\sigma), \iota_s(Underflow)) = False$$
$$\Rightarrow \quad [\![Dup_s]\!](\sigma) = \Delta_{+1}^{PC}(Load_s(Fetch_s(\sigma), \sigma))$$

It should be emphasised that we do not wish to trivialise the error cases which are important and informative. On restoring the missing error-propagating information to our specifications, we would find that errors would not arise and propagate had we subjected the instructions to some suitable prior analysis (such as that provided in practice by the JVM bytecode verifier). The convention we adopt allows us to treat the dynamic semantics of the JVM with greater clarity.

Filtering As we indicated in Section 2.2, we typically need to impose additional constraints on a specification to define the set of well-formed programs of a language. We shall perform this task by adding a filtering step to the specifications we have introduced. Such filters allow us to define the typically occurring constraints of

distinctness: that elements of a list be distinct from each other;
disjointness: that two lists are disjoint from each other;
completeness: that every element of one list is present in another.

For an axiomatisation of these filters, see Stephenson [1996], Rees *et al.* [1998]. In this paper, we shall simply indicate that we need to apply a filter by prefixing a specification name with "*F*", as in *FCP*, *FTABLE*, etc., and listing which of the properties given above that the filter captures.

3   An Abstract Model of the JVM

To axiomatise the semantics of JVM programs (Java bytecodes), we first build a high-level specification of the JVM in this section which abstracts away any features that could be classed as implementation-dependent. On this architecture that we produce, we describe the semantics (in Section 4) of a set of abstract instructions.

We start in Section 3.1 by presenting an overview of the JVM, concentrating in particular on its architecture. Then in Section 3.2, we describe the abstractions that we have employed in this model, and in Section 3.3, specify the architecture of the abstract machine. Finally, we specify its instruction set in Section 3.4; we devote the whole of Section 4 to specifying the semantics of these instructions.

3.1   Overview of the JVM

The JVM displays characteristics typical of both high- and low-level virtual machines. This hybridisation is intentional, in that the JVM has been designed to be at a sufficiently low level of abstraction so that it can be efficiently executed (by interpretation, compilation or direct execution), whilst being at a sufficiently high level to enable it to be architecturally neutral.

These considerations are reflected in many aspects of the JVM's design. For instance, the JVM, like many abstract machines for high-level languages, but unlike many abstract machines for low-level languages (and many traditional hardware implementations), is a stack-based machine.

Our concern in this paper is that of the essential structure of the JVM: to perform this analysis, we model an abstracted version of the JVM which pays no attention to any implementation-dependent features. We can then reinstate these features to produce a model of the concrete JVM.

Architecture We illustrate the architecture of the abstract JVM in Figure 2 (see Section 3.2 for a description of how this model abstracts from the actual JVM).

First though, we outline the principle components of the JVM and describe their purpose. The JVM has all the characteristics of the classical von Neumann architecture discussed in Section 2.2:

Programs The programs are stored in the *Method Area*. A program for the JVM is low-level in the sense that programs can only be constructed by the sequential composition of instructions. However, the code is designed to support object-oriented structuring: the code is split into classes, each of which defines a set of methods that can be applied to instantiations of a class.

Memory The JVM's memory is termed the *Heap*. Here the class instantiations are stored. Note that the values of the variables that constitute an instantiation can be shared either amongst all the instantiations of a class (static fields) or are tied to particular instances of a class (non-static fields).

ALU The *Operand Stack* and the *Local Variables* of the JVM together constitute its ALU. The operand stack is used as a temporary storage area to calculate the value (if any) that a method computes. The local variables store the parameters that are passed to methods, together with variables that are local to a method.

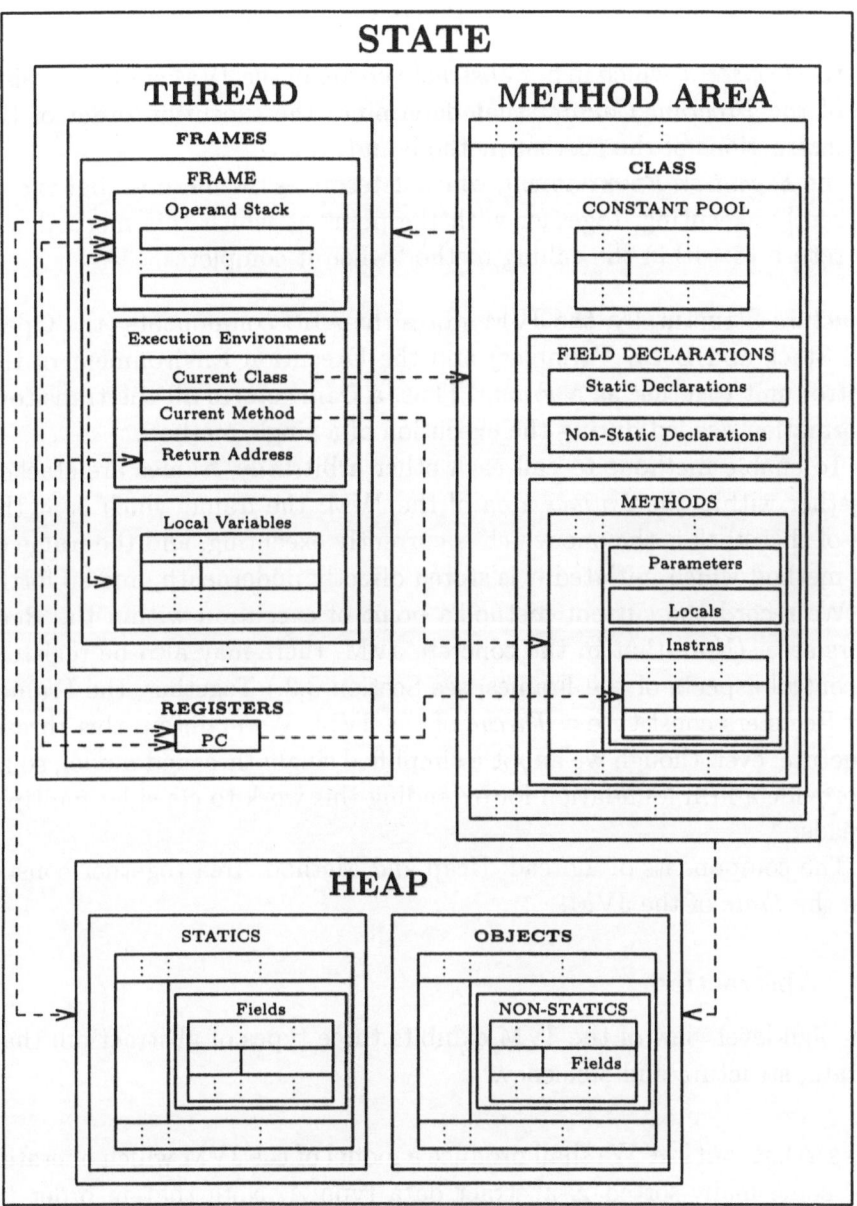

Fig. 2. The architecture of our abstract JVM. The dotted arrows indicate the flow of data between components

Control Unit The control unit of the JVM is split between two areas:

(*i*) the *Registers*, which in our abstract version of the JVM simply consists of the *Program Counter* that determines the execution order of the instructions of the current method; and

(*ii*) the *Execution Environment*, which determines the method that is currently executing, together with the point at which this method will return to within the calling method when it completes.

Structure Structurally, the JVM stores the ALU components (the Operand Stack and Local Variables) and the Execution Environment of the control unit together as a *Frame*. Thus, a frame stores all the transitory information needed during the execution of a single method.

To enable methods to call each other arbitrarily, frames are stacked together within the *Frames* area of the JVM; the frame which is at the top of this stack is the one which is currently executing, and the frame of the method which initiated it is stored directly underneath, and so forth.

We record the current method's point of execution within the Registers area. (Note that in the concrete JVM, there may also be registers to control aspects of the Frames; see Section 3.2.) Together, the Frames and Registers constitute a *Thread* of the JVM. We maintain this thread structure, even though we adopt a simplified single-threaded model, so as to provide a firm foundation for extending this work to consider multiple threads.

The components of Thread, Heap and Method Area together constitute the *State* of the JVM.

3.2 Abstraction

Our high-level view of the JVM exhibits three types of abstraction: that of data, structure and efficiency.

Data Abstraction We shall produce a model of the JVM which operates over some many-sorted Σ-abstract data type A. Note that in order to model the flow-of-control instructions that the JVM has, we shall presume that A specifies a Boolean- and Naturals-standard algebra.

We shall assume that we have a specification for the abstract data type A that

(*i*) imports specifications *INSTRN_INDEX* and *OBJECT_INDEX* for indexing sets which have sort sets *instrn_index* and *object_index*, respectively;

(*ii*) for each sort $s \in S$, determines the equality function

$$Equals_s : s \times s \to bool$$

on elements;

(*iii*) for each sort $s \in S$ and word $w \in S^*$ with $\Sigma_{w,s} \neq \emptyset$, defines the operations

$$Apply_{w,s} : fun_{w,s} \times list(S) \to s_{error}$$

on the set of functions of the data type A, so that $Apply_{w,s}(f, L)$ returns the result of applying the function f to the arguments given in the list L if this is all well-typed, and otherwise returns an error; and

(*iv*) for each sort $s \in S$, defines a default value

$$DefaultValue_s :\to s$$

associated with the sort s.

In order to incorporate the syntax of A into the instructions, we shall assume that we have a specification

$$SIGNATURE(\Sigma)$$

of the signature Σ of A, (for example, Rees *et al.* [1998]).

In addition, we shall also abstract away completely from how this data is represented. We shall simply consider that the abstract JVM is able to store, transfer and manipulate values of the data type A.

Structure Abstraction We shall abstract away from how we implement the different data structures that we use to store the components of the JVM. We can split this idea into three different applications.

Firstly, the internal stack of the concrete JVM is commonly implemented as an array of values, with a pointer (stored in a register) to the value which is the current top of the stack. We shall remove this implementation-dependent feature, and simply specify stacks using the *STACK* data type of Section 2.3.

Secondly, the internal stack of the concrete JVM is used to store three different types of information (the operand values, the execution environment and the local variables). In order to differentiate between these elements, the concrete JVM is commonly implemented using two registers. In our abstract model though, we shall simply consider that these are different structures which we can project out of the state.

Thus, our abstract JVM has just one register (PC) which controls the execution order of the instructions, and the execution environment does not have to perform the rôle of maintaining the internal stack that it typically does in implementations of the JVM.

Thirdly, we shall employ the *TABLE* data structure of Section 2.3 to allow access to values through some location mechanism. We shall consider that we have such indices (for example, the names of variables or constants) by which we can access the locations in which we store these values.

Efficiency Abstraction As the JVM is a practical model of computation, it has efficient versions of the most commonly deployed instructions (in addition to the _quick variants, which we do not consider in this paper). For example, the most basic type of load instructions require the location of the local variable to be specified; the more efficient versions of this instruction are specific to individual locations, so eliminating the need to store and retrieve this information.

As we are interested in modelling functionality rather than efficiency, these efficient versions of instructions have no part to play in our abstract model, (and indeed, our architectural abstractions prevent us from being able to consider such instructions). Later though in Section 5, we shall describe how we can model the effect of these efficient versions on the JVM when we have a more concrete model of the JVM (which uses positions rather than names to locate values).

3.3 Architectural Specification

We need to construct a specification for the architecture of our abstract JVM illustrated in Figure 2. In fact, this is now a straightforward task given our generic specification structures of Section 2 and the abstractions listed in Section 3.2. We illustrate the architecture of our specification for the structure of the abstract JVM in Figure 3.

Notation For convenience, we introduce projection and alteration functions that operate directly on each aspect of the JVM. For example, we define the operations

$$\Pi^{PC} : jvm\_state \rightarrow instrn\_index$$
$$\Delta^{PC} : instrn\_index \times jvm\_state \rightarrow jvm\_state$$

to allow us to access and change respectively, the value of the program counter by:

253

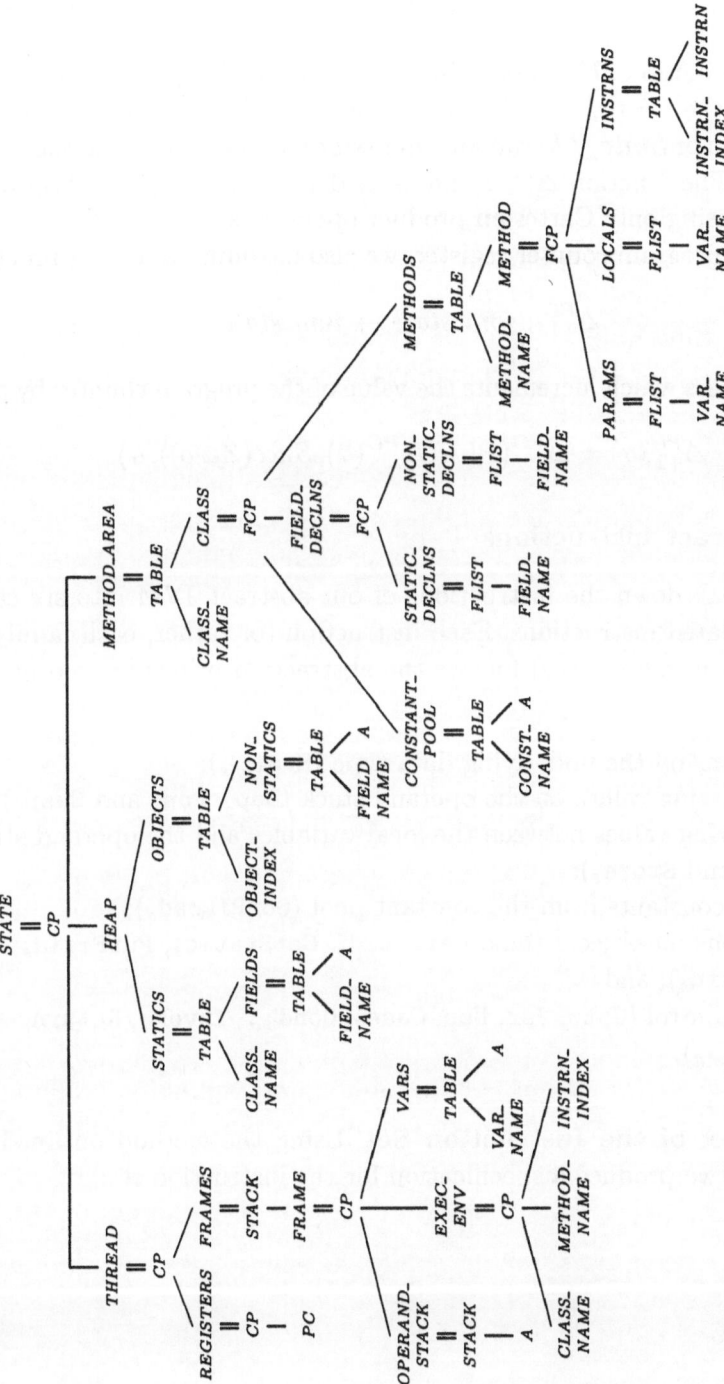

Fig. 3. The specification architecture of our abstract JVM. (For typographical reasons, we have omitted to indicate the reliance of a specification on the underlying abstract data type A or its signature Σ.

$$\Pi^{PC}(\sigma) = \pi^{PC}(\pi^{Registers}(\pi^{Thread}(\sigma)))$$
$$\Delta^{PC}(i,\sigma) = \delta^{Thread}(\delta^{Registers}(\delta^{PC}(i, \Pi^{Registers}(\sigma)), \Pi^{Thread}(\sigma)), \sigma)$$

Thus, the function Π^{PC} works by repeatedly applying projection functions from the Cartesian product specification of Section 2.3, as each of the elements of *State*, *Thread* and *Registers* are Cartesian products (see Figure 3). The function Δ^{PC} is similarly defined (although slightly more involved), using only Cartesian product operations.

For the program counter register, we also introduce a further function

$$\Delta_{+1}^{PC} : jvm\_state \to jvm\_state$$

for conciseness which increments the value of the program counter by one:

$$\Delta_{+1}^{PC}(\sigma) = \Delta^{PC}(Plus(\Pi^{PC}(\sigma), Succ(Zero)), \sigma)$$

3.4 Abstract Instructions

We can break down the instructions of our abstract JVM into six categories of related instructions. Each instruction (or rather, each family of instructions in most cases) follows the abstraction principles laid out in Section 3.2:

(*i*) operations on the underlying data type ($\text{Eval}_{w,s}$);
(*ii*) manipulating values on the operand stack (Dup_s, Pop_s and Swap_s);
(*iii*) transferring values between the local variables and the operand stack (Load_s and Store_s);
(*iv*) loading constants from the constant pool (ConPlLoad_s);
(*v*) operations on objects (New, GetField_s, GetStatic_s, PutField_s and PutStatic_s); and
(*vi*) flow-of-control (Goto, Jsr, Nop, Case_s, $\text{Cond}_{w,s}$, Invoke, Return_s and Return_{void}).

The Syntax of the Instruction Set Using the method outlined in Section 2.2, we produce a specification for the instruction set:

specification	$INSTRN(\Sigma)$	
import	$SIGNATURE(\Sigma), CONST\_NAME, CLASS\_NAME,$	
	$FIELD\_NAME, METHOD\_NAME, VAR\_NAME,$	
	$INSTRN\_INDEX$	
sorts	$instrn$	
constants	Nop :	$\rightarrow instrn$
	New :	$\rightarrow instrn$
	$Return_{void}$:	$\rightarrow instrn$
	$\ldots, Return_s$:	$\rightarrow instrn, \ldots$
	$\ldots, Dup_s$:	$\rightarrow instrn, \ldots$
	$\ldots, Pop_s$:	$\rightarrow instrn, \ldots$
	$\ldots, Swap_{s,s'}$:	$\rightarrow instrn, \ldots$
operations	Goto :	$instrn\_index \rightarrow instrn$
	Jsr :	$instrn\_index \rightarrow instrn$
	Invoke :	$class\_name \times method\_name$
		$\times list(var\_name) \rightarrow instrn$
	$\ldots, Case_s$:	$s \times list(s \times instrn\_index)$
		$\times instrn\_index \rightarrow instrn, \ldots$
	$\ldots, Cond_w$:	$fun_{w,bool} \times instrn\_index$
		$\rightarrow instrn, \ldots$
	$\ldots, Eval_{w,s}$:	$fun_{w,s} \rightarrow instrn, \ldots$
	$\ldots, Load_s$:	$var\_name_s \rightarrow instrn, \ldots$
	$\ldots, Store_s$:	$var\_name_s \rightarrow instrn, \ldots$
	$\ldots, ConPlLoad_s$:	$const\_name_s \rightarrow instrn, \ldots$
	$\ldots, GetField_s$:	$field\_name_s \rightarrow instrn, \ldots$
	$\ldots, GetStatic_s$:	$class\_name \times field\_name_s$
		$\rightarrow instrn, \ldots$
	$\ldots, PutField_s$:	$field\_name_s \rightarrow instrn, \ldots$
	$\ldots, PutStatic_s$:	$class\_name \times field\_name_s$
		$\rightarrow instrn, \ldots$
equations		

The Syntax of Programs As we shall explain in Section 4.7, we create programs from the instruction set by forming tables of individual instructions, labelled by an appropriate indexing scheme (which we specify by *INSTRN_INDEX*). Onto this context-free superset of the syntax, we have to impose some additional constraints on the language to ensure that it satisfies some non-context-free properties; for example that any branch instruction refers to an instruction within the same method.

We now define the semantics of these instructions.

4 Semantics of the Abstract JVM

Using the operations provided by the architecture specification framework illustrated in Figure 3, we define the semantics of the individual instructions of the abstract JVM given in Section 3.4.

This will allow us to define the semantics of abstract JVM programs; recall from Section 2 that to perform this task, we just need to define a next-state function. For this machine, we define our next-state function

$$Next : jvm\_state \rightarrow jvm\_state$$

by

$$Next(\sigma) = [\![Fetch^{Instrn}(\sigma)]\!](\sigma)$$

so that $Next(\sigma)$ locates and executes the current instruction on the state σ. (We define the function $Fetch^{Instrn}$ that performs this location service in Section 4.7.)

4.1 The Operand Stack

As the JVM is a stack-based architecture, rather than being register-based, the operand stack is the hub of all activities concerning the application of functions to data. The data to be manipulated comes from, and is distributed to, the various repositories within the JVM: load instructions deposit values onto the operand stack, and store instructions retrieve values.

Structure At our high level of abstraction, we model the operand stack as a stack of values from the abstract data type A:

$$OPERAND\_STACK(A) = STACK(A)$$

Transferring Values We can either load a value onto the operand stack, or we can fetch a value from the operand stack and store it elsewhere.

Loading Values onto the Operand Stack A load instruction places a copy of a value stored in a location of the JVM on the top of the operand stack. In particular, there are instructions to load values from:

- the local variables (Section 4.2);
- dynamically created objects that are stored in the heap (Section 4.8); and
- the constant pool (Section 4.7).

We shall split the action of these instructions into two principle components:

(i) first, we fetch the value from the specified location, and then
(ii) we place this value onto the operand stack.

We exploit the independence of action (ii) to produce more modular specifications before dealing with the different fetching operations of action (i).

To load a value onto the operand stack, we define a function

$$Load_s : s \times jvm\_state \to jvm\_state$$

so that $Load_s(v, \sigma)$ pushes the value v onto the top of the operand stack of the state σ:

$$Load_s(v, \sigma) = \Delta^{OpStack}(Push_s(v, \Pi^{OpStack}(\sigma)), \sigma)$$

Fetching Values from the Operand Stack The store instructions work in a similar fashion, but this time we transfer a value from the operand stack to elsewhere. Again, we split the action of the store instructions into that of fetching and storing (but note that we have no instructions to store values in the constant pool, as by their nature these elements are static).

In order to fetch an item from the operand stack, we need to be able to determine the top element of a stack and to remove it. Thus, we need to use the functions Top_s and Pop_s of the generic stack specification; for ease of notation we introduce functions

$$Fetch_s : jvm\_state \to s_{stack\_under flow}$$
$$Remove_s : jvm\_state \to jvm\_state$$

that work directly on states:

$$Fetch_s(\sigma) = Top_s(\Pi^{OpStack}(\sigma))$$
$$Remove_s(\sigma) = Pop_s(\Pi^{OpStack}(\sigma))$$

Notation To aid the clarity of later definitions, we extend each of our operations $Load_s$, $Fetch_s$ and $Remove_s$ to operate on lists with the functions

$$Load^w : list(S) \times jvm\_state \to jvm\_state_{error}$$
$$Fetch^w : jvm\_state \to list(S)_{stack\_underflow}$$
$$Remove^w : jvm\_state \to jvm\_state$$

which are all simply defined by recursion over lists, except that in addition, the function $Load^w$ checks the types of the list of arguments that it is presented with.

Manipulating the Operand Stack We have three types of instructions in the JVM to manipulate the operand stack; we can pop values from the stack, and because the JVM is stack-based we have instructions to swap and duplicate values on the stack.

We pop elements from the operand stack with the instruction

$$\text{Pop}_s :\to instrn$$

by:

$$[\![\text{Pop}_s]\!](\sigma) = \Delta^{PC}_{+1}(Remove_s(\sigma))$$

We can swap the top two values (of sorts s and s' respectively) around on the operand stack with the instruction

$$\text{Swap}_{s,s'} :\to instrn$$

by removing them both from the stack, and then pushing them back on in the reverse order:

$$[\![\text{Swap}_{s,s'}]\!](\sigma) = \Delta^{PC}_{+1}(Load^{s' \cdot s}(Lst_{s'}(Fetch_{s'}(Remove_s(\sigma)),$$
$$Lst_s(Fetch_s(\sigma), EmptyList))),$$
$$Remove^{s \cdot s'}(\sigma))$$

We can duplicate the top value on the operand stack with the instruction

$$\text{Dup}_s :\to instrn$$

by:

$$[\![\text{Dup}_s]\!](\sigma) = \Delta^{PC}_{+1}(Load_s(Fetch_s(\sigma), \sigma))$$

Performing Calculations The JVM operates by applying the functions of the underlying data type to arguments which are stored on the operand stack.

We define the instruction

$$\mathtt{Eval}_{w,s} : fun_{w,s} \to instrn$$

so that $[\![\mathtt{Eval}_{w,s}(f)]\!](\sigma)$ applies the function $f : w \to s$ to the arguments stored on the top of the operand stack, and replaces these values with that of the result:

$$[\![\mathtt{Eval}_{w,s}(f)]\!](\sigma) = \Delta_{+1}^{PC}(Load_s(Apply_{w,s}(f, Fetch^w(\sigma))), Remove^w(\sigma))$$

4.2 The Local Variables

We use the local variables area of the JVM to store the values of parameters that are passed to methods, together with the values of variables that are local to a method. For this reason and because the JVM is a stack-based architecture, the only instructions acting on local variables are to transfer values between the local variables and the operand stack.

Structure We model the local variables as a table indexed by the names of the variables (be they parameters or local variables), and storing their values:

$$VARS(A) = TABLE(VAR\_NAME(S), A)$$

where $VAR\_NAME(S)$ specifies a set of variable names, which are typed with the sort set S of the underlying data type A.

Retrieving Local Variables To retrieve values from local variables, we define a function

$$Fetch_s^{Vars} : var\_name_s \times jvm\_state \to s_{uninitialised}$$

so that $Fetch_s^{Vars}(x, \sigma)$ fetches the value that is stored in the local variable x of the state σ:

$$Fetch_s^{Vars}(x, \sigma) = Read_s(x, \Pi^{Vars}(\sigma))$$

Now we can define the instruction

$$\mathtt{Load}_s : var\_name_s \to instrn$$

so that $[\![\mathtt{Load}_s(x)]\!](\sigma)$ places a copy of the value stored in the local variable x on the top of the operand stack of the state σ:

$$[\![\mathtt{Load}_s(x)]\!](\sigma) = \Delta_{+1}^{PC}(Load_s(Fetch_s^{Vars}(x, \sigma), \sigma))$$

Storing Local Variables Similarly, we define a function

$$Store_s^{Vars} : s \times var\_name_s \times jvm\_state \to jvm\_state$$

so that $Store_s^{Var}(v, x, \sigma)$ stores the value v in the local variable x of the state σ:

$$Store_s^{Vars}(v, x, \sigma) = \Delta^{Vars}(Store_s(v, x, \Pi^{Vars}(\sigma)))$$

We can now define the instruction

$$\texttt{Store}_s : var\_name_s \to instrn$$

so that $[\![\texttt{Store}_s(x)]\!](\sigma)$ transfers the value from the top of the operand stack to the local variable x of the state σ:

$$[\![\texttt{Store}_s(x)]\!](\sigma) = \Delta_{+1}^{PC}(Store_s^{Vars}(Fetch_s(\sigma), x, Remove_s(\sigma)))$$

4.3 The Execution Environment

Within each frame, the execution environment stores information about the method currently executing (the method and class), together with information (the return instruction address) about the point where the previous method was interrupted to initiate the current method.

Structure We store this information in the execution environment as a Cartesian product:

$$EXEC\_ENV$$
$$= CP(CLASS\_NAME, METHOD\_NAME, INSTRN\_INDEX)$$

where $CLASS\_NAME$ specifies a set of class names, $METHOD\_NAME$ a set of method names, and $INSTRN\_INDEX$ the indexing set for the instructions.

Setting the Execution Environment We operate on the execution environment with a function

$$SetEnv : class\_name \times method\_name \times jvm\_state \to jvm\_state$$

so that $SetEnv(c, m, \sigma)$ sets the execution environment up with the class c and method m as the new current values, together with the instruction address of where to return to (the instruction following the current one):

$$SetEnv(c, m, \sigma)$$
$$= \Delta^{ExecEnv}(v^{ExecEnv}(c, m, Plus(\Pi^{PC}(\sigma), Succ(Zero))), \sigma)$$

We set the environment upon the invocation of a method as we shall now see in the next section.

4.4 Frames

A frame collects together the operand stack (on which we store the values of (partial) computations), the execution environment (that we use to restore information to another frame when we have completed the execution of the current method), and the set of local variables (in which we store the values of local variables and parameters of methods).

Structure We model an individual frame as a Cartesian product of the operand stack, the execution environment and the local variables:

$$FRAME(A) = CP(OPERAND\_STACK(A), EXEC\_ENV, VARS(A))$$

We stack individual frames on top of each other to form the frames of the JVM:

$$FRAMES(A) = STACK(FRAME(A))$$

The current frame is that which is at the top of this stack.

Invoking methods When a method is invoked, we have to push a new frame onto the stack of frames and we have to store information about the point of interruption so that we can correctly resume the old method when the new method completes.

To create a new frame, we need to introduce a function

$SetVars$:
$$class\_name \times method\_name \times list(var\_name) \times jvm\_state \rightarrow vars$$

that will deal with the passing of parameters to a newly invoked method. In particular, $SetVars(c, m, L, \sigma)$ loads the current values of the list L of variables into the table $VARS$ of variables that are declared as parameters by the method m of the class c. Note that this function also checks the types of the lists L of variables with the declared list of parameters.

We define the instruction

$$\text{Invoke} : class\_name \times method\_name \times list(var\_name) \rightarrow instrn$$

so that $[\![\text{Invoke}(c, m, L)]\!](\sigma)$ invokes the method m of the class c on the values that are stored in the local variables specified in the list L:

$$
\begin{aligned}
[\![\text{Invoke}&(c, m, L)]\!](\sigma) \\
&= \Delta^{PC}(StartIndex, \Delta^{Frames}(Push_{frame}(v^{Frame}(EmptyStack, \\
&\qquad\qquad\qquad\qquad\qquad\qquad\qquad SetEnv(c, m, \sigma), \\
&\qquad\qquad\qquad\qquad\qquad\qquad\qquad SetVars(c, m, L, \sigma)), \\
&\qquad\qquad\qquad\qquad\qquad \Pi^{Frames}(\sigma)), \sigma))
\end{aligned}
$$

(where *StartIndex* gives the first value of the indexing set used to locate program instructions).

Returning from methods When we return from a method, we pop the completed frame off the top of the stack of frames, taking care to push the value from the top of the operand stack of the completed frame onto the cleared operand stack of the reinstated frame. Finally, we restore the value of the program counter from the execution environment; we define this action with an instruction

$$\textbf{Return}_s :\rightarrow instrn$$

by:

$$
\begin{aligned}
&[\![\textbf{Return}_s]\!](\sigma) \\
&= \Delta^{PC}(\Pi^{ReturnInstrn}(\sigma), \\
&\qquad Load_s(Fetch_s(\sigma), \\
&\qquad\qquad \Delta^{OpStack}(\ EmptyStack, \\
&\qquad\qquad\qquad \Delta^{Frames}(Pop_{Frame}(\Pi^{Frames}(\sigma)),\sigma))))
\end{aligned}
$$

Void methods do not return any value. We return from a void method with the instruction

$$\textbf{Return}_{void} :\rightarrow instrn$$

which we define by:

$$
\begin{aligned}
[\![\textbf{Return}_{void}]\!](\sigma) = \Delta^{PC}(\Pi^{ReturnInstrn}(\sigma), \\
\Delta^{OpStack}(EmptyStack, \\
\Delta^{Frames}(Pop_{Frame}(\Pi^{Frames}(\sigma)),\sigma)))
\end{aligned}
$$

4.5 Registers

As we explained in Section 3.2, we only have one register, that of the program counter, in our abstract model of the JVM. This register controls which instruction we execute next.

Being a low-level language, the JVM has basic flow-of-control mechanisms to conditionally or unconditionally alter the value of the program counter or to execute a subroutine, as well as the high-level flow-of-control mechanisms of invoking or returning from methods described in Section 4.4.

Structure We consider that the program counter register only stores the address of the particular instruction of a given method and class that we are to execute next. (Recall from Section 4.3, that we store the information about the method and class in the execution environment to maintain links with the concrete JVM).

We structure the registers as a Cartesian product

$$REGISTERS = CP(PC)$$

containing the single program-counter element.

Unconditional Flow-of-Control The simplest flow-of-control mechanism is provided by the unconditional instructions of Goto and Nop, and also that of the Jsr instruction which is a more structured version of Goto.

The Nop instruction has no effect on the state other than to increment the program counter. This is trivial to model:

$$[\![\text{Nop}]\!](\sigma) = \Delta_{+1}^{PC}(\sigma)$$

The Goto instruction simply specifies the next instruction to be executed by providing a new program counter address relative to the current instruction. We define

$$\text{Goto} : instrn\_index \rightarrow instrn$$

so that $[\![\text{Goto}(i)]\!](\sigma)$ changes the value of the program counter of the state σ by an offset i:

$$[\![\text{Goto}(i)]\!](\sigma) = \Delta^{PC}(Plus(\Pi^{PC}(\sigma), i), \sigma)$$

The jump-to-subroutine instruction

$$\text{Jsr} : instrn\_index \rightarrow instrn$$

adds a given offset to a program counter, but so that execution can resume after the subroutine has completed, the address of the instruction following the jump-to-subroutine instruction is pushed onto the operand stack:

$$[\![\text{Jsr}(i)]\!](\sigma) = \Delta^{PC}(Plus(\Pi^{PC}(\sigma), i),$$
$$Store_{instrn\_index}(Plus(\Pi^{PC}(\sigma), Succ(Zero)), \sigma))$$

Conditional Flow-of-Control A more flexible flow-of-control mechanism is provided by the conditional instruction

$$\text{Cond}_w : fun_{w,bool} \times instrn\_index \to instrn$$

so that $[\text{Cond}_w(f, i)](\sigma)$ alters the program counter by the offset i if the predicate $f : w \to bool$ applied to the arguments which are stored on the top of the operand stack evaluates to true, and otherwise the program counter is simply incremented by one:

$$Apply_{w,bool}(f, Fetch^w(\sigma)) = True$$
$$\Rightarrow \quad [\text{Cond}_w(f, i)](\sigma) = \Delta^{PC}(Plus(\Pi^{PC}(\sigma), i), Remove^w(\sigma))$$

$$Apply_{w,bool}(f, Fetch^w(\sigma)) = False$$
$$\Rightarrow \quad [\text{Cond}_w(f, i)](\sigma) = \Delta^{PC}_{+1}(Remove^w(\sigma))$$

We also have an extended conditional instruction

$$\text{Case}_s : s \times list(s \times instrn\_index) \times instrn\_index \to instrn$$

so that $[\text{Case}_s(k, L, d)](\sigma)$ searches the list L of pairs of matches and offsets for the first occurrence of a match equal to the key k, and returns the corresponding offset. If no such match is found, then the default offset d is used.

In order to maintain the useful notion that each instruction can be completed within one time step, we introduce a function

$$Case_s : s \times list(s \times instrn\_index) \times instrn\_index \times jvm\_state \to jvm\_state$$

to describe the semantics of the instruction Case_s. We define $Case_s$ by:

$$Case_s(k, Empty, d, \sigma) = \Delta^{PC}(Plus(\Pi^{PC}(\sigma), d), \sigma)$$
$$Equals_s(k, m) = True$$
$$\Rightarrow \quad Case_s(k, Lst((m, i), L), d, \sigma) = \Delta^{PC}(Plus(\Pi^{PC}(\sigma), i), \sigma)$$
$$Equals_s(k, m) = False$$
$$\Rightarrow \quad Case_s(k, Lst((m, i), L), d, \sigma) = Case_s(k, L, d, \sigma)$$

Then, we can define

$$[\text{Case}_s(k, L, d)](\sigma) = Case_s(k, L, d, \sigma).$$

4.6 Single Threads

We can regard the threads area of the JVM as the control centre of the machine. It determines the order of the instructions that are executed, and it stores the intermediate results of computations that are initiated by these instructions.

Structure For simplicity, we just consider a single-threaded model. The thread of a state performs calculations on data; we store the results of such calculations in the objects on the heap. In particular, a thread consists of a program counter register that tells us which instruction we are to execute next, and a stack of frames which we use to store values needed in the calculation of the execution of methods.

We model a thread as a Cartesian product of the registers and the frames:

$$THREAD(A) = CP(REGISTERS, FRAMES(A))$$

4.7 The Method Area

The method area of the JVM stores all the information pertaining to the classes of the Java bytecode programs. We record all the fields that are declared by the methods of a class, together with the actual program instructions.

Structure In the method area we store the instructions that we execute. We structure the method area as a table of classes indexed by the class names:

$$METHOD\_AREA(A) = TABLE(CLASS\_NAME, CLASS(A))$$

Within each class entry we store

(*i*) the constant pool, where we store the constants of the class;
(*ii*) the declarations of the fields that the class uses; and
(*iii*) the methods of the classes, which include the actual program instructions.

Thus,

$$CLASS(A)$$
$$= FCP(CONSTANT\_POOL(A), FIELD\_DECLNS(S), METHODS(\Sigma))$$

where the filter we need to apply is that of checking that all the constants and fields used in a method have been declared in the class in which it resides (an example of a completeness filter), and that these two entities are disjoint from each other.

Field Declarations We declare all the fields of a class before we use them in the instructions; we store the values of the fields on the heap. There are two types of field: statics (per-class fields) and non-statics (per-object fields).

Structure We first split the fields into the statics and non-statics:

$$FIELD\_DECLNS(S)$$
$$= FCP(STATIC\_DECLNS(S), NON\_STATIC\_DECLNS(S))$$

where the filter we apply ensures that the static and non-static field declarations are disjoint from each other. Within each of these components, we represent the fields as a list of the field names:

$$STATIC\_DECLNS(S) = FLIST(FIELD\_NAME(S))$$
$$NON\_STATIC\_DECLNS(S) = FLIST(FIELD\_NAME(S))$$

where $FIELD\_NAME(S)$ specifies a set of field names which we type with the sort set S of the underlying data type A, and in both cases we ensure that the lists contain no repetitions.

The Constant Pool We store the constants of the classes within the constant pool. (As our model is so abstract, this is all we need store in our constant pool.)

Structure We structure the constant pool as a table indexed by the constant names, and storing their values:

$$CONSTANT\_POOL(A) = TABLE(CONST\_NAME(S), A)$$

where $CONST\_NAME(S)$ specifies a list of constant names which we type with the sort set S.

Loading from the Constant Pool To retrieve values from the constant pool, we define a function

$$Fetch_s^{ConstantPool} : const\_name_s \times jvm\_state \rightarrow s_{uninitialised}$$

so that $Fetch_s^{ConstantPool}(c, \sigma)$ returns the constant c that is stored in the constant pool of the state σ:

$$Fetch_s^{ConstantPool}(c, \sigma) = Read_s(c, \Pi^{ConstantPool}(\sigma))$$

This allows us to define the instruction

$$\texttt{ConPlLoad}_s : const\_name_s \rightarrow instrn$$

so that $[\![\texttt{ConPlLoad}_s(c)]\!](\sigma)$ places a copy of the value of the constant c from the constant pool on the top of the operand stack.

$$[\![\texttt{ConPlLoad}_s(c)]\!](\sigma) = \Delta_{+1}^{PC}(Load_s(Fetch_s^{ConstantPool}(c, \sigma), \sigma))$$

The Methods We store the program instructions of the JVM within the methods section of the classes.

Structure We structure the program code by initially storing the instructions for each method in a table

$$INSTRNS(\Sigma) = FTABLE(INSTRN\_INDEX, INSTRN(\Sigma))$$

indexed by *INSTRN_INDEX*; this indexing scheme provides an isomorphic copy of the natural numbers with the constant *StartIndex* and functions *Succ* and *Plus*.

The filter that we need to apply here is that any conditional or unconditional branching instructions refer to an instruction within the table, i.e., branching instructions can only direct execution to instructions within the same method. This type of filter is an example of a check for completeness.

With each method we associate its variables (local and parameter):

$$METHOD(\Sigma)$$
$$= FCP(PARAMETERS(S), LOCALS(S), INSTRNS(\Sigma))$$

where
$$PARAMETERS(S) = FLIST(VAR\_NAME(S))$$
specifies the parameters and

$$LOCALS(S) = FLIST(VAR\_NAME(S))$$

the local variables of methods as lists of variable names. Note that we apply filters to check that the parameters and locals are disjoint from each other and that both exhibit the property of distinctness.

Then we store the individual methods in a table indexed by the method names:

$$METHODS(\Sigma)$$
$$= TABLE(METHOD\_NAME(S \cup \{void\}), METHOD(\Sigma))$$

where *METHOD_NAME*$(S \cup \{void\})$ specifies a set of method names which we type to indicate the return type of the method using the set S of the signature Σ, or if the method does not return a value, we indicate this with the sort *void*.

Operations The only operation on the bytecodes is that of accessing the individual instructions. We define a function

$$Fetch^{Instrn} : jvm\_state \rightarrow instrn$$

so that $Fetch^{Instrn}(\sigma)$ returns the instruction of the JVM that we are to execute next on the state σ:

$$
\begin{aligned}
Fetch^{Instrn}(\sigma) \\
= Read_{instrn}(\Pi^{PC}(\sigma), \\
Read_{method}(\Pi^{CurrentMethod}(\sigma), \\
Read_{class}(\Pi^{CurrentClass}(\sigma), \Pi^{MethodArea}(\sigma))))
\end{aligned}
$$

4.8 The Heap

Objects are created dynamically as instances of classes and are stored on the heap.

We can load and store values in fields of objects. We can also create objects, but in our high-level view of the JVM we shall not consider any aspect of memory reclamation.

Structure We store dynamic structures in the form of objects on the heap. At this level of abstraction, we regard the heap as a storage area for two types of information: we separate out the per-object information from the per-class information:

$$HEAP(A) = CP(STATICS(A), OBJECTS(A))$$

Each class is associated with one set of static fields; we store these static fields as a table indexed by the class names, and storing the fields:

$$STATICS(A) = TABLE(CLASS\_NAME, FIELDS(A))$$

In turn, we store the fields as a table indexed by the field names and storing their values:

$$FIELDS(A) = TABLE(FIELD\_NAME(S), A)$$

Each class may have an arbitrary number of objects associated with it. Hence, we store the objects in a table containing the non-static fields and indexed by some scheme (specified by $OBJECT\_INDEX$) that uniquely identifies each object:

$$OBJECTS(A) = TABLE(OBJECT\_INDEX, NON\_STATICS(A))$$

In addition, we require that we can generate a fresh reference upon request with a function

$$NewRef : jvm\_state \to object\_index$$

whereby

$$Read_{non\_statics}(NewRef(\sigma), \Pi^{Objects}(\sigma)) = Uninitialised_{non\_statics}.$$

As with the static fields, we store the non-static fields as a table indexed by the field names and storing their values:

$$NON\_STATICS(A) = FIELDS(A) = TABLE(FIELD\_NAME(S), A).$$

Creating Static Instances When we create an object, it is as the instance of some class, each of which has a unique name.

Recall from Section 4.7, that we declare all the types of the fields of a class within the method area, and that we split the declarations into the static and non-static fields. When we create an instance of the class statics, we initialise all the fields to their default values with the function

$$Default : list(field\_name) \to fields$$

which is an extension of the function $DefaultValue_s$ discussed in Section 3.2.

We store the static instance of a class with a function

$$StoreStatics : jvm\_state \to jvm\_state$$

so that $StoreStatics(\sigma)$ places an instance of the static variables of the current class on the heap, if it has not already been stored:

$$Equals(Read_{fields}(\Pi^{CurrentClass}(\sigma), \Pi^{Statics}(\sigma)),$$
$$Uninitialised_{fields}) = False$$
$$\Rightarrow StoreStatics(\sigma) = \Delta^{Statics}(Store_{fields}(\Pi^{CurrentClass}(\sigma),$$
$$Default(\Pi^{StaticDeclns}(\sigma))),$$
$$\sigma)$$

$$Equals(Read_{fields}(\Pi^{CurrentClass}(\sigma), \Pi^{Statics}(\sigma)),$$
$$Uninitialised_{fields}) = True$$
$$\Rightarrow StoreStatics(\sigma) = \sigma$$

Creating Objects As with the static fields, we initialise all the non-static fields of a newly created object to their default values with the function $Default$. We define a function

$$StoreNonStatics : jvm\_state \rightarrow jvm\_state$$

so that $StoreNonStatics(\sigma)$ places an instance of the non-static variables of the current class on the heap:

$$StoreNonStatics(\sigma)$$
$$= \Delta^{Objects}(Store_{non\_statics}(NewRef(\sigma),$$
$$Default(\Pi^{NonStaticDeclns}(\sigma))), \sigma)$$

Now we can define the instruction

$$\text{New} :\rightarrow instrn$$

so that $[\![\text{New}]\!](\sigma)$ places an object on the heap of the current class and stores the index to the object on the top of the operand stack:

$$[\![\text{New}]\!](\sigma) = \Delta^{PC}_{+1}(Load_{object\_index}(NewRef(\sigma),$$
$$StoreStatics(StoreNonStatics(\sigma))))$$

Loading from Objects We have two instructions to load field values: one for static fields, and the other for non-static fields.

We define the function

$$\text{GetField}_s : field\_name_s \rightarrow instrn$$

so that $[\![\text{GetField}_s(f)]\!](\sigma)$ loads the value of the field f of the object that is on the heap at the location determined by the top element of the operand stack:

$$[\![\text{GetField}_s(f)]\!](\sigma)$$
$$= \Delta^{PC}_{+1}(Load_s(Read_s(f, Read_{non\_statics}(Fetch_{object\_index}(\sigma),$$
$$\Pi^{Objects}(\sigma))),$$
$$Remove_{object\_index}(\sigma)))$$

The process for loading static fields, i.e., fields of class instances is very similar: we define the instruction

$$\text{GetStatic}_s : class\_name \times field\_name_s \rightarrow instrn$$

so that $[\![\text{GetStatic}_s(c, f)]\!](\sigma)$ places a copy of the static field f of the class c on the top of the operand stack by:

$$[\![\text{GetStatic}_s(c, f)]\!](\sigma)$$
$$= \Delta^{PC}_{+1}(Load_s(Read_s(f, Read_{fields}(c, \Pi^{Statics}(\sigma))), \sigma))$$

Storing in Objects Similarly, we have two instructions to store field values, depending on whether they are static or non-static.

To store non-static field values, we first introduce a function

$$Store_s^{Field} : s \times field\_name_s \times object\_index \times jvm\_state \rightarrow jvm\_state$$

so that $Store_s^{Field}(v, f, o, \sigma)$ stores the value v of the field f of the object at position o on the heap:

$$
\begin{aligned}
&Store_s^{Field}(v, f, o, \sigma) \\
&= \Delta^{NonStatics}(Store_s(v, f, Read_{non\_statics}(o, \Pi^{Objects}(\sigma))), \sigma)
\end{aligned}
$$

We define the instruction

$$\mathtt{PutField}_s : field\_name_s \rightarrow instrn$$

so that $[\![\mathtt{PutField}_s(f)]\!](\sigma)$ transfers the second item of the operand stack into the field f of an object which is determined by the top item of the operand stack:

$$
\begin{aligned}
&[\![\mathtt{PutField}_s(f)]\!](\sigma) \\
&= \Delta_{+1}^{PC}(Store_s^{Field}(Fetch_s(Remove_{object\_index}(\sigma)), \\
&\qquad\qquad f, Fetch_{object\_index}(\sigma), Remove^{object\_index \cdot s}(\sigma)))
\end{aligned}
$$

The act of storing a static field with the instruction

$$\mathtt{PutStatic}_s : class\_name \times field\_name_s \rightarrow instrn$$

follows similarly:

$$
\begin{aligned}
&[\![\mathtt{PutStatic}_s(c, f)]\!](\sigma) \\
&= \Delta_{+1}^{PC}(\Delta^{Statics}(Store_s(Fetch_s(\sigma), f, Read_{fields}(c, \Pi^{Statics}(\sigma))), \\
&\qquad Remove_s(\sigma)))
\end{aligned}
$$

5 Modelling the Concrete JVM

Having specified the behaviour of our abstract JVM, we can now turn our attention to what would be required to model the concrete JVM. This process is a mixture of reducing the level of abstraction that we introduced, together with addressing the simplifications made to our model.

5.1 The Underlying Data Structures

In our abstract model of the JVM, we just considered that it computed over some arbitrary abstract data type A. To model the concrete JVM (CJVM), we have to instantiate A with an appropriate data type.

As will be the case in dealing with the concretisation of other features of the abstract JVM (AJVM), we shall find it helpful to add the details required in a step-wise manner. Thus, we consider the underlying data structures, then the underlying data type as a computational entity, and finally the representation of the data.

The Specification Structures The specification structures of Section 2.3 also provide a suitable framework for the CJVM. We simply need to instantiate the underlying data type with appropriate concrete abstract data types (as indicated below) in most cases.

To model implementations of the CJVM though, (i.e., to remove yet another layer of abstraction), more radical work (although essentially just exercises in data structures) is required; for example, the operand stack of the JVM is typically implemented as an array with a register recording the current top of the stack.

The Underlying Data Type As can be seen from Figure 4, we take the data type A over which the AJVM computes and instantiate it so that it is constructed from the primitive types of *BYTE, INT, SHORT, LONG, CHAR, RETURN_ADDRESS* (which we termed *INSTRN_INDEX* in the AJVM), and *REFERENCE* (which we termed *OBJECT_INDEX* in the AJVM).

We can then model each of these components at decreasing levels of abstraction.

Data Representation In order for Java to be portable, the CJVM specifies how the data types are represented:

- `byte`, `short`, `int` and `long` are signed two's complement integers (of sizes 8 bit, 16 bit, 32 bit and 64 bit, respectively);
- `char` as unsigned two's complement integer (of size 16 bit);
- `float` and `double` are IEEE 754 floating point numbers (of sizes 32 bit and 64 bit, respectively); and
- `returnaddress` and `reference` are stored using 16 bits.

To maintain the benefits that our abstract models have introduced, it would be beneficial to model the JVM's computation:

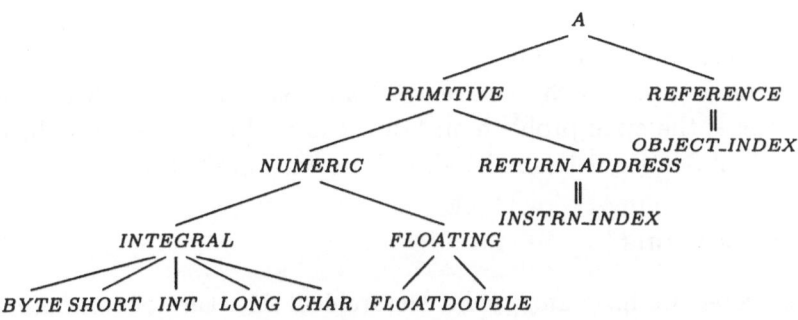

Fig. 4. Structure of the underlying data type.

(*i*) first using a completely abstract notion of word;

(*ii*) then using the JVM's abstract notion of word, where one word is sufficiently large to store values of `byte`, `short`, `int`, `float`, `reference` and `returnaddress`, and two words are sufficiently large to store `long` and `double`; and

(*iii*) finally at bit-level.

5.2 Dealing with the Remaining Simplifications

Furnishing our model with concrete structures will not yield a full specification of the JVM; we still have to deal with the simplifications that we introduced into our model. These simplifications fall into two categories: those that we have omitted so that we do not obscure the essential structure of the JVM, and those which are problematical to deal with.

In the first category fall instructions which are provided for: (*i*) implementation efficiency reasons, (*ii*) exception handling and (*iii*) type checking.

We can only consider efficient versions of instructions at a concrete level where the local variables are indexed by (relative) addresses, rather than the abstract notion of names used in the AJVM. Then it is a simple matter to extend the instruction set to include specifications of the semantics of `load` and `store` instructions which have an implicit index.

We omitted details regarding the throwing and catching of exceptions in the AJVM as this is essentially an extension of method invocation.

We also neglected to deal with issues in any way associated with type checking, which we have deliberately underplayed in this document. For example: we have not made any distinction between classes with regard to interfaces or access restrictions; we have not considered the `checkcast` instructions; and we have not dealt with method resolution.

The major area which we have not dealt with is that of multithreading, which raises the open problem of: "How can we lift the general algebraic approach of Section 2 to model a machine with multithreading?"

6   Conclusions

In this paper, we have analysed a hierarchical structure of computer systems using algebraic methods. This algebraic modelling has been much studied at Swansea: at the microprocessor level (Harman and Tucker [1997] and Fox and Harman [1998]) through abstract models of computation to high-level languages Stephenson [1996] and a study of hierarchical discrete-space, discrete-time systems (Poole *et al.* [1998]). This allows for an analysis of the correctness of implementation to be considered within a unified framework with the aim of supporting trusted compilation.

The Java programming language is an ideal vehicle for our programme of constructing a unified formal path from high-level languages to hardware, as it employs an abstraction mechanism in the form of the Java Virtual Machine for its implementation. Thus, the gap between Java and the JVM is smaller (and therefore more tractable) than between Java and a more physically detailed hardware model.

Work has already been performed in proving the correctness of a smaller skeletal compiler from a simple **while** language to an idealised machine model (Unlimited Register Machine) and has shown to be feasible (the proof has been performed by hand — Stephenson [1996]). In addition, this intermediate stepping stone of the JVM will allow more modular proofs to be constructed of the analysis of any particular implementation.

In this paper, we have concentrated on considering the specification of a case study of the Java Virtual Machine. We have shown that our specification techniques are capable of handling such a large example in a unified, comprehensive and practical fashion. The feasibility of specifying the JVM is, we feel, only made possible by exploiting all the possible abstractions we can make.

Acknowledgments

I wish to thank J V Tucker for encouraging me to investigate the Java Virtual Machine, and who together with N A Harman, M Haveraaen and D Ll L Rees provided useful comments and suggestions on this work.

I also thank the referees of this paper for spurring me on to fully applying the abstractions which have drawn out the underlying structure of the machine.

References

Bergstra and Tucker [1987]
  J A Bergstra and J V Tucker. Algebraic Specifications of Computable and Semicomputable Data Types. *Theoretical Computer Science*, 50:137–181, 1987.
Börger and Schulte [1998]
  E Börger and W Schulte. Defining the Java Virtual Machine as Platform for Provably Correct Java Compilation. In *Proceedings of the 23rd International Symposium on the Mathematical Foundations of Computer Science*, LNCS 1450, pages 17–35. Springer-Verlag, 1998.
Cohen [1997]
  R M Cohen. The Defensive Java Virtual Machine Specification. Technical Report Draft Version Alpha 1, Computational Logic Inc., May 1997. Available at: http://www.cli.com/software/djvm.
Davidson and Fraser [1984]
  J W Davidson and W Fraser. Code Selection through Object Code Optimization. *ACM Transactions on Programming Languages and Systems*, 6(4):505–526, 1984.
Fox and Harman [1998]
  A C J Fox and N A Harman. Algebraic Models of Superscalar Microprocessor Implementations: A Case Study, 1998. In this volume.
Freund and Mitchell [1998]
  S N Freund and J C Mitchell. A Type System for Object Initialization in the Java^{TM} Bytecode Language. In *ACM Conference on Object-Oriented Programming, Systems, Languages and Applications*. ACM Press, 1998. To appear.
Goguen and Meseguer [1992]
  J A Goguen and J Meseguer. Order-Sorted Algebra I: Equational Deduction for Multiple Inheritance, Overloading, Exceptions and Partial Operations. *Theoretical Computer Science*, 105(2):217–273, 1992.
Goguen et al. [1977]
  J A Goguen, J W Thatcher, E G Wagner, and J B Wright. Initial Algebra Semantics and Continuous Algebras. *Journal of the ACM*, 24:68–95, 1977.
Goldberg [1998]
  A Goldberg. A Specification of Java Loading and Bytecode Verification. In *Proceedings of the 5th ACM Conference on Computer and Communications Security*. ACM Press, 1998. To appear.
Gosling [1995]
  J Gosling. Java Intermediate Bytecodes. *SIGPLAN Notices*, 30(3):111–118, 1995.
Harman and Tucker [1996]
  N A Harman and J V Tucker. Algebraic Models of Microprocessors: Architecture and Organisation. *Acta Informatica*, 33:421–456, 1996.
Harman and Tucker [1997]
  N A Harman and J V Tucker. Algebraic Models of Microprocessors: The Verification of a Simple Computer. In V Stavridou, editor, *Proceedings of the 1995 IMA Conference on Mathematics for Dependable Systems*, pages 135–170. Oxford University Press, 1997.

Hartel *et al.* [1998]

P H Hartel, M J Butler, and M Levy. The Operational Semantics of a Java Secure Processor. In J Alves-Foss, editor, *Formal Syntax and Semantics of Java^{TM}*, LNCS. Springer-Verlag, 1998. To appear.

Haveraaen and Wagner [1995]

M Haveraaen and E G Wagner. Guarded Algebras and Data Type Specification. Technical Report 108, Department of Informatics, University of Bergen, Norway, 1995.

Kamperman and Walters [1993]

J F T Kamperman and H R Walters. ARM — Abstract Rewriting Machinery. In *Proceedings of Computer Science in the Netherlands (CSN '93)*, pages 193–204. Stichting Mathematische Centrum, 1993.

King [1994]

A King. *Inside Windows 95*. Microsoft Press, 1994.

Landin [1964]

P J Landin. The Mechanical Evaluation of Expressions. *Computer Journal*, 6:308–320, 1964.

Lindholm and Yellin [1997]

T Lindholm and F Yellin. *The Java Virtual Machine Specification*. Addison-Wesley, 1997.

Liu [1996]

C Liu. *Smalltalk, Objects, and Design*. Manning Publications, Ashland, Ohio, 1996.

Meinke and Tucker [1992]

K Meinke and J V Tucker. Universal Algebra. In S Abramsky, D M Gabbay, and T S E Maibaum, editors, *Handbook of Logic in Computer Science*, volume I, pages 189–411. Oxford University Press, 1992.

Nori *et al.* [1981]

K V Nori, U Ammann, K Jenson, H H Nageli, and C Jacobi. Pascal-P Implementation Notes. In D W Barron, editor, *Pascal — The Language and its Implementation*, pages 125–170. Wiley, 1981.

Poole *et al.* [1998]

M J Poole, J V Tucker and A V Holden. Hierarchies of Spatially Extended Systems, 1998. In this volume.

Pusch [1998]

C Pusch. Formalizing the Java Virtual Machine in Isabelle/HOL. Technical Report TUM-I9816, Technische Universität München, Munich, Germany, June 1998. Available at: http://www.in.tum.de/~pusch/.

Qian [1998]

Z Qian. A Formal Specification of Java Virtual Machine Instructions for Objects, Methods and Subroutines. In J Alves-Foss, editor, *Formal Syntax and Semantics of Java^{TM}*, LNCS. Springer-Verlag, 1998. To appear.

Rees *et al.* [1998]

D Ll L Rees, K Stephenson, and J V Tucker. The Reporting and Correcting of Syntax Errors in an Algebraic Environment. Technical report, Department of Computer Science, University of Wales Swansea, 1998. In preparation.

Rus [1971]

T Rus. ΣS-Algebra of a Formal Language. *Société des Sciences Mathématiques de la République Socialiste de Roumaine Bulletin Mathématique*, 15(2):227–235, 1971.

Seawright and MacKinnen [1979]

L H Seawright and R A MacKinnen. VM/370 — A Study of Multiplicity and Usefulness. *IBM Systems Journal*, 18(1):4–17, 1979.

Stata and Abadi [1998]

R Stata and M Abadi. A Type System for Java Bytecode Subroutines. In *Proceedings of the 25th ACM Symposium on Prinicples of Programming Languages*, pages 149–160. ACM Press, 1998.

Stephenson [1996]

K Stephenson. *An Algebraic Approach to Syntax, Semantics and Compilation*. PhD thesis, Department of Computer Science, University of Wales Swansea, 1996.

Strong *et al.* [1958]

J Strong, J Olsztyn, J Wegstein, O Mock, A Tritter, and T Steel. The Problem of Programming Communication with Changing Machines: A Proposed Solution. *Communications of the ACM*, 1(8):12–18 and 1(9): 9–15, 1958.

van Deursen *et al.* [1996]

A van Deursen, J Heering, and P Klint, editors. *Language Prototyping: An Algebraic Specification Approach*, volume 5 of *AMAST Series in Computing*. World Scientific Publishing, 1996.

Warren [1983]

D H D Warren. An Abstract Prolog Instruction Set. Technical Note 309, Artifical Intelligence Center, SRI International, 1983.

Grid Protocol Specifications *

Jan A. Bergstra[1,2] and Alban Ponse[1]

[1] University of Amsterdam, Programming Research Group, Kruislaan 403,
NL-1098 SJ Amsterdam, The Netherlands.
http://www.wins.uva.nl/research/prog/.
[2] Utrecht University, Department of Philosophy, P.O. Box 80126,
NL-3508 TC Utrecht, The Netherlands.
http://www.phil.uu.nl/eng/home.html

Abstract. A grid protocol models concurrent computation, and consists of one or more modules repeatedly performing parallel I/O and computation. We provide several concise specification formats and correctness results on (external) I/O behaviour, and illustrate our approach by examples.

Note: Some of the results described in this paper were published earlier in [BHP97]; other results were established by students in the '96/'97 course Process Algebra II delivered at the University of Amsterdam [BJM97], and in a master's thesis [Pou97].

1 Introduction

This paper surveys work done on specification and analysis of "grid protocols". It is based on [BHP97], in which a simple class of these protocols is introduced, and on the papers [BJM97,Pou97], both of which deal with extensions.

A *Grid protocol* models concurrent computation in a grid-like architecture. This type of protocols is based on Synchronous Concurrent Algorithms (SCAs) as developed by Tucker *et al.* [TT94]). Our motivation to follow this approach can be illustrated by the following citation (*op. cit.*):

> "many specialised models of computation possess the essential features of SCAs, including systolic arrays, neural networks, cellular automata and coupled map lattices. The parallel algorithms, architectures and dynamical systems that comprise the class SCAs have many applications, ranging from their use in special purpose devices [...] to computational models of biological and physical phenomena."

* Partially sponsored by Esprit Working Group 8533 NADA — New Hardware Design Methods.

A grid protocol consists of *modules*, i.e., data processing units that can cooperate with each other or the environment by passing values (terminology taken from *op. cit.*). This cooperation can be modeled in various ways. In this paper we consider value-passing by synchronization (communication actions). A module has fixed incoming and outgoing channels or ports, modeling the connection with either one of the network's modules, or with some external device. Furthermore, it has an associated function. The current value of a module is either initial or computed from its function on the values received via its input ports. In terms of behaviour, a module repeatedly performs *parallel* execution of input and output actions, each of which operates on a distinct channel. Having executed all its I/O actions (Input/Output), the module updates its current value by application of its function to the newly received value(s). As an example, consider the module M in Fig. 1.

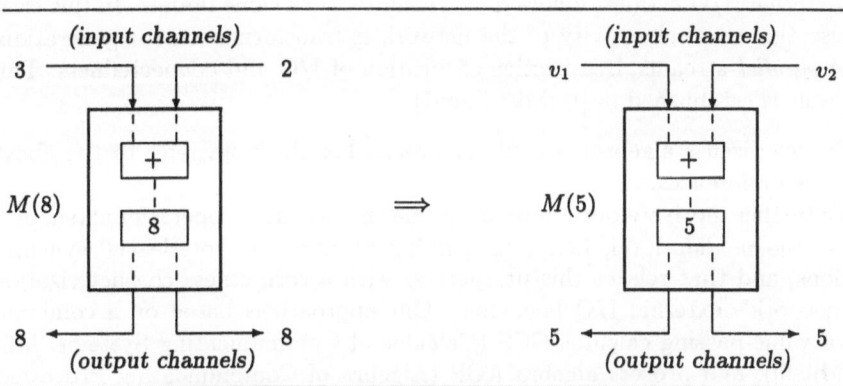

Fig. 1. Example of the operation of a single module.

In this figure, module M has current value 8, notation $M(8)$ (displayed at the left-hand side). This value can be sent along the two output channels, while values 3 and 2 are ready to be received along the two input channels. The function of this example module is to add the values received, thus the next current value will be 5 (available at the output channels), and new values v_1 and v_2 can be received. After this parallel I/O behaviour the module has evolved into $M(5)$. A straightforward, recursive specification of M's behaviour is

$$M(d) = (\| \text{ I/O value-passing actions}) \cdot M(e + f)$$

in case d is the current value, and values e and f are received as new input values. Throughout the paper, we stick to the convention that modules are depicted by rectangular blocks, with input channels coming in at the top and output channels leaving from the bottom.

A grid protocol can be a network of processors or (groups of) points of measure in some physical phenomenon, for example a hardware device or a vibrating string. In this paper we focus on modeling and characterization of grid protocols in process algebra. We offer some specification formats, and provide for each of these a general result on the external behaviour of the network (*characterization*). We come up with two characterization results on the external behaviour of grid protocols. These imply both corectness and freedom of deadlock:

1. In the case that all modules and internal channels of the network form a connected graph and the external behaviour is located at *one* single module, we obtain a simple characterization result: the order of the (internal) synchronizations is not relevant and the network's external behaviour — *stream* transformation or generation — is determined by a prefix of I/O actions, followed by a simultaneous value update. This result is established in [BHP97].

2. In the case that all modules are synchronized by a device that keeps the modules in pace, the operation of the network is characterized by a prefix of (external) I/O actions, followed by a simultaneous value update. In this case, also the external activity of the network is transformation (or generation) of *parallel* streams, irrespective of location of I/O and connectedness. This result is established in [BJM97,Pou97].

We do not discuss algebraic details or proofs. For these we refer to the above mentioned references.

We further motivate our approach as one that yields an operational perspective on the *module* level, i.e., value-passing by arbitrary interleaved synchronizations, and that relates this perspective with a correctness characterization of a network's external I/O behaviour. Our approach is based on a combination of value-passing calculus CCS (Calculus of Communicating Systems, Milner [Mil89]), and process algebra ACP (Algebra of Communicating Processes, Bergstra and Klop [BK84,BK85,BW90]). Main ingredients are *early read* actions, in which a variable can get instantiated via communication (value-passing), and the *process prefix*, a generalization of Milner's action prefix, introduced in [BB94]. With these ingredients, a concise notation of parallel input is possible.

Structure of the paper. In the next section we introduce value-passing, process prefixes and early read actions. In Section 3, we give a specification format for (finitary) connected networks with I/O located at one port, and discuss a characterization result. In the next section (4) we introduce a second class of grid protocols: *Beating Grid Protocols*. These networks are controlled by a *Beat*-process, i.e., a synchronization device that keeps parallel I/O of the whole network in phase. For this class we consider two types of *Beat*-processes, and state a general characterization result. In Section 5 we consider as an example an approximation of solutions of the one-dimensional *wave equation*, which can be modeled either as a connected grid protocol, or a beating grid protocol. Finally, in Section 6 we give some conclusions. An appendix gives a brief introduction to $\mathrm{ACP}^{\tau}(A, \gamma)$, the process algebraic approach underlying this paper.

Acknowledgements. Jos van Wamel and Gerard Kok are thanked for many contributions and discussions, especially concerning Section 5.1. Furthermore, Egbert-Jan van Buiten, Merijn de Jonge, Ramin Monajemi, and Marco Pouw are thanked for their contributions in establishing specification and verification of beating grid protocols. Didier Caucal and Kethil Stoelen are thanked for valuable comments.

2 Data and some Process Algebra

In this section we explain *value-passing*, the basic communication mechanism in grid protocols. Furthermore, we introduce early reads and process prefixing, and show that these form a concise notation for the mechanics of parallel value-passing. On the fly we recall some process algebra.

2.1 Actions, Value-Passing, and Generalized Merge

Actions are the most basic processes we deal with. Furthermore, we consider handshaking communication between actions: the simultaneous occurrence of two actions fuses together to a new action. Such an action is often called a communication action, and we assume both the set of actions, and the communications as parameters of our theory. If two actions a and b communicate to action c, we can use the *communication merge* $|$ and write

$$a \mid b = c,$$

and in case we are not particularly interested in c, we also say that a and b synchronize. If a and b do not communicate, we write

$$a \mid b = \delta,$$

where δ is a symbol expressing deadlock or inaction. The communication merge is a commutative and associative operation on processes.

We adopt a simple specification paradigm for processes parameterized with data, which originates from μCRL [GP95]. As grid protocols process data, we demand computability and decidability of all data involved (in the sense of [BT95]). Data parameterization is used in actions, sums, and communications.

In order to specify value-passing, let i, j be channel identifiers. Action $r_i(t)$ models the act of *receiving* the particular value t along channel i. Action $s_j(t)$ models the *sending* of data value t along port j. Here t may also be a product of data values. Let for instance r_i and s_j be typed as actions that can carry values of type $\mathbb{N}$ (the natural numbers), and of type $\mathbb{N}^2$, respectively. So $r_i(0), r_i(1), ..., s_j(0,0), s_j(0,1), ...$ are considered actions.

A first example of a data-parametric sum is the expression

$$\sum_{v:\mathbb{N}} (r_i(v)),$$

denoting a process that for an arbitrary value n of $\mathbb{N}$ can once perform action $r_i(n)$, after which it terminates. Note that the type of the variable v is declared *in* the scope of the $\sum$-operation. This expression represents the infinite summation

$$r_i(0) + r_i(1) + r_i(2) + \cdots$$

where the commutative and associative operation $+$ is called *alternative composition* or *choice*, and defines the execution of one of its operands. However,

$$x + \delta = x.$$

(So in context of alternative composition, δ behaves as inaction.) Alternative composition binds weakest of all binary operations.

A typical form of data-parametric sums concerns the combination with *sequential composition*: $x \cdot y$, or simply xy represents process x followed by y. For example,

$$\sum_{v:\mathbb{N}} (r_i(v) \cdot s_j(2v, v+1))$$

represents the infinite summation

$$r_i(0) \cdot s_j(0,1) + r_i(1) \cdot s_j(2,2) + r_i(2) \cdot s_j(4,3) + \cdots.$$

The operation $\cdot$ is associative, and defines the sequential execution of its operands. However,

$$\delta \cdot x = \delta.$$

(So, $a \cdot \delta$ deadlocks after execution of a.) Sequential composition binds strongest of all binary operations. Furthermore, note that

$$x(y+z) \neq xy + xz.$$

(For example, in case $x = y = a$ and $z = \delta$, the leftmost process equals aa, whereas the rightmost process can deadlock with $a\delta$.) On the other hand, we do have

$$(x+y)z = xz + yz.$$

A form of repeated sequential composition, employed in the specification of grid protocols, is *no-exit iteration*, introduced in [Fok97] and defined by

$$x^\omega = x \cdot (x)^\omega.$$

For data-parametric sums, axioms and a proof rule are defined in [GP91c,GP94b]. In particular, these comprise α-conversion and axioms to change its scope. We adopt the convention that $\sum_{...} (\_)$ binds strongest of all operations, for example

$$\sum_{v:\mathbb{N}} (r_i(v) \cdot s_j(2v, v+1))^\omega = (\sum_{v:\mathbb{N}} (r_i(v) \cdot s_j(2v, v+1)))^\omega.$$

As for data-parametric communications, we assume that the communications in Table 1, defining *send-read communication*, are the only ones defined.

283

Table 1. Send-read communication for value-passing, $a, b \in A$.

$$a \mid b = \begin{cases} c_i(t) & \text{if } \{a, b\} = \{r_i(t), s_i(t)\} \\ \delta & \text{otherwise.} \end{cases}$$

Data-parametric sums distribute over the communication merge $\mid$, provided no new bindings arise. Also $+$ distributes over $\mid$. For example,

$$r_i(2) \mid (s_i(2) + s_j(2,2)) = r_i(2) \mid s_i(2) + r_i(2) \mid s_j(2,2) = c_i(2) + \delta = c_i(2),$$
$$(r_i(1) + r_i(2)) \mid s_i(2) = c_i(2),$$
$$\textstyle\sum_{v:\mathbb{N}}(r_i(v)) \mid s_i(2) = \sum_{v:\mathbb{N}}(r_i(v) \mid s_i(2)) = c_i(2).$$

With help of send-read communication and *encapsulation* one can easily model value-passing (cf. [Mil89]). Here encapsulation is defined by an operation that renames all actions in H into δ,

$$\partial_H(a) = \begin{cases} \delta & \text{if } a \in H, \\ a & \text{otherwise.} \end{cases}$$

Furtmermore, encapsulation distributes over $\cdot$, $+$, and $\sum_{\ldots}(\text{-})$.

Encapsulation does not distribute over merge operations, and can be used to enforce communication between concurrent processes, such as value-passing communications. Rather than considering processses $P \mid Q$ of which the first action must be a communication between P and Q, concurrent execution of P and Q is specified as

$$P \parallel Q,$$

where the merge operator $\parallel$ is defined by ACP-axiom (CM1)

$$x \parallel y = (x \mathbin{\lfloor\!\lfloor} y + y \mathbin{\lfloor\!\lfloor} x) + x \mid y.$$

Here $\mathbin{\lfloor\!\lfloor}$, *leftmerge*, is an auxiliary operation that requires that the first action performed stems from the left operand. It is axiomatized by

(CM2) $\quad a \mathbin{\lfloor\!\lfloor} x = a \cdot x$

(CM3) $\quad ax \mathbin{\lfloor\!\lfloor} y = a(x \parallel y)$

(CM4) $(x + y) \mathbin{\lfloor\!\lfloor} z = x \mathbin{\lfloor\!\lfloor} z + y \mathbin{\lfloor\!\lfloor} z$

where a is an action, δ, or τ (a constant explained below). So in $P \parallel Q$, the first action comes either from P, from Q, or is a communication between P and Q.

Now, for a small, typical example on value-passing involving encapsulation, consider

$$R = \textstyle\sum_{v:\mathbb{N}}(r_i(v) \cdot s_j(2v, v + 1))^\omega,$$

a process that is willing to receive any natural k along channel i, then sends the pair $(2k, k+1)$ along channel j, and then resumes this behaviour. Assume that R is executed in parallel with

$$s_i(5) \cdot S,$$

a process that initially sends the value 5 along channel i. The value-passing of 5 from $s_i(5) \cdot S$ to R along channel i can be represented by

$$\partial_{\{r_i, s_i\}}(R \parallel s_i(5) \cdot S)$$

where we adopt the notation $\partial_{\{r_i, s_i\}}$, only mentioning the identifiers r_i, s_i, from μCRL. Hence, single $r_i(n)$ and $s_i(n)$ actions cannot occur and are thus enforced to communicate. We derive

$$\partial_{\{r_i, s_i\}}(R \parallel s_i(5) \cdot S) = \partial_{\{r_i, s_i\}}(\textstyle\sum_{v: \mathbb{N}}(r_i(v) \cdot s_j(2v, v+1)) \cdot R \parallel s_i(5) \cdot S)$$
$$= c_i(5) \cdot \partial_{\{r_i, s_i\}}(s_j(10, 6) \cdot R \parallel S),$$

where the second identity follows from the axioms of $\mathrm{ACP}^\tau(A, \gamma)$ and those for data-parametric sums. So, the *value-passing* in this example is modeled by the execution of the communication action $c_i(5)$ and the resulting process is $\partial_{\{r_i, s_i\}}(s_j(10, 6) \cdot R \parallel S)$. In the setting of μCRL, a detailed treatment of this value-passing format can be found in [GK95].

The distinction between internal (unobservable) and external (observable) behaviour is modeled with the hiding operation τ_I, where I is a set of (internal) actions. This operation renames the actions in I into τ, the silent action:

$$\tau_I(a) = \begin{cases} \tau & \text{if } a \in I, \\ a & \text{otherwise}, \end{cases}$$

and distributes over $\cdot$, $+$, and $\sum_{\dots}(\_)$. For the constant τ, an important axiom is $x \cdot \tau = x$.

Grid protocols are specified as the concurrent composition of a finite number of modules, and for readability it makes sense to use the *generalized merge*

$$\left[\left\Vert_{i \in I} P_i \right. \right]$$

which abbreviates the expression $(P_{i_1} \parallel P_{i_2} \parallel \dots \parallel P_{i_n})$ for $I = \{i_1, i_2, \dots, i_n\}$ a non-empty, finite set of indices. This notation can be justified by commutativity and associativity of the $\parallel$ operation. If I is a singleton, say $I = \{i_1\}$,

$$\left[\left\Vert_{i \in \{i_1\}} P_i \right. \right] = P_{i_1}.$$

We often write $\left[\left\Vert_{i=1}^{n} P_i \right. \right]$ rather than $\left[\left\Vert_{i \in \{1, \dots, n\}} P_i \right. \right]$.

The following result follows easily by induction on n, exploiting $\tau x \parallel y = \tau(x \parallel y)$ and $x\tau = x$, and is typical for the process algebraic reasoning that underlies our characterization results.

Lemma 2.1.1. $x \left(\left[\left\Vert_{i=1}^{n} \tau y_i \right. \right] \parallel z \right) = x \left(\left[\left\Vert_{i=1}^{n} y_i \right. \right] \parallel z \right).$

2.2 Parallel Input: Early Reads and Process Prefix

Let D be some data type. We introduce the binary operation *process prefix* and *early read actions* as a means to provide concise notation for parallel input. Let i be a channel or port identifier, and v a variable of type D. Then

$$er_i(v); x = \sum_{v:D}(r_i(v) \cdot x)$$

is the axiom scheme that introduces the early read action $er_i(v)$ and the operation ;, the process prefix. This identity is a μCRL-like interpretation of the early read axiom in [BB94]. It is meant that v may occur in process x, e.g.,

$$er_i(v); s_j(v) = \sum_{v:D}(r_i(v) \cdot s_j(v))$$

is an expression without free data-variables, and so is

$$er_i(v); s_j(t) = \sum_{v:D}(r_i(v) \cdot s_j(t))$$

for t a closed term of type D.

Remark 2.2.1. The axiom scheme above reflects Milner's translation of the basic CCS term $a(x).E$ into the value-passing CCS term

$$\sum_{v \in V} a_v.E\widehat{\{v/x\}}$$

where V is the value set and $\widehat{}$ the translation function [Mil89].

Let A_{er} be the extension of A (the set of atomic actions) with early read actions for any action $r_i : D_1 \times ... \times D_n$ declared over A. Axioms for process prefixing are given in Table 2. The axiom PP4 is considered to be parameterized with the type of the r_i action. Note that for the er actions we use *globally* typed variables.

Table 2. Early input and process prefixing, $a \in A$.

(PP1) $\delta; x = \delta$		(PP4) $er_k(v); x = \sum_{v:D}(r_k(v) \cdot x)$
(PP2) $\tau; x = \tau \cdot x$		(PP5) $(x + y); z = x; z + y; z$
(PP3) $a; x = a \cdot x$		(PP6) $(x \cdot y); z = x; (y; z)$

By the send-read communication paradigm (see Table 1) we have that $er_i(v) \mid a = \delta$ for all $a \in A_{er}$. This is used in the following example, in which parallel input is unraveled (v, w variables of some type D):

$$(er_i(v) \parallel er_j(w)); s_l(F(v, w))$$
$$\overset{(CM1)}{=} (er_i(v) \parallel\!\!\!\!- er_j(w) + er_j(w) \parallel\!\!\!\!- er_i(v) + er_i(v) \mid er_j(w)); s_l(F(v, w))$$
$$\overset{(CF2)}{=} (er_i(v) \cdot er_j(w) + er_j(w) \cdot er_i(v) + \delta); s_l(F(v, w))$$
$$\overset{(PP5)}{=} (er_i(v) \cdot er_j(w)); s_l(F(v, w)) + (er_j(w) \cdot er_i(v)); s_l(F(v, w))$$
$$\overset{(PP6)}{=} er_i(v); (er_j(w); s_l(F(v, w))) + er_j(w); (er_i(v); s_l(F(v, w))).$$

Applying axiom PP4 to the last expression yields that

$$(er_i(v) \parallel er_j(w)); s_l(F(v, w)) = \begin{cases} \sum_{v:D}(r_i(v) \cdot \sum_{w:D}(r_j(w) \cdot s_l(F(v, w)))) \\ + \\ \sum_{w:D}(r_j(w) \cdot \sum_{v:D}(r_i(v) \cdot s_l(F(v, w)))), \end{cases}$$

showing conciseness of notation with early read actions and process prefix. Observe that in case we replace w by v,

$$(er_i(v) \parallel er_j(v)); s_l(F(v, v)) = \begin{cases} \sum_{v:D}(r_i(v) \cdot \sum_{v:D}(r_j(v) \cdot s_l(F(v, v)))) \\ + \\ \sum_{v:D}(r_j(v) \cdot \sum_{v:D}(r_i(v) \cdot s_l(F(v, v)))). \end{cases}$$

This example models *non-deterministic* input along one of the channels i, j, yielding send-action $s_l(F(k, k))$ with k being the value received. In the peculiar case that the channel identifier j is replaced by i, we find that

$$(er_i(v) \parallel er_i(w)); s_l(F(v, w)) = \begin{cases} \sum_{v:D}(r_i(v) \cdot \sum_{w:D}(r_i(w) \cdot s_l(F(v, w)))) \\ + \\ \sum_{w:D}(r_i(w) \cdot \sum_{v:D}(r_i(v) \cdot s_l(F(v, w)))) \end{cases}$$

models the sending of either $s_l(F(j, k))$ or $s_l(F(k, j))$ if values j and k are sent along i. Finally,

$$(er_i(v) \parallel er_i(v)); s_l(F(v, v)) = (er_i(v) \cdot er_i(v)); s_l(F(v, v))$$

describes the situation in which the first inputed value along channel i is neglected, and the second one instantiates $F(v, v)$.

Remark 2.2.2. We stress that the process

$$\sum_{v:D}(\sum_{w:D}((r_i(v) \parallel r_j(w))s_l(F(v, w))))$$

does *not* model parallel input: if for example $D = \{0, 1\}$,

$$\sum_{v:D}(\sum_{w:D}((r_i(v) \parallel r_j(w))s_l(F(v, w)))) = \begin{aligned} &(r_i(0) \parallel r_j(0)) \cdot s_l(F(0, 0)) + \\ &(r_i(0) \parallel r_j(1)) \cdot s_l(F(0, 1)) + \\ &(r_i(1) \parallel r_j(0)) \cdot s_l(F(1, 0)) + \\ &(r_i(1) \parallel r_j(1)) \cdot s_l(F(1, 1)). \end{aligned}$$

So, upon reading the first value along channel i or j, the choice for the second read action is already fixed.

Furthermore, τ_I and ∂_H-applications also apply to er-actions via axiom PP4, using the μCRL axioms that state that these applications commute with the $\sum$-operation. For instance,

$$\partial_{\{r_i\}}(er_i(v); P_1 + er_j(w); P_2)$$
$$= \partial_{\{r_i\}}(\textstyle\sum_{v:D}(r_i(v)P_1)) + \partial_{\{r_i\}}(\textstyle\sum_{w:\mathbb{N}}(r_j(w)P_2))$$
$$= \textstyle\sum_{v:D}(\partial_{\{r_i\}}(r_i(v)P_1)) + \textstyle\sum_{w:\mathbb{N}}(\partial_{\{r_i\}}(r_j(w)P_2))$$
$$= \textstyle\sum_{v:D}(\delta) + \textstyle\sum_{w:\mathbb{N}}(r_j(w)\partial_{\{r_i\}}P_2)$$
$$= \delta + er_j(w); \partial_{\{r_i\}}(P_2)$$
$$= er_j(w); \partial_{\{r_i\}}(P_2).$$

3 Modules and Connected, single-I/O Networks

In this section we propose a specification format for *connected networks*. Such a network consists of *modules*, elementary data processing units which may have feedback. Next we introduce *connected networks* as a format for the parallel execution of such modules. Our modeling is based on [TT94], in which SCAs (Synchronous Concurrent Algorithms) are analyzed.

3.1 Modules

A module M_i has a (current) value d, a fixed (positive) number n of input channels $i_1, ..., i_n$, and a fixed (positive) number m of output channels $o_1, ..., o_m$. Channels have unit bandwidth and are unidirectional; this corresponds with our format for value-passing as discussed in the previous section. We first consider a setting with only one data type D. Computation in M_i is modeled by a (total) value function $F_i : D^n \rightarrow D$. The complete operation of module $M_i(d)$ can be described as follows:

$$M_i(d) = \left(\left[\mathbin{\overset{n}{\underset{j=1}{\|}}} er_{i_j}(v_j) \right] \| \left[\mathbin{\overset{m}{\underset{j=1}{\|}}} s_{o_j}(d) \right] \right) ; M_i(F_i(v_1, ..., v_n)). \tag{1}$$

Unfortunately, this definition presupposes that M_i has no *feedback*, i.e. that $\{i_1, ..., i_n\} \cap \{o_1, ..., o_m\} = \emptyset$ because early read actions do not communicate (otherwise, the value in question would get lost). So for the particular case that M_i also has a feedback channel f, its definition should be something like

$$M_i(d) = \left(\left[\mathbin{\overset{n}{\underset{j=1}{\|}}} er_{i_j}(v_j) \right] \| \left[\mathbin{\overset{m}{\underset{j=1}{\|}}} s_{o_j}(d) \right] \right) ; M_i(F_i(d, v_1, ..., v_n)), \tag{2}$$

where the first argument of F_i models the feedback. This has two disadvantages: we lose uniformity of specification, and the feedback action is not explicit, only its effect is. As can be expected, we allow at most one feedback channel per module.

Because uniformity of specification is particularly useful in proving correctness, we adopt a "low level specification format" of modules, and obtain (1) as a derivable identity. Because feedback is an explicit, but hidden action in our specification format, we postpone the derivable variant of (2) till after the introduction of the operation of *networks*. Module $M_i(d)$ as described above is defined by means of two iterative processes. The first one of these defines the *receive*-part Rec_i of the module (modeling its read actions), the second its *send*-part $Send_i(d)$ (ready to send the value d along the ports $o_1, ..., o_m$). These two parts communicate along some channel i, internal to module M_i, and are also used to model computation of F_i. More precisely, communication of a value $F_i(d_1, ..., d_n)$ by (internal) action $c(F_i(d_1, ..., d_n))$ can only take place if all parallel read actions of Rec_i have been executed, and if also $Send_i(d)$ has performed all its (parallel) send actions $s_{o_j}(d)$. This yields the following specification and picture of $M_i(d)$:

$$M_i(d) = \tau_{\{c_i\}} \circ \partial_{\{r_i, s_i\}}(Rec_i \parallel Send_i(d)),$$

$$Rec_i = \left(\left[\mathop{\parallel}_{j=1}^{n} er_{i_j}(v_j) \right] ; s_i(F_i(v_1, ..., v_n)) \right)^\omega ,$$

$$Send_i(d) = \left[\mathop{\parallel}_{j=1}^{m} s_{o_j}(d) \right] \cdot Send_i,$$

$$Send_i = \left(er_i(v); \left[\mathop{\parallel}_{j=1}^{m} s_{o_j}(v) \right] \right)^\omega .$$

In case M_i has no feedback, i.e., $\{i_1, ..., i_n\} \cap \{o_1, ..., o_m\} = \emptyset$, it follows that $M_i(d)$ has a process prefix

$$(er_{i_1}(v_1) \parallel ... \parallel er_{i_n}(v_n) \parallel s_{o_1}(d) \parallel ... \parallel s_{o_m}(d))$$

(this is a consequence of Theorem 3.3.3). After having read certain values $d_1, d_2, ..., d_n$ along channels $i_1, ..., i_n$, and having sent d along ports $o_1, ..., o_m$, the module's current value is updated to $F_i(d_1, ..., d_n)$ by a value-passing communication along channel i, renamed into the silent action τ. After this, the next process prefix is ready to be performed:

$$(er_{i_1}(v_1) \parallel ... \parallel er_{i_n}(v_n) \parallel s_{o_1}(F_i(d_1, ..., d_n)) \parallel ... \parallel s_{o_m}(F_i(d_1, ..., d_n))) .$$

For readability, we introduce the following abbreviation for synchronization and abstraction over some port i: we further write

$$P \parallel_i Q \quad \text{instead of} \quad \tau_{\{c_i\}} \circ \partial_{\{r_i, s_i\}}(P \parallel Q).$$

Henceforth, $M_i(d) = Rec_i \parallel_i Send_i(d)$.

Because the specific typing of the read and send actions is not relevant, except that the function F_i must be compatible with it, we further consider a many-sorted setting. We assume that each variable is uniquely typed.

3.2 Connected Networks

A network is a finite collection of modules, in which the read/send connections respect the typing of the corresponding read and send actions. A general restriction is that there is *at most one* channel for transmission between any two modules M_i and M_j. In particular, we do not allow merging of channels, or more than one feedback channel per module (case $i = j$). Note that branching of channels is modeled by taking different send actions. In this section we consider *connected* network specifications of the form

$$\tau_I \circ \partial_H \left(\left[\parallel_{i=1}^{n} M_i(d_i) \right] \right).$$

Here, connectedness refers to the graph which has the modules as nodes, and the (undirected) channels as arcs. In the specification above, the ∂_H application models value-passing synchronizations between modules $M_1, ..., M_n$, and the τ_I application models hiding of the resulting communication actions. We further say that the *I/O* of a network denotes its *external* actions, i.e., read or send actions that have no communication partner within the network. A network is *single-output* if its I/O consists of exactly one output action, which will be referred to as

$$s_{out}(...).$$

Below we recall an example taken from [BHP97] for computing a Fibonacci sequence using a connected single-output network consisting of modules M_1 and M_2. This example also illustrates the particular way we deal with *feedback*.

Example 3.2.1. *Consider the following network in which all values to be passed are of type* $\mathbb{N}$*, and in which a channel name* ij *indicates that values are transmitted from module* M_i *to module* M_j*:*

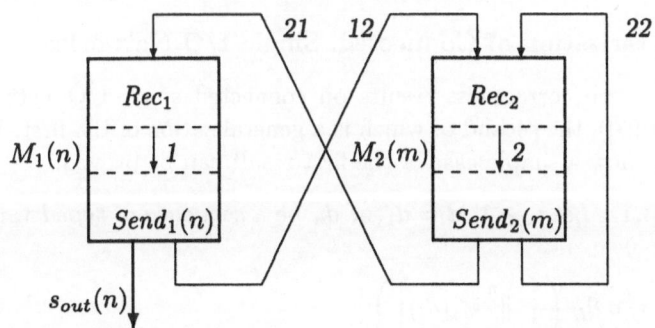

We can specify these modules by the following two iterative processes $M_1(n)$ and $M_2(m)$:

$$M_1(n) = Rec_1 \parallel_1 Send_1(n),$$
$$Rec_1 = (er_{21}(v); s_1(v))^\omega,$$
$$Send_1(n) = (s_{out}(n) \parallel s_{12}(n)) \cdot Send_1,$$
$$Send_1 = (er_1(v); (s_{out}(v) \parallel s_{12}(v)))^\omega,$$

and

$$M_2(m) = Rec_2 \parallel_2 Send_2(m),$$
$$Rec_2 = ((er_{12}(v_1) \parallel er_{22}(v_2)); s_2(v_1 + v_2))^\omega,$$
$$Send_2(m) = (s_{21}(m) \parallel s_{22}(m)) \cdot Send_2,$$
$$Send_2 = (er_2(v); (s_{21}(v) \parallel s_{22}(v)))^\omega.$$

Let $I = \{c_{21}, c_{12}, c_{22}\}$ and $H = \{r_{21}, s_{21}, r_{12}, s_{12}, r_{22}, s_{22}\}$. The Fibonacci Network

$$\tau_I \circ \partial_H(M_1(1) \parallel M_2(1))$$

computes the ordinary Fibonacci sequence $1, 1, 2, 3, 5, 8, \ldots$ as the values of its consecutive s_{out}-actions:

$$\tau \cdot \tau_I \circ \partial_H(M_1(1) \parallel M_2(1))$$
$$= \tau \cdot s_{out}(1) \cdot s_{out}(1) \cdot s_{out}(2) \cdot s_{out}(3) \cdot s_{out}(5) \cdot s_{out}(8) \cdot \ \cdots$$

where the leftmost τ's smooth the difference between the networks first possible actions: either $s_{out}(1)$ or τ resulting from some internal value-passing. A different characterization is given by the equation

$$\tau \cdot \tau_I \circ \partial_H(M_1(n) \parallel M_2(m)) = \tau \cdot s_{out}(n) \cdot \tau_I \circ \partial_H(M_1(m) \parallel M_2(n + m)),$$

from which it is immediately clear that $\tau \cdot \tau_I \circ \partial_H(M_1(1) \parallel M_2(1))$ computes the Fibonacci sequence. This equation can easily be grasped from the picture above; its correctness follows from Theorem 3.3.1 presented in the following section.

3.3 Characterization of Connected, Single-I/O Networks

In this section two correctness results on connected single-I/O networks are recalled ([BHP97]), the second of which is a generalization of the first. We show by an example how a simple case of the first result can be proved.

Theorem 3.3.1. Let $n \geq 1$, $\boldsymbol{d} = d_1, \ldots, d_n$ be a sequence of typed values, and let

$$N(\boldsymbol{d}) = \tau_I \circ \partial_H \left(\left[\parallel_{i=1}^n M_i(d_i) \right] \right)$$

be a network that is connected and single-output, where M_1 is the output-module. Then

$$\tau \cdot N(d) = \tau \cdot s_{out}(d_1) \cdot N(F_1(d_1), ..., F_n(d_n))$$

where F_i is the value function of module M_i, and d_i abbreviates $d_{i_1}, ..., d_{i_k}$ whenever F_i computes on the values of modules $M_{i_1}, ..., M_{i_k}$, respectively.

For the case $n = 1$, the proof of the theorem is trivial. We spell out a most simple instance. This also shows how a derivable variant of (2)—i.e., a data-parametric definition of a module with feedback—would look like.

Example 3.3.2. *Consider the following network $N(d)$ where $d \in \mathbb{N}$, containing one module*

$$M_1(d) = Rec_1 \parallel_1 Send_1(d)$$

that generates a stream:

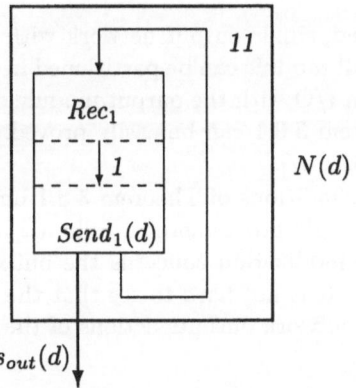

Here

$$Rec_1 = \sum_{v:\mathbb{N}}(r_{11}(v) \cdot s_1(v+1))^\omega,$$
$$Send_1 = \sum_{v:\mathbb{N}}(r_1(v)(s_{11}(v) \parallel s_{out}(v)))^\omega,$$
$$Send_1(d) = (s_{11}(d) \parallel s_{out}(d)) \cdot Send_1.$$

Let $H = \{r_{11}, s_{11}\}$. The behaviour of $\partial_H(Rec_1 \parallel_1 Send_1(d))$ can be analyzed as follows:

$$\begin{aligned}
\partial_H(M_1(d)) &= \partial_H(Rec_1 \parallel_1 Send_1(d)) \\
&= c_{11}(d) \cdot \partial_H(s_1(d+1) \cdot Rec_1 \parallel_1 s_{out}(d) \cdot Send_1) \\
&\quad + s_{out}(d) \cdot \partial_H(Rec_1 \parallel_1 s_{11}(d) \cdot Send_1) \\
&= c_{11}(d) \cdot s_{out}(d) \cdot \partial_H(s_1(d+1) \cdot Rec_1 \parallel_1 Send_1) \\
&\quad + s_{out}(d) \cdot c_{11}(d) \cdot \partial_H(s_1(d+1) \cdot Rec_1 \parallel_1 Send_1) \\
&= c_{11}(d) \cdot s_{out}(d) \cdot c_1(d+1) \cdot \partial_H(Rec_1 \parallel_1 Send_1(d+1)) \\
&\quad + s_{out}(d) \cdot c_{11}(d) \cdot c_1(d+1) \cdot \partial_H(Rec_1 \parallel_1 Send_1(d+1)).
\end{aligned}$$

Let $I = \{c_{11}\}$, then it follows from the derivation above that the one-module network

$$N(d) = \tau_I \circ \partial_H(M_1(d))$$

for some $d \in \mathbb{N}$ satisfies

$$N(d) = \tau \cdot s_{out}(d) \cdot N(d+1) + s_{out}(d) \cdot N(d+1).$$

Hence

$$\tau \cdot N(d) = \tau \cdot s_{out}(d) \cdot N(d+1),$$

expressing that $\tau \cdot N(d)$ outputs the infinite stream

$$\tau \cdot s_{out}(d) \cdot s_{out}(d+1) \cdot s_{out}(d+2) \cdot \;\cdots.$$

In general, a connected, single-output network with more than one module, all modules but the output module can be partitioned in a number of connected sub-networks that perform I/O with the output module only. From this perspective, the correctness Theorem 3.3.1 can be easily proved. The reader interested in a proof is referred to [BHP97].[1]

We can relax the conditions of Theorem 3.3.1 under which the execution of a network satisfies a single process prefix, followed by a recursive update of its data state. A first generalization concerns the output actions of a connected, single-output network. It is not hard to see that the previous correctness result is preserved if such a network outputs actions of the form

$$s_{out}(F(d))$$

for some function F rather than $s_{out}(d)$. We call this *output modification* of the *out*-channel.

A second generalization concerns *additional* external output of the network. Assume a network

$$N(\boldsymbol{d}) = \tau_I \circ \partial_H \left(\left[\big\|_{i=1}^{n} M_i(d_i) \right] \right)$$

has more than one output channel, and that I is such that all extra output channels not located at the I/O module are hidden. Then $N(\boldsymbol{d})$ is *single*-I/O if all its I/O activity (its collection of external read and send actions) stems from a single module, the I/O-*module*. Our most general result on the class of connected network is the following: [2]

---

[1] We remark that the last condition in the definition of Rec_l, i.e., $m \in R_l \setminus R' \Rightarrow x_m \in D_{j_m}$, should be skipped.

[2] Cf. [BHP97], though we exploit the Expansion Theorem and alphabet axioms (both recalled in the Appendix) to obtain a nicer formulation.

Theorem 3.3.3. *Let* $n \geq 1$, $\boldsymbol{d} = d_1, ..., d_n$ *be a sequence of typed values, and let*

$$N(\boldsymbol{d}) = \tau_I \circ \partial_H \left(\left[\|_{i=1}^{n} M_i(d_i) \right] \right)$$

be a network that is connected and single-I/O, where M_1 *is the I/O-module and Extern is the set of indices of the I/O channels. (Notice that Extern $\neq \emptyset$ and may hide output from non-I/O-modules.)*

Then

$$\tau \cdot N(\boldsymbol{d}) = \tau \cdot \left[\|_{i \in Extern} a_i(x_i) \right] \; ; \; \tau_I \circ \partial_H \left(\left[\|_{i=1}^{n} M_i(F_i(\boldsymbol{d}_i)) \right] \right)$$

where

1. *Function* F_i *is the value function of module* M_i,
2. *For* $i > 1$, $\boldsymbol{d}_i$ *abbreviates* $d_{i_1}, ..., d_{i_k}$ *whenever* F_i *computes on the values of modules* $M_{i_1}, ..., M_{i_k}$, *respectively,*
3. *For* $i \in Extern$, *either* $a_i(x_i) \equiv s_i(G_i(d_1))$ *where* G_i *is the output modification of channel* i, *or* $a_i(x_i) \equiv er_i(v_i)$,
4. *Sequence* $\boldsymbol{d}_1$ *is defined similar, except for its Extern-coordinates (see the clause 3).*

This result gives way to regarding networks as *stream transformers*, be it that the I/O connection is located at a single module. In particular, this allows one to connect single-I/O networks with each other while preserving a simple correctness characterization. We apply this theorem in Section 5.

4 Beating Grid Protocols

In some cases the restriction to single-I/O networks is too strong. If for example one wants to model the operation of a simple *SR*-latch in process algebra (or *RS* Flip-Flop, cf. Section 5.1.2 in [TT94]), we obtain a network with multi-I/O. Below we depict an *SR*-latch in two typical states: irrespective of the value b, output at Q is 0, respectively 1. The components below symbolize *nor*-ports (where $nor(x, y) = 1 - max(x, y)$).

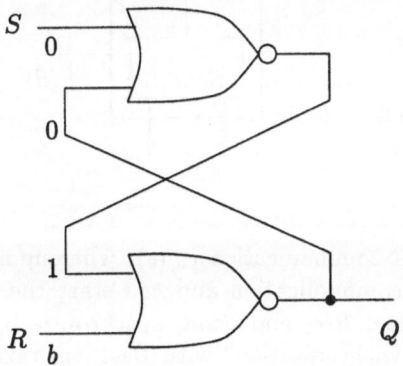
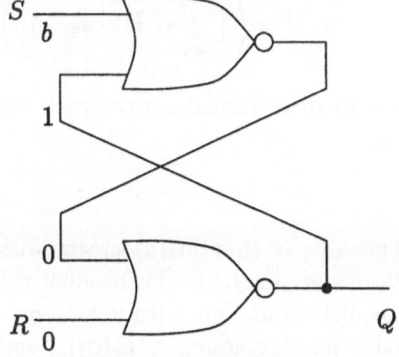

The format for connected networks discussed in the previous section does not comply to the intended operation of this network: it does not imply that S is evaluated before R starts its second evaluation. In this section we obtain the following type of characterization for *multi-I/O networks*, expressing that the I/O is performed *per cycle*:

$$\tau \cdot N(d) = \tau \cdot ((\| \text{ all I/O value-passing actions}) \; ; \; N(F_i(d_i)))$$

i.e., we want to view network operation in a similar way as module operation, performing I/O in consecutive phases. A way to achieve this is to assume a global synchronization device, the *Beat* process. We consider two different options for the definition of such a device.

4.1 Synchronized Modules

We follow the approach described in Section 3.1, but extend module specification with two external synchronization points with a *Beat* process, and one extra internal synchronization point. Another difference is that we associate a unique variable with *each* input channel:

$$M_i(d) = Rec_i \|_i Send_i(d),$$

$$Rec_i = \left(r_i \left(\left[\overset{n}{\underset{j=1}{\|}} er_{i_j}(v_{i_j}) \right] ; s_i(F_i(v_{i_1}, ..., v_{i_n})) \right) \right)^\omega,$$

$$Send_i(d) = r_{b_i}(s) \cdot s_i \cdot \left[\overset{m}{\underset{j=1}{\|}} s_{o_j}(d) \right] \cdot Send_i,$$

$$Send_i = \left(er_i(v_i); \left(r_{b_i}(e) \cdot r_{b_i}(s) \cdot s_i \cdot \left[\overset{m}{\underset{j=1}{\|}} s_{o_j}(v_i) \right] \right) \right)^\omega.$$

and

$$Beat = \left(\left[\overset{n}{\underset{i=1}{\|}} s_{b_i}(s) \right] \cdot \left[\overset{n}{\underset{i=1}{\|}} s_{b_i}(e) \right] \right)^\omega,$$

or

$$Beat = \left(\left[\overset{n}{\underset{i=1}{\|}} s_{b_i}(s) \cdot s_{b_i}(e) \right] \right)^\omega,$$

provided we consider a network with n modules.

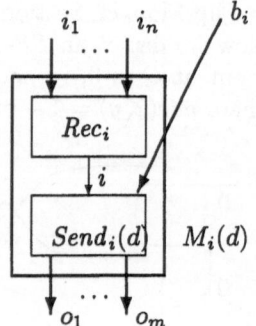

The idea is that $M_i(d)$ starts with a *Beat*-communication $c_{b_i}(s)$, whereupon Rec_i and $Send_i(d)$ synchronize with a c_i-communication and can start their parallel input and output actions. After this, Rec_i and $Send_i$ synchronize by value-passing action $c_i(F_i(d_i))$, and "end-synchronization" with *Beat* can take place by a $c_{b_i}(e)$ communication, by which the module evolves into $M_i(F_i(d_i))$. In the following section we further explain the synchronization actions between M_i and *Beat*.

4.2 Networks with a Beat

Again a network is a collection of modules as defined above, in which the read/send connections respect the typing of the read and send actions. As in the previous section we adopt the restriction that there is *at most one* channel for transmission of data from a module to a module (but feedback is allowed). For an n-module network, we consider two different definitions for the *Beat* process as given above. So, the action $s_{b_i}(s)$ gives module M_i permission to start its parallel I/O, and $s_{b_i}(e)$ signals end of this activity. By definition of send-read communication, these actions yield communications $c_{b_i}(s)$ and $c_{b_i}(e)$. Note that the second definition of *Beat* is most liberal, as it covers each execution of the first one. (The converse is not true: *all* $s_{b_j}(s)$ actions must take place before an $s_{b_i}(e)$ action can occur.)

In this section we consider network specifications of the form

$$\tau_I \circ \partial_H \left(\left[\overset{n}{\underset{i=1}{\|}} M_i(d_i) \right] \| \textit{Beat} \right),$$

in which the ∂_H application models value-passing synchronizations between modules $M_1, ..., M_n$ and *Beat*, and the τ_I application models hiding of the resulting communication actions. In this case, the rhythm of the *Beat* guides the operation of the network.

Below we give an example for computing the operation of an *SR*-latch using a beating grid protocol.

Example 4.2.1. *SR-Latch. Consider the following network in which all data to be transmitted are in $\{0,1\}$. A channel name ij indicates that values are transmitted from module M_i to module M_j: We put the branching of output of the R, Q-module explicit in the module (corresponding with the restriction that channels have bandwidth 1):*

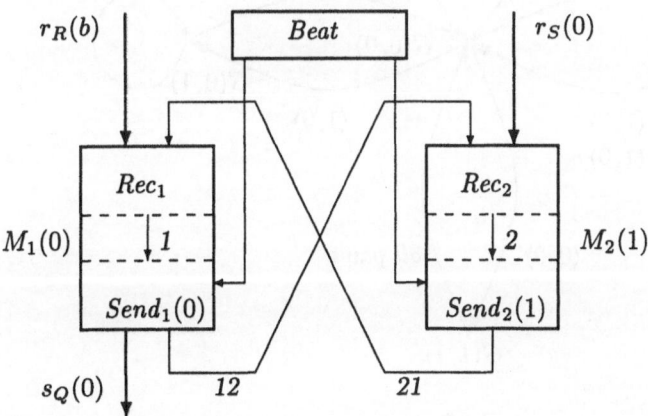

The precise specification of $M_1(b_1)$ and $M_2(b_2)$ is as follows:

$$M_1(b_1) = Rec_1 \parallel_1 Send_1(b_1),$$
$$Rec_1 = (r_1 \cdot [(er_R(v_R) \parallel er_{21}(v_{21})); s_1(nor(v_R, v_{21}))])^\omega,$$
$$Send_1(b_1) = r_{b_1}(s) \cdot s_1 \cdot (s_Q(b_1) \parallel s_{12}(b_1)) \cdot Send_1,$$
$$Send_1 = (er_1(v); [r_{b_1}(e) \cdot r_{b_1}(s) \cdot s_1 \cdot (s_Q(v) \parallel s_{12}(v))])^\omega,$$

$$M_2(b_2) = Rec_2 \parallel_2 Send_2(b_2),$$
$$Rec_2 = (r_1 \cdot [(er_S(v_S) \parallel er_{12}(v_{12})); s_2(nor(v_S, v_{12}))])^\omega,$$
$$Send_2(b_2) = r_{b_2}(s) \cdot s_2 \cdot s_{21}(b_2) \cdot Send_2,$$
$$Send_2 = (er_2(v); [r_{b_2}(e) \cdot r_{b_2}(s) \cdot s_2 \cdot s_{21}(v)])^\omega.$$

Let $I = \{c_{21}, c_{12}\}$ and $H = \{r_{21}, s_{21}, r_{12}, s_{12}\}$. We argue that

$$\tau_I \circ \partial_H(M_1(0) \parallel M_2(1) \parallel Beat)$$

computes the operation of an *SR-latch* per two cycles. First we analyze the behaviour of

$$G(b_1, b_2) \stackrel{\text{def}}{=} \tau_I \circ \partial_H(M_1(b_1) \parallel M_2(b_2))$$

in a graphical style. The characterization theorem for beating grid protocols, which we present below, yields that

$$\tau \cdot G(b_1, b_2) = \tau \cdot ((er_R(c_1) \parallel er_S(c_2) \parallel s_Q(b_1)); G(nor(b_2, c_1), nor(b_1, c_2))).$$

In order to further analyze this behaviour we use a graphical style, deleting τ-steps and only showing the input-value pairs $\langle c_R, c_S \rangle$. The output value b_1 of $s_Q(b_1)$ is characterized as the first value of $G(\_,\_)$:

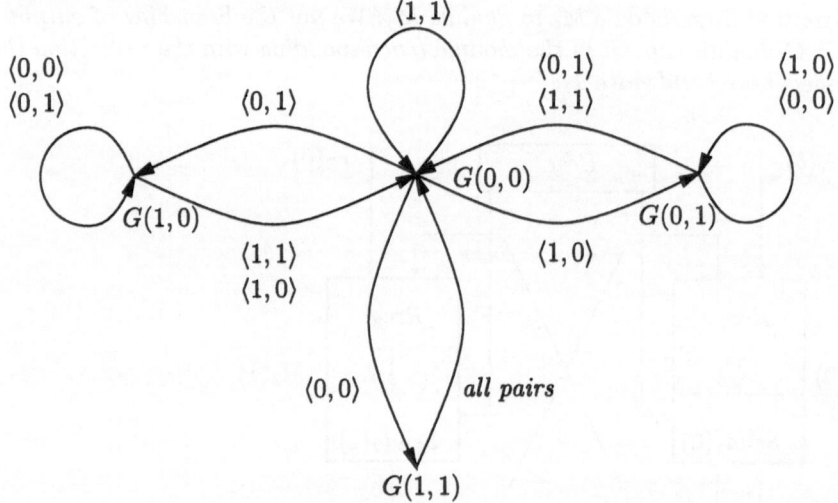

As argued in [TT94], the SR-latch behaviour can be traced back if one assumes that input is offered twice per cycle to the network. Let $L(b_1, b_2)$ represent the appropriate G-states, and use the following coding of input pairs:

set   for $\langle 0,1 \rangle \cdot \langle 0,1 \rangle$ (output 1 at Q)

reset for $\langle 1,0 \rangle \cdot \langle 1,0 \rangle$ (output 0 at Q)

hold   for $\langle 0,0 \rangle \cdot \langle 0,0 \rangle$ (output at Q the same as in the previous cycle)

Then $L(0,0)$ has the intended behaviour, as follows from the behaviour of $G(0,0)$ as analyzed above:

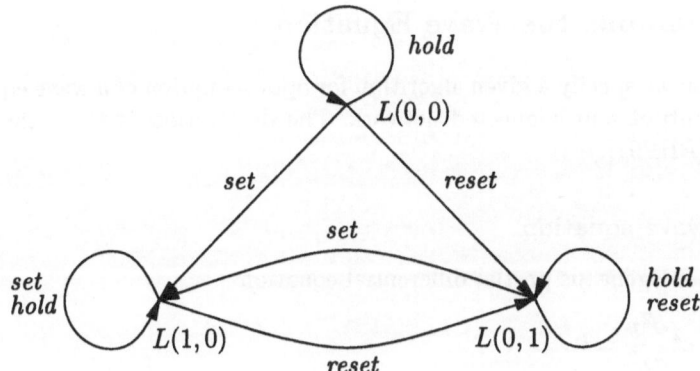

So, $L(1,0)$ is the set-state, $L(0,1)$ is the reset-state, and also $L(0,0)$ is considered as possible initial state.

4.3   Characterization of Beating Grid Protocols

In this section we state our final correctness results on networks. As before, we allow *output modification* of the external output-actions.

Theorem 4.3.1. *Let $n \geq 1$, $d = d_1, ..., d_n$ be a sequence of typed values, and let*

$$N(d) = \tau_I \circ \partial_H \left(\left[\big\|_{i=1}^n M_i(d_i) \right] \| \text{ Beat} \right)$$

be a beating grid protocol, with synchronized modules. Furthermore, let Beat be defined in one of the following ways:

1. $Beat = \left(\left[\big\|_{i=1}^n s_{b_i}(s) \right] \cdot \left[\big\|_{i=1}^n s_{b_i}(e) \right] \right)^{\omega}$,

2. $Beat = \left(\left[\big\|_{i=1}^n s_{b_i}(s) \cdot s_{b_i}(e) \right] \right)^{\omega}$.

Then

$$\tau \cdot N(d) = \tau \cdot \left[\big\|_{i \in Extern} a_i(x_i) \right] ; \tau_I \circ \partial_H \left(\left[\big\|_{i=1}^n M_i(F_i(d_i)) \right] \| \text{ Beat} \right),$$

where

1. *Extern $\neq \emptyset$ is the set of indices of the I/O channels,*
2. *Function F_i is the value function of module M_i,*
3. *For $i \in Extern$, either $a_i(x_i) \equiv s_i(G_i(d_i))$ where G_i is the output modification of channel i, or $a_i(x_i) \equiv er_i(v_i)$,*
4. *The sequence d_i abbreviates $a_{i_1}, ..., a_{i_{k_i}}$ whenever F_i computes on input channels $i_1, ..., i_{k_i}$.*

Various inductive proofs of this result [BJM97,Pou97] use a second characterization that covers the case that a network has *no* external connections. We apply this characterization result in the next section.

5 An Example: the Wave Equation

In this section we specify a given algorithm for approximation of a wave equation in a single-output and connected network. The description of this example is taken from [BHP97].

5.1 The wave equation

The linear homogeneous partial differential equation

$$\frac{\partial^2 y}{\partial t^2} - c^2 \frac{\partial^2 y}{\partial x^2} = 0$$

is known in wave mechanics as the *one-dimensional wave equation*; it describes transversal propagation along the x-coordinate or *amplitude* $y(x, t)$ of a wave. This equation models for instance vibrations in a string, where it is required that the tension in the string is approximately constant. The constant c is defined by $\sqrt{T/\rho}$, where T is the tension in the string and ρ the string mass per unit of length. In solutions $y(x, t)$ the constant c is interpreted as the propagation velocity of the wave in transversal direction.

In order to solve the wave equation, boundary and initial conditions are needed. As boundary conditions we assume that $y(0, t) = y(l, t) = 0$ for $t \geq 0$, i.e. that the string is fixed in $x = 0$ and $x = l$. With these boundary conditions a string amplitude at some time t, as a function of x, may be graphically represented as in Fig. 2.

In case we have $y(x, 0)$ and $\partial y/\partial t|_{t=0}$ given as initial conditions for $0 \leq x \leq l$, it is possible to derive an approximation of $y(x, \Delta t)$, where Δt is a very small time interval. The values $y(x, 0)$ and $y(x, \Delta t)$ are used for the initialization of an algorithm that numerically solves the wave equation.

Let N be a natural number, and $\Delta x = l/N$ a very small length interval. We define

$$F(z_1, z_2, z_3, z_4) = 2z_1 - z_2 + (c\frac{\Delta t}{\Delta x})^2(z_3 - 2z_1 + z_4),$$

and

$$y_i(t + \Delta t) = F(y_i(t), y_i(t - \Delta t), y_{i-1}(t), y_{i+1}(t)).$$

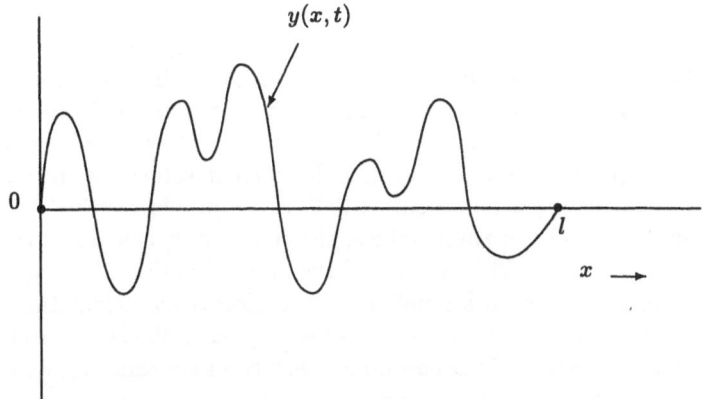

Fig. 2. A string amplitude at time t.

From numerical analysis it is known that $y_i(t)$ approximates $y(i\Delta x, t)$ for $1 \leq i \leq N - 1$, and $t \geq 2\Delta t$ (see e.g. [Smi65,FJL$^+$88]). Therefore, the above equation for $y_i(t + \Delta t)$ may serve as a basis for numerical approximation of solutions of the wave equation.

Now an algorithm for calculating wave amplitudes $y_i(t)$ may be designed which uses one processor per *sample point* on the x-axis, i.e., one for every i and one for each boundary. As a result the calculations for the string amplitude at some *sample moment* t will be carried out by $N + 1$ processors in parallel. In fact, $N - 1$ processors will suffice, since the values at the sample points $i = 0$ and $i = N$ are already known from the boundary conditions.

In the next section we specify a connected, single-output grid protocol that models this approximation. For simplicity we assume that Δx and Δt are given, and that there is no interaction between a user of the algorithm and the algorithm itself; the algorithm just produces an infinite stream of outputs. Of course we need a criterion for correctness; we require that the algorithm outputs approximations of the total string amplitudes on the successive sample moments:

$$y(0), y(\Delta t), y(2\Delta t), ...$$

where $y(t)$ abbreviates $y_0(t), ..., y_N(t)$. Other requirements are that the algorithm contains no deadlocks or livelocks, so that it is always able to proceed. We will see from one simple equation on the external behaviour of the algorithm that these three requirements are satisfied. This equation immediately follows from the correctness theorems presented earlier.

5.2 Grid Protocols modeling the Wave

In the previous section we established the following equation for the calculation of the value of coordinate y_i at time $t + \Delta t$:

$$y_i(t + \Delta t) = F(y_i(t), y_i(t - \Delta t), y_{i-1}(t), y_{i+1}(t)).$$

Modeling this approximation as a grid protocol obscures explicit reference to *time*. All that is left is that computation of the amplitudes at time $t + \Delta t$ depends on the amplitudes at time t and time $t - \Delta t$, and that our protocol is modeled in such a way that *all* outputted amplitudes are computed in consecutive phases. So any reference to time t must be interpreted as to a certain computation phase.

The equation above shows that the current values (at time t) of coordinates y_i, y_{i-1}, and y_{i+1} are needed, as well as the previous value (at time $t - \Delta t$) of coordinate y_i. Given these values, the function F calculates the new value (at time $t + \Delta t$) of y_i. When we model the approximation of the wave equation as a grid protocol, we need a number of processors, each calculating the consecutive values of one or more coordinates as floating reals. We choose to let one processor calculate the values of one coordinate. For $N+1$ coordinates, we thus define $N+1$ processors $P_0, ..., P_N$. Each processor P_i $(0 < i < N)$ needs the following input:

- the output of processor P_{i-1},
- the output of processor P_i (itself),
- the output of processor P_{i+1}, and
- the *previous* output of processor P_i (itself).

Naturally, processors P_0 and P_N do not need input at all. However, for reasons of uniformity we also use channels from P_1 to P_0 and from P_{N-1} to P_N. The last item above requires that we store the output of each processor for one time slot. This is, however, not possible in a single module. We solve this problem by splitting each processor P_i into a calculating module M_i and a delay module D_i. The delay module does nothing more than storing the output value of the calculating module for one time slot. After that, this value is sent back to the calculating module. We can now state that the input of each module M_i $(0 < i < N)$ should be:

- the output of module M_{i-1},
- the output of module M_i (itself),
- the output of module M_{i+1}, and
- the output of module D_i.

This can be visualized as follows:

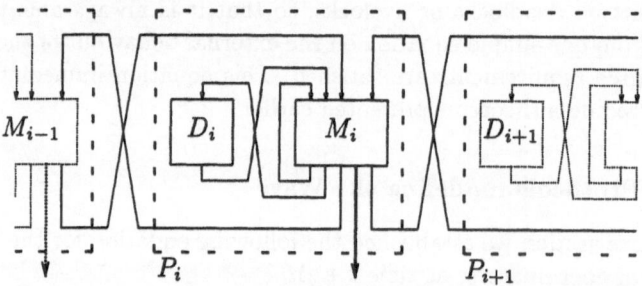

We can proceed in two ways:

1. We can define a *connected*, single-output grid protocol. Here an additional output module transmits the values of all 'processors', and hence acts as a synchronizing device,
2. We can define a single-output *beating* grid protocol, collecting output directly from the 'processors' described above.

We describe the first alternative in detail. It should be immediately clear how to model the second approach. Now that we have composed a grid protocol modeling the wave equation, we can start writing a specification in the early-read format. This is not difficult: just read what happens from the picture. To start with, we specify the D_i $(0 < i < N)$ modules:

$$D_i(e) = \tau_{\{c_{(D_i)}\}} \circ \partial_{\{r_{(D_i)}, s_{(D_i)}\}} (RD_i \parallel SD_i(e))$$
$$RD_i = (er_{(M_i, D_i)}(v); s_{(D_i)}(v))^\omega$$
$$SD_i = (er_{(D_i)}(v); s_{(D_i, M_i)}(v))^\omega$$
$$SD_i(e) = s_{(D_i, M_i)}(e) \cdot SD_i.$$

Here, $er_{(M_i, D_i)}(v)$ and $s_{(D_i, M_i)}(v)$ stand for an early read or a send action on the ports connecting M_i and D_i. Note that (M_i, D_i) is the port from M_i to D_i and (D_i, M_i) the port from D_i to M_i. The actions $er_{(D_i)}(v)$ and $s_{(D_i)}(v)$ stand for an early read or a send action on the internal port of the concerning module.

Likewise, we specify the modules M_i, using the following shorthands:

$$In_i = (er_{(M_i, M_i)}(v_1) \parallel er_{(D_i, M_i)}(v_2) \parallel er_{(M_{i-1}, M_i)}(v_3) \parallel er_{(M_{i+1}, M_i)}(v_4))$$
$$O_i(x) = (s_{(M_i, M_i)}(x) \parallel s_{(M_i, D_i)}(x) \parallel s_{(M_i, M_{i-1})}(x) \parallel s_{(M_i, M_{i+1})}(x) \parallel s_{(M_i, O)}(x))$$

Now,

$$M_i(d) = \tau_{\{c_{(M_i)}\}} \circ \partial_{\{r_{(M_i)}, s_{(M_i)}\}} (R_i \parallel S_i(d))$$
$$R_i = \left(In_i \; ; \; s_{(M_i)}(F(v_1, v_2, v_3, v_4))\right)^\omega$$
$$S_i = \left(er_{(M_i)}(v) \; ; \; O_i(v)\right)^\omega$$
$$S_i(d) = O_i(d) \cdot S_i.$$

The port (M_i, O) is the actual output port of the processor, leading to an output module O.

The processors P_i $(0 < i < N)$ can now be defined as follows:

$$P_i(d, e) = M_i(d) \parallel D_i(e),$$

with d and e the initial values of coordinate y_i ($y_i(\Delta t)$ and $y_i(0)$, respectively).

For $N + 1$ coordinate pairs, $N - 1$ of these processors are coupled together, the outer ones also using two border processors (which are simple modules). The output of all the calculating modules M_i $(0 \le i \le N)$ in the processors is sent to output module O. This module collects the computed values of all processors and bundles them in a vector. This bundling is somewhat arbitrary; alternatively O may send its output in parallel to the environment. In a picture:

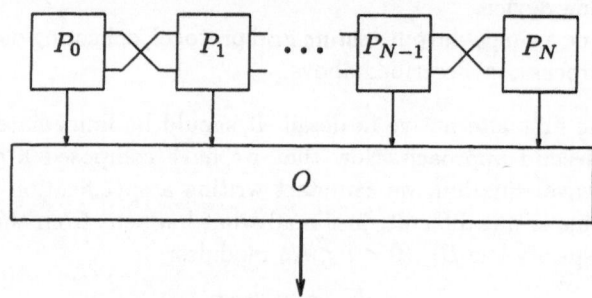

As one can see from this picture, the first and the last processor only communicate with their neighbor and the output module O. The specification of these two processors is, therefore, very simple:

$$P_0(d) = \tau_{\{c_{(P_0)}\}} \circ \partial_{\{r_{(P_0)}, s_{(P_0)}\}}(R_0 \parallel S_0(d))$$
$$R_0 = (er_{(M_1, P_0)}(v); s_{(P_0)}(0))^\omega$$
$$S_0 = (er_{(P_0)}(v); (s_{(P_0, M_1)}(v) \parallel s_{(P_0, O)}(v)))^\omega$$
$$S_0(d) = (s_{(P_0, M_1)}(d) \parallel s_{(P_0, O)}(d)) \cdot S_0$$

$$P_N(d) = \tau_{\{c_{(P_N)}\}} \circ \partial_{\{r_{(P_N)}, s_{(P_N)}\}}(R_N \parallel S_N(d))$$
$$R_N = (er_{(M_{N-1}, P_N)}(v); s_{(P_N)}(0))^\omega$$
$$S_N = (er_{(P_N)}(v); (s_{(P_N, M_{N-1})}(v) \parallel s_{(P_N, O)}(v)))^\omega$$
$$S_N(d) = (s_{(P_N, M_{N-1})}(d) \parallel s_{(P_N, O)}(d)) \cdot S_N.$$

Note that P_0 and P_N need not to be split in a calculating and a delay module. Since we describe a wave through a string with both ends tight, the output value of processors P_0 and P_N will remain zero all the time:

$$P_0(d, e) = P_0(0) \quad \text{and} \quad P_N(d, e) = P_N(0).$$

The only thing left to specify is the output module O. Let $\boldsymbol{d} = d_1, ..., d_N$, then

$$O(\boldsymbol{d}) = \tau_{\{c_{(O)}\}} \circ \partial_{\{r_{(O)}, s_{(O)}\}}(RO \parallel SO(\boldsymbol{d}))$$
$$RO = \left(\left(\left[\parallel_{i \in \{0, N\}} er_{(P_i, O)}(v_i)\right] \parallel \left[\parallel_{i=1}^{N-1} er_{(M_i, O)}(v_i)\right]\right); s_{(O)}(\boldsymbol{v})\right)^\omega$$
$$SO = (er_{(O)}(\boldsymbol{w}); s_{out}(\boldsymbol{w}))^\omega$$
$$SO(\boldsymbol{d}) = s_{out}(\boldsymbol{d}) \cdot SO.$$

Now the algorithm can be specified by the parallel composition of O and all processors P_i:

$$\text{WAVE}(k) = \tau_{\{c_p\}} \circ \partial_{\{r_p, s_p\}} \left(\begin{array}{l} O(\boldsymbol{y}(k \cdot \Delta t)) \\ \| \\ \left[\underset{i=0}{\overset{N}{\|}} P_i(y_i((k+1) \cdot \Delta t), y_i(k \cdot \Delta t)) \right] \end{array} \right),$$

$$\text{WAVE} = \text{WAVE}(0),$$

with $y_i(0), y_i(\Delta t)$ $(i = 0, ..., N)$ arbitrary initial values, and p ranging over the following set of ports:

$$\{(M_i, M_j), (M_i, D_i), (D_i, M_i), (M_i, O) \mid 0 < i, j < N\} \cup$$
$$\{(P_0, M_1), (M_1, P_0), (P_0, O), (M_{N-1}, P_N), (P_N, M_{N-1}), (P_N, O)\}.$$

The external behaviour of the algorithm can then be expressed by

$$\tau \cdot \text{WAVE} = \tau \cdot s_{out}(\boldsymbol{y}(0)) \cdot s_{out}(\boldsymbol{y}(\Delta t)) \cdot s_{out}(\boldsymbol{y}(2\Delta t)) \cdot \cdots.$$

This follows from Theorem 3.3.1, which gives the following characterization of our specification:

$$\tau \cdot \text{WAVE}(k) = \tau \cdot s_{out}(\boldsymbol{y}(k \cdot \Delta t)) \cdot \text{WAVE}(k+1).$$

A beating grid protocol modeling this algorithm need not depend on a synchronizing output module like O defined above. By Theorem 4.3.1 we cam omit O and view the send-actions to O as external. For the resulting protocol WAVE' protocol one has a choice in the definition of its ouput values: either those of M_i, yielding

$$\tau \cdot \text{WAVE}' = \tau \cdot \left(\left[\underset{i=0}{\overset{N}{\|}} s_{M_i, O}(y_i(\Delta t)) \right] \right) \cdot \left(\left[\underset{i=0}{\overset{N}{\|}} s_{M_i, O}(y_i(2\Delta t)) \right] \right) \cdot \ldots$$

not giving output at time 0, or reading the values from the D_i modules instead. In the latter case, the modules M_i lose their output action $s_{M_i, O}(..)$, and the D_i should get an extra output action $s_{D_i, O}(..)$. We then obtain output also at time 0, and hence the two (required) initial configurations of the string (at time 0 and Δt).

6 Conclusions

It appears that early read and process prefix form a useful extension to ACP-based specification formalisms. Grid protocols—intended to model parallel computation—are considered for two types of architectures:

- Strongly connected networks in which I/O is located at one module. Here internal computation need not proceed in lock step. By connectedness and I/O interface located at one module, I/O proceeds in lock step.

– Networks in which modules need only be strongly connected to a synchronizing device: the *beat* (for instance a global clock). Both I/O and internal
actions, i.e., all parallel activity, proceed in lock step.

Future work concerns a more formal treatment of substitution, extensions in
the field of asynchronous networks, and establishing a precise relationship with
protocol specification and verification in μCRL.

We finish with some remarks on the proposed specification format for grid
protocols, comprising early reads, process prefix and no-exit iteration. It is not
essential whether one uses full μCRL or some other data-parametric, recursive
specification format, or the extension of ACP with data and no-exit iteration ω
as presented in this paper. Restricting all occurring types of networks to single-
module networks, one finds by the characterization results that an identity such
as

$$M(d) = \left[\underset{I/O}{\|}\ actions \right] ; M(F(\boldsymbol{v}))$$

can just as well be regarded as the (data-parametric) *specification* of a module.
In that case, transformation to the specification format as discussed before (with
ω and distinctive read and send parts) yields a specification in which characterization is relatively easy to prove. Note that the μCRL perspective yields two
basic types of modules, both in the setting without and with a beat process:
those *without* feedback, as displayed above, and those *with* feedback, having a
value-update of the form $F(d, \boldsymbol{v})$ (and the possibility of an initial τ-step if one
cares to model the feedback as explicit activity, which from an operational point
of view seems best). In the specification format discussed in this paper feedback
is treated in the same way as other value-passings, which seems a preferable sort
of modeling.

Finally, one can show that for the internal communication actions it is sufficient to assume that all outputs are in parallel; input may have a fixed order.
Because all internal output is performed in parallel this cannot raise any deadlock, which also is a consequence of the characterization results: both approaches
reduce to the same external characterization. This appears to be useful for (more)
efficient proto-typing of grid protocols (cf. [Hil96,Pou97]).

References

[BB94]   J.C.M. Baeten and J.A. Bergstra. On sequential composition, action prefixes
and process prefix. *Formal Aspects of Computing*, 6(3):83–98, 1994.
[BBK87]   J.C.M. Baeten, J.A. Bergstra, and J.W. Klop. Conditional axioms and α/β
calculus in process algebra. In M. Wirsing, editor, *Formal Description of
Programming Concepts – III, Proceedings of the 3rd IFIP WG 2.2 working
conference*, Ebberup 1986, pages 53–75, Amsterdam, 1987. North-Holland.
[BHP97]   J.A. Bergstra, J.A. Hillebrand, and A. Ponse. Grid protocols based on synchronous communication, *Science of Computer Programming*, 29:199–233,
1997.

[BJM97]   E. van Buiten, M. de Jonge, and R. Monajemi. Beating Grid Protocols, PAII-thesis, University of Amsterdam, 1997.

[Pou97]   M. Pouw. Beating Grid Protocols, Master's Thesis, Utrecht University, 1997.

[BK84]   J.A. Bergstra and J.W. Klop. The algebra of recursively defined processes and the algebra of regular processes. In J. Paredaens, editor, *Proceedings 11th ICALP*, Antwerpen, volume 172 of *Lecture Notes in Computer Science*, pages 82–95. Springer-Verlag, 1984. An extended version appeared in [PVV95], pages 1–25, 1995.

[BK85]   J.A. Bergstra and J.W. Klop. Algebra of communicating processes with abstraction. *Theoretical Computer Science*, 37(1):77–121, 1985.

[BT84]   J.A. Bergstra and J.V. Tucker. Top down design and the algebra of communicating processes. *Science of Computer Programming*, 5(2):171–199, 1984.

[BT95]   J.A. Bergstra and J.V. Tucker. Equational specifications, complete term rewriting systems, and computable and semicomputable algebras. *Journal of the ACM*, 42(6):1194–1230, 1995.

[BW90]   J.C.M. Baeten and W.P. Weijland. *Process Algebra*. Cambridge Tracts in Theoretical Computer Science 18. Cambridge University Press, 1990.

[FJL+88] G. Fox, M. Johnson, G. Lyzenga, S. Otto, J. Salmon, and D. Walker. *General Techniques and Regular Problems*, volume 1 of *Solving Problems on Concurrent Processors*. Prentice-Hall International, 1988.

[Fok97]   W.J. Fokkink, Axiomatizations for the perpetual loop in process algebra. In P. Degano, R. Gorrieri, and A. Marchetti-Spaccamela, editors, *Proc. 24th Colloquium on Automata, Languages and Programming - ICALP'97*, pages 571–581. Lecture Notes in Computer Science Vol. 1256, Springer-Verlag, Berlin, 1997.

[GK95]   J.F. Groote and H. Korver. A correctness proof of the bakery protocol in μCRL. In [PVV95], pages 63–86, 1995.

[GP91c]   J.F. Groote and A. Ponse. Proof theory for μCRL. (Extended version.) Report CS-R9138, CWI, Amsterdam, 1991.

[GP94b]   J.F. Groote and A. Ponse. Proof theory for μCRL: a language for processes with data. In D.J. Andrews, J.F. Groote, and C.A. Middelburg, editors, *Proceedings of the International Workshop on Semantics of Specification Languages*, pages 232–251. Workshops in Computing, Springer-Verlag, 1994.

[GP95]   J.F. Groote and A. Ponse. The syntax and semantics of μCRL. In [PVV95], pages 26–62, 1995.

[Hil96]   J.A. Hillebrand. A simple language for the specification of grid protocols (working title). Technical Report, Programming Research Group, University of Amsterdam, to appear.

[Kle56]   S.C. Kleene. Representation of events in nerve nets and finite automata. In *Automata Studies*, pages 3–41. Princeton University Press, 1956.

[Mil89]   R. Milner. *Communication and Concurrency*. Prentice-Hall International, Englewood Cliffs, 1989.

[PVV95]   A. Ponse, C. Verhoef, and S.F.M. van Vlijmen, editors. *Algebra of Communicating Processes, Utrecht 1994*, Workshops in Computing. Springer-Verlag, 1995.

[Smi65]   G.D. Smith. *Numerical Solution of Partial Differential Equations*, Oxford University Press, 1965.

[TT94]   B.C. Thompson and J.V. Tucker. Equational specification of Synchronous Concurrent Algorithms and architectures (Second Edition). Report CSR 15-94, University of Wales, Swansea, 1994.

Appendix

In this appendix we recall some basic process algebra (without explicit use of data): the system $\text{ACP}^\tau(A, \gamma)$, standard concurrency, and no-exit iteration. Furthermore, we recall expansion and alphabet axioms, all of which are essential for specification and verification of grid protocols.

The process algebraic framework $\text{ACP}^\tau(A, \gamma)$ (ACP with branching bisimulation) has two parameters: a set A of constants modeling atomic actions, and a (partial) binary, commutative and associative *communication function* γ on A, defining which actions communicate. Furthermore there are constants δ (deadlock or inaction) and τ (silent step). Process operations in $\text{ACP}^\tau(A, \gamma)$ are alternative composition or choice (+), sequential composition ($\cdot$), parallel composition or merge ($\|$), left and communication merge ($\|\!\_$ and $|$, used for the axiomatization of $\|$), encapsulation (∂_H), and hiding (τ_I). We mostly suppress the $\cdot$ in process expressions, and brackets according to the following precedences: $\cdot > \{\|, \|\!\_, |\} > +$. Process expressions are subject to the axioms of $\text{ACP}^\tau(A, \gamma)$, displayed in Table 3 ($x, y, z, \ldots$ ranging over processes). Note that + and $\cdot$ are associative.

We provide a slightly modified version of $\text{ACP}(A, \gamma)$ (i.e., the axioms A1–7, CF1,2 and CM1–8), comprising commutativity of $\|$ and $|$, defined by the (new) axiom CMC (Communication Merge is Commutative). As a consequence, the symmetric version of CM5 and CM8, i.e. CM6 and CM9 respectively, are left out (cf. [BW90]). Furthermore, we adopt associativity of $\|$ and $|$. Commutativity and associativity of these operations is known as Standard Concurrency [BT84], and is referred to as SC.

In this paper we only considered two-party communication or *handshaking* (see [BT84]), which is axiomatized by $x \mid y \mid z = \delta$.

We give some informal explanation on the use of process algebra. Often, + is used as an operation facilitating analysis rather than as a specification primitive: concurrency is analyzed in terms of sequential composition, choice and communication. Verification of a concurrent system $\partial_H(C_1 \| \ldots \| C_n)$ generally boils down to representing the possible executions with + and $\cdot$, having applied left-merge ($\|\!\_$), communication merge, and encapsulation (∂_H, by which communication between components C_i can be enforced). After renaming internal activity to the silent, unobservable action τ with help of the hiding operator τ_I (also called 'abstraction'), this may yield a simple and informative specification of external behaviour. For a detailed introduction to $\text{ACP}^\tau(A, \gamma)$ and SC we refer to [BW90].

In order to describe iterative, non-terminating processes we use the unary operation $\_^\omega$, *perpetual loop* or *no-exit iteration*, for which NEI1 in Table 3 is the defining axiom. This operation is introduced by Fokkink in [Fok97]. In that paper, several completeness results are established, among which the fact that BPA (axioms A1–A5) with NEI1 and RSP^ω characterizes strong bisimilarity. (The 'missing' axiom NEI2 concerns the empty process ϵ, and reads $(x + \epsilon)^\omega = x^\omega$.) It should be remarked that RSP^ω is not sound in the setting with the silent step τ. For example, each process $\tau \cdot P$ satisfies

$$\tau \cdot P = \tau \cdot \tau \cdot P,$$

though $\tau \cdot P = \tau^\omega$ is of course a very undesirable identity.

Table 3. Axioms of $\mathrm{ACP}^\tau(A, \gamma)$ and for no-exit iteration, where $a, b \in A_{\delta,\tau}$, $H, I \subseteq A$.

(A1)	$x + y = y + x$		(B1)	$x\tau = x$	
(A2)	$x + (y + z) = (x + y) + z$		(B2)	$x(\tau(y + z) + y) = x(y + z)$	
(A3)	$x + x = x$				
(A4)	$(x + y)z = xz + yz$				
(A5)	$(xy)z = x(yz)$				
(A6)	$x + \delta = x$				
(A7)	$\delta x = \delta$				
(CF1)	$a \mid b = \gamma(a, b)$ if $\gamma(a, b)\downarrow$				
(CF2)	$a \mid b = \delta$ \qquad otherwise				
(CM1)	$x \parallel y = (x \mathbin{\underline{\parallel}} y + y \mathbin{\underline{\parallel}} x)$		(D1)	$\partial_H(a) = a$ if $a \notin H$	
	$\qquad + x \mid y$		(D2)	$\partial_H(a) = \delta$ if $a \in H$	
(CM2)	$a \mathbin{\underline{\parallel}} x = ax$		(D3)	$\partial_H(x + y) = \partial_H(x) + \partial_H(y)$	
(CM3)	$ax \mathbin{\underline{\parallel}} y = a(x \parallel y)$		(D4)	$\partial_H(xy) = \partial_H(x) \cdot \partial_H(y)$	
(CM4)	$(x + y) \mathbin{\underline{\parallel}} z = x \mathbin{\underline{\parallel}} z + y \mathbin{\underline{\parallel}} z$				
(CMC)	$x \mid y = y \mid x$		(TI1)	$\tau_I(a) = a$ if $a \notin I$	
(CM5)	$ax \mid b = (a \mid b)x$		(TI2)	$\tau_I(a) = \tau$ if $a \in I$	
(CM7)	$ax \mid by = (a \mid b)(x \parallel y)$		(TI3)	$\tau_I(x + y) = \tau_I(x) + \tau_I(y)$	
(CM8)	$(x + y) \mid z = x \mid z + y \mid z$		(TI4)	$\tau_I(xy) = \tau_I(x) \cdot \tau_I(y)$	
(NEI1)	$x^\omega = x \cdot (x)^\omega$		(NEI3)	$\partial_H(x^\omega) = (\partial_H(x))^\omega$	
(RSP$^\omega$)	$x = y \cdot x \implies x = y^\omega$		(NEI4)	$\tau_I(x^\omega) = (\tau_I(x))^\omega$	

The proofs of the characterization results as described in this paper employ the *Expansion Theorem* (cf. [BW90]). This theorem holds in the setting of handshaking:

$$\text{for } n \geq 3: \quad \left[\left\|_{i=1}^{n} P_i \right] = \sum_{j=1}^{n} P_j \, \right\|\!\!\right\|\!\!\left[\left\|_{i \in \{1,\ldots,n\}\setminus\{j\}} P_i \right] + \sum_{j=2}^{n} \sum_{k=1}^{j-1} (P_j \mid P_k) \, \right\|\!\!\right\|\!\!\left[\left\|_{i \in \{1,\ldots,n\}\setminus\{j,k\}} P_i \right].$$

Also, a lot if (intermediate) results depend on application of *alphabet axioms*. Under certain conditions the scope, or the action set of τ_I or ∂_H applications can be changed, depending on the alphabet of a process. In Table 4 we give some axioms to determine the alphabet of process P, notation $\alpha(P)$. Except for AB6, these axioms stem from [BBK87].

Table 4. Alphabet axioms, $a \in A$.

(AB1)	$\alpha(\delta) = \emptyset = \alpha(\tau)$		(AB4)	$\alpha(ax) = \{a\} \cup \alpha(x)$
(AB2)	$\alpha(a) = \{a\}$		(AB5)	$\alpha(x + y) = \alpha(x) \cup \alpha(y)$
(AB3)	$\alpha(\tau x) = \alpha(x)$		(AB6)	$\alpha(x^{\omega}) = \alpha(x)$

Starting from the alphabet of a process, the *conditional alphabet axioms* in Table 5 (also taken from [BBK87]) give conditions for changing either scope or action sets I, H of τ_I and ∂_H applications. Here $B \mid C$ for $B, C \subseteq A$ denotes the set $\{a \in A \mid a = \gamma(b,c) \text{ for some } b \in B, c \in C\}$.

Table 5. Conditional alphabet axioms, $H, I \subseteq A$.

(CA1)	$\alpha(x) \mid (\alpha(y) \cap H) \subseteq H$	$\implies$	$\partial_H(x \parallel y) = \partial_H(x \parallel \partial_H(y))$
(CA2)	$\alpha(x) \mid (\alpha(y) \cap I) = \emptyset$	$\implies$	$\tau_I(x \parallel y) = \tau_I(x \parallel \tau_I(y))$
(CA3)	$\alpha(x) \cap H = \emptyset$	$\implies$	$\partial_H(x) = x$
(CA4)	$\alpha(x) \cap I = \emptyset$	$\implies$	$\tau_I(x) = x$

The Computational Description of Analogue System Behaviour

Peter T. Breuer, Natividad Martínez Madrid, and Carlos Delgado Kloos

Área de Ingeniería Telemática, Universidad Carlos III de Madrid
Butarque 15, E–28911 Leganés, Madrid, Spain.
Tel/Fax: +34(1)624-9953/9430, Email: ptb@it.uc3m.es

Abstract. The aim of this chapter is to define a simple analogue hardware description language L and give it a sound semantics that supports formal reasoning about its properties.

The syntax of L is that of a *hybrid* programming languages but the semantics has been derived from the analogue signal semantics of the upcoming IEEE VHDL-AMS extension to the IEEE standard digital hardware description language, VHDL [1].

L will here be given two semantics. Firstly, what may be termed an *exact*, or *hardware*, semantics and secondly an *aproximation*, or *simulation*, semantics. The simulation semantics is computable and the hardware semantics is not. It will be shown that the simulation semantics approximates the hardware semantics in a well-defined sense. This property is a "no surprises" guarantee with respect to simulation for the language.

1   Introduction

The forthcoming discussion will be motivated by means of a small puzzle: an ideal *operational amplifier* is an electronic device that monitors two continuously varying input signals x_1, x_2 without disturbing them and, insensitive to loading, produces an amplified difference signal on its single output y. The natural way for a computer simulation to represent the amplifier in this open loop configuration is as a simple, causal, input-to-output computation (Fig. 1).

$$y(t) = \beta \int_0^{+\infty} (x_1(t-\tau) - x_2(t-\tau))h(\tau)\mathrm{d}\tau \tag{1}$$

$$\stackrel{\triangle}{=} \beta h^*(x_1 - x_2)(t)$$

in which $h(t)$ is the impulse response of the amplifier and it is zero for negative times. * is the convolution operator Usually the impulse response is taken to be a decaying exponential with gradient μ:

$$h(\tau) = \begin{cases} \mu e^{-\mu\tau}, & \tau \geq 0 \\ 0, & \tau < 0 \end{cases} \tag{2}$$

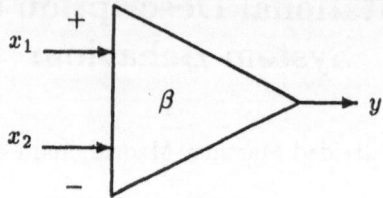

Fig. 1. The open loop operational amplifier computes its output y causally from its inputs.

and for the amplifier to be useful, the amplification β has to be greater than 1. A value of several thousand is normal.

Computational simulations of the amplifier do the integration numerically, using an approximation grid on the discrete points of which x, h and y are evaluated (3).

$$y(t_{i+1}) = \beta \sum_{j=0}^{\infty} (x_1(t_{i-j}) - x_2(t_{i-j}))h(t_j)(t_{j+1} - t_j) \qquad (3)$$

But that computation produces strange results if the simulation output is fed back in negative phase to its input, putting the amplifier in the classical closed loop (*follower*) configuration (Fig. 2, Eqn. 4).

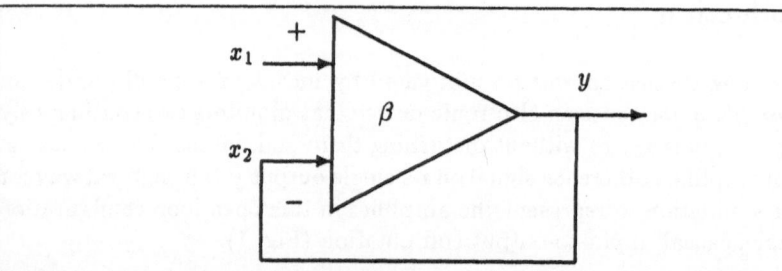

Fig. 2. The closed loop operational amplifier feeds its output back to its negative input.

$$y(t_{i+1}) = \beta \sum_{j=0}^{\infty} (x_1(t_{i-j}) - y(t_{i-j}))h(t_j)(t_{j+1} - t_j) \qquad (4)$$

In this physical configuration, the amplifier output should follow the input faithfully, lagging by an amount related to the lag observed in the open loop configuration. However, that is not the behaviour that is observed from the simulation. Moreover, it is not an artifact of simulation. The integral equation (5) that corresponds to the simulation is unstable – it only has solutions that grow unboundedly in time.

$$y(t) = \beta \int_0^\infty (x_1(t - \tau) - y(t - \tau))h(\tau)\mathrm{d}\tau \tag{5}$$

It can be shown that causal solutions to (5) must have the form (6)

$$y = \beta h^* x_1 - (\beta h^*)^2 x_1 + (\beta h^*)^3 x_1 \mp \dots \tag{6}$$

In this series, contributions from longer and longer ago in the input x_1 have a greater and greater effect on the output y, and that is quite contrary to physical intuition. The output does not have a Fourier spectrum even when the input signal is very well-behaved (zero for negative times, bounded, with bounded absolute and square integrals over time, and with a Fourier spectrum).

Since the open-loop amplifier is simulated correctly, the conclusion to be drawn from failure to simulate the closed loop amplifier given a simulation of the open loop amplifier is:

1. either *the closed-loop amplifier cannot be simulated compositionally in terms of simulations of the open loop amplifier and a feedback wire*;
2. or *the behaviour of the open-loop amplifier is not represented adequately by its impulse response h, or the feedback wire behaviour is likewise not adequately represented*;
3. or *the method of composing descriptions of components to get a description of the whole is as set out here is not correct.*

It is the second item in this list that is correct. The amplifier is capable of many more behaviours than given by the causal equation (1). The full set is described by a differential equation (7) to which (1) with $h(t) = \mu e^{-\mu t}$ is the solution in the open loop case:

$$\frac{\mathrm{d}y}{\mathrm{d}t} = -\mu(y - \beta(x_1 - x_2)) \tag{7}$$

The equation (7) may be understood by supposing that a "perfect" open loop amplifier impulse response is given by the Dirac delta centered at zero:

$$y = \beta(x_1 - x_2)$$

and that momentary departures from this ideal may be expected in a real amplifier under the application of rapidly changing external signals that the output cannot follow quite rapidly enough. In the event of such a departure, a "restoring force" acts to restore the ideal and it applies itself to y in proportion μ to the departure $y - \beta(x_1 - x_2)$, with opposite sign.

In the closed loop case, the equation (7) then becomes

$$\frac{dy}{dt} = -\mu(y - \beta(x - y)) \tag{8}$$

with solution:

$$y(t) = \frac{\beta}{1 + \beta} \int_0^t x(t - \tau)\lambda e^{-\lambda \tau} d\tau, \qquad \lambda = \mu(1 + \beta) \tag{9}$$

that describes a lagging follower, as expected. Physically, the constant $\mu = 1/RC$, where R and C are respectively the internal resistance and capacitance of an equivalent circuit for the amplifier (Fig. 3). The component represented by the circle in the Figure is an infinite impedence voltage generator.

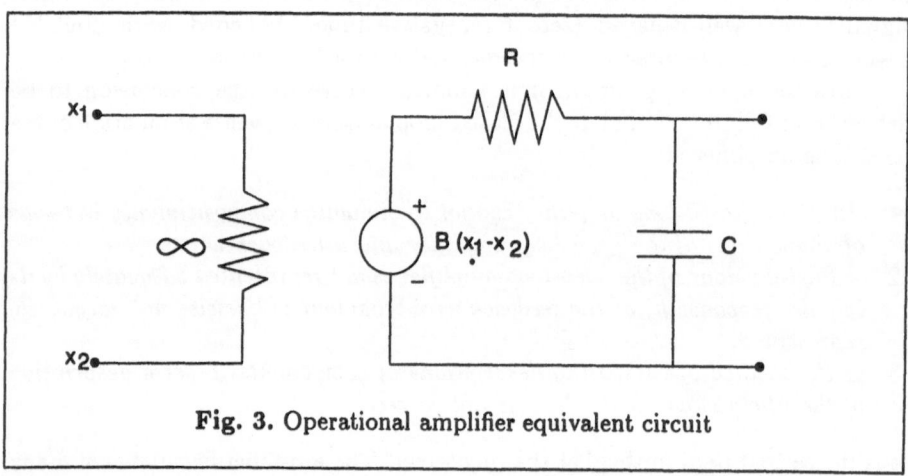

Fig. 3. Operational amplifier equivalent circuit

Any network of classical components each of whose voltages and currents satisfies a linear second order differential equation may be represented by a matrix of simple first order differential equations in the voltages and currents in the network, calculated by Kirchoff's laws (the sum of the currents entering a circuit node is zero, the voltage felt at a node is the same for all the components touching it). So we may infer that:

1. *a complete circuit behaviour is described by differential equations that are composed from the differential equations describing its components behaviours;*

2. *and analogue component behaviour is represented adequately through differential equations;*

3. *and differential equations are composed by identifying their shared variables.*

The use of differential equations to describe physical systems is a classical modelling method. It is only with the advent of computers that it has become more usual to model physical systems as computations, and it comes as a surprise to computational scientists that computation is not neccessarily an adequate substrate for the representatuon of the operational amplifier.

Section 3 sets out the concrete syntax of a small language L that can capture descriptions of circuits via differntial equations. To represent changes in the governing equations, the language permits computations to decide which to apply at any moment in time. The language is a cut-down version of the upcoming mixed-signal extension – called VHDL-AMS – to the IEEE standard digital hardware description language VHDL [1].

It will be shown that although small, L can express the constructs of VHDL-AMS that it explicitly lacks. It is also capable of expressing the atomic constructs of hybrid programming languages. The latter have developed from foundations in computer science and aim to provide a rigorous basis for the development of real time systems controlled by software. VHDL-AMS has developed from efforts by the hardware community to codify their existing designs as computer models. The separate aims and backgrounds of these two communties have given rise to very different development tracks that may nevertheless be converging.

The aim of this chapter is to provide

1. a non-computational semantics for the core language, given in terms of classical solutions to differential euqations;
2. for each constant of precision δ, a computational semantics for the core language, in domain theoretic terms;
3. a demonstration that as δ tends to zero, that the computational semantics tends to the classical semantics given first in a well-defined way.

The computational domain of in which these discussions are set is presented in Section 4.

In Section 5 a nonstandard evaluation of logic is set out in which truth is a real valued quantity. This is appropriate for real-valued problems. The logic will be used in implementing the small description lanauage that is defined in Section 3, and an ideal semantics for which is given in Section 6. The semantics is a set of state-space trajectories for the system being described, each of which is a piecewise smooth function of time.

Section 7 sets out the computable approximating semantics for the language, based on a discrete grid of time points, and shows that the approximate state descriptions tend to the ideal descriptions, this fulfilling a "no surprises" contract. Section 8 describes an implementation of the approximating semantics and gives some experimental results.

2   A Computational Approach

In the following section a way of representing switched analogue circuits as *hybrid programs* will be set out. A hybrid program is an imperative program that switches state between different regimes governed by different differential equations according to the resulst of certain computations. For examplem, the operational amplifier will be represented by the process code:

```
proc amp(in: x_1, x_2; out: y) {
    y = 0;
    wait until false with
        dy/dt = μ * (y - β * (x_1 - x_2)) ;
}
```

Note that the signals x_1 and x_2 are called by reference – they are updated by an exterior process whilst this process runs. The intention is that when this process is called with parameters

```
amp(x, y; y)
```

then it should automatically behave as the closed loop amplifier is supposed to behave – as a faithful signal follower.

3 Language

The precise syntax of the small language illustrated by the **amp** process is given below. There are only two forms of atomic statement; assignment and **waits**:

$Circuit$ $::= Process^*$

$Process$ $::= Pid$ (**in**: Var^* ; **out**: Var^*) {
            [**var** Var^* ;] $Statement$
            }

$Statement ::= Var = Expr$;
         | **wait until** $Elog$ **with** Eqn^* ;
         | **if** $Elog$ **then** $Statement$ **else** $Statement$ **fi** ;
         | **while** $Elog$ **do** $Statement$ **od** ;
         | $Statement^*$

$Expr$ $::= Float \mid Var \mid Expr + Expr \mid \dots$

$Elog$ $::=$ **true** $\mid$ **false** $\mid Elog$ **or** $Elog \mid \dots \mid Expr = Expr \mid \dots$

Eqn $::= \mathbf{d}\, Var/\mathbf{dt} = Expr$

The usual syntactic restrictions apply. Only declared variables may be referred to in a process body. A variable may be an **in** variable (imported) or an **out** variable (exported) or a **var** variable (local), but not any two simultaneously. A variable may be an **out** variable of only one (and exactly one) process. Only a local variable or an exported variable may be the subject of a differential equation or an assignment. The special implicitly imported variable t stands for time and is governed by the differential equation

$$\mathbf{dt/dt} = 1$$

A "process" is a piece of syntactic sugar. It serves only to provide a protected name space for its local variables. If x is the name of a local variable of p, then it accesses a global location p.x but the language syntax protects against access via the latter name. A process usually corresponds to a circuit component and its variables correspond to voltage or current values at interior points in the circuit.

A circuit consists of several processes (i.e., components) running in parallel. Each of these processes writes via its exported variables to possibly many listening processes. Communication is 1-many. All writes are non-blocking in the sense that the listener need not agree to receive a change of state in its imported variable for the change to take place. No cooperation between processes is implied by communication. The listening process may take no notice of its input. As such, the language has similarities to VHDL [1] and Verilog rather than to CSP. Indeed, the language is intended to be a cut-down version of the proposed VHDL-AMS mixed-signal extension to VHDL currently in final draft before the IEEE.

Blocking takes place within each process while it waits for an exit condition in a `wait` statement. This is the same as the `until` semantics used by Esterel, except that local state is not held constant during the `wait`, but instead develops according to the associated differential equations.

This little language is intended to approximate a subset of the upcoming VHDL-AMS standard (see [3] for a proposed denotational semantics). It has all the essential features of that language apart from *scheduling* and the distinction that VHDL-AMS makes between *quantities* and *signals*. Quantities in VHDL-AMS are analogue values and are governed by differential equations. They correspond to the variables we have used here. Signals in VHDL-AMS are the concept inherited from the old VHDL (digital) standard and are intended to represent digital signals: they admit only abrupt changes from one signal level to another at predefined discrete times. Therefore they are not governed by differential equations – or rather are governed by an implicit equation $dx/dt = 0$ that aserts that they remain constant between discrete time points. Becuase of this, their characteristics can by and large be emulated by the use of quantities governed by $dx/dt = 0$. The only area in which their behaviour is not straightforward to emulate is *scheduling*.

In VHDL, changes to a signal value can be scheduled for a future time. In the language that we have set up here, explicit scheduling is not provided for, but one can signal a helper process to begin a wait that terminates at the scheduled time and launches an interrupt. The command "x <= 1 after 5" in VHDL is equivalent to the command "x_delay=5; x_val=1; x_req=1; wait until x_ack = 1; x_req = 0" here, when the helper process contains the following code:

```
in  x_val, x_delay, x_req;
var val, delay;
out x_ack;
wait until x_req = 1;  /* wait on schedule attempt  */
while x_req = 1; do    /* repeat until timed exit    */
    val  = x_val;      /* grab scheduled value       */
```

```
    delay = x_delay      /* grab scheduled delay      */
    x_ack = 1;           /* acknowledge scheduling    */
    wait until x_req = 0;
    wait until delay = 0 or x_req = 1 with d delay/dt = -1;
done                     /* exit at scheduled time    */
x = val;                 /* make scheduled  assignment */
```

This helper process has been constructed to also treat signal *preemptions* correctly. Preemption is the classical VHDL semantics for scheduling. A scheduled signal change may be preempted by a new scheduling request that has been launched after the original request. The new request may assert a new delay or a new scheduled value. The second scheduling request, not the first, is the one that is eventually always honoured – unless it too is preempted before it matures. Even if the second request has asked for a longer delay, the second request is honoured and the first is discarded.

The absence of an explicit interrupt facility in the language here has made the helper process code more complicated than it otherwise need have been. The loop in the code is only there to check to see if an exit from the innermost wait occurred because of an interrupt or because of the maturation of the timer that had been set at entry. If the exit occurs early, then it is because of a rescheduling attempt and new timer and scheduled values must be set before reentering the wait state. The absence of subroutines and macros is not helpful either. But the language has been deliberately constructed in minimalist style in order that it lend itself to study the more easily.

It must be concluded from the above code fragment that explicit scheduling is not a necessary part of the language from the point of view of its expressive power, but it clearly is necessary from the point of programming convenience. However, it is not clear that scheduling remains necessary as a simulation technique, once the framework includes analogue quantities governed by differential equations. Scheduling a delay is a way of modelling real analogue device performance characteristics in a digital environment. It is now possible to model the performance more exactly, by means of differential equations. So it may not be necessary to include scheduling constructs in an analogue hardware description language, just as it is not necessary to provide explicit mechanisms for monitors or spinlocks, or other concepts familiar from parallel computer programming languages.

Another construct missing from the language is a class of *nondeterministically delayed and preemptible imperatives*. In this language all imperatives apart from wait take zero time to execute. But frequently it is necessary to model real systems in which a reaction may take some time to trigger, or in which a triggered but delayed action may abort if the trigger condition is not maintained for long enough. Such a construct is typically encountered in hybrid programming languages. If the triggering condition e is maintained for t_{min} then the action a may choose to fire at t_{min} (but not before). If the condition is maintained for t_{max} then the action must fire (at t_{max}). If the condition is maintained for $t_{min} \leq t < t_{max}$

then the action chooses to fire or not nondeterministically at t. Once fired the condition e is irrelevant. The construct may be described as

if e persists to t_{min} then a before t_{max}

and it may be emulated by the following code fragment, supposing access to a function or input signal random(t) that can provide a varying boolean feed:

```
wait until not e or t >= tmin with ...
                                  /* current equations */
if t >= tmin then
   wait until not e or random(t) or t >= tmax with ...
                                  /* current equations */
   if t >= tmax or random(t) then a; fi;
fi;
```

Nondetermism is not neccessary for a valid implementation, but it would be more satisfactory in practice. In any case, the code fragment shows that imperative actions that possess a duration, and even those that may be preempted, may be constructed from the toy language constructs given here.

4 Semantic Domains

The basic domain in which all quantities will take their values is the reals, augmented with $\perp$ and $\top$.

Statements of the hardware description language will have the semantics of a dependent *path*. A path is a piecewise smooth trajectory through state space with support a closed interval of time. A path assigns two real ordinates to every point of its support, the *left* and *right* values, representing limits from the right and left. The paths followed by programs are dependent on the paths followed by the external variables:

$$Semantics = Path \rightarrow Path$$
$$Path \quad = \bigsqcup_{a,b \in \Re} ([a,b] \rightarrow (State, State)) \times \{\sqrt{}, \perp\} \cup \{\perp\}$$
$$State \quad = Id \rightarrow \Re \cup \{\perp, \top\}$$
$$Time \quad = [0, \infty)$$

States assign an augmented real value to every identifier. $\perp$ denotes the undefined value, to be thought of as meaning "every and any real value is possible here," and $\top$ denotes an error: "no real value is possible here." A state will be said to be "in error" if any of its values is equal to $\top$, but we will not identify the error states together.

The topology of the reals is extended to $\Re \cup \{\perp, \top\}$ by letting the neigbourhoods of $\perp$ be all sets that include $\perp$. Thus $\perp$ is uniquely the unique limit of any sequence that eventually always is $\perp$,

Similarly, the neighbourhoods of $\top$ are all sets that include $\top$, and $\top$ is uniquely the unique limit of any sequence that eventually always is $\top$.

The notations y^-, y^+ denote the left and right values at t in the support of a path f with in which we will say that $f\,t\,x = y = (y^-, y^+)$. That is

$$\pi_1(f\,t)\,x = y^-$$
$$\pi_2(f\,t)\,x = y^+$$
$$(y^-, y^+) = y$$

and we use y^0 for the average value, and write $f^0\,t\,x = y^0$, $f^-\,t\,x = y^-$, $f^+\,t\,x = y^+$:

$$y^0 = \frac{y^- + y^+}{2}$$
$$y^- = \lim_{\tau \to t^-} f^0\,\tau\,x$$
$$y^+ = \lim_{\tau \to t^+} f^0\,\tau\,x$$

These domains all have all finite limits: *State* is the full domain of total functions, with the pointwise refinement ordering; *Path* is a domain of partial functions – each function has a *support* on which it is defined. A support is a contiguous interval $[a, b]$ of the time line

$$Time = [0, \infty)$$

A path either terminates (signified by a $\sqrt{}$ symbol) or is prepared to continue (signified by $\bot$). In the latter case it is a *partial* path. A terminating path refines another terminating path if its support is exactly the same and it refines the first pointwise on the support. Otherwise one path refines another only if the latter is partial and has an equal or shorter support, and there is pointwise refinement on the common initial segment of the supports.

We define the functions *initial* and *final* on paths, which obtain the initial and final state and time:

Definition 1.

$$initial\,f = (f^-\,t_0, t_0)$$
$$final\,f = (f^+\,t_1, t_1)$$

where $dom\,f = [t_0, t_1]$

Note that the pointwise meet $f \sqcap g$ of two continuous paths f and g is continuous. If the limit $f\,t_i$, $g\,t_i$ as the t_i approach t is not a real number, then it must be $f\,t = \bot$ or $\top$ and/or $g\,t = \bot$ or $\top$. In this case the limit is eventually always achieved by the sequence, and so $(f \sqcap g)\,t_i$ will either eventually always be $f\,t_i$, or eventually always be $g\,t_i$.

This definition is required for the semantics of parallelism. Putting two processes in parallel signifies calculating the path $f \sqcap g$. If the paths disagree with real values at a point t, then the parallel composition $f \sqcap g$ has an error at t. I.e. if $f\,t \neq g\,t$ and $f\,t$, $g\,t \neq \bot$, then $(f \sqcap g)\,t = \top$.

Returning now to the language L: to get the semantics $[s_1; s_2$ of a pair of statements s_1, s_2 in sequence, we will eventually put the path that we get from $[s_1]$ in sequence with the path we get from $[s_2]$, given the final state of the first path as initial.

Assignment statements will have a semantics as a special sort of path. They take no time to execute, and as such are sited at particular points in time, at which they cause a discontinuous change in state. They can be regarded as triples of time points and pairs of before/after states:

$$Discontinuity \subseteq Path$$
$$Discontinuity = (Time, State, State)$$

The representation of (t, σ_-, σ_+) in $Path$ is $(\{(t, (\sigma_-, \sigma_+))\}, \sqrt{})$.

A discontinuity (t, σ_-, σ_+) can abut a path with support $[t_0, t]$ terminating in a right state σ_- and the combination produces a path with the same support but terminating in a right state σ_+. Two triples based at the same time point can likewise be combined.

5 Logic

We will evaluate logical propositions in a truth domain

$$\Omega = \Re^{\pm\infty}$$

consisting of all the real numbers and $\pm\infty$, not only the boolean $\{T, F\}$. This is appropriate to problems that deal with continuously varying values.

In this domain the more positive a result is, the more false it is, and the more negative a result is, the more true it is! To get a grip on this, we define the positive and negative parts of this intepretation of logic separately. Both parts evaluate into $\Re_0^{+\infty}$, and then the whole evaluation is the difference:

$$[-] :: Elog \to \Omega$$
$$[x] = [x]_+ - [x]_-$$

In the positive interpretation we get the degree of falsity of a condition, and in the negative interpretation we get the degree of truth.

Falsity		Truth	
$[x \text{ and } y]_+$	$= \max [x]_+ [y]_+$	$[x \text{ and } y]_-$	$= \min [x]_- [y]_-$
$[x \text{ or } y]_+$	$= \min [x]_+ [y]_+$	$[x \text{ or } y]_-$	$= \max [x]_- [y]_-$
$[\text{not } x]_+$	$= [x]_-$	$[\text{not } x]_-$	$= [x]_+$
$[\text{true}]_+$	$= 0$	$[\text{true}]_-$	$= +\infty$
$[\text{false}]_+$	$= +\infty$	$[\text{false}]_-$	$= 0$
$[u < v]_+$	$= \max (u - v)\ 0$	$[u < v]_-$	$= \max (v - u)\ 0$
$[u = v]_+$	$= abs(u - v)$	$[u = v]_-$	$= 0$

Universal and existential quantification will be implemented via sup and inf.

Falsity	Truth
$[\forall x\|p.q]_+ = \sup\{\min\ [p]_-\ [q]_+\}$	$[\forall x\|p.q]_- = \inf\{\max\ [p]_+\ [q]_-\}$
$[\exists x\|p.q]_+ = \inf\{\max\ [p]_+\ [q]_+\}$	$[\exists x\|p.q]_- = \sup\{\min\ [p]_-\ [q]_-\}$

It is easy to prove by induction that the positive interpretation is positive when the negative interpretation is zero and vice versa:

Proposition 2.

$$[x]_+ > 0 \rightarrow [x]_- = 0$$
$$[x]_- > 0 \rightarrow [x]_+ = 0$$

so that only one of $[x]_+$, $[x]_-$ is ever positive at a time. Hence $[x]_+ = \max\ [x]\ 0$ *is* the positive part of $[x]$ and $[x]_- = -\min\ [x]\ 0$ *is* the negative part of $[x]$.

This means that negation is $[\text{not }x] = -[x]$ and therefore that implication is $[x \rightarrow y] = \min\ [y]\ (-[x])$.

One of the useful aspects of this interpretation is that it is, excluding the quantifier interpretation and adding the point at infinity, continuous and piecewise differentiable in any free variables.

If quantifiers are taken into account, then the interpretation is still continuous (and piecewise smooth) provided that the atomic statements are continuous (and smooth) in *all* variables simultaneously. For example, consider $[\forall t|t < t'.t < 1]_+$. The interpretation depends on the interpretation of $t < t'$ and $t < 1$, which are $t' - t$ and $1 - t$ respectively. These interpretations are bi-continuous in t and t', and the interpretation of the quantified statement is

$$\sup\{\min\ (t - t')\ (1 - t)\} = (1 - t')/2$$

and is continuous (and piecewise smooth) as a result. It is possible to use this interpretation with generic numerical methods that find the zeros of continuous and piecewise differentiable functions.

If a result is classically true, then it evaluates to a negative number here, and if it is classically false, then it evaluates to a positive number:

Proposition 3.

$$x\ is\ true \rightarrow [x] \leq 0$$
$$x\ is\ false \rightarrow [x] \geq 0$$

The only possibility of getting 0 simultaneously both from the negative and positive evaluations is when the state lies exactly on the boundary of an underlying inequality or equality. A modification to the interpretation of equality could make the conditions mutually exclusive, but at the cost of introducing discontinuities on a set of measure zero.

To this substructure we add the notation used earlier for left and right limits. A proposition $p(t)$ that depends on time t and which evaluates into this real-valued truth domain may take different values close to t on its left and on its right on any particular path:

$$[p]^-(t) = \lim_{\tau \to t^-} [p(\tau)]$$
$$[p]^+(t) = \lim_{\tau \to t^+} [p(\tau)]$$

In particular, the idea that a path is continuous at a point t in variables x may be expressed as

$$\exists y.[x = y]^- \wedge [x = y]^+$$

or

$$[\exists y.x^- = y \wedge x^+ = y] = -abs(x^- - x^+)/2 \geq 0$$

Proposition 4. $[\exists y.(x^- = y \wedge x^+ = y)]$ *evaluates as false (i.e., < 0) precisely at the points t on a path where it is discontinuous in x.*

When dealing with predicates p that vary continuously along a path, one derived property that is of particular interest is the fact that the time domain over which they take at least a given truth value extends further to the right than the point of first evaluation:

$$[p(t)] > a \to \exists \delta t > 0. \forall \tau \in [t, t + \delta t).[p(\tau)] > a$$

(and equally for $[p(t)] < a$). This property of predicates will be called *sharpness*:

Definition 5. A property p is *sharp* on a path f, if (1) whenever it has a truth value more than a at t, it has at least the value a through a small interval to the right of t, (2) whenever it has a truth value less than a at t, it has at most that value through a small interval to the right of t.

A sharp property is one which holds in intervals of the shape $[a, b)$. I.e., anywhere that the property is true to a certain degree, it is true to that degree also for a short interval to the right. And similarly for falsity.

This is a weaker requirement than continuity. For example, the function

$$\begin{cases} 1, t \in [2n, 2n+1) \\ 0, t \in [2n+1, 2n+2) \end{cases}$$

is sharp but not continuous.

Proposition 6. *All continuous properties are sharp.*

Sharpness for predicates generalizes a classical property of boolean predicates over a finite state machine with real world inputs: a boolean predicate is sharp if whenever it is true, it stays true for a while, and whenever it is false, it stays false for a while. I.e.

$$p(t) \quad \rightarrow \exists \delta t > 0. \forall \tau \in [t, t + \delta t).p(\tau)$$
$$\neg p(t) \rightarrow \exists \delta t > 0. \forall \tau \in [t, t + \delta t).\neg p(\tau)$$

This classical property reflects the behaviour of a finite state machine given time varying inputs. The machine cannot examine its inputs with infinite precision because looking at decimals takes instruction cycles, and arbitrarily many may be required in principle to distinguish between $0.99999\ldots9$ and $0.1000\ldots1$. So a computer that guarantees to progress must, in a given state, stop looking at decimals somewhere, and then is insensitive to variations of finer precision. So the computer holds the outputs it controls momentarily constant in the face of such variations. Putting it another way, once it is in a given state it cannot leave that state for some small positive interval of time.

If the outputs of the computer are a combination of its internal state and continuously varying external factors, however, then all that can be said is that the outputs are locally continuous. They consist of picewise continuous fragments. The intervals of continuity are precisely closed-open intervals of the shape $[a, b)$. At the right hand edge of the intervals the computer "wakes up" to the fact that something has changed and changes its state abruptly, leading to a discontinuous change in the output. The edges of the intervals do not cluster anywhere provided that the computer never goes into an infinite loop.

Sharpness of predicates captures the latter state of affairs exactly: Note first that any function that is piecewise continuous with the pieces consisting of a sequence of abutting closed-open intervals $[a_i, a_{i+1})$ that cover the whole real line is sharp (by the definition of sharp).

Conversely, we can show that *sharp* as stated here is equivalent to the notion of *continuity* when the domain space has the topology generated by the base of neighbourhoods $[t, t')$ of t. This is because, in that topology, limits are necesarily downgoing limits $t_i \rightarrow t^-$. So continuity over that topology means exactly that a function turns downgoing limits into limits. It follows easily from the definition of sharp that a sharp function turns downgoing limits into limits. Hence:

Proposition 7. *A sharp function is precisely a continuous function when the time domain is given the topology in which the closed-open intervals $[t, t')$ are a base of neighbourhoods for t.*

Continuity over this topology means preservation of downgoing limits. Clearly both classically continuous functions and functions piecewise continuous over abutting intervals $[a_i, a_{i+1})$ preserve these limits. There are no more candidate functions whose points of discontinuity do not cluster to the right.

6   Semantic Functions

The semantics described loosely earlier may be formalized as follows. Let ';' be the semantic operator that combines abutting paths (and discontinuities), the first one of which is terminating:

$$(;) :: Path \to Path \to Path$$
$$f_{a,b}; g_{b,c} = h_{a,c}, \quad f^+ b \sqsubseteq g^- b$$
$$where \quad h^\pm t \;=\; \begin{cases} f^\pm t, & t \in [a,b) \\ g^\pm t, & t \in (b,c] \end{cases}$$
$$\left. \begin{matrix} h^- t \\ h^+ t \end{matrix} \right\} \;=\; \begin{cases} g^+ b \\ f^- b \end{cases}, \quad t = b \tag{10}$$

The termination attribute of the result is summarized in the following table:

$(;)$	$\checkmark$	$\perp$
$\checkmark$	$\checkmark$	$\perp$
$\perp$	$-$	$-$

The semantic function will evaluate statements to paths on the variables in scope predicated on the path of the external variables.

$$[-] :: Statement \to Semantics \tag{11}$$

Let μ be the least fixpoint operator in the *Semantics* domain. I.e. it finds the least invariant path transformer:

$$\mu :: ((Path \to Path) \to Path \to Path) \to Path \to Path$$
$$\mu \, F f_0 = \perp \sqcup F \, (const \perp) f_0 \sqcup F^2 (const \perp) f_0 \sqcup \ldots$$

and identify the trajectories that a system $dv/dt = e$ may take given external trajectories f via the following predicate.

Definition 8. Let $\mathcal{O}(f, g, b, v, e)$ be the predicate ("oracle") that says that

- g_{t_0,t_1} is a path satisfying the equations $dv/dt = e$ on the interval (t_0, t_1) starting with initial state and time $(\sigma_0, t_0) = initial \, f$;
- $g|_{\overline{v}} = f|_{\overline{v}}$ (equality on variables not among v) on this interval;
- $g|_v \sqsupseteq f|_v$ (refinemet on variables among v) on this interval;
- $t_1 \ge t_0$ is the first point in time on the path at which the conditions b become true (i.e. $f \, t_1 \, b \le 0$).

That is:

$$\mathcal{O}(f, g, b, v, e)$$
$$iff$$
$$t_1 = \sup\{t \mid t \ge t_0, \; \forall \tau \in (t_0, t). \; \lim_{\tau' \to \tau} \frac{g \, \tau' \, v - g \, \tau \, v}{\tau' - \tau} = g \, \tau \, e, \; g \, \tau \, b \ge 0\}$$

The important property of this predicate (for a particular set of equations $dv/dt = e$ and condition b) is that, given the classical uniform topology on the function spaces:

1. the path described by the variables v is uniquely and continuously and causally determined by the starting conditions of the variables v in σ_0 at t_0 in f *plus* the path in f taken by the variables other than v referenced by e (i.e., imported external variables);

2. the stopping time t_1 is uniquely and continuously determined by the initial condition of the variables v in σ_0 at t_0 in f *plus* the path in f taken by the variables other than v referenced by b and e over $[t_0, t)$.

Causality here means the absence of dependence on the state at future times. This type of dependence may not be true for all sets of differential equations, but it will be true for those that we treat.

Using the nonstandard interpretation of logic set out in Section 5, these conditions mean precisely that

1. $[\mathcal{O}(t_0, t_1, \sigma_0, f, b, v, e)]$ is a real continuuous function of its real and functional parameters, using the appropriate topology (real and uniform, respectively).

2. $[\mathcal{O}(t_0, t_1, \sigma_0, f, b, v, e)]$ is dependent only on the portion of f restricted to $[t_0, t_1]$.

The defined action of a state σ on a variable v has been taken to extend naturally to expressions e and conditions b in the above. That is, $f\, t\, e$ is the evaluation of the state $\sigma = f\, t$ on the expression e in the natural way (interpreting + as addition, and so on, and taking arithmetic operations and comparators to be strict; $\perp + 5.4321 = \perp$, etc.), and $f\, t\, b$ is the evaluation of the state $\sigma = f\, t$ on the condition b using the real-valued logic of Section 5. Then we may express the semantics of the language as follows:

$$[p_1 \ldots p_n]f_0 = [p_1]f_0 \sqcup \ldots \sqcup [p_n]f_0$$

$$[p\,(\ldots)\{\ \mathbf{var}\ v_1 \ldots v_n; s\ \};]f_0 = [s(p.v_1/v_1, \ldots, p.v_n/v_n)]f_0$$

$$[s_1 \ldots s_n]f_0 = [s_1]f_0; \ldots; [s_n]f_{n-1}$$
$$\text{where } f_i = (t_i, \sigma_i, \bot); f_{i-1}|_{[t_i,\infty)}$$
$$\text{and } (\sigma_i, t_i) = final([s_i]f_{i-1})$$

$$[v = e;]f_0 = f_0 \oplus \{(t_0, \sigma_0, \sigma_0')\}$$
$$\text{where } \sigma_0' v = \sigma_0 \oplus \{(v, \sigma_0 e)\}$$
$$\text{and } (\sigma_0, t_0) = initial\ f_0$$

$$[\mathbf{wait\ until}\ b\ \mathbf{with}\ dv/dt = e;]f_0 = f_1$$
$$\text{where } \mathcal{O}(f_0, f_1, b, v, e)$$

$$[\mathbf{if}\ b\ \mathbf{then}\ s_1\ \mathbf{else}\ s_2\ \mathbf{fi};]f_0 = [s_1]f_0,\ \text{if}\ [b](\sigma_0, t_0) < 0$$
$$[s_2]f_0,\ \text{if}\ [b](\sigma_0, t_0) > 0$$
$$\text{and } (\sigma_0, t_0) = initial\ f_0$$

$$[\mathbf{while}\ b\ \mathbf{do}\ s\ \mathbf{od};]f_0 = \mu F\ f_0$$
$$\text{where } F\pi\ f_0 = (t_0, \sigma_0, \sigma_0),\ \text{if}\ [b](\sigma_0, t_0) > 0$$
$$(\pi \circ [s])f_0,\ \text{otherwise}$$
$$\text{where } (\sigma_0, t_0) = initial\ f_0$$

This semantics uses the facts that

1. paths are defined to give values (possibly $\bot$) to all variables. I.e. paths are total functions;
2. paths give the value $\bot$ to variables which they have not assigned a value to, which allows us to put paths in parallel via meet of paths.

If a process p can engage in a path f and it is compatible with a path g that process q can engage in in the sense that there is a common refinement $h \sqsupseteq f, g$, then h will be a possible path for p in parallel with q.

A process p has the semantics of the code it contains, after replacing references to the local variables v with references to unique globals $p.v$.

Sequences of code have the semantics of the set of all possible valid juxtapositions of paths taken from each set in sequence.

One of the consequences of this semantics is that all the possible paths in a circuit must terminate if all the possible paths in any circuit component (i.e., process) terminate. The circuit dies if any of its components dies.

Another consequence is that if a process can loop infinitely often without making infinite time progress, then the path that results is undefined after the limit time that the computation approaches.

7 Approximation

At this point we will construct a second semantics for the language, using a time grid with intervals of no greater size than a fixed constant δ

$$Time_\delta = \ldots t_{-1}, t_0, t_1, \ldots$$

with $t_i < t_{i+1} < t_i + \delta$, $t_i \to \pm\infty$ as $i \to \pm\infty$.

The "paths" f that we will now consider will still be functions through the continuous time space but they will be completely determined by the points on $Time_\delta$; between any two such points they will constantly take the right value of the left-hand point, which will be the left value of the right hand point:

$$Path_\delta = \{f \in Path \mid \forall t, i.\ t \in (t_i, t_{i+1}) \to f^+ t = f^- t = f^+ t_i = f^- t_{i+1}\}$$

So these paths are square-shaped curves. They inherit the refinement ordering on $Path$.

The only points at which discontinuities may be defined are the gridpoints:

$$Discontinuity_\delta = (Time_\delta, State, State)$$

and in general the semantics of statements will be a set of a δ-grid paths:

$$Semantics_\delta \subseteq \{Path_\delta\}$$

Likewise we use a version of the oracle predicate that delivers a result that is based on the time grid. It gives an exit time t exactly on the last grid point immediately before the condition b is first satisfied on the path f.

$$\mathcal{O}_\delta(t_{i_0}, t_{i_1}, \sigma_0, f, b, v, e)$$
$$\textit{iff}$$
$$f(t_{i_0}) = \sigma_0,\ t_{i_1} = \sup\{t_i \mid i \geq i_0,\ \forall \iota \in [i_0, i). \tfrac{f\, t_{\iota+1}\, v - f\, t_\iota\, v}{t_{\iota+1} - t_\iota} = f\, t_\iota\, e,\ f\, t_\iota\, b \geq 0\}$$

Then the semantic function may be defined with only minor alterations with respect to that given earlier:

$$[p_1 \ldots p_n]_\delta = [p_1]_\delta \sqcup \ldots \sqcup [p_n]_\delta$$
$$[p\ (\ldots)\{\ \mathbf{var}\ v_1 \ldots v_n; s\ \};]_\delta = [s(p.v_1/v_1, \ldots, p.v_n/v_n)]_\delta$$
$$[s_1 \ldots s_n]_\delta = \{f_1; \ldots; f_n \mid f_1 \in [s_1]_\delta, \ldots, f_n \in [s_n]_\delta\}^\dagger$$
$$[v = e;]_\delta = \{(t_i, \sigma, \sigma') \mid \sigma' v = \sigma \oplus \{(v, \sigma e)\}\}^\dagger$$
$$[\mathbf{wait\ until}\ b\ \mathbf{with}\ dv/dt = e;]_\delta = \{f_{t_i, t_j} \mid \mathcal{O}_\delta(t_i, t_j, f\, t_i, f, b, v, e)\}^\dagger$$
$$[\mathbf{if}\ b\ \mathbf{then}\ s_1\ \mathbf{else}\ s_2\ \mathbf{fi};]_\delta = \{f_{t_i, t_j} \in [s_1]_\delta \mid f\, t_i\, b \leq 0\}^\dagger$$
$$\sqcap\ \{g_{t_i, t_j} \in [s_2]_\delta \mid g\, t_j\, b \leq 0\}^\dagger$$
$$[\mathbf{while}\ b\ \mathbf{do}\ s\ \mathbf{od};]_\delta = \mu_\delta F$$
$$\text{where } F\pi = \{(t_i, \sigma, \sigma) \mid \sigma\, b > 0\}^\dagger$$
$$\sqcap\ \{f_{t_i, t_j}; g_{t_j, t_k} \mid f\, t_i\, b \leq 0, f_{t_i, t_j} \in [s]_\delta, g_{t_j, t_k} \in \pi\}^\dagger$$

There are several questions of interest here. Is every path f in the standard semantics of a statement the classical limit of paths f^δ in the semantics derived from sufficently small δ-grids? Can one chose arbitrary δ-grids? If a process is deterministic in the sense that its standard semantics yields a principal set $\{f\}^\dagger$ once all inputs have been defined, then is it the case that f is the unique classical limit of paths f^δ? The first of these questions is easy to decide (see the proposition that follows), but first a counter-example: if a path varies gently but exits from the gentle variation at a given threshold and jumps suddenly to a new value, such as for example, in

$$
\begin{aligned}
x &= 0, \ t \leq 0 \\
\frac{dx}{dt} &= \begin{cases} 1, & 0 < t < 1 \\ 0, & t > 1 \end{cases} \\
x &= 0, \ t \geq 1
\end{aligned}
$$

(a single sawtooth), then on a grid in which the last gridpoint before $t = 1$ is $t_i < 1 < t_{i+1}$, the approximation inevitably must make the jump to zero at t_i and not t, and hence will introuce an error of size approximately 1 throughout the small interval $(t_i, 1)$. This means that convergence cannot be uniform, but it will be pointwise. Moreover, convergence will be uniform "almost everywhere" in the sense that it will be uniform excluding only neighbourhoods of a set of nowhere dense points.

A suitable program to generates the sawtooth path above is

```
...
wait until t>0 with dx/dt = 1;
x = 0;
wait until false with dx/dt = 0;
```

(for example).

Proposition 9. *Every proper finite initial segment of a path $f \in [s]$ is the (pointwise) limit of paths $f^\delta \in [s]_\delta$ as $\delta \to 0$ for a suitable choice of δ-grids.*

Proof: WLOG, assume that f has infinite time support. Given f, choose grids t^δ which include at least all the time points $t_{i,j}$ at which the processes p_j that generated f entered and left **wait** statements. Let the grid points of t^δ be (ordered as) t_k^δ. Since f was generated by processes that made infinite progress in time, these points do not cluster anywhere. f is smooth at all points not amongst the $t_{i,j}$.

For any choice of the f^δ given suitable grids as described, let t be the earliest time point at which $f^\delta(t) \not\to f(t)$ as $\delta \to 0$. We can include control path markers in the state to ensure that this is also the first point t at which the control path followed by the f^δ deviates from the control path followed by f in any of the p_j.

Suppose first that t falls at a point when f is strictly within all wait statements of nonzero duration (i.e., t is strictly between the t_k^δ that are $t_{i,j}$s). Say $t_{i_j,j} < t < t_{i_j+1,j}$. Then by hypothesis the states $s^\delta = f^\delta\, t_{i_j,j}$ on entry to the waits at $t_{i_j,j}$ (being earlier) converge to the states $s = f\, t_{i_j,j}$ as $\delta \to 0$. Also by hypothesis the path fragments $f_{t_{i_j,j},t}$ between entry to the waits and t are the pointwise limits of the corresponding f^δ fragments. Since f is smooth at t, the convergence is to a continuous (indeed, smooth) function on the closed interval, and hence is uniform.

The approximating oracle function determines the approximating exit time τ' from each wait statement in each process p_j continuously in terms of the state at entry to the wait at τ and the path segment $f^\delta_{\tau,\tau'}$ followed by the imported variables v_j during the wait. As the state at τ tends to the state at $t_{i_j,j}$ in p_j and the path fragments of f^δ converge uniformly to the fragments $f_{\tau,t}$, so the exit time τ' tends to $t_{i_j+1,j}$ in each process p_j. In particular it tends to some value greater than $t + \epsilon$, for suitable choice of $\epsilon > 0$. Since the development of the paths is governed by differential equations on the intervals $t_{i_j}, t + \epsilon$, the state at t in f^δ is the limit of the states to the left on the path. These tend to the states on f, and therefore $f^\delta\,t$ tends to $f;t$.

Now consider the case when t falls at the exit point $t_{i_j+1,j}$ of a wait statement in process p_j. Then the processes p_j that generated f may have engaged in computation to determine the state at that point. They could not have entered an infinite loop or they would not have progressed beyond t, and by hypothesis, they have. So the state of f at t is the result of finitely many computations in zero time since exiting a wait statement in at least one contributing process. The argument of the last paragraph may be used to conclude that the state at the exit from the wait statement (if any) depended continuously on the path up till then (if there is no preceding wait, then we are at the beginning of the program and the state is fixed). Now, a finite number of computations can only examine the state variables at exit from the wait to a certain fixed accuracy, and the computation thereafter will be invariant once the state is determined to within that accuracy. Therefore taking a sufficiently small δ that f^δ is sufficiently close that the variables on exit from the wait are within the accuracy examined, the state at t will be determined as closely as may be required.

The result in the case when f does not have infinite time support comes by choosing an arbitrary proper initial support $[0, t]$ (on which f is generated by at most a finite number of computations) and choosing the grid as before on this interval and extending it arbitrarily to the right and left.

□

On any finite closed set of intervals that does not include the points $t_{i,j}$ at which the exact path enters and exits wait statements, the convergence, being pointwise and to a piecewise continuous limit, is uniform.

This result is adequate, but it does depend on the good behaviour of the differential equations involved. Can the δ-grids be chosen arbitrarily? If the grid is constructed not with respect to f, then it can only be guaranteed to have points that fall close to but not on the entries and exits from wait statements of the processes that construct f.

In these circumstances, the semantics of the oracle predicate ∅ says that wait statements for the approximations f^δ will exit at the grid point immediately before the exit condition becomes true. For small enough δ this means only a small disturbance with respect to f. We can argue as in the proof of the proposition above that the processes that generated f are computational and therefore cannot use infinite precision, and as soon as the disturbances generated are below this level of precision, then the control flow that generates f^δ will be the same as the control flow that generates f over any proper finite initial segment of f. So, yes,

Proposition 10. *Every proper finite initial segment of a path $f \in [s]$ is the (uniform) limit of paths $f^\delta \in [s]_\delta$ as $\delta \to 0$ for arbitrary choice of small enough δ-grids.*

It cannot in general be known in advance how small is "small enough" for δ. That means that we cannot know beforehand what degree of numerical precision is required to compute a path accurately over a given time interval. The calculation may have to be done again with greater precision. It is not even clear how to check that the computed path is accurate.

The arguments in the preceding propositions showed that control flow is determined in a fine enough δ-grid. In conjunction with the determinacy of the exit state and time in a wait statement, this shows that the limits refered to are unique.

Proposition 11. *If there is a principal path $\{f\}^\dagger = [s]$ then the approximations $f \in [s]_\delta$ converge to it uniquely (and uniformly on any finite proper initial segment of its support).*

The existence of a limit for the approximating paths in $[s]_\delta$ seems to imply that the limit is in $[s]$.

It also seems to be the case that the language semantics is deterministically functional, despite being couched nondetermistically. In a future work, it should be possible to demonstrate that the parallelism in this language is benign. Only one process writes to each shared variable. This does not on its own mean that the value is determined because data dependency loops $a = b; b = a$ may exist. However, each approximating semantics for the language inserts an implicit delay in the evaluation of external variables during the solution of differential equations, because they use a variant of the formula

$$f(t + \delta) = f(t) + \frac{\mathrm{d}f}{\mathrm{d}t}\delta$$

in which only old values are used to calculate the new. So the approximating semantics must be deterministic.

8   Experiments

An interpreter has been built for this language in the functional language *Gofer* [2]. The interpreter works with a fixed δ-grid.

In experiments we have found that it is not very important to have a small δ so long as the solutions to the differential equation sets are relatively smooth (in the sense of only slowly changing, i.e. having a small second derivative). Once at least quadratic approximation is used in the numerical approximation routines that trace the state space trajectories, then the deviation "in flight" from the correct trajectory is very small. Of great importance, however, is the accurate calculation of the entry and exit times to the wait statements. A small inaccuracy can have very large effects, and it has been found necessary to interpolate one extra grid point dynamically at the exit of each wait, using a combination of Newton-Raphson prediction and interval-halving to determine the time of exit accurately.

For example, consider an analogue circuit that simulates the flight $s(t)$ of a bouncing ball. It may be written as the following program:

```
ball (out: s=1, v=0) {
  var g = 9.8, a = 0.1;
  while true do
    wait until s<0 with dv/dt = -g - sign(v) * a * v²
                        ds/dt = v;
    v = -v;
    s = 0;
  od;
}
```

This program essentially introduces the flight equation under gravity

$$\frac{d^2s}{dt^2} = -g$$

with a modification $\pm av^2$ that allows for air resistance. The air resistance acts against the direction of motion and is proportional to the square of the velocity. Whenever the ball bounces on the ground, the velocity reverses exactly. The bounce is perfectly elastic.

The in-flight trajectory deviates slightly but smoothly from a perfect parabola. One may calculate that the ball should lose a fraction ah of its energy hg to air resistance on each journey to ground from height h, and approximately the same loss should occur again on the way up from ground to the peak of the next bounce.

Inaccuracies in the calculation of the trajectory are cumulative. For example, using a tangential linear approximation at each step of the numerical integration between grid points on the way up in the bounce will put the ball significantly higher than it should be (the curve is convex) at each step but get the velocity approximately right, with the net result that the ball loses less energy than it should on the way up. The total error is proportional to the grid size. A grid of 0.08 may produce about a 30% overbounce. But almost all this numerical error is mended by using quadratic approximation instead of linear approximation at each step.

Of more significance is the error introduced by being late or early in detecting the exact point at which the ball hits the floor. The ball is travelling fast there so a small time error causes a large velocity error. The program assumes that the timing of the exit from the wait statement is exactly right and just reflects the velocity ("**v** = −**v**;"), while moving the ball through space ("**s** = 0;"). But, given that the exit is taken too early and that the ball is still above the floor then, this lowers the potential energy of the ball without increasing the kinetic energy to compensate. Because the velocity is high, the ball may be far from the floor when the magic move occurs, which means a large change in the energy. The net result is a large underbounce from being early on the exit from the wait (and a large overbounce from being late).

To reduce the timing error, we have successfully used Newton-Raphson style iteration to locate the onset of the condition $s < 0$. We use the nonstandard interpretation of [**s** < 0] from Section 5 to get a real-valued "degree of falsity" for the condition, and follow the curve of falsity against time to its nearest next zero. The curve is piecewise smooth so it is amenable to this method. Once located, the time point is added to the current grid. This seems to result in very satisfactory precision with very little extra calculation. The state space trajectory is shown in Fig. 4.

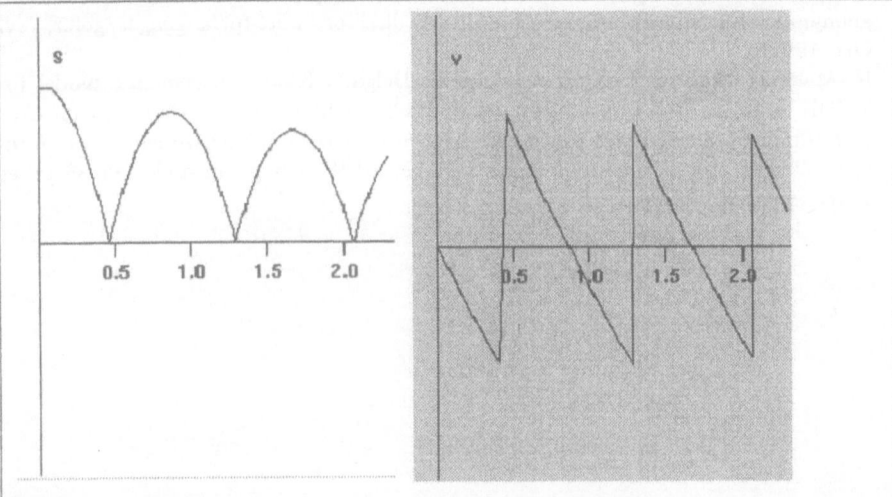

Fig. 4. The velocity v and height above ground s against time of a ball bouncing elastically under gravity with air resistance, as described by the analogue process `ball`. Initial height $s = 1.0$.

9 Conclusion

A minimal analogue process description language has been designed. It is a hybrid programming language that is capable of describing all analogue circuits that are defined in terms of state-switched differential equations. The language has been given a well defined classical semantics in which every process corresponds to a set of possible piecewise smooth paths through state space. Approximate semantics have been defined, each based on a particular discrete grid of time points. Each approximate semantics is computable exactly on a standard computer. It has been shown that, under reasonable assumptions on the behaviour of the differential equations involved, the approximate trajectories computed for the system converge uniformly to the ideal trajectories on any proper initial segment.

The discussion has been motivated by the desire to understand first if and then why the description of the classical operational amplifer as a simple computational input-output causal reactive system is impossible.

References

1. IEEE. *IEEE Standard VHDL Language Reference Manual. ANSI/IEEE STD 1076-1993.* Institute of Electrical and Electronic Engineers, New York, 1994.
2. Mark P. Jones. Introduction to Gofer. Technical report, Department of Computer Science, Yale University, USA, September 1991. (part of the Gofer distribution, anonymous ftp from ftp.cs.nott.ac.uk in the directory nott-fp/languages/gofer, rev. Oct. 1994).
3. N. Martínez Madrid, P.T. Breuer, and C. Delgado Kloos. A semantic model for VHDL-AMS. In Hon F. Li and David K. Probst, editors, *Proc. Conference on Correct Hardware Design and Verification Methods, CHARME'97; Advances in Hardware Design and Verification*, pages 106–126. IFIP; Chapman and Hall, October 1997. Montreal, Canada.

Reasoning about Imperfect Digital Systems

Keith Hanna

Computing Laboratory
University of Kent, UK

Abstract. In order to realise digital systems that operate at high speeds or that have very low power consumptions, it is necessary to work directly at the analog level of abstraction, that is, in terms of analog electronic components such as resistors and transistors. Although the external behaviour of such circuits can be described digitally, their internal operation can only be explained by working at the analog level and by taking account of both voltages and currents.

This chapter describes how existing methods of specification and formal verification of digital systems can be extended so as to encompass such analog designs in a fully rigorous manner.

1 Introduction

The usual, idealised approach to digital design is summarised in Fig. 1:

- The starting point is a *requirements specification*. This can be a predicate, *req*, describing the desired relation between the signals at the terminals of the desired implementation.
- The process of *synthesis* (typically informal) leads to an *implementation*, often presented in the form of a gate schematic.
- The process of *behavioural extraction* yields a derived specification, *imp*, of the behaviour of the implementation.
- The process of *verification* compares the predicates *req* and *imp* to determine if the implementation is *correct*.

As a very simple example, consider the design of an Exclusive-Or gate. The predicate *req* will be

$$req: \mathbb{B}^2 \times \mathbb{B} \to prop$$
$$req\ ((x,y),z) \triangleq (z = (x \oplus y))$$

(where $\mathbb{B} \triangleq \{t, f\}$ is the type of ideal, steady-state digital signals and *prop* is the type of propositional logic truth values).

- Synthesis might yield the gate schematic shown in Fig. 2.

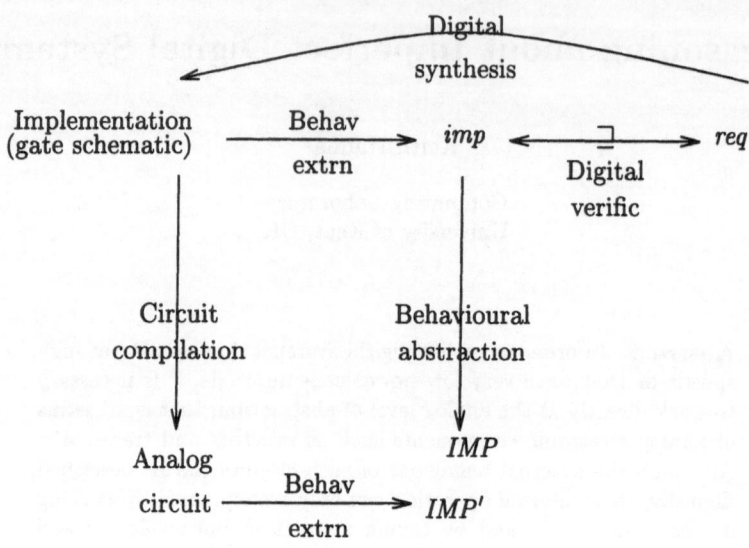

Fig. 1. Idealised digital design process

– Behavioural extraction would then yield the derived specification

$$imp: \mathbb{B}^2 \times \mathbb{B} \to prop$$
$$imp\ ((x,y),z) \stackrel{\wedge}{=}$$
$$\exists u,v,w: \mathbb{B}.$$
$$or\ ((x,y),u) \wedge and\ ((x,y),v) \wedge$$
$$not\ (v,w) \wedge and\ ((u,w),z)$$

– The verification condition is

$$\forall x,y,z: \mathbb{B}.\ imp\ ((x,y),z) \Rightarrow req\ ((x,y),z)$$

or, in higher-order form, $imp \sqsupseteq req$.

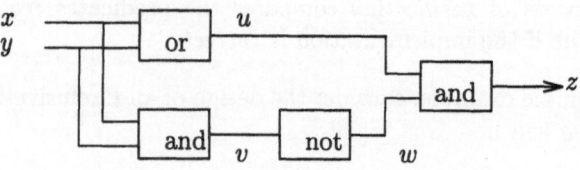

Fig. 2. A typical implementation of Exclusive-Or

It is the task of the fabricator of the devices (in general, a different person than the user of the devices) to ensure that the devices function in such a way as to guarantee that when the *analog* signals at their terminals are viewed through the appropriate abstraction function, they do, in fact, satisfy the predicate *imp*. Doing this involves ensuring that the functions and predicates round the square in this diagram commute (that is, that *IMP'* ⊒ *IMP*). In general, this is guaranteed only provided the digital circuit obeys certain (technology-specific) *design rules*.

Limitations There are two major limitations with this approach to specification and verification. Firstly, compositionality has not been considered, and this leads to obvious anomolies. For example, the back-to-front gate schematic shown in Fig. 3 equally satisfies the above verification condition. Secondly, and of greater significance, this approach does not cover *optimised*

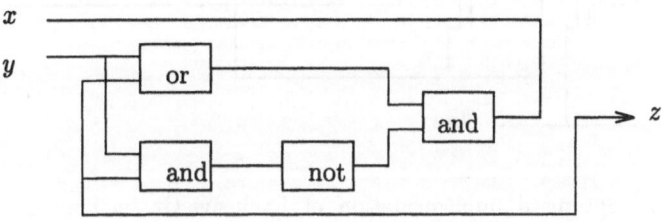

Fig. 3. An unsatisfactory implementation of Exclusive-Or

implementations. In practice, designers usually need to optimise an implementation with respect to speed, power consumption or area. For instance, an optimised implementation of *req* might instead use the circuit shown in Fig. 4. Such an implementation, which makes use of *pass-transistor logic*, is very fast, consumes very little power and occupies a very small area.

Reasoning about the behaviour of implementations involving pass-transistor logic, or even those involving *tristate logic* (as widely used in implementing bidirectional busses) is much more difficult than reasoning about the properties of *pure* logic circuitry for three reasons:

– The property of *directionality* is not present. Causality in such implementations is *adirectional* and there is no notion of *input* and *output*.
– To understand the operation of the circuit, both voltages *and currents* need to be considered.
– There is no *a priori* reason why any of the signals (including the 'output' signal) should be at well-defined digital levels.

Informally, the behaviour of implementations involving tristate gates or *wired-or* gates is determined by "summing the drives" and then using a "resolution function" to convert the summed drive to a logic level. For example, the combination of drives of a *weak pullup* in parallel with a *strong pulldown* and three *high impedances* would resolve to a *low* logic level.

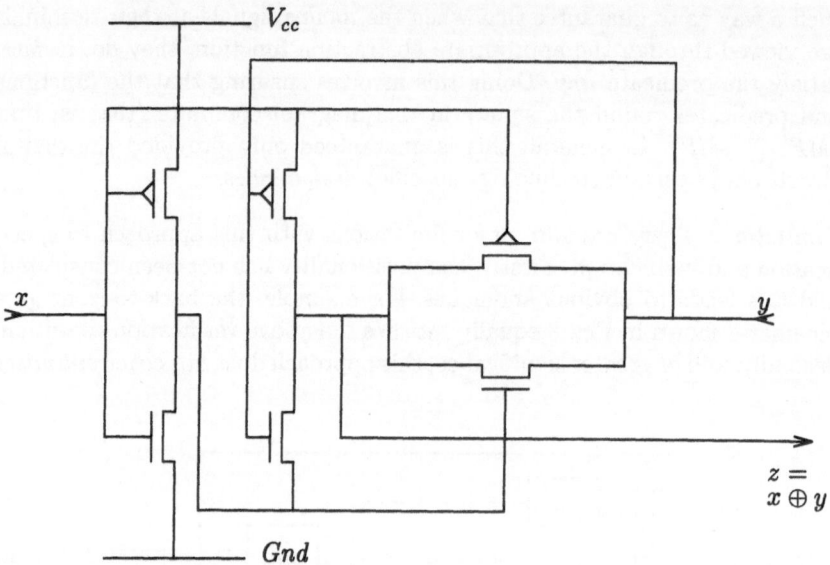

Fig. 4. An optimised implementation of Exclusive-Or, making use of pass-transistor logic.

Conclusion The design process for analog-level implementations of this general kind is more accurately described by Fig. 5 (or by an amalgam of both diagrams if the implementation involves both analog and digital components):

- As before, the starting point is a requirements specification, *req*, described at the *digital* level of abstraction.
- Synthesis yields an *analog* circuit (maybe with tristate gates, pullup resistors and pass transistors present).
- Behavioural extraction yields a derived specification, *IMP*, involving both voltages *and currents*, and described at the *analog* level of abstraction.
- *Behavioural abstraction* maps the digital-level requirements specification, *req*, to a corresponding specification, *REQ*, described at the analog level.
- The verification condition is now $IMP \sqsupseteq REQ$.

In this paper, we show how the well-established techniques of specification and verification at the digital level can be extended so as to encompass the analog level as well, and how behaviours at the digital and analog levels can be related. The approach inherits and builds upon concepts introduced in [1, 2, 4, 6, 8, 9, 10] but goes significantly further in generality and rigour.

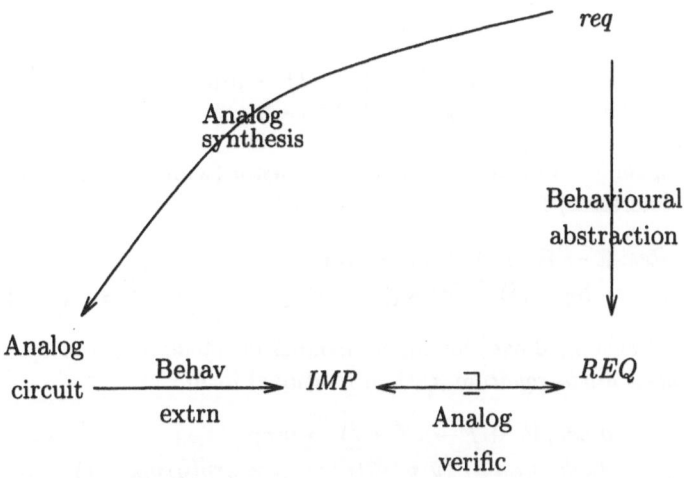

Fig. 5. Design process, for analog implementations

2 Analog specifications

We take a *behavioural specification* for an analog component as being a predicate on the signals, both voltage and current, at its terminals. Such a specification can be either *static* or *dynamic* according as to whether the signals are steady-state levels or time-varying waveforms. In general, a relational specification does not uniquely describe a device's observable behaviour; rather, it defines a subset of possible behaviours.

Notation We treat analog physical quantities as reals ($\mathbb{R}$). For clarity, we introduce type synonyms of V (for voltages) and I (for currents), both equivalent to $\mathbb{R}$.

2.1 Examples (static specifications)

We illustrate these concepts with a series of examples.

The specification, *voltage*, for an *ideal voltage source* is defined as

$$voltage\colon V \to (V \times I) \to prop$$
$$voltage\ v_1\ (v,i) \triangleq (v = v_1)$$

The specification of the dual concept, an *ideal current source*, is

$$current\colon I \to (V \times I) \to prop$$
$$current\ i_i\ (v,i) \triangleq (i = i_1)$$

The specification, *short*, for a *short circuit* is $short \triangleq voltage\ 0$, and the specification for the dual concept, an *open circuit*, is $open \triangleq current\ 0$.

The specification, *res*, for an *ideal resistor*, is

$$res: \mathbb{R} \to (V \times I) \to prop$$
$$res\ r\ (v,i) \triangleq (v = i \times r)$$

The specification, *Res*, for an *actual resistor* (which is specified to within a given tolerance) is

$$Res: \mathbb{R} \to \mathbb{R} \to (V \times I) \to prop$$
$$res\ r_1\ tol\ (v,i) \triangleq \exists r: \mathbb{R}.(|r - r_1| \leq tol \times r_1) \wedge (res\ r\ (v,i))$$

The specification, *diode*, for an *ideal junction diode*, is given by the well-known *ideal diode equation*, cast in relational form

$$diode: V \to I \to (V \times I) \to prop$$
$$diode\ v_{th}\ i_{sat}\ (v,i) \triangleq (i = i_{sat} \times exp(v/v_{th} - 1))$$

A looser version of the same specification for describing the behaviour of an *actual junction diode* is

$$Diode\ V^2 \to I^2 \to (V \times I) \to prop$$
$$Diode\ (v_{th1}, v_{th2})\ (i_{sat1}, i_{sat2})\ (v,i) \triangleq$$
$$\exists v_{th}, i_{sat}.$$
$$(v_{th1} \leq v_{th} \leq v_{th2}) \wedge (i_{sat1} \leq i_{sat} \leq i_{sat2}) \wedge$$
$$diode\ v_{th}\ i_{sat}\ (v,i)$$

Here, the arguments v_{th1}, v_{th2} and i_{sat1}, i_{sat2} define the lower and upper bounds for the parameters v_{th} and i_{sat} of an ideal diode.

2.2 Examples (dynamic specifications)

The same approach extends naturally to cover the specification of dynamic behaviours. To express time, we introduce a type synonym, T, (for time), equivalent to $\mathbb{R}$, and we treat *waveforms* (that is, time-varying signals) as functions defined on T.

Any static specification may be lifted to a dynamic one simply by asserting that the static specification holds at all instants of time. For instance, the ideal diode specification defined above can be lifted to a dynamic specification, *diode'*, defined by

$$diode': V \to I \to (T \to V) \times (T \to I) \to prop$$
$$diode'\ v_{th}\ i_{sat}\ (u,j) \triangleq \forall t: T.\ diode\ v_{th}\ i_{sat}\ (u\ t)\ (j\ t)$$

Many devices have behavioural specifications that are inherently dynamic, typically taking the form of a differential equation. To describe such equations, we use the *differentiation* function, $D: (\mathbb{R} \to \mathbb{R}) \to (\mathbb{R} \to \mathbb{R})$ that takes a differentiable function to its differential. For instance, the value of $D\ sin$ is cos.

An example of a device with an inherently dynamic specificaton is an *ideal capacitor*. Its specification, *cap*, is parameterised by its capacitance:

$$cap: \mathbb{R} \to (T \to V) \times (T \to I) \to prop$$
$$cap \ c \ (u, j) \triangleq \forall t: T. \ j \ t = c \times (D \ u) \ t$$

(that is, the instantaneous current is equal to the capacitance times the rate of change of voltage).

2.3 Operations on specifications

Many useful operations can be defined on specifications. Some apply to any kind of specification, others are specific to specifications involving voltages and currents.

Lattice operations We overload the usual propositional connectives ($\wedge$, $\vee$, $\Rightarrow$, etc.) and the two propositional truth values (T and F) so that they also apply to predicates (ie, specifications) of any arity. Thus, we have, for any type S and for any predicates p and q defined on S, the following operations:

$$(p \wedge q) \ x \triangleq p \ x \wedge q \ x$$
$$(p \vee q) \ x \triangleq p \ x \vee q \ x$$
$$(p \Rightarrow q) \ x \triangleq p \ x \Rightarrow q \ x$$
$$\mathsf{T} \ x \triangleq \mathsf{T}$$
$$\mathsf{F} \ x \triangleq \mathsf{F}$$

We also define a partial ordering on predicates by

$$(\sqsupseteq): (S \to prop) \times (S \to prop) \to prop$$
$$p \sqsupseteq q \triangleq \forall x: S. \ p \ x \Rightarrow q \ x$$

(Read $p \sqsupseteq q$ as 'p is at least as strong a specification as q.)

Composition of components Given a set of components, the voltages and currents at their terminals will, by definition, obey the individual specifications of each one separately and so will obey the conjunction of them all taken together. In addition, the overall circuit will impose the usual conservation constraints (currents summing to zero, etc).

The act of *hiding* a node for an analog circuit involves two conceptually distinct operations:

- *Disconnecting* it, that is, asserting that there will be a zero net current, and
- *Disregarding* it, that is, ignoring the voltage present at the node.

The first is carried out by substitution, the second by existential quantification. For example, if *spec* is the specification of an $n + 1$ terminal component, then the specification, *spec'*, of the component with the last terminal hidden is

$$spec' \; (v_1, i_1, \ldots, v_{n-1}, i_{n-1}) \triangleq$$
$$\textbf{let } i_n = 0 \textbf{ in } \exists v_n. \; spec \; (v_1, i_1, \ldots, v_n, i_n)$$

Serial and parallel composition Using the above rules, we can define a combinator, ++ , that takes the specifications, p and q, of a pair of 2-terminal components and yields the specification, p ++ q, of their *serial composition*:

$$(\text{++}) : (V \times I \to prop)^2 \to (V \times I \to prop)$$
$$(p \text{ ++ } q) \; (v, i) \triangleq \exists v_1, v_2. \; p \; (v_1, i) \wedge q \; (v_2, i) \wedge v_1 + v_2 = v$$

Likewise, we can define the dual notion, the combinator || for *parallel composition*:

$$(\|) : (V \times I \to prop)^2 \to (V \times I \to prop)$$
$$(p \| q) \; (v, i) \triangleq \exists i_1, i_2. \; p \; (v, i_1) \wedge q \; (v, i_2) \wedge i_1 + i_2 = i$$

Identities The device specifications and combinators described above satisfy a number of useful identities. For example:

- The combinator || is commutative and associative, and has *open* as its unit:
  $$p \| q = q \| p, \qquad p \| (q \| r) = (p \| q) \| r, \qquad p \| open = p.$$
- The dual combinator, ++ , is likewise commutative and associative, and has *closed* as its unit.
- Voltage and current souces, when appropriately composed, add linearly:
  voltage v_1 ++ *voltage* v_2 = *voltage* $(v_1 + v_2)$,
  current i_1 || *current* i_2 = *current* $(i_1 + i_2)$,

2.4 Correctness

The condition that an implementation with a derived specification *imp* is a *correct* implementation of a given requirements specification, *req*, is that any tuple, x, of signals that satisfy the derived specification should also satisfy the requirements specification. That is, the implementation is correct if the following *verification condition* holds:

$$\forall x. \; imp \; x \Rightarrow req \; x$$

that is, if $imp \sqsupseteq req$.

As a simple example, the serial composition of an ideal 20Ω resistor and a 27Ω one is a correct implementation of a requirements specification for a $50\Omega \pm 10\%$ actual resistor, since

$$\forall v, i. \; (res \; 20 \text{ ++ } res \; 27) \; (v, i) \Rightarrow Res \; 0.1 \; 50$$

3 Rectilinear specifications

In general, a behavioural specification of an analog component is an entirely arbitrary predicate on the voltages and currents at its ports. This means both that it can be difficult to validate (ie, confirm that it captures the intended notion) and that there will not be any decision procedures available to aid reasoning about it.

We have, however, observed that, for analog implementations of *digital* devices, the task of establishing correctness (and other useful properties) *only relies upon having a relatively coarsely quantified approximation to these analog behaviours*. We exploit this fact by restricting the class of specifications we consider to a syntactically defined subset of all possible specifications. As we shall demonstrate, by a judicious choice of this subset, we can simplify the task of reasoning about correctness (and related properties) to a point where it becomes computationally decidable, *without any significant loss in the range of implementations that can be proven correct*.

In this section we discuss *rectilinear specifications*, a restricted form of specification that meets this requirement. We term a specification *rectilinear* if:

- Its atomic formulae are restricted to (in)equalities involving at most one parameter; and
- No bound variable occurs in more than one atomic formula in which a parameter is present[1].

The graph of a rectilinear specification consists of regions bounded by hyperplanes which are parallel to the coordinate axes.

The class of rectilinear specifications is closed under the propositional connectives and quantification, and so the derived specification of a circuit whose components are specified by rectilinear specifications will itself be rectilinear.

3.1 Examples

Bipolar junction diode Consider a rectilinear specification for a bipolar junction diode (a component widely used in implementations of digital devices). From the point of view of the digital designer, its behaviour can be specified as the conjunction of four subspecifications. These cover each of the following characteristic modes of operation:

1. When it is reverse biassed (or *hard off*);
2. When it is forward biassed, but not yet conducting significantly;

---

[1] This restriction prevents bound variables being used to implicitly allow more than one parameter to figure in an atomic formula as, for instance, in a (non-rectilinear) specification like: $spec\ (v, i) \triangleq \exists v'.\ (v' = v) \wedge (v' = i \times r)$.

3. When it is forward biassed and conducting an indeterminate amount; and

4. When it is forward biassed and conducting strongly (or *hard on*).

This leads (see Fig. 6) to a rectilinear specification of the form:

$diode_{rl}\ v_1\ v_2\ i_1\ i_2\ i_3\ (v,i) \triangleq$

$$((v < 0) \Rightarrow (i_1 \leq i \leq 0))\ \wedge$$
$$((0 \leq v \leq v_1) \Rightarrow (0 \leq i \leq i_2))\ \wedge$$
$$((v_1 \leq v \leq v_2) \Rightarrow (0 \leq i))\ \wedge$$
$$((v_2 \leq v) \Rightarrow (i_3 \leq i))$$

Notice that the overall specification consists of a conjunction of four sub-

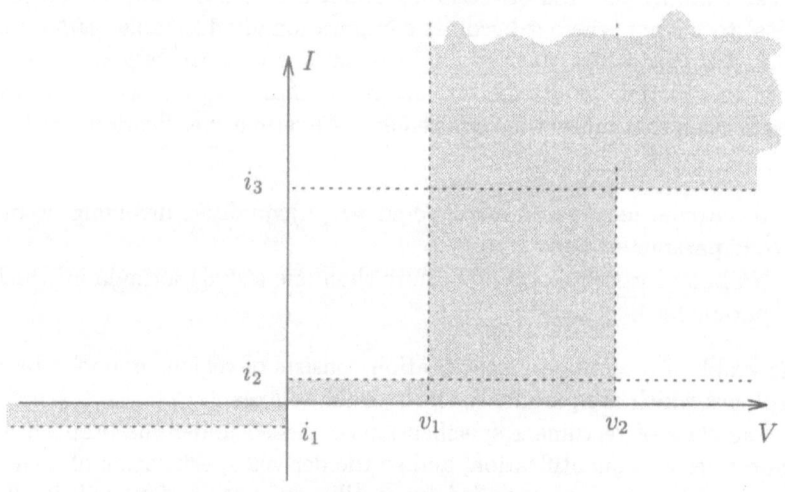

Fig. 6. Graph of a rectilinear specification of a junction diode.

specifications, and that each subspecification consists of an implication whose hypothesis delimits a region of the parameter space within which the consequent constrains the allowable range of behaviours.

This specification can be specialised to give the specification obeyed by a typical silicon signal junction diode:

$$typical\_diode \triangleq diode\quad 0.3\quad 0.6\quad -10^{-6}\quad 10^{-6}\quad 0.01$$

Bipolar junction transistor Digital circuits make use of both *bipolar junction transistors* (BJTs) and *field effect transistors* (FETs). In general, the former are more difficult to reason about since their control electrode (generally the base) imposes a significant current loading on the circuit (by contrast, the gate electrode of a FET can be considered to be an open circuit). The examples given in this chapter all refer to BJTs.

The description of the behaviour of a BJT [7] is generally partitioned into four modes (*forward active, saturation, cutoff* and *reverse active*) according to the relative polarities of its three electrodes. In TTL technologies (described later), all four modes of behaviour can occur. From the perspective of an analog designer, its detailed behaviour in each of these modes of behaviour is complex. However, just as with the diode, a broad-brush, conservative approximation to each mode of behaviour turns out to provide sufficient information to characterise its behaviour from a digital perspective. For example, when a typical BJT is operating in the *cutoff* mode (as defined by both its junctions being reverse biassed), the current through its collector electrode can simply be characterised as being between zero and 1nA; no further precision is necessary.

The specification for each of the four modes of operation of a BJT takes the form of an implication, with the hypothesis defining a region in the operating space and the conclusion specifying its behaviour in that region. The overall specification is then simply the conjunction of these partial specifications.

4 Specification at the digital level

Our aim in this section is to formulate specifications, at the digital level of abstraction, for the steady-state behaviour of ordinary gates. This apparently trivial task needs to be handled with care in order to avoid inconsistency arising when these specifications are related to the corresponding ones at the analog level of abstraction. We illustrate the approach by considering the specification for a 2-input And gate.

Our starting point is the set $\mathbb{B} = \{t, f\}$ of *ideal* digital signal levels to which we add a third element, n, to allow *non-digital* signal levels to be represented, giving the set $\mathbb{T} \triangleq \{t, n, f\}$ of *non-ideal* signal levels.

Since the output of an And gate with signals of t and n at its inputs could be any of t, n or f, a *relational* description is required; a functional one would involve arbitrary overspecification. The specification, a predicate on the tuple of signals at the inputs and output of the gate, is of type

$$andReq \colon \mathbb{T}^2 \times \mathbb{T} \to prop$$

Evidently, it needs to be compatible with the Boolean algebra function $and \colon \mathbb{B}^2 \to \mathbb{B}$. The weakest relation on $\mathbb{T}^2 \times \mathbb{T}$ with this property is

$$andReq_1\left((x, y), z\right) \triangleq \mathbf{if}\ (x \neq n) \wedge (y \neq n)\ \mathbf{then}\ z = and\ (x, y)$$

In practice, however, designers invariably assume a stronger specification than this; they also assume the characteristic non-strict property that f acts as a zero element:

$$andReq_2 \ ((x, y), z) \triangleq (x = \mathsf{f}) \vee (y = \mathsf{f}) \Rightarrow (z = \mathsf{f})$$

Taking the conjunction of these two predicates yields the overall specification for an And gate:

$$andReq \triangleq andReq_1 \wedge andReq_2$$

This can equivalently be expressed as

$$
\begin{aligned}
andReq \ ((x, y), z) \triangleq \\
((x = \mathsf{t}) \wedge (y = \mathsf{t}) \Rightarrow (z = \mathsf{t})) \quad &\wedge \\
((x = \mathsf{f}) \vee (y = \mathsf{f}) \Rightarrow (z = \mathsf{f})) &
\end{aligned}
$$

Relational specifications for other types of gate can be derived in a similar way. For example, the specification for a Nand gate is

$$
\begin{aligned}
&nandReq \colon \mathbb{T}^2 \times \mathbb{T} \to prop \\
&nandReq \ ((x, y), z) \triangleq \\
&\quad ((x = \mathsf{t}) \wedge (y = \mathsf{t}) \Rightarrow (z = \mathsf{f})) \quad \wedge \\
&\quad ((x = \mathsf{f}) \vee (y = \mathsf{f}) \Rightarrow (z = \mathsf{t}))
\end{aligned}
$$

5 Analog level behaviours

We now describe how the specifications of digital devices can be formulated at the analog level (where both voltages *and* currents are involved), how the specifications of implementations can be derived, and how correctness conditions are expressed. We illustrate the discussion with examples based on TTL (transistor-transistor logic), a technology based on bipolar junction transistors (and therefore a challenging one to handle formally).

5.1 Specification at the analog level

We begin by describing how device specifications expressed at the digital level of abstraction (such as the Nand gate specification just defined) can be mapped down to the analog level of abstraction. There are two aspects that have to be considered: the *abstraction function* that defines the relation between signals at each of these levels and the *loading predicates* that define the loading a gate is allowed to impose on its environment and the amount of drive it can supply to its environment.

Voltage abstraction function The voltage abstraction function relates analog voltage levels to digital signal levels. For a standard TTL technology (and assuming the *true-as-high* convention) voltages below 0.4V represent false and ones above 2.4 represent true. Thus, the abstraction function for TTL is:

$$a: V \to \mathbb{T}$$
$$a\ v \overset{\wedge}{=} \quad \textbf{if } v < 0.4 \textbf{ then f else}$$
$$\textbf{if } v > 2.4 \textbf{ then t else}$$
$$\textsf{n}$$

Voltage-only device specifications Using the abstraction function, a device specification defined at the digital level can be mapped down to a voltage specification at the analog level (notice the contravariance: whilst the abstraction function maps analog signals up to digital ones, it maps digital specifications *down to* analog ones).

As an example, the digital-level Nand gate specification, *nandReq*, defined earlier, maps to the analog-level specification, *NandReq*, defined by

$$NandReq: V^2 \to V \to prop$$
$$NandReq\ (v_1, v_2)\ v \overset{\wedge}{=} nandReq\ ((a\ v_1), (a\ v_2))\ (a\ v)$$

This specification, however, does not adequately characterise the behaviour we require of a gate since it makes no reference to current flows. For instance, it implies that forcing a Nand gate's *output* terminal low would unconditionally *prevent* either of its inputs terminals from going low. Such a device would be rather difficult to realise. To obviate such difficulties, it is necessary to take account of currents as well as voltages.

Loading of transistor-transistor logic (TTL) We refer to the relation between the voltage and current at a device's terminals as the *load* it imposes (or, equivalently, as the *drive* it can supply). There are two aspects of a digital device's behaviour that we need to be able to characterise:

– The load an input terminal is allowed to impose on the gate's environment. We use a predicate

$$unitLoad: (V \times I) \to prop$$

to characterise this. A definition of this predicate for a standard TTL input terminal is shown in Fig. 7(a).
– The drive an output terminal is required to be able to supply to the gate's environment whilst still maintaining the intended digital signal level (that is, whilst still satisfying the gate's voltage-only specification). We use a predicate

$$stdLoading: (V \times I) \to prop$$

to characterise this. A definition of this predicate for a standard TTL output terminal is shown in Fig. 7(b).

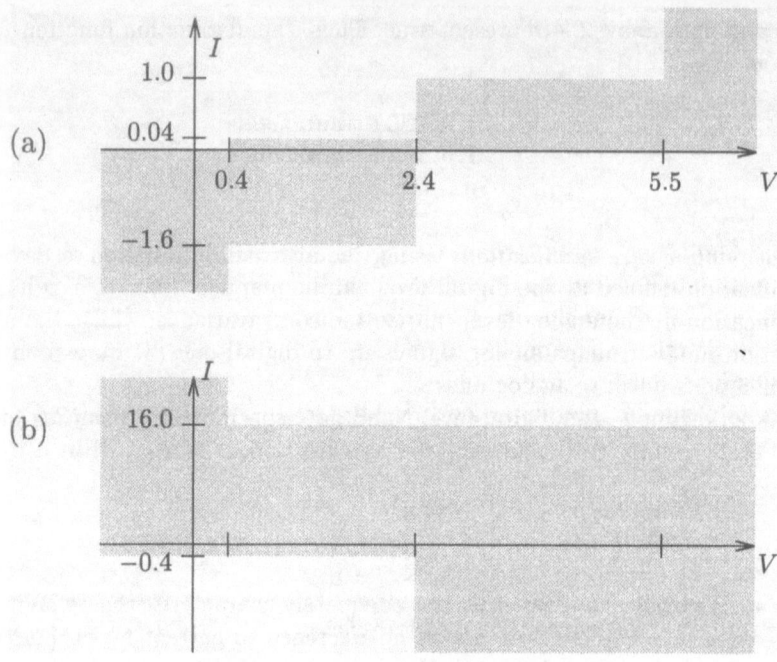

Fig. 7. Definitions for (a) the load a TTL input terminal is allowed to impose, and (b), the drive a TTL output terminal is required to be able to supply. (Note that currents here are shown in mA.)

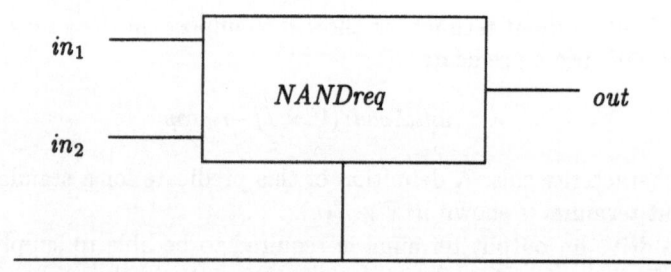

Fig. 8. Interface for analog-level specification of a Nand gate

Using these two loading predicates, we can now define behavioural specifications at the analog level. For example, the specification for a Nand gate (with terminals as shown in Fig. 8) takes the form:

$$NANDreq: (V \times I)^2 \to (V \times I) \to prop$$
$$NANDreq\ ((v_{in_1}, i_{in_1}), (v_{in_2}, i_{in_2}))\ (v_{out}, i_{out}) \stackrel{\triangle}{=}$$
$$\quad unitLoad\ (v_{in_1}, i_{in_1})\ \wedge\quad unitLoad\ (v_{in_2}, i_{in_2})\ \wedge$$
$$\quad (stdLoading\ (v_{out}, i_{out}) \Rightarrow NandReq\ (v_{in_1}, v_{in_2})\ v_{out})$$

This specification states that the load a Nand gate imposes on each of its input terminals must satisfy the *unitLoad* specification and that, provided the load the environment imposes on the output terminal satisfies the *stdLoading* specification, the voltages on the gate's input and output terminals will satisfy the voltage-only specification for a Nand gate.

5.2 Implementation at the analog level

A typical TTL implementation for a Nand gate is shown in Fig. 9. Assuming

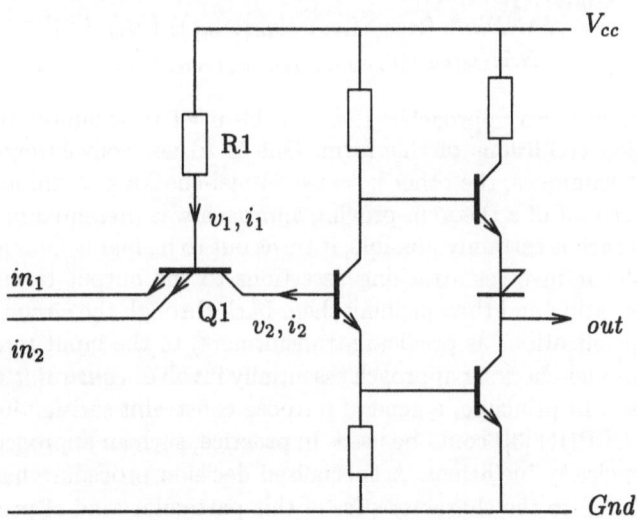

Fig. 9. A typical implementation, in TTL technology, of a Nand gate.

that $Q1$ is the specification for transistor Q1, $R1$ the specification for resistor R1, and so on, the derived specification for this circuit[2] takes the

---

[2] A complete derived specification for a similar circuit is given in the Appendix.

form:

$$NANDimp: (V \times I)^2 \to (V \times I) \to prop$$
$$NANDimp \ ((v_{in_1}, i_{in_1}), (v_{in_2}, i_{in_2})) \ (v_{out}, i_{out}) \triangleq$$
$$\exists v_1, v_2, \dots, v_n : V.$$
$$\exists i_1, i_2, \dots, i_m : I.$$
$$Q1 \ (v_{in_1}, i_{in_1}, v_{in_2}, i_{in_2}, v_1, i_1, v_2, i_2) \land$$
$$R1 \ (V_{cc} - v_1, i1) \land$$
$$\dots$$

(That is, the voltages and currents at the terminals of each device obey the behavioural specification for the device and, in addition, the currents sum to zero at nodes and voltage differences sum to zero round closed paths.)

5.3   Verification at the analog level

The verification condition asserting that the behaviour of this circuit satisfies the behavioural specification for a Nand gate is simply $NANDimp \sqsupseteq NANDreq$, or, in first-order form:

$$\forall v_{in_1}, v_{in_2}, v_{out} : V.$$
$$\forall i_{in_1}, i_{in_2}, i_{out} : I.$$
$$NANDimp \ ((v_{in_1}, i_{in_1}), (v_{in_2}, i_{in_2})) \ (v_{out}, i_{out}) \quad \Rightarrow$$
$$NANDreq \ ((v_{in_1}, i_{in_1}), (v_{in_2}, i_{in_2})) \ (v_{out}, i_{out})$$

There are two approaches that can be used to establish the truth of verification conditions of this form. One is to use conventional theorem-proving techniques, the other is to use model-checking techniques.

An account of a theorem-proving approach was presented in [5]. Whilst this approach is certainly possible, it turns out to be highly labour-intensive. Essentially it involves attaching assertions to the output terminals of an implementation and then pushing them back through the circuit (using the device specifications as predicate transformers) to the input terminals.

The model-checking approach essentially involves *constraint satisfaction* techniques. In principle, a general purpose constraint satisfaction program (such as CLP(R) [3]) could be used. In practice, such an approach turns out to be hopelessly inefficient. A specialised decision procedure has therefore been tailored to the characteristics of this particular kind of problem.

6   Decision procedure

The verification condition we wish to establish is of the form

$$\forall e. \ imp[e] \Rightarrow req[e]$$

where:

- e is the tuple of *external* variables (for instance, in the verification condition for the Nand gate (above), the tuple comprises the variables $v_{in_1}, \ldots, i_{out}$);
- $imp[e]$ is the derived specification of the implementation;
- $req[e]$ is the requirements specification.

In general, a derived specification, will be of the form $\exists i.\ implem[e, i]$ where i is a tuple of *internal* variables in the implementation (for instance, the variables $v_1, \ldots, v_n$ and $i_1, \ldots, i_m$ in the *NANDimp* specification). Thus, the verification condition can be cast in the form

$$\forall e.\ (\exists i.\ implem[e, i]) \Rightarrow req[e]$$

By moving the existential quantifier to the outer level (where it becomes a universal), and then by replacing the universal quantifier by a negated existential formula, the verification condition can be cast in the form

$$\neg \exists e, i.\ implem[e, i] \wedge \neg req[e]$$

By using simple propositional reasoning, the body of this formula can then be expressed in disjunctive normal form:

$$\neg \exists e, i.\ \phi_1[e, i]) \vee \ldots \vee \phi_n[e, i]$$

where each subformula ϕ_j is a conjunction of literals, and each literal is a simple linear (in)equality in the external and internal variables.

Finally, by distributing the existential quantifier over the disjunction, the verification condition is converted to the form

$$\neg((\exists e, i.\ \phi_1[e, i]) \vee \ldots \vee (\exists e, i.\ \phi_n[e, i]))$$

The verification condition can now be established simply by showing that each of the n formulae, $\phi_1[e, i], \ldots, \phi_n[e, i]$, has no feasible solution.

6.1 Practical implementation

An algorithm to implement the above decision procedure has been written in Haskell (a widely used functional programming language). The algorithm takes as its input a set of definitions of the behaviours of the primitive components (resistors, diodes, transistors) and a statement of the verification condition (an example is shown in the Appendix), and goes through the following steps:

1. The input, which syntactically takes the form of a single formula (structured by liberal use of let bindings), is parsed. This yields an abstract representation of the verification condition.
2. Beta reduction is used to eliminate all let bindings, that is, to replace locally defined names with their definitions and symbolically evaluate all applications.

3. Any existential quantifiers present in the hypothesis of the formula are moved outwards to the top level (where they become universal quantifiers). In turn, all universals are rewritten as negated existentials.

4. The body of the formula is converted to disjunctive normal form and the existential quantifiers are distributed over the disjunction.

5. Each separate disjunct (which itself corresponds to a conjunction of literals, each one of which is a linear inequality) is converted to a standard linear-programmming matrix form.

6. Each such set of matrices is submitted for analysis to a standard Fortran linear-programming library routine (routine E04MBF in the NAG library). This routine quickly determines whether the set of inequalities has a feasible solution.

If none of the sets of inequalities is found to have a feasible solution, then the original verification condition is true. Conversely, if a feasible solution is found, then this solution provides a counterexample demonstrating the falsity of the verification condition.

In addition to the steps outlined above, the algorithm also incorporates a number of optimisations. For instance, in step (5), a quick test for the presence of opposing literals (that is, pairs of the form $\ldots \wedge (x > a) \wedge \ldots \wedge (x < a) \wedge \ldots$) allows many subformulae to be eliminated without the need for submission to the linear-programming routine.

7 Conclusions

The overall aim of the work described here has been to extend existing predicate-logic based methods used for specifying and verifying systems defined at the "ideal digital" level of abstraction down to the analog level. This allows digital systems that (perhaps in order to gain speed or economise on power consumption) have been implemented in part at the analog level to be specified and reasoned about with the same degree of certainty and transparency as those implemented wholly at the digital level.

The method described is straightforward; it simply involves using predicates to characterise the behaviour of analog components in terms of the voltages and currents at their terminals. A central tenet of the approach is that these characterisations should be *conservative* approximations to the actual behaviours. Based on detailed studies, in particular of implementations of TTL technology, it has been found that these approximations can be remarkably weak and yet still capture enough of the essential behavioural properties of an analog device to allow successful verification at the digital level of abstraction. Perhaps this should come as no surprise; after all, digital designers habitually reason at the analog level simply in terms of devices being 'on' or 'off' and of voltage levels being 'high' or 'low', and so on.

An algorithm for checking the verification conditions that arise with this approach has been programmed and has been used to verify, automatically, simple TTL circuits. The computational time the algorithm takes has, however, been found to increase sharply with circuit complexity. At present it is not clear whether the computational task is an inherently hard one or whether a different algorithm would be less sensitive to circuit size. Irrespective of the algorithm used, one approach to limit the computational time is to partition an implementation into a set of smaller ones by introducing intermediate specifications (in effect, lemmas). This seems to be the approach the human designer uses when confronted with a complex implementation.

8 Acknowledgments

This work was partially sponsored by ESPRIT (under Grant 8533) and by the UK EPSRC (under grant GR/J/78105).

References

[1] David A. Basin. Verification of combinational logic in Nuprl. In Miriam Leeser and Geoffrey Brown, editors, *Hardware Specification, Verification and Synthesis: Mathematical Aspects*, volume 408 of *LNCS*, pages 333–357. Springer Verlag, 1990.

[2] Geoffrey M. Brown and Miriam E. Leeser. From programs to transistors: Verifying hardware synthesis tools. In Miriam Leeser and Geoffrey Brown, editors, *Hardware Specification, Verification and Synthesis: Mathematical Aspects*, volume 408 of *LNCS*, pages 129–15. Springer Verlag, 1990.

[3] Eugene C. Freuder and Alan K. Mackworth, editors. *Constraint-based reasoning*. MIT/Elsevier, 1994.

[4] Mike Gordon, Paul Loewenstein, and Moshe Shahaf. Formal verification of a cell library. In L. J. M. Claesen, editor, *VLSI Design Methods II*, pages 409–417. Elsevier Science Publishers B.V., 1990.

[5] Keith Hanna. Reasoning about Real Digital Circuits. In *Proc Higher Order Logic Theorem Proving and its Applications*. Springer-Verlag, 1994.

[6] C. A. R. Hoare. A theory for the derivation of combinational C-mos circuit designs. *Theoretical Computer Science*, 90:235–251, 1991.

[7] D. A. Hodges and H. G. Jackson. *Analysis and design of digital integrated circuits*. McGraw-Hill, 1983.

[8] T. Melham. *Higher Order Logic and Hardware Verification*. Cambridge University Press, 1993.

[9] Robert E. Shostak. Formal verification of circuit designs. In T. Uehara and M. Barbacci, editors, *Computer Hardware Description Languages and their Applications*, pages 13–30. North-Holland, 1983.

[10] Daniel Weise. Constraints, abstraction and verification. In Miriam Leeser and Geoffrey Brown, editors, *Hardware Specification, Verification and Synthesis: Mathematical Aspects*, volume 408 of *LNCS*, pages 25–39. Springer Verlag, 1989.

9 Appendix

Here is a simple example of an input to the verification condition checking algorithm. Overall, it consists of a single formula, the verification condition to be verified, viz $\forall u, v, i, j.\ imp\ u\ i\ v\ j\ \Rightarrow req\ u\ i\ v\ j$. This is prefixed with a number of let bindings that define the predicates *imp* (the derived specification of the proposed implementation, a two-stage transistor buffer) and *req* (a simple requirement specification). In turn, these bindings are prefixed by bindings that define predicates such as *res* (for resistors), *diode* and *trans* (for NPN bipolar junction transistors). Throughout, currents and voltages are expressed in amps and volts.

Note: in the interests of brevity, some of the bindings have been edited out, but all follow a similar pattern.

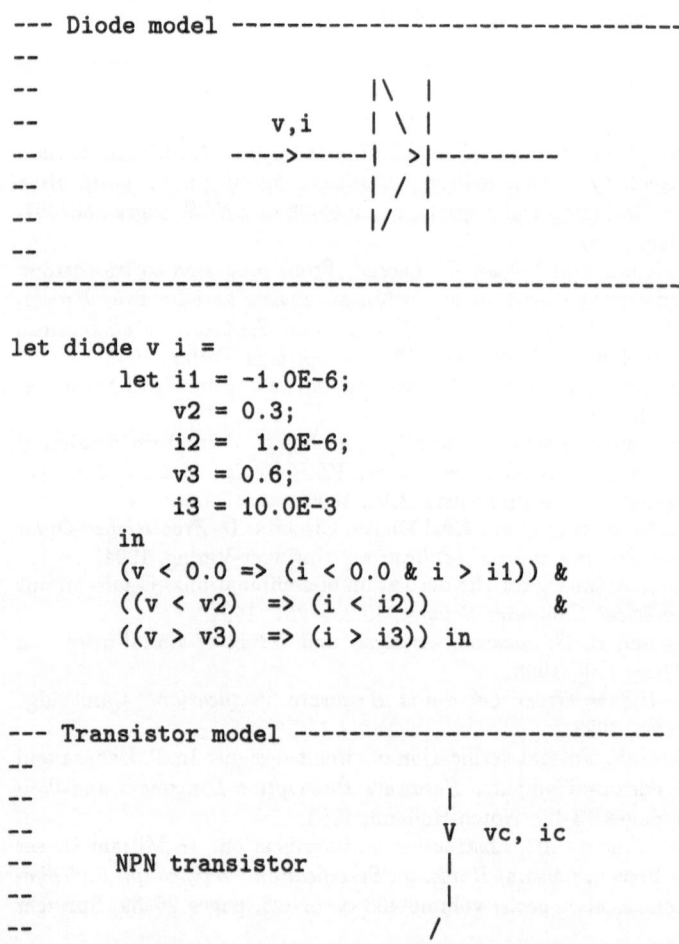

```
--- Diode model ----------------------------------
--
--                         |\ |
--                   v,i   | \ |
--                  ---->-----|  >|---------
--                         | / |
--                         |/  |
--
--------------------------------------------------
```

```
let diode v i =
        let i1 = -1.0E-6;
            v2 = 0.3;
            i2 =  1.0E-6;
            v3 = 0.6;
            i3 = 10.0E-3
        in
        (v < 0.0 => (i < 0.0 & i > i1)) &
        ((v < v2)  => (i < i2))           &
        ((v > v3)  => (i > i3)) in
```

```
--- Transistor model -----------------------------
--
--                         |
--                         V  vc, ic
--        NPN transistor   |
--                         |
--                        /
--                       |/
```

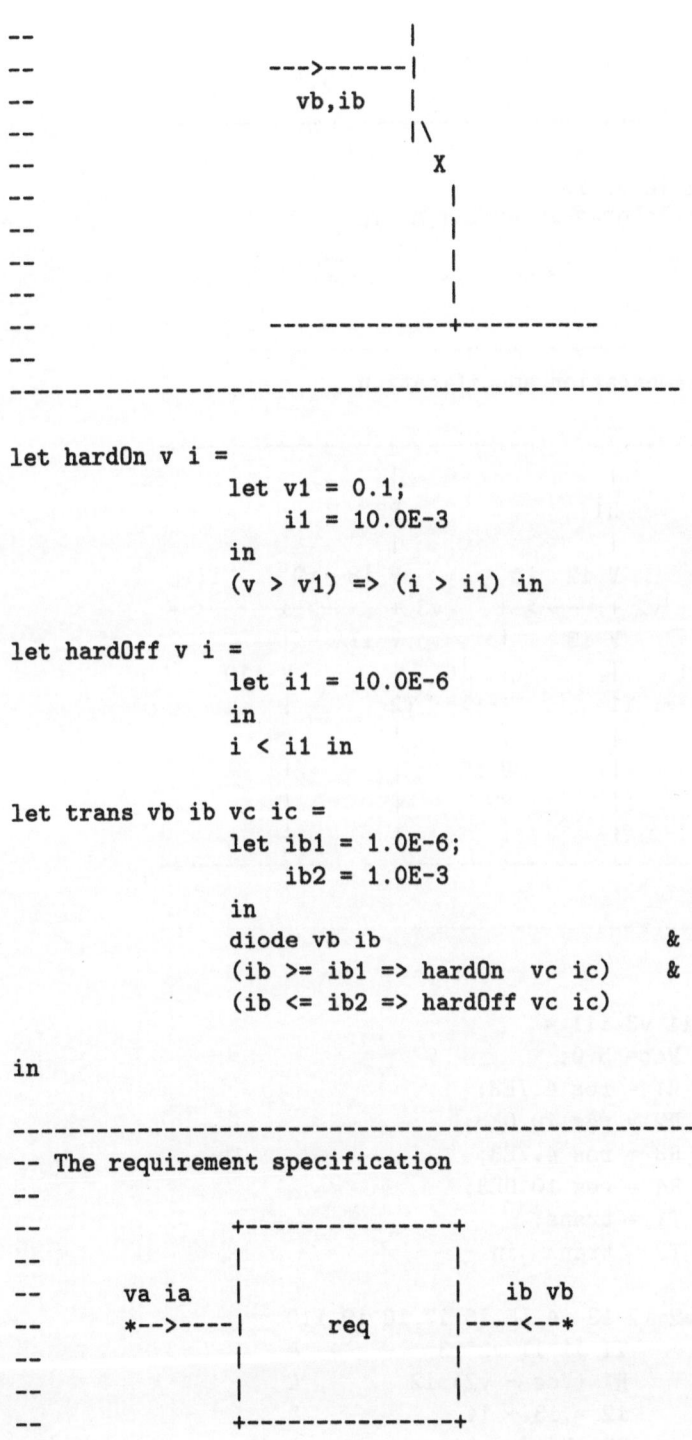

```
--                           |
--               --->------|
--               vb,ib  |
--                       |\
--                          X
--                       |
--                       |
--                       |
--                       |
--               --------------+----------
--
--
--------------------------------------------------
```

```
let hardOn v i =
              let v1 = 0.1;
                  i1 = 10.0E-3
              in
              (v > v1) => (i > i1) in

let hardOff v i =
              let i1 = 10.0E-6
              in
              i < i1 in

let trans vb ib vc ic =
              let ib1 = 1.0E-6;
                  ib2 = 1.0E-3
              in
              diode vb ib                        &
              (ib >= ib1 => hardOn  vc ic)    &
              (ib <= ib2 => hardOff vc ic)

in
```

```
--------------------------------------------------
-- The requirement specification
--
--               +----------------+
--               |                |
--     va ia  |                | ib vb
--     *-->----|     req        |----<--*
--               |                |
--               |                |
--               +----------------+
--                        |
```

```
--                          |
--          +-------+-------+-------+-------+-------+-
--
-- ---------------------------------------------------
```

```
let req  va ia vb ib =
         ia > 1.0E-3 => vb < 1.0  in
```

```
-- ---------------------------------------------------
-- The implementation specification
--
--          +-------+-------+-------+-------+-------+-
--              |               |               Vcc
--             R1              R3
--              |               |
--              V i2  i4        V i8  i9      i11
--          v2 +----->-+    v3 +----->-+------<-*
--              V i3   |        V i7   |
--        i1    |      |  i6    |      V i10
--        *->--- T1    +-->-- T2       |
--        v1    |      |       |      R4
--              |      V i5    |       |
--              |      R2      |       |
--              |      |       |       |
--          +-------+-------+-------+-------+-------+-
--
-- ---------------------------------------------------
```

```
let imp v1 i1 v3 i11 =
        let Vcc= 5.0;
            R1 = res 4.7E3;
            R2 = res 10.0E3;
            R3 = res 4.7E3;
            R4 = res 10.0E3;
            T1 = trans;
            T2 = trans  in

        ?v2 i2 i3 i4 i5 i6 i7 i8 i9 i10.
            T1 v1 i1 v2 i3          &
            R1 (Vcc - v2) i2        &
            i2 = i3 + i4            &
            R2 v2 i5                &
```

```
T2 v2 i6 v3 i7          &
R3 (Vcc - v3) i8        &
i8 = i7 + i9            &
R4 v3 i9                &
i9 + i11 = i10          in
```

```
--------------------------------------------------
-- The Correctness Criterion
--------------------------------------------------
```

```
! u v i j.
    imp u i v j => req u i v j
```

Formal Verification and Hardware Design with Statecharts *

Jan Philipps   Peter Scholz

Technische Universität München, Institut für Informatik
D-80290 München, Germany
Email: {philipps,scholzp}@in.tum.de

Abstract. Statecharts extend the concept of Mealy Machines by parallel composition, hierarchy, and broadcast communication. While Statecharts in principle are widely accepted in industry, some semantical concepts, especially broadcasting, are still contested. In this contribution, we present a Statechart dialect that includes the basic concepts of the language and present a formal, relational semantics for it. We show that this semantics can be used for both formal verification by model checking and hardware synthesis.

1 Introduction

Statecharts [12] are a visual specification language proposed for specifying reactive systems. They extend conventional state transition diagrams with structuring and communication mechanisms. These mechanisms allow the description of large and complex systems. Due to this property and their support by a number of tools, Statecharts have become quite successful in industry. The full Statecharts language, however, contains many mechanisms that cause problems concerning both their syntax and semantics. An overview of these problems can be found in [28].

In this paper, we describe a dialect of Statecharts, called μ-Charts. In contrast to Statecharts as defined by Harel [12] but similar to Argos [18, 19], μ-Charts can be clearly decomposed into subcharts. Thus, they can be developed in a fully modular way by simply sticking them together. μ-Charts are restricted to the most essential constructs. The basic components are sequential, nondeterministic automata. μ-Charts can be composed in parallel and hierarchically decomposed.

Argos and the approach followed in [14] provide steps in the same direction. Our work extends their approaches in many respects.

---

*   This work has been partially sponsored by the NADA Esprit Working Group 8533 and the BMBF project "KorSys".

First, Argos does not offer data variables. Second, although Argos also uses an explicit feedback operator for communication it does not generate causality chains for signals as we do. Instead, it simply computes the set of broadcast signals by solving signal equations. In our semantics, however, each system step consists of a number of micro steps. In each such micro step further signals for broadcasting in the current system step are added until a fixed point is reached. In every single micro step we check whether the set of broadcasting signals is consistent.

Furthermore, for Argos in [19] non-determinism is introduced by using external prophecy signals. This is different to the approach we follow. In our semantics, those prophecies are not necessary since non-determinism is treated internally.

Finally, while in the Statechart version described in [14] data variables are available, it is not possible at all to construct larger charts by simply sticking components together as in Argos or μ-Charts.

Although μ-Charts are powerful enough to describe large and complex reactive systems, we assign a concise, formal semantics to them. It is given in a fully mathematical way, based on the specification methodology FOCUS. Therefore, we can mix pure functional FOCUS specifications [5, 11, 23] with μ-Charts. The main intention of this paper is to demonstrate

- how to restrict and modify the syntax of traditional Statecharts [12] in order to get a modular specification language,
- that μ-Charts are not a toy language but can be used to specify, verify, and implement practical systems.

Since our semantics is based on the relational μ-calculus, we do not only define a theoretical semantics, but can also apply existing μ-calculus verification tools as a basis for hardware generation and model checking.

This contribution is structured as follows. Section 2 gives an informal introduction to our language. Syntax and semantics are explained in detail in Section 3 and 4, respectively. In Section 5 we outline how the μ-calculus encoding can be used for formal verification. Finally, in Section 6 we present a hardware design scheme using μ-Charts.

2 Introduction to μ-Charts

Before we formally describe syntax and semantics of our dialect we first give some brief informal explanations together with an example, a central locking system for cars.

2.1 Motivation

A μ-Chart is a specification of a component in a reactive system that demonstrates a cyclic behavior. In each cycle, an input is read, an output is emitted, and the component state may change. In this respect, μ-Charts are similar to ordinary Mealy machines: they have a finite set of states, an initial state, an input and output alphabet, and a transition relation defined over current state, input signal, output signal and next state.

For reactive systems, the input alphabet can be regarded as a set of signals generated by the systems' environment that are relevant for the operation of the system. Similarly, the output alphabet usually consists of events that influence the future behavior of the environment.

The time between two cycles is non-zero and finite [1]. Between two cycles in the environment more than one event can occur that might be of interest to the system. The idea is then that the signals for all these events are collected in a set, and this set is used as input to the component. The output is then also defined to be a set of signals. Syntactically, this means that transition labels are not simply signal pairs, but consist of a Boolean expression that characterizes triggering input signal sets, and a set of output signals. Of course, the reaction itself in practice also consumes time, and, theoretically, events in the environment could be lost if they occurred during the system reaction. If, however, the system is sufficiently fast in comparison to the environment, we can disregard the reaction delay, and arrive at the synchronous time model illustrated in Figure 1. Since system reactions are assumed to be infinitely fast, they just divide time flow into finite intervals; at each interval border there is a system reaction where input is read and output produced.

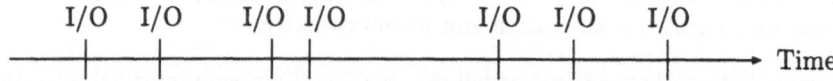

Figure 1. Synchronous time model

Even when input and output is generalized to sets of signals, however, Mealy machines are not practical as a specification formalism for reactive systems. The reason is simply that using state machines for specifications often yields diagrams that are too large to be written down or comprehended. For this reason, Statecharts were suggested by Harel in [12]; they combine the operational notions of Mealy machines with graphical devices to concisely describe large state spaces.

Basically, Statecharts are defined inductively as follows:

- A Mealy machine where input and output alphabet are generalized to powersets is a Statechart.
- The parallel composition of two Statecharts is a Statechart. Parallel composition is the main technique to reduce the number of states needed for the specification.
- A Mealy machine, where one state is replaced with a Statechart is itself a Statechart. This construction is called *hierarchical decomposition*, and is the main technique to reduce the number of transition arrows needed for the specification.

In the rest of this section, we explain parallel composition and hierarchical decomposition in more detail.

Parallel composition and communication. The main technique to reduce complexity in the specification is the parallel composition of two or more state machines. The state space of the parallel composition is the product of the state spaces of the sub-state machine, yet the size of the specification grows only linearly.

Intuitively, the components composed in parallel operate independently: for each input signal set, each component makes a transition and emits an output signal set. The output of the composition is the union of the component outputs.

Unfortunately, only rarely can a component be specified by the independent composition of smaller specifications. In practice, the state machines composed in parallel should be able to communicate. To avoid the clutter resulting from communication channel names, broadcast communication can be introduced. Whenever a state machine emits an output signal, it is visible to the other machines; there it can then cause further outputs, and so on. Thus, communication can lead to chain reactions of machine transitions. Only the result of the chain reaction with the accumulated output is then the visible reaction of the system.

Together with our synchronous time model, communication can cause causality conflicts. For example, assume that a machine M_1 produces an output b if and only if it receives input a, machine M_2 produces output a only if it receives input b, and machine M is the parallel composition of M_1 and M_2 with internal communication of a and b. When neither a nor b is input from the environment, should the output of M be the set $\{a, b\}$ or the empty set?

Plausible semantical definitions of communication are quite intricate, and they are the major difference between the various Statechart dialects found in the literature. The communication semantics of our dialect μ-Charts is defined in Section 4.7.

Hierarchical decomposition. The second technique to reduce the complexity of a specification is the introduction of hierarchy: Groups of states with common transitions can be gathered in a sub-chart (Figure 2). This way, the number of transitions needed for a specification can be reduced.

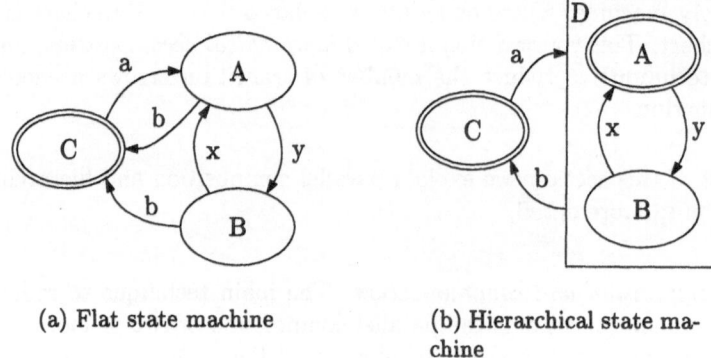

(a) Flat state machine (b) Hierarchical state machine

Figure 2. Hierarchical decomposition

In μ-Charts, as in most Statechart dialects, however, hierarchical decomposition is not only employed to cluster states with identical transitions. In addition, hierarchy is also used to model preemption. Our semantics realizes weak preemption. Weak preemption means that the sub-chart still has the chance to fire a transition before becoming inactive whenever the corresponding master withdraws the control. Although weak preemption can be used to model strong preemption the converse is not true; strong preemption can be derived from weak preemption by signal negation. Thus, we choose weak preemption as default mechanism because it is the more general concept [2].

Hierarchical decomposition, too, gives rise to interesting semantical questions. For example, what should be the proper behavior when the signal necessary to leave the hierarchy is produced within it?

2.2 Example

Figure 3 shows how the ideas of the previous section can be made concrete. The example models the central locking system of a two-door car. Table 1 gives an overview of the signals used. The signals marked external are inputs from the environment to the system, those marked internal are signals that are produced by the system; they are the system's output.

Our central locking system consists essentially of three main parts: CONTROL and the two door motors. These parts are composed in parallel. Locking and unlocking the doors leads to complex signal interactions. The default configuration of the system is that all doors are unlocked (UNLD) and both motors are OFF. Now the driver can lock the car either from outside by turning the key or from inside by pressing a button. Both actions generate the external signal c. The CONTROL unit generates the internal signals ldn and rdn and enters its locking state LOCKG, which is decomposed by the automaton in Figure 4.

Instantaneously, influenced by ldn and rdn, respectively, both motors begin to lock the doors by entering their DOWN states. Those states are decomposed by the sequential automata pictured in Figure 5. Thus, the motors are additionally in their START states. As the speed of the motors depends on external influences like their temperature, each motor either needs one or two time units to finish the lowering process. Only when both have sent their ready messages lmr and rmr, the CONTROL enters the BOTH state and produces the signal $ready$. The effect of this signal is twofold: on the one hand the CONTROL terminates itself immediately and enters the LOCKED state. On the other hand also both motors are triggered by this signal and are switched OFF.

In our syntax communication is expressed by an explicit feedback operator. It is graphically indicated by the box on the bottom of Figure 3.

Whenever the crash signal occurs and the ignition is on, the CONTROL changes from the NORMAL mode to the CRASH mode and generates the signals lup and rup.

Signal	Meaning	Source
crash	Crash sensor	External
o	Opened with external key	External
c	Closed with external key	External
ignition	Ignition on	External
lmr	Left motor ready	Internal
rmr	Right motor ready	Internal
lup	Left motor up	Internal
ldn	Left motor down	Internal
rup	Right motor up	Internal
rdn	Right motor down	Internal
ready	Un-/Locking process ready	Internal

Table 1. Signals used in the locking system

Note that our sequential automata may contain nondeterminism. Nondeterminism is introduced whenever there are two transitions from a single state with nonexclusive trigger conditions. In our example, for instance, the automaton MOTORLEFT contains nondeterminism: if both signals ldn and lup are input while the automaton is in state OFF, the transition to DOWN or the transition to UP may be taken.

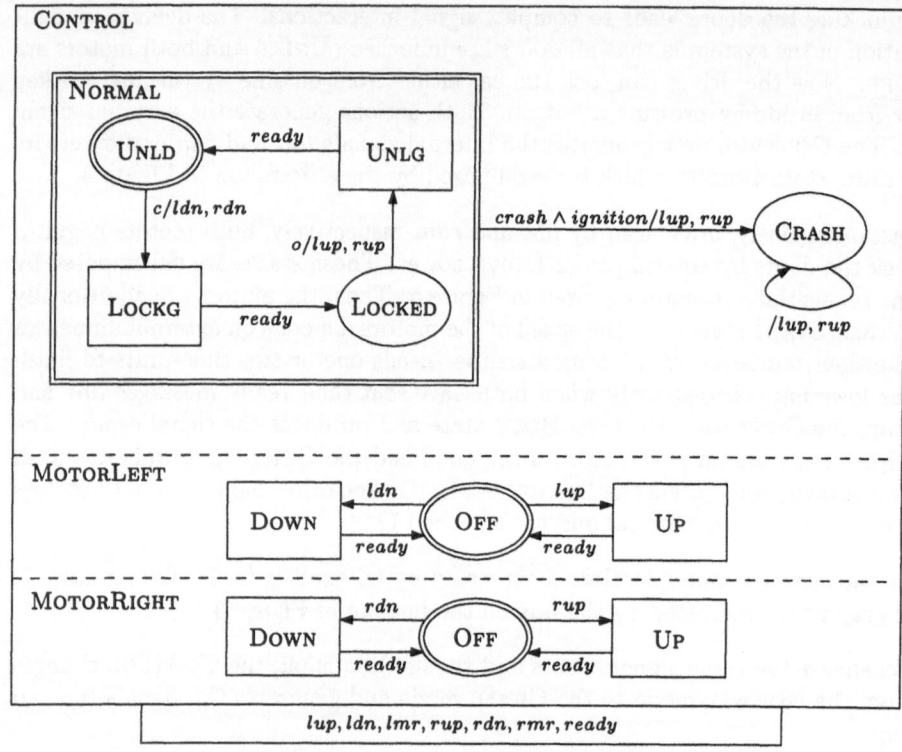

Figure 3. Central locking system

3 Syntax

In this section, we formally define a textual syntax for μ-Charts. It corresponds to the graphical syntax used in the central locking system example in Section 2. The language μ-Charts is based on Mini-Statecharts, as first presented in [21] and later refined in [24, 25, 27]. We only repeat those concepts that are a prerequisite for the extension to nondeterminism and assume the reader to be familiar with the principles of hierarchical, interacting state machines.

Throughout this paper, M denotes a set of signal names, *States* a set of state names, and *Ident* a set of identifier names for sequential automata. For any chart, only a finite number of signal, state, and automata names can be used; $\wp(X)$ denotes the set of finite subsets of some set X.

In addition to the constructs used in the example, we allow sequential automata to have local (state) variables. Transition actions may then consist of simple imperative programs.

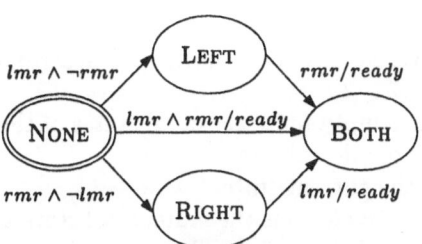

Figure 4. Decomposition of LOCKG and UNLG

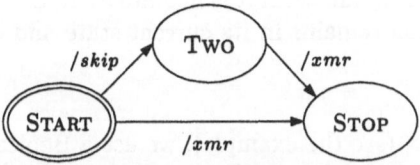

Figure 5. Decomposition of DOWN and UP, $x \in \{l, r\}$

Hence, let V be a set of local integer-valued variables. Note that local variables were not needed in the specification of the central locking system. V has to be disjoint from the sets introduced so far. The other syntactic sets associated with a simple language for transitions (borrowed from [30] and adapted for our purposes) are: integers Int, truth values $Bool = \{\text{true}, \text{false}\}$, arithmetic expressions $Aexp$, Boolean expressions $Bexp$, and commands Com.

The set of μ-Charts S is defined inductively. A μ-Chart is either a sequential automaton, a parallel composition of two μ-Charts, the decomposition of a sequential automaton's state by another μ-Chart, or the result of a feedback construction for broadcasting. The inductive steps are motivated and defined in Sections 3.1 to 3.3.

3.1 Sequential Automata

Sequential automata $\text{Seq}(N, V_l, \beta_d, \Sigma, \sigma_d, \sigma, \delta)$ are the basic elements of our Statechart dialect. They consist of:

1. $N \in Ident$ is the unique identifier of the automaton.
2. $V_l \subseteq V$ is a set of local variables of the automaton. All variables in V_l can only be read or written by operations on transitions of the automaton itself. Other automata do not have any read or write access on them.

3. Whenever the automaton is initialized, that is, starts in its default state σ_d, also every local variable in V_l is initialized according to the initialization function $\beta_d : V_l \rightarrow \mathbb{Z}$.
4. $\Sigma \subseteq States$ is a nonempty finite set of all states of the automaton.
5. $\sigma_d \in \Sigma$ represents the default state.
6. $\sigma \in \Sigma$ represents the current state.
7. $\delta : \Sigma \times \wp(M) \rightarrow \wp(\Sigma \times Com)$ is the finite, total state-transition relation that takes a state and a finite set of signals and yields a set of next states paired with a finite set of commands. If this set contains more than one pair, the automaton is nondeterministic; if the set is empty, the automaton cannot react to the current input when it is in state σ. In the latter case, we assume that the automaton remains in its current state and does not produce any output signals.

In our concrete syntax (see the example), we use a Boolean term t instead of a set of signals $x \in \wp(M)$ as trigger. It is straightforward to translate a partial transition function that deals with arbitrary Boolean terms as trigger conditions into a set-valued total function (see for example [27]).

A transition takes place in exactly one time unit (see Section 2.1). In a specification with several automata working in parallel, more than one automaton can make a transition; all transitions taken in parallel automata are assumed to occur in the same time unit. Note, however, that every single sequential automaton only is allowed to make one transition in one instant. The set of all system actions in one time unit is called a *step*.

Transition Syntax In this section, we introduce the syntax of μ-Charts with local variables and value-carrying signals. In this paper, we only consider integer numbers as data values; however, the language can easily be extended to other datatypes and operators.

In presenting the syntax of our transition language we will follow the convention that $n \in Int$, $X \in V$, $E \in M$, $a \in Aexp$, $b \in Bexp$, and $c \in Com$. Note that Boolean expressions are only used in commands and not as trigger conditions. Arithmetic/Boolean expressions and commands are formed by:

$$a ::= n \mid X \mid a_1 \text{ binop } a_2$$
$$b ::= \text{true} \mid \text{false} \mid a_1 \text{ equ } a_2 \mid a_1 \text{ leq } a_2 \mid \text{ not } b \mid b_1 \text{ and } b_2$$
$$c ::= \text{skip} \mid X := a \mid E \mid \text{if } b \text{ then } c_1 \text{ else } c_2 \text{ fi} \mid c_1, c_2$$

Here binop stands for any of the usual binary operations on integers, such as addition or multiplication. As usual, if b then c fi is an abbreviation for if b then c else skip fi, and single skip commands can be omitted. For example in Figure 7 we simply write $s \wedge \neg r$ and r instead of $s \wedge \neg r/\text{skip}$ and r/skip, respectively.

The meaning of Boolean and arithmetic expressions is straightforward whereas the meaning of commands needs some explanation. $X := a$ assigns the value of the arithmetic expression a to the variable X. In this context, X is local with respect to the automaton that contains the transition. E generates the pure signal E as output in the current instant. E is said to be *present* in the current step only. In the very next step, E is absent again unless it is generated afresh. The if-then-else construct is used as usual.

The command c_1, c_2 stands for the parallel composition of the two commands c_1 and c_2. This construct has to be treated with some care. In traditional Statecharts, when two or more commands want to change the same variable in the same step so-called race conditions [13] can occur, which have to be detected by Statemate's simulation and dynamic test tools because the values of the variables are unknown before runtime.

In previous work [24, 25], to get a more deterministic behavior, we chose sequential execution $c_1; c_2$ instead of parallel composition. However, the program counter needed for sequential execution makes both hardware implementation and formal verification more complex.

As a consequence, we have now decided to realize a compromise between the two above mentioned approaches. Instead of the sequential composition $c_1; c_2$ proposed in [24, 25] we use the parallel composition c_1, c_2 as in [13], but avoid race conditions by the *weak Bernstein condition.*

Bernstein's condition demands that each common location must not occur on the left-hand-side of an assignment. In our context possible locations are local variables. Possible assignments are of the form $X := a$. The following composition is an example: "$X := 1$, if $X = 2$ then $Y := 3$ else $Y := 4$", abbreviated by c_1, c_2. The unique common variable of c_1 and c_2 is X. However, in c_1 we have a write access to X and therefore c_1, c_2 does not fulfill Bernstein's condition. Such commands are not valid with respect to this condition in our setting. Note that a procedure that decides whether a command is valid or not is based on the syntax only and can easily be implemented and therefore is part of the static analysis.

Note further that Bernstein's condition implies commutativity, i.e. commutativity is a weaker condition than Bernstein's. Hence, the meaning of parallel composed commands does not depend on their sequential ordering.

Example As an example of a μ-Chart with local variables we consider a three-digit stopwatch. Each digit is implemented as a seven-segment display as shown if Figure 6. The stopwatch is part of a benchmark collection for hardware design and verification [17]. The corresponding μ-Chart specification is shown in Figure 7. Note that although we used the variable name X in four different automata, all variables with this name are local with respect to the automaton in which they occur. As a consequence, as all variables are local, we do not have to require Bernstein's condition to be fulfilled in case of parallel composition.

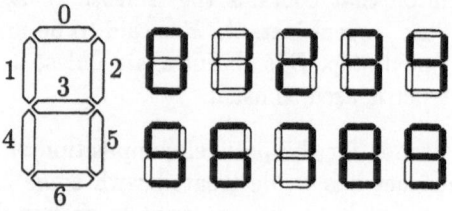

Figure 6. Seven segment display

The stopwatch is controlled by two buttons: "start/stop" (s) and "reset" (r). Table 2 provides an overview over the signals in use. The watch is started by pressing the start/stop button. Then the display shows the time that has elapsed, where the rightmost display (LO) shows tenths of seconds and the remaining two (MED and HI) show seconds and tens of seconds, respectively. Thus, the watch can display times from 00.0 up to 99.9 seconds.

Signal	Meaning	Source
s	Start/Stop	External
r	Reset	
time	Tenths of seconds	Internal
med	Seconds	
low	Tens of seconds	

Table 2. Signals used in the stopwatch

The stopwatch is driven by a 1 MHz external clock, hence every 100,000 clock pulses the lowest digit on the display increases by one, if it is less than nine; otherwise, it is reset to zero, and the medium digit increases by one. When the reset button is pressed, the watch returns to its OFF state, and the display shows 00.0. If however, instead of the reset button, the start/stop button is pressed again, the watch stops counting until this button is pressed again. The stopwatch in Figure 7 is modeled with five sequential automata: $S_{Stopwatch}$, S_{Timer}, S_{Hi}, S_{Med}, and S_{Low}. They are composed as follows (the textual syntax of the subsequent example is explained in the following sections):

Dec $S_{Stopwatch}$ by $\varrho_{Stopwatch}$
$\qquad \varrho_{Stopwatch}(\text{OFF}) = \text{NoDec}$

$$\varrho_{Stopwatch}(\text{ON}) = \text{Feedback}(\text{And}(S_{Display}, S_{Timer}), \{time\})$$
$$S_{Digits} = \text{Feedback}(\text{And}(S_{Hi}, S_{Med}, S_{Low}), \{med, low\})$$

The watch contains two basic control states: ON and OFF. The former is decomposed into two parallel components, namely display and timer:

$$\text{And}(S_{Display}, S_{Timer})$$

There are two feedback constructions for broadcast communication: one around $S_{Display}$, and one around the decomposed ON state.

The external clock signal does not appear in the specification. Instead, we assume that it is this clock signal that causes the steps of a system, and thus determines the time model for the specification.

3.2 Parallel Composition

If S_1 and S_2 are elements of the set S then their parallel composition denoted by the syntax

$$\text{And }(S_1, S_2)$$

is in S, too. There are no syntactic restrictions on this composition. In the graphic notation parallel components are separated by splitting a box into components using dashed lines [12].

In our framework, parallel composition does not imply broadcast communication between the subcharts. Both subcharts operate independently; communication is introduced by an explicit feedback operator (see Section 3.3).

Informally, the parallel composition of μ-Charts behaves as S_1 and S_2 in synchrony. Generated signals of the parallel components are joined. The parallel composition is commutative and associative. We therefore write $\text{And }(S_1, \ldots, S_n)$ to denote $n \in \text{IN}$ nested parallel μ-Charts.

3.3 Broadcast Communication

Parallel composition is used to construct independent, concurrent components. To allow interaction of such components, our language provides a broadcast communication mechanism. In [12], for example, this mechanism already is integrated in the parallel composition of Statecharts. There, broadcasting is achieved by feeding back all generated signals to all components. This means that there exists an *implicit* feedback mechanism at the outermost level of a Statechart. Unfortunately, this implicit signal broadcasting leads to a non-compositional semantics. We avoid this problem by adding an *explicit* feedback operator.

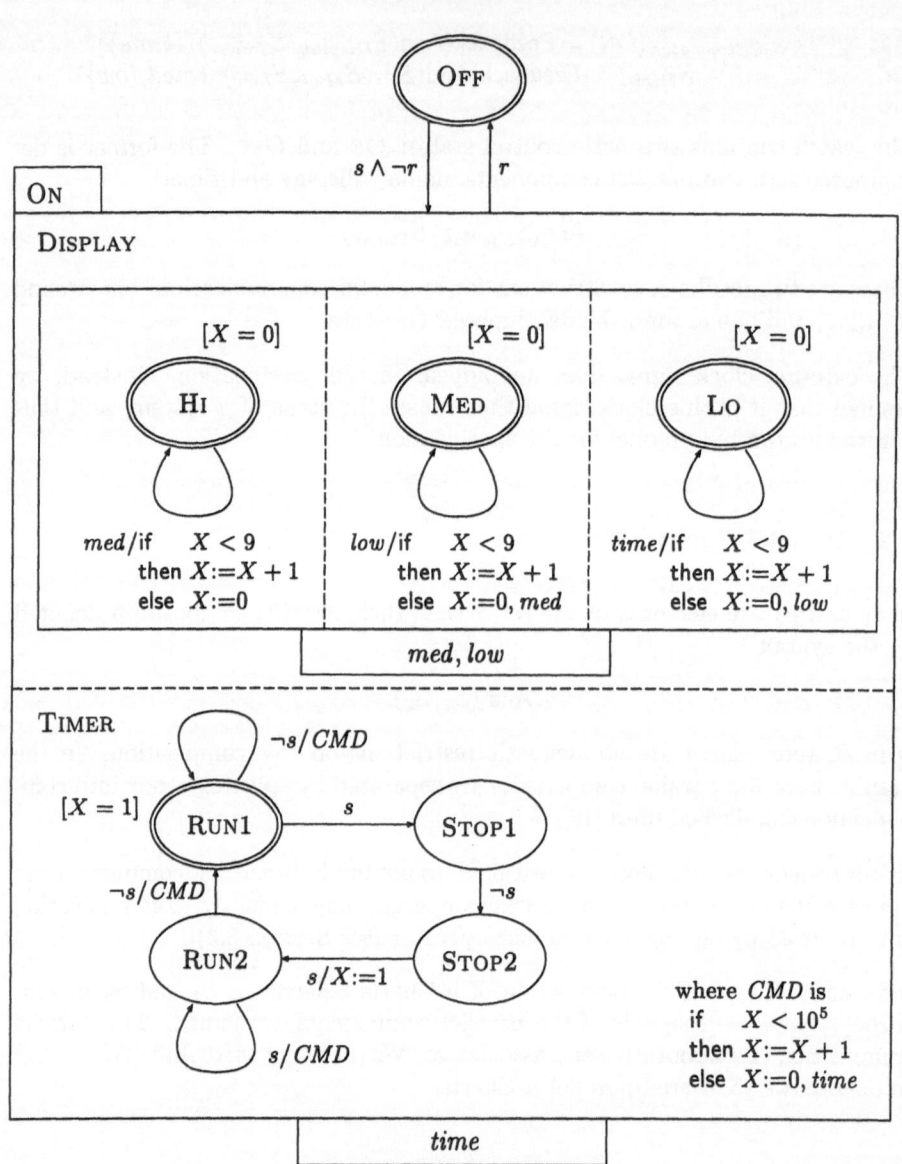

Figure 7. Stopwatch

In the literature, different semantic views of the feedback mechanism can be found [28]. For the deterministic version of our language [21, 24, 27], we provided different syntactic constructs with different communication timings. We believe that for nondeterministic, abstract specifications *instantaneous feedback* is the proper concept, since it is better suited for behavioral refinement. Hence, we present only this operator here.

Suppose that $S \in \mathcal{S}$ is in an arbitrary μ-Chart and $L \in \wp(M)$ is the set of signals which should be fed back, then the construct

$$\text{Feedback } (S, L)$$

is also in $\mathcal{S}$. Graphically, the feedback construction is denoted with a box below the μ-Chart S. This box contains the signals L that are fed back.

Instantaneous feedback follows the perfect synchrony hypothesis of Berry [1]; this demands that an action and the event causing this action occur at the same instant of time. Therefore, the signals in z generated by chart S are instantaneously intersected with the signals L to be fed back and then joined with the external signals x. This signal set $x \cup (z \cap L)$ is passed to S at the same instant.

3.4   Hierarchical Decomposition

The concept of hierarchically structuring the state space is essential for State-charts. In our Statechart dialect, hierarchy is introduced by replacing states of a sequential automaton (the *master*) with arbitrary charts (the *slaves*). This replacement is expressed by a finite, partial function ϱ, which is defined for those states σ of the master that are further decomposed. The decomposition function ϱ yields the refining slave-chart. Suppose that $\mathsf{Seq}(N, V_l, \beta_d, \Sigma, \sigma_d, \sigma, \delta)$ is a sequential automaton, then hierarchical decomposition is denoted by

$$\mathsf{Dec}(N, V_l, \beta_d, \Sigma, \sigma_d, \sigma, \delta) \text{ by } \varrho$$

where $\varrho : \Sigma \to \mathcal{S}$. Like other formal Statechart semantics [14, 18, 19], the approach presented here has no history states. It is possible to extend our semantics along the lines of [21]. Due to space limitations we omit this extension here. Throughout this paper, we assume that the slave is always re-initialized when leaving it.

4   Semantics

In this section, we introduce the transition relation for a μ-Chart. It is defined inductively following the syntactical structure of the language. The transition relations presented here are based on the semantics as presented in [22]. μ-Charts are synchronized by a global, discrete clock. Each transition relation formally denotes the relationship between two system configurations, i.e. the set of all currently valid control states of all sequential automata between two subsequent instants.

4.1 Transition Semantics

To define the denotational semantics of transitions we first need a valuation ε as a total function $\varepsilon : V \to \mathbb{Z}$. The set of all valuations is denoted by $\mathcal{E}$. Note that $\mathcal{E}$ contains total functions: variables have a defined value at every single time point, whereas signals have proper values only when they are present. With this background we are able to define the semantic functions:

$$\mathcal{A}[\![.]\!] : Aexp \to (\mathcal{E} \to \mathbb{Z})$$
$$\mathcal{B}[\![.]\!] : Bexp \to (\mathcal{E} \to \mathbb{B})$$
$$\mathcal{C}[\![.]\!] : Com \to (\wp(M) \times \mathcal{E} \to \wp(M) \times \mathcal{E})$$

where $\mathbb{B} = \{tt, ff\}$. We define the denotation of an arithmetic expression as follows:

$$\mathcal{A}[\![n]\!]\varepsilon = n$$
$$\mathcal{A}[\![X]\!]\varepsilon = \varepsilon(X)$$
$$\mathcal{A}[\![a_1 \text{ binop } a_2]\!]\varepsilon = \mathcal{A}[\![a_1]\!]\varepsilon \text{ binop } \mathcal{A}[\![a_2]\!]\varepsilon$$

The denotation of a Boolean expression is also defined inductively:

$$\mathcal{B}[\![\text{true}]\!]\varepsilon = tt$$
$$\mathcal{B}[\![\text{false}]\!]\varepsilon = ff$$
$$\mathcal{B}[\![a_1 \text{ equ } a_2]\!]\varepsilon = \mathcal{A}[\![a_1]\!]\varepsilon = \mathcal{A}[\![a_2]\!]\varepsilon$$
$$\mathcal{B}[\![a_1 \text{ leq } a_2]\!]\varepsilon = \mathcal{A}[\![a_1]\!]\varepsilon \leq \mathcal{A}[\![a_2]\!]\varepsilon$$
$$\mathcal{B}[\![\text{not } b]\!]\varepsilon = \neg \mathcal{B}[\![b]\!]\varepsilon$$
$$\mathcal{B}[\![b_1 \text{ and } b_2]\!]\varepsilon = \mathcal{B}[\![b_1]\!]\varepsilon \wedge \mathcal{B}[\![b_2]\!]\varepsilon$$

The definition of $\mathcal{C}[\![c]\!]$ for commands c is a bit more complex than the definitions of $\mathcal{A}[\![.]\!]$ and $\mathcal{B}[\![.]\!]$:

$$\mathcal{C}[\![\text{skip}]\!](x, \varepsilon) = (x, \varepsilon)$$
$$\mathcal{C}[\![X := a]\!](x, \varepsilon) = \text{let } n = \mathcal{A}[\![a]\!]\varepsilon \text{ in } (x, \varepsilon[n/X])$$
$$\mathcal{C}[\![E]\!](x, \varepsilon) = (x \cup \{E\}, \varepsilon)$$
$$\mathcal{C}[\![c_1, c_2]\!](x, \varepsilon) = \mathcal{C}[\![c_2]\!](\mathcal{C}[\![c_1]\!](x, \varepsilon))$$
$$\mathcal{C}[\![\text{if } b \text{ then } c_1 \text{ else } c_2 \text{ fi}]\!](x, \varepsilon) = \begin{cases} \mathcal{C}[\![c_1]\!](x, \varepsilon) & \text{if } \mathcal{B}[\![b]\!]\varepsilon = tt \\ \mathcal{C}[\![c_2]\!](x, \varepsilon) & \text{otherwise} \end{cases}$$

Here we write $\varepsilon[n/X]$ for the function obtained from ε by replacing its value in X by n. Note that because of the commutativity of the parallel composition we could also have defined $\mathcal{C}[\![c_1, c_2]\!](x, \varepsilon) = \mathcal{C}[\![c_1]\!](\mathcal{C}[\![c_2]\!](x, \varepsilon))$.

4.2 Preliminaries

Steps and System Reactions. Like other Statechart dialects, μ-Charts is a synchronous language based on a discrete time model. A run of a μ-Chart system consists of a sequence of *steps*. At each step, the system receives a set of signals from the environment. Upon receipt of this input set, the system produces a set of output signal, and may change its state. The output signals are assumed to be generated in the same instant as the input signals are received. A signal is said to be *present* in a given instant, if it is either input from the environment or generated by the system in this instant. Otherwise, it is said to be *absent*.

Avoiding Multiple Transitions in one Step. As we deal with instantaneous feedback, more than one transition of different sequential automata can fire simultaneously. However, every single automaton only can make one step in one instant, i.e. no two consecutive transitions in a sequential automaton are taken in a step. This informal requirement has to be formalized in the automaton's transition relation. Furthermore, we have to ensure that only one branch of a nondeterministic choice in an automaton is taken in a step.

Both restrictions can be ensured using additional signals. For each sequential automaton $\mathsf{Seq}(N, V_l, \beta_d, \Sigma, \sigma_d, \sigma, \delta)$ we introduce a signal $\copyright_N$. Informally, this is a copyright on transitions of the automaton signaling that N has already made a step. When the signal is not present, the automaton may yet make a transition, whereupon it will generate $\copyright_N$. If $\copyright_N$ is already present, the automaton has to stay in its current state. The need for this signal will become clearer later when we introduce broadcast communication. The copyright signals are introduced in the following way. Each transition with label c/y of N is modified such that:

- The trigger condition c is strengthened by conjoining $\neg\copyright_N$ to it.
- The action set y is extended by $\copyright_N$.

We assume all signals $\copyright_N$ to be disjoint from signals in M and define $M_\copyright$ by $M \cup \{\copyright_N \mid N \in Ident\}$.

Negation in Trigger Expressions. Negation in trigger expressions can lead to some tricky causality problems. For example, what would be the semantics of a transition labeled $\neg a/a$? Some Statecharts semantics simply disallow Statecharts with causality problems. They require a static analysis of the chart, which might reject charts that do not really have causality conflicts. This is for instance the approach taken by Argos [18] or the reactive programming language Esterel [3].

We handle these conflicts semantically. In case of a causal conflict, the transition is simply not taken. We accomplish this through *oracle signals* that predict the presence or absence of a given signal in a step. For each signal a that occurs negatively in the trigger of a transition, we introduce a new signal $\tilde{a}$ that replaces a in the trigger part of a transition label. We define $\widetilde{M}$ to be $M \cup \{\tilde{a} \mid a \in M\}$. However, oracle signals can cause the following two inconsistencies:

- A signal a is generated by the system or input from the environment, although the oracle forecasts its absence. In other words, a is in the signal set, but not $\tilde{a}$.
- A signal a that is predicted to be present, is neither input nor generated by the system. In other words, $\tilde{a}$ is in the signal set, but not a.

The requirement to avoid these inconsistencies is formally expressed by:

$$Consistence(x, y, o) \equiv (\bigwedge_{s \in x \cup y} s \in o) \land (\bigwedge_{s \in o} s \in x \cup y)$$

where x, y, and o denote the sets of input, output, and oracle signals respectively. This technique is similar to that used in the bottom-up evaluation of logic programs with negation as presented in [16]. For a detailed discussion of this topic the interested reader is referred to [22].

4.3 Configurations

Configurations $c = (\gamma, \varepsilon) \in C$ are defined inductively. Each configuration has a control part γ and a data part ε. The configuration of a sequential automaton is simply the tuple of its current control and data state. To denote the configuration of an And-chart And (S_1, S_2) we use a tuple[1] $(\gamma_1, \varepsilon_1, \gamma_2, \varepsilon_2)$, where $(\gamma_1, \varepsilon_1)$ and $(\gamma_2, \varepsilon_2)$ are the configurations of the parallel components S_1 and S_2, respectively. The configuration of Feedback (S, L) is simply the configuration of S.

For hierarchical decomposition we need a slightly more subtle notation. The master is decomposed into $n =_{df} |\text{dom } \varrho|$ slaves, where dom ϱ denotes the domain of the partial function ϱ. The configurations of these slaves are denoted by $c_1, \ldots, c_n$, whereas the configuration of the master is denoted by c_m. The overall configuration of

$$\text{Dec}(N, V_l, \beta_d, \Sigma, \sigma_d, \sigma, \delta) \text{ by } \varrho$$

is then the $(n + 1)$-tuple $(c_m, c_1, \ldots, c_n)$.

---

[1] Or $((\gamma_1, \varepsilon_1), (\gamma_2, \varepsilon_2))$ more precisely. However, we omit parentheses whenever the meaning is clear from the context.

In the sequel, we will formulate the transition relations for every single syntactic construct of the μ-Charts language. We have two different categories of predicates: one for initialization and one for the transition step from one configuration to the following. These predicates have the type:

$$Init_S : C \to Bool$$

$$Trans_S : C \times \wp(M_{\mathbb{C}}) \times C \times \wp(M_{\mathbb{C}}) \times \widetilde{M} \to Bool$$

for every μ-Chart S. A predicate $Trans_S(c, x, c', y, o)$ is true whenever the current configuration of S is c and S can, stimulated by the input signal set x, reach the subsequent configuration c' in exactly one instant while producing the output signal set y. The set o includes those oracles that are needed for the treatment of negative signals in S.

4.4 Sequential Automata

Initially, a sequential automaton $S =_{df} \mathsf{Seq}(N, V_l, \beta_d, \Sigma, \sigma_d, \sigma, \delta)$ is in its default configuration (σ_d, β_d). For an input signal set x coming from the environment, S generates a set y of output signals and changes its configuration from (γ, ε) to (γ', ε'):

$$Init_S((\gamma, \varepsilon)) \equiv (\gamma = \sigma_d) \wedge \forall X \in V_l : \varepsilon(X) = \beta_d(X)$$

$$Trans_S((\gamma, \varepsilon), x, (\gamma', \varepsilon'), y, o) \equiv \exists com \in Com : (\gamma', com) \in \delta(\gamma, x \cup o) \wedge$$
$$(y, \varepsilon') = \mathcal{C}[\![com]\!](x, \varepsilon)$$

Note that we omit parentheses for tuples whenever the context allows.

4.5 Parallel Composition

The tuple (c_1, c_2) is the initial configuration of chart $S =_{df} \mathsf{And}\ (S_1, S_2)$ whenever c_1, c_2 are the initial configurations of charts S_1, S_2, respectively:

$$Init_S((c_1, c_2)) \equiv Init_{S_1}(c_1) \wedge Init_{S_2}(c_2)$$

The formal semantics is defined by the following case distinction, which yields three mutually exclusive cases. An And-chart can perform a step when at least one of the subcharts makes a step.

$$Trans_S((c_1, c_2), x, (c'_1, c'_2), y, o) \equiv$$
$$(\exists y_1, y_2. Trans_{S_1}(c_1, x, c'_1, y_1, o) \wedge$$
$$Trans_{S_2}(c_2, x, c'_2, y_2, o) \wedge y = y_1 \cup y_2) \vee$$
$$(\not\exists y_2, c. Trans_{S_2}(c_2, x, c, y_2, o) \wedge$$
$$Trans_{S_1}(c_1, x, c'_1, y, o) \wedge c'_2 = c_2) \vee$$
$$(\not\exists y_1, c. Trans_{S_1}(c_1, x, c, y_1, o) \wedge$$
$$Trans_{S_2}(c_2, x, c'_2, y, o) \wedge c'_1 = c_1)$$

The first conjunction represents the case when both charts S_1 and S_2 can react in their current configurations c_1 and c_2 on the current signals x. In this case the overall reaction is simply denoted by the logical conjunction of both transition predicates $Trans_{S_1}$ and $Trans_{S_2}$. The other two conjunctions are true whenever only one of S_1 or S_2 can react on the current stimuli in its current configuration. Should none of the three terms be true, the overall transition predicate $Trans_S$ is false, i.e. S cannot react at all.

4.6 Hierarchical Decomposition

A decomposed chart $S =_{df} \text{Dec}(N, V_l, \beta_d, \Sigma, \sigma_d, \sigma, \delta)$ by ϱ is in its initial configuration iff the master $A =_{df} \text{Seq}(N, V_l, \beta_d, \Sigma, \sigma_d, \sigma, \delta)$ and all existing n slaves $\text{dom}\, \varrho =_{df} \{\sigma_1, \ldots, \sigma_n\} \subseteq \Sigma$ are in their initial configurations:

$$Init_S((c_m, c_1, \ldots, c_n)) \equiv Init_A(c_m) \wedge \bigwedge_{i=1}^n Init_{S_i}(c_i)$$

where for all $i = 1, \ldots, n$ the mapping ϱ is defined by $\varrho(\sigma_i) = S_i$. To define the step relation for the decomposition, we distinguish four mutually exclusive cases. The first case occurs whenever the current state c_m ($c_m = (\sigma_m, \varepsilon_m)$) of the master is refined by a slave S_i (in this case $\varrho(\sigma_m)$ is defined, i.e. $\sigma_m \in \text{dom}\, \varrho$ and $\varrho(\sigma_m) = S_i$), and both A and S_i can react. All other currently non-active slaves keep their current configuration $\bigwedge_{j \neq i} c_j = c'_j$. Generated signals of both master and active slave are collected: $y = y_s \cup y_m$. Note that whenever the transition predicate $Trans_A$ of the master is true, the slave is initialized through the predicate $Init_{S_i}(c'_i)$. This first case is formally denoted by:

$$Trans_S^1((c_m, c_1, \ldots, c_n), x, (c'_m, c'_1, \ldots, c'_n), y, o) \equiv$$
$$\exists y_m, y_s, c.Trans_A(c_m, x, c'_m, y_m, o) \wedge$$
$$\sigma_m \in \text{dom}\, \varrho \wedge S_i = \varrho(\sigma_m) \wedge Trans_{S_i}(c_i, x, c, y_s, o) \wedge$$
$$y = y_s \cup y_m \wedge Init_{S_i}(c'_i) \wedge \bigwedge_{j \neq i} c_j = c'_j$$

Here both master and slave can react on the current set of input stimuli. In this case, the master *preempts* the slave's reaction. Our semantics deals with weak preemption: so the slave still can terminate its current action, i.e. generate all output signals y_s. However, even then it will be re-initialized.

Whenever the master's current configuration $c_m = (\sigma_m, \varepsilon_m)$ is not decomposed ($\sigma_m \notin \text{dom}\, \varrho$), all slaves stay in their current configurations ($\bigwedge_{i=1}^n c_i = c'_i$) and only the master itself reacts:

$$Trans_S^2((c_m, c_1, \ldots, c_n), x, (c'_m, c'_1, \ldots, c'_n), y, o) \equiv$$
$$Trans_A(c_m, x, c'_m, y, o) \wedge \sigma_m \notin \text{dom}\, \varrho \wedge \bigwedge_{i=1}^n c_i = c'_i$$

If, however, a slave exists but is not able to make a step, again only the master reacts but now the current slave S_i is initialized and all other slaves do not change their configuration:

$$Trans_S^3((c_m, c_1, \ldots, c_n), x, (c'_m, c'_1, \ldots, c'_n), y, o) \equiv$$
$$Trans_A(c_m, x, c'_m, y, o) \wedge \sigma_m \in \text{dom } \varrho \wedge S_i = \varrho(c_m) \wedge$$
$$\nexists y_s, c'_s. Trans_{S_i}(c_i, x, c'_s, y_s, o) \wedge Init_{S_i}(c'_i) \wedge \bigwedge_{j \neq i} c_j = c'_j$$

Finally, if the master cannot react, but the current slave S_i can, we have:

$$Trans_S^4((c_m, c_1, \ldots, c_n), x, (c'_m, c'_1, \ldots, c'_n), y, o) \equiv$$
$$\nexists y_m, c'_m. Trans_A(c_m, x, c'_m, y_m, o) \wedge$$
$$\sigma_m \in \text{dom } \varrho \wedge S_i = \varrho(\sigma_m) \wedge \bigwedge_{j \neq i} c_j = c'_j \wedge Trans_{S_i}(c_i, x, c'_i, y, o)$$

Overall, the complete transition relation is the disjunction of these cases:

$$Trans_S((c_m, c_1, \ldots, c_n), x, (c'_m, c'_1, \ldots, c'_n), y, o) \equiv$$
$$Trans_S^1((c_m, c_1, \ldots, c_n), x, (c'_m, c'_1, \ldots, c'_n), y, o) \vee$$
$$Trans_S^2((c_m, c_1, \ldots, c_n), x, (c'_m, c'_1, \ldots, c'_n), y, o) \vee$$
$$Trans_S^3((c_m, c_1, \ldots, c_n), x, (c'_m, c'_1, \ldots, c'_n), y, o) \vee$$
$$Trans_S^4((c_m, c_1, \ldots, c_n), x, (c'_m, c'_1, \ldots, c'_n), y, o)$$

The predicate $Trans_S$ is false iff neither master nor slave can react to the current input.

4.7 Broadcast Communication

The initialization predicate for $S = \mathsf{Feedback}(R, L)$ is defined as:

$$Init_S(c) \equiv Init_R(c)$$

The transition relation $Trans_S$ is built up from a number of auxiliary predicates. As we deal with a chain reaction when defining the semantics of the instantaneous feedback, we have to fix the termination of this reaction. It terminates when in the current configuration c the chart S cannot react any more on the current input stimuli x:

$$Term_S(c, x, o) \equiv \nexists y, c'. Trans_R(c, x, c', y, o)$$

The predicate $Cone_S$ constructs the set of all intermediate points in the chain reaction by the μ-calculus formula:

$$Cone_S(c, x, c', y, o) \equiv$$
$$\mu \Psi. (Trans_R(c, x, c', y, o) \vee$$
$$\exists x', y', y'', c''. \Psi(c, x, c'', y'', o) \wedge Trans_R(c'', x', c', y', o) \wedge$$
$$x' = x \cup (y'' \cap L) \wedge y = y' \cup y'')$$

In order to verify whether $Cone_S(c, x, c', y, o)$ yields true we have to verify whether either of the two following cases is true. The first alternative is that c and c' represent two subsequent configurations, i.e. c' is reachable from c in one step: $Trans_R(c, x, c', y, o)$. Otherwise, it has to be verified whether c and c' can be reached via an intermediate configuration c''. All reachable configurations from c are computed by applying the least fixpoint operator μ on predicate Ψ. Note that the external stimuli x are available during the whole chain reaction and that only those internal signals which occur in L can be fed back: $x' = x \cup (y \cap L)$. The overall transition relation of S is then defined as:

$$Trans_S(c, x, c', y, o) \equiv$$
$$Cone_S(c, x, c', y, o) \wedge Term_S(c', x \cup (y \cap L), o) \wedge Consistence(x, y, o)$$

As already mentioned, the oracle signals in o nondeterministically predict the absence or presence of signals in a step. This prediction is needed for the proper treatment of negative trigger expressions in sequential automata. Of course, such a guess might lead to inconsistencies, if in fact a signal predicted to be present is neither input from the environment, nor generated by the system, or vice versa. Such inconsistencies are detected with the predicate $Consistence$ defined in Section 4.2. They can only occur with instantaneous feedback of a signal that can be generated in one subchart, and whose absence is checked in another subchart.

The transition relations defined above are partial. When a chart cannot react to its current input, the relation is undefined. Intuitively, in this case however the chart should stay in its current configuration. The execution of a chart S is therefore defined over the following, total step relation:

$$Step_S(c, x, c', y) \equiv$$
$$\exists o.Trans_S(c, x, c', y, o) \vee$$
$$\forall c'', y'', o.\neg Trans_S(c, x, c'', y'', o) \wedge c = c' \wedge y = \emptyset$$

For each chart, there is only a finite number of control states and a finite set of input and output signals. Thus, this transition relation can be efficiently represented by BDDs [6]. BDDs have a long tradition in the fields of logic minimization, test pattern generation, and symbolic model checking as we show in the next section.

A finite characterization of the initial state of a μ-Chart, $Init_S(c)$, can be derived similarly. Thus, the semantics for every component of a system specification is represented by two BDDs: one characterizes the initial states of the component, and the other the step relation. Since the semantics of μ-Charts is compositional, the BDDs for each chart can be computed from the BDDs of its subcharts.

5 Formal Verification

In the last section, we defined the semantics of μ-Charts in terms of the relational μ-calculus. Recently, several verification tools for this calculus have been developed [4, 7]. For our work, we used the μ-calculus model checker μ-cke. In this section, we show how a specification in μ-Charts can be encoded in μ-cke, and how the encoding can be used for property verification.

5.1 The Verifier μ-cke

The input language of μ-cke is similar to the programming language C. Currently, the supported data types include Booleans, enumerations, bounded intervals of the natural numbers, and algebraic products that are defined with a construct "class" that is similar to "struct" in C.

Relations are defined as boolean-valued functions. In the μ-calculus, the least and greatest fixpoint operators are used to recursively define relations. As in C, μ-cke permits recursion by writing the relation's name in the right-hand side of the relation's definition. In addition, the keywords mu or nu have to precede the definition to indicate whether the least or greatest fixpoint is intended.

Currently, μ-cke does not support non-Boolean functions or types corresponding to the algebraic sum (union in C).

Internally, μ-cke uses BDD algorithms to evaluate formulas. The variable ordering for the BDDs is computed automatically, but it is possible to give "hints" in the input files about the ordering and interleaving of variables. There exist commands to arrange variables in sequential (x < y) or interleaved (x ~+ y) ordering.

5.2 Encoding

We implemented a small translator from μ-Charts to the input language of μ-cke. The translator is written in Perl [29], and the definition of a μ-Chart is just a file with Perl declarations. The translation is performed top-down following the hierarchical structure of the μ-Chart. For each construct a configuration data type, an initialization predicate, and a transition relation is defined.

In the following, we present some parts of the translation of the example in Section 2.2.

Signals. For both the external and internal signals that occur in the specification, a single type is defined. While two separate types might seem more natural, the single type helps with the variable ordering used by μ-cke, and makes the internal representation more efficient. Note that for each sequential automaton a copyright signal is introduced. Whenever a signal s is present, the corresponding Boolean variable v_s equals to true, otherwise to false.

```
class Signals {
/* Internal and external signals: */
        bool crash;             bool o;             bool c;
        bool ignition;          bool ready;         bool lmr;
        bool rmr;               bool ldn;           bool rdn;
        bool lup;               bool rup;

/* Copyright signals: */
        bool CR_Control;        bool CR_Normal;
        bool CR_Lockg;          bool CR_Unlg;
        bool CR_MotorLeft;      bool CR_MotorRight;
        bool CR_DownLeft;       bool CR_DownRight;
        bool CR_UpLeft;         bool CR_UpRight;
};
```

Oracles. The locking system contains two internal signals, *lmr* and *rmr* (see automata for locking and unlocking), that are referenced negatively. Thus, we need two oracle variables. The translator introduces a new type for these oracles, and defines a predicate for consistence:

```
class Oracles {
  bool lmr;
  bool rmr;
};

bool Consistence(Signals i, Signals o, Oracles orc)
(
  ((i.lmr | o.lmr) -> orc.lmr) &
  ((i.rmr | o.rmr) -> orc.rmr) &

  (orc.lmr -> (i.lmr | o.lmr)) &
  (orc.rmr -> (i.rmr | o.rmr)) &
);
```

Sequential automata. For each sequential automaton, two state types are introduced. One, the vertex, is an enumeration type that represents the control state. The second type is a product type for the chart's complete configuration. In addition to the control state, it contains the data state components. Since the locking system is specified without data states, this type consists of just the vertex.

In addition, two predicates are defined:

- The first predicate characterizes the initial configuration of the automaton. Initial configurations restrict the control state to the default state of the automaton, and could also restrict the data components, if used.

- The second predicate defines the transition relation over the current configuration s, the successor configuration t, input and output signal sets i and o, and the oracle set orc. The relation is a disjunction of the individual transition conditions, together with a condition that restricts the automaton's outputs.

Note the three expressions after the transition relation's header: these are variable ordering hints for μ-cke. They indicate that the variables for current and successor configuration, as well as the input and output signal variables should be interleaved. Moreover, the input (and thus also the output) variables come strictly before the configurations. Nothing is said about the oracle variables — thus, the checker is free to use its heuristics for their positioning.

```
enum MotorleftVertex {
    Down_Motorleft, Off_Motorleft, Up_Motorleft
};

class MotorleftState {
    MotorleftVertex c;
};

bool MotorleftInit(MotorleftState s)
    (s.c = Off_Motorleft);

bool MotorleftTrans(MotorleftState s, Signals i, MotorleftState t,
                    Signals o, Oracles orc) s ~+ t, i ~+ o, i < s
(
  ((s.c = Off_Motorleft & t.c = Down_Motorleft &
    i.ldn & !i.CR_Motorleft & o.CR_Motorleft) |
   (s.c = Off_Motorleft & t.c = Up_Motorleft &
    i.lup & !i.CR_Motorleft & o.CR_Motorleft) |
   (s.c = Off_Motorleft & t.c = Down_Motorleft &
    !i.lup & !i.ldn & !i.CR_Motorleft & o.CR_Motorleft) |
   (s.c = Off_Motorleft & t.c = Off_Motorleft &
    i.CR_Motorleft & !o.CR_Motorleft) |

   (s.c = Down_Motorleft & t.c = Off_Motorleft &
    i.ready & !i.CR_Motorleft & o.CR_Motorleft) |
   (s.c = Down_Motorleft & t.c = Down_Motorleft &
    !i.ready & !i.CR_Motorleft & o.CR_Motorleft) |
   (s.c = Down_Motorleft & t.c = Down_Motorleft &
    i.CR_Motorleft & !o.CR_Motorleft) |
```

```
    (s.c = Up_Motorleft & t.c = Off_Motorleft &
     i.ready & !i.CR_Motorleft & o.CR_Motorleft) |
    (s.c = Up_Motorleft & t.c = Up_Motorleft &
     !i.ready & !i.CR_Motorleft & o.CR_Motorleft) |
    (s.c = Up_Motorleft & t.c = Up_Motorleft &
     i.CR_Motorleft & !o.CR_Motorleft))

/* Besides CR_Motorleft no other other output is possible: */

    & !crash & !o & !c & !ignition & !ready & !lmr & !rmr
    & !ldn & !rdn & !lup & !rup & !CR_Control & !CR_Normal
    & !CR_Lockg & !CR_Unlg & !CR_MotorRight & !CR_DownLeft
    & !CR_DownRight & !CR_UpLeft & !CR_UpRight
);
```

Parallel composition and hierarchical decomposition. For brevity we skip the remaining two constructs of μ-Charts. Given the semantics of Section 4, the translation is straightforward, but the resulting code is quite lengthy.

Broadcast communication. The configuration data type and the initialization predicate for the feedback operator are identical to those of its argument μ-Chart.

```
class TopState {
      ParallelState s;
};

bool TopInit(TopState s)
      ParallelInit(s.s);
```

The transition relation for the feedback operator is defined in terms of an auxiliary relation *cone* that defines the chain reactions. This relation is defined as a least fixpoint construction; a chain reaction is either a single transition of the argument μ-Chart, or a transition from a state already reached in the chain reaction. Here the input and output signals have been copied; this is the logical notation of the set-based definition in Section 4.

```
mu bool TopCone(TopState s, Signals i,TopState t,
                Signals o, Oracles orc) s ~+ t, i ~+ o, i < s
/* Base: */
    ParallelTrans(s.s,i,t.s,o,orc) |
```

```
/* Microstep: */
    (exists Signals oo, Signals ooo, Signals ii, TopState tt . (
        TopCone(s,i,tt,oo,orc) &
        ParallelTrans(tt.s,ii,t.c,ooo,orc) &
        (ii.CR_Control <-> (i.CR_Control | oo.CR_Control)) &
        (ii.crash <-> (i.crash)) &


        ...


        (o.rdn <-> (oo.rdn | ooo.rdn)) &
        (o.lup <-> (oo.lup | ooo.lup)) &
        (o.rup <-> (oo.rup | ooo.rup)));
```

The transition relation checks in addition that the configuration c' reached in the cone predicate is terminal, i.e. $Term_S(c', x \cup (y \cap L), o)$, and that the signal sets built up while reaching them are consistent.

```
bool TopTrans(TopState s, Signals i, TopState t,
              Signals o, Oracles orc) s ~+ t, i ~+ o, i < s
/* Reachable, */
    TopCone(s,i,t,o,orc) &

/* yet terminal configuration: */
    !(exists Signals ii, Signals oo, TopState tt .
        (ParallelTrans(t.s,ii,tt.s,oo,orc) &
        (ii.CR_Control <-> (i.CR_Control | o.CR_Control)) &
        (ii.crash <-> (i.crash)) &


        ...


        (ii.rup <-> (i.rup | o.rup)))) &

    Consistence(i,o,orc);
```

Again, the predicate definitions are annotated with hints for the variable ordering.

System reactions. We have seen how the step semantics of a μ-Chart can be encoded in μ-cke. For verification, however, we need the behavior at the level of system reactions. From the transition semantics we obtain the reaction semantics by existentially quantifying the oracles. Thus, we implicitly handle all guesses. If there is no oracle such that there is a valid transition, the μ-Chart's successor configuration is defined to be equal to the current configuration, and all output signals are absent.

```
   bool LockingSystemReact(LockingSystemState s, Signals i,
            Signals o, LockingSystemState t) s ~+ t
 (exists Oracles orc.
        !i.lmr & !i.rmr & !i.ldn & !i.rdn & !i.lup & !i.rup &
        !i.CR_Control & !i.CR_Normal & !i.CR_Doorstate &
        !i.CR_Motorleft & !i.CR_Motorright &
        LockingSystemTrans(s,i,orc,o,t)) |

 (s = t & !o.crash & ... & !o.CR_Motorright);
```

5.3   Model Checking

For property verification, we also formulate the property to be proven in the relational μ-calculus. Simple properties such as invariants can be straightforwardly expressed in μ-calculus; others are usually easier expressed in the more readable temporal logics CTL, CTL^* or LTL, and then schematically translated into the μ-calculus. A translation of the branching-time logic CTL into μ-calculus is described in [20], translations of CTL^* and also LTL can be found in [8].

Here we just look at the simple verification whether a given configuration is reachable. Reachability can be defined as a least fixpoint with the following formula:

```
   mu bool reachable(LockingSystemState s)
      LockingSystemInit(s) |
      (exists Signals i, Signals o, LockingSystemState r.
            reachable(r) &
            LockingSystemReact(r,i,o,s));
```

A similar formula with a largest fixpoint operator nu could be used to check for invariance of a property.

The μ-cke encoding can also be used to check a specification for determinism. In μ-cke, this condition is formulated as follows:

```
   forall Signals i, Signals o1, Signals o2,
         LockingSystemState s, t1, t2 .
      (reachable(s) &
      LockingSystemReact(s,i,o1,t1) &
      LockingSystemReact(s,i,o2,t2))
         -> (o1 = o2 & t1 = t2);
```

Note that here we first calculate the reachable configurations of the specification; thus, our condition is stronger and more precise than the syntactic determinism checks of, say, the Argos compiler. On the other hand, the calculation of reachable states can be computationally expensive for larger specifications, especially when local data states are used.

6 Hardware Generation

In this section we present a hardware implementation scheme for μ-Charts. In contrast to the tool Statemate [15], we aim at a *direct* implementation, and not at compilation to VHDL code. Two previous approaches for direct hardware implementations of a Statecharts-like language were presented by Drusinsky in [9, 10]. The first one implemented a Statechart as a network of communicating finite state machines. Especially for small and medium-sized systems this scheme introduces considerable communication overhead; in addition, the author admits that it is difficult to implement correctly.

In the second approach, he suggested realizing a Statechart as a single logic block. However, it is not clear how this approach scales to larger specifications. Neither of these two approaches is based on a formal semantics. Of course, in principle, a very low-level semantics is given in form of hardware logic. However, it is not possible to formally verify properties like compositionality of this type of semantics. Properties of this kind are, for instance, important if one wants to support the designer with formal refinement rules that help her or him in incrementally developing a specification [26]. Moreover, neither approach allows for specifying systems with data states.

Our implementation scheme is based on the formal semantics introduced in the previous sections; in particular, implementations are generated from the same transition relations that are used for formal verification of μ-Charts with symbolic model checkers. While our scheme also avoids the communication overhead of communicating components, the implementations can naturally be divided into smaller logic blocks, each of them responsible for the value of a single output signal bit.

As synchronous hardware allows only deterministic implementations, we restrict ourselves to deterministic μ-Charts in this chapter. With the techniques of Chapter 5 it is easy to check that a μ-Chart is deterministic.

6.1 Symbolic Encoding of μ-Charts

In Chapter 4 we presented the formal step semantics of μ-Charts. It has been shown that the step semantics of a given μ-Chart S can be described as a finite transition relation

$$Step_S(x, c, y, c')$$

where x and y are finite encodings of the input x and output signals y. The current and next system configuration are encoded in c and c', respectively. A similar predicate $Init_S(c)$ for initialization has been formulated.

These predicates are used for the hardware implementation according to Figure 8. The input to the logic block consists of the external inputs x, the finite encoding of the current system state (including control c and data state ε), and a reset wire. The logic block has system output y and the new system state encoding c' as output. In addition to this combinational logic block, we need a state register for the control and data states and an external clock that triggers the μ-Chart steps.

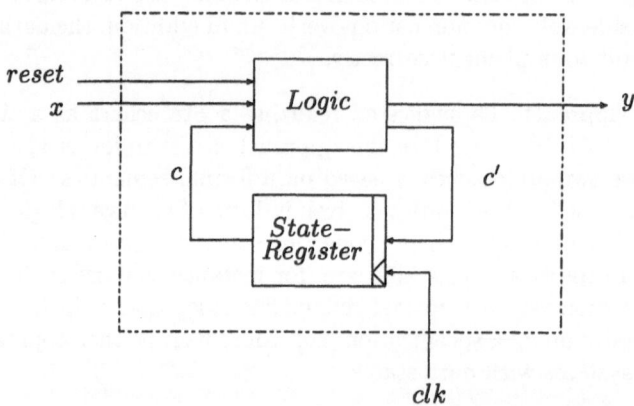

Figure 8. Hardware implementation scheme

The logic block is derived in the following way. The transition relation $Steps$ is converted to a family of Boolean functions, one for each output signal y_i, and one for each bit in the encodings of the control and data states. The Boolean functions for a bit are derived from the transition relation $Steps$ by existentially quantifying the other output signals. This operation can, for instance, be efficiently carried out with BDDs. The conversion to Boolean functions is possible, since for hardware generation we restrict ourselves to deterministic μ-Charts. The check for whether a μ-Chart is deterministic can also be performed on the transition relation $Steps$.

As shown in Figure 9, the individual Boolean functions can be implemented separately. In this figure, thick lines represent bundles of signals, whereas single bit connections are drawn as thin lines.

Each Boolean function for an output signal contains an abstraction of the complete specification. This is the reason why our implementation scheme does not require explicit communication between the logic blocks. The abstraction contains those aspects of the complete system specification that are needed to calculate the signal's value — neither more nor less. This is the reason why the individual Boolean functions can be represented with comparatively small BDDs, much smaller than the complete transition relation $Steps$.

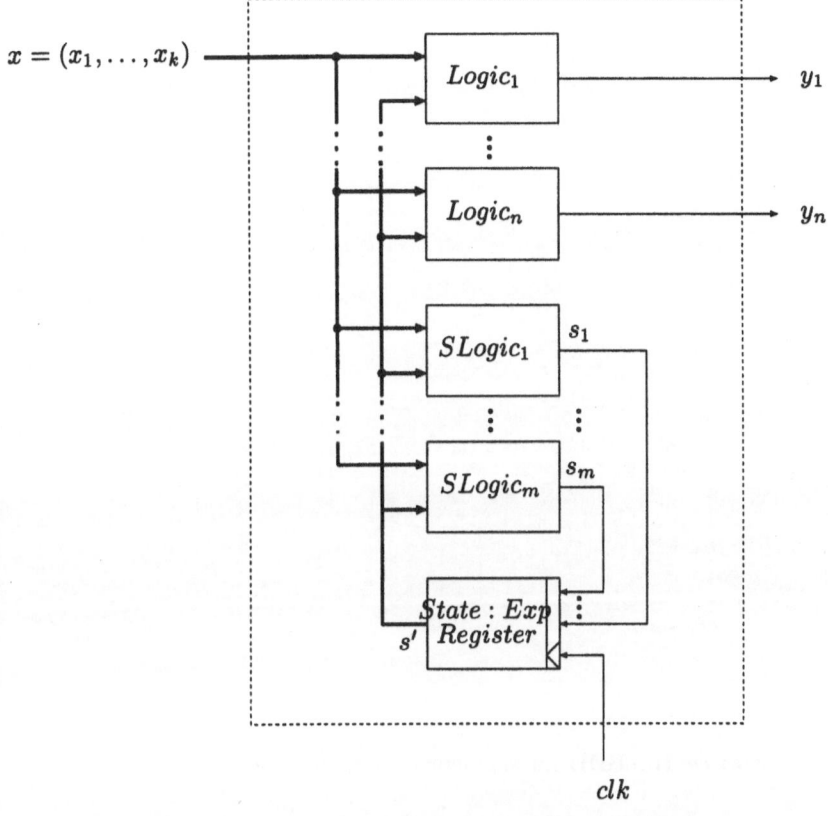

Figure 9. Distributed implementation

6.2 Stopwatch Example

In this section, we apply our implementation technique to the stopwatch example. Since only a finite subset of integers is used for the data states in the example, we can encode them with BDDs. For the clock counter in the subchart TIMER, we employ the standard binary encoding for integers between 0 and 100,000; this requires 17 bits. We could represent the ten values for the digit displays using 4-bit integers, but instead we have chosen a direct encoding of the seven segments for each digit. This allows us to use a slight variation of the implementation scheme: instead of dedicated output signals for the segments, we use the state encoding itself to drive the display.

Since the watch consists of five sequential automata, two parallel compositions, and two feedback constructions, there are nine initialization and nine transition relations. The top level relations, that are those of Dec $S_{Stopwatch}$ by $\varrho_{Stopwatch}$ are the ones used for hardware generation. The transition relation is then converted to a family of Boolean functions.

386

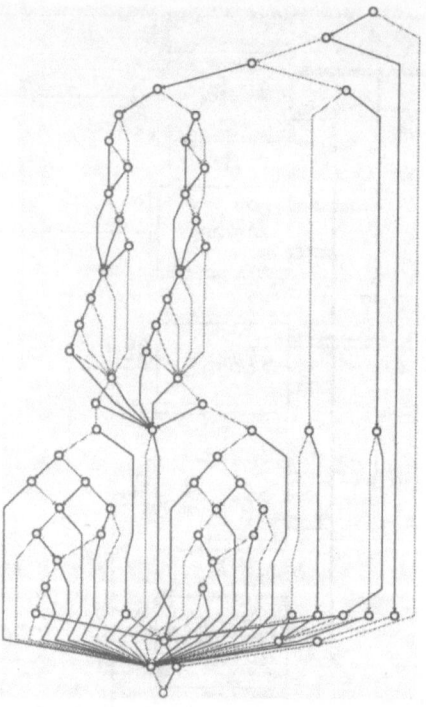

Figure 10. BDD for segment 0 of display Lo

Figure 10 shows the BDD for segment 0 of the lowest digit. With 66 nodes, the BDD is quite small. It is not possible, in general, to predict the BDD sizes for a given μ-Chart. We can, however, calculate the number of bits needed to encode the data and control states, and thus the width of the state register:

$$bits(\mathsf{Seq}(N, V_l, \beta_d, \Sigma, \sigma_d, \sigma, \delta)) = \lceil ld(|\Sigma|)\rceil + \lceil ld(\sum_{X \in V_l} range(X))\rceil$$

$$bits(\mathsf{And}\ (S_1, S_2)) = bits(S_1) + bits(S_2)$$

$$bits(\mathsf{Feedback}\ (S, L)) = bits(S)$$

$$bits(\mathsf{Dec}(N, V_l, \beta_d, \Sigma, \sigma_d, \sigma, \delta)\ \text{by}\ \varrho) = bits(\mathsf{Seq}(N, V_l, \beta_d, \Sigma, \sigma_d, \sigma, \delta)) +$$
$$max\{bits(\varrho(\sigma))\ |\ \sigma \in \Sigma \wedge \varrho(\sigma) \neq \mathsf{NoDec}\}$$

In the stopwatch example we have $ld(2) = 1$ flipflop for the automaton $S_{Stopwatch}$, $ld(4) + \lceil ld(10^5)\rceil = 2 + 17 = 19$ for S_{Timer}, and $3 \cdot (7 + 1) = 24$ for S_{Digits}. As mentioned, we directly use the encoding of the local states to control the seven segment displays and so avoid additional logic to decode the logic for each segment out of a four bit state. Altogether we need a 44 bit wide register.

Referring to Figure 9 again, the register width is the constant m, in our example

44. The constant k is the number of external input signals. In the stopwatch example, $k = 2$ since the only inputs are for the two buttons on the watch. Finally, n is the number of output signals. In the example, n should be $3 \cdot 7 = 21$ for the three seven segment displays. However, since we directly use the state encoding as outputs for the display, our example gives $n = 0$, since there are no other outputs of the system. Thus, for the example 44 BDDs have to be implemented. Note that *low*, *med*, and *time* are internal signals for broadcasting only. Their use is implicitly modeled in the Boolean functions.

7 Conclusion

The Statechart dialect presented in this paper offers instantaneous feedback and nondeterminism. We have shown how to deal with both concepts formally and demonstrated that model checking for specifications with instantaneous chain reactions is possible. We demonstrated our approach by an example. The results presented in Section 5 show that it is difficult to place trust in a formal specification without proving central system properties.

We expect that in our framework larger specifications can be verified than in approaches without instantaneous feedback. The reason is that in the feedback definition intermediate configurations that occur only during chain reactions are hidden through the fixpoint construction. With other communication mechanisms, these intermediate configurations remain visible. Moreover, we believe that specifications with instantaneous broadcasting are more concise than those written in e.g. the Statemate dialect.

Finally, it remains to be seen whether BDD-based symbolic verification techniques are indeed the best approach for model checking μ-Charts. For instance, in our example only 22 configurations are reachable. It is possible that non-symbolic techniques are more efficient for μ-Chart specifications. However, the high-level input language of μ-cke turned out to be very helpful for rapid prototyping of our language definition, semantics, and verification approach.

Furthermore, we have presented a hardware implementation scheme for μ-Charts. Our hardware implementation scheme is directly based on the formal semantics of μ-Charts. This semantics rests upon the same semantics as the one used for model checking. When local data states are restricted to finite types, the step relations can be translated immediately into BDDs. These BDDs can be implemented as combinational logic. As BDDs are based on the Shannon normal form (SNF) and some programmable hardware units like field programmable gate arrays are based on the disjunct normal form (DNF) it may be useful to transform BDDs to DNF before implementing them on hardware.

In addition to the logic, only a register and an external clock is needed. The register size can be calculated a priori.

Future work will focus on the further development of a formal refinement calculus [26] that supports correctness by construction, on software generation, and on hardware/software codesign.

References

1. G. Berry. Real Time Programming: Special Purpose or General Purpose Languages. *Information Processing 89*, 1989.
2. G. Berry. Preemption in Concurrent Systems. In *Foundations of Software Technology and Theoretical Computer Science : 13th Conference Bombay, India, December 15-17*, volume 761 of *Lecture Notes in Computer Science*, pages 72 – 93. Springer, 1993.
3. G Berry and G. Gonthier. The Esterel Synchronous Programming Language: Design, Semantics, Implementation. Technical Report 842, INRIA, 1988.
4. A. Biere. μ-cke — Efficient μ-Calculus Model Checking. Number 1254 in Lecture Notes in Computer Science, pages 468–471, 1997.
5. M. Broy, F. Dederichs, C. Dendorfer, M. Fuchs, T. Gritzner, and R. Weber. The Design of Distributed Systems An Introduction to FOCUS - Revised Version. Technical Report TUM-I9202-2, Technische Universität München, Fakultät für Informatik, TUM, 80290 München, Germany, January 1993.
6. R. E. Bryant. Graph Based Algorithms for Boolean Function Manipulation. *IEEE Transactions on Computers*, 8(C-35):677–691, 1986.
7. M.-M. Corsini and A. Rauzy. Symbolic Model Checking and Constraint Logic Programming: A Cross-Fertilization. ESOP'94, pages 180–194, 1994.
8. M. Dam. CTL* and ECTL* as Fragments of the Modal μ-Calculus. Number 126 in Theoretical Computer Science, 1994.
9. D. Drusinsky-Yoresh. Using Statecharts for Hardware Description and Synthesis. Number 8 in IEEE Transactions on Computer-Aided Design, pages 798–807, 1989.
10. D. Drusinsky-Yoresh. A State Assignment for Single-Block Implementation of State Charts. Number 10 in IEEE Transactions on Computer-Aided Design, pages 1569–1576, 1991.
11. R. Grosu and K. Stølen. A Denotational Model for Mobile Point-to-Point Dataflow Networks. Technical Report SFB 342/14/95 A, Technische Universität München, Fakultät für Informatik, 80290 München, Germany, 1995.
12. D. Harel. Statecharts: A Visual Formalism for Complex Systems. *Science of Computer Programming*, 8:231–274, 1987.
13. D. Harel and A. Naamad. The Statemate Semantics of Statecharts. *ACM Transactions On Software Engineering and Methodology*, 5(4):293–333, 1996.
14. J.J.M. Hooman, S. Ramesh, and W.P. de Roever. A Compositional Axiomatization of Statecharts. *Theoretical Computer Science*, 101:289–335, 1992.
15. i-Logix Inc., Three Riverside Drive, Andover, MA 01810, U.S.A., http://www.i-logix.com. *Languages of Statemate*, 1990.
16. K. Inoue, M. Koshimura, and R. Hasegawa. Embedding Negation as Failure into a Model Generation Theorem Prover. In D. Kapur, editor, *CADE-11*, number 607 in Lecture Notes in Artificial Intelligence, pages 400–415, 1992.
17. T. Kropf. Benchmark Circuits for Hardware-Verification. In R. Kumar and T. Kropf, editors, *Theorem Provers in Circuit Design*, volume 901 of *Lecture Notes in Computer Science*, pages 1–12. Springer-Verlag, 1994.

18. F. Maraninchi. Operational and Compositional Semantics of Synchronous Automaton Compositions. In W.R. Cleaveland, editor, *Proceedings CONCUR'92*, volume 630 of *Lecture Notes in Computer Science*, pages 550 – 564. Springer-Verlag, 1992.

19. F. Maraninchi and N. Halbwachs. Compositional Semantics of Non-deterministic Synchronous Languages. In Riis Nielson, editor, *Programming languanges and systems - ESOP'96, 6th European Symposium on programming*, volume 1058 of *Lecture Notes in Computer Science*. Springer-Verlag, 1996.

20. K. L. McMillan. *Symbolic Model Checking*. PhD thesis, Carnegie Mellon University, 1993.

21. D. Nazareth, F. Regensburger, and P. Scholz. Mini-Statecharts: A Lean Version of Statecharts. Technical Report TUM-I9610, Technische Universität München, D-80290 München, 1996.

22. J. Philipps and P. Scholz. Compositional Specification of Embedded Systems with Statecharts. In *TAPSOFT'97: Theory and Practice of Software Development*, volume 1214 of *Lecture Notes in Computer Science*. Springer-Verlag, 1997.

23. B. Schätz and K. Spies. Formale Syntax zur logischen Kernsprache der Focus-Entwicklungsmethodik. Technical Report TUM-I9529, Technische Universität München, Fakultät für Informatik, 80290 München, Germany, 1995.

24. P. Scholz. An Extended Version of Mini-Statecharts. Technical Report TUM-I9628, Technische Universität München, D-80290 München, 1996.

25. P. Scholz. A Light-Weight Formalism for the Specification of Reactive Systems. In *XXIII-rd Seminar on Current Trends in Theory and Practice of Informatics (SOFSEM'96), Milovy, Slovakia*, volume 1175 of *Lecture Notes in Computer Science*, pages 425 – 432, 1996.

26. P. Scholz. A Refinement Calculus for Statecharts. In *Proccedings of the "ETAPS/FASE'98, Lisbon (Portugal), March 30 - April 03, 1998"*, volume 1382 of *Lecture Notes in Computer Science*. Springer, 1998.

27. P. Scholz, D. Nazareth, and F. Regensburger. Mini-Statecharts: A Compositional Way to Model Parallel Systems. 1996. 9th International Conference on Parallel and Distributed Computing Systems (PDCS'96), Dijon, France.

28. M. von der Beeck. A Comparison of Statecharts Variants. In H. Langmaack, W.-P. de Roever, and J. Vytopil, editors, *Proc. Formal Techniques in Real–Time and Fault–Tolerant Systems (FTRTFT'94)*, volume 863 of *Lecture Notes in Computer Science*, pages 128–148. Springer, 1994.

29. L. Wall, T. Christiansen, R.L. Schwartz, and S. Potter. *Programming Perl*. O'Reilly, 1996.

30. G. Winskel. *The Formal Semantics of Programming Languages*. The MIT Press, 1993.

An Exercise in Conditional Refinement

Ketil Stølen[1] and Max Fuchs[2]

[1] OECD Halden Reactor Project, Institute for Energy Technology, P.O.Box 173,
N-1751, Halden, Norway
[2] BMW AG, FIZ EG-K-3, D-80788, München, Germany

Abstract. This paper is an attempt to demonstrate the potential of conditional refinement in step-wise system development. In particular, we emphasise the ease with which conditional refinement allows boundedness constraints to be introduced in a specification based on unbounded resources. For example, a specification based on purely asynchronous communication can be conditionally refined into a specification using time-synchronous communication.

The presentation is built around a small case-study: A step-wise design of a timed FIFO queue that is partly to be implemented in hardware and partly to be implemented in software. We first specify the external behaviour of the queue ignoring timing and synchronisation. This overall specification is then restated in a time-synchronous setting and thereafter refined into a composite specification consisting of three sub-specifications: A specification of a time-synchronous hardware queue, a specification of an asynchronous software queue, and a specification of an interface component managing the communication between the first two. We argue that the three overall specifications can be related by conditional refinement. By further steps of conditional refinement additional boundedness constraints are introduced. We explain how each step of conditional refinement can be formally verified in a compositional manner.

1 Introduction

Requirements imposing upper bounds on the memory available for some data structure, channel, or component are often programming language or platform dependent. Such requirements may for instance characterise the maximum number of messages that can be sent along a channel within a time unit without risking malfunction because of buffer overflow. Clearly, this number may vary from one buffer to another depending on the type of messages it stores, and the way the buffer is implemented.

One way to treat such boundedness constraints is to introduce them already at the most abstract level — in other words, in the requirement specification. However, this option is not very satisfactory, for several reasons. The boundedness constraints:

- considerably complicate the specifications; as a result, the initial understanding of the system to be designed is often reduced;

- reduce the set of possible implementations; this makes the reuse of specifications more difficult;
- complicate formal reasoning; this means it becomes more difficult to verify the correctness of refinement steps;
- are often not known when the requirement specifications are written; for instance, at this stage in a system development, it is often not decided which implementation language(s) to use and on what sort of platform the system is to run.

We conclude that any development method requiring that boundedness constraints are introduced already in the requirement specification, is not very useful from a practical point of view. However, since any computerised system is based on bounded resources, we need concepts of refinement supporting the transition from specifications based on unbounded resources to specifications based on bounded resources. This paper advocates the flexibility of conditional refinement for this purpose. We define conditional refinement for a specification language based on streams. A specification in this language is basically a relation between input and output streams. Each stream represents a complete communication history for a channel. To formalise timing properties we use what we call timed streams. Timed streams capture a discrete notion of time. The underlying communication paradigm is asynchronous message passing. The ideas of this paper can be adapted to other specification languages, as well. For example, [14] formulates a notion of conditional refinement in SDL (see also [7]).

The remainder of the paper is organised as follows: In Sect. 2 we introduce the basic concepts and notations; in Sect. 3 we give three different specifications of a FIFO queue; in Sect. 4 we formally define conditional refinement and explain how the specifications from Sect. 3 can be related by this concept; in Sect. 5 we conditionally refine the FIFO queue specified in Sect. 3 into a more concrete specification with additional boundedness constraints; in Sect. 6 we give a brief summary and relate our approach to other approaches known from the literature; in App. A we formulate three rules that can be used to verify the refinement steps mentioned above; in App. B we prove that these three rules are sound.

2 Basic Concepts and Notations

Streams model the communication histories of channels. We use both *timed* and *untimed streams*. A timed stream is a finite or infinite sequence of messages and *time ticks*. A time tick is denoted by $\sqrt{}$. The time interval between two consecutive ticks represents the least unit of time. A tick occurs in a stream at the end of each time unit.

An infinite timed stream represents a *complete communication history*, a finite timed stream represents a *partial communication history*. Since time never halts, we require that any infinite timed stream has infinitely many ticks.

By M^∞, $M^{\pm}$ and $M^{\underline{\omega}}$ we denote respectively the set of all infinite timed streams, the set of all finite timed streams, and the set of all finite and infinite timed streams over the set of messages M.

We also work with streams without ticks, referred to as untimed streams. By M^∞, M^* and M^ω we denote respectively the set of all infinite untimed streams, the set of all finite untimed streams, and the set of all finite and infinite untimed streams over the set of messages M. In the sequel, M denotes the set of all messages. Since $\sqrt{}$ is not a message, we have that $\sqrt{} \notin M$.

By N we denote the set of natural numbers; by N_∞ and N_+ we denote $N \cup \{\infty\}$ and $N \setminus \{0\}$, respectively. Given $A \subseteq M \cup \{\sqrt{}\}$, streams $r, s \in M^\omega \cup M^{\underline{\omega}}$, $t \in M^{\underline{\infty}}$ and $j \in N_\infty$:

- $\langle \rangle$ denotes the empty stream.
- $\#r$ denotes the length of r: ∞ if r is infinite, and the number of elements in r otherwise. Note that time ticks are counted. For example, the length of a stream consisting of infinitely many ticks is ∞.
- $r.j$ denotes the jth element of r if $1 \leq j \leq \#r$.
- $\langle a_1, a_2, .., a_n \rangle$ denotes the stream of length n, whose first element is a_1, whose second element is a_2, and so on.
- $A \circledS r$ denotes the result of filtering away all messages (ticks included) not in A. For example:

$$\{a, b\} \circledS \langle a, b, \sqrt{}, c, \sqrt{}, a, \sqrt{} \rangle = \langle a, b, a \rangle$$

- $r \frown s$ denotes the result of concatenating r and s. For example: $\langle c, c \rangle \frown \langle a, b \rangle = \langle c, c, a, b \rangle$. If r is infinite then $r \frown s = r$.
- r^j denotes the result of concatenating j copies of the stream r.
- $r \sqsubseteq s$ holds iff r is a prefix of or equal to s.
- $t \downarrow_j$ denotes the prefix of t characterising the behaviour until time j; this means that $t \downarrow_j$ denotes t if j is greater than the number of ticks in t, and the shortest prefix of t containing j ticks, otherwise. Note that $t \downarrow_\infty = t$, and also that $t \downarrow_0 = \langle \rangle$.
- $\overline{t}$ denotes the result of removing all ticks in t. Thus, $\overline{\langle a, \sqrt{}, b, \sqrt{} \rangle \frown \langle \sqrt{} \rangle^\infty} = \langle a, b \rangle$.

A timed infinite stream is *time-synchronous* if exactly one message occurs in each time interval. Time-synchronous streams model the pulsed communication typical for synchronous digital hardware working in fundamental mode. Since, in this case, exactly one message occurs in each time interval, no information is gained from the ticks; the ticks can therefore be abstracted away; the result is an untimed infinite stream. To facilitate time abstraction in the time-synchronous case, the $\downarrow$ operator is overloaded to untimed infinite streams: For any stream $s \in M^\infty$ and $j \in N_\infty$, $s \downarrow_j$ denotes the prefix of s of length j.

3   Specification of a FIFO Queue

Elementary specifications are basically relations on streams. These relations are expressed by formulas in predicate calculus. This section introduces three formats for elementary specifications: The *time-independent*, the *time-dependent* and the *time-synchronous format*. We first specify the external behaviour of a FIFO queue in the time-independent format, a format tuned towards asynchronous communication. This specification is thereafter reformulated in the time-synchronous format; this format is particularly suited for the specification of digital hardware components communicating in a synchronous (pulsed) manner. Thereafter, we give a composite specification of the FIFO queue consisting of three elementary specifications: A *hardware queue* written in the time-synchronous format, a *software queue* written in the time-independent format, and an *interface component* written in the time-dependent format; the latter manages the communication between the first two.

3.1 Time-Independent Specification

The elementary specification below describes a FIFO queue.

```
══FIFO═══════════════════════════════════ time_independent ══
  in    u : G
  out   v : D
  ────────────────────────────────────────────────────────
  asm   Req_Ok(u)
  ─ ─ ─ ─ ─ ─ ─ ─ ─ ─ ─ ─ ─ ─ ─ ─ ─ ─ ─ ─ ─ ─ ─ ─ ─ ─ ─ ─ ─
  com   FIFO_Beh(u, v)
```

FIFO is the name of the specification. Ignoring the dashed line, the specification FIFO is divided in two main parts by a single horizontal line. The upper part declares the *input* and *output channels* distinguished by the keywords in and out. Hence, FIFO has one input channel u of type G and one output channel v of type D. D is the set of all data elements. What exactly these data elements are is of no importance for this paper and therefore left unspecified. A request is represented by Req. It is assumed that $Req \notin D$. G is defined as follows:

$$G \equiv D \cup \{Req\}$$

Thus, data elements and request are received on the input channel; the queue replies by sending data elements. We often refer to the identifiers naming the channels as *channel identifiers*.

The lower frame, referred to as the *body*, describes the allowed input/output history. It consists of two parts: An *assumption* and a *commitment* identified by the keywords asm and com, respectively. The assumption describes the intended input histories — it is a pre-condition on the input histories. The commitment describes the output histories the queue is allowed to produce when the input history fulfills the assumption. Both the assumption and the commitment are described by formulas in predicate calculus. In these formulas u and v are free variables of type G^ω and D^ω, respectively; they represent the communication histies of the channels they name. That u and v represent untimed streams (and, for instance, not timed infinite streams, as in the time-dependent case) is specified by the keyword **time_independent** in the upper right-most corner.

Assumption The assumption is expressed by an auxiliary predicate

$Req\_Ok(a)$

This predicate states that for any prefix b of the untimed stream a, the number of requests in b is less than or equal to the number of data elements in b. Formally:

$$\boxed{\begin{array}{l} \underline{\text{Req\_Ok}} \\[4pt] a \in M^\omega \cup M^\infty \\ \hline \forall b \in M^\omega \cup M^{\underline{\omega}} : b \sqsubseteq a \Rightarrow \#(\{Req\} \text{\scriptsize Ⓢ} b) \leq \#(D \text{\scriptsize Ⓢ} b) \end{array}}$$

Thus, the assumption of FIFO formalises that, at any point in time, the number of received requests is less than or equal to the number of received data elements; in other words, the environment is assumed never to send a request when the queue is empty. Note that a is of type $M^\omega \cup M^\infty$ and not just G^ω ($\subseteq M^\omega$). This supports the reuse of Req_Ok in other contexts. Hence, the definition of the auxiliary predicate Req_Ok is independent from the specification FIFO in the sense that Req_Ok can be exploited also in other specifications.

Commitment Also the commitment employs an auxiliary predicate

$FIFO\_Beh(a, b)$

This predicate requires that the stream of data-elements sent along b is a prefix of the stream of data elements sent along a (first conjunct), and that the number of data elements in b is equal to the number of requests in a (second conjunct). Formally:

$$\boxed{\begin{array}{l} \underline{\text{FIFO\_Beh}} \\[4pt] a, b \in M^\omega \cup M^\infty \\ \hline D \text{\scriptsize Ⓢ} b \sqsubseteq (D \text{\scriptsize Ⓢ} a) \wedge \#D \text{\scriptsize Ⓢ} b = \#(\{Req\} \text{\scriptsize Ⓢ} a) \end{array}}$$

Thus, the commitment of FIFO requires that the data elements are output in the FIFO order, and that each request is replied to by the transmission of exactly one data-element.

The semantics of elementary specifications is defined formally in Sect. 4.2.

3.2 Time-Synchronous Specification

The time-independent format employed in the previous section is well-suited to specify software components communicating asynchronously. To describe hardware applications communicating in a time-synchronous (pulsed) manner, we use the time-synchronous format as in this section. We now restate FIFO in a time-synchronous setting. Time-synchronous communication is modelled as follows: In each time unit exactly one message is transmitted along each channel. For the case that the time-synchronous FIFO queue or its environment have no "real" message to transmit, a default message Dlt is used. It is assumed that $Dlt \notin G$. We define:

$$G_{Dlt} \equiv G \cup \{Dlt\}, \qquad D_{Dlt} \equiv D \cup \{Dlt\}$$

FIFO can then be restated in the time-synchronous format as follows.

```
═FIFO_TS ═══════════════════════════════ time_synchronous ═
  in    i : G_Dlt
  out   o : D_Dlt
  ───────────────────────────────────────────────────────
  asm   Req_Ok(i)
  - - - - - - - - - - - - - - - - - - - - - - - - - - - - -
  com   FIFO_Beh(i, o)
```

The keyword in the upper right corner implies that the channel identifiers in the body represent infinite untimed streams instead of untimed streams of arbitrary length as in FIFO. The filtration with respect to D in the definitions of the two auxiliary predicates of the previous section makes their reuse in $FIFO_{TS}$ possible.

3.3 Composite Specification

We have presented elementary specifications written in the time-independent and the time-synchronous format. As already mentioned, there is also a time-dependent format. The time-dependent format is tuned towards asynchronous communication. It differs from the time-independent format in that it allows timing requirements to be expressed. We now use all three formats for elementary specifications to describe a composite FIFO queue that is partly to be implemented in hardware and partly to be implemented in software.

As illustrated by Fig. 1, the queue consists of three components, namely a hardware queue specified by HWQ, a software queue specified by SWQ, and an interface component specified by INTF. The interface component is needed as a converter between the time-synchronous hardware component and the asynchronous software component.

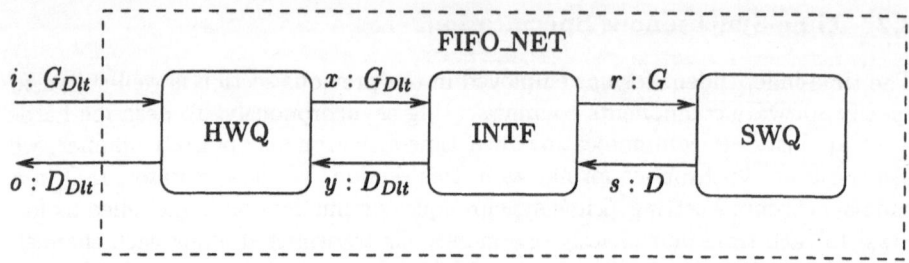

Fig. 1. Decomposed FIFO Queue

The hardware queue has only a bounded amount of internal memory: It can never store more than W_h data elements at the same point in time. To avoid memory overflow it may forward data elements and requests to the software queue. The software queue is in principle unbounded. The external behaviour of INTF and SWQ composed should be that of $FIFO_{TS}$.

Hardware Queue The hardware queue communicates in a time-synchronous manner: In each time-unit the hardware queue receives exactly one message on each input channel (can be understood as an implicit environment assumption) and outputs exactly one message along each output channel. The hardware queue is specified as follows.

═══HWQ ══════════════════════════════ time_synchronous ═══
in $\quad i : G_{Dlt}; \; y : D_{Dlt}$
out $\quad o : D_{Dlt}; \; x : G_{Dlt}$
asm $\quad Req\_Ok(i) \land FIFO\_Beh(x, y)$
com $\quad FIFO\_Beh(i, o) \land Req\_Ok(x) \land Bnd\_Hwm(i, y, o, x, W_h)$

The first conjunct of the assumption is the same as in $FIFO_{TS}$; the same holds for the first conjunct of the commitment. The second conjunct of the assumption implies that the hardware queue guarantees correct behaviour only as long as the software queue (composed with the interface component) behaves like a FIFO queue. The second conjunct of the commitment requires the hardware queue to use the software queue correctly, namely by sending requests only when the software queue has at least one data element to send in return. The third conjunct imposes the boundedness requirement on the number of messages that can be stored by the hardware queue: At any point in time, the number of data elements in the hardware queue is less than or equal to W_h, where W_h is some constant of type natural number. The auxiliary predicate Bnd_Hwm is formally defined as follows.

```
┌─ Bnd_Hwm ──────────────────────────────────────────────
│
│  $a, b \in G_{Dlt}{}^{\infty}$;  $c, d \in D_{Dlt}{}^{\infty}$;  $t \in \mathbb{N}$
│ ────────────────────────────────────────
│
│  $\forall j \in \mathbb{N}: \#D\,\text{Ⓢ}\,(a{\downarrow}_j) + \#D\,\text{Ⓢ}\,(b{\downarrow}_j) - [\#D\,\text{Ⓢ}\,(c{\downarrow}_j) + \#D\,\text{Ⓢ}\,(d{\downarrow}_j)] \le t$
│
└─────────────────────────────────────────────────────────
```

Interface Component The interface component communicates time-synchronously on the channels x and y. However, since the communication on the channels s and r is asynchronous, it cannot be specified in the time-synchronous format. As will be clear when we define specifications semantically in Sect. 4.2, time-synchronous communication cannot be captured in the time-independent format; this means that the time-dependent format is required.

The interface component is specified as follows.

```
══ INTF ══════════════════════════════════════ time_dependent ══
   in    $x : G_{Dlt}$;  $s : D$
   out   $y : D_{Dlt}$;  $r : G$
 ──────────────────────────────────────────────────────────────
   asm   $Time\_Synch(x) \wedge Req\_Ok(x)$
 - - - - - - - - - - - - - - - - - - - - - - - - - - - - - - - -
   com   $Eq(x, r, G) \wedge Time\_Synch(y) \wedge Eq(s, y, D)$
 ────────────────────────────────────────────────────────────────
```

The keyword in the upper right corner specifies that INTF is time-dependent. In that case, the channel identifiers in the body represent timed infinite streams.

The first conjunct of the assumption restricts the input on the channel x to be time-synchronous; this is expressed by an auxiliary predicate defined formally as follows.

```
┌─ Time_Synch ────────────────────────────────────────────
│
│  $a \in M^{\infty}$
│ ──────────────
│
│  $\forall j \in \mathbb{N}: \#M\,\text{Ⓢ}\,(a{\downarrow}_j) = j$
│
└─────────────────────────────────────────────────────────
```

Due to this assumption, the input frequency on x is bounded — a fact which may simplify the implementation of the specification.

The task of the interface component is to convert the time-synchronous stream x into an ordinary timed stream r and to perform the opposite conversion with respect to s and y. This conversion can, of course, introduce additional delays. The second conjunct of the commitment makes sure that y is time-synchronous; the first and third conjunct employ an auxiliary predicate Eq to describe what it means to forward correctly. It is defined formally as follows.

$$
\begin{array}{|l|}
\hline
\text{Eq} \\
\hline
a, b \in M^{\infty};\ A \in \mathbb{P}(M) \\
\hline
A \circledS a = A \circledS b \\
\hline
\end{array}
$$

Thus, *Eq* requires that the streams a and b are identical when projected on the set of messages A. For any set S, $\mathbb{P}(S)$ yields the set $\{T \mid T \subseteq S\}$.

Software Queue The specification of the software queue is expressed in terms of FIFO and substitution of channel identifiers:

$$\text{SWQ} \equiv \text{FIFO}[u \mapsto r, v \mapsto s]$$

The interpretation is as follows: The specification SWQ is equal to the specification obtained from FIFO by replacing its name by SWQ, the channel identifier u by r and the channel identifier v by s.

Composite Specification The three specifications HWQ, INTF and SWQ can be composed into a composite specification describing the network illustrated by Fig. 1 as follows.

$$
\begin{array}{|l l|}
\hline
\text{FIFO\_NET} \\
\hline
\text{in} & i : G_{Dlt} \\
\text{out} & o : D_{Dlt} \\
\text{loc} & x : G_{Dlt};\ r : G;\ y : D_{Dlt};\ s : D \\
\hline
(o, x) := \text{HWQ}(i, y) \quad (y, r) := \text{INTF}(x, s) \quad (s) := \text{SWQ}(r) \\
\hline
\end{array}
$$

The keyword loc distinguishes the declarations of the four local channels from the declarations of the external input and output channels. The body consists of the three component specifications introduced above represented as nondeterministic assignments with the output channels to the left and the input channels to the right. We require that the sub-specifications of a composite specification have disjoint sets of output identifiers. The semantics of composite specifications is defined formally in Sect. 4.3.

Both elementary and composite specifications are required to have disjoint sets of external input and output identifiers. In the composite case, the local channel identifiers must be different from the external channel identifiers. A composite specification is time-dependent, time-independent or time-synchronous depending on whether its elementary specifications are all time-dependent, time-independent or time-synchronous, respectively. Any other composite specification is *mixed*.

4 Refinement

The composite specification FIFO_NET is a conditional refinement of the elementary specification FIFO$_{TS}$, and FIFO$_{TS}$ is a conditional refinement of the elementary specification FIFO. In this section we argue the correctness of this claim by mathematical means. For this purpose, we first describe a schematic translation of any specification into the time-dependent format; then we define the semantics of elementary and composite time-dependent specifications in a more mathematical manner and introduce two concepts of conditional refinement.

4.1 Schematic Translation into Time-Dependent Format

The time-independent and time-synchronous formats can be understood as syntactic sugar for the time-dependent format. In fact, any specification written in the time-independent or the time-synchronous format can be schematically translated into a by definition semantically equivalent time-dependent specification. For any time-independent elementary specification S, let $\mathbb{TD}(S)$ denote the time-dependent specification obtained from S by replacing the keyword time_independent by time_dependent and any occurrence of any channel identifier c in the body of S by $\overline{c}$. $\mathbb{TD}(S)$ captures the meaning of the time-independent specification S is a time-dependent setting.

Any elementary time-synchronous specification S can be translated into a by definition semantically equivalent time-dependent specification $\mathbb{TD}(S)$ by performing exactly the same modifications as in the time-independent case and, in addition, extending the assumption with the conjunct $Time\_Synch(i)$ for each input channel i, and the commitment with the conjunct $Time\_Synch(o)$ for each output channel o.

For any time-dependent elementary specification, we define $\mathbb{TD}(S) \equiv S$. If S is composite then $\mathbb{TD}(S)$ is equal to the result of applying $\mathbb{TD}$ to its component specifications.

For any elementary time-dependent specification S, by I_S, O_S, A_S and C_S we denote the set of typed input streams, the set of typed output streams, the assumption and the commitment of $\mathbb{TD}(S)$, respectively; we say that (I_S, O_S) is the *external interface* of S. If S is a composite specification we use I_S, O_S, L_S to denote the set of typed input, output and local streams of $\mathbb{TD}(S)$, respectively. For example, with respect to FIFO_NET of Sect. 3.3, we have

$$I_{\text{FIFO\_NET}} = \{i \in G_{Dlt}{}^\infty\}$$

$$O_{\text{FIFO\_NET}} = \{o \in D_{Dlt}{}^\infty\}$$

$$L_{\text{FIFO\_NET}} = \{x \in G_{Dlt}{}^\infty, r \in G^\infty, y \in D_{Dlt}{}^\infty, s \in D^\infty\}$$

Let V be a set of typed streams $\{v_1 \in T_1^\infty, \ldots, v_n \in T_n^\infty\}$ and P a formula. We define

$$\forall V : P \equiv \forall v_1 \in T_1^\infty; \ldots; v_n \in T_n^\infty : P$$

$$\exists V : P \equiv \exists v_1 \in T_1^\infty; \ldots; v_n \in T_n^\infty : P$$

4.2 Semantics of Elementary Time-Dependent Specifications

As already explained, there is a schematic translation of any time-independent or time-synchronous specification into the time-dependent format.

To capture the semantics of elementary time-dependent specifications, we introduce some helpful notational conventions. Let P be a formula whose free variables are among and typed in accordance with

$$V \equiv \{v_1 \in T_1^\infty, \ldots, v_n \in T_n^\infty\}$$

Hence, P is basically a predicate on timed infinite streams. By $P\!\downarrow_j$ we characterise the "prefix of P at time j". $P\!\downarrow_j$ is a formula whose free variables are among and typed in accordance with V. $P\!\downarrow_j$ holds if we can find extensions $v_1', \ldots, v_n'$ of $v_1\!\downarrow_j, \ldots, v_n\!\downarrow_j$ such that P' holds. Formally, for any $j \in \mathbb{N}_\infty$, we define $P\!\downarrow_j$ to denote the formula

$$\exists v_1' \in T_1^\infty; \ldots; v_n' \in T_n^\infty : v_1\!\downarrow_j \sqsubseteq v_1' \wedge \ldots \wedge v_n\!\downarrow_j \sqsubseteq v_n' \wedge P'$$

where P' denotes the result of replacing each occurrence of v_j in P by v_j'. Note that $P\!\downarrow_\infty = P$. $P\!\downarrow_\infty$ has been introduced for the sake of convenience: It allows certain formulas, like the one below characterising the denotation of a specification, to be formulated more concisely. On some occasions we also need the prefix of P at time j with respect to a subset of free variables $A \subseteq V$; we define $P\!\downarrow_{A:j}$ to be equal to $P\!\downarrow_j$ if the free variables $V \setminus A$ are interpreted as constants.

The *denotation* $[\![\, S \,]\!]$ of an elementary time-dependent specification S is defined by the formula:

$$\forall j \in \mathbb{N}_\infty : A_S\!\downarrow_j \Rightarrow C_S\!\downarrow_{I_S:j}\!\downarrow_{O_S:j+1}$$

Informally, S requires that:

partial input $(j < \infty)$: The output is in accordance with the commitment C_S until time $j + 1$ if the input is in accordance with the assumption A_S until time j;

complete input $(j = \infty)$: The output is always in accordance with the commitment C_S if the input is always in accordance with the assumption A_S. Note that

$$(A_S\!\downarrow_\infty \Rightarrow C_S\!\downarrow_{I_S:\infty}\!\downarrow_{O_S:\infty+1}) \Leftrightarrow (A_S \Rightarrow C_S)$$

This one-unit-longer semantics, inspired by [1], requires a valid implementation to satisfy the commitment at least one time unit longer than the environment satisfies the assumption. This is basically a causality requirement: It disallows "implementations" that falsify the commitment because they "know" that the environment will falsify the assumption at some future point in time. Since no real implementation can predict the behaviour of the environment in this sense, we do not eliminate real implementations. Note that the assumption may refer to the output identifiers; this is often necessary to express the required assumptions about the input history (see HWQ in Sect. 3.3).

4.3 Semantics of Composite Time-Dependent Specifications

The denotation of a composite specification is defined in terms of the denotations of its component specifications. Let S be a composite specification whose body consists of m specifications

$$S_1, \ldots, S_m$$

Its denotation $[\![S]\!]$ is characterised by the formula

$$\exists L_S : [\![S_1]\!] \wedge \ldots \wedge [\![S_m]\!]$$

As explained in Sect. 4.1, L_S is the set of typed local streams in $\mathbb{TD}(S)$. To simplify the formal manipulation of composite specifications, we define $S_1 \otimes \ldots \otimes S_m$ to denote the composite specification S whose set of typed input, output and local streams are defined by

$$I_S \equiv (\cup_{j=1}^{m} I_{S_j}) \setminus (\cup_{j=1}^{m} O_{S_j})$$

$$O_S \equiv (\cup_{j=1}^{m} O_{S_j}) \setminus (\cup_{j=1}^{m} I_{S_j})$$

$$L_S \equiv (\cup_{j=1}^{m} I_{S_j}) \cap (\cup_{j=1}^{m} O_{S_j})$$

and whose body consists of the m specifications $S_1, .., S_m$ (represented in the form of nondeterministic assignments). For instance, FIFO_NET of Sect. 3.3 is equal to $\text{HWQ} \otimes \text{INTF} \otimes \text{SWQ}$.

It can be shown (see [6]) that if the component specifications are all realizable by functions that are contractive with respect to the Baire metric then the composite specification is also realizable with respect to such a function. Hence, when specifications are all realizable in this sense then there is at least one fixpoint when they are composed.

4.4 Two Concepts of Conditional Refinement

Consider two specifications S_1 and S_2, and a formula B whose free variables are all among (and typed in accordance with) $I_{S_2} \cup O_{S_2}$.

The specification S_2 is a *behavioural refinement* of the specification S_1 with respect to the *condition B*, written[1]

$$S_1 \leadsto_B S_2$$

if

$$I_{S_1} = I_{S_2}, \qquad O_{S_1} = O_{S_2}, \qquad \forall I_{S_1}; \, O_{S_1} : B \wedge [\![\, S_2 \,]\!] \Rightarrow [\![\, S_1 \,]\!]$$

Behavioural refinement allows us to make additional assumptions about the environment since we consider only those input histories that satisfy the condition; moreover, it allows us to reduce under-specification since we only require that any input/output-history of S_2 is also an input/output-history of S_1, and not the other way around.

That the external interfaces of the two specifications are required to be the same is often inconvenient. We therefore also introduce a more general concept that characterises conditional refinement with respect to an interface translation (see Fig. 2). Assume that U and D are specifications such that

$$(I_{S_2} \setminus I_{S_1}) = I_U, \quad (I_{S_1} \setminus I_{S_2}) = O_U, \quad (O_{S_1} \setminus O_{S_2}) = I_D, \quad (O_{S_2} \setminus O_{S_1}) = O_D$$

The specification S_2 is an *interface refinement* of the specification S_1 with respect to the condition B, the *upwards relation U* and the *downwards relation D*, written

$$S_1 \overset{(U,D)}{\leadsto}_B S_2$$

if

$$U \otimes S_1 \otimes D \leadsto_B S_2$$

U translates input streams of S_2 to input streams of S_1; D translates output streams of S_1 to output streams of S_2 (in both cases, ignoring streams with identical names). Both the upwards and the downwards relations are defined as specifications, but these specifications are not to be implemented. Their task is to record design decisions with respect to the external interface.

Let DS (for dummy specification) represent the specification whose external interface is empty $(\{\}, \{\})$. We may then define behavioural refinement in terms of interface refinement as follows

$$S_1 \leadsto_B S_2 \equiv S_1 \overset{(\mathrm{DS},\mathrm{DS})}{\leadsto}_B S_2$$

We define the following short-hands

$$S_1 \leadsto S_2 \equiv S_1 \leadsto_{\mathrm{true}} S_2, \qquad S_1 \overset{(U,D)}{\leadsto} S_2 \equiv S_1 \overset{(U,D)}{\leadsto}_{\mathrm{true}} S_2$$

---

[1] In the same way as we distinguish between three formats for elementary specifications, we could also distinguish between three formats for conditions. $[\![\ ]\!]$ could then be overloaded to conditions in the obvious manner. However, to keep things simple, we view any condition as a formula whose free variables represent timed infinite streams.

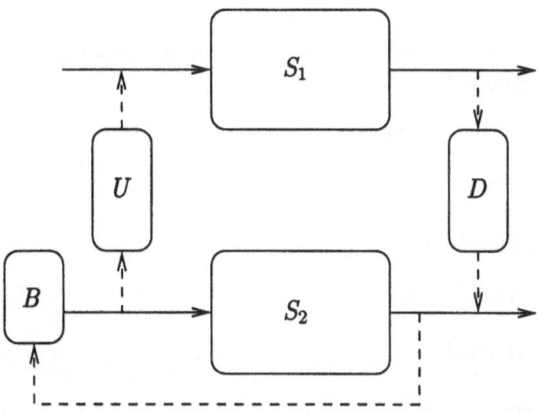

Fig. 2. Interface Refinement

Behavioural refinement is "transitive" in the following sense

$$S_1 \leadsto_{B_1} S_2 \wedge S_2 \leadsto_{B_2} S_3 \Rightarrow S_1 \leadsto_{B_1 \wedge B_2} S_3$$

Interface refinement satisfies a similar property (see App. A).

4.5 Correctness of the FIFO Decomposition

We first argue that $FIFO_{TS}$ is an interface refinement of FIFO; thereafter, that FIFO_NET is a behavioural refinement of $FIFO_{TS}$. This allows us to deduce that FIFO_NET is an interface refinement of FIFO. We base our argumentation on deduction rules formulated in App. A and proved sound in App. B.

Since the external interfaces of FIFO and $FIFO_{TS}$ are different, behavioural refinement is not sufficient; it is not just a question of renaming channels, we also have to translate time-synchronous streams with Dlt elements into streams without. The upwards and downwards relations are formally specified as follows.

$=U_{FIFO}=$		time_dependent $=$
in	$i : G_{Dlt}$	
out	$u : G$	
com	$u = (G \cup \{\sqrt{}\}) \circledS i$	

$=D_{FIFO}=$		time_dependent $=$
in	$v : D$	
out	$o : D_{Dlt}$	
com	$v = (D \cup \{\sqrt{}\}) \circledS o$	

Since in this particular case there are no assumptions to be imposed, the assumptions have been left out. It follows straightforwardly by the definition of behavioural refinement that

$$\text{FIFO} \overset{(U_{\text{FIFO}}, D_{\text{FIFO}})}{\leadsto}_{B_{\text{FIFO}}} \text{FIFO}_{\text{TS}} \tag{1}$$

where

$$B_{\text{FIFO}} \equiv Time\_Synch(i)$$

The next step is to show that

$$\text{FIFO}_{\text{TS}} \leadsto \text{FIFO\_NET} \tag{2}$$

(2) is equivalent to

$$\text{FIFO}_{\text{TS}} \leadsto \text{HWQ} \otimes \text{INTF} \otimes \text{SWQ} \tag{3}$$

Let

$$\text{FIFO}'_{\text{TS}} \equiv \text{FIFO}_{\text{TS}}[i \mapsto x, o \mapsto y]$$

Since $\leadsto$ is reflexive, (2) follows by the transitivity and modularity rules (see App. A.1, A.2) if we can show that

$$\text{FIFO}_{\text{TS}} \leadsto \text{HWQ} \otimes \text{FIFO}'_{\text{TS}} \tag{4}$$

$$\text{FIFO}'_{\text{TS}} \leadsto \text{INTF} \otimes \text{SWQ} \tag{5}$$

Both (4) and (5) follow by the decomposition rule (see App. A.3). (1), (2) and the transitivity rule give

$$\text{FIFO} \overset{(U_{\text{FIFO}}, D_{\text{FIFO}})}{\leadsto}_{B_{\text{FIFO}}} \text{FIFO\_NET} \tag{6}$$

Thus, FIFO_NET is a conditional interface refinement of FIFO.

5 Imposing Additional Boundedness Constraints

The composite specification FIFO_NET does not impose constraints on the response time of the components: Replies can be issued after an unbounded delay. Moreover, the software queue was assumed to be unbounded. Since any computerised component has a bounded memory, this is not realistic. In fact, in FIFO_NET also the interface component is required to have an unbounded memory, since there is no upper bound on the message frequency for the channel s, and the communication on the channel y is time-synchronous. In this section, we show that the composite specification FIFO_NET can be refined into another composite specification FIFO_NET$_B$ in which response time constraints are imposed, and where additional environment assumptions make both the software queue and the interface component directly implementable. The response time constraints are informally described as follows:

- The hardware queue has a required delay of exactly T_h time units. Hence, it is required to reply to a request exactly T_h time units after the request is issued.
- The interface component has a required delay of not more than T_i time units when forwarding messages from the hardware queue to the software queue. Note that the delay can be less than T_i time units. Thus, the delay is not fixed as in the case of the hardware queue.
- The interface and the software queue together have a maximal delay of $T_s + 2 * T_i$ time units, where $*$ is the operator for multiplication. Any reply to a request made by the hardware queue is to be provided within this range of time. The software queue needs maximally T_s time units; the remaining $2 * T_i$ time units can be consumed by the interface.

T_h, T_i and T_s are all constants of type natural number. That the interface component and the software queue together have a maximal delay of $T_s + 2 * T_i$ time units does not mean that the interface component has a maximal delay of T_i time units when messages are forwarded from the software queue to the hardware queue. In fact, such a requirement would not be implementable. To see that, first note that the software queue may send an unbounded number of data elements within the same time unit. Assume, for example, that $T_i = 1$, and that the software queue sends three data elements in the nth time unit. Since the communication on y is time-synchronous, the interface component needs at least three time units to forward these messages along y thereby breaking the requirement that no data element should be delayed by more than one time unit. In fact, for the forwarding from the software queue to the hardware queue, the requirement below is sufficient:

- If at some point in time there are exactly e data elements that have been sent by the software queue, but not yet forwarded to the hardware queue, then the interface component will forward these data elements within the next $T_i + (e - 1)$ time units.

If the interface component satisfies this requirement then the hardware queue is guaranteed to receive a reply to each request within $T_s + 2 * T_i$ time units. To see that, first note that the communication on x is time-synchronous. Together with the timing constraints imposed on the communication along r and s this implies that if e messages are received within the same time unit on the channel s then not more than one of these, namely the first, can be received with the maximal delay of $T_i + T_s$ time units with respect to the corresponding request on x; the second cannot be delayed by more than $T_i + T_s - 1$ time units, and so on.

The constraint on the size of the internal memory is described informally as follows:

- The FIFO queue is not required to store more than W_f data elements, where W_f is a constant of type natural number. Since the hardware queue can store W_h data elements, this means that the software part does not have to store more than $W_f - W_h$ data elements. Obviously, it holds that

$$W_h < W_f$$

Since the communication along x is time-synchronous, and the interface component has a maximal delay of T_i time units, the software queue will never receive more than T_i requests within one time unit on the channel r. This means that $T_i * T_s$ is an upper-bound on the number of data elements that can be sent by the software queue along the channel s within one time-unit.

5.1 Hardware Queue

The hardware queue is once more specified in the time-synchronous format. The only modification to the external interface is that the output channel o is renamed to w. This renaming is necessary since we want to translate o into w with the help of a downwards relation, and we require specifications (and thereby downwards relations) to have disjoint sets of input and output identifiers.

$==$HWQ$_B$$========================$ time_synchronous $==$

in $i : G_{Dlt}; \; y : D_{Dlt}$

out $w : D_{Dlt}; \; x : G_{Dlt}$

---

asm $Req\_Ok(i) \wedge FIFO\_Beh(x, y)$

  $Bnd\_Rsp(x, y, T_s + 2 * T_i, \{Req\}, D) \wedge Bnd\_Qum(i, T_h, W_f)$

- -

com $Exact\_Rsp(i, w, T_h) \wedge Req\_Ok(x) \wedge Bnd\_Hwm(i, y, w, x, W_h)$

  $Bnd\_Qum(x, T_s + 2 * T_i, W_f - W_h)$

Throughout this paper: Line-breaks in assumptions and commitments represent logical conjunction. The two first conjuncts of the assumption have been inherited from HWQ; the same holds for the second and third conjunct of the commitment. Clearly, the hardware queue can only be required to fulfil its response time requirement as long as the two other components fulfil their response time requirements; the third conjunct of the assumption therefore requires the two environment components to reply to a request made by the hardware queue within $T_s + 2 * T_i$ time units. The auxiliary predicate Bnd_Rsp is formally defined as follows.

$\_Bnd\_Rsp\_$

$a, b \in M^\infty \cup M^{\underline{\infty}}; \; t \in \mathbb{N}; \; A, B \in \mathbb{P}(M)$

$\forall j \in \mathbb{N} : \#[A \circledS (a{\downarrow}_j)] \leq \#[B \circledS (b{\downarrow}_{j+t})]$

The fourth conjunct of the assumption makes sure that the FIFO queue is never required to store more than W_f data elements; the second parameter is needed since there is a delay of T_h time units between the transmission of a request and the output of the corresponding data element. The auxiliary predicate Bnd_Qum is formally defined as follows.

__ Bnd_Qum _____

$a \in M^\infty \cup M^{\underline{\infty}}; \ t, n \in \mathbb{N}$

$\forall j \in \mathbb{N} : \#[D \circledS (a{\downarrow}_{j+t})] - \#[\{Req\} \circledS (a{\downarrow}_j)] \leq n$

The fourth conjunct of the commitment formalises a similar requirement for the output along the channel x; note that this requirement is slightly stronger than it has to be since, for simplicity, we do not allow the hardware queue to exploit that the software part may reply in less than $T_s + 2 * T_i$ time units.

The first conjunct of the commitment represents both a strengthening and a weakening of the corresponding conjunct in HWQ. It employs an auxiliary predicate $Exact\_Rsp$ that is formally defined as follows.

__ $Exact\_Rsp$ _____

$a \in G_{Dlt}{}^\infty; \ b \in D_{Dlt}{}^\infty; \ t \in \mathbb{N}$

$\forall j \in \mathbb{N}_+ : a.j = Req \Rightarrow b.(j + t) = (D \circledS a).(\#[\{Req\} \circledS (a{\downarrow}_j)])$

$Exact\_Rsp$ is a strengthening of $FIFO\_Beh$ in the sense that the reply is output with a delay of exactly t time units: If the jth message of the input stream a is a request then the $(j+t)$th message of the output stream b is the nth data element received on a, where n is the number of requests among the j first elements of a. $Exact\_Rsp$ is a weakening of $FIFO\_Beh$ in the sense that for any j such that $a.j \neq Req$, nothing is said about b at time $j + t$ except that the message output is an element of D_{Dlt}.

Correctness of Refinement Step Since the timed hardware queue may output an arbitrary data element in any time unit $j + T_h$ for which $i.j \neq Req$, it follows that HWQ$_B$ is not a behavioural refinement of HWQ. However, we may find a downwards specification D$_{HWQ}$, such that

$$\text{HWQ} \overset{(\text{DS}, \text{D}_{\text{HWQ}})}{\underset{\text{B}_{\text{HWQ}}}{\leadsto}} \text{HWQ}_B \qquad (7)$$

where

$$\text{B}_{\text{HWQ}} \equiv Bnd\_Rsp(x, y, T_s + 2 * T_i, \{Req\}, D) \wedge Bnd\_Qum(i, T_h, W_f)$$

D$_{HWQ}$ can be defined as follows.

$$
\begin{array}{l}
\rule{0pt}{0pt}\!=\!\mathrm{D_{HWQ}}\!=\!\!\!=\!\!\!=\!\!\!=\!\!\!=\!\!\!=\!\!\!=\!\!\!=\!\!\!=\!\!\!=\!\!\!=\!\!\!=\!\!\!=\!\text{time\_synchronous}\!= \\
\end{array}
$$

in $o : D_{Dlt}$
out $w : D_{Dlt}$
com $\forall j \in \mathbb{N} : o.j \neq Dlt \Rightarrow w.j = o.j$

The correctness of (7) follows straightforwardly by the definition of interface refinement.

5.2   Interface Component

The interface component is once more specified in the time-dependent format.

$$=\mathrm{INTF_B}=\!\!\!=\!\!\!=\!\!\!=\!\!\!=\!\!\!=\!\!\!=\!\!\!=\!\!\!=\text{time\_dependent}=$$

in $x : G_{Dlt}$; $s : D$
out $y : D_{Dlt}$; $r : G$
asm $Time\_Synch(x) \wedge Req\_Ok(x) \wedge Bnd\_Frq(s, T_i * T_s)$
$Bnd\_Qum(x, T_s + 2 * T_i, W_f - W_h)$
com $Eq(x, r, G) \wedge Time\_Synch(y) \wedge Eq(s, y, D) \wedge Bnd\_Rsp(x, r, T_i, G, G)$
$Weak\_Rsp(s, y, T_i) \wedge Bnd\_Qum(r, T_s, W_f - W_h)$

The two first conjuncts of the assumption and the three first conjuncts of the commitment restate INTF. The third conjunct of the assumption imposes a bound on the number of data elements that can be received during one time unit on s (see Page 16). The auxiliary predicate Bnd_Frq is defined as follows.

Bnd_Frq
$a \in M^\infty$; $t \in \mathbb{N}$
$\forall j \in \mathbb{N} : (\#\overline{a\!\downarrow_{j+1}} - \#\overline{a\!\downarrow_j}) \leq t$

Constraints similar to the fourth conjunct of the assumption and the sixth conjunct of the commitment have already been discussed in connection with $\mathrm{HWQ_B}$. The fourth conjunct of the commitment requires that the conversion from x to r does not lead to a delay of more than T_i time units; the fifth imposes a weaker timing constraint on the communication in the other direction: If at some point in time there are exactly e data elements that have been sent on s but not yet forwarded along y, then the interface component will forward these e data elements within the next $T_i + (e - 1)$ time units.

the number of received data elements on the channel s is larger than the number of data elements sent on y, then at least one data element is forwarded along y within the next time unit (see explanation on Page 16). This requirement is formalised by the auxiliary predicate *Weak_Rsp* as follows.

$$
\boxed{
\begin{array}{l}
\text{\underline{\quad Weak\_Rsp\quad}} \\[4pt]
a, b \in M^\infty;\ t \in \mathbb{N} \\[6pt]
\hline
\\[-6pt]
\forall j, e \in \mathbb{N} : \# \overline{D \circledS a\!\downarrow_j} - \# \overline{D \circledS b\!\downarrow_j} = e \Rightarrow \# \overline{D \circledS b\!\downarrow_{j+t+(e-1)}} > \# \overline{D \circledS a\!\downarrow_j}
\end{array}
}
$$

Correctness of Refinement Step Since the only difference between INTF and INTF_B is that both the assumption and the commitment have additional constraints, it follows straightforwardly that

$$\text{INTF} \rightsquigarrow_{\text{B}_{\text{INTF}}} \text{INTF}_B \tag{8}$$

where

$$\text{B}_{\text{INTF}} \equiv Bnd\_Frq(s, T_i * T_s) \land Bnd\_Qum(x, T_s + 2 * T_i, W_f - W_h)$$

5.3 Software Queue

The software queue is specified in the time-dependent format as follows.

$$
\boxed{
\begin{array}{l}
\text{\text==SWQ}_B \text{\==========\quad time\_dependent \==} \\[4pt]
\text{in}\quad r : G \\
\text{out}\quad s : D \\[6pt]
\hline \\[-6pt]
\text{asm}\quad Req\_Ok(r) \land Bnd\_Qum(r, T_s, W_f - W_h) \land Bnd\_Frq(r, T_i) \\[6pt]
\text{- -} \\[2pt]
\text{com}\quad FIFO\_Beh(r, s) \land Bnd\_Rsp(r, s, T_s, \{Req\}, D) \land Bnd\_Frq(s, T_i * T_s)
\end{array}
}
$$

SWQ_B differs from SWQ in that both the assumption and the commitment have additional conjuncts. The assumption has been strengthened to make sure that the software queue is never required to store more than $W_f - W_h$ data elements at the same point in time and never receives more than T_i messages within the same time unit. The additional conjuncts of the commitment require that the software queue replies to requests within T_s time units, and never sends more than $T_i * T_s$ messages along s within the same time unit.

Correctness of Refinement Step Since SWQ_B differs from SWQ only in that the assumption and the commitment have additional conjuncts, it follows trivially that

$$\text{SWQ} \rightsquigarrow_{\text{B}_\text{SWQ}} \text{SWQ}_\text{B} \tag{9}$$

where

$$\text{B}_\text{SWQ} \equiv Bnd\_Qum(r, T_s, W_f - W_h) \wedge Bnd\_Frq(r, T_i)$$

5.4 Composite Specification

The three elementary specifications presented above can be composed into a new composite specification as follows.

FIFO_NET$_\text{B}$
---
in $i : G_{Dlt}$

out $w : D_{Dlt}$

loc $x : G_{Dlt};\ r : G;\ y : D_{Dlt};\ s : D$

$(w, x) := \text{HWQ}_\text{B}(i, y)\quad (y, r) := \text{INTF}_\text{B}(x, s)\quad (s) := \text{SWQ}_\text{B}(r)$

Correctness of Refinement Step It must be shown that

$$\text{FIFO} \overset{(\text{U}_\text{FIFO}, \text{D}_\text{FIFO} \otimes \text{D}_\text{HWQ})}{\rightsquigarrow}_{\text{B}_\text{FIFO} \wedge \text{B}_\text{FIFO}'}\ \text{FIFO\_NET}_\text{B} \tag{10}$$

where

$$\text{B}_\text{FIFO}' \equiv Bnd\_Qum(i, T_h, W_f)$$

By (6) and the transitivity rule it is enough to show that

$$\text{FIFO\_NET} \overset{(\text{DS}, \text{D}_\text{HWQ})}{\rightsquigarrow}_{\text{B}_\text{FIFO}'}\ \text{FIFO\_NET}_\text{B} \tag{11}$$

(11) follows by the modularity rule (see App. A.2).

6 Conclusions

This paper builds on earlier research, both by us and others: In particular, the notion of interface refinement is inspired by [3]; the notion of conditional refinement is investigated in [13]; similar concepts have been proposed by others (see for example [1]); the one-unit-longer semantics is adapted from [1]; the particular form of decomposition rule is discussed in [12]; the specification style has been taken from [4].

Specification languages based on the assumption/commitment paradigm have a long tradition. In fact, this style of specification was introduced with Hoare-logic [8]. The pre-condition of Hoare-logic can be thought of as an assumption about the initial state; the post-condition characterises a commitment any correct implementation must fulfil whenever the initial state satisfies the pre-condition. Well-known methods like VDM [10] and Z [11] developed from Hoare-logic. VDM employs the pre/post-style. In Z the pre-condition is stated implicitly and must be calculated. Together with the more recent B method [2], VDM and Z can be seen as leading techniques for the formal development of sequential systems. In the case of concurrency and nonterminating systems the assumption/commitment style of Hoare-logic is not sufficiently expressive. The paradigm presented in this paper is directed towards systems in which interaction and communication are essential features. Our approach is related to [1]. In contrast to [1] we work in the setting of streams and asynchronous message passing.

Conditional refinement is a flexible notion for relating specifications written at different levels of abstraction. Conditional refinement supports the introduction of boundedness constraints in specifications based on unbounded resources; in particular:

- Replacing purely asynchronous communication by time-synchronous communication.
- Replacing unbounded buffers by bounded buffers.
- Imposing additional boundedness constraints on the size of internal memories.
- Imposing additional boundedness requirements on the timing of input messages.

Conditional refinement is a straightforward extension or variant of well-known concepts for refinement [9, 10]. Traditional refinement relations typically allow the assumption to be weakened and the commitment to be strengthened modulo some translation of data structure. Conditional refinement allows both the assumption and the commitment to be strengthened; however, any strengthening of the assumption is recorded in a separate condition.

There are several alternative, not necessarily equivalent, ways to define conditional refinement. For instance, the directions of the upwards and downwards relations could be turned around. In that case we get the following definition of interface refinement

$$S_1 \stackrel{(D,U)}{\rightsquigarrow}_B S_2 \equiv S_1 \rightsquigarrow_B D \otimes S_2 \otimes U$$

where B is a constraint on the external interface of S_1. Alternatively, by allowing B to refer to the external interfaces of both S_1 and S_2 we could formulate the upwards and downwards relations within B. Which alternative is best suited from a pragmatic point of view is debatable.

According to [5], hardware/software co-design is the simultaneous design of both hardware and software to implement a desired function or specification. The presented approach should be well-suited to support this kind of design:

- It allows the integration of purely asynchronous, hand-shake (see [13]) and time-synchronous communication in the same composite specification.
- It allows specifications based on asynchronous communication to be refined into specifications based on time-synchronous communication, and vice-versa.

7 Acknowledgements

The authors have benefited from discussions with Manfred Broy on this and related topics.

References

1. M. Abadi and L. Lamport. Conjoining specifications. *ACM Transactions on Programming Languages and Systems*, 17:507–533, 1995.
2. J.R. Abrial. *The B Book: Assigning Programs to Meaning*. Cambridge University Press, 1996.
3. M. Broy. Compositional refinement of interactive systems. Technical Report 89, Digital, SRC, Palo Alto, 1992.
4. M. Broy and K. Stølen. Focus on system development. Book manuscript, June 1998.
5. K. Buchenrieder, editor. *Third International Workshop on Hardware/Software Codesign*. IEEE Computer Society Press, 1994.
6. R. Grosu and K. Stølen. A model for mobile point-to-point data-flow networks without channel sharing. In *Proc. AMAST'96, Lecture Notes in Computer Science 1101*, pages 504–519, 1996.
7. O. Haugen. *Practitioners' Verification of SDL Systems*. PhD thesis, University of Oslo, 1997.
8. C. A. R. Hoare. An axiomatic basis for computer programming. *Communications of the ACM*, 12:576–583, 1969.
9. C. A. R. Hoare. Proof of correctness of data representations. *Acta Informatica*, 1:271–282, 1972.
10. C. B. Jones. *Systematic Software Development Using VDM*. Prentice-Hall, 1986.
11. J. M. Spivey. *Understanding Z, A Specification Language and its Formal Semantics*. Volume 3 of *Cambridge Tracts in Theoretical Computer Science*. Cambridge University Press, 1988.
12. K. Stølen. Assumption/commitment rules for data-flow networks — with an emphasis on completeness. In *Proc. ESOP'96, Lecture Notes in Computer Science 1058*, pages 356–372, 1996.
13. K. Stølen. Refinement principles supporting the transition from asynchronous to synchronous communication. *Science of Computer Programming*, 26:255–272, 1996.
14. K. Stølen and P. Mohn. Measuring the effect of formalization. In *Proc. SAM'98*, Informatik Bericht Nr. 104, pages 183–190. Humboldt-Universität zu Berlin, 1998.

A Three Rules

In this paper we use several rules. Some of these rules are very simple and therefore not stated explicitly. For example, to prove (1) of Sect. 4.5 we need a rule capturing the definition of behavioural refinement. Three less trivial rules are formulated below; in App. B we prove their soundness. Any free variable is universally quantified over infinite timed streams of messages typed in accordance with the corresponding channel declaration.

A.1 Transitivity Rule

$$B \wedge [\, U_2 \,] \wedge [\, D_2 \,] \Rightarrow B_1$$

$$B \Rightarrow B_2$$

$$[\, U_1 \,] \wedge [\, U_2 \,] \Rightarrow [\, U \,]$$

$$[\, D_1 \,] \wedge [\, D_2 \,] \Rightarrow [\, D \,]$$

$$S_1 \overset{(U_1,D_1)}{\rightsquigarrow}_{B_1} S_2$$

$$S_2 \overset{(U_2,D_2)}{\rightsquigarrow}_{B_2} S_3$$

$$S_1 \overset{(U,D)}{\rightsquigarrow}_{B} S_3$$

Some intuition:

- Premises 1 and 2 make sure that the overall condition B is stronger than B_1 and B_2.
- Premise 3 makes sure that the upwards relation obtained by connecting U_2 and U_1 is allowed by U.
- Premise 4 makes sure that the downwards relation obtained by connecting D_1 and D_2 is allowed by D.
- Premises 5 and 6 are illustrated by Fig. 3.

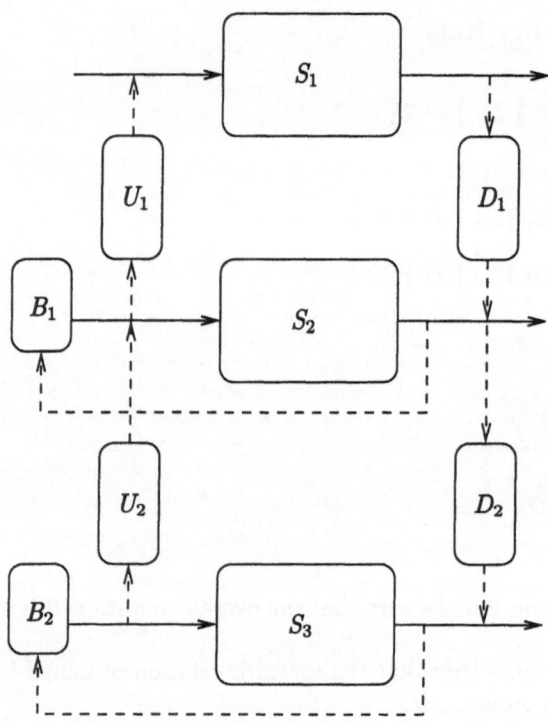

Fig. 3. Illustration of the Fifth and Sixth Premise in the Transitivity Rule

A.2 Modularity Rule

$$\wedge_{i=1}^{n}(B_i \Rightarrow !O_{U_i} : [\![U_i]\!])$$

$$\exists I_{\otimes_{i=1}^{n}S_i};\ L_{\otimes_{i=1}^{n}S_i};\ O_{\otimes_{i=1}^{n}S_i} : \wedge_{i=1}^{n}([\![U_i]\!] \wedge [\![D_i]\!])$$

$$(\wedge_{i=1}^{n}[\![U_i]\!]) \Rightarrow [\![U]\!]$$

$$(\wedge_{i=1}^{n}[\![D_i]\!]) \Rightarrow [\![D]\!]$$

$$B \wedge (\wedge_{i=1}^{n}[\![S_i']\!]) \Rightarrow \wedge_{i=1}^{n} B_i$$

$$\wedge_{i=1}^{n}(S_i \overset{(U_i,D_i)}{\rightsquigarrow}_{B_i} S_i')$$

$$\otimes_{i=1}^{n} S_i \overset{(U,D)}{\rightsquigarrow}_{B} \otimes_{i=1}^{n} S_i'$$

$!V : P$ holds if there is a unique V such that P holds. Some intuition:

- Premise 1 makes sure that for each concrete input history such that B_i holds, the upwards relation U_i allows exactly one abstract input history. Hence, each concrete input history that satisfies the condition is related to exactly one abstract input history, but the same abstract input history can be related to several concrete input histories.
- Premise 2 makes sure that the conjunction of the downwards and upwards relations is consistent.
- Premise 3 makes sure that the upwards relation described by the conjunction of the n upwards relations U_i is allowed by the overall upwards relation U.
- Premise 4 makes sure that the upwards relation described by the conjunction of the n downwards relations D_i is allowed by the overall downwards relation D.
- Premise 5 makes sure that the assumptions made by the n B_i's are fulfilled by the composite specification consisting of the n specifications S_i' when the input from the overall environment satisfies B.

A.3 Decomposition Rule

$$A \Rightarrow A_1\!\downarrow_0 \wedge A_2\!\downarrow_0$$

$$\forall j \in \mathbb{N} : A \wedge C_1\!\downarrow_{I_1:j}\!\downarrow_{O_1:j+1} \wedge C_2\!\downarrow_{I_2:j}\!\downarrow_{O_2:j+1} \Rightarrow A_1\!\downarrow_{j+1} \wedge A_2\!\downarrow_{j+1}$$

$$A \wedge \langle C_1 \rangle \wedge \langle C_2 \rangle \Rightarrow (A_1 \wedge (C_1 \Rightarrow A_2)) \vee (A_2 \wedge (C_2 \Rightarrow A_1))$$

$$\forall j \in \mathbb{N}_\infty : A\!\downarrow_j \wedge C_1\!\downarrow_{I_1:j}\!\downarrow_{O_1:j+1} \wedge C_2\!\downarrow_{I_2:j}\!\downarrow_{O_2:j+1} \Rightarrow C\!\downarrow_{I:j}\!\downarrow_{O:j+1}$$

$$S \rightsquigarrow S_1 \otimes S_2$$

$\langle P \rangle$ denotes the upwards closure of P; formally $\langle P \rangle \equiv \forall j \in \mathbb{N} : P \downarrow_j$. S is a specification with assumption A, commitment C, and external interface (I, O). As illustrated by Fig. 4, the relationship between S_1 / S_2 and

$$A_1, C_1, (I_1, O_1) / A_2, C_2, (I_2, O_2)$$

is defined accordingly. As explained in detail in App. B.3, the correctness of the decomposition rule follows by induction. Some intuition:

- Premise 1 makes sure that the component assumptions A_1 and A_2 hold at time 0.
- Premise 2 makes sure that the component assumptions A_1 and A_2 hold at time $j + 1$ if the component commitments C_1 and C_2 hold at time $j + 1$.
- Premise 3 is concerned with liveness in the assumptions. This premise is not required if both A_1 and A_2 are upwards closed.
- Premise 4 makes sure that the overall commitment C holds at time $j + 1$ if the component commitments C_1 and C_2 hold at time $j + 1$.

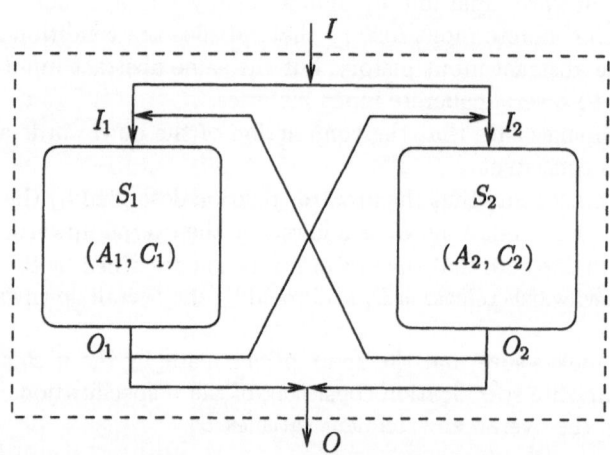

Fig. 4. Network Represented by $S_1 \otimes S_2$

B Soundness of Rules

In this appendix we prove that the three rules formulated in App. A are sound. Any free variable is universally quantified over infinite timed streams of messages typed in accordance with the corresponding channel declaration.

B.1 Transitivity Rule

Given

$$B \wedge [\, U_2 \,] \wedge [\, D_2 \,] \Rightarrow B_1 \tag{12}$$

$$B \Rightarrow B_2 \tag{13}$$

$$[\, U_1 \,] \wedge [\, U_2 \,] \Rightarrow [\, U \,] \tag{14}$$

$$[\, D_1 \,] \wedge [\, D_2 \,] \Rightarrow [\, D \,] \tag{15}$$

$$S_1 \overset{(U_1, D_1)}{\rightsquigarrow}_{B_1} S_2 \tag{16}$$

$$S_2 \overset{(U_2, D_2)}{\rightsquigarrow}_{B_2} S_3 \tag{17}$$

It must be shown that

$$S_1 \overset{(U, D)}{\rightsquigarrow}_B S_3 \tag{18}$$

(18) is equivalent to

$$B \wedge [\, S_3 \,] \Rightarrow [\, U \otimes S_1 \otimes D \,] \tag{19}$$

To prove (19), assume there are I_{S_3}, O_{S_3} such that

$$B \tag{20}$$

$$[\, S_3 \,] \tag{21}$$

(13), (20) imply

$$B_2 \tag{22}$$

(17), (21), (22) imply

$$[\, U_2 \otimes S_2 \otimes D_2 \,] \tag{23}$$

(23) implies there are O_{U_2}, I_{D_2} such that

$$[\, U_2 \,] \tag{24}$$

$$[\, S_2 \,] \tag{25}$$

$$[\, D_2 \,] \tag{26}$$

(12), (20), (24), (26) imply

$$B_1 \tag{27}$$

(16), (25), (27) imply

$$[\, U_1 \otimes S_1 \otimes D_1 \,] \tag{28}$$

(28) implies there are O_{U_1}, I_{D_1} such that

$$[\ U_1 \ ] \tag{29}$$

$$[\ S_1 \ ] \tag{30}$$

$$[\ D_1 \ ] \tag{31}$$

(14), (24), (29) imply

$$[\ U \ ] \tag{32}$$

(15), (26), (31) imply

$$[\ D \ ] \tag{33}$$

(30), (32), (33) imply

$$[\ U \otimes S_1 \otimes D \ ] \tag{34}$$

The way (34) was deduced from (20), (21) implies (19).

B.2 Modularity Rule

Given

$$\wedge_{i=1}^{n}(B_i \Rightarrow !O_{U_i} : [\ U_i \ ]) \tag{35}$$

$$\exists I_{\otimes_{i=1}^{n} S_i}; \ L_{\otimes_{i=1}^{n} S_i}; \ O_{\otimes_{i=1}^{n} S_i} : \wedge_{i=1}^{n}([\ U_i \ ] \wedge [\ D_i \ ]) \tag{36}$$

$$(\wedge_{i=1}^{n}[\ U_i \ ]) \Rightarrow [\ U \ ] \tag{37}$$

$$(\wedge_{i=1}^{n}[\ D_i \ ]) \Rightarrow [\ D \ ] \tag{38}$$

$$B \wedge (\wedge_{i=1}^{n}[\ S_i' \ ]) \Rightarrow \wedge_{i=1}^{n} B_i \tag{39}$$

$$\wedge_{i=1}^{n}(S_i \overset{(U_i, D_i)}{\leadsto}_{B_i} S_i') \tag{40}$$

It must be shown that

$$\otimes_{i=1}^{n} S_i \overset{(U, D)}{\leadsto}_{B} \otimes_{i=1}^{n} S_i' \tag{41}$$

(41) follows if we can show that

$$B \wedge [\ \otimes_{i=1}^{n} S_i' \ ] \Rightarrow [\ U \otimes (\otimes_{i=1}^{n} S_i) \otimes D \ ] \tag{42}$$

To prove (42), assume there are $I_{\otimes_{i=1}^{n} S_i'}, L_{\otimes_{i=1}^{n} S_i'}, O_{\otimes_{i=1}^{n} S_i'}$ such that

$$B \tag{43}$$

$$\wedge_{i=1}^{n}[\ S_i' \ ] \tag{44}$$

(39), (43), (44) imply

$$\wedge_{i=1}^{n} B_i \tag{45}$$

(40), (44), (45) imply

$$\wedge_{i=1}^{n}[\ U_i \otimes S_i \otimes D_i\ ] \tag{46}$$

(46) implies

$$\wedge_{i=1}^{n} \exists O_{U_i}, I_{D_i} : [\ U_i\ ] \wedge [\ S_i\ ] \wedge [\ D_i\ ] \tag{47}$$

(35), (36), (47) imply there are $I_{\otimes_{i=1}^{n} S_i}, L_{\otimes_{i=1}^{n} S_i}, O_{\otimes_{i=1}^{n} S_i}$ such that

$$\wedge_{i=1}^{n}[\ U_i\ ] \tag{48}$$

$$\wedge_{i=1}^{n}[\ S_i\ ] \tag{49}$$

$$\wedge_{i=1}^{n}[\ D_i\ ] \tag{50}$$

(37), (38), (48), (50) imply

$$[\ U\ ] \tag{51}$$

$$[\ D\ ] \tag{52}$$

(49), (51), (52) imply

$$[\ U \otimes (\otimes_{i=1}^{n} S_i) \otimes D\ ] \tag{53}$$

The way (53) was deduced from (43), (44) implies (42).

B.3 Decomposition Rule

Given

$$A \Rightarrow A_1\!\downarrow_0 \wedge A_2\!\downarrow_0 \tag{54}$$

$$\forall j \in \mathbb{N} : A \wedge C_1\!\downarrow_{I_1:j}\!\downarrow_{O_1:j+1} \wedge C_2\!\downarrow_{I_2:j}\!\downarrow_{O_2:j+1} \Rightarrow A_1\!\downarrow_{j+1} \wedge A_2\!\downarrow_{j+1} \tag{55}$$

$$A \wedge \langle C_1 \rangle \wedge \langle C_2 \rangle \Rightarrow (A_1 \wedge (C_1 \Rightarrow A_2)) \vee (A_2 \wedge (C_2 \Rightarrow A_1)) \tag{56}$$

$$\forall j \in \mathbb{N}_\infty : A\!\downarrow_j \wedge C_1\!\downarrow_{I_1:j}\!\downarrow_{O_1:j+1} \wedge C_2\!\downarrow_{I_2:j}\!\downarrow_{O_2:j+1} \Rightarrow C\!\downarrow_{I:j}\!\downarrow_{O:j+1} \tag{57}$$

It must be shown that

$$S \rightsquigarrow S_1 \otimes S_2 \tag{58}$$

(58) is equivalent to

$$[\ S_1 \otimes S_2\ ] \Rightarrow [\ S\ ] \tag{59}$$

(59) is equivalent to

$$(\forall j \in \mathbb{N}_\infty : A_1\!\downarrow_j \Rightarrow C_1\!\downarrow_{I_1:j}\!\downarrow_{O_1:j+1}) \wedge$$

$$(\forall j \in \mathbb{N}_\infty : A_2\!\downarrow_j \Rightarrow C_2\!\downarrow_{I_2:j}\!\downarrow_{O_2:j+1})$$

$$\Rightarrow \tag{60}$$

$$(\forall j \in \mathbb{N}_\infty : A\!\downarrow_j \Rightarrow C\!\downarrow_{I:j}\!\downarrow_{O:j+1})$$

(60) is equivalent to

$$\forall j \in \mathbb{N}_\infty :$$

$$A\!\downarrow_j \wedge$$

$$(\forall j \in \mathbb{N}_\infty : A_1\!\downarrow_j \Rightarrow C_1\!\downarrow_{I_1:j}\!\downarrow_{O_1:j+1}) \wedge$$

$$(\forall j \in \mathbb{N}_\infty : A_2\!\downarrow_j \Rightarrow C_2\!\downarrow_{I_2:j}\!\downarrow_{O_2:j+1})$$

$$\Rightarrow \tag{61}$$

$$C\!\downarrow_{I:j}\!\downarrow_{O:j+1}$$

To prove (61), assume there are $I, L_{S_1 \otimes S_2}, O, l$ such that

$$A\!\downarrow_l \tag{62}$$

$$\forall j \in \mathbb{N}_\infty : A_1\!\downarrow_j \Rightarrow C_1\!\downarrow_{I_1:j}\!\downarrow_{O_1:j+1} \tag{63}$$

$$\forall j \in \mathbb{N}_\infty : A_2\!\downarrow_j \Rightarrow C_2\!\downarrow_{I_2:j}\!\downarrow_{O_2:j+1} \tag{64}$$

There are two cases to consider. Assume

$$l < \infty \tag{65}$$

(54), (55), (62), (63), (64) and induction on j imply

$$j \le l \Rightarrow A_1\!\downarrow_j \wedge A_2\!\downarrow_j \tag{66}$$

(63), (64), (66) imply

$$C_1\!\downarrow_{I_1:l}\!\downarrow_{O_1:l+1} \wedge C_2\!\downarrow_{I_2:l}\!\downarrow_{O_2:l+1} \tag{67}$$

(57), (62), (67) imply

$$C\!\downarrow_{I:l}\!\downarrow_{O:l+1} \tag{68}$$

The way (68) was deduced from (62), (63), (64) proves (61) for the case that (65) holds. Assume

$$l = \infty \tag{69}$$

By the same inductive argument as above

$$\langle C_1 \rangle \wedge \langle C_2 \rangle \tag{70}$$

(56), (62), (69), (70) imply

$$(A_1 \wedge (C_1 \Rightarrow A_2)) \vee (A_2 \wedge (C_2 \Rightarrow A_1)) \tag{71}$$

(63), (64), (71) imply

$$C_1 \wedge C_2 \tag{72}$$

(57), (62), (69), (72) imply

$$C \tag{73}$$

The way (73) was deduced from (62), (63), (64) proves (61) for the case that (69) holds.

Deductive Hardware Design: A Functional Approach*

Bernhard Möller

Institut für Informatik, D-86135 Augsburg, Germany

Abstract. The goal of deductive design is the systematic construction of a system implementation starting from its behavioural specification according to formal, provably correct rules. We use *Haskell* to formulate a functional model of directional, synchronous and deterministic systems with discrete time. The associated algebraic laws are then employed in deductive hardware design of basic combinational and sequential circuits as well as a brief account of pipelining. With this we tackle several of the IFIP WG 10.5 benchmark verification problems. Special emphasis is laid on parameterization and re-usability aspects.

1 Introduction

1.1 Deductive Design

The goal of deductive design is the systematic construction of a system implementation, starting from its behavioural specification, according to formal, provably correct rules. The main advantages are the following.

First, the resulting implementation is correct by construction. Moreover, implementations can be constructed in a modular way: in the first stage, the main emphasis lies on *correctness*, while in further stages transformations can be used to *increase efficiency*.

Second, the rules can be formulated schematically, independent of the particular application area; hence they are re-usable for wide classes of similar problems.

Third, being formal, the design process can be assisted by machine. This helps avoiding clerical errors and disallows "cheating" during the derivation. Moreover, a formal derivation also serves as a record of the design decisions that went into the construction of the implementation. It is an explanatory documentation and eases revision of the implementation upon modification of the system specification.

Note that we do not view deductive design as alternative to, but complementary to verification. In fact, usually transformational derivations will be interleaved with verification of lemmas needed on the way. Conversely, verification

---

* This research was partially sponsored by Esprit Working Group 8533 NADA - New Hardware Design Methods.

may benefit from incorporation of standard reduction strategies based on algebraic laws. Some authors even subsume verification approaches under deductive design (see eg. [15]).

There is a variety of approaches to deductive design in our narrower sense, eg. refinement calculus, program extraction from proofs and transformational programming. We shall follow the latter approach (see e.g. [7,33]) and use mainly equational reasoning, algebraic laws, structural induction and fixpoint induction for recursive definitions.

We exemplify deductive hardware design in the particular area of *directional*, *synchronous* and *deterministic* systems with *discrete time*. Directionality means that input and output are clearly distinguished. As for synchronicity we assume that our systems are clocked, in particular, that the clock period is long enough that all submodules stabilize their output within it.

The approach generalizes with varying degrees of complexity to adirectional systems, asynchrony, non-determinacy or continuous time. Adirectionality, as found eg. in buses, may be modeled better in a relational than in a functional setting, handshake communication may more adequately be treated by formal systems based on CCS, CSP or ACP as presented eg. in [2,23,22].

We show deductive design of basic combinational and sequential circuits, notably systolic ones, and give a brief transformational account of pipelining. Special emphasis is laid on parameterization and re-usability aspects.

1.2 The Framework

We model hardware functionally in *Haskell*. The reasons for this are the following.

First, functional languages support various views of streams directly, eg. through lazy lists or functions from time to data as first-class objects.

Second, polymorphism allows generic formulations and hence supports re-use.

Third, since all specifications are executable, direct prototyping is possible.

Fourth, functional languages are being considered for their suitability as bases of modern hardware description languages. Examples are — in historical order — Hydra [32], MHDL [34] (unfortunately abandoned), Lava [3,35], HAWK [9, 26,18] and SLDL [36] (which is still in the requirements definition phase). Many other approaches to hardware specification and verification also use higher-order concepts to good advantage (see e.g. [16]).

Finally, a transformation system ULTRA for the *Gofer* sublanguage of *Haskell* is being constructed at the University of Ulm [39]. It is an adaptation of the system CIP-S [6]. A prototype version of ULTRA has been used to formally check most of the laws and derivations in our paper (which originally were done with paper and pencil) by machine. While the overall derivations were found to be correct, a number of minor errors and missing side conditions were discovered. The set of transformation rules obtained in this way can be re-used for further derivations that now, of course, should take place directly on the system.

Of course, transformational derivation of circuits is not a new idea (see e.g. [19,21,11,12]). What we view as novel is the exploitation of the full power of Haskell for specifying circuits at a purely "mathematical" level that is far removed from that of concrete hardware. This leads to very simple and concise specifications. An approach that is close to this spirit is presented in [5], using, however, a purely mathematical language that is not directly executable.

At the same time, by taking a high-level algebraic approach we are able to keep the derivations from that level to the actual implementation level surprisingly short. This is partially due to the fact that the problems of wiring do enter into our derivations at a very late stage and hence do not clutter the essential steps.

By exploiting the polymorphism of *Haskell* we can use part of the algebra for a uniform treatment of combinational and sequential circuits. An essential subalgebra is network algebra as investigated eg. in [37].

The introduction of small but very effective sets of algebraic laws for special subproblem areas such as the treatment of delay and slowdown make the approach particularly streamlined. Some of these laws correspond to manipulations of layout graphs; whenever appropriate, we therefore perform the derivations at the graphical level to make them easier to grasp.

The approach has also been used quite successfully in teaching the essentials of hardware to first-year students (who, of course, had been exposed to the *Gofer* sublanguage of *Haskell* in the beginning of the year).

A brief review of the essential concepts of *Haskell* and a notational extension that are used in this paper can be found in the Appendix.

Part I: Combinational Circuits

2 A Model of Combinational Circuits

We start with the simple case of combinational circuits. While this avoids some of the complexity of dealing with streams, it already allows us to introduce a substantial part of the underlying algebra, which will be re-used for the stream case. Moreover, in an extended case study, we introduce the main ingredients of the transformational approach, viz. the unfold/fold strategy, generalization, parameterization, abstraction and re-use of designs. All this will reappear in the stream-based treatment of sequential circuits.

2.1 Functions as Modules

A combinational module will be modeled as a function taking a list of inputs to a list of outputs. This function reflects the behaviour at one clock tick. This mirrors the underlying assumption of synchrony: the complete list of inputs must be available before the output can be computed. Strictly speaking, this conflicts with the lazy semantics of *Haskell*; however, we shall employ such functions only in contexts where the difference between eager and lazy semantics does not matter.

Using lists of inputs and outputs has the advantage that the basic connection operators can be defined independent of the arities of the functions involved. The disadvantage is that we need uniform typing for all inputs/outputs, since *Haskell* does not allow heterogeneous lists.

So we assume some basic type a that is the direct sum of all data types involved, such as integers, Booleans, bytes etc. All our definitions will be polymorphic in that type a. Then a function f describing a module with m inputs and n outputs will have the type f :: Module with

```
type Module = [a] -> [a]
```

However, f will be defined only for input lists of length m and always produce output lists of length n. Assuming

```
[o1,...,on] = f [i1,...,im]
```

we represent such a module diagrammatically as

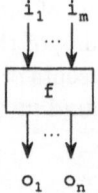

We now discuss briefly the role of functions as modules of a system. In a higher-order language such as *Haskell* there are two views of functions:

- as routines with a body expression that depends on the formal parameters, like in first-order languages;
- as "black boxes" which can be freely manipulated by higher-order functions (combinators).

The latter view is particularly adequate for functional hardware descriptions, since it allows the direct definition of various composition operations for hardware modules.

However, contrary to other approaches we do not reason purely at the combinator level, i.e. without referring to individual in/output values. While this has advantages in some situations, it can become quite tedious in others. So we prefer to have the possibility to switch.

The basis for showing equality of two expressions that yield functions as their values is the extensionality rule

$$f = g \text{ iff } fx = gx \text{ for all } x \ .$$

Many algebraic laws we use are equalities between functions, interpreted as extensional equalities.

Example 2.1. Function composition is defined in *Haskell* by

```
(f . g) x  =  f (g x)
```

with polymorphic combinator

```
(.) :: (b -> c) -> (a -> b) -> a -> c
```

A fundamental law is associativity of composition:

```
(f . g) . h  =  f . (g . h)
```

□

2.2 Modeling Connections

We shall employ two views of connections between modules:

- that of "rubber wires, represented by formal parameters or implicitly by plugging in subexpressions as operands;
- that of "rigid wires", represented by special routing functions which are inserted using basic composition combinators.

Contrary to other approaches (e.g. [19, 21]) we proceed in two stages:

- We start at the level of rubber wiring to get a first correct implementation.
- Then we (mechanically) get rid of formal parameters by combinator abstraction to obtain a version with rigid wiring.

This avoids introducing wiring combinators at too early a stage and carrying them through all the derivation in an often tedious manner.

In drawing diagrams we shall be liberal and use views in between rubber and rigid wiring. In particular, we shall use various directions for the input and output arrows. So input arrows may not only enter at the top but also from the right or from the left; an analogous remark holds for the output arrows.

Example 2.2. An operation we use in several examples below is that of *splicing* two modules together along one wire. This means that one output wire of the second module serves as an input to the first module. This can eg. be used for passing carries from one module to the next. It is modeled by

```
splice :: Int -> Module -> Module -> Module
```

defined as

```
splice m f g  (xs++[c]) =  f (take m xs ++ [u]) ++ us
    where (u:us) = g (drop m xs ++ [c])
```

Assume now

```
xs = [x1,...,xm,x(m+1),...,xn]
[u1,u2,...,up] = g [x(m+1),...,xn,c]
[v1,v2,...,vk] = f [x1,...,xm,u1]
```

Then we may depict `splice m f g xs` as

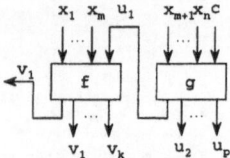

We straighten and move some wires to obtain the following form:

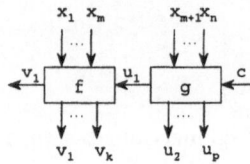

$\square$

Lemma 2.3. *Splicing is associative in the following sense:*

```
(f 'splice m' g) 'splice (m+k)' h =
    f 'splice m' (g 'splice k' h)
```

Moreover, the identity `id` *on singleton lists is left and right neutral w.r.t.* `splice`.

Associativity is essential in that it shows that the functional model adequately describes the graphical and layout views of hardware: there are no "parentheses" in circuits, and hence the mathematical model should not depend on parenthesization.

2.3 Wire Bundles

Often we need to deal with wire bundles. In the case of circuits for binary arithmetic operators it is usually assumed that the wires for the single bits of the two operands are interleaved (or *shuffled*) in the following fashion:

$$y_0 \quad y_1 \quad y_2 \qquad\qquad y_{n-3} \quad y_{n-3} \quad y_{n-3}$$
$$x_0 \quad x_1 \quad x_2 \quad \cdots \quad x_{n-3} \quad x_{n-2} \quad x_{n-1}$$

So the bits for one operand occur at even positions in the overall list of inputs, those for the other one at odd positions. To extract the corresponding sublists we use

```
evns xs = [ xs !! i | i <- [0..length xs -1], even i ]
```

$$x_0 \qquad x_1 \qquad x_2 \qquad \cdots \qquad x_{n-3} \quad x_{n-2} \quad x_{n-1}$$

```
odds xs  =  [ xs !! i | i <- [0..length xs -1], odd i ]
```

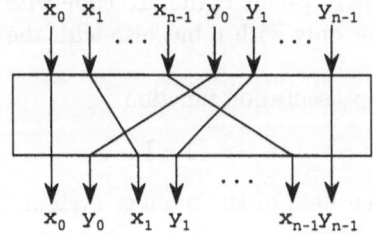

Recursive versions of these functions are

```
evns [] = []
evns (x:xs) = x : odds xs
odds [] = []
odds (x : xs)  = evns xs
```

The converse is **shuf** k which shuffles two lists of length k, say xs and ys, into one list of length 2*k.

Following our general principle that every module takes *one* list of inputs, we have to concatenate ys and zs into one list xs. Then shuf is specified by

```
(shuf n xs) !! (2*i)    =  xs !! i
(shuf n xs) !! (2*i+1)  =  xs !! (n+i)
```

for length xs == 2*n and i <- [0..n-1]. This is an implicit specification; the patterns on the left hand side are not legal *Haskell* patterns. However, the clauses of this specification will be used as algebraic laws in derivations. An explicit version is

```
shuf n xs
  | length xs == 2*n  =  ileave (take n xs) (drop n xs)

ileave [] [] = []
ileave (y : ys) (z : zs) = y : (z : ileave ys zs)
```

3 Numbers and Their Representation

We now briefly leave the field of circuits. As a preparation for the derivation of some basic arithmetic circuits we need some definitions concerning the representation of natural numbers w.r.t. a base p. To simplify matters we use the nonnegative part of the *Haskell* type Int for treating natural numbers; a different possibility would be the definition of a recursive data type

```
data Nat = Zero | Succ Nat
```

We avoid this, since it would necessitate a lengthy redefinition of all arithmetic operators.

To characterize p-adic digits we use the auxiliary predicate

```
below :: Int -> Int -> Bool
n 'below' m    =   0 <= n && n < m
```

Then d is a p digit iff d 'below' p. Lists of length k consisting only of p-adic digits are characterized by

```
digits :: Int -> Int -> [Int] -> Bool
digits p k xs  =   length xs == k  &&  all ('below' p) xs
```

Now we define representation and abstraction functions between (the nonnegative part of) Int and lists of p-adic digits. To cope with bounded word length, we parameterize them not only with p but also with the number of digits to be considered.

First we define the representation function

```
code :: Int -> Int -> Int -> [Int]
```

Its first argument p is the base of the number system; for n > 0 the result of code p k n is defined only for p > 1. The second argument k is the number of digits we want to consider. An exact representation with k digits is only possible for numbers n with n 'below' p^k. Hence for other numbers n the result of code p k n is undefined. Otherwise it is the p-adic representation of n in k digits precision, padded with leading zeros if necessary). The definition reads

```
code p 0     0 =  []
code p (k+1) n =  code p k (n 'div' p)  ++  [n 'mod' p]
```

Example 3.1.   code 2 5 24   = [1, 1, 0, 0, 0]
    code 2 7 24   = [0, 0, 1, 1, 0, 0, 0]

□

For the corresponding abstraction function

```
deco :: Int -> Int -> [Int] -> Int
```

the result of deco p k xs is the number represented by the list xs of p-adic digits. Again k is the number of digits expected; the result is undefined if xs has a length different from n. The definition reads

```
deco p 0     []  =  0
deco p (k+1) xs  =  (deco p k (init xs)) * p + last xs
```

These particular abstraction and representation functions have been introduced in [13]. They are useful in that they admit induction/recursion over the parameter k. They enjoy pleasant algebraic properties:

Lemma 3.2. *The functions* code *and* deco *are inverses of each other:*

```
deco p k (code p k n)  =  n    <==   n 'below' p^k
code p k (deco p k xs) = xs    <==   digits p k xs
```

Moreover, we have the decomposition/distributivity properties

```
code p (j+k) (m * p^k + n)  =  code p j m ++ code p k n
   <==    m 'below' p^j  &&  n 'below' p^k
deco p (j+k) (xs ++ ys)  =  (deco p j xs) * p^k + deco p k ys
   <==    digits p j xs  &&  digits p k ys
```

By the sign <== we mean logical implication from right to left; it is not part of official *Haskell.*

These properties are verified by structural induction over the lists involved using the following properties of div and mod (see [13]):

Lemma 3.3. *Assume that* p>0.

```
x  =  x 'div' p * y + x 'mod' p

(x+y) 'mod' z  =  y 'mod' z                       <==  (x 'mod' z) = 0
(x+y) 'div' z  =  x 'div' z + y 'div' z           <==  (x 'mod' z) = 0

(x 'div' p^m) 'div' p^n  =  x 'div' p^(m+n)
(x 'mod' p^m) 'mod' p^n  =  x 'mod' p^(min m n)
(x 'mod' p^m) 'div' p^n  =
        (x 'div' p^n) 'mod' p^(max 0 (m-n))
(x 'div' p^m) 'mod' p^n  =  (x 'mod' p^(m+n)) 'div' p^m
```

4 Development of an Adder

As our first case study we derive several adders. This tackles one of the IFIP verification benchmarks [20]. Moreover, in this example we demonstrate the basic techniques and strategies of deductive design by transformation.

We specify a generic adder function

```
add :: Int -> Int -> [Int] -> [Int]
```

The first parameter is the base for the number representation, the second the number of digits we treat. For the specification we assume that the list zs is the shuffle of the digit lists for the two summands, ie. that digits p (2*k) zs holds. Then we specify

```
add p k zs  =  code p (k+1) (deco p k (evns zs) +
                             deco p k (odds zs)  )
```

The length k+1 for the result list serves to accommodate a possible overflow digit. We illustrate this by a diagram, using temporarily Dig as the subtype of Int comprising the p-adic digits:

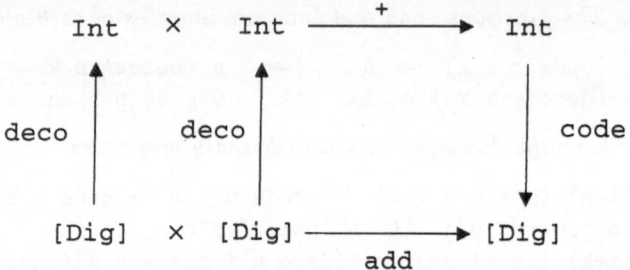

This specification does not yet provide a particular adding algorithm which could be directly taken as the description of an abstract layout. It clearly separates "what" from "how" and allows quite different implementations, such as carry-ripple and carry-lookahead adders. This will be exploited in later stages of our derivation.

4.1 The Unfold/Fold Strategy

Our first goal is now to derive an inductive (recursive) version of **add** that does no longer refer to **deco** and **code** and uses only operations on single digits.

The derivation is driven by the recursion structure of the abstraction and representation functions. It follows a general strategy that can be partly automated, eg. by transformation tactics in ULTRA, and, in the present case, does not require great amounts of intuition. This classical *unfold/fold strategy* (see e.g. [33]) consists of the following steps:

– Unfold the definitions of **deco** and **code**.
– Simplify and rearrange.
– Fold with the definition of **add** to get recursive calls.

The derivation follows the case analysis of **deco** and **code**.
For k=0 we calculate

```
    add p 0 []
=   { unfold add }
    code p 1 (deco p 0 [] + deco p 0 [])
=   { unfold deco, neutrality of 0 }
    code p 1 0
=   { unfold code }
    code p 0 (0 'div' p) ++ [0 'mod' p]
=   { arithmetic and unfold code }
    [] ++ [0]
=   { neutrality of [] }
    [0]
```

This is the termination case; here the overflow digit is 0.

For k > 0 we calculate, assuming xs = evns zs and ys = odds zs,

```
    add p (k+1) (zs ++ [x,y])
```
=   { unfold add }
```
    code p (k+2) (deco p (k+1) (xs ++ [x]) +
    deco p (k+1) (ys ++ [y]) )
```
=   { unfold deco }
```
    code p (k+2) ((deco p k xs)*p + x + (deco p k ys)*p + y )
```
=   { arithmetic }
```
    code p (k+2) ((deco p k xs + deco p k ys)*p + x + y)
```
=   { unfold code }
```
    code p (k+1) (z 'div' p) ++ [z 'mod' p]
    where z = deco p k xs + deco p k ys)*p + x + y
```
=   { by Lemma 3.3 }
```
    code p (k+1) (deco p k xs + deco p k ys + (x + y) 'div' p)
    ++ [(x + y) 'mod' p]
```

This expression is *almost* foldable. However, in the call to code we have the additional summand (x + y) 'div' p, so that we are stuck!

4.2   Generalization

A strategy that frequently helps when direct folding is not possible is *generalization*. It works in two stages.

- First one introduces additional parameters, which may be completely new ones or abstractions of constants in the original specification. These constants may even be "invisible" neutral elements which need to be made explicit first.
- Then one uses the additional degrees of freedom to make the derivation go through.

The original problem is then solved by instantiating the solution for the generalized problem; this is also known as *embedding* the original problem into the generalized one. This strategy is well-known from inductive proofs: there one frequently needs to generalize the induction hypothesis to make the proof go through.

In the case of our adder we introduce a parameter for the extra summand that prevented the folding. The generalized specification reads

```
    cadd p k (xs ++ [c])  =
        code p (k+1) (deco p k (evns xs) + deco p k (odds xs) + c)
```

If one wishes to interpret this, then the new parameter c is the carry. But note that it has been introduced purely formally, "without thinking", as part of the generalization strategy! In fact, this strategy can again be partly automated.

The original problem is retrieved via the embedding

```
add p k xs   =   cadd  p k (xs ++ [0])
```

Now we can replay the derivation for cadd. This results in

```
cadd p 0 [c] = [c]
cadd p (k+1) (xs ++ [x,y,c]) =
        cadd p k (xs ++ [(x+y+c) 'div' p]) ++ [(x+y+c) 'mod' p]
```

We need to ensure that the expression $(x+y+c)$ 'div' p always yields a proper digit. The maximal values for x and y are $p-1$. In this case we have $x+y+c = p + (p+c-2)$ so that the quotient by p is at least 1. Since 1 is the only digit that exists in all number systems, notably the binary system, we have to guarantee that the quotient does not exceed 1. Hence we need the additional assertion c 'below' 2. Fortunately, this assertion is preserved as an invariant of the recursion, ie. if it holds for c it also holds for the new carry $(x+y+c)$ 'div' p. We forego a formal treatment of assertions here and refer to [28] instead.

4.3 Modularization

The resulting expression for the recursive case is very complex. We structure it by packing the two expressions for the last digit and the new carry in cadd into a function fa defined by

```
fa p [x,y,c] = [(x+y+c) 'div' p, (x+y+c) 'mod' p]
```

$$x \quad y$$

$$(x+y+c) \text{ 'div' } p \longleftarrow \boxed{\text{fa } p} \longleftarrow c$$

$$(x+y+c) \text{ 'mod' } p$$

Of course, fa is the full adder function. But note again that this is introduced purely formally!

Now we may use splicing (cf. Section 2.2) to obtain

```
cadd p (k+1)   =   splice (2*k)  (cadd p k)  (fa p)
```

$$2*k \quad \cdots$$

$$\longleftarrow \boxed{\text{cadd } p \ k} \longleftarrow \boxed{\text{fa } p} \longleftarrow$$

$$\cdots \quad k$$

For fixed n we may now unwind the recursion to obtain the well-known regular design of the carry ripple adder:

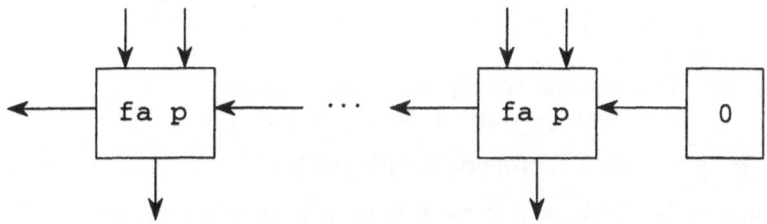

The associativity of splicing is essential here; it allows this "parenthesis-free" graphical layout. Based on the decomposition properties for code and deco we can also show a decomposition property for cadd :

Lemma 4.1. cadd p (k+m) = splice (2*k) (cadd p k) (cadd p m)

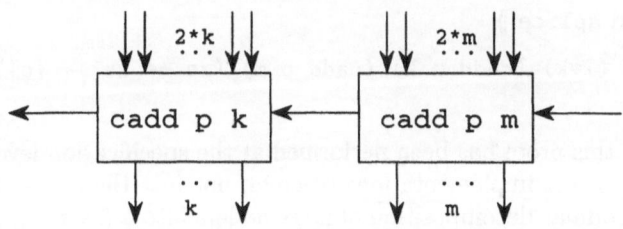

Proof. Consider a list zs ++ zs' ++ [c] with length zs = 2*k and length zs' = 2*m and set

```
xs  = evns zs,  ys  = odds zs,
xs' = evns zs', ys' = odds zs'
```

Then we calculate

        cadd p (k+m) (zs ++ zs' ++ [c])

=   {[unfold cadd]}

        code p (k+m+1) (deco p (k+m) (xs ++ xs') +
                         deco p (k+m) (ys ++ ys') + c)

=   {[by Lemma 3.2]}

        code   p (k+m+1)
             ((deco p k xs) * p^m + deco p m xs' +
               (deco p k ys) * p^m + deco p m ys' + c)

=   {[arithmetic]}

        code   p (k+m+1)
               ((deco p k xs + deco p k ys + d) * p^m + r)
        where (d,r) = (z `div`p^m, z `mod` p^m)

```
                z = deco p m xs' + deco p m ys' + c
=    { by Lemma 3.2, property 3 }

   code p (k+1) (deco p k xs + deco p k ys + d) ++
   code p m r
   where  (d,r) = (z 'div'p^m, z 'mod' p^m)
              z = deco p m xs' + deco p m ys' + c

=    { by Lemma 3.2, property 3 with j=1 }

   code p (k+1)(deco p k xs + deco p k ys + d) ++ us
   where (d:us) = code p (m+1)
                       (deco p m xs' + deco p m ys' + c)

=    { fold cadd }

   cadd p k (xs ++ ys ++ [d] ++ us)
   where (d:us) = cadd p m (xs' ++ ys' ++ [c])

=    { fold splice }

   splice (2*k) (cadd p k) (cadd p m) (zs ++ zs'++ [c])
```

□

Note that this proof has been performed at the specification level and hence holds for all correct implementations of cadd, not just the carry ripple adder! This allows modular decomposition of large adders into a (carry ripple) splicing of smaller ones, say 4-bit modules, which may even be heterogeneous. Again the associativity of splicing is essential here. Here we have a typical combination of parameterization and modularization.

It should also be noted that

```
fa p [x,y,c]  =  cadd p 1 [x,y,c]
```

so that the carry ripple design can also be seen as the result of an iterated application of Lemma 4.1.

4.4 Abstraction

We now review the derivation to find the algebraic laws that were used in it. We abstract from the particular case of addition and define a general function

```
digrep :: (Int -> Int -> [Int] -> [Int]) ->
          Int -> Int -> [Int] -> [Int]
```

The idea is that, given a function f :: Int -> Int -> [Int] -> [Int], the module digrep f p k (zs ++ [c]) takes a list zs, that consists of the shuffled p-adic representations of two natural numbers m and n, and a "carry" c. From these inputs it computes a p-adic representation of the value f applied to m, n and c. Besides its "proper" parameters m, n and c, the function f takes into account the base p and number k of relevant digits. Assuming that digits p (2*k + 1) (zs ++ [c]) holds, we specify

```
digrep f p k (zs ++ [c])  =
    f p k [deco p k (evns zs), deco p k (odds zs), c]
```

To retrieve the adder function, we have to set, for m,n 'below' p^k,

```
f p k [m,n,c]  =  code p (k+1) (m+n+c)                    (*)
```

For the base case k=0 we calculate

```
    digrep f p 0 [c]
=   { unfold digrep }
    f p 0 [deco p 0 [], deco p 0 [], c]
=   { unfold deco }
    f p 0 [0, 0, c]
```

For the inductive case we could now also replay the derivation of cadd for digrep. However, as the remark at the end of Section 4.3 shows, it is more advantageous to head for a decomposition property of digrep. By analyzing the proof of Lemma 4.1 we can find a sufficient condition on f that makes the proof go through in general. Following [17] we call f *factorizable* if

```
f p (j+k) [m*p^k+q, n*p^k+r, c]  =
    ((f p j) 'splice 2' (f p k)) [m,n,q,r,c]
```

holds for all natural numbers j,k,m,n,p,q,r. Now Lemma 4.1 generalizes to

Theorem 4.2 (Factorization Theorem). Let f be factorizable. Then

```
digrep f p (k+m)  =
    (digrep f p k) 'splice (2*k)' (digrep f p m)
```

*Proof.*digrep f p (k+m) (zs ++ zs' ++ [c])

```
=   { unfold digrep }
    f p (k+m) [ deco p (k+m) (xs++xs'),
                deco p (k+m) (ys++ys'), c ]
=   { unfold deco }
    f p (k+m) [ (deco p k xs)*p^m + deco p m xs',
                (deco p k ys)*p^m + deco p m ys', c ]
=   { factorizability }
    splice  2 (f p k) (f p m)
            [ deco p k xs, deco p k ys,
              deco p m xs', deco p m ys', c ]
=   { unfold splice }
    f p k [deco p k xs, deco p k ys, d] ++ us
```

```
     where (d:us) = f p m [deco p m xs', deco p m ys', c]
=    {[ fold digrep twice ]}
     digrep f p k (zs ++ [d]) ++ us
     where (d:us) = digrep f p m (zs'++[c])
=    {[ fold splice ]}
     splice (2*k) (digrep f p k) (digrep f p m)
     (zs ++ zs' ++ [c])
```

□

This is in fact Hanna's Factorization Theorem (see again [17]), which gives a general scheme for correct implementations of iterative arithmetic circuits. The proof of Lemma 4.1 contains a section that uses Lemma 3.2 to show that (*) above defines a factorizable f; the remainder is isomorphic to the proof of Theorem 4.2.

Using this theorem and the fact that digrep f p 1 = f p 1 we can unwind digrep f p k into a regular layout:

Corollary 4.3. *For* k > 0 *we have*

```
digrep f p k  =  foldr1 (splice 2) (copy k (f p 1))
```

Here we use the standard *Haskell* functions foldr1 and copy. The function foldr1 takes a binary operator and a non-empty list and combines all list elements by that operator, associating them to the right. A call copy k x produces a list consisting of k copies of x.

Another instance of digrep is a comparator circuit, described by

```
digrep f p k
   where  f p k [m,n,c] =  [eq m n  /\  c]      (**)
```

Here,

```
eq m n  =  if m == n then 1 else 0
b /\ c  =  b*c
```

so that we have numerical representations of the usual Boolean operations. It is straightforward to show that the function f in (**) is indeed factorizable. To obtain a comparator circuit, we have to instantiate c appropriately, viz. by the neutral element 1 of /\, and to unwind the specification using the Factorization Theorem. This results in

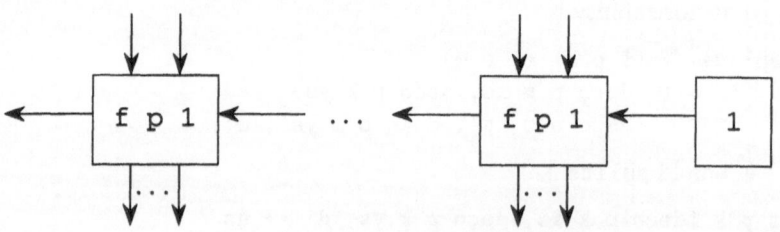

4.5 Re-Use of a Design: Successor (Counting)

Next we want to derive a counter circuit, ie. an implementation of the successor function on digit representations. The specification reads

```
succ :: Int -> Int -> [Int] -> [Int]
succ p k xs  =  code p (k+1) (deco p k xs + 1)
```

This is quite similar to the adder specification. We therefore try to re-use the adder design. Formally we need to reduce succ to add; this is done by making the hidden neutral element 0 of addition visible so that we have a second operand for addition. We calculate:

```
    succ p k xs

=   { unfold succ }

    code p (k+1) (deco p k xs + 1)

=   { neutrality of 0 }

    code p (k+1) (deco p k xs + 0 + 1)

=   { fold deco }

    code p (k+1) (deco p k xs + deco p k (copy k 0) + 1)

=   { fold cadd }

    cadd p k (shuf k (xs ++ copy k 0) ++ [1])
```

Although this is a first correct implementation, it is too inefficient. The fact that in the unwound version we have calls of the form fa [x,0,c] may be used to simplify the design. Define an auxiliary function

```
    ha [x,c]  =  fa [x,0,c]  =  [(x+c) 'div' p , (x+c) 'mod' p]
```

Of course, ha is the half adder function. But again it has been introduced purely formally.

The simplified design looks as follows:

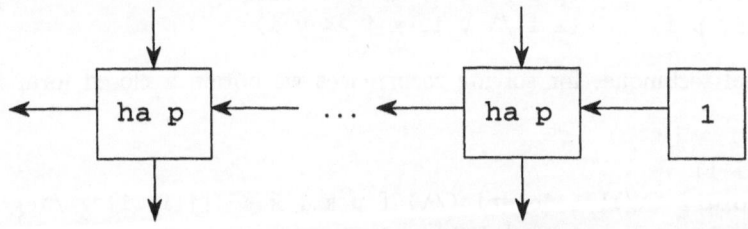

4.6 Specialization: Base 2

For p=2 we obtain the usual representations

```
ha 2 [x,c]  =  [x /\ c,  x >< c]

fa 2 [x,y,c]  =  [ d \/ e,  z]
   where [d,u]  =  ha 2 [x,y]
         [e,z]  =  ha 2 [u,c]
```

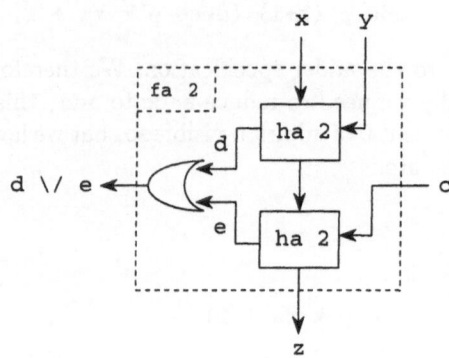

Here, /\, \/ and >< are again the arithmetic representations of the Boolean operations on base 2 digits with >< denoting exclusive or.

4.7   The Carry Lookahead Adder and Hybrid Adders

It is well known that the carry ripple adder is time-inefficient, since the length of the longest path through the design (along which the carries ripple) is proportional to the number of digits processed. So there have been various proposals to speed up the carry computation. One idea is to compute the carries in parallel with the sums; this leads to the carry lookahead adder which we want to derive formally now.

Let the modules in the carry ripple adder be numbered from the right starting with 0 and let $x\ i$, $y\ i$ and $c\ i$ be the i-th input digits and carries (where c 0 is some given value).

From the carry ripple design we read off the recurrence equation

```
c (i+1)    =  (p i /\ c i) \/ g i  where
(g i, p i) =  (x i /\ y i, x i >< y i)
```

By usual techniques for solving recurrences we obtain a closed form for the carries:

```
c (i+1) =
   foldr1 (\/)[ ( foldr1 (/\) [ p k | k <- [j+1..i] ) /\ g j |
              j <- [-1..i] ]
   where g (-1)  =  c 0
```

For reasons of space we draw the picture of the carry lookahead computation only for 3 digits:

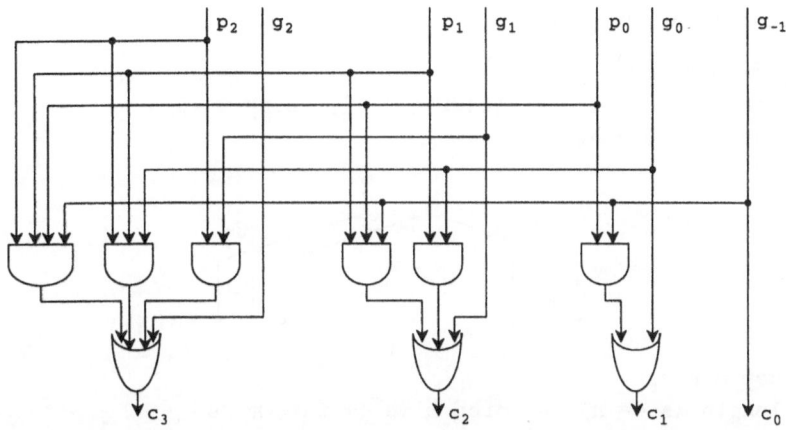

Using this form of carry computation results in a circuit in which the path length is independent of the number of digits processed. This gain is bought at the expense of a maximal fan-in that is proportional to the number of digits. So for electrical reasons this design is meaningful only for small numbers of digits, say 4 or 8. But from our above decomposition property we know that we may connect several carry lookahead adders in a carry ripple fashion to obtain a correct adder which will then be faster by a factor 4 or 8 than the original pure carry ripple adder.

5   More About Wiring

So far we have mostly described connections using the rubber view of wires ("logical connection"). We now sketch how to step from the logical connection to a topology with rigid wires, crossings and fan-out.

Note, however, that many approaches start at this level and have to carry the complications of wiring all through the derivation. This is tedious and obscures the essential steps.

5.1   Basic Wiring Elements

The basic wiring elements are a straight wire, modeled by the identity function, the fan-out of degree 2 (fork), the crossing (swap) and the sink:

```
id    [x]    =  [x]
fork  [x]    =  [x,x]
swap  [x,y]  =  [y,x]
sink  [x]    =  []
```

These operations can be extended to wire bundles in a straightforward way:

```
bfork m n xs
| length xs == n   =  foldr (++) [] (copy m xs)
-- undefined otherwise
```

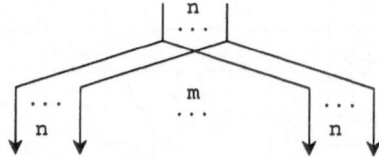

```
bswap m n xs
| length xs == n   =  drop m xs ++ take m xs
-- undefined otherwise
```

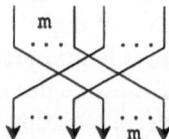

The identity `id` is predefined polymorphically by `id y = y` and hence does not need to be extended to wire bundles. The sink can be handled by setting generally `sink xs = []`. We will discuss other versions later.

Finally, we have the invisible module `ide` with 0 inputs and 0 outputs:

```
ide [] = []
```

5.2 Sequential and Parallel Composition

Sequential composition simply is reverse function composition. We are a bit sloppy here about the arities of the functions and simply define

```
(f |> g) xs   =   g (f xs)
```

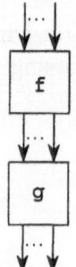

For parallel composition we need to supply the respective operator with the number k of inputs to be routed to the left module; the remaining ones are routed to the right module:

```
par k f g xs  =  f (take k xs) ++ g (drop k xs)
```

By the definition of take and drop this works even if k > length xs: in that case f gets the full list xs whereas g only gets the empty list []. Here is the diagram for par k f g:

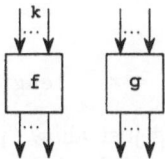

Conventional polymorphism is too weak to model parallel composition more adequately. To avoid the necessity of uniformly typing all list elements one would need an extension to "tuples as first-class citizens" with concatenation of tuple types and also of tuples as primitive operations. However, this might lead to problems with automatic type checking. Therefore we have chosen the simple approach above.

We abbreviate par 1 by the infix operator | | |.

5.3   Basic Laws (Network Algebra I)

All semantic models for graph-like networks should enjoy a number of natural properties which reflect the abstraction that lies in the graph view. A systematic account of these properties has been given in [37].

Associativity:

```
f  |> (g |> h)  =  (f |> g) |> h
(f 'par m' g) 'par (m+k)' h  =  f 'par m' (g 'par k' h)
```

Abiding Law I:

```
(f |> g) 'par m' (h |> k)  =  (f 'par m' h) |> (g 'par n' k)
   <==  n = length (f (take m xs))
```

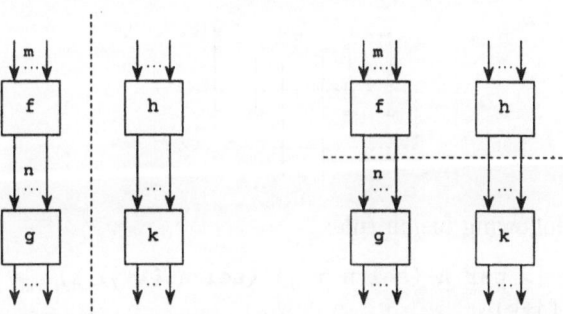

Neutrality:

```
id |> f  =  f  =  f |> id
(f 'par m' ide) xs  =  f xs   <==   length xs = m
ide 'par 0' f  =  f
```

Involution:

```
(swap |> swap) xs  =  xs  <==   length xs  =  2
```

Whereas associativity and abiding just allow "parenthesis-free layouts", use of neutrality or involution means simplification/complexification of abstract layouts.

5.4 Selection

Using parallel composition we can now give alternative definitions for block identity and sink:

```
bid n = foldr (|||) ide (copy n id)
```

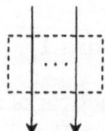

```
bsink n = foldr (|||) ide (copy n sink)
```

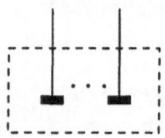

Based on this we define selection nets:

```
sel n i j =
      par i (bsink i) (parj (bid j)  (bsink (n-j-i)))
```

for 0 <= i <= n and 0 <= j <= (n-i).

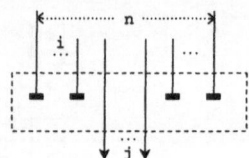

We have the following fusion rule:

```
(bfork 2 n) |> par n (sel n i j) (sel n (i+j) k)  =
    sel n i (j+k)
```

5.5 Recursions for the Bundle Operations

Using sequential and parallel composition we can reduce the bundle operations
to the primitives.

Example 5.1. The bundle operation `bswap m n` swaps its first m inputs with
the following n ones. It is defined by the equations

```
       bswap m 0   =  ide
       bswap 0 n   =  id
       bswap 1 1   =  swap
bswap k (k+m+n)    =  par (k+m) (bswap k (k+m)) (bid n)  |>
                      par m (bid m) (bswap k (k+n))
```

□

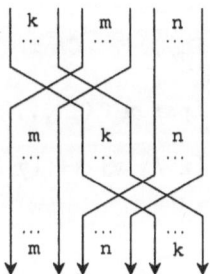

5.6 Combinator Abstraction

We have already discussed the need to pass from rubber wiring to rigid wiring.
This is achieved by eliminating all formal parameters from functional expressions
in favour of parallel and sequential composition and the basic wiring elements.
This is analogous to the process of λ-abstraction in combinatory logic (see eg.
[1]). Therefore we term this operation *combinator abstraction*.

We use the following simplified syntax for *Haskell* expressions:

```
expr ::= parid | (opid expr ... expr) | (expr ++ ... ++ expr)
```

Here we suppose that `parid` produces the admissible identifiers for formal parameters, whereas `opid` produces the admissible operators such as `div` or `(+)`.

For each expression E we now want to construct a composed module `CA E` (CA
stands for combinator abstraction) that computes the corresponding function on
a list of inputs to produce a list of outputs.

For its definition, we need the list `ID E` of the formal parameters occurring
in expression E. This list is organized in textual order of appearance of the
parameters and kept repetition free. It is inductively defined as follows:

```
ID x = [x]
ID (op e1 ... en)    = remdups ([op] ++ ID e1 ++ ... ++ ID en)
ID (e1 ++ ... ++ en) = remdups (ID e1 ++ ... ++ ID en)
```

Here `remdups` removes duplicates, preserving the leftmost occurrence of each item in a list:

```
remdups [] = []
remdups (x : xs) = x : remdups [y | y <- xs, y /= x]
```

Suppose now an expression E all formal parameters of which occur in the repetition free list [x0,...,xn-1]. Then the combinator abstraction CA E of E will take a list of n inputs to produce a corresponding list of outputs. It is defined by induction over the structure of E. To ease the definition, we introduce an auxiliary definition of CA op where op is an opid.

```
CA xi  = sel n i 1
CA op  = \xs -> [ op (xs!!0) ... (xs!!(k-1))]
     if  op :: t0 -> ... tk-1 -> t
CA (op E1 ... Em) =
   (CA (E1 ++ ... ++ Em)) |>  CA f
CA (E1 ++ ... ++ Em)  =
   bfork m n |> (CA E1 'par n' ( ... 'par n' CA Em))
```

Example 5.2. Suppose E = ([x /\ y] ++ [y >< x]). Then

```
CA E =
   bfork 2 2 |>
   (bfork 2 2 |> ((sel 0 1 'par 2' sel 1 1) |> CA /\) 'par 2'
    bfork 2 2 |> ((sel 1 1 'par 2' sel 0 1) |> CA ><))          )
```

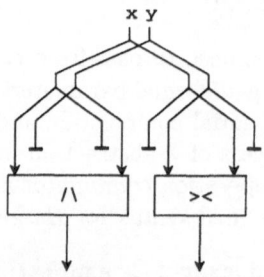

This can, of course, be simplified to

bfork 2 2 |> ((bid 2 |> CA /\) 'par 2' (swap |> CA ><))

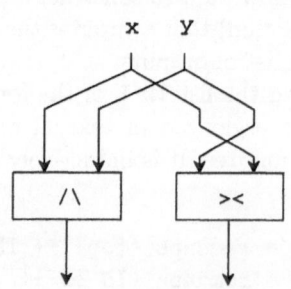

□

The basic rules above lead to circuits involving very high fan-outs. More refined rules avoid this, e.g.

```
CA (E ++ F)  =  CA E1  'par k'  CA En
```

if ID (E ++ F) = ID E ++ ID F, ie. if the sublists of formal parameters are disjoint and in order, and k = length (ID E).

5.7 A Further Example: Shuffling

Recall the specification of the shuffle operation from Section 4.2:

```
(shuf k xs) !! (2*i)    =  x !! i
(shuf k xs) !! (2*i+1)  =  x !! (k+i)
```

for length xs == 2*k and i <- [0..k-1].

Some calculation yields the following inductive version:

```
shuf 0      =  id
shuf 1      =  id
shuf (k+1)  =
    (par 1 id (par k (cshiftl k) id) ) |> ( par 2 id (shuf k))

cshiftl k  =  foldr1 (splice 2) (copy k swap)
```

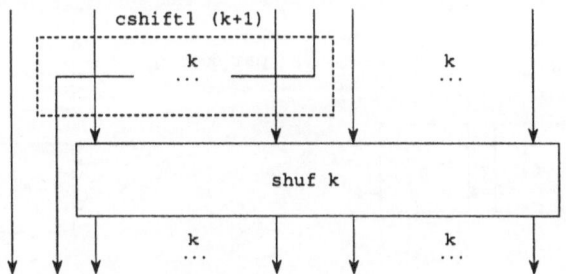

For further details on wiring we refer to [19, 31].

Part II: Sequential Hardware

6 A Model of Streams

A frequently used model of sequential hardware is that of stream transformers. Streams are used to model the temporal succession of values on the connection wires, whereas the modules are functions from (bundles of) input streams to (bundles of) output streams.

In this paper we deal with discrete time only. Even this leaves several options how to represent streams. One possibility would be to define

```
type Stream a = [a]
```

Since *Haskell* employs a lazy semantics, this allows finite as well as infinite streams. Time remains implicit, but can be introduced using the list indexing operation.

We use a version which explicitly refers to time:

```
type Time = Int
type Stream a = Time -> a
```

This will carry over easily to real time. On the other hand, this does not directly support finite streams. They would have to be modeled by functions that become eventually constant, preferably yielding only the pseudo-value **undefined** after the "proper" finite part.

7 Networks

Again we model bundles of inputs and outputs by lists, this time of streams. By polymorphism we can re-use all our connection primitives, such as |>, par, fork, swap and splice and their laws for stream transformers.

Our diagrams will now be drawn sideways:

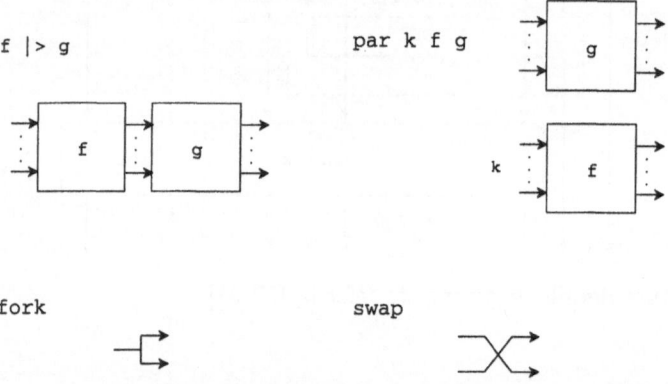

The input/output streams are numbered from bottom to top in the respective lists.

7.1 Lifting and Constant

To establish the connection with combinational circuits we need to iterate their behaviour in time. To this end we introduce liftings of operations on data to streams. A "unary" operation takes a singleton list of input data and produces a singleton list of output data. This is lifted to a function from a singleton list of input streams to a singleton list of output streams. It is the analogue of the apply-to-all operation **map** on lists. We define

```
lift1 :: (a -> b) -> [Stream a] -> [Stream b]
lift1 f [d]  =  [\t -> f (d t)]
```

Alternatively, since streams are functions themselves, the lifting may also be expressed using function composition:

```
lift1 f [d]  =  [f.d]
```

Similarly, we have for binary operations

```
lift2 :: (a -> a -> b) -> [Stream a] -> [Stream b]
lift2 g [d,e]   =  [\t -> g (d t) (e t)]
```

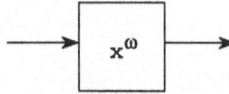

The inscriptions of the boxes follow notationally the view of infinite streams of functions used in [29].

Another useful building block is a module that emits a constant output stream. For convenience we endow it with a (useless) input stream. So this module actually is a combination of a sink and a source. We define

```
cnst :: a -> [Stream b] -> [Stream a]
cnst x   =   lift1 (const x)
```

Here const is a predefined *Haskell* function that produces a constant unary function from a value.

7.2   Initialized Unit Delay

To model memory of the simplest kind we use a unit delay module. Other delays such as inertial delay or transport delay can be modeled similarly. For a value x the stream transformer (x >-) shifts its input stream by one time unit; at time 0 it emits x as the initial value:

```
(>-) :: a -> [Stream a] -> [Stream a]
(x >- [d])  =  [e]
  where  e t  |  t == 0  =  x
             |  t > 0  =  d (t-1)
```

We now state laws for pushing delays through larger networks. They allow for each circuit constructor to shift delay elements from the input side to the output side or vice versa under suitable change of the initialization value. These laws are used centrally in our treatment of systolic circuits.

Lemma 7.1 (Delay Propagation Rules). *If* f *is strict, ie. undefined whenever its argument is, then*

```
(x>-) |> lift1 f   = lift1 f  |> ((f x) >-)
```

If g *is doubly strict, ie. is undefined whenever both its argument are, then*

```
((x>-) ||| (y>-)) |> lift2 g  = lift2 g  |> ((g x y)>-)
```

Moreover,

```
(x>-)               |> cnst y = cnst y |> (y>-)
((x>-) ||| (y>-))   |> swap   = swap    |> ((y>-) ||| (x>-))
(x>-)               |> fork   = fork    |> ((x>-) ||| (x>-))
```

These rules can be given in pictorial form as

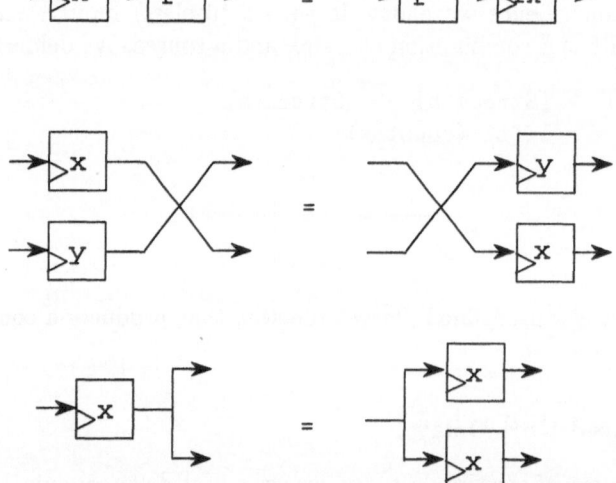

For propagation through |> and ||| we may use associativity of |> and the abiding law.

These simple laws are quite effective as will be seen in later examples. In our derivation of systolic circuits we actually use them in the direction from right to left to shift delays from outputs to inputs.

8 Example: The Single Pulser

To show our algebra at work we will treat a single pulser. This is another of the IFIP verification benchmarks [20]. The informal specification requires the module to emit a unit pulse whenever a pulse starts in its input stream.

8.1 Formal Specification

We model this by a transformer of streams of Booleans. A *pulse* is a maximal time interval on which a stream is constantly True. First we formally characterize those time points at which a pulse starts by

```
startPulse :: Stream Bool -> Time -> Bool
startPulse d t  = d t  && ( t==0 || not(d (t-1)) )
```

Note that by `Time -> Bool = Stream Bool` we may view `startPulse` also as a stream transformer.

Now we can give the formal specification of the pulser:

```
pulser [d]  =  [ \t -> startPulse d t ]
```

Equivalently, by extensional equality,

```
pulser [d]  =  [ startPulse d ]
```

8.2 Derivation of a Pulser Circuit

For t = 0 we calculate

```
    startPulse d 0
```
=   {| unfold startPulse |}
```
    d 0 && ( 0==0 || not (d (0-1)) )
```
=   {| Boolean algebra |}
```
    d 0
```

For t > 0 we have

```
    startPulse d t
```
=   {| unfold startPulse |}
```
    d t && ( t==0 || not (d (t-1)) )
```
=   {| t > 0 and Boolean algebra |}
```
    d t && not (d (t-1))
```
=   {| fold >- |}
```
    d t && not (e t) where [e] = x >- [d].
```

for arbitrary x. Now we try to choose the initialization value x such that

```
    startPulse d t  =  d t  &&  not (e 0)
```

holds also for t=0, ie.

```
    d 0 = d 0  &&  not x
```

This is satisfied for all values d 0 iff x = False.

Now combinator abstraction and simplification yields

```
pulser = fork |> ( ((False >-) |> lift1(not)) ||| id )
               |> lift2 (&&)
```

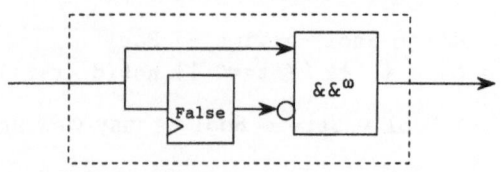

9 Feedback

For describing systems with memory we need another essential ingredient. It is the very general concept of feeding back some outputs of a module as inputs again. This allows, in particular, the preservation of a value for an arbitrary period, ie. storing of values.

9.1 The Feedback Operation

Given a module f :: Module the module feed k f results from f by feeding back the last k outputs to the last k inputs:

```
feed ::  Int  -> Module -> Module

feed k f xs  =  codrop k ys
   where ys  =  f (xs ++ cotake k ys)

cotake n xs  =  drop (length xs - n) xs
codrop n xs  =  take (length xs - n) xs
```

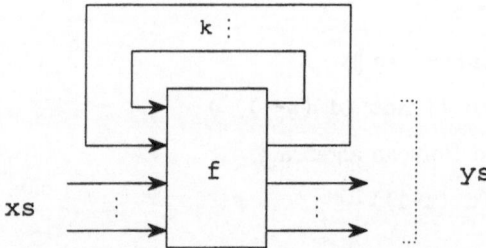

Note the recursive definition of ys that reflects the flowing back of information. This recursion is well-defined by the lazy semantics of *Haskell*.

9.2 Properties of Feedback (Network Algebra II)

The feedback operation enjoys a number of algebraic laws which show that it models the rubber wire abstraction correctly. For a systematic exposition see again [37].

Stretching wires:

Assume that f is defined only for input lists of length m and that g always produces output lists of length n+k. The we have

f |> feed k g |> h   =   feed k ((f 'par m' id) |> g |> (h 'par n' id))

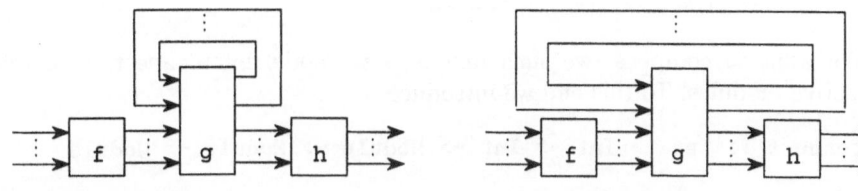

Abiding law II:

f 'par n' feed k g   =   feed k (f 'par n' g)

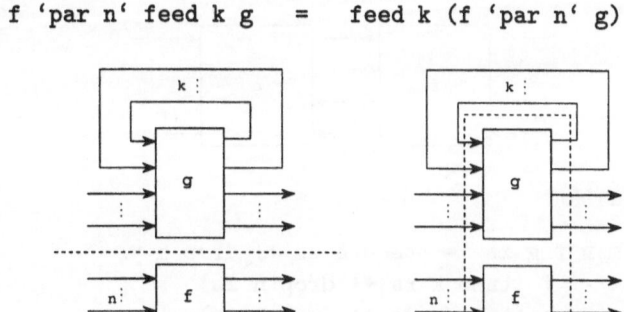

Shifting a module:

Assume that f is defined only for input lists of length m+k and always produces output lists of length n+k and that g is defined only for input lists of length k and always produces output lists of length k. Then we have

feed k (f |> (id 'par n' g))   =   feed k ((id 'par m' g) |> f)

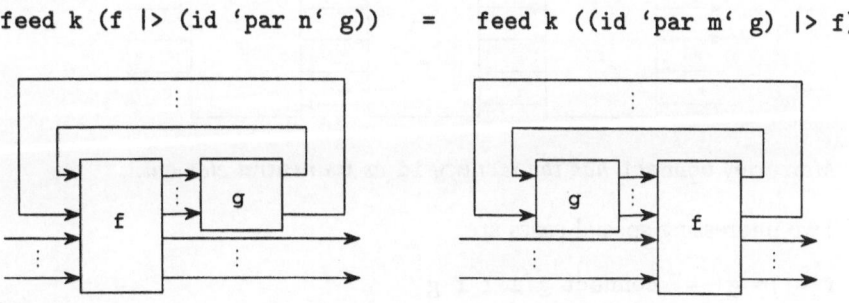

9.3 Interconnection (Mutual Feedback)

In more complex designs it may be convenient to picture a module f with inputs and outputs distributed to both sides:

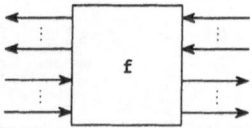

We want to compose two such functions to model interconnection of the respective modules. To this end we introduce

```
connect :: Int -> Int -> Int -> Module -> Module -> Module
```

The three Int-parameters in connect k m n f g are used similarly as for splicing: they indicate that k inputs are supposed to come from the left neighbour of f, that m wires lead from f to g, and that n outputs go to the right neighbour of g.

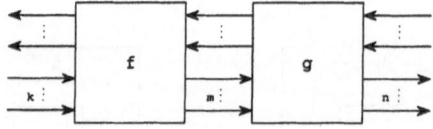

We define therefore

```
connect k m n f g xs  =  take n zs ++ drop m ys
   where ys  =  f (take k xs ++ drop n zs)
         zs  =  g (take m ys ++ drop k xs)
```

This involves a mutually recursive definition of ys and zs which again is well-defined by the lazy *Haskell* semantics.

Lemma 9.1. *Interconnection is associative in the following sense:*

```
(f 'connect k m n' g) 'connect k n p' h   =
   f 'connect k m n' (g 'connect k m p' h)
```

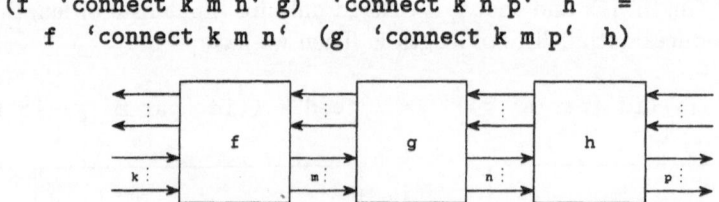

Moreover, connect *has the identity* id *as its neutral element.*

Two interesting special cases are

```
f =||= g  =  connect 1 1 1 f g
```

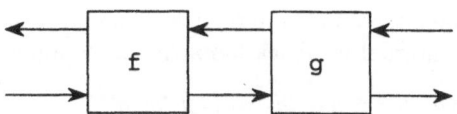

and

f =| g = connect 1 1 0 f g

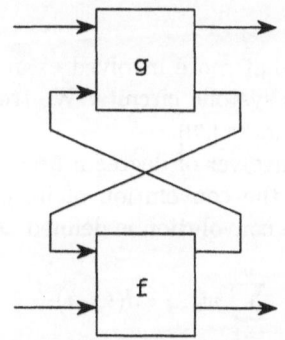

The symbols have been chosen such that they indicate the places of the external wires of the resulting circuits: whereas f =||= g has external wires on the left and on the right, f =| g has them only on the left. The operator =||= is also known as mutual feedback ⊗ (see eg. [4]). The corresponding network can be depicted as

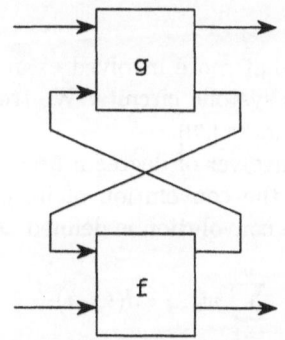

Using a suitable torsion of the network we can relate interconnection to feedback:

```
f =||= g  =
    feed 1 ( (id ||| swap)  |>
            (f 'par 2' id) |> (id ||| swap) |>
            (g 'par 2' id) |> (id ||| swap)     )
```

With the help of this connection, the proof of associativity of connect can be given using purely the laws of network algebra. Hence the lemma is valid for all models of network algebra, not just our particular one.

In special cases the interconnection reduces to simple sequential composition, thus eliminating the internal feedback loop. As an example we state

Lemma 9.2. *Suppose that* f *has the special form*

```
f  =  (fork ||| id) |> (id ||| h)
```

Then

```
f =| g  =  fork |> (id ||| g) |> h
```

Pictorially,

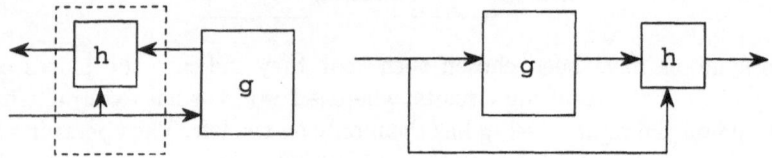

10   A Convolver

We want to tackle a somewhat more involved example now. In particular, we want to prepare the way to systolic circuits. We treat a convolver, another of the IFIP verification benchmarks [20].

A non-programmable convolver of degree n uses n fixed weights to compute at each time point t >= n the convolution of its previous n inputs by these weights. Mathematically the convolution is defined as

$$\sum_{i=1}^{n} w_{n-i} * d(t-i) ,$$

where d is the input stream and the w_j are the weights. Convolution is used eg. in digital filters.

10.1   Specification

Using list comprehension, the above mathematical definition can be directly transcribed into a *Haskell* specification. For convenience we collect the weights into another stream w. Then the convolver is specified by

```
conv :: Stream Int -> Int -> [Stream Int] -> [Stream Int]
conv w n [d]  =
   [ \t -> if t < n
              then undefined
              else sum [ w (n-i) * d (t-i) | i <- [1..n] ] ]
```

It should be clear that the problem generalizes to arbitrary compositions of fold and apply-to-all operations. Since we have taken such an abstraction step already in Section 6.4, we do not want to repeat this here.

10.2 About Error Handling

We have modeled non-initialization by the pseudo-value undefined. However, it turns out that the only essential assumption about undefined that goes into the derivation is the strictness property

```
x + undefined = undefined
```

This could also be achieved by introducing an additional error element using *Haskell*'s facilities for defining variant record types and adapting addition accordingly:

```
data Error a  =  Proper a | Err
instance Num a => Num (Error a) where
   Proper x + Proper y  =  Proper (x+y)
   _ + _  =  Err
```

Similarly definitions would be given for the other arithmetic operations. Since this is somewhat cumbersome, though, we have chosen the above method.

10.3 Derivation of a Convolver Circuit

We now want to derive from the formal specification a regular layout described, as in the case of the adder, by a recursion. The obvious parameter to drive the recursion is the number n of terms in the sum, since the summation function is defined recursively itself and we can carry over its recursion structure to the convolver circuit.

The base case is n = 0. For t >= 0 and [e] = conv w 0 d we calculate

```
    e t
=   { specification of e }
    sum [ w (0-i) * d (t-i) | i <- [1..0] ]
=   { definition of intervals }
    sum [ w (0-i) * d (t-i) | i <- [] ]
=   { definition of list comprehension }
    sum []
=   { definition of sum }
    0
```

Hence conv 0 = cnst 0 with cnst defined as in Section 7.1.

We now perform the induction step. For t >= n+1 and [e] = conv w (n+1) d we obtain

```
  e t
=   { specification of e }
  sum [ w (n+1-i) * d (t-i) | i <- [1..n+1] ]
=   { splitting the interval, definition of sum }
  w n * d (t-1) + sum [ w (n+1-i) * d (t-i) | i <- [2..n+1] ]
=   { index transformation }
  w n * d (t-1) + sum [ w (n+1-(j+1)) * d (t-(j+1)) | j <- [1..n] ]
=   { arithmetic }
  w n * d (t-1) + sum [ w (n-j) * d (t-1-j) | j <- [1..n] ]
=   { fold conv }
  w n * d (t-1) + c (t-1)
  where [c] = conv w n d
```

Now combinator abstraction, together with Lemma 9.2, yields

```
conv w (n+1)  =   (cell w n) =| (conv w n)
cell w k      =   (fork ||| id) |> (id ||| h)
h w k         =   (lift1 ((w k) *) ||| id) |>
                  (lift2 (+)) |> (undefined >-)
```

This recursive formation law for the basic convolver can be depicted as follows, where ⊥ stands for undefined:

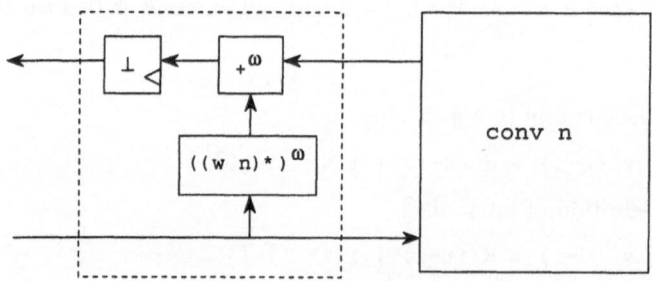

10.4 Unwinding the recursion

For fixed n > 0 we obtain again a regular design:

```
conv w n =
   (foldr1 (=||=) [ cell w k | k <- [1..n] ]) =| cnst 0
```

After simplification of the rightmost cell this yields

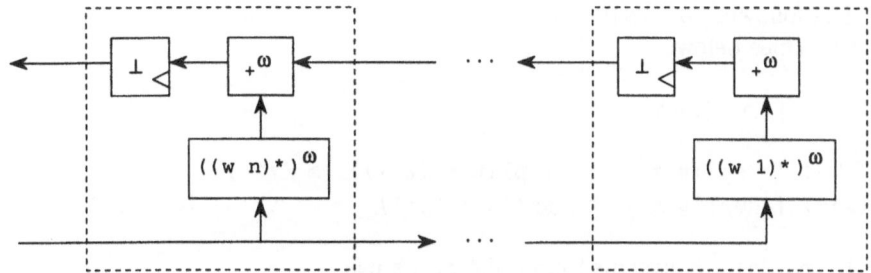

10.5 Towards a Systolic Version

A circuit is *combinational* if it uses only lifted operations and sequential or parallel composition. In a clocked circuit, the clock period is determined by the stabilization time of the circuit which depends on its longest combinational path.

In systolic circuits one tries to minimize the clock period by making the combinational modules involved quite small. Then the clock period can be kept relatively short, namely it can be taken as the maximum of the stabilization times of the combinational submodules involved. Since there is, however, no general rule for calling a combinational module "small" the precise definition of systolism avoids such a notion. Rather, a circuit is called *systolic* (cf. [24, 25, 14]) if there is at least one delay element along every connection wire between any of its combinational modules. A related but somewhat different notion of systolism is used in the field of massively parallel systems; however, there no explicit delay elements are employed.

We want to obtain a systolic version of our convolver. Hence we have to introduce additional delay elements.

11 Speedup by Slowdown

The technique to introduce delays formally is slowdown (see e.g. [24, 25, 21]). The k-fold slowed down version of a circuit works on k interleaved streams. So each of these is processed at rate k slower than in the original circuit.

11.1 Interleaved Streams

To talk about the component streams of such a "multistream" we introduce

```
split k j d t = d (k*t + j)
```

So `split k j d` is the j-th of the k component streams where numbering starts with 0 again. Eg. `split 2 0 d` and `split 2 1 d` consist of the values in d at even and odd time points, respectively. Then d can be considered as an alternating interleaving of these. The interleaving of k=4 streams may be depicted as follows:

The following properties of `split` are useful for proving the slowdown propagation rules below:

Lemma 11.1. *We have*

```
(x>-) |> split k 0  =  (split k (k-1)) |> (x>-)
(x>-) |> split k j  =  split k (j-1)              (0 < j < n)
```

To interleave k streams from a list `ss` we use

```
ileave k ss t  =  (ss !! (t 'mod' k))(t 'div' k)
```

Provided that `length ss >= k`, we have

```
split k j (ileave k ss)  =  ss !! j
```

A special case is the interleaving of k copies of the same stream:

```
rep k d =  ileave k (copy k d)
```

The above property yields

```
split k j (rep k d)  =  d
```

11.2 The Slowdown Function

Now the slowdown function is specified implicitly by

```
(slow k f ) |>  split k j    =    (split k j)  |> f
```

Here `f` is an arbitrary function on streams, not just a lifted unary operation. In particular, `f` may look at all the history of a stream. By this definition, `slow k f s` may be considered as splitting `s` into k substreams, processing these individually with `f` and interleaving the result streams back into one stream. From the specification the following proof principle is evident:

Lemma 11.2. *If for a function* h *and all* j *in* [1..k] *we have*

```
h |> split k j  = (split k j) |> f
```

then h = slow k f.

For easier manipulation we want to obtain an explicit version of `slow`. Since by definition of `split`

```
split k j (slow k f s) t'  =  slow k f s (k*t' + j)      (*)
```

we have conversely

```
    slow k f s t

=   { definition of 'div' and 'mod' }

    slow k f s (k*(t 'div' k) + t 'mod' k)

=   { by (*) }

    split k (t 'mod' k) (slow k f s) (t 'div' k)

=   { specification of slow }

    f (split k (t 'mod' k) s) (t 'div' k)
```

In sum,

```
    slow k f s t  =  f (split k (t 'mod' k) s) (t 'div' k)
```

11.3 Slowdown Algebra

The function `slow` distributes nicely through our circuit building operators:

Lemma 11.3. *We have*

```
    slow k (x >-)        =    foldr (|>) id (copy k (x >-))
    slow k (cnst x)      =    cnst x
    slow k (f |>    g)   =    slow k f   |>     slow k g
    slow k (f |||  g)    =    slow k f   |||   slow k g
    slow k (f =||= g)    =    slow k f   =||=  slow k g
    slow k (f =|   g)    =    slow k f   =|    slow k g
    slow k (feed m f)    =    feed m (slow k f)
```

This means that the k-fold slowed down version of a circuit results by replacing each delay element by k identical delay elements. A further useful propagation law for `slow` is given by

Lemma 11.4. *Suppose that* (x>-) |> f = f |> (y>-). *Then also*

```
    (x>-) |> slow k f  =  (slow k f) |> (y>-)
```

12 A Systolic Convolver: The 2-Slow Convolver

Using k-fold slowdown we can interleave k streams or pad one stream with dummy elements by merging it with constant streams of dummies. The latter approach is usually taken in verification approaches to the systolic convolver: one uses slowdown by 2 and is interested only in the stream values at odd time points; at even time points eg. the value 0 is used.

We want to derive a systolic convolver by deductive design. We leave the decision whether to use proper interleaving or padding open; both can be achieved by suitable embeddings of the original conv function into the slowed down one defined by

```
sconv n  =  slow 2 (conv n)
```

Now, employing the delay propagation rules, we push the second delay introduced by the slowdown through the various modules. We perform the derivation pictorially:

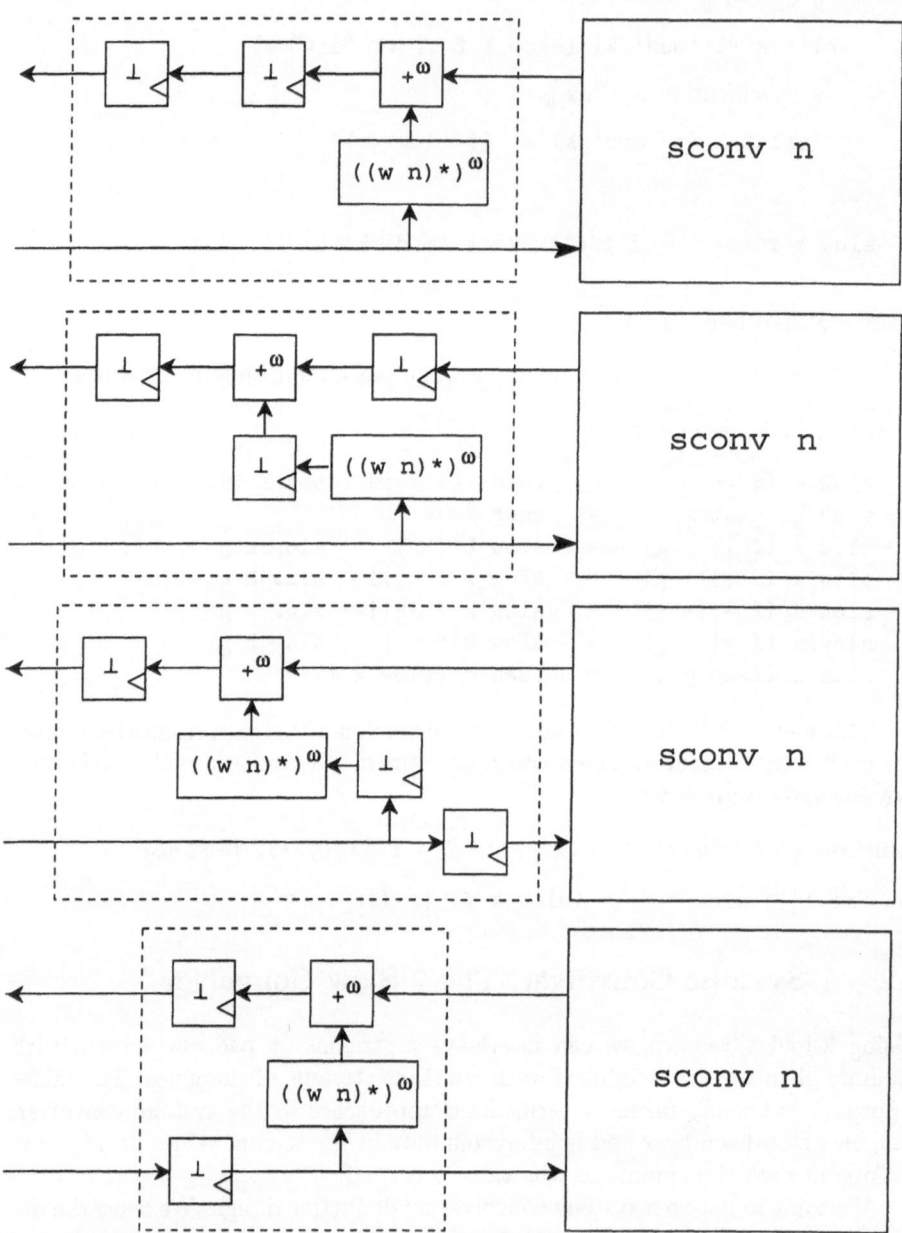

The step of pushing the delay through sconv w n is justified by Lemma 11.4. Unwinding the recursion again we obtain a regular systolic design:

```
sconv w n  =
   (foldr1 (=||=) [scell w k  |  k <- [1..n]]) =| cnst 0
scell w k  =   (undefined >-) |> (fork ||| id) |> (id ||| h)
h w k      =   (lift1 ((w k) *) ||| id) |>
               (lift2 (+)) |> (undefined >-)
```

This simplifies into

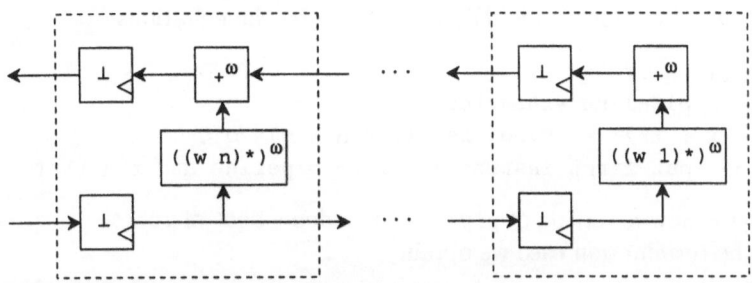

Of course, the techniques we have developed do not only apply to the convolver, but are of general interest for the derivation of systolic implementations
of circuits. As a further case study, a systolic recognizer for regular expressions
is developed in [30].

The derivations have been fairly short; the underlying technique is applicable quite generally. Moreover, the semantical basis is simple. So our approach
compares favourably with verification approaches in this area (see eg. [27, 38]).

13 Pipelining

As a final example we want to leave the level of circuits and step up to questions
about microprocessor architectures. To exemplify our approach in that area, we
give a brief account of the essence of pipelining.

We use a set a of instruction addresses, a set i of instructions and a set s of
machine states. Assume, moreover, a function

```
fetch :: a -> s -> i
```

that obtains the instruction stored under an address in the current state and a
function

```
exe ::  i -> s -> s
```

for executing an instruction in a state to yield a new state. The fetch/execute-
cycle of a machine can then be defined by the function

```
run ::  [a] -> s -> s
run [] q  =  q
run (x : xs) q  =  run  xs  (exe (fetch x q) q)
```

We now want to uncouple the fetch and execute phases so that they can be done in parallel. This is done by a suitable embedding into a function that has as parameters an instruction to be performed currently and a list of addresses of further instructions:

```
pipe :: [a] -> i -> s -> s
pipe xs j q  =  run  xs  (exe j q)
```

The original function run is reduced to pipe by the equations

```
run []  q = q
   --  pipeline exhausted
run (x : xs) =  pipe xs  (fetch x q)  q
   --  put first instruction into pipeline and run that
```

The goal is now a version of pipe that is independent of run.

As the termination case we obtain

```
pipe [] j q  =  exe j q
```

To derive the recursive case we need the central assumption for the correctness of the version of pipelining we treat here. We stipulate that execution of an instruction does not change the contents of the program memory. This means that the program has to be kept in a part of the memory that is administered in a read-only fashion. This assumption can be expressed formally as

```
fetch a (exe j q)  =  fetch a q            (*)
```

for all a,j,q. With this assumption we calculate

```
     pipe (x : xs) j q
=    { unfold pipe }
     run (x : xs) (exe j q)
=    { unfold run }
     run xs (exe (fetch x q') q')
     where q' = exe j q
=    { by (*) }
     run xs (exe (fetch x q) q')
     where q' = exe j q
=    { fold pipe }
     pipe xs (fetch x q) (exe j q)
```

This means that fetching the next instruction can be done in parallel with executing the current one.

Note that the derivation is completely polymorphic; no assumptions are made about the types a, s and i. The only assumption is the validity of equation (*).

In particular, the transformation can be iterated to obtain pipelines with several stages if **exe** can be decomposed into further subfunctions.

Further investigations here will concern transformational derivations of realistic pipeline processors such as formally treated in [8].

14 Conclusion

We have seen a number of essential ingredients of deductive hardware design:

- algebraic reasoning,
- parameterization,
- modularization,
- re-use of designs and derivations,
- precise determination of initialization values.

Special emphasis was laid on parameterization and re-usability aspects.

The major novel ingredients and achievements in this work are the following:

- specification at the level of predicate logic, not necessarily algorithmic yet,
- a clearer disentangling of the abstract idea of an algorithm from the concrete layout that realizes it,
- in particular, introduction of wiring operators in a late stage of the derivations, thus avoiding a lot of burden and clutter,
- a simpler approach to retiming that avoids the concept of anti-delays.

The case studies include several of the IFIP WG10.5 Benchmark Verification Problems. Next to dealing with basic combinational and sequential circuits, a very simple treatment of systolic circuits has been achieved. Finally, concerning higher-level hardware concepts, an easy formal account of pipelining became possible.

The switch to formalizing the specifications and derivations using the functional programming language *Haskell* brought many advantages. The polymorphism of this language allows the use of Ştefănescu's network algebra and other algebraic laws uniformly both at the levels of combinational and sequential circuits. Also fixpoint induction and related proof principles can be applied directly. Moreover, many derivations can be performed in a polymorphic way abstracting from concrete applications and hence achieving much better re-usability. Last, but not least, the derivations could be formally checked using the ULTRA transformation system.

Further elaboration of this approach will mainly concern deductive design in the large, asynchronous systems and other notions of time.

Acknowledgement: Many helpful remarks on this paper were provided by F.K. Hanna, J. Philipps, P. Scholz, G. Ştefănescu and, notably, T. Häberlein who checked the laws and derivations of this paper using the ULTRA system. I am most grateful to T. Ehm for his competent and patient assistance in incorporating the figures into the text.

References

1. H.P. Barendregt: Functional programming and lambda calculus. In: J. van Leeuwen (ed.): Handbook of theoretical computer science. Vol. B: Formal models and semantics. Amsterdam: Elsevier 1990, 321–363

2. J.A. Bergstra, A. Ponse: Grid protocol specifications. In: B. Möller, J.V. Tucker (eds.): Prospects for hardware foundations. Lecture Notes in Computer Science **1546**. Berlin: Springer (this volume)

3. P. Bjesse, K. Claessen, M. Sheeran, S. Singh: Lava: hardware design in Haskell. Proc. ACM International Conf. Functional Programming '98, Baltimore (to appear).

4. M. Broy, G. Ştefănescu: The algebra of stream processing functions. Institut für Informatik, TU München, Report TUM-I9620, 1996

5. R. Boute: A declarative formalism supporting hardware/software codesign. In: J. Rozenblit, K. Buchenrieder (eds.): Codesign — computer-aided software/hardware engineering. Piscataway: IEEE Press 1995, 41–66

6. F.L. Bauer, H. Ehler, A. Horsch, B. Möller, H. Partsch, O. Paukner, P. Pepper: The Munich project CIP. Volume II: The program transformation system CIP-S. Lecture Notes in Computer Science **292**. Berlin: Springer 1987

7. F.L. Bauer, B. Möller, H. Partsch, P. Pepper: Formal program construction by transformations - Computer-aided, Intuition-guided Programming. IEEE Transactions on Software Engineering 15, 165-180 (1989)

8. E. Börger, S. Mazzanti: A correctness proof for pipelining in RISC architectures. DIMACS Technical Report 96-22, July 1996

9. B. Cook, J. Launchbury, J. Matthews: Specifying superscalar microprocessors in Hawk. In: B. Möller, M. Sheeran (eds.): Proceedings of the Workshop FTH '98 — Formal Techniques for Hardware and Hardware-Like Systems, Marstrand, June 19, 1998. Chalmers Institute of Technology, Göteborg, 1998

10. C. Delgado Kloos: Semantics of digital circuits. Lecture Notes in Computer Science **285**. Berlin: Springer 1987

11. C. Delgado Kloos, W. Dosch: Efficient circuits as implementations of nonstrict functions. In: G. Jones, M. Sheeran (eds.): Designing correct circuits. London: Springer 1991, 212–230

12. C. Delgado Kloos, W. Dosch: Transformational development of circuit descriptions for binary adders. In: M. Broy, M. Wirsing (eds.): Methods of programming. Lecture Notes in Computer Science **544**. Berlin: Springer 1991, 217–237

13. C. Delgado Kloos, W. Dosch, B. Möller: Design and proof of multipliers by correctness-preserving transformation. In P. Dewilde, J. Vandewalle (eds.): Proc. IEEE International Conference on Computer Systems and Software Engineering CompEuro 92. IEEE Computer Society Press 1992, 238-243

14. S. Even, A. Litman: On the capabilities of systolic systems. Math. Sytems Theory 27, 3-28 (1994)

15. M. Fourman: Proof and design. In: M. Broy (ed.): Deductive program design. NATO ASI Series. Series F: Computer and Systems Sciences, Vol. 152. Berlin: Springer 1996, 397–439

16. M.J. Gordon: Why higher-order logic is a good formalism for specifying and verifying hardware. In: G.J. Milne, P.A. Subrahmanyam (eds.): Formal aspects of VLSI design. North-Holland 1986

17. K. Hanna, N. Daeche, M. Longley: Specification and verification using dependent types. IEEE Trans. Softw. Eng. 16:9, 949-964 (1990)

18. HAWK — Specifying, Verifying, and Simulating Microprocessors. Web page under http://www.cse.ogi.edu/PacSoft/Hawk/

19. G. Hotz, B. Becker, R. Kolla, P. Molitor: Ein logisch-topologischer Kalkül zur Konstruktion integrierter Schaltungen. Informatik - Forschung und Entwicklung 1, 28-47 and 72-82 (1986)

20. IFIP 94/97: IFIP WG 10.5 Verification Benchmarks. Web document under http://goethe.ira.uka.de/hvg/benchmarks.html

21. G. Jones, M. Sheeran: Circuit design in Ruby. In: J. Staunstrup (ed.): Formal methods for VLSI design. Elsevier 1990, 13-70

22. M.B. Josephs: Formal derivation of a loadable asynchronous counter. In: J. Jeuring (ed.): Mathematics of Program Construction. Lecture Notes in Computer Science **1422**. Berlin: Springer 1998, 234-253

23. M.B. Josephs, A.M. Bailey: The use of SI-Algebra in the design of sequencer circuits. Formal Aspects of Computing **9**, 395-408 (1997)

24. C.E. Leiserson, J.B. Saxe: Optimizing synchronous systems. J. VLSI and Computer Systems 1, 41-68 (1983)

25. C.E. Leiserson, J.B. Saxe: Retiming synchronous circuitry. Algorithmica 6, 5-35 (1991)

26. J. Matthews, J. Launchbury, B. Cook: Microprocessor specification in Hawk. 1998 International Conference on Computer Languages (Chicago)

27. K. Meinke, J. Steggles: Specification and verification in higher order algebra: a case study of convolution. In: J. Heering, K. Meinke, B. Möller, T. Nipkow (eds.): Higher order algebra, logic and term rewriting. Lecture Notes in Computer Science **816**. Berlin: Springer 1994, 189-222

28. B. Möller: Assertions and recursions. In: G. Dowek, J. Heering, K. Meinke, B. Möller (eds.): Higher order algebra, logic and term rewriting. Second International Workshop, Paderborn, Sept. 21-22, 1995. Lecture Notes in Computer Science **1074**. Berlin: Springer 1996, 163-184

29. B. Möller: Ideal stream algebra. In: B. Möller, J.V. Tucker (eds.): Prospects for hardware foundations. Lecture Notes in Computer Science **1546**. Berlin: Springer (this volume)

30. B. Möller: An algebraic approach to systolic circuits. Institut für Informatik der Universität Augsburg, Report 1998-01, January 1998. Also in: B. Möller, M. Sheeran (eds.): Proceedings of the Workshop FTH '98 — Formal Techniques for Hardware and Hardware-Like Systems, Marstrand, June 19, 1998. Chalmers Institute of Technology, Göteborg, 1998

31. P. Molitor: A survey on wiring. J. Inf. Process. Cybern. EIK 27, 3-19 (1991)

32. J. O'Donnell: From transistors to computer architecture: teaching functional circuit specification in Hydra. In: P.H. Hartel, R. Plasmeijer (eds.): Functional programming languages in education. Lecture Notes in Computer Science **1022**. Berlin: Springer 1995, 195-214

33. H.A. Partsch: Specification and transformation of programs - A formal approach to software development. Berlin: Springer 1990

34. D.L. Rhodes: Analog modeling using MHDL. In: J.-M. Bergé (ed.): Current issues in electronic modeling, Issue #2 "Modeling in analog design. Kluwer 1995

35. S. Singh: Lava. Web page under http://www.dcs.gla.ac.uk/ satnam/lava/main.html

36. System level design language. Web page under
http://www.intermetrics.com/SLDL/
37. G. Ştefănescu: Algebra of flownomials. Institut für Informatik der TU München, Report TUM-I9437, 1994
38. J. Steggles: Parameterised higher-order algebraic specifications. In: M. Hanus, J. Heering, K. Meinke (eds.): Algebraic and Logic Programming. Lecture Notes in Computer Science **1298**. Berlin: Springer 1997,76–97
39. W. Schulte, T. Vullinghs: ULTRA: A Useful and Lean Transformation System. Fakult"at f"ur Informatik, Technical Report. Universit"at Ulm 1998 (to appear)

Appendix: Essential Constructs of *Haskell*

Basic Types and Functions

For those not familiar with *Haskell*, we briefly repeat its essential elements. Basic types are Int for the integers and Bool for the Booleans with elements True and False. Exponentiation is written in the form x^n. The operations of conjunction and disjunction are denoted by && and ||, resp. These are the semi-strict versions evaluating their arguments from left to right, ie. satisfying

```
x && y  =  if x then y    else False
x || y  =  if x then True else y
```

The type of functions taking elements of type a as arguments and producing elements of type b as results is a -> b. The fact that a function f has this type is expressed as f :: a -> b.

Function application is denoted by juxtaposing function and argument, separated by at least one blank, in the form f x. Functions of several arguments are mostly used in curried form f x1 x2 ... xn. In this case f has the higher-order type f :: t1 -> (t2 -> ... (tn -> t) ...) or, abbreviated, f :: t1 -> t2 -> ... tn -> t (the arrow -> associates to the right, whereas function application associates to the left).

Functions are defined by equations of the form f x = E or as (anonymous) lambda abstractions. Instead of $\lambda x.E$ one uses the notation \x -> E.

A two-place function f :: a -> b -> c may also be used as an infix operator in the form x `f` y; this is equivalent to the usual application f x y. Eg. instead of div x y one may also write x `div` y. To formulate a number of expressions and properties in a more readable way we use a small notational extension of this: we also use larger expressions (that do not contain the backquote) between backquotes as infix operators. Eg. for

```
zipWith :: (a -> b -> c) -> [a] -> [b] -> [c]
```

we may then write xs `zipWith (+)` ys for the componentwise addition of lists xs and ys.

For a binary operator ?, by supplying only one of its arguments one obtains a *residual function* or *operator section* of the form

```
(x ?)  =  \y -> x ? y  or  (? y) = \x -> x ? y
```

Case Distinction and Assertions

Haskell offers several possibilities for doing case distinctions. One is the usual if then else construct. To avoid cascades of ifs, a function may also be defined in a style similar to the one used in mathematics. The notation is

```
f x
| C1        =    E1
...
| Cn        =    En
```

The result is the value of the first expression Ei for which the corresponding Ci evaluates to True. If there is none, the result is undefined.

We shall also use this to make functions intentionally partial in order to enforce assertions about their parameters (see [28]).

To avoid partiality one can use the predefined constant otherwise = True and add a final clause

```
| otherwise  =    En+1
```

Yet another way of case distinction is provided by defining a function through argument patterns. Several equations indicate what a function does on inputs that have certain shapes. The equations are tried in textual order; if no pattern matches the current argument, the function is again undefined at that point.

Example 14.1. By the equations

```
f 0 = 5
f 1 = 7
```

the function f :: Int -> Int is defined only for argument values 0 and 1. □

Lists

The type of lists of elements of type a is denoted by [a]. The list consisting of elements x1,...,xn is written as [x1,...,xn]; in particular, [] is the empty list. Concatenation is denoted by ++. Prefixing an element to a list is denoted by the colon operator:

```
x:xs = [x] ++ xs
```

The function length returns the length of a list. The ith element of list xs is selected by the expression xs!!i (where numbering starts with 0).

A list may be split into two parts using the functions

```
take, drop :: [a] -> Int -> [a]
```

For non-negative integer k the list take k xs consists of the first k elements of xs if k <= length xs and of all of xs if k > length xs. For negative k the expression take k xs is undefined. The list drop k xs results by removing take k xs from the front of xs. Hence one always has

```
take k xs ++ drop k xs = xs
```

A very useful specification feature is list comprehension in the form

```
[ f x | x <- L, px]
```

where L is a list expression, f some function on the list elements and p a Boolean function. The symbol <- may be viewed as a leftward arrow and pronounced as "drawn from" or as a form of element sign. In this latter view, the expression is the list analogue of the usual set comprehension $\{f\,x | x \in S, p\,x\}$. The meaning of the list comprehension expression [f x | x <- L, p x] is again a list, constructed as follows:

− The elements of list L are scanned in left-to-right order.
− On each such element x the test p is performed.
− If p x = True, f x is put into the result list.
− Otherwise, x is ignored.

The list [m,m+1,...,n] of integers may be denoted by the shorthand [m..n]. The right bound n may be omitted; then the expression denotes the infinite list [m, m+1, ...].

A useful operation on non-empty lists is the folding of their elements using a binary operator f :: :

```
foldr1 f [x1,...,xn]  =  f x1 (f x2 ... (f  xn-1 xn)...)
```

Eg. foldr1 (+) s computes the sum of all elements of s. The function foldr1 itself has the type (a -> a -> a) -> [a] -> a.

A variant of foldr1 that also copes with empty lists is foldr; it uses an additional argument e that specifies the value for empty lists. The defining equations read

```
foldr f e []  =  e
foldr f e [x] ++ xs = f x (foldr f e xs)
```

Based on foldr one can define a universal quantifier over lists. For a predicate p :: a -> Bool one has

```
all p xs  =  foldr (&&) True [p x | x <- xs ]
```

So all p xs yields True iff p x yields True for all x in xs.

Lecture Notes in Computer Science

For information about Vols. 1–1463
please contact your bookseller or Springer-Verlag

Vol. 1498: A.E. Eiben, T. Bäck, M. Schoenauer, H.-P. Schwefel (Eds.), Parallel Problem Solving from Nature – PPSN V. Proceedings, 1998. XXIII, 1041 pages. 1998.

Vol. 1499: S. Kutten (Ed.), Distributed Computing. Proceedings, 1998. XII, 419 pages. 1998.

Vol. 1501: M.M. Richter, C.H. Smith, R. Wiehagen, T. Zeugmann (Eds.), Algorithmic Learning Theory. Proceedings, 1998. XI, 439 pages. 1998. (Subseries LNAI).

Vol. 1502: G. Antoniou, J. Slaney (Eds.), Advanced Topics in Artificial Intelligence. Proceedings, 1998. XI, 333 pages. 1998. (Subseries LNAI).

Vol. 1503: G. Levi (Ed.), Static Analysis. Proceedings, 1998. IX, 383 pages. 1998.

Vol. 1504: O. Herzog, A. Günter (Eds.), KI-98: Advances in Artificial Intelligence. Proceedings, 1998. XI, 355 pages. 1998. (Subseries LNAI).

Vol. 1505: D. Caromel, R.R. Oldehoeft, M. Tholburn (Eds.), Computing in Object-Oriented Parallel Environments. Proceedings, 1998. XI, 243 pages. 1998.

Vol. 1506: R. Koch, L. Van Gool (Eds.), 3D Structure from Multiple Images of Large-Scale Environments. Proceedings, 1998. VIII, 347 pages. 1998.

Vol. 1507: T.W. Ling, S. Ram, M.L. Lee (Eds.), Conceptual Modeling – ER '98. Proceedings, 1998. XVI, 482 pages. 1998.

Vol. 1508: S. Jajodia, M.T. Özsu, A. Dogac (Eds.), Advances in Multimedia Information Systems. Proceedings, 1998. VIII, 207 pages. 1998.

Vol. 1510: J.M. Zytkow, M. Quafafou (Eds.), Principles of Data Mining and Knowledge Discovery. Proceedings, 1998. XI, 482 pages. 1998. (Subseries LNAI).

Vol. 1511: D. O'Hallaron (Ed.), Languages, Compilers, and Run-Time Systems for Scalable Computers. Proceedings, 1998. IX, 412 pages. 1998.

Vol. 1512: E. Giménez, C. Paulin-Mohring (Eds.), Types for Proofs and Programs. Proceedings, 1996. VIII, 373 pages. 1998.

Vol. 1513: C. Nikolaou, C. Stephanidis (Eds.), Research and Advanced Technology for Digital Libraries. Proceedings, 1998. XV, 912 pages. 1998.

Vol. 1514: K. Ohta, D. Pei (Eds.), Advances in Cryptology – ASIACRYPT'98. Proceedings, 1998. XII, 436 pages. 1998.

Vol. 1515: F. Moreira de Oliveira (Ed.), Advances in Artificial Intelligence. Proceedings, 1998. X, 259 pages. 1998. (Subseries LNAI).

Vol. 1516: W. Ehrenberger (Ed.), Computer Safety, Reliability and Security. Proceedings, 1998. XVI, 392 pages. 1998.

Vol. 1517: J. Hromkovič, O. Sýkora (Eds.), Graph-Theoretic Concepts in Computer Science. Proceedings, 1998. X, 385 pages. 1998.

Vol. 1518: M. Luby, J. Rolim, M. Serna (Eds.), Randomization and Approximation Techniques in Computer Science. Proceedings, 1998. IX, 385 pages. 1998.

1519: T. Ishida (Ed.), Community Computing and Support Systems. VIII, 393 pages. 1998. (Subseries LNAI).

Vol. 1520: M. Maher, J.-F. Puget (Eds.), Principles and Practice of Constraint Programming - CP98. Proceedings, 1998. XI, 482 pages. 1998.

Vol. 1521: B. Rovan (Ed.), SOFSEM'98: Theory and Practice of Informatics. Proceedings, 1998. XI, 453 pages. 1998.

Vol. 1522: G. Gopalakrishnan, P. Windley (Eds.), Formal Methods in Computer-Aided Design. Proceedings, 1998. IX, 529 pages. 1998.

Vol. 1524: G.B. Orr, K.-R. Müller (Eds.), Neural Networks: Tricks of the Trade. VI, 432 pages. 1998.

Vol. 1525: D. Aucsmith (Ed.), Information Hiding. Proceedings, 1998. IX, 369 pages. 1998.

Vol. 1526: M. Broy, B. Rumpe (Eds.), Requirements Targeting Software and Systems Engineering. Proceedings, 1997. VIII, 357 pages. 1998.

Vol. 1528: B. Preneel, V. Rijmen (Eds.), State of the Art in Applied Cryptography. Revised Lectures, 1997. VIII, 395 pages. 1998.

Vol. 1529: D. Farwell, L. Gerber, E. Hovy (Eds.), Machine Translation and the Information Soup. Proceedings, 1998. XIX, 532 pages. 1998. (Subseries LNAI).

Vol. 1530: V. Arvind, R. Ramanujam (Eds.), Foundations of Software Technology and Theoretical Computer Science. XII, 369 pages. 1998.

Vol. 1531: H.-Y. Lee, H. Motoda (Eds.), PRICAI'98: Topics in Artificial Intelligence. XIX, 646 pages. 1998. (Subseries LNAI).

Vol. 1096: T. Schael, Workflow Management Systems for Process Organisations. Second Edition. XII, 229 pages. 1998.

Vol. 1532: S. Arikawa, H. Motoda (Eds.), Discovery Science. Proceedings, 1998. XI, 456 pages. 1998. (Subseries LNAI).

Vol. 1533: K.-Y. Chwa, O.H. Ibarra (Eds.), Algorithms and Computation. Proceedings, 1998. XIII, 478 pages. 1998.

Vol. 1538: J. Hsiang, A. Ohori (Eds.), Advances in Computing Science – ASIAN'98. Proceedings, 1998. X, 305 pages. 1998.

Vol. 1540: C. Beeri, P. Buneman (Eds.), Database Theory – ICDT'99. Proceedings, 1999. XI, 489 pages. 1999.

Vol. 1541: B. Kågström, J. Dongarra, E. Elmroth, J. Waśniewski (Eds.), Applied Parallel Computing. Proceedings, 1998. XIV, 586 pages. 1998.

Vol. 1542: H.I. Christensen (Ed.), Computer Vision Systems. Proceedings, 1999. XI, 554 pages. 1999.

Vol. 1543: S. Demeyer, J. Bosch (Eds.), Object-Oriented Technology ECOOP'98 Workshop Reader. 1998. XXII, 573 pages. 1998.

Vol. 1544: C. Zhang, D. Lukose (Eds.), Multi-Agent Systems. Proceedings, 1998. VII, 195 pages. 1998. (Subseries LNAI).

Vol. 1546: B. Möller, J.V. Tucker (Eds.), Prospects for Hardware Foundations. Survey Chapters, 1998. X, 468 pages. 1998.

Vol. 1548: A.M. Haeberer (Ed.), Algebraic Methodology and Software Technology. Proceedings, 1999. XI, 531 pages. 1999.